EVENTS IN PSYCHOLOGY		EVENTS IN HISTORY
Gilbert's *de Magnete;* Bacon	16 ┬ 00	Descartes Born
Montaigne		Copernicus's *De Revolutionibus*
		Reformation
Erasmus	15 ┼ 00	Columbus, Savonarola
		Fall of Constantinople
	14 ┼ 00	Leipzig University Founded
		Black Death Petrarch
Ockham	13 ┼ 00	
Siger of Brabant		School of Siger Condemned
		First English Parliament
Bonaventure, Aquinas		Magna Carta
	12 ┼ 00	
		University of Bologna Founded
Abelard	11 ┼ 00	Wine Distilled to Make Brandy
		Battle of Hastings
Ibn-Sīnā	10 ┼ 00	Vikings Reach North America
	┬ 500	
		Rome Falls
Augustine	┼ 400	Alaric Sacks Rome
		Battle of Adrianople
		Maya Develop Day-Count Calendar
	┼ 300	
		Roman Empire Divided
Plotinus	┼ 200	
Galen's Treatises		First Alchemical Writings
		Marcus Aurelius
Epictetus	┼ 100	
		Colosseum Built
		Steam Power Observed
		Battle of Actium
	A.D. ┼ 1	
		Julius Caesar Assassinated
Lucretius		
	100 ┼	Chinese Invent Collar Harness
		Judas Maccabeus Frees Temple
	200 ┼	
		Chinese Bureaucracy Develops
		Great Wall of China Begun
Zeno		
Diogenes Epicurus	300 ┼	
Pyrrho Aristotle		Alexander the Great Founds Alexandria
		Celts Begin Maiden Castle
Plato	400 ┼	
Democritus Socrates		Parthenon Completed
Empedocles, Protagoras		
Parmenides		Battle of Thermopylae
Alcmaeon, Heraclitus	500 ┼	
Thales	600 ┴ B.C.	First Date in History: May 28, 585 B.C.—Battle Between Medes and Lydians Interrupted by Solar Eclipse Predicted by Thales

EVENTS IN PSYCHOLOGY   **EVENTS IN HISTORY**

Events in Psychology	Date	Events in History
Bain's *Emotions and the Will*	18 — 60	Darwin's *Origin of Species*
Spencer's *Principles of Psychology*		
Helmholtz Measures Reaction Time		
	18 + 50	1848: Year of European Revolutions
J.S. Mill		Darwin's First Abstract of Theory of Evolution
	18 + 40	
Comte		
	18 + 30	Darwin Sails on *Beagle*
Galls's *On the Functions of the Brain*	18 + 20	Faraday's Research on Magnetism
Magendie-Bell Law		
J. Mill		
		War of 1812
	18 + 10	
		University of Berlin (1st Research University)
Malthus's *Essay on Population*	18 + 00	Rosetta Stone Found
Stewart's *Psychology of the Human Mind*	17 + 90	French Revolution
Bentham's *Principles of Moral Legislation*		
Kant's *Critique of Pure Reason*	17 + 80	
Mesmer's *Discovery of Animal Magnetism*		American Revolution
Hume's *Inquiry Concerning Human Understanding*		
	17 + 70	
		Watt's Steam Engine
	17 + 60	
		Helvetius's *Essays on Mind* Condemned
Condillac's *Treatise on Sensations*		
Hartley's *Observations on Man*	17 + 50	*Observations* is First English Work Using Term "Psychology"
La Mettrie's *L'Homme Machine*		
		American Philosophical Society
	17 + 40	
Hume's *Treatise of Human Nature*		
		Algaretti's *Newtonianism for the Ladies*
Berkeley	17 + 30	First Tracheotomy
	17 + 20	South Sea Bubble Collapses
	17 + 10	First Practical Steam Engine
Newton's *Optics*	17 + 00	Yale Founded
		Epsom Salts
Locke's *Essay Concerning Human Understanding*	16 + 90	English Glorious Revolution
Newton's *Principia Mathematica*		
		Halley's Comet
Leibniz	16 + 80	
		Greenwich Observatory Founded
Spinoza	16 + 70	
		Great Fire of London
Pascal	16 + 60	English Restoration
		Pascal's and Fermat's Letters on Probability
Hobbes's *Leviathan*	16 + 50	
		Invisible College Meets
Pascal Invents Calculating Machine		
	16 + 40	
Descartes's *Rules for the Direction of the Mind*		Harvard Founded
	16 + 30	Kepler Dies
Harvey Announces the Circulation of the Blood		
	16 + 20	Plymouth Rock
	16 + 10	King James Bible
		Jamestown Established
Galileo	16 — 00	Bruno Burnt as Heretic

A History
of Psychology

FOURTH EDITION

A History of Psychology

Main Currents in Psychological Thought

Thomas Hardy Leahey
Virginia Commonwealth University

Prentice Hall International, Inc.

© 1997, 1992, 1987, 1980 by Prentice-Hall, Inc.
Simon & Schuster/A Viacom Company
Upper Saddle River, New Jersey 07458

Printed in the United States of America

10 9 8 7 6 5 4 3 2 1

ISBN 0-13-802737-4

Prentice-Hall International (UK) Limited, London
Prentice-hall of Australia Pty. Limited, Sydney
Prentice-Hall Canada Inc., Toronto
Prentice-Hall Hispanoamericana, S. A., Mexico
Prentice-Hall of India Private Limited, New Delhi
Prentice-Hall of Japan, Inc., Tokyo
Simon & Schuster Asia Pte. Ltd., Singapore
Editora Prentice-Hall do Brasil, Ltda., Rio de Janeiro
Prentice-Hall, Inc., Upper Saddle River, New Jersey

Elizabeth, who came in the middle the first time,
and
Grace, who helped through it all, four times.

Photo Credits

Contents

From the Preface to the First Edition

SOME WORDS TO THE STUDENT

Human beings make history—political, military, social, and scientific. In the history of science, ideas are especially important, for science is a changing collection of ideas to which short-lived human beings make contributions. This is not to deny that human personalities and institutions play a role in shaping science; but it is to say that the history of science can be written and studied in more than one way. One may choose to study the history of a science as a succession of great scientists and their major contributions to the field. Or one may study the history of a science as an institution, recording the founding of laboratories and the intellectual genealogies of the generations of scientists. Or, finally, one may study the history of a science solely as a collection of scientific concepts that evolve over time, paying relatively little attention to the personal histories of the scientists who formulate the concepts or the laboratories that put them to the test. Since historians have only limited space at their disposal, the historian cannot practice all three kinds of scientific history, no matter how desirable that might be. This book contains practically no institutional history, which is probably the least developed aspect of the history of psychology. Instead, we will focus our attention on the leading psychological *concepts* as they have evolved since the earliest days of recorded human history. To help organize our study of these concepts and how they have changed, I have chosen to consider the leading exponents of different psychological systems during each historical era. Although little will be said about the personal backgrounds of these people, concentration of them will help pull together concepts into competing viewpoints on the nature of human nature and will prevent us from diffusing our efforts.

Another important option is open to a historian of science. Older histories of the sciences were generally *internal* histories considering the development of the technical ideas of each science independent of the broader intellectual and social context in which the science operated. More recently, histories of the sciences have tended to be *external* histories considering the outside intellectual and social context and its effects on the development of the science. For the most part, this book tends to be externalistic. Psychology is a young science, with only a short history of technical concepts: Before the nineteenth century, psychological ideas were always part of some other field—philosophy, biology, or politics. Moreover, since psychology studies human nature—on which everyone has opinions—-it is particularly subject to influence by larger social and intellectual currents. Such is not the case in other sciences. For example, physics has over its long history become so abstruse that society has little *intellectual* influence on it, although both physics and psychology are profoundly affected as institutions by the degree of support given by society at large.

No historian can be neutral to the subject matter. Historians must care about it enough to want to understand it and to make it come alive for others. Historians must be fair; they must weigh argument and counterargument; and finally, they must choose. Historians must choose some facts over others, for they cannot record everything. They must choose to discuss some thinkers and not others, for not all are equally great—although greatness is hard to define. Historians must choose some concepts over others, for some have survived while others have become extinct. They must choose some interpretation to put on the facts, events, people, and concepts written about, for history is an understanding of the past.

The purpose of this book and of the course for which you are using it is to give you a chance to work out your own point of view. The concepts and issues you learn about in content course do not exist in a vacuum. They arose and existed in a particular historical context. The questions asked in today's research are the outcome of a historical process and the answer given contributes to that process. The opportunity and *history* and *systems* gives you is a chance to see the historical context and the historical process, to reflect on psychology as it is—and on your own experiences as a student of psychology.

Erik Erikson describes adolescence as a search for identity, a necessary prerequisite to a productive adult life. Identity is achieved through reflections on one's past and present and through making a decision on where to go and what to do with one's life. Your reflection on psychology's past and present state is an important part of finding your identity within psychology. You should come away from your experience not with a list of names, dates, and events, but with an understanding of what psychology is and of your own relation to it. You should not be a passive recorder of a monotonous march of yours, but rather an explorer of the past and great minds. The first task is dull and bloodless; the second is an adventure and full of life.

My most important acknowledgment goes to my wife, Grace. She read every word, compiled the index, and made numerous improvements, large and small, to the writing of the book. Without her efforts the manuscript would have been awkward and unclear. My second acknowledgment is to William Brewer, my mentor in graduate school, who never demanded technical specialization to the detriment of broad philosophical and historical ideas about psychology.

Thomas Hardy Leahey
Richmond, Virginia

From the Preface to the Second Edition

One of the fragments of the Greek poet Archilochus goes, "The fox knows many things, but the hedgehog knows one big thing." The distinguished historian of ideas Sir Isaiah Berlin uses this cryptic fragment to represent

> . . . one of the deepest differences which divide writers and thinkers, and it may be, human beings in general. For there exists a great chasm between those, on the one side [the hedgehogs], who relate everything to single central vision . . . a single, universal organizing principle in terms of which alone all that they are and say has significance—and, on the other side [the foxes], those who pursue many ends, often unrelated and often contradictory, connected, if at all, only in some *de facto way*. . . .*

Dante was a hedgehog; Shakespeare a fox. Plato, who devised an ideal Republic, was a hedgehog; Socrates, the gadfly on the rump of the state, was a fox. When I wrote the first edition of this book I thought I was a hedgehog, a rationalist, albeit at times an uncomfortable one. I have found out, however, that I am a fox, and am happy to be so.

Richard Rorty, in his *Philosophy and the Mirror of Nature,*† distinguishes capital-P *Philosophy* from small-p *philosophy*. Capital-P Philosophers are philosophy's hedgehogs. Their ambition is to make Philosophy the first and foundational discipline for all other disciples, providing the first principles upon which scientists and humanists build. Small-p philosophers, on the other hand, are philosophy's foxes, critically examining the ideas of their times, offering comments they hope are illuminating and instructive, but offering no foundational vision of their own, because they believe there is no foundation to be had. Plato, as a rationalist hedgehog, was a Philosopher; his teacher, Socrates the fox, was a philosopher. We might modify

---

* *The hedgehog and the fox* (New York, Toughstone, c. 1954).
† (Oxford: Blackwell, 1980).

Rorty's division and distinguish Psychologists and psychologists. Capital-P Psychologists are the system builders, envisioning psychology unified under a single set of principles. Small-p psychologists, by contrast, believe that humanlife is too messy, the influences on human behavior too diverse, the differences between people as animal-machines and people as social-humans too great ever to be encompassed by a single point of view. The Psychologist is distressed at psychology's permanent quarrels and dreams of psychology as a genuine and accepted science. The psychologist enjoys psychology's permanent quarrels, believes they can never be resolved, and is skeptical that psychology as a whole can ever become a science. When I wrote the first edition of this book I wanted to be a Philosopher, and hoped that Psychology was possible, although I had my doubts. Having discovered I am a fox, I have become a philosopher, and think that unified, scientific psychology is a pipe dream. Becoming a fox has been liberating, for it is better to be a fox than a fox who thinks he's a hedgehog and gets depressed.

Foxes make better historians, because they attend to the daily contradictions and concrete reality of life as people live it, and are not carried away by sweeping generalities that erase the specificities of history. Hedgehog historians are wont to paint over the contradictions and grit of life with a glossy, superficial sheen of abstractions. The hedgehog, if he or she notices the messiness of history at all, is likely to be downcast by people's inconsistencies and cross-purpose, especially if he or she is a historian of science, which thinks itself a rational enterprise. The fox is at home with history's disorder and confusion, and tries to tell an instructive and entertaining tale of human life. I became a fox, a philosopher, and a psychologist by writing, with my wife, Grace (*Psychology's Occult Doubles: Psychology and the Problem of Pseudoscience**). There I set out (she was always more skeptical) to find the essence of science, believing that even if other fields are too self-contradictory to have an essence, science it not, having some central method or attitude apart from its substantive concepts. However, at the end I concluded that science is only a set of beliefs held by scientists, and that all but two beliefs have changed over the centuries. The older, dating back to the ancient Greeks, is naturalism, explaining the world without reference to supernatural entities or events. Hence "creation science" is an oxymoron, because even if creationism is true (which I don't believe), it cannot be part of science. The second belief, defining modern science, comes from Newton and says that science explains events as outcomes to timeless, universal natural *laws*. These beliefs, however, merely define science as a Western social institution; they are not essential Truths.

Having become a fox, and agreeing with Giambattista Vico that "The useful historians are not those who give general descriptions of facts and explain them by reference to general conditions, but those who go into the greatest detail and reveal the particular cause of each event," I have tried to write a more strongly narrative history than before, more chronological and less conceptually driven. Thus the great influence of Kuhn in the first edition has been largely purged. Kuhn has been used to tidy up psychological history under a tidy hedgehoggian scheme of mentalist paradigm replaced by behaviorist paradigm replaced by cognitive paradigm. I now believe that there never has been a paradigm in psychology, and to think so obliterates vital differences between thinkers lumped together in a supposed shared "paradigm." I

* (Chicago, Nelson-Hall, 1983).

From the Preface to the Second Edition

have also expanded the coverage of twentieth-century psychology by linking changes in psychology to social changes. These is a whole new chapter on the rise of applied psychology and psychologists' involvement with social issues. I have included material on clinical psychology, because it is a major—perhaps the major—way psychology affects society.

Thomas Hardy Leahey
Richmond, Virginia

Preface to the Fourth Edition

This fourth edition contains no great surprises, but continues the evolution of *A History of Psychology* and its companion, *A History of Modern Psychology,* toward greater narrative drive, a more critical sensibility, and the greater interlocking of developments in psychology and society.

The biggest changes were forced on me by the publisher's desire for a shorter book. Through a series of accidents, Prentice-Hall did not realize until too late that the manuscript of the third edition of *A History of Psychology* was too long by about a chapter. They kept the page length down by expanding the page size and making the text more dense, but they told me to shorten the next manuscript quite severely. I achieved part of this goal by going through the entire manuscript and editing it. I hope that in addition to reducing the book's length I have made it more readable.

However, minor cuts throughout the text did not meet my editor's demands. I then chose to reorganize and make more drastic cuts to the last three chapters, which cover psychology since World War II. I will not make the same changes to the next edition of *A History of Modern Psychology.* I have chosen to make the two books more different than they have been in the past. While in *A History of Psychology* I still bring the story of psychology up to the present, there is, and will remain, much more detail available in *A History of Modern Psychology.* Professors wishing to spend more time on the recent past might consider adopting *A History of Modern Psychology* instead of *A History of Psychology.* I myself teach History and Systems of Psychology in two versions. In the fall semester, I use *A History of Psychology* and go from the Greeks to the early twentieth century. In the spring, I use *A History of Modern Psychology* and go from mid-nineteenth century to the present.

Consequently, changes to the content of the fourth edition of *A History of Psychology* focus on periods where the two texts do not overlap. From the standpoint of writing, the oldest chapter in the book was the one on the Classical World, which remained virtually unchanged since the first edition. After many years of desuetude, the field of history of classical philosophy began to revive in the past decade, and so I scrapped and completely rewrote Chapter 2. My treatment is now more of a real narrative than a collection of potted summaries of philosophers' ideas, and I have broadened the scope of my treatment to include ethical and political/social aspects of philosophical psychology as well as the cognitive issues on which I concentrated originally. One other chapter, Chapter 4, on the seventeenth century, has been significantly reworked, though not completely rewritten. The greatest changes are in my treatment of Descartes, which was greatly influenced by the recent biography by Gary Gaukroger, and by criticisms of the Cartesian approach to the mind by modern philosophers, especially in Daniel Dennett in his *Consciousness Explained*. In addition to revisiting Descartes' philosophy, I try to connect it, as Gaukroger does, to wider developments in religious thought in the seventeenth century. Other minor changes occur throughout the book, including updates of recent developments such as the drive for prescription privileges for clinical psychologists.

By the way, I had an odd author's experience connected with the first edition. In a 1996 episode of the TV show *X-Files* concerning gargoyles, Agent Mulder goes to a library to do some research. While watching the show, I suddenly noticed that on the top of a pile of books next to Mulder was a copy of *A History of Psychology*'s first edition! I confirmed my sighting by freezing the tape in my VCR. I had achieved a very small two seconds of fame.

I hope that adopters and students will think this new edition of *A History of Psychology* an improvement on its predecessors, as I do, and that it will continue to meet with success.

If you have comments, good or bad, or errors to bring to my attention, I may be reached at the Internet address listed below. Every author wishes to touch his or her readers, and reactions, even if unfavorable, are therefore welcome.

Thomas Hardy Leahey
Richmond, Virginia
tleahey@vcu.edu

PART I

BACKGROUND TO PSYCHOLOGY

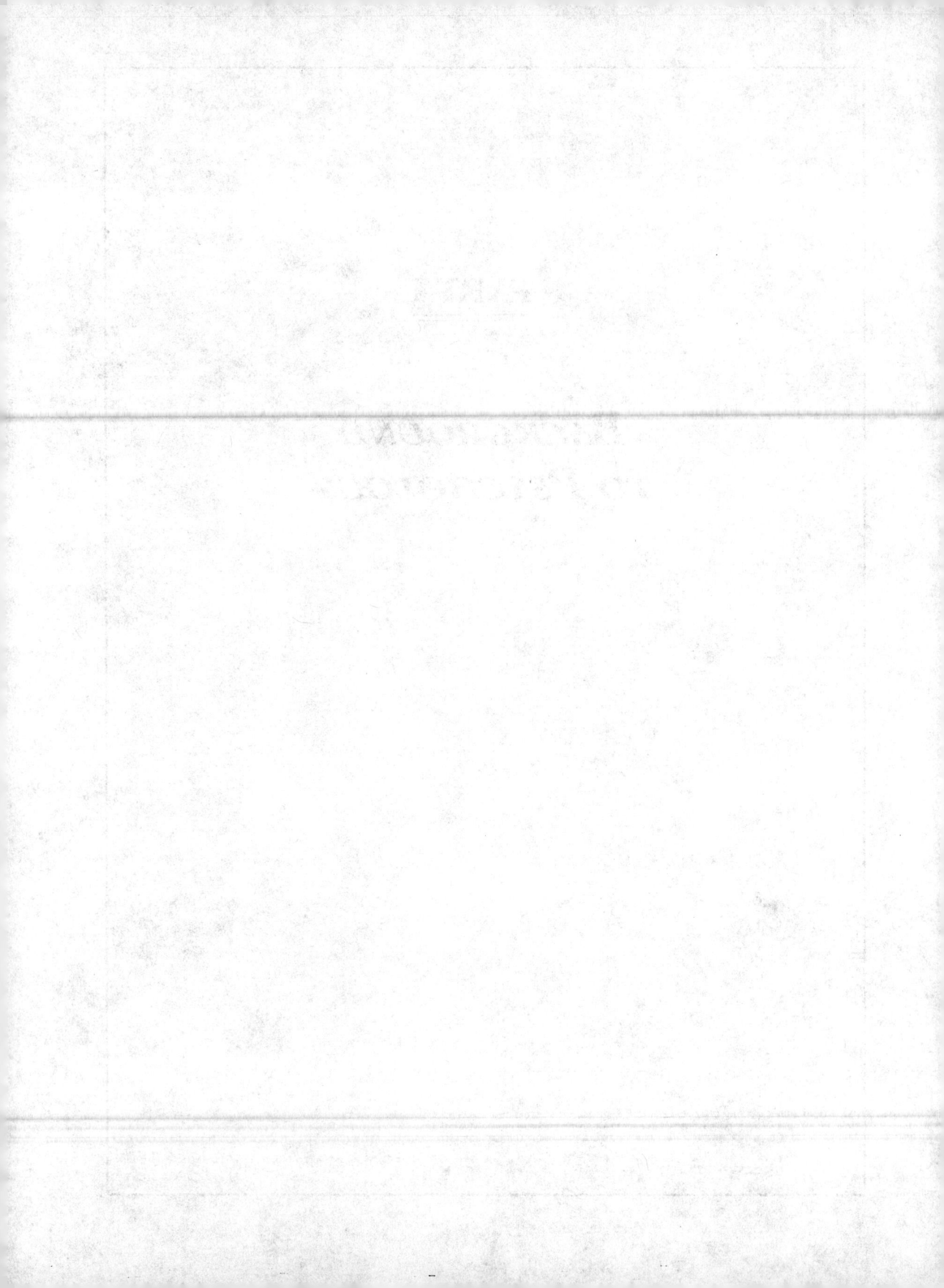

1 *Psychology, History, and Science*

Wilhelm Wundt, the founder of scientific psychology, in his laboratory. Wundt and others based their work on experimentation and close links to the physiology of the nervous system. They could only dream of the Decade of the Brain, when technological advances made the study of mind/brain an achievable reality.

INTRODUCTION

Plato observed that philosophy begins in wonder. Science also begins in wonder—wonder at the inner workings of nature—and all sciences, including psychology, were originally part of philosophy. Over the centuries, the special sciences gradually became independent of philosophy. Psychology was one of the last of the special sciences to separate from the parent, remaining part of philosophy until the nineteenth century. The founders of psychology were philosophers as well as psychologists, and even today psychology retains close ties with philosophy.

For centuries, the history of psychology was the history of much of philosophy, especially the fields of philosophy of mind, epistemology, and ethics. *Psychology* means *psyche–logos,* literally, the study of the soul. Philosophers and religious teachers around the world have wrestled with the nature of the soul, a topic known to philosophers as philosophy of mind. Does the soul exist? What is its nature? What are its functions? How is it related to the body? While psychologists resist the term *soul,* preferring the less religiously loaded term *mind,* they have continued to address these vexing questions. Even psychologists who define psychology not as the study of the mind but as the study of behavior have differing answers to them.

Since the time of the ancient Greeks, philosophers have inquired into how human beings know the world. This enterprise is called *epistemology,* from the Greek words *episteme* (knowledge) and *logos* (discourse). Asking how human beings know the world involves questions about sensation, perception, memory, and thinking—the whole realm of what psychologists call *cognitive psychology.*

Ethics is the third area shared by philosophers (and religious thinkers) with psychology. Although ethics is centrally concerned with how people ought to act, practical ethics depends on a conception of human nature. Are people by nature good? What motives do people have? Which ones are wholesome and which should be repressed? Are people social by nature? Is there a common good life all humans ought to live? Such questions are profoundly psychological and can be informed by scientific research on human nature. Ethical concerns manifest themselves in many areas of psychology. In *scientific psychology,* we find them in the studies of motivation and emotion, social behavior, and sexual behavior. *Applied psychology,* whether in business, industry, or government, or in individual clinical and counseling psychology, is deeply involved in human ethics. People come to psychologists wanting to be happier or more productive, seeking the psychologist's scientifically informed help. The psychologist's knowledge of motivation, emotion, learning, and memory give him or her the tools to change behavior, but the psychologist must not be merely the client's accomplice. A business consulting psychologist may need to tell a client that he or she is the problem in the company, and no ethical psychologist would teach a con artist how to improve his or her self-presentation skills. Science is traditionally value-neutral in pursuing the secrets of nature, but, as Francis Bacon said, "Knowledge is power," and the tools of the applied scientist must be rightly used.

Although the conceptual foundations of psychology are to be found in philosophy, the inspiration for the creation of an independent science of psychology came from biology. The idea that the functions philosophers and others ascribed to the mind in fact depended on underlying processes of the brain had been fitfully entertained since Greek times but had attained the status of a conviction by the mid-nineteenth century. The founders of psychology hoped that, by taking a path to the mind through physiology, what had been speculative philosophy and religion might become naturalistic science. A younger branch of biology—evolution—also shaped the founding of scientific psychology. Especially in Britain and America, philosophers and psychologists began to ask what the mind was good for in the struggle for existence that was evolution by natural selection. Why should we be conscious at all? Were animals conscious? These new questions would disturb, yet animate, psychologists from the beginning. Therefore, we will be concerned not just with the abstract questions of philosophy, but with the growing understanding of the brain and nervous system from the Classical era to the present.

In this decade of the brain, the early psychologists' hopes regarding physiology deserve especial respect. They hoped that psychological processes could be linked to physiological ones; yet, for most of the twentieth century, psychology turned away from the path through physiology. Today, however, armed with twenty-first century techniques for imaging the brain, psychologists have returned to the original psychological quest. At the same time, the new field of evolutionary psychology has returned to asking the ultimate questions about human nature (Wright, 1994).

UNDERSTANDING SCIENCE

Although the definition of psychology's subject matter has always been controversial, from the nineteenth century onward there has been general agreement that psychology is, or at least ought to be, a science. The nature of science—what psychology aspires to be—is a good starting point for understanding it.

Explanation

You are sitting in an airplane about to take off. A child in front of you has a helium balloon floating on a string. A man across the aisle—who turns out to be a physicist—strikes up a conversation with the child by asking which way the balloon will go when the plane accelerates toward its takeoff: toward the back of the plane or toward the front? The physicist claims it will move to the front, but the child says it will move toward the back, and the passengers agree—the steward bets a free drink that the child is right. The plane takes off, and the balloon moves toward the front of the plane. The physicist savors his triumph with a glass of champagne.

Why did the balloon go in such an unexpected direction?

People expect science to answer *why* questions like this one. However, observers of science have had a hard time agreeing on what constitutes scientific explanation.

The modern style of scientific explanation began with Isaac Newton and the Scientific Revolution. Newton defined *scientific enterprise* as the search for a small number of mathematical laws from which one could deduce observed regularities in nature. His domain was the physics of motion, which he proposed to explain in terms of three laws of motion and a law of gravity, and he showed how his laws could precisely account for the movement of the bodies in the solar system. As an example of the Newtonian style of explanation (Cohen, 1980), we will take the law of gravity: Between any two bodies there is a mutually attracting force whose strength is inversely proportional to the square of the distance between them. Newton was criticized by his contemporaries for failing to provide any mechanism to explain how gravity worked; to them, action at a distance between two objects smacked of magic. Newton, however, replied, *"Hypotheses non fingo,"* "I do not feign [propose] hypotheses." Newton refused, in other words, to explain his principle of gravity; for him, it was sufficient to postulate a force from which one could predict the motions of the heavenly bodies.

With Newton began a new philosophy for understanding nature that was later codified in an extreme form by Auguste Comte (1798–1857) and his followers, the *positivists*. Comte believed that because science worked so well, its methodology should be adopted by other forms of human endeavor, and he founded the philosophy of science by attempting to distill the essence of science into a formula others could use.

For Comte and the positivists who followed him, science worked because of the Newtonian style of remaining as close as possible to the observable facts and as far as possible from hypothetical explanations. For positivism, then, the basic job of science is *description* rather than explanation. Scientists were supposed to closely observe nature, looking for regular occurrences and reliable correlations. On the basis of their observations, scientists would propose scientific *laws,* such as Newton's law of gravity. Extending Newton's reluctance to frame hypotheses, positivists understood scientific laws to be mathematical summaries of past observations rather than truths of nature.

From the first function of science, description, ideally summarized as laws, came the second function, *prediction.* Using Newton's law of gravity and his three laws of motion, scientists could predict future events, such as eclipses and the return of comets. Finally, prediction from laws made *control* of nature possible. Using Newton's laws, engineers could calculate the thrust required to throw satellites into precise orbits around the earth and send probes to the distant planets. Knowledge, as Francis Bacon said, is power, and control was the ultimate rationale for science in the positivist's philosophy. Comte looked forward to the scientific rule of society, and the desire to apply scientific psychological expertise to Comte's project played an important role in shaping twentieth-century psychology.

Description, prediction, and control were the only three functions assigned to science by the first positivists. They regarded the human desire for explanations—answers to *why* questions—as a dangerous temptation to indulge in metaphysical and even theological speculation. Science worked, they said, by austerely eschewing hypotheses and explanations and sticking, as so many fictional detectives say, to the facts. However, in 1948, the contemporary era of philosophical understanding of explanation began with the publication of "Studies in the Logic of Explanation" by two logical positivists, Carl Hempel and Paul Oppenheim. Their "epoch-making" (Salmon, 1989) paper showed a way of incorporating an explanatory function for science within the positivist framework, and, despite its age and defects, the Hempel–Oppenheim model of explanation remains the starting point for all subsequent studies of explanation in science.

Hempel and Oppenheim proposed that scientific explanations could be regarded as logical arguments in which the event to be explained, the *explanandum,* could be deduced from the *explanans,* relevant scientific laws and the observed initial conditions. So a physicist would explain a solar eclipse by showing that, given the relative position of sun, moon, and earth sometime before the eclipse, one could use Newton's laws of motion and gravity to deductively predict their arrival into an eclipse-producing alignment. Since Hempel and Oppenheim said that explanations are deductions from scientific laws, their scheme is called the *deductive-nomological* (from the Greek *nomos,* law) model of explanation. It is also called the *covering-law* model of explanation, since an explanation shows how an event is subsumed, or covered, under some set of scientific laws.

Certain features of the Hempel–Oppenheim model should be noted. First, it makes explicit an anciently understood and universally acknowledged feature of explanation that I will call the Iron Law of Explanation: *The explanandum may not be contained explicitly or implicitly in the explanans.* Violation of this rule renders an explanation null and void on grounds of circularity. An example borrowed from the French playwright Molière may be used to illustrate a circular explanation. Imagine asking "Why does Somitol make me sleepy?" and receiving the reply "Because it possesses the soporific power!" At first glance, this appears to be an explanation of one thing (sleepiness) in terms of another (soporific power), and indeed, stated forcefully in an advertisement, it might be able to pass itself off as one. However, when we learn that "soporific" means "sleep-inducing," we see that the proffered explanation is empty because it says, in effect, Somitol makes you sleepy because it makes you sleepy. The explanandum, causing sleep, was implicitly contained in the explanans, so the explanation was circular.

Although the Iron Law of Explanation may seem straightforward, following it is not easy. It is tempting to label a phenomenon—especially with a fancy-sounding name like "soporific power"—and then think one has gained an explanation. Ancient doctors, having observed the sleep-inducing properties of various substances, may have inferred the presence of a soporific power capable of putting people to sleep. This may be a first step toward understanding the pharmacology of sleep, but it is not an explanation. Much of the positivists' animus toward explanation derived from the historical fact that people often fooled themselves into accepting explanations of just this sort, inferring powers—and demons and angels and gods—from patterns of events that were then thought to have been explained. By rigorously separating explanandum and explanans, the Hempel–Oppenheim model of explanation makes the Iron Law clearer and perhaps easier to follow.

A more controversial feature of the deductive-nomological model is its assimilation of explanation to prediction. In the Hempel and Oppenheim view, explanation of an event consists in showing that it could have been predicted. Thus, an astronomer *predicts* an eclipse in the year 2010 but *explains* one in 1010. In each case, the procedure is the same—applying the laws of motion to the state of the sun, moon, and earth, and demonstrating the inevitability of the eclipse. However, the thesis that explanation and prediction are symmetrical runs into important problems. Consider, for example, that one could deduce the occurrence of an eclipse from the laws of motion applied to the positions of sun, moon, and earth a month after the eclipse as well as from the conditions a month before. Or, consider a flagpole and its shadow. If one knows the height of the flagpole and the position of the sun, one can deduce and so predict the length of the shadow from the laws governing light and the rules of geometry, and it seems reasonable to say that we have thereby explained the length of the shadow. By the same token, if we know the length of the shadow, we can deduce and so predict the height of the flagpole, but surely the length of the shadow does not explain the height of the flagpole. Drops in barometric pressure predict storms but do not cause them.

A final important feature of the Hempel and Oppenheim model of explanation is that it views explanations as logical arguments: The scientist deduces (and so predicts) an event from a set of premises. Because scientific laws are regarded by positivists simply as human inventions—summaries of past observations—they are not thought to govern nature and so do not cause anything to happen. Strictly speaking, for the positivist, Newton's laws of motion and gravity do not cause or bring about eclipses; they merely allow us to deduce their future occurrence.

The Hempel–Oppenheim approach to scientific explanation, and its descendants, carefully avoid questions about the real causal structure of nature, preferring to focus instead on how we can predict and control nature. Usable knowledge need not pretend to be profound or true. Although how aspirin works is only now being understood, physicians have long prescribed it to relieve pain, swelling, and fevers. With Newton, who refused to worry about why his laws of motion were true, positivists demand of scientific explanations only that they work, not that they reveal why they work. Discomfited by the shortcomings of the positivist approach, some philosophers want science to probe deeper, telling us not merely how nature works as it does, but why it works as it does.

The main rival to the positivist approach to explanation is the *causal* approach (e.g., Salmon, 1984). Its starting point is the various failures of the Hempel–Oppenheim model, especially the differences between explanation and prediction previously listed. From the causal perspective, the key shortcoming of any epistemic treatment of understanding is viewing explanation as an argument deducing a conclusion logically from premises (Railton, 1989). The reason the deduction of an eclipse from the conditions holding afterward is not an explanation is that causes cannot follow effects, and so a pattern in the solar system can only explain what comes later, not what came before. Similarly, although we can deduce the height of a flagpole from the length of its shadow, shadows cannot cause anything, and so they should not be cited in explanations; in contrast, objects blocking rays from the sun causally cast shadows. Finally, although we would never predict and expect a rare event from the laws of quantum physics, surely quantum physics can explain the causes of the rare event after it has occurred. The mere existence of a predictive regularity is not the same as a law of nature, no matter how reliable and useful the regularity may be. The generalization "When the barometer drops, a storm will occur" states a useful correlation, not a causal law of nature.

More importantly for the explanation of human behavior, we intuitively accept explanations that cite no laws at all. When in the last chapter of a murder mystery the detective unravels the crime, explaining who did it, how, and why, he or she will not invoke laws of nature. Instead, he or she will show how a series of particular, unique events led, one after the other, to the commission of murder. We feel satisfied to learn that Lord Poobah was murdered by his son to pay his gambling debts, but there is no law of nature saying "All (or even most) sons with gambling debts will kill their fathers." Much explanation in everyday life and in history is of this type, connecting events in a causal sequence without the mention of laws. Even if one assumes there are laws of history, we do not know what they are, but we can nevertheless explain what happens in history. Not all explanations, then, fit the covering-law model.

From the causal perspective, the positivists' fear of falling into metaphysics and their consequent unwillingness ever to stray beyond the facts have led them to miss the point of science and to ignore important intuitions about the nature of explanation. Instead of shunning it, the causalist embraces metaphysics, arguing that the goal of science is to penetrate the causal structure of reality and discover—not just invent—the laws of nature. Science is successful, they say, because it is more or less right about how nature works, and it gains predictive power and control from being true, not from being logically organized. Science protects itself from the positivists' bugaboo—superstition—by rigorously testing every hypothesis and challenging every theory.

Nevertheless, the causal view has weaknesses that critics are quick to point out (Kitcher, 1989). How, they ask, can we ever be certain we have grasped the causal structure of the world when it lies, everyone concedes, beyond the reach of observation?

Because we cannot directly verify our hunches about real causes, they are a metaphysical luxury that need not be indulged, no matter how tempting. More serious is explicating the notion of cause itself. The causalists appeal to intuitions about causation, but they have, by their own admission (Salmon, 1989), provided no theory about what causes are, how they work, and how we may legitimately infer them from evidence. Absent such a general treatment of a difficult concept, critics say, the causal view of explanation remains psychologically appealing but not philosophically compelling. The debate between the causal and epistemic accounts of scientific explanation is not over.

There is a third, *pragmatic,* perspective on explanations that sometimes seems to be a rival to the first two but is emerging as an important adjunct to them. Pragmatists begin from the observation that explanations are answers to *why* questions asked in a specific context by a specific questioner. The nature of an acceptable answer will therefore be conditioned by social and personal factors as well as logical and scientific ones. For example, the question "Why is the sky blue?" will have a range of acceptable answers, depending on the context in which it is asked, the social relationship of the questioner and explainer, and the prior level of understanding of both. A small child will be happy with the explanation "Because it's the prettiest color for a sky." An older child asking his or her parent might be told something general about the bending of light, with perhaps a reference to prisms. The same child in a science class might be given a more detailed explanation involving frequencies of light and how they are refracted through the atmosphere. In college, students in a physics class would learn the precise mathematics of refraction involved. With the exception of the first, none of these explanations is wrong—what makes them different is the context in which the question is asked, the expectations of the questioner, and a judgment by the explainer as to what an appropriate explanation would be.

What is true about this example is true about the history of science as well. As scientific understanding of a problem advances, explanations of it change too. The understanding of AIDS moved from identifying the syndrome, to figuring out it was a sexually transmitted disease, to discovering it was virally transmitted and by what virus, to today's detailed explanation of how the HIV retrovirus inhabits and subverts human T-4 cells. What counts as an explanation varies with historical, social, and personal context, and any general theory of explanation must accommodate this fact.

We may now bring together the three approaches to explanation by returning to the problem of the wrong-way balloon (Salmon, 1989). There are both causal and positivist explanations of the balloon's wrong-way motion. The causal explanation describes the balloon moving to the front of the plane as resulting from the disturbed movement of air in the cabin. As the plane takes off, it moves relative to the molecules of air in the cabin. As the rear wall collides with them, they are pitched forward, generating a pressure gradient to the front that carries the balloon with it. This causal explanation cites no laws, referring instead to the real physical interaction of air molecules and the walls of the plane. The positivist explanation subsumes the balloon's forward movement under a general law of nature in relativity theory. According to relativity, acceleration has the same effects as gravity. In normal earth atmosphere, helium balloons rise away from the center of gravity. Therefore, under acceleration (as in our plane), a helium balloon will move away from the base of acceleration. Finally, the explanations our victorious physicist would give to his fellow passengers would pragmatically vary with the questioner; the child, the steward, a college student, and a philosopher would be given different explanations.

So there is some hope that the various perspectives on explanation we have surveyed may be less contrary to one another than is usually supposed, because they focus on different aspects of explanation (Salmon, 1989). The causal model is a bottom-up approach, focusing on specific events and their specific mechanical causes. The epistemic model is a top-down approach, taking the broadest view of science as dedicated to finding the most general and most simple unified picture of nature possible. Finally, the pragmatic model focuses on explanations in context, attempting to explicate how specific questions are given appropriate answers.

Realism

Although there may be some hope for a rapprochement between the epistemic and causal models of explanation, there remains an important and perhaps unresolvable dispute between them concerning the status of reference in science to unobserved entities. The positivist movement began by rejecting as metaphysical foolishness the inferring of causes and entities lying behind our observations of nature. In contrast, the advocates of the causal view accept the metaphysical challenge of laying bare the hidden structures of nature and therefore accept scientists' inferences to nonobserved entities and processes that cause the events we see.

The dispute may be historically illustrated by the late nineteenth-century debate between atomists and antiatomists. Since the late eighteenth century, widespread acceptance had been gained by the theory that various observable phenomena such as the behavior of gases and the regularities governing the combination of chemical elements could best be explained by supposing that objects were composed of infinitesimally small particles called atoms. Yet, how to interpret the concept of atoms remained unclear. In one camp were the positivists, led in this battle by the distinguished physicist Ernst Mach (1838–1916), who argued that because atoms could not be seen, belief in their existence was faith, not science; he said atoms should be regarded at best as hypothetical fictions whose postulation made sense of data but whose existence could not be confirmed. The atomic camp was led by Russian chemist Dmitri Mendeleev (1834–1907), who believed atoms were real things whose properties and interactions explained the regularities of the periodic table he had invented.

Mendeleev's view is a *realist* view of inferred entities and processes: Behind observations lies a realm of unseen but real things about which science theorizes; observations are regarded as evidence for the underlying causal structure of the universe. Mach's positivist view is an *antirealist* view of science, regarding observations themselves as the only things science need explain. Antirealists come in agnostic and atheistic brands (Newton-Smith, 1981; Salmon, 1989). The atheists are *instrumentalists* who regard all inferred entities as false; the agnostics are *constructive empiricists* (van Frassen, 1980) who say we simply cannot tell whether our inferences are correct or not.

At stake is the possibility of attaining truth in science. According to van Frassen (1980), realists say that "science aims to give us, in its theories, a literally true story of what the world is like; and acceptance of a scientific theory involves the belief that it is true." On the other hand, according to antirealists, "science aims to give us theories which are empirically adequate [the laws cover the phenomena]; and the acceptance of a theory involves as belief only that it is empirically adequate."

Disagreement over realism lies at the heart of the positivist versus causalist dispute about explanation, and is the most difficult issue to resolve not only in philosophy of science but in science itself. Most people are probably realists at heart, but quantum physics threatens to establish antirealism as a correct account not only of the world as we observe it, but also of the universe, paradoxical as that sounds. How can the universe be really unreal? It is well known that, according to quantum physics, the exact position and momentum of a subatomic particle cannot be determined. The mainstream view in physics is that particles *do not possess* actual locations and momenta, so that, in accordance with the epistemic model of explanation, physical theories are descriptions of our measurements and can be nothing more. As Niels Bohr wrote, "*There is no quantum world.* There is only an abstract quantum description" (Herbert, 1985, p. 17).

On the other hand, one might follow the realist Einstein and assert that particles have genuine positions and momenta, and that our inability to determine both at the same time is a failure of human measurement, not a property of nature. As Einstein said, "God does not play dice with the universe." On this view, contemporary quantum theory is fatally flawed and must and will be replaced by a theory that uncovers the deeper hidden variables lying behind the abstract quantum description. A review of the relevant evidence is out of place here, but recent findings support Bohr rather than Einstein, suggesting that if there is a reality behind observation it is a very strange one, with every event in the universe potentially instantaneously connected to every other event (Herbert, 1985). The debate between realists and antirealists continues (Kitcher and Salmon, 1989).

Theories

Science explains the world with theories, whether they are regarded as true (the causalist–realist view) or merely useful (the positivist–antirealist view). However, the study of the nature of scientific theories is the least settled area of philosophy of science today (Savage, 1990). Savage (1990) identifies three broad approaches to theories, with many variations within: (1) the *syntactic view,* holding that theories are axiomatized collections of sentences; (2) the *semantic view,* holding that theories are counterfactual models of the world; and (3) a view we will call *naturalism,* holding that theories are amorphous collections of ideas, values, practices, and exemplars. From this mélange, I have chosen to discuss four issues of particular relevance to psychology. First, I will discuss the grandaddy of syntactic views, the Received View on Theories, which has greatly influenced psychology. Second, I will briefly consider the semantic view of theories as models, which will take us to the final topic of this section—theory testing. The naturalistic viewpoint will be taken up in the following section on rationality.

The Syntactic Approach to Theories: Logical Positivism

At the end of the nineteenth century, the positivism of Comte and Mach was melded with advances in logic and mathematics to produce the movement called *logical positivism,* which dominated the philosophy of science for several decades. So great was its influence that it became known as the Received View on Theories (Suppe, 1977). The atomists had won the debate over the existence of atoms. The heirs to Comte and Mach, the logical positivists, therefore had to concede that, despite philosophical scruples, science could incorporate unseen, hypothetical concepts into its theories, and they attempted to show how it could be done without lapsing into the dangerous practices of metaphysics. Doing so, they set out a recipe for science that has had great influence.

Logical positivists divided the language of science into three sets of terms: *observation terms, theoretical terms,* and *mathematical terms.* Unsurprisingly, the logical positivists gave absolute priority to observation terms. The fundamental task of science remained description; observation terms referred to directly observable properties of nature and were taken to be unproblematically true. The bedrock of science was *protocol sentences*—descriptions of nature that contained only observation terms. Putative generalizations from the data—candidate laws of nature—were *axioms* that contained only theoretical terms connected by logico-mathematical terms.

The use of theoretical terms such as "atom" or "magnetic field" raised the issue of realism and, for logical positivists, the dangerous lure of metaphysical inference. They preserved the antirealism of earlier positivism by denying that theoretical terms referred to anything at all. Instead, theoretical terms were said to be given meaning and epistemological significance via *explicit,* or, more familiarly, *operational definitions.* Operational definitions were the third sort of sentences recognized by the logical positivists—mixed sentences containing a theoretical term and an observation term to which it was linked. The resulting picture of science resembles a layer cake. On the bottom, representing the only reality for positivists, were observation terms; on top were purely hypothetical theoretical terms organized into axioms; in between were sandwiched the operational definitions connecting theory and data:

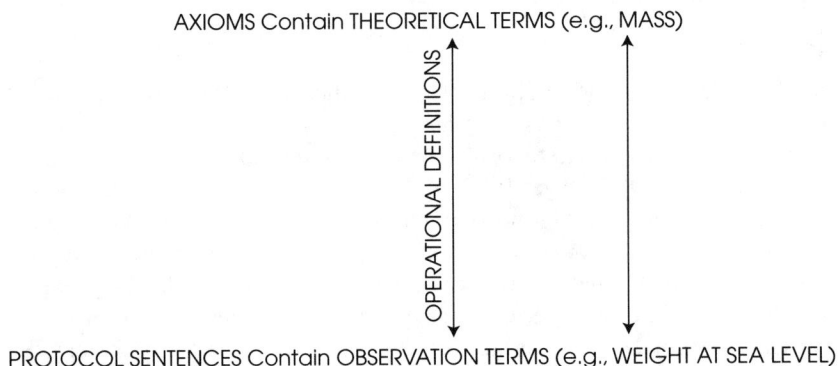

AXIOMS Contain THEORETICAL TERMS (e.g., MASS)

OPERATIONAL DEFINITIONS

PROTOCOL SENTENCES Contain OBSERVATION TERMS (e.g., WEIGHT AT SEA LEVEL)

Let us take an example from physics to clarify the Received View. An important axiom in classical physics is $F = M \times A$, force equals mass times acceleration. Force, mass, and acceleration are theoretical terms. We do not observe them directly, but we must define them in terms of something we do observe—often, by some procedure—which is why operational definitions are so called. For example, mass is defined as weight of an object at sea level. Thus, in the Received View, theories are sentences (axioms) whose terms are explicitly defined by reference to observation terms. Note that, for the Received View, as for any antirealist philosophy of science, observations do not provide *evidence for* the existence and properties of inferred entities, but they *define* those entities by fiat.

The Received View leads naturally to the Hempel and Oppenheim model of explanation. The laws of nature are theoretical sentences from which we logically deduce phenomena, or, more precisely, observation sentences. As we shall see, psychology from 1930 to the 1960s was greatly influenced by the rigorous formal ideals of logical positivism, and it remains influenced to the present by the concept of operational definition.

The Received View on Theories runs into a number of difficulties, including those besetting its deductive nomological account of explanation. The deepest difficulty with the Received View is its absolute separation of theory and data. Positivists always took it for granted that science was based on observation and that observation was entirely independent of theory. However, the positivist conception of perception was simplistic. At the very least, it's impossible to observe everything all the time; one must have some prior notion of what to observe in a given situation, some idea of which events are important and which are irrelevant, so that the significance of an event is determined by a theory. Moreover, psychologists have demonstrated how perception is influenced by people's expectations and values, so we know perception is never the immaculate process the positivists thought it was. Indeed, we may turn the positivist view on its head and regard the guiding of observation by theory as a virtue instead of as a sin. The point may be illustrated by a passage from the Sherlock Holmes story "Silver Blaze." We see the theoretically guided master detective triumph over the positivist policeman:

> Holmes then [descended] into the hollow, . . . [and] stretching himself upon his face and leaning his chin upon his hands he made a careful study of the trampled mud in front of him.
>   "Halloa!" said he, suddenly, "what's this?" It was a wax vesta [a sort of match], half burned, which was so coated with mud that it looked at first like a little chip of wood.
>   "I cannot think how I came to overlook it," said the Inspector, with an expression of annoyance.
>   "It was invisible, buried in the mud. I only saw it because I was looking for it."
>   "What! You expected to find it?"
>   "I thought it not unlikely."

Here we see the importance of having a theory that tells investigators for what to look. Holmes found the match because he had formed a theory of the crime that led him to expect it, while the police—who had no theory—failed to find the match despite meticulous searching. To the fact-gatherer, all facts are equally meaningless and meaningful. To the theoretically guided researcher, each fact assumes its proper place in an overall framework.

The Semantic Approach to Theories

For a rival approach to the Received View, we may turn to the semantic approach to theories (e.g., Suppe, 1989). The semantic approach builds on some highly technical developments in modern logic, but, for our purposes, the semantic approach is important for the central role it assigns to models in science, and the resulting indirect relationship between scientific theories and the world they purport to explain. The semantic approach regards theories as abstract mathematical structures that apply not to the world as it is but to an idealized world purged of irrelevant considerations.

From a theory, the scientist constructs a *model* of reality, a highly idealized, partial simulation of the world. It describes what the world would be like if the theory behind it were true and if the variables found in it were the only ones involved in behavior. The physical theory of particle mechanics, for example, describes a block sliding down an inclined plane as a system of three frictionless, dimensionless, point-masses—one each for the block, the plane, and the earth. In the real world, these bodies are extended in space and there is friction between block and plane; in the model, such irrelevant or complicating factors disappear. Thus, the model is a simplified, idealized version of reality, which is all a theory can cope with. It is important to realize how limited a scientific theory is. It purports to explain only some phenomena, and only some aspects of these. A scientific theory is not about the real world as we experience it, but about abstract, idealized models. The real world, unlike the model, is much too complex to be explained by a theory. To take a psychological example, a theory of paired associate learning describes an ideal learner as untroubled by neurosis or motivational factors—which of course are determinants of the memory-performance of actual subjects.

These models give science enormous power. First, they free the scientist from the impossible task of describing all of reality, which, because of its infinite complexity, will never conform to theory. Models allow the scientist to imagine how the world is and to try out and refine theories before coping with the world. Many of the greatest experiments in physics were thought-experiments never carried out in actuality. Einstein built his theory of relativity on many such experiments.

Second, these idealized theories and models enable the scientist to make powerful and wide-ranging explanations of observed phenomena. The model embodies certain *ideals of natural order,* descriptions of an idealized world (Toulmin, 1961). These descriptions, although not observed, provide the basis for explaining that which is observed.

Newton's theory, for example, provides this ideal of natural order: all natural motion of objects through space is in a straight line that continues forever. Such motion cannot be observed. Motion that does not conform to this ideal is explained as being a result of other factors. For example, a ball rolling across grass quickly comes to rest, but we say the motion would have gone on forever except for friction. The scientist does not *explain* the ideal of natural order, but rather uses it (and other factors) to explain phenomena that do not conform to the ideal, such as the stopped ball. Scientific explanation is always indirect and metaphorical. The scientist can only describe what the world would be like if a theory were true, and then explain why the world is not really like that.

Rationality

The ancient Greeks defined the human being as the rational animal, but since the time of Freud this definition has seemed increasingly suspect. Science, however, is one institution that seemed to meet the Greek ideal, its success apparently proclaiming it the paragon of rationality. The issue of the rationality of science is important because since rationality, like morality, is a *normative* concept. Being moral and rational is something people ought to be, and, over the years, philosophers have tried to establish standards of rationality to which people can be held accountable in the same way they are held accountable for moral or immoral conduct. The potential danger in abandoning standards of rationality is the same as in abandoning standards of morality: If either goes, how are we to be saved from anarchy, tyranny, and ignorance? How are we to know right from wrong and good from bad? If *science* is not rational, is anything?

Traditional philosophies of science, such as positivism and logical positivism, accepted the rationality of science and took it upon themselves to spell out the rational methodology of science in formal, logical detail. Moreover, the positivists' picture of science was *content-free:* They assumed that there is a single, logical structure to science whatever the historical period and whatever the science. Yet, the more we examine the history of science, the less it seems to be a purely rational affair following an abstract, changeless, content-free methodology. Scientists are human beings, and, despite rigorous training, their perceptual and reasoning skills are subject to the same constraints and errors as other people's. Scientists are trained in and work within a community of scientists who share historically changing goals, values, and standards. In science, as in other walks of life, what seems eminently rational to one person seems like foolishness to another.

These general considerations suggest that perhaps logical positivism was deeply mistaken to look for a formally logical account of science. Since the early 1960s, a movement in metascience has been afoot that challenges—even denies—the assumption that science is defined by a constitutive rationality that sets it apart from other forms of human activity. Because it regards science as an institution to be examined empirically rather than dictated to philosophically, this new movement is called the *naturalistic approach* to science, and it incorporates philosophers, historians, sociologists, and psychologists of science. There are many ways of conducting a naturalistic approach to science, and in this section I will discuss three: (1) the *Weltanschauung theorists,* led by Thomas S. Kuhn, who have exerted direct influence on psychology in the past three decades; (2) the theorists who regard science as a matter of intellectual *evolution* along Darwinian lines; and (3) the content-oriented framework of competing scientific *themata.* Then we will take up rationalist responses to the naturalist challenge.

The Naturalistic Approach to Theories: Kuhn and Paradigms

The most dramatic challenge to the rational model of science is mounted by metascientists who regard science as a socially constituted *form of life,* as Ludwig Wittgenstein defined it (see Chapter 13). A human culture constitutes a form of life, and it shapes our perception and behavior in ways of which we are often unaware. We absorb values, practices, and ideals with little or no explicit teaching, and we take them for granted as much as we do the air we breathe. When anthropologists study a culture, they try to penetrate and describe the hidden worldview, or *Weltanschauung,* shared by its members, and to show how it works and how it changes over time. Some naturalistic students of science propose to take an anthropologist's and historian's approach to science and capture the worldviews—and revolutions in worldview—of science.

The fullest expression of the *Weltanschauung* approach to science was given by historian Thomas Kuhn in his *Structure of Scientific Revolutions* (1970). Kuhn describes the history of science as a repeating cycle of stages and provides an account of how scientific practice is shaped by deep assumptions of a worldview of which working scientists may be only dimly aware. One of Kuhn's innovations was to stress the social nature of science. Science is practiced by communities of scientists, not by isolated men and women. To understand working science, then, we must understand the scientific community and its shared norms, which together constitute what Kuhn calls *normal science.*

For scientific research to be progressive, the scientific community in a particular research area must agree on certain basic issues. Its members must agree on the goals of their science, on the basic characteristics of the real world relevant to their subject, on what counts as a valid explanation of phenomena, and on permissible research methods and mathematical techniques. Kuhn calls this agreed-on worldview a *paradigm*. Given agreement on these issues, scientists can proceed to analyze nature from a collective, unified standpoint; without such agreement, each researcher would have his or her own standpoint, and there would be much fruitless discussion at cross-purposes. The traditional architectural metaphor for science may be modified to clarify this point. A building must be constructed according to a plan and on a firm foundation. Until the blueprints and the foundation have been decided on, there can be no construction, no progress. Only when the plans are agreed on can construction begin.

Paradigms, by settling unanswerable metaphysical questions, free the researcher to get on with the puzzle-solving work of science. Just as one can solve a jigsaw puzzle because one knows what the picture looks like, scientists know from the paradigm approximately what nature is like; thus, all that remains is to work out the details.

During periods of normal science, experiments do not test the paradigm but are attempts to solve puzzles posed by the paradigm. If a scientist fails to solve a puzzle, the failure is the scientist's, not the paradigm's. Consider what happens in your own laboratory courses. You follow all the instructions, but the "correct" results do not always occur. When you inform your instructors, they do not tear their hair and cry, "All our theories are wrong!" On the contrary, they assume that you must have erred at some point, and they give you a poor grade. This same thing occurs to scientists in normal science. The scientific community recognizes certain puzzles as ripe for solution, and—except in extraordinary circumstances—when a scientist tackles one of these problems, it is the scientist and his or her theories that are on trial, not the unstated paradigm.

Within normal science, research is progressive, as puzzle after puzzle is solved. However, Kuhn claims that normal science is just one phase of scientific development. A paradigm is a specific historical achievement in which one or a few scientists establish a new scientific style based on an outstanding success in understanding nature. Paradigms also break down and get replaced when they cease to work well in guiding the research of a community. A science's first paradigm arises out of a prescientific phase in that science's history, and paradigms are periodically replaced during scientific revolutions.

Scientific change, according to Kuhn, is not always gradual and continuous. There are times when a science undergoes radical change in a short period of time—change so radical that those who were great individuals beforehand often become forgotten antiques, and concepts and issues that previously occupied scientists' minds simply disappear. Such change seems to constitute revolution rather than evolution and depends on principles beyond those of variation, selection, and retention. Kuhn (1959) proposes that the replacement of the ancient earth-centered cosmology of Ptolemy by the sun-centered cosmology of Copernicus constituted such a revolution, and some observers think psychology has had its own revolutions.

The picture of science drawn by Kuhn and his followers has proven controversial. Kuhn has helped direct scholars' attention to the actual history of science, rather than to idealized versions of it. However, studies of scientific history have rendered mixed judgments on the adequacy of Kuhn's model of scientific change, especially regarding the existence of revolutions (Gutting, 1980). Some historians find little evidence that any science has ever changed in a revolutionary manner (Laudan, 1980), and Kuhn himself has rather backed off from his revolutionary claims (Kuhn, 1977). On the other hand, one of the most distinguished living historians of science, I. Bernard Cohen (1985), elaborates on Kuhn's theme through close case studies of successful, unsuccessful, real, and purported revolutions in science, and he regrets that Kuhn has retracted so much. The adequacy of Kuhn's specific historical model is unresolved, although most would concede that he has shown that an understanding of science must incorporate historical, social, and personal influences lying outside scientific methodology.

Within philosophy, *Weltanschauung* approaches have been assaulted for their apparent depiction of science as an irrational enterprise. For example, Kuhn suggests that rival paradigms cannot be rationally compared, making adherence to a paradigm more a matter of faith than of evidence. However, historical and philosophical works have shown that rival viewpoints have been rationally evaluated even during times of deep crisis, using rational criteria such as simplicity, adequacy of the available evidence, and research fruitfulness. Again, Kuhn has backed away from his revolutionary claims, often saying he was misunderstood (Kuhn, 1970, Postscript). But both retractions have made Kuhn's theses much less exciting and rather more conventional. There is not much left of the *Weltanschauung* thesis, except the valuable notion that scientists work in communities to which they are socialized during training, and that the values they learn shape their thinking and research.

Naturalistic Approaches to Theories: Evolutionary Epistemology

Another naturalistic account of science applies Darwin's theory of evolution to the history of science (e.g., Toulmin, 1972). Species evolve over time by the process of natural selection. Individuals possessing variant traits are produced by mutation and genetic recombination. Successful variants grow up and reproduce themselves, and unsuccessful variants die out. Given enough time, natural selection can completely alter the body and behavior of a species into something altogether new. Indeed, human beings are descended from the first single-celled animals. Although the rate of evolution may vary, there are no revolutions in the history of nature.

Perhaps sciences evolve by natural selection among ideas. Individual scientists seeking to improve their science propose variant concepts that they hope will be accepted by the scientific community. The community debates new ideas and subjects them to empirical tests. Concepts that win acceptance are selected and passed to the next generation of scientists through textbooks and instruction; ideas that are not accepted become extinct. Over time, the stock of concepts accepted by a scientific community may be completely changed by this process of natural scientific selection. However, there are no scientific revolutions in the evolutionary model. There may be periods of relatively rapid conceptual evolution, but such periods are not revolutions because the usual processes of variation, selection, and retention account for both fast and slow evolution.

Naturalistic Approaches to Theories: Themata

One possible problem with both Kuhn's and evolutionists' analyses of science is that they are not naturalistic enough. Each of them respects the history of science more than does his or her methodological adversaries, but each nevertheless seems to extract a methodological story from his or her studies. A truly naturalistic alternative might stop looking for underlying processes and, instead, look at the substantive commitments that guide scientific research. Gerald Holton (1973, 1978, 1984) has done this with his analysis of scientific *themata*. Themata are metatheoretical, even metaphysical, commitments that motivate and guide scientists' work and often come in pairs. In physics, for example, one ancient opposing pair of themata is the belief that the universe can be analyzed into a small number of discrete parts versus the belief that there are no ultimate parts, that the universe is a continuum. Each theme can be traced back at least to ancient Greece, and neither is yet triumphant (Herbert, 1985).

The concept of themata is content-based. In Holton's scheme, there is no constant underlying scientific process beyond physicist Percy Bridgman's formulation: "The scientific method is doing one's damnedest, no holds barred" (Holton, 1984, p. 1232). Rather, science is shaped by the beliefs scientists hold about the nature of the world. Sometimes, opposing themata come into sharp conflict, and one may become overwhelmingly dominant for a time, giving a picture of stable normal science punctuated by revolutions. On the other hand, themata endure; so there are no real revolutions, ensuring that the science of today is entirely continuous with the science of yesterday and even of the distant past. As to rationality, science has no special method. People are rational; they try to come to a reasonable understanding of each other—their political and personal arrangements, their art, and so on. Scientific reason is simply human reason applied to nature, and, within science, reason is guided by historical themata that commit scientists to certain ways of work.

Science and Pseudoscience: What Is the Difference?

Perhaps the most determined and influential of the new rationalists are rooted in philosophy of science that began in the same time and place as logical positivism. Since its beginning, this philosophy has been centrally concerned—even obsessed—with demonstrating the rationality of science and separating science cleanly from superstition and metaphysics, namely the *falsificationism* of Sir Karl Popper (1902–1994), originally of Vienna and later of the London School of Economics.

Popper erected his philosophy of science on the search for a *demarcation criterion* by which to separate true science from false, or pseudo-, science (Popper, 1963). Like the positivists, he believed that science was a preeminently rational affair and that there must exist some firm methodological rule that constitutes scientific rationality. In Vienna, when Popper was a young man, many systems of thought put themselves forward as sciences, including relativity theory and psychoanalysis. Popper wanted to know which claims to take seriously and which to dismiss. He approached the problem by looking at clear-cut cases of science, such as Newtonian physics, and clear-cut cases of pseudoscience, such as astrology, trying to figure out the difference between them. Positivists stressed the *confirmability* of theories as the test of their scientific status. That is, from a theory with properly worked out operational definitions, we can deduce predictions whose confirmation lends credence to the theory. Pseudoscientific or metaphysical theories will not be able to operationally define their terms and so will not be able to derive predictions of events and support their claims. Good theories pile up confirmations; poor ones do not.

Popper saw, however, that things were not so simple. Pseudosciences can claim many confirmations. The astrologer can point to predictions verified—raises awarded, girlfriends won—and can defend failed predictions by employing escape clauses such as neglected influences from minor planets. Nor did confirmability help with the uncertain cases, such as relativity or psychoanalysis; both could claim confirmation of their theories time after time.

In fact, by listening to psychoanalysts and comparing them to Einstein, Popper was led to formulate a demarcation methodology. Popper discovered that no matter what difficulties a case seemed to raise for psychoanalysis, a good analyst, like a good astrologer, could always reinterpret it to fit analytic theory. At the same time, shortly after World War I, an expedition was mounted to test one of relativity's predictions—that light bends in the presence of a gravitational field. From photographs of stars near the edge of the sun, taken during a total eclipse, astronomers found that light rays were bent as Einstein's theory required. Although at first glance this successful test appeared consistent with the logical positivists' confirmation requirement, Popper found in it a decisive difference between relativity and psychoanalysis: Both could claim confirmation of their theory, but only relativity risked *falsification*. The important thing about Einstein's prediction was not that it might prove true, but that it might prove false. There were some events that relativity, admittedly, could not explain. In contrast, psychoanalysis—like astrology—could readily explain everything. In other words, according to Popper, scientific rationality consists not in seeking to be proved right but in allowing for the possibility of being proved wrong—in sticking one's neck out and risking being beheaded by a fact.

However, Popper's simple demarcation criterion of falsifiability runs into two difficulties, and acknowledgment of them has guided the philosophies of his followers in their pursuit of a criterion of scientific rationality. First, theories are never defeated by single, decisive experiments; and second, theories compete with each other as well as with nature. Single experiments cannot decide the fate of a theory because every experiment is based on certain methodological assumptions that have nothing to do with the theory itself. Any single experiment may be flawed by choosing the wrong apparatus, sampling the wrong subjects, mishandling the statistical methods, or making some other mistake. In short, the truth of a theory may almost always be defended against falsified data by attacking the validity of those data. Additionally, Popper assumed that science was a two-sided contest between a theory and the world, but possession of a theory is so important that scientists prefer having a poor theory to having none at all. Scientific research is not a two-sided contest between a theory and the world, but a three-sided contest between two rival theories and the world.

Combining these points, the problem for the Popperian philosopher becomes formulating a methodology by which scientists rationally choose one theory's developing *research program* over another (Lakatos, 1970). The criterion developed by Lakatos and, following him, by Larry Laudan (1977) is *problem-solving success*. Lakatos and Laudan regard science as primarily a problem-solving—or, as Kuhn would say, puzzle- and anomaly-solving—enterprise. Rather than a single theory being tested by a single experiment, as Popper originally proposed, research programs constructed around a theory attempt to solve a series of problems over time. The rational scientist should then adopt the program solving the most problems with the fewest ad hoc appeals to methodological escape routes, while fruitfully proposing new problems that it can address.

The main problem with Lakatos's proposal is that it virtually ignores everything that naturalism has established—namely, that science is shaped by historical, social, and personal forces, not by impersonal methodology. For example, Lakatos (1970) claims that the history of science ought primarily to be rational reconstruction. That is, the historian should tell how an achievement ought rationally to have come about, and indicate only in the footnotes how things really did go, criticizing history for its deviation from the path of true reason. To preserve scientific rationality—and, as he seems to think, Western civilization—from "contemporary religious maniacs" (Lakatos, 1971), Lakatos resorts to fairy-tale history, apparently expecting that knowledge of the history of their discipline would turn scientists into lunatics. One of Lakatos's own rational reconstructions, of Niels Bohr's early work on the atom, "is an historical parody that makes one's hair stand on end" (Holton, 1978, p. 106).

Laudan's view has been criticized for its antirealism (Newton-Smith, 1981). If theories are merely conveniences and not potentially true descriptions of the world, it becomes difficult to give a firm definition of a problem and problem solution. Newton-Smith writes, "Unless truth plays a regulative role [in science], we can each select on the basis of our whims our own set of sentences which are statements of problems for us just because we so choose to regard them. We each then erect our own theories for solving these problems. Never mind how the world is, just solve your own problems!" (1981, p. 190). And so we are back to anarchy in science, the very state from which Lakatos and Laudan claimed to save us.

As with the other issues we have canvassed, the issue of whether and how science is rational remains unresolved. The anarchist–naturalist view had its heyday in the freewheeling 1960s; today's naturalists adopt more modest, less romantic poses (see, e.g., the essays collected in Nersessian, 1987). At the same time, rationalists no longer aim to lay down statute law for scientists the way Lakatos did, but they seek a more modest role for normative philosophy of science (e.g., Nersessian, 1987). Some methodologically inclined philosophers hope that developments in statistics—especially concerning Bayes's theorem, which tells how to revise beliefs in hypotheses given evidential findings—may offer a new foundation for rationalism (Savage, 1990).

Reduction and Replacement

What happens when two theories deal with the same phenomena? One possibility is *reduction*. Science explains the world at different levels of explanation; higher levels deal with large objects and forces, lower levels deal with smaller objects and forces. In their attempt to get a unified picture of nature, scientists try to reduce larger theories to more elementary—more basic—theories, showing that the truth of the higher theory is a consequence of the truth of the more basic theory. The reduced theory is still considered valid and useful at its level of explanation. On the other hand, sometimes a theory is simply wrong, and gets *replaced* or eliminated by a superior rival.

The reduction relation may be illustrated by the reduction of the classical gas laws to the kinetic theory of gases and the reduction of Mendelian genetics to molecular genetics. Physicists in the eighteenth century determined that the pressure, volume, and temperature of gases were interrelated by a mathematical equation called the *ideal gas law*: $P = V \times T$. Using this law—a paradigmatic example of a covering law—physicists could describe, predict, control, and explain the behavior of gases in precise and useful ways. One of the early triumphs of the atomic hypothesis was the kinetic theory of gases, which gave a causal explanation of the ideal gas law. The kinetic theory held that gases (like everything else) were made up of billiard-ball-like atoms, whose degree of excitation—movement—was a function of energy, particularly heat. The ideal gas law predicted, for example, that if we heat the air in a balloon it will expand, and if we cool the air it will deflate (placed in liquid nitrogen, it deflates to nothing). The kinetic theory explains why. As we heat air, the particles that compose it move around more, bouncing into the skin of the balloon, pushing it outward in expansion. As we cool air, the atoms slow down, striking the balloon's skin less vigorously, and if they slow down enough, there will be no pressure at all. The kinetic theory shows why the ideal gas law works by postulating an underlying causal mechanism, and so it is said that the ideal gas law is *reduced* to the kinetic theory. In principle, we could do away with the gas law, but we keep it as valid and useful in its range of application. It is still a scientific theory, but it has been unified with a broader conception of the universe.

A similar story may be told about Mendelian genetics. Mendel proposed the existence of a unit of hereditary transmission, the *gene,* which was entirely hypothetical. Mendel's concept provided the basis for population genetics, but no one ever saw a gene or knew what one might look like. However, in the early 1950s, the structure of DNA began to be unraveled, and it emerged that it was the bearer of hereditary traits. As molecular genetics has progressed, we have learned that coding sequences on the DNA model are the real "genes," and they do not always behave in the simple ways that Mendel thought. Nevertheless, Mendelian genetics remains valid for its purposes—population genetics—but, like the ideal gas law, has been reduced to and unified with molecular genetics.

In the case of reduction, the older theory is recognized as still scientific and as usefully valid within its sphere of application; it simply takes a subsidiary place in the grand scheme of science. The fate of a replaced theory, on the other hand, is very different. Often, it turns out that an old theory is simply wrong and cannot be woven into the extending tapestry of scientific theory. In this case, it is abandoned and replaced by a better theory. The Ptolemaic theory of the heavens, which placed the earth at the center of the universe and described the sun, moon, and stars as revolving in complex and unlikely circles around it, was accepted by astronomers for centuries because it gave a usefully precise account of the motions of heavenly objects. Using it, they could describe, predict, and explain events such as eclipses. Despite its descriptive and predictive powers, after a long struggle the Ptolemaic view was shown to be hopelessly wrong, and it was replaced with the Copernican system, which placed the sun at the center with the rest of the solar system revolving around it. Like an old paradigm, the Ptolemaic view died off, eliminated from science.

The question of reduction or replacement is especially important in psychology. By taking the path through physiology, psychologists tried to link psychological processes to physiological processes. But if we have a theory of some psychological process and in fact discover the underlying physiological process, will the psychological theory be reduced or replaced? Some observers believe that psychology is fated to disappear like Ptolemaic astronomy. Others hold that psychology will be reduced to physiology, becoming an outpost of biology, but some optimists among them think that at least some of human psychology can be neither reduced nor replaced by neurophysiology. We shall find that the relation of psychology to physiology has been an uneasy one.

Psychology of Science

The most recent discipline to contribute to the study of science is psychology (Gholson, Shadish, Niemeyer, and Houts, 1989; Tweney, Mynatt, and Doherty, 1981). The field is new, embracing approaches to science from traditional psychology, such as describing the personality of the creative scientist (e.g., Simonton, 1989), to recent psychology, such as applying to science the program evaluation techniques developed for business and government (Shadish, 1989). Without doubt, however, the most active area in the psychology of science is in applying concepts of cognitive psychology to understanding the research and theorizing of scientists (e.g., Giere, 1988; Thagard, 1988; Tweney, 1989).

No overarching perspective has emerged from the cognitive study of science, but the work of Ryan Tweney (e.g., 1989) may be taken as an example. Tweney has experimentally studied scientific reasoning in nonscientists and historically studied case studies of actual science. In the first line of research (e.g., Mynatt, Doherty, and Tweney, 1978), subjects interact with a computer-generated reality, conducting experiments to discover the laws governing motion in their alternate universe. The main object is to find out the degree to which people use positivist confirming and Popperian disconfirming strategies, and which strategy proves more effective. In 1989, Tweney examined the reasoning of the physicist Michael Faraday as he formulated his theory of magnetic fields. Various concepts from cognitive science, including schemas, scripts, heuristics, and production systems are employed to represent how Faraday tested hypotheses and gradually built up the body of knowledge about magnetism and electricity that culminated in his postulation of magnetic fields and the description of their behavior.

The psychology of science represents a naturalistic approach to understanding science, and as such it is open to the charges of relativism and anarchy that have been leveled at Kuhn (Gholson et al., 1989). Philosophers tend to assume that psychology's role is merely to explain deviations from rationality, not rationality itself (Heyes, 1989). Surely, however, the philosophers' view is both simplistic and imperialistic. Rational thought is a psychological process, and it is therefore reasonable to think that it can be empirically studied in a naturalistic fashion without undermining its normative claims (Leahey, 1992). The fruits of psychology of science are yet to be harvested, but we need not worry that science's rationality must thereby be unmasked.

PSYCHOLOGY AND SCIENCE

Psychology without Science

For thousands of years, men and women got along without benefit of scientific psychology. Moreover, even in those parts of the world that have taken up psychological terms such as "libido," "reinforcement," and "feedback," mind and behavior are explained outside the theories proposed by psychologists in the past hundred years. Psychology has flourished without science: People effectively describe, predict, explain, and even control their behavior without knowing any so-called science at all. More than other sciences, therefore, scientific psychology meets existing rivals on the field it hopes to conquer. Two of these rivals deserve special attention. One, *dualism,* is deeply appealing and lies at the heart of religious conceptions of behavior; the other, *folk psychology,* is a powerful theory we use every day to explain our own behavior as well as others'. Each presents a distinct challenge to the possibility of scientific psychology.

Dualism is a belief almost universally held around the world. In addition to the natural material world, religions typically posit a supernatural world populated by nonmaterial beings such as a god or gods, angels, and demons. Human beings, and sometimes animals, are regarded as composed of two substances, a nonmaterial supernatural soul contained within and controlling a material natural body. Dualists explain experience and behavior as the result of interaction between the body and its ruling soul.

As we shall find, dualism has been criticized on many grounds, the most important of which is its incompatibility with science. Although science has been defined by philosophers primarily in terms of its methods, science is also committed to one central dogma, naturalism (Leahey & Leahey, 1983). One pair of Holtonian themata that may be used to describe Western intellectual history is naturalism–supernaturalism. Religions give much of what happens in the world a supernatural explanation: God's will, demonic possession, or the decisions of the soul. The aim of science, in contrast, is to explain every event, no matter how large or how small, as the result of natural causes. Psychology as a science thus must reject dualism: Wherever the dualist sees the operation of the soul, the psychologist must see the operation of natural causes. Beginning with the battle between the "Old [religious] Psychology" and the "New [scientific] Psychology" a century ago, psychology as science has been profoundly at odds with psychology as psyche-logos. So deep and thorough is psychology's commitment to naturalism that its indifference, even hostility, to religion is scarcely noticed, save by a small group of religiously inclined psychologists. To a large degree, the history of scientific psychology is a history of the rejection of dualist conceptions of mind and behavior and their replacement by naturalistic ones.

The other framework for explaining behavior before and outside scientific psychology is the simple but powerful system of folk psychology. In everyday life, people explain behavior in a framework of *beliefs* and *desires*. A student will explain her taking a course on History and Systems of Psychology by saying she *desires* to do well on the Graduate Record Examination and *believes* that taking History and Systems just before taking the exam will help her do well on it. Folk psychology works very well and finds little it cannot explain, but it is not clear whether it can be regarded as a scientific, or even potentially scientific, theory of behavior.

One problem concerns the nature of reasons. When we justify an action, we cite reasons for doing it; but reasons are statements connecting beliefs, and it is controversial whether reasons are causes. Reasons connect beliefs logically, not causally. In the previous example, we can formulate the student's reasoning this way:

> If I do well on the GRE, I can go to graduate school in psychology.
>
> I want to go to graduate school in psychology.
>
> If I take History and Systems, I will do well on the GRE.
> _____
>
> Therefore, I should take History and Systems of Psychology.

Her decision is a result of logical deduction, but logical connection between propositions is not the same thing as causal connection between events. Moreover, beliefs, and therefore reasons, have to do mainly with the meanings of events, not their causal structure. The reasoning the student used only makes sense (1) in a cultural place and time that have graduate schools, assessment procedures, and formal classroom teaching, and (2) against a larger set of cultural practices and beliefs about them that are not stated, such as the high prestige assigned professionals with graduate degrees and the salary they command, the idea of employment for pay, the idea and importance of money, and so on, in an enormously large web of concepts. Science, however, is supposed to be about causal patterns that transcend time and place and are part of nature, not culture, and so it is unclear whether folk psychology, with its dependence on historically and culturally constrained reasons, can be a scientific theory. These considerations are the focus of much current debate in philosophical psychology, and we will return to them in Chapter 15. The distinction between reasons and causes was first raised in the context of historical explanation and will be discussed again in the section on historiography, later in this chapter.

Another problem with folk psychology is its appeal to *teleology*. Our student's argument is teleological: It cites a future state (going to graduate school) as a cause of a current behavior (taking History and Systems). However, it is generally accepted in science that causes must precede effects. In Aristotle's science, final (teleological) cause was the most important kind and could be legitimately invoked to explain not only human behavior but animal behavior, plant growth, and the fall of a rock toward the surface of the earth; however, since the time of Newton, science has relentlessly replaced purposive explanations with mechanical ones, leaving teleological explanation of human behavior a strange anomaly in a discipline that calls itself a science. Therefore, citing future events as causes of present ones is automatically suspect in modern science. Purging teleology from science, along with purging dualism, has been another driving force in psychology since the seventeenth century; indeed, the two are connected for it is to the soul that purposes are most usually attributed.

The Scientific Challenges to Psychology

Given the problems of incorporating traditional modes of explaining human mind and behavior within the framework of modern science, it is not surprising that psychology is a confusing enterprise, comprising not only a broad array of research areas but also a diversity of approaches to researching and explaining each one. I would like to simply list here several key problems that will occupy us in the chapters to follow.

- The challenge of *naturalism*. The goal of science is to explain natural things in a natural way, without resorting to supernatural entities or processes, and within a universalizing framework that transcends time, location, history, and culture. Is it possible to explain human mind and behavior this way?

- The challenge of *realism*. Many theories in psychology, such as those of Freud and information processing, infer from behavior unconscious underlying states and processes, such as id and schemas, repression and schema instantiation. Do these states and processes really exist in a realm of the mind that is inaccessible to introspection, or are they convenient fictions, as antirealists would prefer?

- The challenge of *autonomy*. Many thinkers believe the ultimate nature of reality is material, and the ultimate causes of human consciousness and behavior must therefore be physiological. Is psychology autonomous from biology, or are psychological theories doomed to be reduced one day to neurophysiological theories, or, worse, replaced outright, thrown on the scrap heap of history with alchemy and astrology? What fate awaits folk psychology? Teleological explanation? Explanation by reasons?

- The challenge of *explanation*. Scientific explanation stops when we reach laws of nature—ideals of natural order—such as rectilinear motion, which are considered to be ultimate, requiring no explanation themselves. What are psychology's ideals of natural order? What should psychologists accept as ultimate and what should they define as problems to be solved?

These challenges are predicated on a particular style of science that has grown up since the towering achievements of Newton in the seventeenth century. Psychologists have mostly embraced the Newtonian style and indulged in a Newtonian fantasy (Leahey, 1990).

For at least a hundred years, psychology has claimed to be a science. There are three main reasons for this claim. First, human beings are part of the natural world, so it seems logical that natural science should encompass them. Second, by the nineteenth century, when scientific psychology was founded, it seemed no discipline could be respectable were it not a science. Finally, especially in the United States, scientific status was important to psychology's pretensions to social control. Only a discipline that was a science could claim to control behavior and thus contribute to planned social and personal reform. Thus, although mentalists defined psychology as the science of conscious experience, and behaviorists defined it as the science of behavior, they agreed that psychology was, or at least ought to be, a science.

The science that psychologists emulated was physics. Physical science had proved itself the queen of the sciences by its outstanding success. By the second half of the nineteenth century, John Stuart Mill had urged the methods of physics on the moral sciences. As positivism turned into logical positivism, the preeminence of physics increased. The logical positivists based their philosophy of science on a rational reconstruction of physics and claimed that physics was the most fundamental of sciences, to which all other sciences would eventually be reduced.

Thus, psychologists developed "physics envy." Psychologists, assuming that physics was the best science, tried to apply the methods and aims of physics to their subject matter—and felt inadequate when they did not succeed. Physics envy is a hallmark of twentieth-century psychology, especially in America. Psychologists engage in a Newtonian fantasy. One day, their faith says, a Newton will arise among psychologists and propound a rigorous theory of behavior, delivering psychology unto the promised land of science.

In Samuel Beckett's play *Waiting for Godot,* two characters wait for a third who never arrives. Psychologists have been waiting for their Newton for over a century (Leahey, 1990). Will he or she ever arrive? The Newtonian fantasy assumes that a natural science of human beings is possible and that the model of that science is physics. In Chapter 15, we will ask whether these assumptions are reasonable.

PSYCHOLOGY AND HISTORY

History of Science

History is a well-developed discipline with its own professional norms and controversies. I will discuss here only those issues that bear directly on writing a history of psychology.

The most general problem in writing history, especially scientific history, is the tension between reasons and causes in explaining human action. Imagine the investigation of a murder. The police first determine the *cause* of death; that is, they must find out what physical process (for example, the ingestion of arsenic) caused the victim to die. Then investigators must determine the *reason* for the victim's death. They might discover that the victim's husband was having an affair with his secretary, had taken out an insurance policy on his wife, and had bought two air tickets to Rio—suggesting that the husband killed his wife in order to live in luxury with his mistress (who had better take care). Any given historical event may be explained in either or both of two ways, as a series of physical causes or of reasons. In our example, the series of physical causes is: placement of the arsenic in coffee, its ingestion by the victim, and its effect on the nervous system. The series of reasons, of rational acts carried out with intention and foresight, is: purchasing arsenic, putting it in one's intended victim's drink, setting up an alibi, and planning an escape.

Tension arises between rational and causal accounts of human action when it is unclear how much explanatory force to attribute to each. So far in our example, the causal story is relatively trivial, because we know the cause of death, and fixing the guilt seems clear. However, causal considerations may enter into our evaluations of an actor's behavior. During his first term, President Ronald Reagan was shot and wounded by a young man, John Hinckley. There was no doubt that Hinckley fired the bullet and was thereby part of the cause of Reagan's wound, but there were serious doubts about whether Hinckley's act could be explained rationally. The reason advanced for his attack on the president was to win the love of actress Jodie Foster, but this reason seems strange, certainly stranger than murdering one's wife to run off with one's mistress. Moreover, testimony was offered by psychiatrists that Hinckley was psychotic: Tests showed he had abnormal brain X-rays. Taken together, such evidence convinced the jury that Hinckley's shooting of the president had no reasons, only causes involving Hinckley's diseased brain. Thus, he was found not guilty, because where there is no reason there can be no guilt. In cases such as John Hinckley's, we feel the tension between rational and causal explanation at its highest pitch. We want to condemn a proven criminal, but we know we may only direct moral outrage at someone who chose a particular act when he or she could have done otherwise. We recognize that a person with a diseased brain cannot choose what to do and so deserves no blame.

In fact, the tension between reasons and causes arises in explaining every historical action. Caesar's crossing the Rubicon may be described either as a shrewd political move or as a result of his megalomaniacal ambitions to rule the world. One may choose to major in premed because of a desire to help people and make money, or because of an unconscious neurotic need to show that one is just as good as one's older sibling.

In history of science, the tension between reasons and causes is perennial. Science professes to be a wholly rational enterprise. Scientific theories are supposed to be proposed, tested, accepted, or rejected on rational grounds alone. Yet, as Kuhn and others have amply shown, it is impossible to exempt scientists from the causal forces that play a part in determining human behavior. Scientists crave fame, fortune, and love as much as anyone else, and they may choose one hypothesis over another, one line of research among many, because of inner personal causes or outer sociological causes that cannot be rationally defended and may even be entirely unconscious. In every instance, the historian, including the historian of science, must consider both reasons and causes, weighing both the rational merits of a scientific idea and the causes that may have contributed to its proposal—and to its acceptance or rejection.

Traditionally, history of science has tended to overestimate reasons, producing *Whig* history and *presentism*. These failings are shared by other branches of history, too, but are most tempting to the historian of science. A Whig account of history sees history as a series of progressive steps leading up to our current state of enlightenment. A Whig history of science assumes that present-day science is essentially correct, or at least superior to that of the past, and tells the story of science in terms of how brilliant scientists discovered the truth known to us today. Error is condemned in a Whig account as an aberration of reason, and scientists whose ideas do not conform to present wisdom are either ignored or dismissed as fools.

Whig history is comforting to scientists and therefore is inevitably found in scientific textbooks. However, Whig history is fairy-tale history and is increasingly being supplanted by more adequate history of science, at least among professional historians of science. Unfortunately, because it shows scientists as human beings and science as, upon occasion, irrationally influenced by social and personal causes, good history of science is sometimes seen by practicing scientists as undermining the norms of their discipline, and therefore as dangerous. I have written this book in the spirit of the new history of science, trusting, with historian of physics Stephen Brush (1974), that instead of harming science, good history can help young scientists by liberating them from positivist and Whiggish dogma, making them more receptive to unusual and even radical ideas. A large-scale historical survey of the sort I am writing must be to some degree presentist—that is, concerned with how psychology got to be the way it is. This is not because I think psychology today is for the best, as a Whig historian would, but because I wish to use history to understand psychology's current condition. As we shall find, psychology could have taken other paths than it did, but it is beyond the scope of this book to explore what might have been.

An important dimension in history of science is *internalism–externalism*. Whig histories of science are typically internal, seeing science as a self-contained discipline solving well-defined problems by rational use of the scientific method, unaffected by whatever social changes may be occurring at the same time. An internal history of science could be written with few references to kings and presidents, wars and revolutions, economics and social structure. Recent history of science recognizes that, although scientists might wish themselves free of influence by society and social change, they cannot achieve it. Science is a social institution with particular needs and goals within the larger society, and scientists are human beings socialized within a given culture and striving for success within a certain social setting. Recent history of science is therefore externalist in orientation, considering science within the larger social context of which it is a part and within which it acts. The present edition of this book is more externalist than its predecessors, as I have striven even more to place psychology—especially the formally institutional psychology of the past hundred years—within larger social and historical patterns.

An old historical dispute, tied up with reasons versus causes, Whig versus new history of science, and internalism versus externalism, is the dispute between those who see Great Men as the makers of history, and those who see history made by large impersonal forces outside human control. In the latter *Zeitgeist* (German for "spirit of the times") view of history, people are sometimes depicted as little more than puppets.

The Great Man view was eloquently stated by the English writer Thomas Carlyle (1795–1881):

> For, as I take it, Universal History, the history of what man has accomplished in this world, is at bottom the History of the Great Men who have worked here. They were the leaders of men, these great ones; the modellers, patterns, and in a wide sense creators, of whatsoever the general mass of men contrived to do or attain; all things that we see standing accomplished in the world are properly the outer material result, the practical realisation and embodiment, of Thoughts that dwelt in the Great Men sent into the world: the soul of the world's history, it may justly be considered, were the history of these. (Carlyle, 1841/1966, p. 1)

Great Man history is stirring, for it tells of individual struggle and triumph. In science, Great Man history is the story of the research and theorizing of brilliant scientists unlocking the secrets of nature. Because Great Men are revered by later ages for their accomplishments, Great Man history is usually Whiggish and internalist, precisely because it stresses rationality and success, downplaying cultural and social causes of human thought and action.

The opposing view was essentially invented by the German philosopher Georg Wilhelm Friedrich Hegel (1770–1831):

> [O]nly the study of world history itself can show that it has proceeded rationally, that it represents the rationally necessary course of the World Spirit, the Spirit whose nature is indeed always one and the same, but whose nature unfolds in the course of the world. . . . [W]orld history goes on in the realm of the Spirit. . . . Spirit, and the course of its development, is the substance of history. (Hegel, 1837/1953, p. 12)

Zeitgeist history tends to ignore the actions of human beings, because people are believed to be living preordained lives controlled by hidden forces working themselves out through historical process. In Hegel's original formulation, the hidden force was the Absolute Spirit (often identified with God) developing through human history. Spirit has gone out of fashion, but *Zeitgeist* histories remain. Hegel's student, Karl Marx, materialized Hegel's Spirit into economics and saw human history as the development of modes of economic production. Kuhn's model of scientific history is a *Zeitgeist* model, because it posits an entity, the paradigm, that controls the research and theorizing of working scientists.

Because of its emphasis on the inevitability of progress, the *Zeitgeist* conception of history is Whiggish from Hegel's or Marx's perspective. Both Hegel and Marx saw human history directed toward some final end—the ultimate realization of the Spirit or God, or the ultimate achievement of socialism, the perfect economic order—and both viewed historical development as a rational process. Their history is not, however, internalist, because it places the determination of history outside the actions of men and women. The contribution of Hegel and Marx was in inventing externalism, directing historians' attention to the larger context in which people work, discovering that the context of action shapes action in ways at best dimly seen by historical actors themselves. Taking this broad perspective, externalism provides a greater understanding of history. However, contrary to Hegel or Marx, history has no discernible direction. The history of the world, or of psychology, could have been other than it has been. We humans struggle in a semidarkness of social and personal causes; yet, as Freud observed, the still small voice of human reason, not some abstract Reason or economic plan, is finally heard.

Historiography of Psychology

The history and methodology of the field of history are called *historiography*. The historiography of science—of which history of psychology is a part—has passed through two stages (Brush, 1974). In the earlier stage, from the nineteenth century until the 1950s, history of science was mostly written by scientists themselves—typically, older scientists no longer active at the forefront of research. This is not surprising, since one of the special difficulties of writing history of science is that one must be able to understand the details of scientific theory and research in order to chronicle its story. However, beginning in the 1950s, and gaining momentum in the 1960s, a "new" history of science emerged as the field was professionalized. History of science was taken over by men and women trained as historians, although in many cases they had scientific backgrounds; Thomas S. Kuhn, for example, had been a chemist.

History of psychology underwent the same change, although a little later and still incompletely. The classic "old" history of psychology is Edwin G. Boring's magisterial *History of Experimental Psychology,* published first in 1929, with a revised edition in 1950. Boring was a psychologist, a student of introspectionist E. B. Titchener, and the psychology that Boring knew was being superseded by behaviorism and the rise of applied psychology. So, while Boring was by no means retired, he wrote his *History* as an internalist, Whiggish justification of his tradition (O'Donnel, 1979). Boring's book was the standard text for decades, but, beginning in the mid-1960s, the new, professional history of psychology began to replace the old. In 1965, a specialized journal appeared, *Journal of the History of the Behavioral Sciences,* and the American Psychological Association approved formation of a Division (26) for the History of Psychology. In 1967, the first graduate program in history of psychology was begun at the University of New Hampshire, under the direction of Robert I. Watson, founder of the *Journal* (Furomoto, 1989; Watson, 1975). The development of the "new history of psychology" gathered steam in the 1970s and 1980s, until, in 1988, Laurel Furomoto could declare it fully matured and demanded its incorporation into the psychological curriculum. We should note that the change is incomplete. Although the text you are reading is one of the few to be influenced by the new history of psychology (Furomoto, 1989), I am a psychologist with no training in history.

Much more, than who writes it, is involved in the change from the old history of science (and psychology) to the new. This change coincides with a longer-term movement in historiography from "old history" to "new history" (Furomoto, 1989; Himmelfarb, 1987). "Old history" was "history from above"; it was primarily political, diplomatic, and military, concentrating on great people and great events. Its form was the narrative, telling readable stories—frequently written for a broadly educated public, not just other historians—of nations, men, and women. "New history" is history from below; it attempts to describe, even recreate in words, the intimate lives of the anonymous mass of people neglected by the old history. As Peter Stearns has put it, "When the history of menarche is widely recognized as equal in importance to the history of monarchy, we [new historians] will have arrived" (quoted by Himmelfarb, 1987, p. 13). Its form is analytic rather than narrative, often incorporating statistics and analytic techniques borrowed from sociology, psychology, and other social sciences.

The "new history" is very much *Zeitgeist* history, depreciating the role of the individual and seeing history as made by impersonal forces, not the actions of men and women. Although the new history focuses on ordinary lives, it depicts men and women as victims of forces they do not control. Contingency is denied, as the new history is described by perhaps its foremost practitioner, French historian Fernand Braudel:

> So when I think of the individual, I am always inclined to see him imprisoned within a destiny in which he himself has little hand, fixed in a landscape in which the infinite perspectives of the long term stretch into the distance both behind him and before. In historical analysis, as I see it, rightly or wrongly, the long term always wins in the end. Annihilating innumerable events—all those which cannot be accommodated in the main ongoing current and which are therefore ruthlessly swept to one side—it indubitably

limits both the freedom of the individual and even the role of chance. (Quoted by Himmelfarb, 1987, p. 12)

The new history of psychology is described by Furomoto (1989):

The new history tends to be critical rather than ceremonial, contextual rather than simply the history of ideas, and more inclusive, going beyond the study of "great men." The new history utilizes primary sources and archival documents rather than relying on secondary sources, which can lead to the passing down of anecdotes and myths from one generation of textbook writers to the next. And finally, the new history tries to get inside the thought of a period to see issues as they appeared at the time, instead of looking for antecedents of current ideas or writing history backwards from the present context of the field. (p. 16)

Apart from its call for greater inclusiveness in writing history, Furomoto's description of the new history of psychology actually describes good traditional history as well.

Although the new history has become mainstream history, it has provoked, and continues to provoke, controversy (Himmelfarb, 1987). Most upsetting to traditional historians is the abandonment of narrative for analysis, the denial of contingency, and the rejection of the efficacy of human action. A backlash in favor of narrative and in appreciation of contingency and the importance of individuals has recently appeared. For example, James M. McPherson (1988), in his splendid *Battle Cry of Freedom,* adopted narrative as the only mode of history that could do justice to his topic, the American Civil War, and in the end concluded that human will and leadership—Lincoln's political skill and Grant's and Sherman's generalship—won the war for the North.

Where in the spectrum of old to new history does the present book fit? It is true that I have been influenced by and have used the new history of psychology in writing my book, but it is not entirely *of* the new history. I feel the greatest affinity for the traditional history of ideas and have not generally sought to find the causes of psychology's development in the biographies of psychologists. I believe that history is a humanity, not a science, and that when historians lean on the social sciences, they are leaning on weak reeds. I agree with Matthew Arnold that the humanities should concern themselves with the best (and most important) that has been said and done. Finally, I agree with English historian G. R. Elton that history "can instruct in the use of reason." I have tried, then, to write as narrative a history as the material allows, focusing on the leading ideas in psychological thought and aiming to instruct the young psychologist in the use of reason in psychology.

Let us now set out, carrying as few preconceptions as we can get away with, on our 2,500-year tour of psychology's fascinating zoo.

BIBLIOGRAPHY

The literature on philosophy of science is large. A good recent survey is David Oldroyd, *The arch of knowledge* (New York: Methuen, 1986). A slightly older and more technical survey, but one that is widely cited as a definitive one up to its time, is found in Frederick Suppe's long introduction to his *Structure of scientific theories* (1977). *Science and philosophy: The process of science* (Dordrecht, The Netherlands: Martinus Nijhoff, 1987), edited by Nancy J.

Nersessian, contains a selection of papers by leading philosophers of science, written for non-specialists. Many of the issues and approaches mentioned in the present text are discussed and represented in Nersessian's volume. Wesley Salmon's *Scientific explanation and the causal structure of the world* (Minneapolis: University of Minnesota Press, 1989) provides an outstanding comprehensive history of the problem of scientific explanation by one of the area's leading lights; Salmon is a realist, and in the same volume his friend Kitcher gives a lengthy summation of the antirealist perspective. The realism–antirealism issue is given an interesting treatment by Arthur Fine in "Unnatural attitudes: Realist and instrumentalist attachments to science," *Mind* (1986, *95:* 149–79). Fine argues that both viewpoints are flawed by mirror-image failings: "metaphysical inflationism" and "epistemological inflationism," respectively. For realism in physics, see Nick Herbert (1985), *Quantum reality* (New York: Doubleday, 1985), a wonderful introduction to modern quantum physics and its many deep puzzles. The Received View on theories is fully explicated and criticized in Suppe's introduction, already mentioned. C. W. Savage, *Scientific theories* (Minneapolis: University of Minnesota Press, 1990), contains a collection of essays (preceded by Savage's summary of all of them) on modern approaches to scientific theory, especially Bayesian considerations, and a recent paper by Kuhn that still pushes incommensurability. W. H. Newton-Smith, *The rationality of science* (London: Routledge & Kegan Paul, 1981), provides a general treatment of and argument in favor of the rationalist view of science. Ronald N. Giere, "Philosophy of science naturalized," *Philosophy of Science* (1885, *52:* 331–56), argues for the opposite point of view. The most recent statement of an evolutionary framework for understanding the history of science is David Hull, *Science as a process: The evolutionary account of the social and conceptual development of science* (Chicago: University of Chicago Press, 1988). Empirical studies of science, including psychology of science, from the seventeenth century to the present are collected in R. Tweney, C. Mynatt, and D. Doherty, *On scientific thinking* (New York: Columbia University Press, 1981). A forceful set of arguments for, plus case studies of, psychology of science may be found in Gholson et al. (1989). Essays applying philosophy of science to psychology include Barry Gholson and Peter Barker, "Kuhn, Lakatos and Laudan: Applications in the history of physics and psychology," *American Psychologist* (1985, *40:* 744–69); Peter Manicas and Paul Secord, "Implications for psychology of the new philosophy of science," *American Psychologist* (1983, *38:* 399–414); and Joseph Margolis, Peter Manicas, Rom Harre, and Paul Secord, *Psychology: Designing the discipline* (Oxford, England: Basil Blackwell, 1986).

Useful studies in philosophy of psychology include several surveys: Neil Bolton (Ed.), *Philosophical problems in psychology* (New York: Methuen, 1979); Mario Bunge and Ruben Ardila, *Philosophy of psychology* (New York: Springer, 1987); Paul Churchland, *Matter and consciousness* (Cambridge, MA: MIT Press, 1988), who focuses on materialism and reductionism/replacement; Fred Dretske, *Explaining behavior: Reasons in a world of causes* (Cambridge, MA: MIT Press, 1988), focusing on reasons and causes; Peter Smith and O. R. Jones, *The philosophy of mind* (Cambridge, England: Cambridge University Press, 1986); and Jenny Teichman, *Philosophy and the mind* (Oxford, England: Basil Blackwell, 1988).

REFERENCES

Boring, E. G. (1929/1950). *A history of experimental psychology,* 2nd ed. New York: Appleton-Century-Crofts.

Brush, S. G. (1974). Should the history of psychology be rated X? *Science 183:* 1164–72.

Carlyle, T. (1841/1966). *On heroes, hero-worship and the heroic in history.* Lincoln: University of Nebraska Press.

Cohen, I. B. (1980). *The Newtonian revolution.* Cambridge, England: Cambridge University Press.

Cohen, I. B. (1985). *Revolution in science.* Cambridge, MA: Harvard University Press.

Furomoto, L. (1989). The new history of psychology. In T. S. Cohen, ed., *The G. Stanley Hall Lecture Series* (Vol. 9). Washington, DC: American Psychological Association.

Gholson, B., Shadish, W. R., Jr., Niemeyer, R., and Houts, A., eds. (1989). *Psychology of science.* Cambridge, England: Cambridge University Press.

Giere, R. N. (1988). *Exploring science: A cognitive approach.* Chicago: University of Chicago Press.

Gutting, G., ed. (1980). *Paradigms and revolutions: Applications and appraisals of Thomas Kuhn's philosophy of science.* South Bend, IN: University of Notre Dame Press.

Hegel, G. W. F. (1837/1953). *Reason in history: A general introduction to the philosophy of history,* trans. R. Hartmann. Indianapolis: Bobbs-Merrill.

Hempel, C. G., and Oppenheim, P. (1948). Studies in the logic of explanation. *Philosophy of Science 15:* 135–75. Reprinted in Hempel, C. (1965). *Aspects of scientific explanation.* New York: Free Press.

Herbert, N. (1985). *Quantum reality. Beyond the new physics.* Garden City, NY: Doubleday.

Heyes, C. M. (1989). Uneasy chapters in the relationship between psychology and epistemology. In B. Gholson, W. R. Shadish, Jr., R. Niemeyer, and A. Houts, eds., *Psychology of science.* Cambridge, England: Cambridge University Press.

Himmelfarb, G. (1987). *The new history and the old.* Cambridge, MA: Harvard University Press.

Holton, G. (1973). *Thematic origins of scientific thought: Kepler to Einstein.* Cambridge, MA: Harvard University Press.

Holton, G. (1978). *The scientific imagination: Case studies.* Cambridge, England: Cambridge University Press.

Holton, G. (1984, November 2). Do scientists need a philosophy? *Times Literary Supplement:* 1231–4.

Kitcher, P. (1989). Explanatory unification and the causal structure of the world. In P. Kitcher and W. S. Salmon, eds., *Scientific explanation. Minnesota studies in the philosophy of science* (Vol. 13). Minneapolis: University of Minnesota Press.

Kitcher, P., and Salmon, W. S., eds. (1989). *Scientific explanation. Minnesota studies in the philosophy of science* (Vol. 13). Minneapolis: University of Minnesota Press.

Kuhn, T. S. (1959). *The Copernican revolution.* New York: Vintage Books.

Kuhn, T. S. (1970). *The structure of scientific revolutions,* rev. ed. Chicago: University of Chicago Press.

Kuhn, T. S. (1977). Second thoughts on paradigms. In F. Suppe, ed., *The structure of scientific theories,* 2nd ed. Urbana: University of Illinois Press.

Lakatos, I. (1970). Falsification and the methodology of scientific research programs. In I. Lakatos and A. Musgrave, eds., *Criticism and the growth of knowledge.* Cambridge, England: Cambridge University Press.

Lakatos, I. (1971). History of science and its rational reconstruction. In R. Buck and R. Cohen, eds., *Boston studies in the philosophy of science.* Dordrecht, The Netherlands: D. Reidel.

Laudan, L. (1977). *Progress and its problems.* Berkeley: University of California Press.

Laudan, R. (1980). The recent revolution in geology and Kuhn's theory of scientific change. In G. Gutting, ed., *Paradigms and revolutions: Applications and appraisals of Thomas Kuhn's philosophy of science.* South Bend, IN: University of Notre Dame Press.

Leahey, T. (1992). The new science of science. Review of Gholson, W. R. Shadish, Jr., R. Niemeyer, and A. Houts (1989), *Contemporary Psychology,* in press.

Leahey, T. H., and Leahey, G. E. (1983). *Psychology's occult doubles: Psychology and the problem of pseudoscience.* Chicago: Nelson-Hall.

McPherson, J. M. (1988). *The battle cry of freedom: The Civil War era.* New York: Oxford University Press.

Mynatt, C. R., Doherty, M. E., and Tweney, R. D. (1978). Consequences of confirmation and disconfirmation in a simulated research environment. *Quarterly Journal of Experimental Psychology 30:* 395–406.

Nersessian, N. J., ed. (1987). *The process of science: Contemporary approaches to understanding scientific practice.* Dordrecht, The Netherlands: Martinus Nijhoff.

Newton-Smith, W. H. (1981). *The rationality of science.* London: Routledge & Kegan Paul.

O'Donnel, J. M. (1979). The crisis of experimentalism in the 1920's: E. G. Boring and his uses of history. *American Psychologist 34:* 289–295.

Popper, Karl. (1963). *Conjectures and refutations: The growth of scientific knowledge.* London: Routledge & Kegan Paul.

Railton, P. (1989). Explanation and metaphysical controversy. In P. Kitcher and W. S. Salmon, eds., *Scientific explanation. Minnesota studies in the philosophy of science* (Vol. 13). Minneapolis: University of Minnesota Press.

Salmon, W. S. (1984). *Scientific explanation and the causal structure of the world.* Princeton, NJ: Princeton University Press.

Salmon, W. S. (1989). Four decades of scientific explanation. In P. Kitcher and W. S. Salmon, eds., *Scientific explanation. Minnesota studies in the philosophy of science* (Vol. 13).. Minneapolis, MN: University of Minnesota Press.

Savage, W. (1990). *Scientific theories. Minnesota studies in the philosophy of science* (Vol. 14). Minneapolis: University of Minnesota Press.

Shadish, W. R., Jr. (1989). The perception and evaluation of quality in science. In B. Gholson, W. R. Shadish, Jr., R. Niemeyer, and A. Houts, eds., *Psychology of science.* Cambridge, England: Cambridge University Press.

Simonton, D. K. (1989). The chance-configuration theory of scientific creativity. In B. Gholson, W. R. Shadish, Jr., R. Niemeyer, and A. Houts, eds., *Psychology of science.* Cambridge, England: Cambridge University Press.

Suppe, F., ed. (1977). *The structure of scientific theories,* 2nd ed. Urbana: University of Illinois Press.

Suppe, F. (1989). *The semantic conception of theories and scientific realism.* Urbana: University of Illinois Press.

Thagard, P. (1988). *Computational philosophy of science.* Cambridge, MA: MIT Press.

Toulmin, S. (1961). *Foresight and understanding.* Princeton, NJ: Princeton University Press.

Toulmin, S. (1972). *Human understanding.* Princeton, NJ: Princeton University Press.

Tweney, R. D. (1989). A framework for the cognitive psychology of science. In B. Gholson, W. R. Shadish, Jr., R. Niemeyer, and A. Houts, eds., *Psychology of science.* Cambridge, England: Cambridge University Press.

Tweney, R. D., Mynatt, C. R., and Doherty, M. E., eds. (1981). *On scientific thinking.* New York: Columbia University Press.

van Frassen, B. C. (1980). *The scientific image.* Oxford, England: Clarendon Press.

Watson, R. I. (1975). The history of psychology as a specialty: A personal view of its first 15 years. *Journal of the History of the Behavioral Sciences 11:* 5–14.

Wright, R. (1994). *The moral animal.* New York: Pantheon.

2 The Classical World
Origins of Philosophy, Science, and Psychology

The Parthenon, one of the most famous buildings in the world. Erected under the rule of Pericles in the days of Socrates and Plato, it expresses the confidence of an imperial civilization at the height of its powers. It was in Greece that the history of secular thought in Western civilization began. Psychology began there in the Greek motto "Know thyself."

BEFORE PHILOSOPHY

The Past Is Another Country

A few years ago, I visited the British Museum in London. As an undergraduate, I had narrowly chosen psychology over archeology as a career, and I was eager to visit the treasures of the past to be found in the Museum. Among of the greatest are the Elgin

Marbles, named after Lord Elgin, a British Hellenophile who brought them back to England for preservation. The Elgin Marbles are large flat slabs of carved stone that were part of the decorative frieze around the top of the Parthenon on the Acropolis in Athens. In the Museum, they are rightly given a large room of their own, mounted high around the walls to give the viewer some sense of the original experience of seeing them. They are indeed marvelous works of art, but I was disappointed by how little about the marbles was told by the Museum's labels. They discussed the purely formal, aesthetic properties of the Marbles, pointing out, for example, how the figures on one echoed the forms on another across the room. They did not reveal what the figures and forms meant, what the people, gods, and animals were doing. At first, I thought this formal approach simply reflected the fact that archeology developed in Europe as a branch of art history and therefore stressed aesthetic appreciation, whereas archeology developed in America as a branch of anthropology and stressed cultural interpretation. The treatment of other artifacts seemed to confirm my hypothesis.

Subsequently, however, I learned that the story was less simple: no one really knows what the Elgin Marbles mean. Traditionally, they are thought to show the Panathenaic Procession. Once a year, the leaders and citizens of Athens staged a grand parade to the Parthenon to honor their city's special god, Athena. However, detailed interpretation remains lacking (Biers, 1987), and some scholars think the marbles commemorate a legendary sacrifice by a mother of her two daughters to gain an Athenian military victory. Had she had sons, they would have died in battle, so she gave her daughters (Adler, 1995). That the Marbles are something of a mystery is especially surprising because the Parthenon is not especially old. The Parthenon whose ruins we see today was erected in the heyday of the "glory that was Greece" era, during the leadership of Pericles (495–429 B.C.E.) and under the guidance of the great sculptor Phidias (500–432 B.C.E.), as a replacement for structures destroyed by Persian invaders. The Greeks were inventing philosophy, science, and history, yet we have no discussions of the meaning of the Parthenon frieze. People rarely write down what they take for granted.

My experience with the Elgin Marbles is an important lesson as we begin our historical journey. The job of any historian is to tell about the past, to bring alive the thoughts and actions of people who lived in earlier times, to see the world as they saw it. Yet, as the title of one book has it, *The Past is Another Country* (Foster, 1988). Often, our grip on the past will be loose, for much quotidian detail is gone forever. We will try to think like Greeks or nineteenth-century German mandarins, and thus improve ourselves as we do by travel. The quest for historical understanding is worth the effort, but the goal of complete understanding will never be reached. No one really knows what the Elgin Marbles mean.

Most elusive of all is the ancient beginning of psychology.

Psychology of the Bronze Age

In his dialogue *Theatetus,* Plato observes that philosophy begins in human wonder, a powerful desire to *understand* the world, not merely to act in it as animals do. Even before human beings began to make written records of their ideas, they took a lively interest in the universe. Archeological investigations (Marshack, 1972) suggest that prehistoric people made records on incised bones representing important astronomical regularities, such as the phases of the moon. These systematic observations could make possible accurate calculation of eclipses and changes in the seasons. The most dramatic, but by no means the only, evidence of early humanity's astronomical sophistication is Stonehenge, which served as both observatory and calculating machine.

Stone monuments and incised bones, however, do not reveal our ancient ancestors' beliefs about human nature, the object of psychology's quest. In the history of Western civilization, our oldest window on psychology is opened by the Homeric poems, the *Iliad* and the *Odyssey*. When Homer wrote the *Iliad* and *Odyssey,* he gave permanent voice to an oral tradition already millennia old, reaching back to the Bronze Age. Because they are tales of love and loyalty, passion and battle, they contain explanations of human behavior, indirectly revealing the oldest folk psychology of which we have record.

One object of ancient wonder was surely the difference between living and nonliving things. Only plants, animals, and humans are born, develop, reproduce, and die; only animals and humans perceive and move about. Cultures and religions all over the world mark this distinction by ascribing to living things a soul that animates their inanimate bodies, producing the functions of life. When the life-spirit is present, the body is alive, and when it departs, the body becomes a corpse. Some, but not all, religions add a second, personal soul, unique to human beings, that is the psychological essence of each person and may survive the death of the body.

At least as recorded by Homer, Bronze Age Greek concepts of the soul are distinctive and, to a modern eye, rather odd (Onians, 1951; Snell, 1960; Bremmer, 1983). To begin with, the *Iliad* and *Odyssey* contain no word designating the mind or personality as a whole. Closest is the word *psuche* (traditionally, but misleadingly, transliterated as *psyche,* and usually translated as soul) from which the field of psychology—the study of (*logos*) the soul (*psuche*)—takes its name. *Psuche* is at least the breath of life, because its departure from a wounded warrior means his death. However, *psuche* is also more than the breath of life but less than the complete individual mind or soul. During sleep or a swoon, it may leave the body and travel around, and it may survive bodily death, but it is never described as being active when a person is awake, and it is never implicated in causing behavior.

Instead, behavior is attributed to several independently operating soul-like entities residing in different parts of the body. For example, the function of *phrenes,* located in the diaphragm, was rationally planning action. On the other hand, *thumos,* in the heart, governed action driven by emotion. *Noos* was responsible for accurate perception and clear cognition of the world, and there were other, less frequently cited mini-souls as well. None of these mini-souls survived the death of the body, giving the afterlife of the Homeric *psuche* a rather bizarre character. Deprived of their body-souls, *psuches* in the afterlife were mental cripples, deprived of feeling, thought, and speech, and incapable even of normal movement. The appearance of the *psuche* was exactly that of the body at death, complete with wounds. Moreover, not every *psuche* went to Hades, because proper burial of the body was felt necessary to effect the transition from life to afterlife. Women, children, adolescents, and the elderly were not ritually buried, so their *psuches* were not believed to survive death, and warriors feared death without burial—for example, by drowning at sea. On the other hand, when buried with honor, a great warrior found an exalted place in the afterlife.

A final aspect of the Bronze Age folk psychology casts a long shadow over Greek philosophical psychology and ethics. The Bronze Age heroic conception of virtue—the good life—meant living honorably by the warriors' code and achieving immortality through great prowess in battle. When the gods offer young Achilles the choice between a long, quiet, private life or a short but glorious life, he chooses what any other Bronze Age man would—the short life of glory won in battle (which did, indeed, make his name immortal).

The Homeric conception of virtue is radically unlike ours in two important respects. First, virtue—*arete*—is an achievement, not a state of being, and second, as a consequence, virtue could be achieved by only a lucky few. Women, children, adolescents, slaves, the poor, and cripples (few of whom were buried) could not achieve virtue because they could not gain glory in battle. Greeks ever walked in fear of fate—*Tyche*—that might keep virtue from them. An accident of birth—being a woman, poor, or a slave—put virtue out of reach. A childhood accident or disease might cripple one, keeping one from achieving glory and, thereby, *arete*. Although the emphasis on glory won in battle was muted, even harshly criticized, in later Classical philosophy, the idea that virtue and the good life could be attained only by an elite and lucky few remained intact until the Hellenistic Age. Today, we tend to think that virtue may belong to anyone, rich or poor, man or woman, athletic or crippled, because we think of virtue as a psychological state of mind, or of the soul, not as a prize to be won by action. Virtue was first so conceived by the therapeutic philosophy of Stoicism in the last centuries B.C.E., and achieved its modern meaning with the advent of Christianity.

ARGUMENT, LAW, AND NATURE: PHILOSOPHY AND PSYCHOLOGY BEGIN

Greek Democracy and the Critical Tradition

It is difficult for people to accept criticism of their ideas or to reflect critically on them. Consequently, many systems of thought are *closed*. Adherents of a closed system of thought believe that they possess truths beyond criticism and improvement. If some criticism is offered, the system is not defended with reason or evidence, but by attacking the character of the critic as somehow defective. Religions may become closed systems when, resting on divinely revealed dogma, they expel (or worse) internal critics as heretics and revile outsiders as wicked infidels. Secular systems of thought may become closed, too; similarly, communists used to reproach each other for "deviation" from the Truth of Marx and persecuted critics as if they were religious heretics. In psychology, psychoanalysis sometimes shows tendencies to intolerance, attacking criticisms as neuroses rather than as potentially legitimate objections.

In democratic Greece, however, intellectual life took a different turn, almost unique in human history. The ancient Greek philosophers were the first thinkers to progress by employing criticism. There, beginning with Thales of Miletus (flourished* 585 B.C.E.), a tradition of *systematic criticism* whose aim was the improvement of ideas came into being. As the philosopher Karl Popper (1965, p. 151) wrote: "Thales was the first teacher who said to his pupils: 'This is how I see things—how I believe that things are. Try to improve upon my teaching.' " Thales did not teach his ideas as a received Truth to be conserved, but as a set of hypotheses to be improved. Thales and those who followed him sought change. They knew that ideas are rarely right, that only by making errors and then correcting them can we progress. In addition, they achieved the fundamental basis of all free discussion, separating the

* The word "flourished" will be given as fl. A person "flourishes" around age forty.

character of persons from the plausibility of their ideas. In an *open* system of thought, ideas are considered on their own, entirely apart from the personality, character, ethnic background, or faith of the person who advances them. Without this separation, argument degenerates into name calling and heresy hunting. The critical attitude is fundamental to both philosophy and science, but it requires overcoming intellectual laziness and the natural feeling of hostility toward critics. Founding a critical tradition of thought was the major achievement of the Greek inventors of philosophy.

The inauguration of the critical tradition of open, impersonal discussion was an achievement—fallen away from but never broken—of the Classical Greek city-state, or *polis*. The Bronze Age Greeks were ruled by semidivine kings whose word was law, and were led by warrior-heroes on horseback who were pursuing personal glory. That Mycenean society crashed and was followed by a centuries-long Dark Age of which we know nothing, memory of the past being kept alive by the oral tradition culminating in Homer. When history begins in the middle of the first millennium B.C.E., we find the *polis* in its infancy. Greek democracy was imperfect by our standards but a great achievement nonetheless. The city was ruled by its free citizens—about 40,000 men at Athens, for example; women, slaves, children, and outsiders were excluded. Decisions were made collectively by the assembly of all citizens, and citizens accused of crimes were tried by juries of 200–400 randomly chosen fellow citizens. War was fought by the *phalanx*—a disciplined body of citizens acting as a unit for the good of all. Citizens were expected to devote themselves to the public life of the *polis;* private life was shunned as unworthy of the free man. So important was participating in the *polis* that most crimes were punished by withdrawal of some political right, such as the right to serve on juries, or to speak in the assembly, or to vote. Greeks citizens of the *polis* would be puzzled by how few Americans vote today.

The critical tradition of philosophy and science was an outgrowth of the democratic *polis* (Vernant, 1982). Instead of simply obeying the orders of a king, democratic Greeks came together to argue over the best course of action, opening the debate to all citizens. Because citizens were equal, charges of bad faith or bad character became unseemly, and ideas were debated on their own merits (Clark, 1992). Law was no longer given by a king who could change it or disregard it at will, but was agreed on and written down, becoming binding on everyone equally. The idea of law governing all people eventually was mirrored in an important scientific idea: natural laws governed natural events, and these laws could be discovered by human minds. This extension of law from the *polis* to nature first appears in Greek myths, wherein the chief god Zeus is subjected to constraints even he cannot escape (Clark, 1992). Free and impartial philosophy and science can flourish only in a free society of laws.

Understanding the Universe: The Naturalists

The specific philosophical and scientific problem Thales addressed was the fundamental nature of reality. Thales proposed that although the world appears to be made up of many different substances (wood, stone, air, smoke, and so forth), there is in reality only one element—water—which takes on many forms. Water can be liquid, gaseous, or solid, and was, Thales proposed, the essential constituent of all things. The name for the single element out of which all things are made was *phusis,* and so those who followed Thales in searching for some such universal element were called *physicists*.

Modern physics continues the search, asserting that all the substances of common experience are really composed of a few elementary particles.

Besides inaugurating a critical tradition, then, Thales began a line of *physical* investigation. In doing so, he moved away from religious or spiritual interpretations of the universe toward *naturalistic* explanations of how things are constituted and how they work. Thus, Thales asserted that the world is within human understanding, for it is made up of ordinary matter and does not reflect the capricious whims of gods. Naturalism is an essential constituent of science, because science seeks to explain things and events without reference to supernatural powers or entities of any kind. In psychology—the study of the soul—naturalism poses a profound challenge to dualistic conceptions of life and human personality. As scientists, psychologists seek to explain animal and human behavior without reference to souls of any sort, bringing them into conflict with an ancient and durable tradition—subscribed to by many psychologists themselves—of faith in a supernatural soul. In the rest of science, Thales' naturalism reigns; in psychology, it remains at odds with dualism. Coming to terms with this tension is a serious problem for contemporary psychology.

Thales' physicist tradition continued with his student Anaximander of Miletus (fl. 560 B.C.E.), who criticized Thales' hypothesis that the *phusis* was water, proposing instead the existence of a *phusis* (the *apeiron*) that was not any recognizable element but was instead something less definite that could take on many forms. Anaximander also anticipated the concept of adaptive evolution later elaborated by Darwin. He observed that human babies are fragile and require prolonged nursing, inferring that human beings' original, primeval form must have been different, sturdier, and presumably more quickly independent, as are most animal infants. To support his thesis, Anaximander appealed to fossils of creatures unknown in his world.

Although he was a poet rather than a philosopher, Xenophanes of Colophon (fl. 530 B.C.E.) broadened the critical and naturalistic traditions by his open assault on Greek religion. Xenophanes maintained that the Olympian gods were simply anthropomorphic constructions, behaving like human beings, lying, stealing, murdering, and philandering. Xenophanes said that if animals had gods, they too would make them in their own images, inventing lion gods, cat gods, dog gods, and so on. Xenophanes' critique is the beginning of the ancient struggle between scientific naturalism and religion that reached its greatest crisis when Darwin proposed the theory of evolution in the nineteenth century.

More directly influential on later philosophers, especially Plato, was Pythagoras of Samos (fl. 530 B.C.E.). Pythagoras was an enigmatic figure, a great mathematician, a philosopher—indeed, he coined the term (Artz, 1980)—and yet the founder of a cult. He is famous for the Pythagorean theorem, and he also formulated the first mathematical law of physics, expressing the harmonic ratios of vibrating strings of different lengths. Mathematics, however, was more than just a tool of science for Pythagoras. It was also a magical key to the cosmos. Pythagoras founded a secret religious sect devoted to mathematics, which they believed held the keys to nature.

In psychology, Pythagoreans drew a sharp distinction between soul and body. Not only could the soul exist without the body, but, going further, the Pythagoreans considered the body a corrupting prison in which the soul was trapped. An important part of the Pythagorean cult teaching concerned purifying the flesh—for example, by dietary restrictions—so the soul could more easily attain truth. As we shall see, in his emphasis on the care of the soul and the purifying and transcendental character of mathematics, Plato was a follower of Pythagoras.

Being and Becoming; Appearance and Reality: Parmenides and Heraclitus

An important intellectual polarity in Western thought has been, and remains, the tension between philosophies of *Being* and of *Becoming*. The first spokesman for Being was Parmenides of Elea (fl. 475 B.C.E.). Parmenides wrote his philosophy as a poem and declared it the inspiration of a goddess, suggesting, as with Pythagoras, that the line between science and religion, philosopher and shaman, was not yet clear and sharp (Clark, 1992). Parmenides' basic thesis was simply stated, "It is." Presumably influenced by the physicists, Parmenides asserted that the underlying permanent reality of the universe was an unchanging substance, a simple and immutable *It:* pure Being. Change—Becoming, to the Greeks—was an illusion of the human mind, because *It* simply is, beyond change or alteration. Expanded by Plato, the philosophy of Being became a moral doctrine asserting that beyond the flux of changing human opinions there are eternal truths and values that exist apart from humanity, truths we should seek and use to guide our lives. These truths exist in a realm of pure Being; they exist changelessly apart from the changing physical world.

Advocates of Becoming, on the other hand, deny that any such truths, or realm of pure being, exist. Instead, the only constant in the universe is change; things never simply *are,* but are always becoming something else. For such thinkers, even moral values can change as the world changes. The Greek spokesman for Becoming was Heraclitus of Ephesus (fl. 500 B.C.E.). Like Parmenides, Heraclitus was still as much seer as philosopher, speaking in metaphorical aphorisms that earned him the nickname "the Obscure." He asserted that the *phusis* was fire. This idea led to the conclusion that there is even less permanence in the world than there seems to be. What looks like a stone is really a condensed ball of ever-changing fire, a reality not unlike the modern physicist's swarm of particles. Heraclitus's most famous aphorism was that no one ever steps in the same river twice. The statement aptly sums up his philosophy, in which nothing in the universe is ever the same twice. Nevertheless, Heraclitus also believed that, although change is the only constant, it is lawful rather than capricious. Regulating change is a dynamic universal harmony that keeps things in an equilibrium of balanced forces. Thus, whatever truth philosophy and science may attain will be truth about change—Becoming—rather than about static things.

Since the time of Parmenides, the struggle between Being and Becoming has been fought by many thinkers. Through Plato, Parmenides' admirer, the philosophy of Being dominated Western thinking, although not without challenge, until modern times. Neoplatonism was the philosophical cornerstone of medieval Christian thought. It was not until the breakdown of the Middle Ages that becoming began to ascend. With Darwin's theory of evolution by random mutation and natural selection, Becoming triumphed in science. This triumph is evident not only in the biological sciences, but even in physics. Thus, quantum theory asserts that we can never know where a particle *is* with certainty, only where it *might be.*

The debate between Being and Becoming was a metaphysical one, but it created an important epistemological difficulty that led to the first theory in psychology. Both Parmenides' philosophy of Being and Heraclitus's philosophy of Becoming imply a sharp difference between *Appearance* and *Reality*. For Parmenides, the Appearance was

Change and the Reality was Being; for Heraclitus, it was the other way round. Parmenides made the distinction explicit, sharply distinguishing a *Way of Seeing* (appearances) from a *Way of Truth* (reality). The proposal that human experience is faulty jolted the Greeks into self-consciousness about how best to search for truth and about the workings of the human mind, especially what today we call the cognitive functions. With regard to the first issue, Parmenides concluded that, because the senses deceive, they should not be trusted, and one should rely on pure logic instead. Thus, was founded the approach to philosophy known as *rationalism,* which after being polished and combined with Being by Plato, would emerge as a powerful general theory of the universe. Concern with the second issue, combined with a desire to claim experience free from error, gave rise to the first theory in psychology and the rival to rationalism, *empiricism.*

The First Protopsychologists: Alcmaeon and Empedocles

When psychology was founded as a science in the nineteenth century, it took what I will call the path through physiology. The new psychology was conceived as the scientific offspring of a fruitful marriage between philosophy of mind and the science of physiology. This marriage—or alliance, as Wilhelm Wundt called it—was reflected in the careers of psychology's main founders, Wundt, William James, and Sigmund Freud. Wundt and James had M.D. degrees and taught physiology, but moved toward philosophy, holding professorial chairs in philosophy and starting laboratories of psychology along the way. Freud, too, was an M.D. and early saw psychology as a branch of neurophysiology, but was learned in and wrote about philosophical issues. All three were thus physician-philosophers. However, long before psychology established itself as a science on the path through physiology, there were physician-philosophers—I shall call them *protopsychologists*—who approached the problems of the mind through the discipline of physiology.

The first appears to have been Alcmaeon of Croton (fl. 500 B.C.E.). Alcmaeon was a physician who practiced some of the earliest dissections. He was also interested in philosophy and directed his attention to understanding perception. He dissected the eye and traced the optic nerve to the brain. Unlike later thinkers, such as Empedocles and Aristotle, Alcmaeon correctly believed that sensation and thought occur in the brain. Alcmaeon also proposed a view of perception that was developed into the first theory in psychology by another physician-philosopher who opposed Parmenides' rejection of the validity of experience.

This protopsychologist, Empedocles of Acragas (fl. 450 B.C.E.), may be regarded as the founder of *empiricism,* the orientation to philosophy that finds truth in appearances and rejects reason as tending to fantasy. Following Alcmaeon, Empedocles believed that the senses are "duct[s] of understanding" through which information about the world travels to the brain (Vlastos, 1991, p. 68), and upon that basis developed a theory of perception that would justify our commonsense reliance on our senses. Empedocles proposed that objects emit effluences that are sense-modality-specific copies of themselves, and they enter the body through the ducts of the senses. Today, we know that smell works this way; our noses respond to certain molecules given off by some things. Empedocles thought this true of all kinds of perception. Unlike Alcmaeon, Empedocles returned to the usual Greek location of the mind in the heart or chest, saying that the effluences get in the bloodstream where they meet and mix in the heart. The agitation of the effluences in the beating of the heart, Empedocles argued, was thinking. His theory, although it sounds absurd today, was an important step for naturalism because it proposed a purely physical basis for mental activity, which was usually attributed to a soul.

Empedocles' views are characteristically empiricist in claiming that we know reality by observing it, specifically by internalizing copies of objects. His theory of cognition, suitably updated, is the most widely held theory in cognitive psychology today. Most cognitive psychologists believe that perceptual processes create mental representations which are in turn the objects of our thinking. Empedocles also shows why empiricists have generally contributed more to psychology than have rationalists. Wishing to demonstrate that the senses are reliable sources of truth, the empiricist needs to provide a theory of perception. The rationalist, on the other hand, simply denies the validity of sensory information, and so can ignore problems of empirical psychology as philosophically irrelevant. At the same time, however, rationalists have helped correct the empiricist tendency to see the mind as no more than a simple piece of clay or a mirror of the world, and have contributed to theories of memory, thinking, decision making, and cognitive development.

The Last Physicists: Atomism

The last classical philosophers to be concerned primarily with the nature of physical reality were Leucippus of Miletus (fl. 430 B.C.E.) and his better-known student, Democritus of Abdera (fl. 420 B.C.E.). After them, philosophers turned to questions about human knowledge, morality, and happiness. As the name of their school implies, the *atomists* proposed an idea that has proven immensely fruitful in physics: that all objects are composed of infinitesimally small atoms. For physics, this has meant that the complexity of substances we find around us can be analyzed as collections of a few particles interacting in mathematically precise ways.

Atomism can be metaphorically extended to psychology, where it has proved to be the most durable of psychological assumptions. Psychological atomism says that complex ideas such as "cathedral" or "psychology" can be analyzed as collections of simpler ideas, or even of sensations, that have been associated together. This assumption has been an integral part of empiricist theories of the mind, and it still, in some form, underlies all psychological systems except Gestalt psychology.

The atomists pushed their hypothesis to its limit, supporting *materialism* and *determinism.* A favorite motto of Democritus was that only "atoms and [the] Void exist in reality." There is no God and no soul, only material atoms in empty space. If only atoms exist, then free will must be an illusion. Leucippus said, "Nothing happens at random; everything happens out of reason and by necessity." The soul and free will are illusions that can be reduced to the mechanical functioning of our physical bodies. Democritus became known as the "Laughing Philosopher" because he laughed at the follies of human beings believing in freedom and struggling against the necessities of Fate.

Atomism served to deepen the divide between *Appearance* and *Reality* and to bolster rationalism. Democritus wrote, "We know nothing accurately in reality, but only as it changes according to the bodily condition and the constitution of those things that impinge upon [the body]" (Freeman, 1971, p. 93), concluding that only reason can penetrate to the reality of the atoms (Irwin, 1989). Democritus adopted a version of Empedocles' theory of cognition. Democritus said that every object gives off special kinds of atoms called *eidola,* which are copies of the object. When these reach our senses, we perceive the object indirectly through its copy. Thus, our thought processes are restricted to putting together or taking apart the *eidola*-images in our brains. Democritus sensed a difficulty in this theory that would bedevil eighteenth-century philosophers after atomism was resurrected by the Scientific Revolution. The *eidola,* and thus our perceptions, are not accurate or precise copies of the objects that emit them. For example, the atoms of Democritus and the atoms of modern physics are without color, yet we see color. The nature and source of such subjective sensations became a key starting point for psychology after 1700. Assessing their validity created a crisis for eighteenth-century philosophy.

Democritus also maintained an ethical doctrine that likewise came to trouble eighteenth-century ethical philosophers and psychologists. A consistent materialism, denying as it does God and the soul, can offer only one guide to the conduct of life: the pursuit of pleasure and the avoidance of pain. This doctrine is called *hedonism.* We find Democritus saying, "The best thing for man is to pass his life so as to have as much joy and as little trouble as may be" (Copleston, 1962, p. 93). This is the logical outcome of naturalism, for it reduces values to our natural bodily experiences of pleasure and pain. To many, however, it is morally offensive, for if an individual's pleasure is the sole criterion of the good, what right has anyone to condemn the happy and successful criminal or tyrant? Such moral concerns were at the heart of Socrates' and Plato's thinking, and Plato once suggested burning Democritus's books. Democritus's own answer to this moral dilemma strikes most people as lame: The greatest pleasure is philosophizing—greater than the obvious physical pleasures—and the happy (good) life is a philosophical one.

Humanism: The Sophists

The key to success in the Athenian *polis* was *rhetoric:* the art of persuasion. Political power depended on effective speech in the assembly, and being a litigious people, Athenian citizens had to argue lawsuits and sit in judgment on juries. Therefore, the ability to make and critically comprehend complex arguments was a skill of great value. Naturally, then, rhetoric became an object of study, a profession, and an expertise to be taught. The Athenian teachers of rhetoric were called *Sophists,* from *sophistes* (meaning "expert") the source of the word "sophisticated." They were the first paid professionals in history, and they represent the beginnings of higher, as opposed to childhood, education (Clark, 1992). The practical concerns of the Sophists mark an important turn in philosophy from concern with the cosmos to concern with human life and how it ought to be lived.

As hired advocates and teachers of rhetoric, the Sophists did not profess a system of philosophy, but certain important philosophical attitudes emerged from their practice. If the Sophists had a central idea, it was stated by Protagoras (approximately 490–420 B.C.E.): "Of all things the measure is man, of things that are that they are, and of things that are not that they are not" (Sprague, 1972). Protagoras's motto is ambiguous, suggesting a range of meanings from the personal through the cultural to the metaphysical. At the center of all of them, however, is *humanism,* a concern with human nature and human living instead of the protoscientific concerns of the naturalists.

On its narrowest personal interpretation, "man is the measure of all things" endorses a *relativistic empiricism,* a humanistic preference for Appearance over Reality. Whatever may be the ultimate constituent of nature—water, fire, or atoms—the world we humans live in is the world as it appears to us in our immediate experience. Truth for us, as a practical matter, will never be the *phusis,* but will be the familiar world of people and things; usable truth lies in Appearances, not a speculative reality. Yet, because truth is in appearances, truth is relative to each perceiver: Each human being is the only qualified judge of how things appear to him or her. Two people may enter the same room, yet to one the room is warm, to the other cool, if the former has been out in a blizzard and the latter downstairs stoking the furnace. Neither perception is incorrect; each is true for its perceiver, and there is no hidden Reality of the matter.

"Man is the measure of all things" carries a cultural, or, to use a term of today, a multicultural meaning in addition to its individual meaning. The Greeks were cultural chauvinists; their word "barbarian," with all of its negative connotations, simply meant non-Greek-speaking. For them, there is only one right way of life—the Greek way— and all others were ways of folly or wickedness. The Sophists challenged Greek thinking on this point, championing a form of *cultural relativism.* Just as each person knows what is true for himself, so cultures may arrange their affairs in any number of equally valid and satisfying ways. Hellenes speak Greek and Romans speak Latin; neither is superior to the other. Greeks worship Zeus, the Anglo-Saxons, Wodan; each is the god of his people.

Finally, "man is the measure of all things" has a metaphysical meaning. If the alleged Reality of nature is unknowable, so, too, are the gods (Luce, 1992). There is no divine truth or god-given law to which human beings are subject. Right and wrong are matters for cultures, not gods, to decide. Science and philosophy ought not waste time on idle speculation about Reality or the gods, but concern itself with practical achievements conducive to human happiness and workable compromises through which humans can live together.

The Sophists' relativism was an important innovation in the history of Western thought, but carried dangers for Greek democracy and for Western social and political thought down to the present. The Sophists sharpened the division between *phusis* (nature) and *nomos* (human law). By considering their way of life the best life, traditional Greeks identified *phusis* and *nomos:* the Greek way of life, their *nomos,* was the best, that is, the natural (*phusis*) way of life, ideally suited to human nature (*phusis*). The Sophists denied this identification, making *nomos* a mere matter of arbitrary convention, a set of equal ways of life lived in different cultures, none superior to another. Indeed, the Sophist Antiphon elevated convention (*nomos*) above nature, saying that human laws bind human nature (*phusis*), presumably in different ways in different cultures.

The danger for Athenian democracy emerged in Plato's lifetime, when the aristocrat Callicles says, in Plato's dialogue *Gorgias* (the name of a Sophist who appears in it), that laws are made by weak and inferior—but more numerous—citizens to fetter the naturally strong and superior ones who ought to rule. De Sade, Nietzsche, and, in some moods, Freud, later agreed. Callicles put his claim into action, participating in an aristocratic coup against Athenian democracy. Ever since the time of the Sophists, the questions of what human nature is and what, if any, way of life is natural to it, have challenged those parts of psychology and philosophy devoted to human happiness. These challenges were first met head-on by Socrates.

Enlightenment and Eudaemonia: Socrates

Much to his own liking, Socrates was a troublesome and troubling figure in his own lifetime and has remained so in the history of Western thought. For conventional

Athenians, Socrates was a troublemaker whose deliberately provocative questions about virtue corrupted their children and undermined their morals. For Christian philosophers, and especially for those still Christian in outlook if not in faith, Socrates was an attractive figure, a poor wandering seeker after virtue who annoyed the smug and the self-righteous and whose reward was execution. Although a citizen of Athens and an admired soldier, Socrates, like Jesus, came from a modest background, being the son of a stone-mason, and challenged the reigning values of the day, whether the aristocrat's love of power and glory or the merchant's love of money. Speaking to the jury that condemned him, Socrates said, "I go about doing nothing but persuading you, young and old, to care not for the body or money in place of it, or so much as, excellence of soul" (*Apology,* 30a, trans. R. E. Allen). For Nietzsche and for the German neo-Pagans of the turn of the century—some of whom turned to that decisive leader Hitler—Socrates and Jesus were evil teachers who clouded the minds of the naturally strong with altruistic morality and bound their hands with manacles of law passed by the weak.

Socrates, it seems, was a dangerous man, but what did he teach? In a sense, nothing. Socrates was a moral philosopher, unconcerned with physics and, though Athenians took him for one, not a Sophist. He was on a self-defined quest for the nature of true virtue and goodness, though he professed not to know what they were. In his teaching, he would closely question a young man or group of young men about some topic related to virtue. What is justice? Beauty? Courage? The Good? Socrates' interlocutors would offer some conventional definition which Socrates would then tear apart with clever and penetrating questions. For example, in the *Gorgias* Callicles defines justice as "the rule of the strong," reflecting his aristocratic birth and Sophistic training (Gorgias was a Sophist). So devastating is Socrates' assault on Callicles' beliefs, however, that Callicles flees rather than give them up. Those who stayed with Socrates came to share his own mental state of *aporia,* or enlightened ignorance. With Socrates, they had to confess they were ignorant about what justice (or whatever virtue was under discussion) really was, but realized they were better off than before because they had been disabused of their conventional, but wrong, beliefs.

Although Socrates taught no positive doctrine, his philosophical approach contained several important innovations. The first was his search for the general nature of the virtues and of virtue itself. Intuitively, we recognize that returning a pencil and establishing a democracy are just acts, but what they have in common—what justice itself as such is—remains elusive. A spectacular sunset and a Mozart symphony are both beautiful, but what they share in common, or what beauty itself is, remains likewise elusive. Moreover, Socrates took his inquiries to a higher level. Justice, beauty, honor, and so on are all good, but what they have in common, or what *good* itself is, remains elusive. In his domain of moral philosophy, Socrates began to try to understand the meaning and nature of general human concepts such as justice and beauty in the abstract. Plato and Aristotle would broaden Socrates' quest from ethics to include the whole range of human concepts in every area, creating the field of *epistemology*—the search for truth itself—a central undertaking of all later philosophy and psychology.

Socrates' method, a special sort of dialogue called the *elenchus,* was innovative as well. Socrates believed that everyone possesses moral truth, even if they are unaware of it. Socrates called himself a "midwife" to knowledge of virtue, bringing it out of people by questions rather than simply describing it to them. So, for example, he would use specific cases to undermine false ideas about virtue. A young man might define courage in Bronze Age fashion, as fighting honorably and fearlessly against one's ene-mies, and Socrates might counter it with something like the Charge of the Light Brigade: Brave but foolish, and bringing death and defeat to one's whole people. Such questions and problems weakened and eventually—for those who stayed—dislodged false beliefs and ended in *aporia*. However, precisely because we can make correct judgments about what is virtuous and what is not, even if we cannot give grounds for our intuitions, Socrates assumed knowledge of virtue is already in us if we but learn to seek it with him and make our latent knowledge conscious and explicit. In some re-spects, the Socratic *elenchus* is the starting point of depth psychotherapies, such as psy-choanalysis. With Socrates, the psychoanalyst maintains that we have learned false beliefs that make us ill, yet we contain somewhere within a liberating truth that can be found by the quest for self-knowledge that is *psychotherapy.*

Like psychoanalysis, Socrates also believed that nothing is worthy of the name knowledge or truth unless we are conscious of it and can explain it. A person might infallibly do good, but for Socrates he was not truly good and worthy unless he could give a rational justification of his actions. In his quest for virtue, Socrates demanded more than good behavior or correct intuitions about right and wrong; he demanded a theory of virtue, the Greek word *theoria,* meaning contemplation, not action. In the *Symposium,* the semi-divine seeress and alleged teacher of Socrates, Diotima, says to him, "Don't you know that right opinion without ability to render an account is not knowledge—how could an unaccountable thing be knowledge . . . . Right opinion . . . is intermediate between wisdom and ignorance?" (202a, trans. R. Allen).

Socrates' requirement that knowledge be an explicitly stated and defended theory was adopted by Plato and became a standard one in Western philosophy, setting it off from other traditions that cultivate intuition and depreciate abstract theory. It has had a powerful effect in psychology, erecting an ideal of theories of mind and behavior that has been continuously aspired to, but never met. In Chapter 15, we will see that Socrates' demand for theory became problematical in the wake of the failures of artifi-cial intelligence and cognitive science. Beginning in the 1960s, cognitive scientists un-dertook to create artificial minds that some hoped would be better than humans'. It proved far more difficult than expected to turn cognitive theory into working intelli-gence, and the biggest pitfall was capturing what humans do intuitively, without thought. Some philosophers and psychologists today have a higher respect for thought-less intuition than they used to, and challenge the ancient Socratic equation of knowl-edge with theory.

Finally, in his concern with virtue, Socrates raised important questions about human motivation. Central problems for any moral philosophy are providing reasons why people should do the right things and explaining why they so often fail to do them. The first problem—why people should be virtuous—was never a difficulty for Greek and Roman philosophers because they assumed, entirely without discussion, that virtue and *eudaemonia* were deeply linked, if not identical. The usual translation of *eudaemonia* into English is "happiness," but *eudaemonia* meant more than the at-tainment of pleasure, though it included pleasure. It meant living well, or flourishing. Like all Greeks, Socrates assumed that the proper end of life was *eudaemonia,* and he believed that being virtuous would guarantee *eudaemonia.* Thus he, and they, assumed that because all people seek happiness, *eudaemonia,* they naturally seek virtue, and there was no need to provide special reasons for doing good as opposed to seeking evil. Plato asserts in the *Symposium* (205a, trans. R. E. Allen), ". . . the happy are happy by possession of good things, and there is no need in addition to ask further for what purpose he who wishes to be happy wishes it. On the contrary, the answer seems final." In their near-identification of happiness and virtue, the Greeks differed sharply from later ethical systems, including Christianity, which urge us to be ethical but warn that pursuing virtue often brings suffering rather than happiness.

Since for Greek and Roman ethical philosophers there was no problem explaining why people seek virtue, they focused instead on the question of why people act badly. If virtue and happiness are almost the same, the existence of bad behavior becomes hard to explain. Because people want to be happy, they therefore ought always to act rightly. Socrates proposed a purely intellectual answer to the problem of evil, maintaining that people act badly only when they are ignorant of the good. His explanation of bad behavior was predicated on the assumption behind the *elenchus:* people know what virtue is, but have acquired false beliefs that mask their knowledge of the good and lead them to do evil. Once someone knows what virtue truly is, he will automatically act correctly. Thus, Callicles, having abandoned his dialogue with Socrates, participated in an aristocratic coup because he remained in the grip of the false belief that justice was the rule of the strong. In Socrates' account, Callicles was not evil, but simply misguided. Had he continued his encounter with Socrates, he would have learned that justice was not the rule of the strong, and would not have sought the overthrow of democracy. For Socrates, knowledge of the good—not a good will or love of virtue— was all that was needed to effect good behavior. Later Greek and Roman ethical philosophers, including Plato himself and especially the early Christians, found Socrates' intellectual solution implausible, because manifestly some people enjoy wrongdoing, and even the virtuous sometimes do wrong while knowing it is wrong. Wrestling with the source of evil in human behavior became an important question for motivational psychology.

THE GREAT CLASSICAL PHILOSOPHIES

Plato: The Quest for Perfect Knowledge

Background

Unlike his teacher, who was the son of a stone-mason, Plato sprang from the aristocratic class that Socrates disdained. When Sparta finally defeated Athens at the end of the long Peloponnesian wars, a clique of aristocrats, including two of Plato's relatives, carried out a short-lived coup against the Athenian democracy. Ironically, when the coup was defeated, Socrates was caught up in the purge of aristocrats and their supporters because so many of them, like Callicles, had been in his circle of students. Socrates was condemned to the death he chose in preference to exile from the city he loved. Plato naturally became disenchanted with political life as he knew it. Aristocrats, even relatives, friends, and students, might selfishly sacrifice the general good to their personal ambition. A democracy might fear and kill a loyal yet critical citizen because he questioned conventional ideas of virtue and sought to know Virtue itself.

Socrates, the first moral philosopher, had tried to find just such an overarching Good. His student, Plato, built on and broadened Socrates' moral concerns, filling Socrates' *aporia* with his own philosophy, the first general philosophical point of view in the history of Western civilization. Plato dedicated his philosophy above all to the pursuit of justice both in the state and in the individual. The Greek word for justice, *dikaiosune,* had a specific, relatively narrow meaning: getting out of life what one fairly deserved, no more and no less. The aristocratic junta was guilty of justice's corresponding vice, *pleonexia,* grasping for more than one is fairly due. In his mature dialogues, Plato tried to lead his students from their conventional understanding of justice to a larger one, doing good for its own sake regardless of one's personal interests.

Cognition: What Is Knowledge?

Socrates had tried to find general definitions of the virtues and of Virtue itself. Plato saw that Socrates' quest was part of a larger, not merely ethical, undertaking— that of finding definitions for any sort of general terms. Just as we can define *courage* apart from particular courageous actions, or *beauty* apart from particular beautiful things or people, so we can define *cat* apart from any particular cats, or *fish* apart from any particular fish.

Talk of cats and fish may seem to make Plato's quest trivial, but that is not the intent here. What sets human beings apart from the animals is that we have the capacity for abstract knowledge, while animals can respond only to the concrete here-and-now. Science, including psychology, searches for general knowledge about how things are everywhere in the universe at any point in time. Psychologists run experiments on small groups of people, but build theories about human nature. In a social psychology experiment, for example, our concern is not why Bob Smith or Susan Jones failed to help a person in distress, but why people at large so often fail to help others in so many situations. Plato was the first thinker to inquire into how knowledge is possible and how it may be justified. In philosophy, he created the field of epistemology—the study of knowledge—which eventually created cognitive psychology.

Modern science, the heir to the empiricist tradition in epistemology that Empedocles inaugurated, justifies its claims to knowledge by citing confirming observations. However, science has learned to live with an ugly fact about generalizations based on past experience: As Plato was the first to point out, what seems true based on today's data may be overturned by tomorrow's. The truth for which Socrates died cannot be so transient, so ugly, Plato thought. Centuries later, looking upon a Classical Grecian urn, John Keats uttered Plato's sentiments:

> When old age shall this generation waste,
> Thou shalt remain, in midst of other woe
> Than ours, a friend to man, to whom thou say'st,
> "Beauty is truth, truth beauty,—that is all
> Ye know on earth, and all ye need to know."

For the Platonist, truth, and hence our knowledge of it, has two overriding characteristics. First, like Keats's Grecian urn that outlasts human generations, a belief is true—is knowledge—only if it is true in all times and all places absolutely. Socrates wanted to know what justice or beauty *is,* apart from just acts and beautiful things, and knowledge of justice or beauty itself would therefore be true of all just acts and beautiful things in the past, now, and forever. Second, though not part of Keats's romantic yearnings, for Plato, as for Socrates, knowledge claims had to be rationally justifiable. A judge who always judges rightly or a connoisseur of impeccable taste does not, for Plato, genuinely know the truth unless he can explain his judgments and by force of argument convince others they are correct.

Unlike the Skeptics (see p. 69), who were also students of Socrates, Plato never questioned Socrates' faith that there was a truth to replace *aporia,* and he accepted earlier philosophers' arguments that sense perception was not the path to knowledge. From Heraclitus, Plato took the belief that the *phusis* was fire, and the conclusion that the physical world was therefore always in a state of becoming. Because the truth Plato sought lay in the realm of Being—eternally and unchangeably true—knowledge of it could not derive from material senses occupied with the changing material world. From the Sophists, Plato took the belief that how the world seems to each person and each culture is relative to each of them. Observation, therefore, is tainted by individual differences and the sort of cultural preconceptions that Socrates had challenged. Truth, then, could not be found in the error-prone processes of perception of the fleeting and imperfect world of ordinary experience.

So far, Plato had not gotten past Socratic *aporia;* Plato was convinced that transcendental truth exists, and that perception was not the path to knowledge. Then, in midlife, Plato studied geometry with the Pythagoreans and was transformed by it, as Thomas Hobbes and Clark Hull would be centuries later. In mathematics, Plato found not only a path to truth but something of the nature of truth itself. Plato came to side with Parmenides and Democritus in holding that the Way of Truth was the inward path of logic and reason rather than the outward path of Seeming, but went beyond them to indicate what truth—Reality—was. In the *Phaedo,* Plato has Socrates conclude, "So when does the soul grasp truth? For whenever she undertakes to investigate anything with the body it is clear that she will be thoroughly deceived by the body. . . . Therefore it is in reasoning, if anywhere, that any reality becomes clearly revealed to the soul" (65b–c, trans. G. Vlastos).

Most of us have, in high school or college, done proofs in geometry, such as of the Pythagorean theorem that the area of a square erected on the hypotenuse of a right-angled triangle is equal to the sum of the areas of squares erected on the other two sides. For Plato, the first revelation of geometry was the notion of proof. The Pythagorean theorem was provably true, a piece of genuine knowledge supported by logical argument rather than observation and measurement. The Socratic requirement that knowledge be justified by reason was satisfied by geometry, because anyone who followed the steps of the proof is compelled to believe the theorem. Geometry vindicated rationalism's claim that logic was the Way of Truth.

Plato went on to assert more, that rationalism was the way to Reality, too. The Pythagorean theorem is true not merely of a triangle drawn by someone doing the proof, or of all the people who have ever done or will do the proof, but of every right-angled triangle. However, given that the Pythagorean theorem is true, and that it is not true simply of triangles drawn by mathematicians, or a mere statistical generalization from a sample of triangles, but is a real universal proof, of what object is it true? Plato asserted that it was true of what he called the *Form of the Right-Angled Triangle,* an eternally existing, perfect right-angled triangle of no particular size.

The idea of Form helped reconcile Being and Becoming and provided a solution for Socrates' questions about the virtues and virtue itself that went beyond ethical philosophy. All right-angled triangles are copies of, and so resemble, the Form of the Right-Angled Triangle, and our knowledge of the Form is thus necessarily true of all of its copies. Forms belong to the realm of Being, subsisting eternally, while their material but ephemeral copies belong to the realm of Becoming. Similarly, in Socrates' ethical realm, every courageous act resembles the *Form of Courage,* every beautiful object resembles the *Form of Beauty,* and every just act resembles the *Form of Justice.* Courage, Beauty, and Justice—being all good—resemble the *Form of the Good.* Genuine knowledge then, which Socrates had sought in the moral domain, was knowledge of the Forms of things, not of things themselves. From a Platonic standpoint, psychologists seek to know the *Form of the Human.* By carefully studying living human beings, who resemble the Form of which they are copies in just the way drawings of right-angled triangles are copies of the Form of the Right-Angled Triangle, psychologists try to formulate knowledge of the human Form itself.

As Plato realized, describing the Forms is difficult, if not impossible, because by their very nature they cannot be displayed. Instead, Plato offered metaphors for the Forms, descriptions of the "child of goodness" rather than Goodness itself (*Republic,* 506e, trans. R. Waterfield). Three of these similes, the *Sun,* the *Line,* and the *Cave* are given in the *Republic.* A fourth, which offers a psychological path to the Forms, the *Ladder of Love,* occurs in the *Symposium*, probably written just before the *Republic.*

In the simile of the Sun, Plato says that the Form of the Good is to the intelligible world of the Forms what the sun is to the physical world of objects, the copies of the Forms. Plato did not think of vision as happening because light entered the eye, as we do today; that conception lay centuries in the future (Lindberg, 1992). Instead, the eye was thought to have a power of seeing by itself. Nevertheless, everyone recognized that light had to be present in order for vision to occur, because it's hard to see at night. The light of the sun was an "other third thing" needed (in addition to the eye and an object) for vision to occur. In the intelligible realm, reason has the power to grasp the Forms as in the physical world the eye has the power to see. However, in the intelligible realm, an "other third thing" is needed to illuminate the Forms, making it possible for reason to know them. Plato says that the "third thing" is the Form of the Good, analogous to the light of the Sun on earth.

The simile of the Sun is followed by the appropriately geometrical metaphor of the Line. Imagine a line (Figure 2–1) divided into four unequal sections,* whose relative length is a measure of its degree of truth. The line is first divided into two large

	OBJECTS	STATES OF MIND
INTELLIGIBLE WORLD	The Good	Intelligence or D Knowledge
	Forms	
	Mathematical objects	C Thinking
WORLD OF APPEARANCES	Visible Things	B Belief
	Images	A Imagining

FIGURE 2–1 Plato's metaphor of the line. (From Cornford, 1945)

* It is famous in philosophy that Plato's line can't be drawn as instructed in the text.

sections. The lower and shorter section stands for the world of Appearances and opinions—beliefs without proof—based on perception. The higher and longer section stands for the world of the Forms and provable knowledge about Them. The world of Appearances line is further divided into segments for the worlds of *Imagining,* the shortest line segment of all, and of *Belief,* next shortest in length.

Apprehension of images is the most imperfect way of knowing. Imagining is the lowest level of cognition, dealing with mere images of concrete objects, such as images cast in water. Plato relegated art to this realm, for when we see a portrait of a man we are seeing only an image, an imperfect copy of a thing. Plato banished art from his Utopian Republic as we wish to banish image polishing from our politicians. Better than looking at images is looking at objects themselves; Plato called this Belief. With the next, longer, section of the line, *Thinking,* we move from mere opinion to real knowledge, beginning with mathematical knowledge. Proofs vouchsafe the truth of mathematical propositions, and the objects of mathematical knowledge are not observable things but Forms themselves.

Mathematics, however, while providing a model of knowledge, was recognized by Plato to be imperfect and incomplete. It is imperfect because mathematical proofs assume things that cannot themselves be proved, falling short of the Socratic ideal of justified knowledge. For example, geometrical proofs—the form of mathematics most developed in Plato's time—depend on acceptance of axioms which themselves are intuitively appealing but unproved, such as the axiom that parallel lines never meet. Plato sensed what later proved correct, that if one changes the axioms, different systems of geometry emerge. To be True in Plato's sense, then, geometry needed metaphysical support, which he provided with the Forms. Mathematics is incomplete because not all knowledge concerns mathematics. Highest in importance were the moral truths sought by Socrates. The highest and longest segment of the line, then, represents the *World of the Forms,* the place of all Truth, mathematical or otherwise. Greatest among the Forms is, naturally, the Form of the Good, the ultimate object of Socrates' and Plato's quest.

The third "child of goodness" in the *Republic* is the most famous, the Allegory of the Cave. Imagine people imprisoned in a deep cave, chained in such a way that they can look only at the back wall of the cave. Behind them is a fire with a short wall between it and the prisoners. Bearers walk along a path behind the wall, holding above it statues of various objects, so that the objects cast shadows on the wall for the prisoners to see. For the prisoners, "the shadows of artifacts would constitute their only reality" (515c).

"Imagine that one of them has been set free and is suddenly made to stand up, to turn his head and walk, and to look toward the firelight" (515c–d). Plato goes on to tell how hard it would be for the liberated prisoner to give up his familiar reality for the greater reality of the fire and the statues. Harder still—he must be "dragged forcibly" through "pain and distress"—is the ascent past the fire out the mouth of the cave and into the world itself and the sun that illuminates it. Ultimately, he would feel joy in his new situation and think with disdain on the life he led, on the honors and glory the cave dwellers coveted as he himself once had. Finally, Plato asks that we imagine the prisoner returning to his old spot in the darkness, not seeing well and knowing the truth. "Wouldn't he make a fool of himself? Wouldn't they [the other cave dwellers] say that he'd come back from his upward journey with his eyes ruined and that it wasn't even worth trying to go up there? And wouldn't they—if they could—grab hold of anyone who tried to set them free and take them up there and kill him?" (517a).

Plato offers the cave as an allegory of the human condition. Each soul is imprisoned in an imperfect fleshly body, forced to look through eyes at imperfect copies of the forms, illuminated by the sun. As the freed prisoner turns his head around from the shadows to reality, Plato asks us to turn our souls around from the ordinary world and undertake the difficult journey to the better world of the Forms, the true Reality of which objects are but shadows. Today, Plato would offer a virtual reality (VR) chamber instead of the metaphor of the cave. In such a chamber, we interact with people and things that appear to be real, but are not. Someone raised in a VR chamber would be living a lie, inside the imagination of another, and Plato would want to rescue that person, and take him or her outside to the world as it is.

The Allegory of the Cave is at once optimistic and pessimistic (Annas, 1981). The optimism lies in the promise that, with effort, we can be liberated from ignorance and illusion. The cave is culture, the web of conventional beliefs the *elenchus* brought into question. Through philosophy and right education, however, we may escape from the cave of opinion of Appearances to the realm of knowledge of Reality. We may know the truth and it shall make us free. The pessimism lies in the difficulty and dangers of the path upward. It is not, Plato says, for everyone; it is only for an elite few whose character can bear its burdens. Most people do not want to be free, he suggests, and will greet their would-be liberators with jeers and even death.

The story is also an allegory of Socrates' life. He once was a political animal and a brave soldier, but caught a vision of Truth which he tried to share with the world to his own cost. Centuries later, when the *Republic* became known to Christians, the Allegory of the Cave and Socrates' life made powerful impressions, striking deep resonances with the story of Christ, who assumed human form, taught the truth, and was executed by disbelieving men.

The fourth metaphor for the Forms, the Ladder of Love in the *Symposium,* describes the love of Beauty, which Plato once said was the easiest path from this world to the Forms, and which inspired the romantic poet Keats. Through the female character Diotima, Plato describes an upward ascent from profane physical love to sacred love of the Form of Beauty itself.

The first rung of the ladder is sexual love, but it must be steered in the right direction by a philosophical guide, as Diotima was said to have led Socrates. The student "begin[s] while still young by going to beautiful bodies; and first, if his guide guides rightly, to love one single body" (201a). Plato's formulation of this first step depends on the conception and practice of male homoerotic love in Athens and much of the Classical world. Greek citizens—all male—spent most of their time together, depreciating home life and deprecating women. In this atmosphere, a well-defined homosexual culture grew up. Established citizens would take as lovers beautiful youths who had just entered puberty but whose beards were not grown and so were not yet citizens themselves. The older man became a mentor and teacher to the youth, and sometimes the relationship would last throughout life. The exact nature of these relationships, especially the kind of physical intimacy that took place, remains controversial. In the highest theory, the relationships were, as our saying goes, "platonic," although there is no question that sexual activity did in fact occur. Socrates, although susceptible to beautiful youths, condemned any sexual liaisons with his students, saying it was always bad for the young man. The *Symposium* ends with the story of Alcibiades, the most beautiful youth of his day and a student of Socrates, recounting the abject failure of his aggressive attempts to seduce Socrates.

In the conception of love in the *Symposium* and most of Plato's works (his last, the *Laws,* in which Socrates is absent, condemns homosexuality outright), love of women was inferior to homosexual love. Love of women leads to procreation of children, seeking immortality through merely physical offspring. Greek men tended to fear women as sexual temptresses who pulled their eyes from better things such as politics, war, or, for Socrates and Plato, philosophy and the pursuit of the Good. Such fear of sexuality passed over into certain strands of Christian thought, where physical pleasure was regarded as distracting men from knowing and worshipping God. Better than physical procreation—being "pregnant with respect to the body"—Plato thought, was being "pregnant in respect to [one's] soul" (209a), seeking immortality in the soul itself and through teaching students, and having intellectual rather than physical heirs.

Having learned to love one beautiful body, the student "next, learn[s] to recognize that the beauty on any body whatever is akin to that on any other body. . . . Realizing this, he is constituted a lover of all beautiful bodies and relaxes this vehemence for one, looking down on it and believing it of small importance. After this, he must come to believe that beauty in souls is more to be valued than in the body" (201b–c). With Socrates, we move beyond the care of the body to the care of the soul, and such a man will teach ugly youths of good soul—Socrates was famously ugly—believing "bodily beauty a small thing" (201c). Now, the teacher introduces the student to other kinds of beauty in practices such as music and art, and in studies such as mathematics and philosophy.

The lovers on Keats's Grecian urn are "forever panting and forever young." For Plato, however, when properly guided, *eros* goes beyond the pantings of physical love to a union with Beauty itself in the realm of the Forms where Truth is Beauty and Beauty in Truth (210e–211d):

> He who has been educated in the things of love up to this point, beholding beautiful things rightly and in due order, will then, suddenly, in an instant, proceeding at that point to the end of things of love, see something marvelous, beautiful in nature: it is that, Socrates, for the sake of which in fact all his previous labors existed.
>
> First, it ever is and neither comes to be nor perishes, nor has it growth nor diminution.
>
> Again, it is not in one respect beautiful but in another ugly, nor beautiful at one time but not at another, nor beautiful relative to this but ugly relative to that, nor beautiful here but ugly there, being beautiful to some but ugly to others.
>
> Nor on the other hand will it appear beautiful to him as a face does, or hands, or anything else of which body partakes, nor as any discourse or any knowledge does, nor as what is somewhere in something else, as in an animal, or in earth, or in heaven, or anything else; but it exists in itself alone by itself, single in nature forever, while all other things are beautiful by sharing in that in such manner that though the rest come to be and perish, that comes to be neither in greater degree nor less and is not at all affected. But when someone, ascending from things here through the right love of boys, begins clearly to see that, the Beautiful, he would pretty well touch the end. For this is the right way to proceed in matters of love, or to be led by another—beginning from these beautiful things here, to ascend ever upward for the sake of that, the Beautiful, as though using the steps of a ladder; from one to two, and from two to all beautiful bodies and from beautiful bodies to beautiful practices and from practices to beautiful studies, and from studies one arrives in the end at that study which is nothing other

than the study of that, the Beautiful itself, and one knows in the end, by itself, what it is to be beautiful. It is there, if anywhere, dear Socrates . . . that human life is to lived: in contemplating the Beautiful itself.

In the *Republic,* the Ladder of Love is elaborated into the lengthy and painstaking form of education laid down for the Republic's philosopher-leaders, the Guardians. As children, they receive the same moralizing form of education as all citizens. Plato proposes carefully censoring literature, including Homer, replacing it with tales crafted by teachers to build proper character. Music, too, is carefully controlled, so only what is perfect and pleasant is heard. Athletics, too, train the body as literature and music train the soul. Only the elite of the noblest souls, however, are selected for higher, academic education. Through philosophy, the Guardian elite are led out of the Cave of Opinion to a knowledge of the Forms, but they are obligated to return to the best cave going, Plato's Republic, and rule disinterestedly out of their inspired wisdom. Only they know what is best for all the citizens of the Republic.

In some other dialogues, a different path to the Forms is described that resembles Socrates' midwifery. From his Pythagorean education and from the Greek religion of Orphism, Plato adopted the idea of *reincarnation.* For example, in the *Phaedrus,* Plato works out a detailed scheme by which souls go through a cycle of reincarnations. Souls are born in heaven, and thus see the Forms before their first incarnation in "the pollution of the walking sepulcher we call a body" (250c, trans. W. Hamilton). The future fate of a soul depends on how virtuous a life it led on earth. At death, souls are brought to judgment. The wicked "go to expiate their sins in places of judgment beneath the earth" (249a) and may come back as beasts. The virtuous, especially those who had been philosophers (who on the third straight incarnation as philosophers, escape the wheel of rebirth), will ascend to the highest reaches of the heavens, and in the train of the gods see the Forms again. The less virtuous ascend less high in heaven and are more quickly reincarnated as lesser humans such as financier (third best) or farmer (seventh).

Thus, "every human soul by its very nature has beheld true being" (250a). In the sepulcher of the body, however, the "beatific vision" of the Forms is forgotten, more in bad people than in good. Knowledge of the Forms may be regained, however. As contemplation of beautiful things leads us to knowledge of Beauty itself because all beautiful things resemble Beauty, so all cats resemble the Form of the Cat, gerbils the Form of the Gerbil, just acts the Form of Justice, and so on for all universal concept terms. Because of the resemblance of things to the Forms that are within us, we can "collect out of the multiplicity of sense-impressions a unity arrived at by a process of reason. Such a process is simply the recollection of things which our soul once perceived when it took its journey with a god . . . gazing upwards toward what is truly real" (249b). Reincarnation explained for Plato how Socrates could hope to be a moral midwife giving birth to knowledge of virtue without explicitly teaching it. Knowledge of virtue, like all knowledge, is latent in the soul, hidden by the body and conventional belief, awaiting the right stimulus to be recollected.

Perhaps the oldest enduring controversy in the history of psychology is the debate between nativism and empiricism, nature and nurture. Plato is the first great exponent of *nativism,* holding that our character and knowledge are innate, being carried by the soul from its vision of the Forms and its lives in previous incarnations. Learning is a process of recollecting to consciousness what we already know but of which we have become ignorant. Later nativists dropped Plato's unscientific belief in reincarnation for evolution and genetics, but the question of how much we are shaped by our inheritance and how much we are shaped by the environment remains.

Motivation: Why Do We Act as We Do?

Plato's theory of cognition of the Forms is metaphysical rather than psychological. His ideas on education have been influential, especially on American education (Annas, 1981), but as a rationalist Plato distrusted the senses and so said little about the (to him) mundane and error-prone processes of perception and memory. However, as a moral psychologist, Plato keenly addressed questions about human motivation. He was the first thinker to try to give an account of why we behave the way we do.

Although Plato accepted the Greek beliefs that happiness (*eudaemonia*) and virtue are intimately connected and that all people naturally seek happiness, he did not accept his teacher's intellectualist moral determinism. Socrates had said that people always do what they believe is morally right, doing evil only out of ignorance of what is good. In the *Republic* and *Phaedrus,* Plato advances a more complex psychology of human motives and human action.

Plato divides the citizens of the Republic into three classes. By virtue of innate greatness of soul and the academic education it merits, the elite Guardians constitute the ruling class. Next in character are the Auxiliaries, who aid the Guardians by acting as soldiers, magistrates, and other functionaries of the Republic. The mass of the citizens make up the least inherently virtuous Productive Class. In a way reminiscent of Homeric psychology, Plato postulates three forms of soul present in every human being that parallel the three classes of citizens. Class membership is determined by which soul rules each citizen.

The highest form of soul, and the only immortal one, is the *rational soul,* located in the head because the soul, being perfect, must be round and must be located in the roundest and highest part of the body. The rational soul rules in the Guardians and is led to the Forms from which it came by their academic education. The second form of soul is the *spirited soul,* located in the chest and dominant in the Auxiliaries. The spirited soul represents the old Homeric virtues, being motivated by glory and fame. Because of its quest for noble things like glory and the immortality of fame, and because it can feel shame and guilt, the spirited soul is superior to the third soul, the *desiring soul,* located in the belly and below. The desiring soul is a disparate grab-bag of irrational wants. Physical desires for food or sex, which we share with animals, are paradigm cases of the appetites of the desiring soul, but desire for money is also located there. It may be best to think of the desiring soul as the pursuit of self-interest. It dominates in the Productive Classes, who are described as unfit to rule precisely because they seek their own interests, not the general interests of the state. Only the Guardians may rule, because their reason places them beyond self-interest.

In the *Phaedrus,* the three forms of soul are given in a famous metaphor later alluded to by a psychologist deeply read in the classics, Sigmund Freud. Plato depicts the personality as a chariot pulled by two horses. One horse is "upright and clean limbed . . . white with black eyes" whose "thirst for honor is tempered by restraint and modesty. He is a friend to genuine renown and needs no whip, but is driven simply by the word of command. The other horse is lumbering, crooked and ill-made . . . wantonness and boastfulness are his companions and he is . . . hardly controllable even with whip and goad" (253d). The first horse is the spirited soul, the second is the desiring soul. The charioteer is the rational soul, which should master the horses and drive them toward the good. Mastering the spirited soul is easy because it knows honor, and therefore, something of virtue. Mastering the desiring soul is nearly impossible; the most strenuous efforts by reason are required to break it utterly. Even when the rational soul thinks it is master, desire springs up in dreams, said Plato, a statement later linked with Freud. In dreams, a person "doesn't stop at trying to have sex with his mother . . . he doesn't hold back from anything, however bizarre or disgusting" (*Republic,* 571d).

For Plato, unlike Socrates, bad behavior may stem from more than ignorance; it may stem from insufficient mastery of the rational over the spirited and desiring souls. Foolish pursuit of honor may lead to disasters such as the Light Brigade. Even worse are the sins committed by giving in to the demands of the body. In the *Phaedrus,* Plato vividly describes the torments of a philosophical lover for a beautiful youth. Reason knows physical consummation of love is wrong, but the desiring horse races headlong into it. Only by the strongest measures, yanking on the reins until the horse's mouth is drenched in blood and beating its haunches until they collapse to the ground, will "the wicked horse abandon its lustful ways" (254e) and submit meekly to the commands of reason.

Plato's analysis of human motivation contains, however, a profound muddle that haunts later philosophical and scientific psychology (Annas, 1981). In his explicitly psychological descriptions of human personality, reason is sharply differentiated from irrational passion. The desiring soul, and to a lesser extent the spirited soul, simply *want,* being incapable of any sort of rational calculation at all; they are all drive and no reason, providing the energy that makes the chariot go. Reason is directive, steering the motivational souls to good ends; it is all reason and no drive, providing direction but not energy.

However, when Plato describes the souls operating in the citizens of his Republic, the picture is more complicated. Citizens of the Productive Class are supposed to be dominated by desire, but they do not dash about in a confused orgy of lust and gratification—they are productive. Merchants must be able to calculate how to buy or make goods that people want how to price and market them. Tailors and shoemakers must be able to design clothes and shoes and properly execute the means to make them. Similarly, Auxiliaries must be able to make and carry out battle plans.

Members of the Productive and Auxiliary classes clearly can calculate means to ends, suggesting that the desiring and spirited souls themselves have some measure of reason, being not mere engines of action. Reason, for its part, does more than merely steering calculation. The souls of the Guardians seek knowledge out of a special kind of *eros,* drawn not to physical bodies but by love of the Good and Beautiful themselves. Reason, then, is more than a calculator; it has a motive of its own: justice.

Later psychological thinkers wrestled with whether motive and reason are distinct or intertwined. Most theorists have favored Plato's official theory. In the Age of Reason, David Hume said that reason is and can only be a slave to the passions (see Chapter 5), capable of steering them but not of initiating action on its own. Freud agreed with Hume but modified Plato's image. The Homeric virtues having been lost by 1900, Freud describes the rational *ego* as a rider struggling to master the horse of the *id,* Plato's desiring soul. Others, however, saw more in feeling than irrational desire. Shortly before Hume, Blaise Pascal wrote that the heart has its reasons that reason does not understand; later, the romantics revolted against cold reason, elevating feeling and intuition over scientific calculation. In our own day, we worry about the triumph of the computer—the very model of Plato's charioteer—and about computer-inspired models of the mind, for which motives to do anything are missing.

Plato's chariot image contains another difficulty of long standing in psychology, called the *homunculus problem* (Annas, 1981). Homunculus means "little man." Plato asks us to imagine that the driver of a person's behavior is the rational soul, a charioteer. He thus invites us to think of the rational soul as a little man inside the head, who steers the behavior of the body and manages the passions of the heart, belly, and genitals the way a charioteer steers the chariot and masters its horses. However, what accounts for the behavior of the little charioteer, reason, inside the head? Has he got inside an even littler charioteer? Who has in turn a still smaller charioteer? And so on, ad infinitum? To explain the behavior of a person by positing a small person inside is not an adequate explanation, because the actions of the inner person, the homunculus, remain unexplained. To what extent Plato is guilty of this mistake is unclear (Annas, 1981), but it is a mistake that will crop up in psychology from Plato's day to our own.

Conclusion

Although Plato began with Socrates, he ultimately went a great deal further, in constructing the first general point of view in philosophy. We must call it a point of view rather than a system, because, unlike Aristotle, Plato did not work out a set of systematically interlocking theories across the whole range of human knowledge. For example, Plato's so-called Theory of the Forms is less a theory in epistemology than a vision, tempting to some people, of a higher reality (Annas, 1981). The Forms appear in different guises in different dialogues, and appear not at all in many. In the late dialogue, the *Thaetetus,* Plato discusses knowledge without mentioning the Forms, and concludes that truth is elusive. That Platonic thought was more a point of view than a system made it easier to assimilate to Christian thought during the Middle Ages. Christians could pick and choose the more otherworldly parts of Plato and identify the realm of the Forms with Heaven.

Plato's ideas resonate with many religions. For example, the basic idea of the Ladder of Love, that one can move toward enlightenment beginning with physical love, is found in the Hindu path of *Kama* (pleasure) and the Buddhist use of love imagery to lead the soul to the light of the *One,* though these Ladders do not involve homosexuality. Many, if not most, world religions teach that, in addition to this physical world, there is an invisible world of spirits. As with love, Brahman Hindus and Buddhists teach that this world is an illusion, *Maya,* and that the soul must have as little to do with it as possible or risk more reincarnations. With Plato, they bid the charioteer of the body to discipline desire, but go beyond metaphor to prescribe practices by which the desiring soul may be broken. In the *Phaedrus,* Plato talks metaphorically about controlling lust for one's beloved. Tantric Yoga and Daoist masters taught how to have sexual intercourse with perfect rational control while withholding orgasm to obtain spiritual strength (*Tantrism*) or personal health (*Daoism*).

Plato's otherworldliness takes us to points on which Plato changed Socrates' teachings in ways Socrates himself might have found disturbing. Once he had his own philosophy to push, Plato discarded the penetrating search of the *elenchus* for dialogues in which "Socrates'" students come off as toadies, saying "Oh yes, wise Socrates," and "It cannot be otherwise." Disdaining wealth and fame, Socrates was unworldly, but he was not otherworldly (Vlastos, 1991). Socrates never mentioned the Forms, and he always meant a virtuous life to be worthwhile in *this* world, not some imagined afterlife. Socrates would converse with, and try to save, the soul of anyone willing to undertake the *elenchus*. Plato was an elitist, reserving academic education for an innately wise ruling class, the Guardians, and, among them, he reserved philosophy only for the mature, over thirty, fearing it would make the young lawless.

Whatever its faults, the Platonic vision has been immensely influential. The twentieth-century philosopher and mathematician Alfred North Whitehead said, "The safest general characterization of the whole Western philosophical tradition is that it consists of a series of footnotes to Plato" (quoted by Artz, 1980, p. 15). Returning a copy of the *Republic* to Ralph Waldo Emerson, a Vermont farmer said, "That book has a great number of my ideas" (quoted by Artz, 1980, p. 16).

At St. John's College, the curriculum consists of reading the great books of Western civilization, and it is said that in their first semester students become either Platonists or Aristoteleans, and that they remain so at least until graduation. It is to Plato's great rival we now turn.

Aristotle: The Quest for Nature

Background

Like Plato, Aristotle (384–322 B.C.E.) came from a wealthy family, but from the remote province of Macedonia, which later became part of Yugoslavia and recently has become an independent nation. His father was a physician to the Macedonian king, and Aristotle was his whole life a biologist even while developing the first systematic philosophy in history. At 17, he went to the Academy to study with Plato, and remained there 20 years, earning the nickname "the Brain" from Plato himself. When Plato died, Aristotle left the Academy and traveled around the Adriatic doing zoological research, until being called by King Phillip II of Macedon to be tutor to his son, Alexander, the later world conqueror. Eventually, Aristotle returned to Athens and founded his own place of learning and research, the *Lyceum*. After Alexander's death in 323, anti-Macedonian feeling prompted Aristotle to flee Athens, fearing that Athenians might "sin twice against philosophy." He died in the town of Chalcis soon after.

The differences between Plato and Aristotle begin with temperament. Plato never developed a genuine system of thought, but in dramatic and provocative dialogues laid out a stirring cosmic vision, and there was clearly about him, as about so many early Greek thinkers, something of the seer and shaman. Aristotle, on the other hand, was first and foremost a scientist, an empirically inclined observer of nature as the rationalist Plato could never be. Whether writing about the soul or ethics, metaphysics or politics, dreams or art, Aristotle was always practical and down to earth. Those works of his that survive are prose treatises, probably his lecture notes. In them, we hear the voice of the first professor, reviewing the literature—fortunately for us, else we would know next to nothing about the naturalists—before advancing his own carefully thought out and often reworked ideas. We never find in Aristotle the otherworldly quasi-mysticism of Plato.

Instead, Aristotle was always concerned with what is *natural*. Unlike Plato, for whom what is real, and therefore natural, exists in heavenly Being rather than on earth, Aristotle, the biologist, looked to this world to define what is. Unlike the Sophists, he drew no sharp line between *phusis* and *nomos,* believing that the human way of life should be built on what was best for human nature. We should not, however, exaggerate the differences between Plato and Aristotle. As Plato built on Socrates, Aristotle built on Plato.

Philosophy of Science

Aristotle worked out a comprehensive philosophical system, including the first psychology. I will restrict my discussion here to his philosophy of science and his psychology. As a working scientist who was also a philosopher, Aristotle painstakingly considered the goals and methods of science, defining in large measure what science would be until the Scientific Revolution of the seventeenth century overthrew Aristotle to create the very different science we know today.

The Four Fashions of Explanation.   Aristotle set out four ways by which to explain things and events. Like Plato, Aristotle tended to focus on the former more than the latter, on understanding what a thing is, rather than on the dynamics of change, which is the focus of modern science.

The most basic conceptual division for Aristotle was between form and matter. Aristotle's conception of matter was very different from ours. Today, we think of matter as coming in distinct types with distinct properties, as in the elements in the atomic table or the list of subatomic particles of quantum physics. However, for Aristotle, precisely because they can be distinguished and defined, such particles are already mixtures of intelligible form and raw matter. In his conception, matter was sheer undifferentiated physical existence. The closest modern parallel is matter as it existed in the first seconds after the Big Bang, before the particles and elements had come into existence. Matter as such was unknowable, said Aristotle; for matter to be knowable—to be an object of science—it has to be joined to form.

Form, of course, is a term Aristotle took from Plato, but characteristically he stripped it of its heavenly existence and demystified it; hence, in Plato it is Form, in Aristotle, form. Form is, most generally, what makes a thing that which it is, defining it and thus making it intelligible to us. The paradigm example of the relation of form and matter is that of a statue. Imagine a bronze statue of the type that stands on Monument Avenue in Richmond, representing a Confederate Civil War general such a Robert E. Lee, or soon, tennis champion Arthur Ashe.

The *matter* of a statue is what it is made of; in the case of a Monument Avenue statue, it is bronze. When the bronze is cast, it takes on form, becoming a likeness of Lee or Ashe. The form makes the statue what it is. The same bronze could be cast as Lee or Ashe: same matter, different form. We can also have the same form in different matter: the figure of Lee or Ashe might be rendered in plaster, clay, or plastic.

Table 2–1   Aristotle's Four Fashions of Explanation

1. Material Cause: The Physical Particularity of a Thing

   Formal: The Why of a Thing, which includes the other three causes.

2. Essential Cause: What a Thing Is

3. Efficient Cause: Processes That Make a Thing or Make It Work

4. Final Cause: The Purpose of a Thing or Event

What makes something a statue of Robert E. Lee or of Arthur Ashe is, then, its form, not its matter, and we know the statue through the form rather than the matter.

Aristotle rejected what he called the *separability of the Forms,* Plato's sometime thesis that the Forms exist in a realm of Being far from our imperfect physical world. His general standpoint was that separate Forms do not explain anything. They are just glorified individuals—perfect, heavenly individuals, true—but individuals nonetheless. There is no reason to think that if an artist casts 100 identical statues there must be a separate heavenly Form of the Statue that they all resemble. Similarly, there may be thousands of cats in the world, but there is no reason to think there's an additional heavenly Form of the Cat, too. Positing one perfect Cat (or statue) really does nothing to explain the nature of the physical cats (or statues) we see. We lose nothing by dropping the separate Forms.

Aristotle's concept of form, however, is more than just shape and is comprised of the other three causes. First, form defines what something is in its essence: *essential cause.* Second, form includes how things come into existence or are made: *efficient cause.* The efficient cause of a bronze statue is the process of casting the metal; of a marble statue, the processing of chipping and polishing a block of marble into the desired shape. Third, form includes the purpose for which a thing exists: *final cause.* Statues are erected to honor a great person and perpetuate his or her memory. Taking all these things together—a thing's shape and essence, its process of creation, and its purpose for being—constitute a thing's form, why it is what it is.

Aristotle's four fashions of cause seem strange to us because we have inherited a quite different conception of causation from the Scientific Revolution. From Aristotle's list, modern science accepts only efficient causation—processes by which objects affect one another through physical forces. Aristotle's other fashions of causation—material, essential, and final—have been redefined or eliminated from the vocabulary of modern science.

We no longer think of matter as a "cause" at all, because modern science strives to explain events, not things. We find it sensible to ask the cause of Bill Clinton's election, but find it odd to ask the cause of Bill Clinton. Modern science has also undermined Aristotle's idea of essential cause. In a Platonic vein, Aristotle thought that essences, like Forms, were fixed and unchanging. Thus, the essential natures of the cat, of the dog, of the horse, while not separate heavenly Forms, were, for Aristotle, still immutable. Evolution, however, teaches that cats, dogs, and horses have changed over time and will continue to change. Form as eternal, unchanging essence does not exist.

Final causes, too, have been dismissed by modern science, at least by natural science. A recurring maxim of Aristotle's was "Nature does nothing to no purpose." Everything and every event, Aristotle thought, happens in part because there is a purpose behind it. If I pick up a stone and let it go, it falls to earth. According to Aristotle, the stone falls to earth because it is striving to return to its natural place in the universe, the earth from which it sprang and to which it belongs. Its movement downward is purposeful and teleological, directed to ward the goal of returning to its proper place in the cosmos. We see its fall as the outcome of efficient causation only, the effect of earth's gravity on the mass of the stone. Much of the simplifying triumph of modern science has been eliminating essential and final causes, showing that efficient causes are the only ones operative in nature. The struggle between efficient and final causes has been especially acute in the biological and social sciences, as we shall see.

Potentiality and Actuality

In Aristotle's conception, everything in the universe (with two exceptions) has both potentiality and actuality. A lump of bronze is actually a lump of bronze, but it is potentially a statue. The two exceptions to the rule of potentiality and actuality are pure matter in Aristotle's sense, and his unmoved mover, whom Christians later identified with God. Sheer matter without form of any kind is pure potentiality, capable of becoming anything, as matter was at the moment of the Big Bang. If there is pure potentiality, Aristotle thought, there must be pure actuality, a being whose potentiality is used up, incapable of further change, perfected; this is the unmoved mover. Because it has no potentiality, the unmoved mover cannot change. Because the unmoved mover is perfect, fully actualized, other things naturally move toward it as their potentiality becomes actuality. The unmoved mover moves by being desired, not through activity of its own, the way a beloved moves a lover by inspiring desire. The more fully actualized a thing is, the nearer it is to the unmoved mover. The striving for actualization creates a grand hierarchy among all things, from perfectly unformed, neutral matter in a state of pure potentiality up to the unmoved mover. Aristotle called this hierarchy the *natural scale,* but later it was called the *Great Chain of Being.*

The fit of the unmoved mover to the Christian God is partial. On the one hand, the unmoved mover is perfect, like God, and we rightly want to be near Him; on the other hand, the unmoved mover is not remotely like a person, and, being incapable of change and thus of any action whatsoever, is not active in history as is the God of the Bible. The unmoved mover is a logical construct demanded by Aristotle's metaphysics, not a God in any traditional sense.

The ideas of potentiality and actuality may be regarded as a creative solution to an important biological problem that was not fully solved until the 1950s. Plant an acorn and it becomes an oak; plant a tomato seed and it becomes a tomato plant; fertilize a human ovum and it becomes a human being. Unlike the casting or chiseling of a statue, these changes are forms of spontaneous development. We don't force the acorn to become an oak the way we force bronze to become a statue. Moreover, development is directed to a predetermined end. Acorns never become tomato plants; tomato seeds never become oaks; and human mothers never give birth to bears.

Something apparently guides the acorn to naturally actualize its potential oak-hood. Today (but only since 1951), we know that what guides biological development is DNA. For Aristotle, however, it was form. The purpose, or final cause, of an acorn is to become an oak, and so the striving of an acorn toward oak-hood is an aspect of its form. Plato's Forms were perfect Objects in the realm of Being. Aristotle's forms, at least in the biological world, are dynamic, directing development and constituting and controlling the life processes of living things.

Psychology

For Aristotle, psychology was the study of the soul, that which differentiates the animate from the inanimate worlds. Aristotle defines the soul as "the form of a natural body having life potentially within it" (*On the Soul,* II, i, 412a20–1). All living things possess soul as their form, and thus it is a living thing's soul that defines its nature, what it is to be that living thing. Soul is the actuality and the actualizing, directing force of any living organism, fulfilling the body's potential *having of life.*

As we will learn later, in the wake of the Scientific Revolution of the seventeenth century, particularly through the work of René Descartes, the relation of soul to body became deeply problematical, but it was not so for Aristotle. Not all things can have souls, according to Aristotle; only those things—the bodies of organisms—that have the potential for life (Burnyeat, 1992). Flesh and blood may have soul as its form, but bronze may not. In the seventeenth century, Descartes would propose that living bodies are machines little different from clocks, making the uniting of souls with only some types of machines a real issue, and ultimately prompting the question of modern artificial intelligence, "Can a computer have a soul?"

As the form of a living thing, soul is thus the essential, efficient, and final cause of an organism. As essential cause, the soul is what defines an animal or plant—a cat is a cat because it has a cat's soul and behaves like a cat. The soul is the efficient cause of bodily growth and movement and of life processes generally. Without soul, the body is not actualized and is dead, mere matter. The soul is also the final cause of an organism, for the body serves the soul and the soul guides its purposive development and activity. To summarize, of any living organism, the material cause is the body of which the living thing is made, and the soul is the form, being the efficient cause of life processes, being the animal's essence, and being the organism's final cause, the purpose of the body.

Aristotle's view of the relation of soul to body is different from Plato's. Because he rejected the separability of the forms, Aristotle rejected the separability of soul and body, the dualism of Plato, the Pythagoreans, or of many religions. The form of a statue is not a separate thing added to bronze to make it a statue. Similarly, as the form of the body, the soul is not a separate thing added to the body. An organism is a unity. Without soul, the body is dead; without body, there is no soul. Aristotle put it this way in *On the Soul,* "That is why we can wholly dismiss as unnecessary the question whether the soul and the body are one: it is as meaningless to ask whether the wax and the shape given to it by the stamp are one" (II. i, 412b6–9).

Aristotle evades the ways of thinking about mind and body ushered in by Descartes. He is not a dualist with Plato, Christianity, or Descartes himself, because Aristotle's soul is not a separate thing made of something other than matter, a thing that may therefore exist without a body. Neither is he the dualist's modern nemesis, a materialist, denying with the atomists the existence of soul altogether, because without a soul a body has no life and no purpose. For Aristotle, the soul is the set of capacities of a living body. Just as seeing is the capacity of the eye, soul is the capacity of the body (Sorabji, 1974/1983). Without an eye, there is no seeing; without a body, there is no soul.

All living things have soul, but there are very different forms of living things, possessing, therefore, different forms of soul. Specifically, Aristotle distinguished three levels of soul appropriate to different levels of actualization on his natural scale. At the lowest level there is the *nutritive soul,* possessed by plants, serving three functions: (1) maintaining the individual plant through nutrition, (2) maintaining the species through reproduction, and (3) directing growth. Animals possess a more complex, *sensitive soul,* which subsumes the nutritive soul's functions while adding others, making it more fully actualized than the nutritive soul. Animals, unlike plants, are aware of their surroundings. They have sensations—hence, "sensitive soul." As a consequence of sensation, animals experience pleasure and pain and so feel desire either to seek pleasure or to avoid pain. There are two further consequences of sensation: first, imagination and memory (since experience can be imagined or recalled); and second, movement as a consequence of desire. Highest in the scale of souls comes the human, or *rational soul,* subsuming the others and adding *mind,* the power to think and have general knowledge.

Structure and Functions of the Rational, Human Soul. According to Aristotle, gaining knowledge is a psychological process that starts with the perception of particular objects and ends with general knowledge of universals, of forms. Aristotle's analysis of the soul can be represented by a diagram showing the faculties of the soul and their interrelationships (Figure 2–2). In many respects, Aristotle's analysis of the sensitive and rational soul resembles that given by modern cognitive psychologists (Nussbaum & Putnam, 1992), and I have anachronistically depicted Aristotle's theory as an information processing flowchart of the type made popular by cognitive psychology.

The five primary senses send information to common sense, which unifies sensations into conscious perception and passes this processed information on to the passive mind, which is imprinted with the objects of perception. These perceptions may persist, creating images. Memory for Aristotle was a species of imagination, for our memories are always concrete images. Material passes into memory as we learn and can be recalled to consciousness later; hence, the flow of information goes both ways. Finally, the contents of the passive mind are acted on by the active mind to produce universal knowledge. We will now consider these functions in more detail. Bear in mind that Figure 2–2 shows both the animal and human souls. Animals possess the faculties, or mental abilities, of sensation, common sense, imagination, and memory. Only mind is unique to the human soul.

Sense Perception. Aristotle writes, "Generally, about all perception we can say that a sense is what has the power of receiving into itself the sensible forms of things without the matter, in the way in which a piece of wax takes on the impress of a signet ring without the iron or gold" (*On the soul,* 4242a 18–20). That is, if I

FIGURE 2-2 The structure of the human (sensitive and rational) soul according to Aristotle.

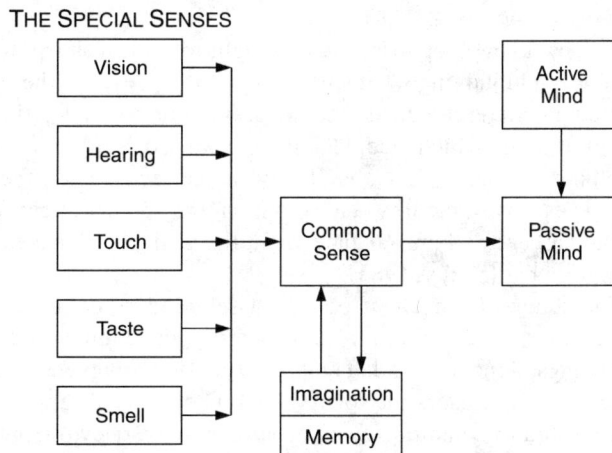

look at a bronze statue, my eye receives the form of the statue without receiving its matter, the bronze. *Perception*—the starting point of knowledge—has to do with form, not matter.

The first stage in perception is the reception of aspects of an object's form by the *special senses*. Each special sense is dedicated to reception of a particular kind of information about objects, which is why these senses are called "special"; a better translation might be "specialized." Aristotle regarded the special senses as passive, simply conforming themselves to the forms of objects, and therefore reliable and unerring.

The Interior Senses.   The information provided by the special senses is passed on to faculties that deal with it in various ways. In the animal soul, these faculties are called the *interior senses* because they are not connected with the outside world, but still are dealing with experienced sensations.

The next stage of perception Aristotle called the faculty of *common sense*. Common sense is an important faculty, being Aristotle's answer to one of the great mysteries of perception, the problem of *sensory integration,* or as it is known in cognitive neuroscience, the *binding problem.* Each special sense detects a specific kind of information about how an object looks, sounds, feels, tastes, or smells. The physical origin of each sense is quite distinct; for example, vision begins with light striking the retina, hearing with sound waves striking the eardrum. The neural path of each special sense into the brain is unique. Yet the world as we experience it is not a jumble of disconnected sensations. We hear sounds coming from objects we see, and we expect objects to be touchable. We experience single objects with multiple facets, not a blooming, buzzing confusion of sense-impressions. Somehow, we integrate the information provided by the special senses by binding together their separate neural pathways into a single mental representation of objects.

Aristotle said the job was done by common sense (Bynum, 1987/1993). It is the place—Aristotle located it in the heart—where the special senses are brought together and coordinated into a single, integrated picture of the world, where the sensations are held together in common. Common sense and the next faculty, *imagination,* are involved in judging what an object is. I see a red spot on a tree, but I must judge whether it is a drop of red paint or a lady bug. Thus, whereas the special sensations are infallible—there can be no doubt that I see a red spot—the judgments of common sense and imagination are fallible interpretations of special sensibles—I may wrongly think I'm seeing a lady bug.

We now know that Aristotle was right to draw a sharp distinction between sensing an object and judging what sort of object it is, because the two mental processes are performed in different parts of the brain. For example, there is the syndrome of *prosopagnosia,* in which people with certain sorts of brain damage (Aristotle was wrong about the heart) lose the ability to see faces. They see the stimuli that correspond to eyes, noses, mouths, and so on, but they do not integrate them into the perception of a face, even a familiar face, as in the well-known case of the man who mistook his wife for a hat (Sacks, 1985).

The coherent images of objects assembled by common sense are passed on in two directions, to imagination and memory in animals and human beings, and, in human beings alone, to mind. The basic function assigned to imagination by Aristotle is the ability to represent the form of an object in its absence, whether just after it has been presented to common sense, or later, after retrieval from memory. Imagination, however, is assigned other functions (Bynum, 1987/1993) that were separated into distinct faculties by medieval physician-philosophers. As already mentioned, imagination is involved in judging what an object is—that is, in inferring from sensation what object is affecting our senses. In addition to this purely cognitive function, imagination is involved in feeling pleasure and pain and in judging whether a perceived object is good or bad for an organism, thereby causing a behavioral response. Thus, a cat sees a mouse and judges that it is good for it, and so it chases the mouse. The mouse, of course, seeing the cat, judges that it is bad for it and runs away.

The final faculty of the sensitive, or animal, soul is *memory*. Aristotle conceived of memory as a storehouse of the images created by common sense and imagination. It is thus the record of an animal's life, available to be recalled by imagination. Aristotle's memory corresponds to what modern cognitive psychologists call *episodic*, or personal, memory—the ability to recall specific events, or episodes, in one's life. The organization of memory is based on *association*, as described in many modern psychological theories. Plato hinted at the concept of the association of ideas in his proposal that, by their resemblance to the innate Forms, perceived objects lead to knowledge. Aristotle, however, discussed the processes of association more fully. Aristotle discussed three laws of association—*similarity, contiguity,* and *contrast.* Similar images are associatively linked, images of contiguous experiences are linked, and opposite images are linked (that is, "hot" usually elicits the association "cold"). He also hinted at the law of *causality*—causally linked experiences remind us of one another.

Cognitive psychologists distinguish episodic memory from *semantic* memory, the ability to recall the definitions of words. Sometimes, semantic memory is called simply "knowledge," because it concerns general ideas (*universals*), not specific events or things (*particulars*). Aristotle, too, separated memory from knowledge, acquisition of the latter being the function of the uniquely human part of the soul, mind, or *nous.*

Mind. The rational part of the human soul Aristotle called *mind.* It is unique to human beings and is capable of acquiring knowledge of abstract universals, as opposed to the knowledge of individuals given in perception. As we experience different members of the same natural type, we note similarities and so form an impression of a universal, which Aristotle believed was always an *image.* As one experiences a multitude of cats, one eventually forms an idea of what the essence of a cat is, an image of a cat that contains only those perceptual features shared by all cats. To borrow Platonic imagery, my memory stores the remembered forms of my cats—Shadow, Theo, and Chessie—but my mind stores the Form of the Cat.

Within the mind there must be, as Aristotle believed there to be throughout nature, a difference between potentiality and actuality. The *passive mind* is potentiality. It has no character of its own, for it can take on the form of experienced objects. Knowledge of universals in the passive mind is actualized, or made manifest, by the operations of the active mind. The *active mind* is pure thought, acting on the contents of the passive mind to achieve rational knowledge of universals. This active mind is quite different from the other parts of the soul. As actuality, it is not acted on; rather, it acts on the contents of the passive mind. For Aristotle, this meant that the active mind was unchangeable—hence, immortal, for death is a form of change. The active mind is, therefore, separable from the body and survives death, unlike the rest of the soul. However, the active mind is not a personal soul, for it is identical in all human beings. It is pure thought and carries nothing away from its sojourn on earth. Knowledge is realized only in the passive mind, which perishes. Active mind corresponds to the processes of abstract thought, passive mind to the contents (Wedin, 1986/1993).

Motivation.   Movement is characteristic of animals and thus is a function of the sensitive soul, which can experience pleasure and pain. All action is motivated by some form of desire, which Aristotle believed involved imagination. In animals, motivation is directed by an image of what is pleasurable, and the animal seeks only present pleasure. Aristotle calls this type of motivation *appetite*. Human beings, however, are capable of reason and so can conceive of right and wrong. Therefore, we can be motivated by desire for what is good or for long-term future benefits. This type of motivation is called *wish*. Animals experience simple motivational conflicts between opposing appetites, but humans have, in addition, the problem of moral choice. Aristotle's view of motivation resembles Freud's, distinguishing between the innate, animalistic pleasure principle, which cares only for immediate pleasure, and the acquired, uniquely human reality principle, which calculates long-term gain.

Ethics

Aristotle erected his ethics squarely on his psychology. Just as there is a natural end to the growth of an acorn—it ought to become a flourishing, big oak tree—so there is a natural, proper goal to human life, namely, human flourishing. Aristotle provided a philosophical basis for the Greek prejudice that there is only one best way of life, only one path to *eudaemonia,* and for the Greek fear of *Tyche.* Just as oak trees have an inherent nature that they naturally tend to fulfill when conditions are favorable, so human beings have a nature that we tend to fulfill when conditions are favorable. Because the human soul is in its essence rational, and therefore capable of virtue, so "human good turns out to be activity of the soul in accordance with virtue" (*Nichomachean Ethics,* 1098a20).

Because the conditions in which a tree or human lives are so important to human flourishing, Aristotle's ethics is at the same time *political science* (Lear, 1988). Aristotle's ethics cum political science attempts to erase the distinction between *phusis* and *nomos* that the Sophists had drawn so sharply. Aristotle famously says that by nature (*phusis*) man is a social, or more precisely, political animal. The natural life for human beings is living in society, and human flourishing, *eudaemonia,* depends, therefore, on living in the right kind of ordered society (*nomos*).

However, the ideal state described by Aristotle, like Plato's Republic, would be rejected, by and large, by modern citizens of the West. As Plato had held, only the wise and virtuous should rule, because only they can set aside personal interest and govern in the interest of the state as a whole. As we might agree, a monarchy might be a good state if the king is wise and benevolent, but a better state is one ruled by law rather than the temporary virtues of a mortal king. Therefore, Aristotle's ideal state is a sort of aristocratic democracy. The citizens of the state participate in ruling it, but most members of the state are not citizens. The citizens of Aristotle's utopia are not the cultivated Guardians of Plato's Republic, but men of independent means who do not work, and who therefore have no personal interests to corrupt their judgment and who have the time to devote to politics. "In the state which is best governed . . . the citizens must not lead the life of artisans or tradesmen, for such a life is ignoble and inimical to virtue. Neither must they be husbandmen [farmers and ranchers], since leisure is necessary both for the development of virtue and the performance of political duties"

(*Politics,* VII.9, 1328b33–1329a2). Such a state contains no Jeffersonian yeoman, and certainly is without the principle of one man, one vote.

In the Europe in which psychology was born, Aristotle's reverence for a leisured elite and disdain for ordinary life and work persisted. Psychology was created in Germany by a self-consciously philosophical elite who wanted it to be a pure science of the human soul. When psychology traveled to America, however, it was profoundly changed by men and women who had long since rejected Aristotle's scale of virtues. In Germany, psychology was part of the elite class's cultivation of *theoria,* the Greek word for philosophical contemplation, which Aristotle held to be the best life of all. In America, psychology was put to work.

THE HELLENISTIC AND ROMAN WORLDS

Aristotle's pupil Alexander the Great changed the Western world forever. He sought to establish a universal empire that brought Greek thought to the world. He failed, but his vision was fulfilled by the less romantic and more practical Romans, who knitted their empire together with common roads, a common language, and a common bureaucracy. The life of the small, democratic *polis* was destroyed, replaced by larger empires. Rootedness in a small parochial community began to be replaced by more universal ideas of citizenship. A Roman Stoic once said that every person is a citizen of two cities, his place of birth, and Rome, center of the known world.

The immediate consequence of Alexander's death, however, was a period of intense and disturbing social change known as the *Hellenistic period,* usually dated from his death to the final conquest of Egypt by Octavian, the future Emperor Augustus, in 30 B.C.E. Until the coming of the *pax Romana,* the eastern Mediterranean was in turmoil. Alexander's imperial center did not hold: his generals carved his hoped-for empire into personal kingdoms that they ruled like gods, and they and their heirs fought incessant wars with each other.

Having lost their beloved *polis,* and discovering that governments could be positively evil, Hellenistic men and women turned away from public life toward the pleasures of private life and home. Rejecting Homeric fame and classical Greek politics, a Stoic said what no older Greek could ever have uttered, that nothing in life can "compare with the companionship of a man and wife" (quoted by Barnes, 1986, p. 373). From a social perspective, the great gainers of the Hellenistic era were women, as the idea of marriage as a contract to beget heirs was replaced by ideas of love and lifelong partnership. The Cynic Crates married for love and lived in full equality with his wife, Hipparchia, in what they called their "dog marriage." Most surprising to traditionalist Greeks, they even went out to dinner together! (Green, 1990).

Psychologically, however, the uncertainties of the Hellenistic epoch were more disturbing. The traditional Greek fear of *Tyche* was strengthened by the travails of life. The leading dramatist of the era, Menander, wrote, "Stop going on about [human] intelligence. . . . It's fortune's intelligence that steers the world. . . . Human forethought is hot air, mere babble" (quoted by Green, 1990, p. 55). As Hellenes turned inward to their homes, they also turned inward to their souls, seeking succor from the misfortunes of the world. The more secular of them sought freedom from upset in philosophy, and the more religious, in traditional worship or in the exotic new religions that flowed from the East into the West. In between was the philosophical religion of Neoplatonism.

Therapeutic Philosophies of Happiness

In a disturbing world, people sought freedom from disturbance, a form of happiness Greeks called *ataraxia*. The Classical Greeks had sought the happiness of *eudaemonia*, human flourishing or living well. Hellenistic Greeks and the Romans who followed them lowered their sights and settled for *ataraxia*, a happiness that was within their own control. As we have learned, Greek *eudaemonia* depends on luck, including living in favorable circumstances. When *Tyche* was unfavorable, as it was during the Wars of Alexander's Successors, *eudaemonia* was placed out of reach. What lay within reach was the ability to quiet one's own soul, to achieve self-mastery and, thus, personal freedom from disturbance, no matter what fortune might bring.

To the rescue rode a new form of philosopher, the philosopher as physician. If the physician as philosopher—figures such as Alcmaeon, Empedocles, or Aristotle—begins the story of psychology as science, the philosopher as physician begins the story of psychology as psychotherapy. The Hellenistic schools of philosophy set out to create and teach a therapy of the soul (Nussbaum, 1994).

One of the most influential of the Hellenistic therapeutic philosophies was *Epicureanism*, founded by Epicurus (341–270 B.C.E.). Epicurus spoke for all the schools when he wrote, "Empty is that philosopher's argument by which no human suffering is therapeutically treated. For just as there is no use in a medical art that does not cast out the sicknesses of bodies, so too there is no use in philosophy, unless it casts out suffering of the soul" (quoted by Nussbaum, 1994, p. 13). Epicureanism is also known as the *philosophy of the garden,* because part of Epicurus's recipe for *ataraxia* is literal withdrawal from the world to live a quiet life of philosophy and friendship. Epicurus taught that happiness was to be found by avoiding all strong passions, including the ups and downs of erotic love, and living simply, avoiding dependence on others or the world. To allay fear of death, Epicurus accepted atomism, teaching that there was no soul and thus no possibility of suffering in the afterlife. There was also a cult-like aspect of Epicureanism. Epicureans addressed Epicurus as "Leader," had to promise to accept all his teachings, and were admonished always to behave "as though Epicurus is watching" (quoted by Green, 1990, p. 620). The success of his Garden also depended on his wealth, the donations that supported the movement, and the slaves who tended him and his circle.

The most controversial of the happiness philosophies was *Cynicism*. Epicureanism was part philosophy and part lifestyle; Cynicism was all lifestyle, and the Cynics were the Hippies of Hellenism. Epicureans withdrew physically from the world, but Cynics remained in the world but not of it. They believed that one should live as naturally as possible, utterly rejecting all worldly conventions, contemptuous of whatever opinions people might have: all *phusis* and no *nomos*. The most famous Cynic was Diogenes (400–325 B.C.E.), whose proud nickname was "The dog," because he lived as dogs live, outside social convention. He would urinate and defecate in public, as dogs did. Found masturbating in the marketplace, his only remark was that he wished hunger could be as easily assuaged. Plato called him "Socrates gone mad." Diogenes proclaimed himself citizen of the world, and said the greatest good was free speech. To the extent that there was a therapeutic philosophy in the Cynics, it resembled Epicurus's advice to reject society, control the emotions, and avoid pleasure. Antisthenes said, "I would rather go mad than experience pleasure" (quoted by Vlastos, 1991, p. 208).

More philosophical than either Epicureanism or Cynicism was the school of *Skepticism,* founded by Pyrrho of Elis (360–270 B.C.E.) and developed by several later heads of Plato's Academy. Like Plato, the Skeptics distrusted sense-perception, but did not believe in the Forms. Therefore, they held that any general conclusions one might reach on the basis of experience might turn out to be wrong in the light of new experience. One might regard Skepticism as developing the non-Platonic side of Socrates, holding that Truth cannot be known, so all we can achieve is a thoughtful state of *aporia.* Once achieved, *aporia* could function as a means of achieving *ataraxia.* If one holds no belief wholeheartedly, then one will never experience the disturbance of finding one was in error.

The most influential of all the therapeutic philosophies was *Stoicism,* founded by Zeno of Citium (333–262 B.C.E.), who taught at the painted colonnade, or *Stoa,* in Athens. Stoicism was a general and genuine philosophy that was developed for centuries by Greeks and Romans. Its appeal was considerable, cutting across social lines; it counted among its adherents both a slave (Epictetus, C.E. 50–138) and an Emperor (Marcus Aurelius, C.E. 121–180), and was effectively the philosophy of the Roman ruling class. In addition to philosophy, the Stoics worked in science and made tremendous advances in logic.

As a therapy of the soul, Stoicism taught two interconnected things: (1) absolute determinism and (2) the complete extirpation of the emotions. Stoics believed that whatever happens in one's life was foreordained to happen. *Tyche* is inescapable. However, we are in control of our mental world, so feeling unhappy about misfortune is our fault and may be corrected with Stoic teaching. Strong positive feelings are also to be avoided because they lead to overvaluation of things and people and, thus, to potential unhappiness should they be lost. These sayings from the *Enchiridion,* or Handbook, of Epictetus convey the flavor of Stoicism.

> V
>
> Men are disturbed not by the things which happen, but by the opinions [Stoics regarded emotions as wrong opinions] about the things: for example, death is nothing terrible, for if it were, it would have seemed so to Socrates; for the opinion about death, that it is terrible, is the terrible thing. When, then, we are impeded or disturbed or grieved, let us never blame others, but ourselves, that is, our opinions. It is the act of an ill-instructed man to blame others for his own bad condition; it is the act of one who has begun to be instructed, to lay the blame on himself; and of one whose instruction is completed, neither to blame another nor himself.

> XVI
>
> When you see a person weeping in sorrow either when a child goes abroad or when he is dead, or when the man has lost his property, take care that the appearance does not hurry you away with it, as if he were suffering in external things. But straightway make a distinction in your own mind, and be in readiness to say, it is not that which has happened that afflicts this man, for it does not afflict another, but it is the opinion about this thing which afflicts the man. So far as words, then, do not be unwilling to show him sympathy, and even if it happens so, to lament with him. But take care that you do not lament internally also.

> XX
>
> Remember that it is not he who reviles you or strikes you, who insults you, but it is your opinion about these things as being insulting. When, then, a man irritates you, you

must know that it is your own opinion which has irritated you. Therefore especially try not to be carried away by the appearance. For if you once gain time and delay, you will more easily master yourself.

XLIV

These reasonings do not cohere: I am richer than you, therefore I am better than you; I am more eloquent than you, therefore I am better than you. On the contrary these rather cohere, I am richer than you, therefore my possessions are greater than yours: I am more eloquent than you, therefore my speech is superior to yours. But you are neither possession nor speech.

LII

In every thing (circumstance) we should hold these maxims ready to hand:
Lead me, O Zeus, and thou O Destiny,
The way that I am bid by you to go:
To follow I am ready.
If I choose not, I make myself a wretch, and still must follow.
But who so nobly yields unto necessity,
We hold him wise, and skill'd in things divine.

In many respects, Stoicism was like Christianity, and its popularity in the Roman Empire aided the reception of, and also influenced, Christian thought. Unlike earlier Greek philosophies, Stoicism was universalist rather than elitist. Anyone, slave or emperor, could aspire to be a Stoic sage. Stoics thought of the universe as a living and divine being, ruled by reason, or *logos,* and permeated by spirit, or *pneuma.* Determinism was easier to accept if one believed that the wise universe was rationally working out an ultimately good plan, and that one's personal happiness was rationally accepting the *logos* of the universe. Like Christian martyrs, Stoics calmly endured pain in the interest of a higher purpose. Humans had spirits, their own *pneumas,* if not souls, although Stoics held that at death one's *pneuma* simply returned to the universe's, so there was for them no personal immortality. *Logos* also means word, and the Gospel of John opens, "In the beginning was the word . . . and the word was God."

Neoplatonism and Mystery Religions

As we have seen, Plato's philosophy had a strong otherworldly pull, and during the Hellenistic period, as Plato's Academy turned to Skepticism, that pull produced the philosophy of *Neoplatonism,* whose best-known spokesman was Plotinus (A.D. 204–270), an Egyptian Greek. Plotinus fully developed the mystical aspect of Platonism, very nearly turning that philosophy into a religion. He described the universe as a hierarchy, beginning with a supreme and unknowable God called *the One.* The One "emanates" a knowable God called *Intelligence,* which rules over Plato's realm of the Forms. From Intelligence serially emanate more divine creatures until we reach humans, whose divine souls are imprisoned in degrading, material bodies. The physical world is an imperfect, impure copy of the divine realm.

Plotinus's concern was to turn his followers' eyes away from the corrupting temptations of the flesh and toward the spiritual world of truth, goodness, and beauty in the realm of the Forms. In his *Enneads,* Plotinus wrote: "Let us rise to [the] model . . . from which [the physical] world derives. . . . Over [it] presides pure Intelligence and incredible wisdom. . . . Everything there is eternal and immutable . . . [and] in a state of bliss." The last phrase makes the change from Platonic philosophy to the ecstatic vision of the religious. Like Stoicism, Neoplatonism helped pave the way for, and shaped, Christian thought. It was through Neoplatonism that Plato's philosophy came to dominate the Middle Ages.

Religion, too, offered a path to *ataraxia,* and sometimes to something more dramatic and ecstatic. The old pagan religions remained lively for centuries into the Christian era, but in Hellenistic and Roman times, many people turned to one or more of the various *mystery religions* that flowed into the Greek and Latin world from the Near East. They were called mystery religions from the word *myster,* meaning a special rite, often held in secret and never revealed to outsiders, through which initiates had to pass in order to become full members of the cult. Three popular ones were the cults of *Magna Mater* (Great Mother), Isis, and Mithras (Artz, 1980).

The cult of Magna Mater began to enter the West from Asia Minor in the 600s B.C.E. Inflamed by jealousy, Magna Mater, the source of life, became infuriated at the infidelity of her lover, Attis, the god of vegetation, and slew him and emasculated him, burying him beneath a pine tree. Then she mourned him and brought him back to life. The seasons of the earth retell the story, as vegetation fades in the Fall, dies in Winter, and returns in the Spring, when the great ceremonies of Magna Mater took place. There was dancing, singing, and music. Aspirants to the priesthood emasculated themselves with stones, repeating Attis's fate and giving their fertility to the Great Mother. Finally, a pit was dug into which initiates dressed in white robes descended. A live bull was held over them and sacrificed. Covered with blood, the initiates crawled out of the pit, being "born again" into the cult of Magna Mater.

Isis, like Magna Mater, was a female goddess. An Egyptian deity, she was sister to Osiris, who gave arts and law to human beings, and who died and was reborn with Isis' help. The cult of Isis involved a daily, weekly, and yearly cycle of rituals, including baptism in holy water, lighting of candles and incense, stately processions, and temples left open so adherents could come in and pray.

Isis appealed especially to women; Mithraism appealed mostly, if not entirely, to men, and was a special favorite of Roman soldiers, who carried it throughout the Roman world. Mithras stemmed from Persia, and was a god of light and enemy of evil, born of a virgin. Mithras is represented as riding and slaying a bull, who represents unrestrained natural power needing to be controlled by people. His birthday was December 25, and the first day of the week was his. Devotees were baptized in water, or later in a bull-slaying ceremony borrowed from Magna Mater. They identified with him by eating a sacred meal of bread and wine, and tried to live, in imitation of Mithras, lives of morality and virtue.

By the fourth century C.E., there was a tendency for all the mystery cults to converge together into a single, monotheistic religion. Ultimately, this was Christianity, based on birth and rebirth, sin and redemption, but public rather than mysterious (Artz, 1980; Lane Fox, 1987).

Early Christian Thought

An important problem for early Christians was how to deal with classical philosophy. Should it be condemned as pagan and necessarily heretical, as St. Jerome (345–420) contended; or should Christians accept those elements of philosophy compatible with faith, as St. Ambrose (340–430) argued? The latter position emerged victorious, and its greatest representative, one of the two greatest teachers of Catholic philosophy, was St. Augustine (354–430). Augustine is the last classic philosopher and the first Christian one, combining Stoicism, Neoplatonism, and Christian faith.

Stoicism, with its emphasis on divine wisdom and human submission, has elements that can be assimilated easily to Christian belief. Even more compatible, however, was Neoplatonism, which was a philosophy evolving into a religion. In the fourth century Christianity was a simple faith, lacking a supporting philosophy. Augustine integrated faith and philosophy into a powerful Christian worldview that would dominate all aspects of medieval thought until the thirteenth century. The following passage illustrates Augustine's Christian Neoplatonism:

> God, of course, belongs to the realm of intelligible things, and so do these mathematical symbols, though there is a great difference. Similarly the earth and light are visible, but the earth cannot be seen unless it is illumined. Anyone who knows the mathematical symbols admits that they are true without the shadow of a doubt. But he must also believe that they cannot be known unless they are illumined by something else corresponding to the sun. About this corporeal light notice three things. It exists. It shines. It illumines. So in knowing the hidden God you must observe three things. He exists. He is known. He causes other things to be known. St. Augustine, *Soliloquies I*

Augustine assimilated a sophisticated if mystical philosophy and created basic Christian theology. In the next chapter, we will look at Augustine's distinctively Christian medieval ideas, for with Augustine we have reached the beginning of the Middle Ages.

CONCLUSION: THE END OF THE ANCIENT WORLD

> I shudder when I think of the catastrophes of our time. For twenty years and more the blood of the Romans has been shed daily . . . the great cities have been sacked and pillaged and plundered by Goths . . . Huns and Vandals. . . . The Roman world is falling; yet we hold up our heads instead of bowing them. St. Jerome, "The Roman World is Falling"

The fall of Rome is usually dated as 476 C.E.. However, culture, art, philosophy, and science went into decline around 200 C.E., a decline that intensified about 300 C.E. There was a brief renaissance under Charlemagne in the middle of the ninth century, but European civilization did not really revive until the twelfth century. Until then, the character of Western thought was shaped by Christianized Neoplatonism. We turn, then, to the medieval world and the changes it brought.

BIBLIOGRAPHY

There are many fine books on the Classical, Hellenistic, and Roman worlds. I shall mention some of the ones I consulted and found useful. On the prehistoric roots of science, Alexander Marshack's *Roots of civilization* (New York: McGraw-Hill, 1972) is fascinating. A convenient survey of ancient Greek life and history is given by Antony Andrew in *The Greeks* (New York: Norton, 1978). The outstanding historian of Greece was M. I. Finley, who published numerous works; a general one is *The ancient Greeks* (Harmondsworth, England: Penguin). See also J. V. A. Fine, *The ancient Greeks* (Cambridge, MA: Harvard University Press), and R. Sealey, *A history of the Greek city states* (Los Angeles: University of California Press). Vernant (1982) is important for the transition from the Bronze to Classical ages.

There are two excellent surveys consisting of compilations of articles by distinguished scholars, A. Kenny, ed., *The Oxford history of Western philosophy* (Oxford, England: Oxford University Press, 1994 on philosophy, and J. Boardman, J. Griffin, and O. Murray, eds., *The Oxford history of the Classical world* (Oxford, England: Oxford University Press, 1986) on the Classical, Hellenistic, and Roman worlds in all their aspects. Harvard University Press has issued 1993 editions of its series on the ancient world, in five volumes: *Early Greece, Democracy and Classical Greece, The Hellenistic world, The Roman republic,* and *The later Roman Empire.*

The study of Greek homosexuality began with Kenneth Dover, *Greek homosexuality* (Cambridge, MA: Harvard University Press, rev. ed. 1989), which is still the place to start. Dover's picture is extended by E. Cantarella, *Bisexuality in the ancient world* (New Haven, CT: Yale University Press). Greatly influential, and controversial, has been Michel Foucault's *The history of sexuality* (New York: Vintage Books, 3 vols., 1978–1986). Dover's and Foucault's books have prompted a stream of works on the "social construction of sexuality," mostly agreeing with and elaborating on their semiofficial position. However, a certain reaction has set in, suggesting that homosexual conduct was not as widely accepted as the Dover–Foucault view says. See D. Cohen, *Law, sexuality and society: The enforcement of morals in Classical Athens* (Cambridge, England: Cambridge University Press).

On Greek psychology, see G. S. Kirk, *The nature of the Greek myths* (Harmondsworth, England: Penguin, 1974); Bruno Snell, *The discovery of the mind: The Greek origins of European thought* (New York: Harper & Row, 1960); R. B. Onians, *The origins of European thought* (Cambridge, England: Cambridge University Press, 1951), and E. R. Dodds, *The Greeks and the irrational* (Berkeley: University of California Press, 1951), which is a classic of Classical scholarship. See also Bernard Knox, *The oldest dead white European males* (New York: Norton, 1993), who rejects the idea that Bronze Age Greeks had no concept of the soul. George Sidney Brett surveys Greek and Hellenistic psychologies in *Psychology: Ancient and modern* (New York: Cooper Square, 1963). Bennett Simon examines Greek ideas about psychopathology in *Mind and madness in ancient Greece: The classical origins of modern psychiatry* (Ithaca, NY: Cornell University Press, 1978).

For the Hellenistic period, see above all Green (1992), a lively and opinionated treatment of that fascinating era in all its dimensions, with copious discussions of philosophy. Also see F. W. Walbank, *The Hellenistic world* (Sussex, England: Harvester, 1981); and Michael Grant, *From Alexander to Cleopatra: The Hellenistic world* (New York: Scribner's, 1982); the latter is especially useful on realism, art, happiness philosophies, and mystery religions; Grant has authored many other works on the ancient world, including *The rise of the Greeks* (1987), *The founders of the Western World* (1990), and *A social history of Greece and Rome* (1992), all published by Scribner's (New York). On Rome, see Donald R. Dudley, *The Romans: 850 B.C.–A.D. 337* (New York: Knopf, 1970). W. K. Klingamann's *The first century: Emperors, gods, and everyman* (New York: HarperCollins, 1990), is a broad survey of world history of the period. Although it is unavoidably out of date, Edward Gibbon's (1776) *Decline and fall of the Roman Empire* still repays study. It is beautifully written, with some biting ironic asides (Gibbon says history is "little more than the register of the crimes, follies and misfortunes of mankind"). Living before the age of professional history, Gibbon can get away with what every historian would like to—omitting, as he often does, everything that is neither "entertaining nor instructive." Penguin Books has published a fine one-volume abridgment of the original (Harmondsworth, England, 1981).

There are several valuable treatments of Classical science. An excellent short but comprehensive work, embracing both science and philosophy, is Giorgio de Santillana, *The origins of scientific thought* (New York: Mentor, 1961). The standard histories of science in this period are George Sarton, *A history of science,* 2 vols. (New York: Norton, 1952); and Marshall Clagett, *Greek science in antiquity* (New York: Collier Books, 1955); Sarton set out to write a history of all science, but he worked so thoroughly that he died before getting past the Hellenistic age. The major younger scholar of Greek science is G. E. R. Lloyd. His *Early Greek science: Thales to Aristotle* (New York: Norton, 1970) is a good short introduction to the field; his *Magic, reason, and experience: Studies in the origin and development of Greek science* (Cambridge, England: Cambridge University Press, 1979) and *Science, folklore, and ideology: The life sciences in ancient Greece* (Cambridge, England: Cambridge University Press, 1983) offer more specialized and technical studies. There are more general histories of science which include the Classical period. Stephan Mason's *A history of the sciences* (New York: Collier Books, 1962) is a useful one-volume history. The most erudite and comprehensive history is Lynn Thorndike's massive and magisterial *History of magic and experimental science,* 8 volumes (New York: Columbia University Press, 1928–58). Another ambitious undertaking is Richard Olson's social history of science: *Science deified and science defied: The historical significance of science in Western culture 3500 B.C.–A.D. 1640* (Berkeley: University of California Press, 1982), with volume II (1990) taking the story to 1820. A recent award-winning book is Lindberg (1992).

Turning to philosophy, there are several comprehensive histories that include the Greek period. I have primarily consulted Frederick Copleston, *A history of philosophy,* 9 vols. (Garden City, NY: Image Books, 1962–77); Jacob Bronowski and Bruce Mazlish, *The western intellectual tradition* (New York: Harper & Row, 1960); and Bertrand Russell, *A history of western philosophy* (New York: Simon & Schuster, 1945). Copleston's history is comprehensive and detailed, though sometimes difficult. Bronowski and Mazlish is less detailed, but more readable. Russell's history must be used with care; it is wonderfully written, but not disinterested. As a brilliant philosopher, Russell discusses his dead colleagues from his own point of view, neglecting, and sometimes distorting, various facets of the thinkers he presents.

There is a wealth of works on the Greek philosophers. Three general works are J. Burnet, *Early Greek philosophy,* 4th ed. (New York: Collins, 1957); A. H. Armstrong, *An introduction to ancient philosophy* (London: Methuen, 1980); and W. K. C. Guthrie's multivolume *History of Greek philosophy* (Cambridge, England: Cambridge University Press), summarized in *The Greek philosophers: Thales to Aristotle* (New York: Harper, 1950). In recent years, the history of philosophy has revived. Two fine works on the Greeks are Irwin (1989) and Luce (1992). The latter is shorter and informally written; the former is deeper and more reflective. More specialized works follow.

The Naturalists.   G. Kirk and K. Raven, *The presocratic philosophers* (Cambridge, England: Cambridge University Press, 1971). Drew Hyland, *The origins of philosophy* (New York: Putnam, 1973). G. Kerferd, *The Sophistic movement* (Cambridge, England: Cambridge University Press, 1980). R. Sprague (1972).

Socrates.   Vlastos (1991) is an outstanding work, the culmination of a lifetime of study of the subject.

Plato.   *The collected dialogues of Plato,* edited by Edith Hamilton and Huntington Cairns (New York: Pantheon, 1961, Bollingen Series LXXI). Georges Grube, *Plato's thought* (Boston: Beacon Press, 1958). Norman Gulley, *Plato's theory of knowledge* (London: Methuen, 1962). Erik Nis Ostenfield, *Forms, matter, and mind* (The Hague, The Netherlands: Martinus Nijhof, 1982). J. E. Raven, *Plato's thought in the making* (Cambridge, England: Cambridge University Press, 1965). T. Robinson, *Plato's psychology* (Toronto: Toronto University Press, 1970). David Ross, *Plato's theory of ideas* (Oxford, England: Oxford University Press, 1951). See also the commentaries to the works cited in the references and Annas (1981), a fine work on the *Republic.*

Aristotle.   *The basic works of Aristotle,* edited by Richard McKeon (New York: Random House, 1941). J. C. Ackrill, *Aristotle the philosopher* (Oxford, England: Oxford University Press, 1980). John Ferguson, *Aristotle* (New York: Twayne, 1972). G. E. R. Lloyd, ed., *Aristotle on mind and the senses* (Cambridge, England: Cambridge University Press, 1978). John H.

Randall, *Aristotle* (New York: Columbia University Press, 1960). David Ross, *Aristotle* (London: Methuen, 1966). Richard Sorabji, *Aristotle on memory* (Providence, RI: Brown University Press, 1972). An excellent recent work that clarified Aristotle for me is Lear (1988). M. Durrant, ed., *Aristotle's* de Anima *in focus* (London: Routledge and Kegan Paul, 1993) contains most of the text of *On the soul* with accompanying reprinted articles about it. A lively, indeed sometimes nasty, controversy has arisen over Aristotle's conception of mind. Martha Nussbaum and Hilary Putnam have argued that Aristotle's idea that soul is to body as form is to matter is essentially identical to the modern thesis of functionalism (first stated by Putnam, and discussed in Chapters 13–15) that mind is to body as program is to computer. Their view was vigorously challenged by classicist Miles Burnyeat (1992), who argues that Aristotle's conception of matter was so different from ours that comparing Aristotle to artificial intelligence is comparing apples to bobsleds. Both viewpoints are represented in Nussbaum and Rorty (1992). I lean toward Burnyeat's view, but have mostly avoided the controversy in the text. Lear (1988) tries to find a middle ground.

Hellenistic/Roman Period. A. Long, *Hellenistic philosophy: Stoics, Epicureans, Skeptics* (London: Duckworth, 1974). Giovanni Reale, *The systems of the Hellenistic age* (Albany, NY: State University of New York Press, 1985). Emile Brehier, *The philosophy of Plotinus* (Chicago: University of Chicago Press, 1958). Ramsey McMullen, *Paganism in the Roman Empire* (New Haven, CT: Yale University Press, 1981). S. Angus, *The mystery religions* (New York: Dover, 1975). Joscelyn Godwin, *Mystery religions in the ancient world* (San Francisco: Harper & Row, 1981). R. Nash, *The light of the mind: St. Augustine's theory of knowledge* (Lexington: The University of Kentucky Press, 1969).

REFERENCES

Adler, J. (Nov. 6, 1995). The gods must be hungry. *Newsweek,* p. 75.

Annas, J. (1981). *An introduction to Plato's Republic.* Oxford, England: Clarendon Press.

Artz, F. B. (1980). *The mind of the Middle Ages,* 3rd ed. Chicago: University of Chicago Press.

Barnes, J. (1986). Hellenistic philosophy and science. In J. Boardman, J. Griffin, & O. Murray, eds. (1986). *The Oxford history of the Classical world.* Oxford, England: Oxford University Press.

Biers, W. R. (1987). *The archaeology of Greece: An introduction,* rev. ed. Ithaca, NY: Cornell University Press.

Bremmer, J. N. (1983). *The early Greek concept of the soul.* Princeton, NJ: Princeton University Press.

Burnyeat, M. F. (1992). Is an Aristotelian philosophy of mind still credible? In M. Nussbaum and A.-O. Rorty, eds., *Essays on Aristotle's* de Anima. Oxford, England: Oxford University Press.

Bynum, T. W. (1987). A new look at Aristotle's theory of perception. *The History of Philosophy Quarterly, 4,* 163–178. Reprinted in M. Durrant, ed. (1993). *Aristotle's* de Anima *in focus,* 90–109. London: Routledge and Kegan Paul.

Clark, S. R. L. (1992). Ancient philosophy. In A. Kenny, ed. (1992). *The Oxford history of Western philosophy,* 1–53. Oxford, England: Oxford University Press.

Cornford, F. (1945). *The Republic of Plato.* Oxford, England: Oxford University Press.

Durrant, M. (Ed.). (1993). *Aristotle's* de Anima *in focus.* London: Routledge.

Foster, S. W. (1988). *The past is another country.* Berkeley: University of California Press.

Freeman, K. (1971). *Ancilla to the presocratic philosophers.* Cambridge, MA: Harvard University Press.

Green, P. (1990). *Alexander to Actium: The historical evolution of the Hellenistic Age.* Los Angeles: University of California Press.

Irwin, T. (1989). *Classical thought. A history of Western philosophy I.* Oxford, England: Oxford University Press.

Lane Fox, R. (1987). *Pagans and Christians.* New York: Knopf.

Lear, J. (1988). *Aristotle: The desire to know.* Cambridge, England: Cambridge University Press.

Lindberg, D. C. (1992). *The beginnings of Western science.* Chicago: University of Chicago Press.

Luce, J. V. (1992). *An introduction to Greek philosophy.* New York: Thames and Hudson.

Marshack, A. (1972). *Roots of civilization.* New York: McGraw-Hill.

Nussbaum, M. (1994). *Therapies of desire: Theory and practice in Hellenistic ethics.* Princeton, NJ: Princeton University Press.

Nussbaum, M., and Rorty, A.-O., eds., (1992). *Essays on Aristotle's* de Anima. Oxford, England: Oxford University Press.

Onians, R. B. (1951). *The origins of European thought: About the body, the mind, the soul, the world, time, and fate.* Cambridge, England: Cambridge University Press.

Plato (1973). *Phaedrus and Letters VII and VIII,* trans. W. Hamilton. London: Penguin.

Plato (1991). *The dialogues of Plato.* Volume II, *The Symposium,* trans. R. E. Allen. New Haven, CT: Yale University Press.

Plato (1993). *Republic,* trans. R. Waterfield. Oxford, England: Oxford University Press.

Popper, K. (1965). Back to the presocratics. *In conjectures and refutations.* New York: Harper & Row.

Sacks, O. (1985). *The man who mistook his wife for a hat.* New York: HarperCollins.

Sorabji, R. (1974). Body and soul in Aristotle. *Philosophy 49,* 63–89. Reprinted in M. Durrant, ed. (1993), *Aristotle's* de Anima *in focus,* 162–196. London: Routledge and Kegan Paul.

Snell, B. (1960). *The discovery of the mind: The Greek origins of European thought.* New York: Harper & Row, 1960.

Sprague, R. (1972). *The older Sophists.* Columbia: University of South Carolina Press.

Vernant, J.-P. (1982). *The origins of Greek thought.* Ithaca, NY: Cornell University Press.

Vlastos, G. (1991). *Socrates: Ironist and moral philosopher.* Ithaca, NY: Cornell University Press.

Wedin, M. V. (1986). Tracking Aristotle's nous. In A. Donegan, A. Perovich, and M. V. Wedin (Eds.), *Human nature and natural knowledge.* Dordrecht, The Netherlands: D. Reidel, 167–197. Reprinted in M. Durrant, ed. (1993), *Aristotle's* de Anima *in focus,* 128–159. London: Routledge and Kegan Paul.

3 Spirituality and Individualism
The Middle Ages and Renaissance

St. Lucy of Syracuse and St. Catherine of Alexandria. During the Middle Ages, St. Catherine was considered the patron saint of philosophy. Desiring to marry her, the pagan Emperor Maxentius (d. 312) set fifty philosophers to refute her Christian faith, but instead she refuted them. Enraged, the Emperor seized Catherine and tortured her to death. Another early martyr, St. Lucy, is broadly associated with Christian enlightenment through her name.

The Middle Ages was the crucible in which our modern Western world was formed, and the Renaissance was the first self-consciously modern period. The medieval period saw the beginning of constitutional democracy, romantic love, individualism, and experimental science. During the Renaissance, learning and scholarship left the confines of the church to become again the property of lay society concerned with humanity's nature and needs rather than God's.

FROM CLASSICAL TO MEDIEVAL: THE EARLY MIDDLE AGES (476–1000)

The Medieval Context

Although tradition sets the date of the end of Classical civilization at A.D. 476, something like the medieval way of life began during the Roman Empire in the late third and fourth centuries. Because of economic decline, small farmers became legally tied to the land, a bond that evolved into serfdom. As the control of Rome over her provinces loosened, local autonomous leadership grew, leading to feudalism. The breakdown of the Roman world was evident as a barter economy began to replace the money economy of the empire; communication broke down; the imperial army became more and more a mercenary army of barbarians rather than a voluntary army of Roman citizens; populations declined; and the Eastern Empire with its own emperor and capital at Constantinople leached treasure and resources from the European, or Western, Empire to preserve its own superior way of life.

These crises were compounded by an extraordinary movement of barbarians into the empire. Early settlers had often come peacefully into the empire, but later invasions were bloody and destructive. Rome itself was sacked in Augustine's time; the Emperor Romulus Augustulus, who fell in 476, was himself only a barbarian usurper. The empire was finally torn asunder by waves of barbarian invaders, each group fleeing the one behind it, seeking stable lives within it. As each group of people settled, the empire became less Roman and universal. Restless movements of such peoples did not end until the Vikings settled in France as Normans around 1000 C.E. What prompted and ended the Barbarian invasions remains unclear.

This extended period of transition from classic to medieval times, from before 475 to about 1000, is sometimes still called the Dark Ages but is better called the early Middle Ages. Although creative thinking declined, there were periods of intellectual development, most notably the Carolingian renaissance under Charlemagne (768–814). New political forms were developed to replace the husk of imperial government. It was even a period of technological advance. For example, the heavy plow and the modern horse-harness were invented, opening new lands for farming and improving the yield from old. Although this period brought economic, demographic, and intellectual decline, a new, creative society was arising from the imperial ashes.

The economy and population began to rise again around 1000, ushering in the high Middle Ages, which lasted to about 1300. This was an enormously creative period in Western civilization. Many Greek works, especially those of Aristotle, were recovered, and philosophical thinking resumed in the twelfth-century Renaissance. The magnificent Romanesque and Gothic churches were constructed. Modern political forms, especially in England, were developing, as was the concept of romantic love and the interest in individuality.

This fertile European culture ended between 1277 and 1350 in the rise of nationalism and in the wake of wars between the embryonic nations, the increasing dogmatism of the church, and the Black Death of 1348 to 1350, which killed no less than one-third of the population of Western Europe. Friedrich Heer calls this the *closed* Europe of the late Middle Ages, in contrast to the intellectually and politically *open* Europe of the previous period. The late Middle Ages lasted into the Renaissance, which began in Italy as early as 1300, but took about two hundred years to reach the north of Europe.

It is against this background of loss and recovery, decline and innovation, that we must understand medieval thinking.

Reason: What, then do you want to know?
Augustine: The very things for which I have prayed.

R: Summarize them concisely.
A: I want to know God and the soul.
R: Nothing else?
A: Nothing else at all.

St. Augustine, *Soliloquia*

Augustine (354–430) was the last great classical philosopher and the first great Christian philosopher. His attitudes dominated medieval philosophy until about 1300. Philosophy was carried out in a context of Christian faith. Augustine wanted only to know God and the soul, and he used faith to justify belief. Medieval humanity turned away from the observable world, full of pain and turmoil, and concentrated on heaven and the soul, both of which could be known through introspection.

The soul could be known by introspection, by seeking within oneself that divine illumination that comes from God, so that to know the soul was to know God. And just as the soul was the representative of God within the self, so spiritual truth could be found in all things. Similarly, every thing and every event symbolized something supernatural and beyond human experience. Just as Plato found in every class noun the symbol of a Form, medieval people found symbols in every aspect of life. The medieval thinker did not want to understand the mind or the world in its own terms, but only as clues to the invisible reality of God in heaven.

Science and philosophy as we know them (or as the Greeks knew them) are impossible in such a context. Being devout, medieval thinkers consciously worked within a religiously defined framework they had no wish to undermine. Most medievals, if accused of heresy, simply concluded they had erred and rethought their views. However, as the Middle Ages progressed—especially after 1277—the boundaries of dogma became more rigid, and the hand of censorship more oppressive. The spirit of many thinkers rebelled, helping to dissolve the medieval synthesis.

The Middle Ages sought a grand synthesis of all knowledge. Because all knowledge was of God, the soul, and the spiritual world, it was believed that knowledge, tradition, and faith could be synthesized into a single, grand, authoritative picture of the universe. This belief, too, broke down after 1300.

Not all Christian thinkers, in whatever time, have accepted any role for secular reason in seeking Godly truth. Augustine had to struggle against ideas of those like Tertullian (160–230), who rejected the classical philosophers. St. Bernard (1091–53) decried excessive *curiosity* about Christian beliefs. In the Renaissance, Savonarola (1452–98) burned heretical books and works of art. All these people emphasized the mystical aspects of Neoplatonism, the immediate inward confrontation of man with God, either through contemplation or reading the scriptures. They rejected natural reason as unnecessary and even dangerous. Fundamentalism and mysticism were important elements not only in Christianity, but in medieval Islam and Judaism, where they triumphed and extinguished philosophical thought. In the Christian West, the thinkers of the later Middle Ages finally drew a line between the ideas of faith and the ideas of reason and observation. This separation of science and philosophy from theology destroyed the medieval synthesis but opened the way to independent secular thought.

Neoplatonism colored every aspect of medieval thinking. All things were symbolic of God's invisible world; visions, prophecies, and magic were everyday parts of life; and, until the Reformation, the Catholic Church let magical practices be (Thomas, 1971). Medieval people structured their world according to earthly hierarchies, reflecting the heavenly one. Just as there was a hierarchy from God to angels to man to animals to matter, so was the church a hierarchy from pope to archbishop to bishop to priest to layperson, and society mirrored it with king, vassal, subvassal, and serf. All the world was doubly structured—every thing, every event was symbolic of the invisible world and found its natural place in a hierarchically structured universe.

Literacy was the preserve of the church. To be literate was almost without exception to be a cleric, and the language of learning was Latin. The church forbade the translation of the Bible into vernacular language, and services were conducted in Latin. The religion of the common people, therefore, was a barely modified paganism. One of the most revolutionary developments of the later Middle Ages was unauthorized translation of the Bible and the rise of vernacular literature.

Thus, medieval knowledge was priestly knowledge. The monasteries carefully preserved past learning and kept historical chronicles. Some priests became the first governmental bureaucrats, bringing order, reason, and literacy to the rule of near-barbarians. The seeds of the future, however, lay in the schools attached to the cathedrals of the twelfth-century Renaissance. These became the first universities, with regularly scheduled courses, lectures, and textbooks, and the most independent thinkers, such as Peter Abelard, were to be found there. In the universities, under the increasing influence of translated Greek works, especially Aristotle's, reason parted ways with faith, producing heresies to be suppressed by the church, and learning began to spread past the control of the church authorities.

We must not overestimate the oppressiveness of the religious framework of thought, especially in the high Middle Ages, nor underestimate its achievement. A modern person would be an alien in those times, but modern thought could not have developed without its medieval predecessors. Before discussing medieval achievements, however, we must consider the achievement of peoples outside Western Christendom: the Jews and Muslims.

Relations between European Christendom and its two great rival religions were, to say the least, ambiguous. It was against Muslims that the Crusades were directed, when, in the early Middle Ages, Islam nearly engulfed Europe. Christendom's relations with the Jews were even more unpleasant. Jews were persecuted with a ferocity rivaling that of the Nazis. They were expelled from England and France; they were forced to live in ghettos and wear distinctive clothing; they were often killed *en masse* by burning down their homes with the inhabitants inside. Without St. Paul's mission to the Gentiles, Christianity might have remained a Jewish sect. Jesus was, of course, a Jew, and his teachings reflect the concerns of Jewish rabbis of the first century B.C.E. Largely because of St. Paul's mission to the Gentiles, Christianity did not remain a Jewish sect.

Both Muslims and the Jews who lived among them made major contributions to the intellectual development of the West. They preserved, and later translated, the works of the ancients, forgotten in Europe. In the early Middle Ages, only the *Timaeus* of Plato and the *Categories* of Aristotle (not their most representative works) were known. By 1200, much of Plato and almost all of Aristotle were available to Christian scholars. The naturalistic works of Aristotle revolutionized the thinking of the West; Aristotle was substituted for Plato as *the* philosopher. Thus, both the Jews and the Muslims greatly enriched the knowledge of European Christendom by preserving and translating the Greek philosophers. This new knowledge was disseminated to European Christendom through Spain and Sicily, where, within Muslim culture, Jews and Muslims lived together in peace.

Philosophers among the Jews and Muslims also made important contributions; their influence often rivals Aristotle's. Maimonides, the greatest Judaic philosopher, was treated with the utmost respect by Thomas Aquinas. Islamic thinkers contributed to mathematics and science as well as philosophy. The two most important Muslims for our purposes were Ibn Sīnā, whose psychological system we will examine later, and Ibn Rushd, whose purified Aristotelianism provoked an intellectual crisis that marked the end of the high Middle Ages.

Unfortunately, Judaic and Islamic philosophy failed to escape the fate so narrowly avoided in Latin Christendom. The conservatives among Jewish and Islamic leaders found the free inquiry of philosophy too dangerous to revealed truth to be tolerated. Philosophy and its works were prohibited, so that after the time of Ibn Rushd (died 1198) there was little independent, nontheological philosophy among Jews or Muslims. As we shall see later in this chapter, similar persecution fell upon Aristotle's teachings in thirteenth-century Europe, but it was not successful in suppressing his writings. In unified, absolutist Islam, thought control could succeed; in politically diverse Europe, it could not.

Islamic Psychology

> He who knows his soul, knows his creator.
>
> Proverb of the Muslim Brethren of Purity

This proverb could stand as the motto of early and high medieval psychology. Augustine, as we have seen, wanted to know God and the soul. He believed that by turning inward and inspecting the soul one could come to know God, who is present in every soul. In Augustine's concept of the unity of Creator and Creation, the three mental powers—memory, understanding, and will—mirror the three beings of the Holy Trinity. Introspective psychology characterized the earliest years of Christian philosophy. A philosopher looked inward to his own soul as a way to know God—not to understand himself as a unique human being, but to find an external order, God's order, to guide one's life. True individualism did not appear until the high Middle Ages, and then it was found largely in popular culture rather than philosophy.

Nevertheless, within the Islamic world, a naturalistic, rather than religious, faculty psychology developed, based on Aristotle. This psychology was originally worked out in a Neoplatonic framework within which Aristotle was interpreted, and it combined an elaboration of Aristotle's psychology with late Roman and Islamic medicine. Over the next two centuries, as Aristotle became better known in Europe, this naturalistic faculty psychology completely replaced the older, Augustinian Neoplatonic psychology.

In the Neoplatonic scheme of things, humans stand midway between God and matter. As a rational animal, a human being resembles God; as a physical being, a human resembles animals and other purely physical creatures. In this view, when allied with Aristotelian faculty psychology, the human mind itself reflects this ambiguous position: The five corporeal senses are tied to the animal body, while the active intellect—pure reason—is close to God. A person is a microcosm reflecting the greater Neoplatonic macrocosm.

Various writers elaborated on Aristotle's psychology by elaborating on the set of faculties possessed by Aristotle's sensitive souls. Because these faculties processed sensory images passed on from the special, or exterior, senses, they were called *inward wits,* or *interior senses.* These were thought to be the exact transition point between body and soul in the chain of being. Such a scheme appears in Islamic, Judaic, and Christian thought in the early Middle Ages. Muslims made the special contribution of placing the discussion in a physiological context. Islamic medicine carried on the Classical medical tradition, and Muslim doctors looked for brain structures that hosted the various aspects of mind discussed by philosophers. The most complete statement of the Aristotelian medical view was made by Abū Ali al-Husayn Ibn Sīnā (980–1037), known in Europe as Avicenna, who was both a doctor and a philosopher and whose works were influential in constructing high medieval philosophy and psychology.

Different lists of mental faculties had been drawn up by commentators on Aristotle before Ibn Sīnā. The five corporeal senses and intellect were not considered mental faculties, a status reserved for the interior senses or faculties. Aristotle had proposed three faculties—common sense, imagination, and memory—although the lines between them were not sharply drawn. Later writers proposed three to five faculties, but Ibn Sīnā produced a list of seven faculties that became the norm. This list presented a Neoplatonic hierarchy, in ascending order, from the faculty closest to the senses (and the body) to the faculty closest to divine intellect. His system of description is outlined in Figure 3–1.

Beginning with the parts of the mind closest to the body, Ibn Sīnā's system discusses the *vegetative soul,* common to plants, humans, and animals (which he treats as did Aristotle), saying that it is responsible for the reproduction, growth, and nourishment of all living things. Next comes the *sensitive soul,* common to people and animals. At its lowest level, it comprises the five *exterior senses* or corporeal senses (again, following Aristotle). The second level of the sensitive soul comprises the *interior senses,* or mental faculties, which are at the border between our animal and angelic natures. They, too, are hierarchically arranged. First comes *common sense,* which (as in Aristotle) receives, unites, and makes conscious the various qualities of external objects perceived by the senses. These perceived qualities are retained in the mind by the second internal sense, *retentive imagination,* for further consideration or later recall. The third and fourth internal senses are the *compositive animal imagination* and the *compositive human imagination,* which are responsible for active, creative use of mental images; they relate together (compose) the images retained by the retentive imagination into such imaginary objects as unicorns. In animals, this process is simply associative; in human beings, it may be creative—hence the distinction of two faculties. The fifth internal sense is *estimation,* a kind of natural instinct for making judgments about the "intentions" of external objects. The dog avoids the stick because it has learned the stick's punishing "intentions." The wolf seeks the sheep for it knows the sheep is edible. This power, similar to the simple conditioning of modern psychologists, "estimates" the value or harm of objects in the animal's world.

The highest internal senses are *memory* and *recollection.* Memory stores the intuitions of estimation. These intuitions are simple ideas of the object's essence, not sensible attributes of the object. Recollection is the ability to recall these intuitions at a later time. The material stored by memory and recalled by recollection is thus not a copy of an object, for this function is performed by the retentive and compositive

RATIONAL SOUL
{
Contemplative Intellect—knows universals
Practical Intellect—manages everyday affairs
}

Appetite
{
Approach pleasure (concupiscible appetite)
Avoid pain (irascible appetite)
}

SENSITIVE SOUL

Interior Senses
{
Recollection—recalls intuitions from memory
Memory—stores intuitions from estimation
Estimation—intuitions about benefit and harm
Compositive human imagination—creative imagination
Compositive animal imagination—combines images
Retentive imagination—image—copies of objects
Common sense—combines the five exterior senses
}

Exterior Senses
{
Vision
Hearing
Touch
Taste
Smell
}

VEGETATIVE SOUL
{
Reproduction
Growth
Nourishment
}

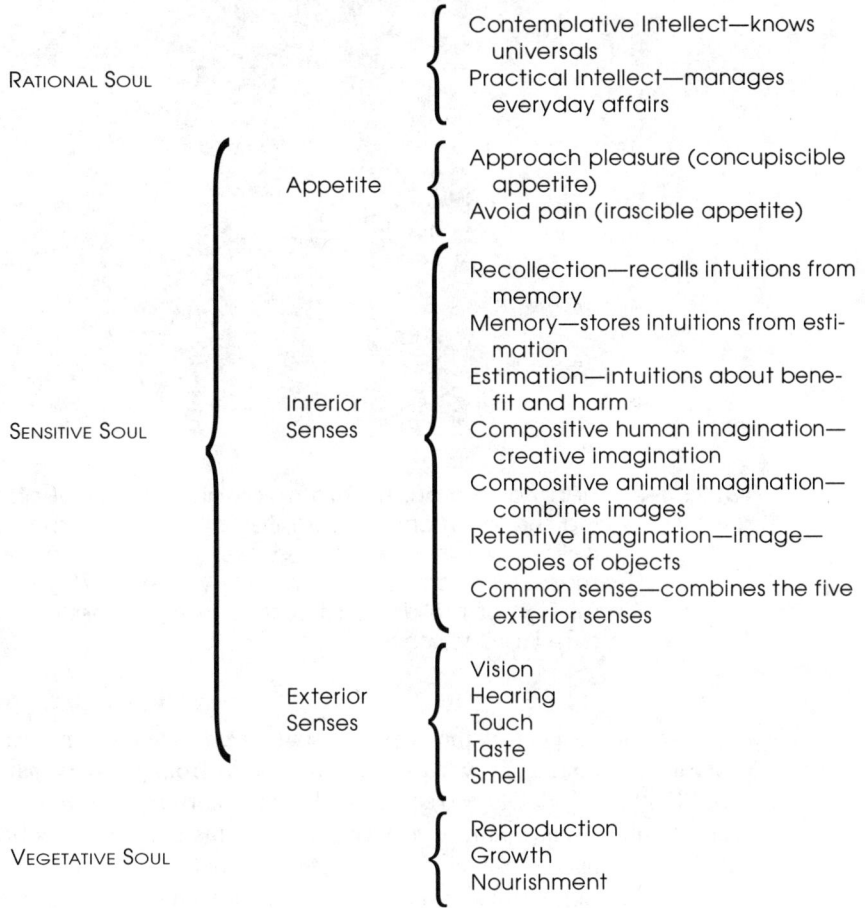

FIGURE 3–1 Ibn Sīnā's faculty psychology.

imaginations. Instead, the material is a set of simple but abstract ideas, or general conclusions, derived from experience. They are not, however, true universals, for only the human mind has the power to form universals.

Ibn Sīnā was a physician, and he tried to combine his explication of Aristotle's philosophical psychology with the traditional, though erroneous, Roman medical tradition stemming from Galen. By speculation, without resort to forbidden dissections, Ibn Sīnā and other Muslim faculty psychologists located the internal senses in different parts—specifically, in the *ventricles,* of the brain. His proposals became standard medical teaching until, in the sixteenth century, Vesalius again practiced dissection and proved Ibn Sīnā's ideas wrong.

Figure 3–2, a simple drawing of a head from a medical textbook of about 1420, shows the location of the four internal senses accepted by most medical writers. The first (front) ventricle contains common sense, which here includes retentive imagination. The second contains human and animal compositive imagination. The third holds estimation. The fourth (rearmost) ventricle contains memory, including recollection.

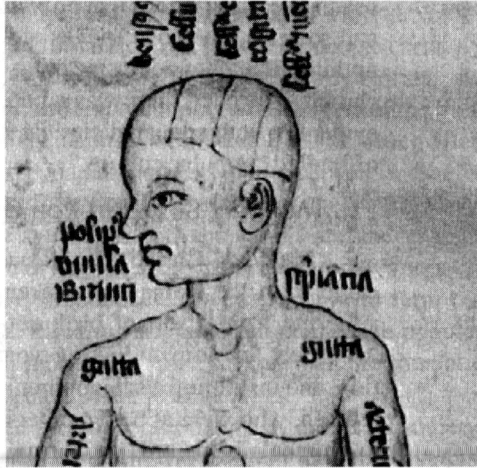

FIGURE 3-2   Head of a man, from a medical textbook of about 1420, showing the locations of four internal senses. From front to back, the cells contain *common sense, imagination, estimation,* and *memory.* (From Clarke and Dewhurst, 1972.) Reprinted by permission of the University of California Press and Wellcome Institute Library, London.

The final aspect of the sensitive soul treated by Ibn Sīnā was motivation. As Aristotle had pointed out, what sets animals apart from plants is that they move themselves. Ibn Sīnā, following Aristotle, called this motive power *appetite,* and it has two forms. Animals sense pain or danger and flee; this may be called *avoidance.* On the other hand, animals sense or anticipate pleasure and move toward it; this is *approach.*

The mental powers and senses so far considered by Ibn Sīnā are tied to the body and brain and are held in common by humans and animals. However, we surpass the animals in our ability to form universal concepts. This is the unique power of the human soul that alone transcends the material body and brain. Ibn Sīnā distinguished two faculties within the human soul: *practical intellect* and *contemplative intellect.* The lower-ranked practical intellect concerns itself with everyday affairs. It regulates the body, maintains good behavior, and protects the contemplative intellect so it may fulfill itself.

The fulfillment of the contemplative intellect is knowledge of universals abstracted from particular sense experiences. In this, Ibn Sīnā followed Aristotle, as he does in further distinguishing active and passive intellect. The contemplative intellect of the human soul is entirely passive (Aristotle's *passive mind*) and has the potential for knowledge, which is actualized by the active intellect, or *agent intellect.* However, Ibn Sīnā set the agent intellect outside the human soul (which Aristotle had not done). A kind of angelic intellect next up in the Neoplatonic hierarchy, it illuminates the contemplative mind and leads it to knowledge of the Forms, as in Plato and Augustine. As we shall see, the doctrine of a separate agent intellect is un-Christian, and its entry into Europe via the Muslim philosopher Ibn Rushd precipitated the intellectual part of the crisis that ended the high Middle Ages.

THE FLOWERING OF MEDIEVAL CIVILIZATION: THE HIGH MIDDLE AGES (1000–1300)

Popular Culture

The high Middle Ages brought many social developments that came to define the modern world: the primacy of law over personal rule; capitalism; the growth of cities. Two closely related developments command our attention, for they expressed important popular psychological attitudes that provided the setting for later theories about human motivation and society. When one speaks of "popular culture" in the medieval context, nothing like the modern meaning is intended, for few people were literate outside the church. However, there was a popular vernacular literature, and a common set of ideas was evident in both educated clerical society and lay society. Together, these can be considered a kind of limited popular culture.

Women, Sex, and Romantic Love

In early Christianity, women were full participants in religion; they preached and often lived in chaste, mixed-sex monasteries. The early Middle Ages were full of strong female figures as capable and powerful as any man. However, as Christianity absorbed Classical culture, it absorbed Roman misogyny and Platonic aversion to sensual pleasure. Marriage was forbidden to priests; women were forbidden to preach or even approach holy relics. They were reduced to second-class status as helpers of men. According to St. Thomas Aquinas, "Woman was created to be man's helpmate, but her unique role is in conception . . . since for other purposes men would be better assisted by other men" (Heer, 1962, p. 322).

One especially strong source of Christian misogyny was St. Jerome (340–420), a Neoplatonist who linked womanhood to the temptation of the flesh. Medieval Christianity looked on sex as sinful, whether inside marriage or out. St. Jerome said (Pagels, 1989, p. 94), "in view of the purity of Christ's body, all sexual intercourse is unclean." Virginity was exalted; the immaculate Virgin Mary was contrasted with Eve the temptress. As the oppression of women grew, the cult of the Virgin spread throughout the Middle Ages and well into modern times, as is evident from the number of churches and schools carrying some variation of the name *Notre Dame*. This focus created an ambivalent attitude toward women. Women at their best were seen as holy vessels of God, yet men feared women as sources of temptation.

Most medieval women lived lives of quiet desperation, but there were two important responses to their oppression. Many women became actively involved in heretical movements. *Albigensianism,* for example, which was more a rival religion than a heresy, put many women in positions of power and influence.

The other response was subtler, more influential, and tied to wider developments in Christendom. It was the invention of courtly love, an artistic and philosophical embroidering of the romantic love experienced by many people in all societies (Jankowiak, 1995). Medieval people certainly were not unaware of sex. It was the major topic of many folk tales, bawdy stories, and fabliaux. It was also the main topic of the goliards—student poets and singers of the high Middle Ages. The most famous collection of their songs is *Carmina Burana,* which often presents a blasphemous glorification of the pagan goddess of love, Venus. She is described in terms such as "Rose of the World," usually reserved for the Virgin Mary. (The rose, incidentally, was widely used as a symbol of both the vagina and the Virgin.)

Among aristocrats, romantic, sexual love was elaborated and incorporated into the emerging idea of knightly honor. Ideally, knights dedicated themselves to the love of one lady, for whom they promised great deeds, and from whom they expected great love. The courtly version of romantic love was to have tremendous popular influence down the ages; today's love songs are echoes of the twelfth-century troubadours' lyrics.

In the vast majority of human societies throughout history, love very rarely formed the basis of all enduring male–female relations. In most cultures, that relationship is formed by more or less forced, indissoluble marriages. Romantic love is usually adulterous, as it was in courtly love. Still, romantic love remains an important element in popular consciousness and psychology. Theories of motivation must reckon with the romantic love, or as Tennov (1979) has called it, *limerence.*

Ultimately, the spreading belief in romantic love (combined with the prosperity to act on it) tended to undermine the corporate nature of medieval society by making the basis of relationships personal feeling rather than appointed status. Gottfried von Strasbourg, in his *Tristan und Isolde,* one of the most enduring romantic love stories, wrote about the lovers' union this way: "Man was there with Woman, Woman there with Man. What else should they be needing?" (Heer, 1962, p. 195). Church, state, and society were dispensed with in favor of the romantic, spiritual, and carnal union of two individuals.

The Growth of Individuality

Gottfried von Strasbourg's statement in a popular thirteenth-century poem stands in total contrast to the rest of medieval society and philosophy. There was little conception of the individual in most of the Middle Ages. The concept was invented during the Middle Ages, but it did not become deeply ingrained in thought until the Renaissance. This is not to say that there were no individuals in the Middle Ages, for those centuries were full of strong and distinctive men and women, but there was no conception of the individual as an important object of concern or study. This lack is part of the Neoplatonic *Zeitgeist* that dictated that the human intellect knows only universals, not individuals. The rational mind of each person thus knows another only as an essence—humanness—not as an individual defined by the characteristics that make each person unique. A person's status as emperor, pope, king, or serf was far more important than status as an individual human being distinct from all others.

Medieval philosophical psychology expressed this attitude. The philosopher-psychologist was interested in the sensitive soul, the will, the imagination, the intellect; medieval theorists had little interest in individual differences in psychological makeup. This Platonic attitude had a long and durable history. Not until the nineteenth century do we find a systematic interest in individual differences, and even then, the founder of psychology, Wundt, was indifferent to them.

Thus, for the birth of the Western conception of individualism, we must look rather in facets of popular culture and religion, such as courtly love. The concept of the individual blossomed forth in many areas during the high Middle Ages: Biographies and autobiographies were written; portraits came to reflect the individual, not merely the person's status; close friendship was encouraged; and literature was increasingly concerned with individual thoughts and feelings rather than with an external narrative of action.

In two areas, individualism did make its way into academic culture—ethics and mystic religion—and even here, the movement began in popular culture. Before the twelfth century, sin was acknowledged but not felt as something personal. Penance was a mechanical procedure for expiating sin. In the twelfth century, however, people began to weigh personal intention in judging transgressions. This attitude was formalized in Peter Abelard's (1079–1142) *voluntaristic ethics,* the motto of which was "Know yourself." Abelard held, contrary to other thinkers, that sin was entirely a matter of intention, not of action. An act is not right or wrong; what is right or wrong is the intention behind the act. Intentions are, of course, intensely personal, so Abelard's ethics were part of the growth of the individual. The medieval Catholic confessional, in which sinners recount their individual sins to a forgiving confessor, was a practical form of psychotherapy (Thomas, 1971).

Mysticism began in popular religion rather than scholastic theology. Not content with the mediation of a priest between self and God, mysticism seeks a direct connection between the two. The way to God is contemplation, not ritual. St. Francis of Assisi (1182–1226), the greatest medieval popular preacher, abandoned wealth and status in favor of communing with God through nature. St. Francis's teaching was individualistic and was perceived, correctly, as subversive by the Catholic Church. He narrowly escaped persecution as a heretic instead of canonization as a saint. Poverty was not an ideal that a rich and worldly church wished to support, and solitary contemplation threatened the complex of rituals the church claimed brought salvation. Only by absorbing St. Francis and his followers could the church avert the threat of the rising consciousness of the individual inherent in mysticism. Thus, the idea of the individual, which would grow to great prominence in the Renaissance, was born in medieval popular culture.

Christian Psychology

The high Middle Ages experienced an intellectual renaissance as the works of Aristotle and other Greek writers, together with Muslim commentary, poured into the West through Spain, Sicily, and Constantinople. Aristotle's philosophy was naturalistic and brought a fresh, unreligious approach to knowledge and humanity that was reconciled with Christian faith only with difficulty. St. Thomas Aquinas, who synthesized faith in God's word and reason as found in Aristotle's philosophy, only narrowly escaped a charge of heresy. This union of Christ and Aristotle, impressive though it was, was relatively sterile. The future belonged to those who, like William of Ockham, divorced faith from reason and pursued only the latter. We will therefore only briefly summarize the psychology of the high Middle Ages.

In the twelfth and thirteenth centuries, there was a great increase in education, and philosophers abounded. We will limit our consideration to the twin peaks of high medieval Christian philosophy: St. Bonaventure (1221–1274) and St. Thomas Aquinas (1225–1274). They stand, respectively, for the two great medieval approaches to knowledge, humanity, and God: the Platonic-Augustinian mystical way, and the Aristotelian-Thomistic way of natural reason constrained by faith.

St. Bonaventure

St. Bonaventure was the great voice of the conservative Platonic-Augustinian philosophy that resisted the introduction of Aristotle into Christian thinking. He took a sharply dualist, Platonic view of soul and body, as did Augustine. To Bonaventure, the soul was much more than the form of the body. The soul and body were two completely distinct substances, and the immortal soul was merely using the mortal body during its earthly existence. The essence of a person was the soul.

The soul was capable of two sorts of knowledge. First, as united with the body, it could have knowledge of the external world. Here, Bonaventure followed the empiricism of Aristotle by denying innate ideas and arguing that we build up universal concepts by abstraction from experienced individual objects. However, like Aquinas, Bonaventure asserted that abstraction alone is insufficient and must be joined to the divine illumination from God if there is to be any true knowledge.

The second source of knowledge, Bonaventure said, belonged to the soul alone: knowledge of the spiritual world, including God. The source of this knowledge was introspection, which discovers the image of God illuminated in the soul, and apprehends God through interior reflection without recourse to sensation. We should emphasize again that this Augustinian introspection did not have as its aim knowledge of a personal self as in psychotherapy, or of human nature as in scientific psychology. Its goal was a vision of God, not persons or humanity.

Bonaventure distinguished four mental faculties: the vegetative faculties, the sensitive faculties, the intellect, and the will. However, Bonaventure spoke of other "aspects" of the soul, which he refused to call faculties but whose inclusion made his system resemble Ibn Sīnā's. For example, he distinguished a "higher" aspect and a "lower" aspect to the intellect, a distinction that resembles Ibn Sīnā's contemplative and practical intellects.

Bonaventure's Platonism was destined to be overtaken and overshadowed by Aquinas's Aristotelianism, which became the official doctrine of the Catholic Church. It lives on in Protestantism, however, which stresses the word of God over reason, and individual communion between each person and God over ritual.

St. Thomas Aquinas

As Aristotle became known in the West, many thinkers struggled to reconcile his scientific naturalism with the teachings of the church. The greatest and most successful of these thinkers was St. Thomas Aquinas. He called Aristotle "The Philosopher," the thinker who demonstrated both the power and the limits of human reason practiced without the word of God. Aquinas adopted Aristotle's system and showed that it was not incompatible with Christianity. In doing so, he stood Aristotle on his head. Where Aristotle stayed close to nature and was silent on God, Aquinas reoriented everything to depend on and reveal God.

To harmonize philosophy and theology, Aquinas distinguished sharply between them, limiting a person's reason to knowledge of the world of nature. Aquinas thus accepted Aristotle's empiricism and the consequence that reason can know only the world, not God. God can be known only by inference. His work can be seen in the world. This is an important moment in the evolution of Western thought. Aquinas said that philosophy and religion were separate; while they were not incompatible, they did not connect. This division ultimately destroyed the medieval synthesis Aquinas worked so hard to achieve. However, Aquinas's philosophy and theology were, in practice if not in theory, intertwined; reason and revelation did make contact. But later thinkers pursued his division of reason and faith to its logical conclusion and destroyed theological metaphysics while giving birth to science.

Aquinas set out to consider all topics, including psychology, philosophically—that is, independent of revelation. In his psychology, he closely followed Aristotle, but he also gave weight to the opinions of Islamic writers, especially Ibn Sīnā. He made few original contributions to Aristotelian psychology but refined and extended the classification of mental aspects given by the Philosopher and his Islamic commentators. Figure 3–3 summarizes Aquinas's picture of mind. As can be seen, most of it is similar to ideas of Aristotle and Ibn Sīnā, and most of the new points are self-explanatory. It will be necessary only to comment on a few unique points.

Aquinas, more than Aristotle or his non-Christian commentators, was concerned with distinguishing persons, who have souls, from animals. This emerges most clearly in his discussions of motivation and the faculty of estimation. Unlike Ibn Sīnā, Aquinas held that there are two kinds of estimation. First, there is *estimation proper,* which is characteristic of animals and not under voluntary control: The lamb *must* flee the wolf it sees to be dangerous; the cat *must* pounce on the mouse. The second kind of estimation is under rational control. Aquinas called it *cogitava,* and it is found only in humans: We flee the wolf, or choose to approach it. One's estimative power is under the control of one's free will, for one chooses and makes judgments instead of simply responding blindly to animal instinct. Just as there are two kinds of estimation, so there are two kinds of motivation or appetite. Sensitive, animal appetite is an unfree, natural inclination to pursue pleasurable objects and avoid harmful ones, and to overcome obstacles

FIGURE 3-3 Aquinas's conception of mind.

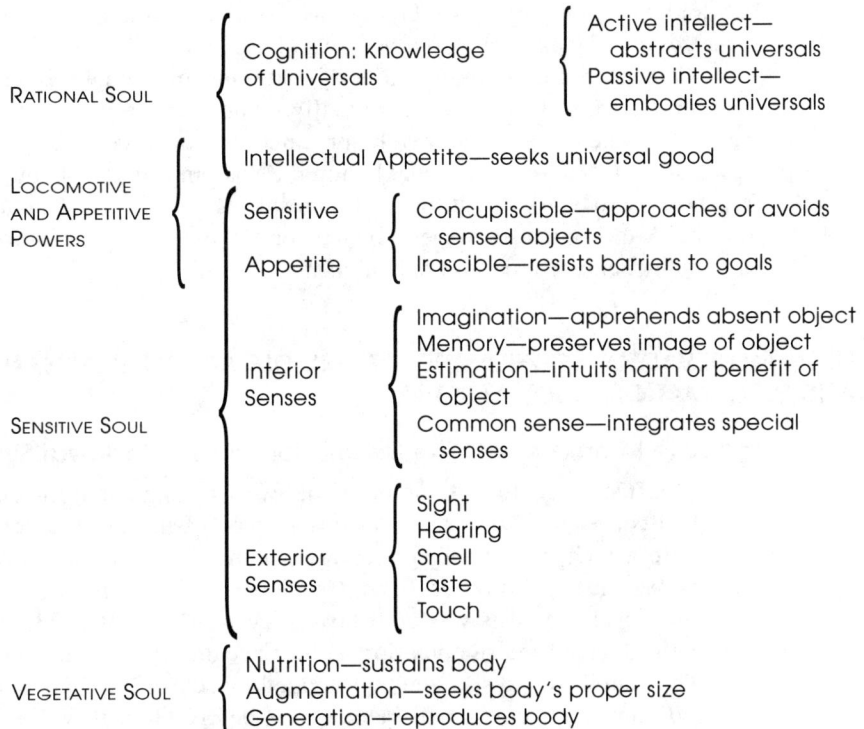

RATIONAL SOUL
  Cognition: Knowledge of Universals
    Active intellect—abstracts universals
    Passive intellect—embodies universals

LOCOMOTIVE AND APPETITIVE POWERS
  Intellectual Appetite—seeks universal good
  Sensitive Appetite
    Concupiscible—approaches or avoids sensed objects
    Irascible—resists barriers to goals

SENSITIVE SOUL
  Interior Senses
    Imagination—apprehends absent object
    Memory—preserves image of object
    Estimation—intuits harm or benefit of object
    Common sense—integrates special senses
  Exterior Senses
    Sight
    Hearing
    Smell
    Taste
    Touch

VEGETATIVE SOUL
  Nutrition—sustains body
  Augmentation—seeks body's proper size
  Generation—reproduces body

to that pursuit. A human being, however, has intellectual appetite, or will, which seeks the general good under the guidance of reason. The animal knows only pleasure or pain; the human knows right and wrong.

Three other changes from Ibn Sīnā may be noted. First, Aquinas dropped compositive imagination as an unnecessary addition to retentive imagination and rational thinking. Second, by making *cogitava*—human estimation—a rationally guided faculty concerned with the outer world, the need for Ibn Sīnā's practical intellect vanished. Finally, Aquinas made the mind whole by returning the active intellect to the human soul. Knowledge is an active product of human thinking, not a gift of divine illumination via the agent intellect.

Despite some Neoplatonic remnants, such as the hierarchic organization of faculties, Aquinas's views stand in sharp contrast to Bonaventure's. Aquinas rejected the Platonic-Augustinian tradition's radical dualism of soul and body. The body is not a tomb, prison, or punishment; nor is it a puppet operated by the soul. A person is a whole, a mind *and* a body. Although the soul is transcendent, its natural place is in a body, which it fulfills and which fulfills it. This got Aquinas into trouble with Neoplatonized Christian orthodoxy, which looked to a disembodied life of bliss in heaven. By stressing the resurrection, when soul and body would be united forever, Aquinas was able to defend his Aristotelean philosophy.

Aquinas also adopted a consistent empiricism. The human mind can have direct knowledge only of what was once in the senses; there are no innate ideas. All thinking requires images. Bonaventure had upheld the Augustinian notion of direct self-knowledge through introspection, which revealed an innate image of God. Aquinas rejected this. All knowledge of the soul or God, and of all things invisible, must be indirect. Direct communion with God or with the essence of ourselves is impossible. We can know God only by examining the world, which is God's work; we can know ourselves only by examining our acts, which are our work.

Aquinas's philosophy was a heroic attempt to reconcile science—Aristotle—with revelation. However, by conceptually separating the two, he was a harbinger of the future, when reason and revelation came into open conflict. Aquinas brought a fresh naturalism to the traditional Platonic Christian framework, but he accepted that framework and worked within it. The resulting edifice is a monument to human thought. A monument, however, commemorates the past. The future of science and psychology belonged to more radical men.

FROM MEDIEVAL TO MODERN: THE LATE MIDDLE AGES, RENAISSANCE, AND REFORMATION (1300–1600)

The Late Middle Ages: The Dissolution of the Medieval Synthesis

By the fourteenth century, the factors that would bring about the end of the Middle Ages had coalesced. The growth of cities, capitalism, and the nation-state eroded feudal life, which finally ended in empty playing at chivalry. A severe economic depression began. Population declined. Crime and violence increased. The death blow to the medieval synthesis was probably the Black Death of 1348, which carried off about a third of Europe's population. People became cynical and pessimistic.

The church was distrusted and divided by schism, and popular preachers emphasized human sinfulness and helplessness before God. It was a period when the medieval confidence in the ability to find a total explanation of the world in unified terms was abandoned and the limits of human reason were acknowledged. We will focus on three intellectual movements that undercut the medieval worldview: empiricism; its offspring, analytic philosophy, which demonstrated the shortcoming of human knowledge; and science, which offered an alternative to the religious conception of the universe.

The Rebirth of Empiricism

Before the scourge of the Black Death, the late Middle Ages were remarkably creative. We will briefly examine the most influential late medieval thinker, William of Ockham (1290–1349, approximately), whose contribution was to revive empiricism, opening up for psychological analysis what had previously been reserved to metaphysics.

Medieval philosophers conflated psychology and ontology, the study of the nature of being or existence. Following Plato, most medieval thinkers believed that something real must correspond to each mental concept. For Plato, that something real was the Forms; for Aristotle, it was real essences; for medievals, it was the Ideas in the mind of God.

For the Greeks and medievals, the only real knowledge was knowledge of universals; indeed, it was asserted that the rational soul, or intellect, had knowledge *only* of universals, not of particular things. Following Aristotle, medievals held that the only certain knowledge was what could be deduced from universal propositions. This attitude persisted even in Aquinas. Although he described the process of abstraction as the way to universal knowledge, and although he held that the intellect knows only what is derived from the senses, he still maintained that the abstracted essences were metaphysically true, that they corresponded to holy Ideas.

Ockham challenged this centuries-old assumption by substituting psychology for metaphysics. He asserted that knowledge begins with acts of "intuitive cognition"—direct, infallible acquaintance with some object in the world. Intuitive cognition does not yield mere opinion, as Plato held; it yields knowledge of what is true and false about the world. From such knowledge of things, it may go on to "abstractive cognition" of universals. But universals exist only as mental concepts; they have no existence outside the mind. These abstract concepts may be either true or false; for example, one may form the concept of a unicorn, which does not exist. Abstractive cognition is thus wholly hypothetical. The touchstone of reality and truth is intuitive cognition. Ockham discarded the metaphysical problem that bedeviled Plato, Aristotle, and the medievals, How can each individual participate in a transcendent essence or form? and substituted the psychological question, How do we form universal concepts, given that we have certain knowledge only of individuals? His answer was that the mind notes similarities among objects, and, based on the similarities, it classifies objects. Thus, universals are logical terms that apply to some objects and not others, and that indicate relations among objects.

Up to this point, Ockham was the truest empiricist of the Middle Ages, for he made observation of the world the test of knowledge. However, Ockham was a Franciscan, and there was an important Augustinian element in his view of the soul. Like Bonaventure and unlike Aquinas, Ockham held that we have direct, introspective, intuitive knowledge of the soul, rather than mere reflection on our acts. The soul can know itself directly, not just indirectly.

Unlike Aquinas and other faculty psychologists, Ockham denied the distinction of soul from its faculties. According to Ockham, the soul does not *have* the faculty of will or intellect. Rather, what we call a faculty is simply a name for a certain kind of mental act. Will describes the soul in the act of willing; intellect describes the soul in the act of thinking. Ockham always sought to simplify accounts as much as possible, ridding them of nonessentials, which is why we speak of "Ockham's razor," although the idea is Aristotle's. Ockham saw faculties as unnecessary reifications of mental acts into mental entities apart from the mind.

Habit was crucial to Ockham's view of the mind. For him, concepts were learned habits, ideas derived from experience. When he rejected the world of universals, whether Platonic Forms or divine Ideas, the status of universals was reduced to habit. These habits are what make possible a person's thinking independent of actually sensed objects. We cannot think about the Forms, for they do not exist. We think instead about derived, habitual concepts; without them, we would be animals, reduced to simple responses to external stimuli. Ockham was the first thinker, but not the last, to put such a burden on habit; but he was not a behaviorist, for to him habits were mental concepts, not bodily responses.

Ockham drew a radical distinction, far more radical than Aquinas's, between faith and reason. Ockham pointed out that there is no ground in experience, or intuitive cognition, for believing we have an immaterial, immortal soul. As far as reason or philosophy goes, the mind may be a perishable entity dependent on the body. It is only from faith that knowledge of the immortal soul comes. This separation of faith and reason greatly weakened theology and metaphysics, but it helped bring science into being.

Analysis and the Limits of Reason

Most medieval philosophers believed, as did the Greeks, in the power of human reason to know eternal Truth. They went further in asserting that God's truth and philosophical truth were one and could be synthesized, as in Aquinas's *Summa Theologica*. The idea was rejected by some mystical clergymen, such as St. Bernard of Clairvaux, who denied that philosophy could say anything about God, who is known through faith alone. Despite the mystics, the general trend of thought before 1300 favored the Greek view.

We saw this earlier in this chapter, when we touched on the problem of universals. Most medievals held to some form of *realism,* a belief that universal human concepts correspond to some enduring Form or essence, conceived by medievals as an Idea in the mind of God. This view was held by Plato, Aristotle, and Aquinas, despite their other differences. A few thinkers, called *nominalists,* maintained that universals were mere puffs of air emitted when we speak names (hence, nominalism). They have no transcendent reality, being nothing more than verbal behaviors. Nominalism was held by a small minority of thinkers.

Analysis of the problem of universal human knowledge led fourteenth-century philosophers to put severe limits on what humans may know. The first step was taken by Peter Abelard (1079–1142), the greatest medieval philosopher before the high Middle Ages (when Aristotle's works were recovered). Like Aristotle, Abelard saw the absurdity of the metaphysical-realist approach, predicating one thing of another thing. According to realists, to say "Socrates is a man" is to relate two things, the living individual Socrates and the heavenly Form of man. Abelard saw that *man* should be considered a label—or better, a *concept* that we apply to some individual. *Man* is a mental concept applied to Socrates, not a separate thing or transcendent Form. For Abelard, concepts were purely mental images or labels, and when we discuss universals we are discussing these mental entities, not eternal Forms. Abelard's account of universals was thus logical and psychological rather than metaphysical. This position, best called *conceptualism,* was a forerunner of Ockham's views (discussed earlier).

In the high Middle Ages, it was thought that human knowledge and Holy Truth were coordinate, that human universals corresponded to the divine Ideas. Abelard and Ockham destroyed this self-confidence. They posed new questions about the bases of human knowledge. If universals do not reflect the divine Ideas, and if they rest on knowledge of individuals, how do we justify our knowledge and show its truth? Before Abelard and Ockham, knowledge was taken for granted; afterward, knowledge had to be justified. Philosophers had to show how knowledge and opinion can be distinguished without reference to God or Forms.

Interestingly, belief in God's omnipotence forced a skeptical attitude on fourteenth-century philosophers. Christian thinkers believe that God is omnipotent, capable of doing anything that is not self-contradictory. Therefore, if you are looking at a tree, God could destroy the tree, but maintain in you the experience of the nonexistent object. If this is so, Christian thinkers must ask how we can be certain of any perception, of any piece of knowledge.

This problem fostered a thoroughgoing critique of human knowledge by fourteenth-century philosophers. The most interesting among them was Nicholas of Autrecourt (born 1300), a follower of Ockham. Like Ockham, he did not see psychology as metaphysics, saying that there are only acts of understanding and volition, not separate faculties of Understanding and Will. Like later empiricists, Autrecourt argued that certain knowledge lies in staying as close to appearances as possible. All we can know is what our senses tell us, so knowledge is grounded in experience, and the best knowledge is that which remains closest to experience. Making a leap from sense perception to Forms, essences, or divine Ideas, he considered illegitimate.

Nicholas of Autrecourt rejected the possibility of divine intervention to maintain an illusion of perception, and he based knowledge on an assumption shared with Ockham: Whatever appears is true. This belief is necessary to any empiricist theory of knowledge, and Ockham held it implicitly. By making it explicit, Autrecourt had to ask whether it is justified. Anticipating American pragmatism, he concluded that we cannot be certain of this assumption but can only hold that it is probably true because it seems more likely than the contrary assumption that whatever appears is false. Autrecourt and others worked out the complications of Ockham's psychological account of universals by close analysis of the grounds of human knowledge. The search for a justification of human knowledge of the external world has continued ever since and is a root problem for modern cognitive science.

In addition to fostering skepticism, Ockham's thoroughgoing empiricism had another consequence. By excluding things of faith from the sphere of observation and reason, empiricism directed human eyes toward observation of the world that could be known, the physical world. Physical science experienced its birth in the fourteenth century.

The Medieval Foundations of Modern Science

> We are not discussing God's miracles; what we have to do is to discuss what is natural in a natural way.
>
> Siger of Brabant (1240–1282)

Science has displaced religion as the pivot of the modern world. Scientific knowledge is taken as the model for all knowledge, and the revolutionary impact of the shift from theology to science is hinted at by the quotation above. God is involved only in miracles, not the ordinary events of everyday life.

The watershed date in ending the Middle Ages is 1277. In that year, the church condemned a school of thinkers at the University of Paris led by Siger of Brabant, who went too far in accepting Aristotle's naturalism in place of Christian dogma. Some of the condemned doctrines were held by Thomas Aquinas. The church leaders felt challenged by Aristotelianism because they correctly saw that it provided an un-Christian, naturalistic, and complete account of nature independent of religious faith. Aquinas struggled to reconcile the Philosopher with Christ, but the church did not accept his synthesis until it became necessary to its very survival during the Reformation. The church's first response was to reject Aristotle and repress his works. It tried to do this in 1210, 1231, and 1272. Despite attempts at repression, however, thoroughgoing Aristotelians were to be found at the University of Paris, and the church finally could not tolerate them; they were condemned, and Siger was arrested. (He was murdered by a madman while under detention in Rome.) Naturalist philosophers were regularly attacked afterward. Nicholas of Autrecourt had to recant and burn his own books.

In this climate, Siger and others after him, like Ockham, began to separate the domains of faith and reason. Only by asserting that the two were separate, that one did not bear on the other, could naturalism be defended as innocuous to Christianity. It was a move that failed in Islam, where philosophy and science were stamped out after promising starts. Europe, however, with its many nations and kings, was too heterogeneous to succumb to dogmatic repression. Ockham's analysis of knowledge successfully separated reason and revelation. But precisely because revelation was not something known by reason, minds turned to study the natural world, and religion became less and less important to European intellectuals; by the Age of Enlightenment, revelation was openly rejected and deism or atheism was adopted.

The immediate result of Ockham's ideas in the fourteenth century was an increased interest in physics. Scientific interests had, in fact, been present before the fourteenth century. We can trace the modern scientific attitude back to Robert Grosseteste (1168–1253) and Roger Bacon (1214–1292), both English Franciscans like William of Ockham. Grosseteste and Bacon each conducted experiments in optics because of their Platonic-Augustinian belief in the primacy of light among the world's elements. Both also stressed the role of mathematics in reaching an understanding of nature. This belief is most important, for mathematization has been the touchstone of science from Galileo through Newton to Einstein.

One attitude Grosseteste and Bacon shared that marks them as distinctly medieval was their desire to harmonize faith and science. After Ockham, however, medieval scientists began to take the claims of religion less seriously and to assert the claims of science more forcefully.

This new attitude emerged in Jean Buridan (approximately 1300–1358) and Nicholas Oresme (1320–1382), the greatest cleric-physicists of the fourteenth century. Both of them worked on the problem of motion, and Oresme nearly formulated the law of inertia. In this, they challenged the authority of Aristotle and laid the groundwork for Galileo. They also argued that the earth rotated, contrary to the prevailing belief that the earth was motionless and circled by the stars, moon, and planets, which were each pushed by an angel. They pointed out that experience did not support the received view that the earth is stationary at the center of the universe. They believed in the power of mathematics and in the possibility of conceiving of the universe mechanically.

Although science was born in the fourteenth century, it needed to be reborn in the seventeenth. When medieval society broke down from economic depression, the Black Death, and the end of feudalism, there was no room for science, and even Renaissance humanists did not value abstract scientific research. It remained for Galileo and Newton to found modern physics, and the connection between medieval and modern science is at best tenuous (Lindberg, 1992).

There is also an important paradox in post-Ockham empiricism. Although Ockham argued that all general knowledge was rooted in particular experience, fourteenth-century medieval scientists did not apply their physical theories to experimental data. Rather, they preferred to argue from everyday experience, from Nicholas of Autrecourt's appearances. They were, in short, *too* empiricist to do good science. Galileo took a more Platonic view of experience by building idealized models of the world and isolating crucial aspects of reality to test them. He saw, as the fourteenth-century empiricists did not, that science must be built on a selective, not a comprehensive, treatment of experience.

Such was the medieval contribution to philosophy, science, and psychology. The medieval world is not one we recognize as our own, for it was deeply religious and fostered a symbolic mentality. The medieval mind was focused on God and universal truth, not on nature and individual experience. This religious-symbolic orientation began to change in the fourteenth century, inaugurating an intellectual crisis that helped bring about the consciously modern worldview of the Renaissance. Because of radical thinkers such as Ockham and Nicholas of Autrecourt, and because the feudal system was no longer viable, society and the life of the mind had to reorganize on a new basis, the individualistic capitalistic world with which we are familiar.

Renaissance and Reformation

What a piece of work is man, how noble in reason,
How infinite in faculty,
In form and moving how express and admirable,
In action how like an angel,
In apprehension how like a god;
The beauty of the world, the paragon of animals.

Shakespeare, *Hamlet*, II, ii, 300–303

The idea of the Middle Ages was invented by the Renaissance. Renaissance thinkers divided world history into three ages: the Classical period of Greece and Rome, which was viewed as a Golden Age of philosophy and art; a Middle Age of ignorance and superstition, which was the Dark Age; and the third age, their own era. The Renaissance was a self-consciously "modern" period that saw itself breaking sharply with the past. This judgment was reaffirmed by the German historian Jakob Burkhardt, who defined the Renaissance as a special creative period crucial to the formation of contemporary society.

Ever since, historians have disputed Burkhardt's acceptance of the self-evaluation of the Renaissance. Today, continuity with the Middle Ages is stressed, and historians speak of a Carolingian renaissance and a twelfth-century renaissance. It has become apparent that Western society has been renewing itself since A.D. 1000, if not earlier.

However, when all this is said, there was unquestionably something historically new but immediately familiar about the Renaissance. One has only to compare a painting by Leonardo da Vinci or Michelangelo with any medieval work to feel the difference. We understand Shakespeare's works far more easily than medieval mystery plays.

The origin of the Renaissance is hard to pin down. A traditional starting point is 1453, when Constantinople fell and Greek-speaking scholars fled to a West that knew only Latin. However, it would be more accurate to date the beginning of the Renaissance to around 1300 in Italy. The first Renaissance man was Francesco Petrarch (1304–1374), most famous today as a poet, but also active in the distinctive Renaissance activities of classical scholarship, education, and history. The Renaissance reached its peak in Italy around 1500, by which time it had spread to Northern Europe. Although the Renaissance is the beginning of modern history, it shares its worldview with the Middle Ages, a worldview that began to be weakened by the Reformation and was dissolved by the Scientific Revolution around 1600.

The nature of the Renaissance is elusive. It contributed nothing to philosophy: There is no first-rate philosopher between Ockham (died 1348) and Descartes (born 1596). It is doubtful how much it contributed to science, for which Renaissance thinkers had little use. Its enduring achievements were in art and politics, by such men as Shakespeare, Leonardo da Vinci, and Machiavelli.

What is most important about the Renaissance is its broad mutation of values, usually called *humanism,* a secularization of the West's understanding of the universe and humanity's place in it. In all spheres, thinking became more human-centered and less God-centered, although religion was never abandoned; and in the sixteenth century, the Reformation dominated all else.

This secularization started modestly with the increased reclamation of the classics, begun by Petrarch. Humanism originally meant the recovery of classical thought and its application to contemporary human problems. We have seen that recovery of the past began in the twelfth century, but the pace accelerated in the fourteenth century, and the outlook changed. The first and most obvious contribution of the humanist efforts was in the recovered works themselves; for example, the whole of Plato became known for the first time. Renaissance scholars also sought to edit the works, to separate text from commentary, to ascribe to each author the correct treatise, and to discover forgeries.

The Renaissance scholar wanted to understand the mind of each classical writer in itself, and in its own historical context. This is the first manifestation of the secularization of philosophy and of an important Renaissance attitude not seen since the Sophists, that truth has many perspectives. Medieval philosophers held to one truth, known perfectly by God, that must be sought by humans. Although they used the classics, medieval philosophers did not want to understand Plato or Aristotle as individual thinkers. They wanted to find God's truth in the ancient writings. Accurate texts were, therefore, unimportant; it did not matter whether the words were those of the original writer or of a later commentator, as long as God's Word could be found. The Renaissance humanists sought human truth rather than divine truth. They wanted to converse with the ancients (to whom they wrote letters), not rummage through works in search of support for revelation.

Although the humanists believed in God and truth, they believed that truth can be seen in many ways, from many individual perspectives. During the Reformation, the northern humanist Disiderius Erasmus (1466–1536) held to this belief despite the fanaticism of Protestants and Catholics alike. He would commit himself to neither camp, despite his initial sympathy for Luther, and he found himself condemned by both sides.

The shift from God-centeredness to human-centeredness appeared in many spheres of life. The state increasingly resisted the temporal claim of the pope to a secular power. Higher education became open to laypeople, not just to clerics. Even religious movements were occasionally led by the laity; Anabaptism, a radical Protestant movement, was started by a German weaver.

We meet in the Renaissance humanists a figure we last met in Greece: the Sophist. Like the humanists, the Sophists were practical educators interested in individual perspectives rather than divine truths. The most important belief of the Sophists was that humanity is the measure of all things. The humanists could not go so far without abandoning Christianity, which none did, but they forcefully pushed Western thought in a secular direction. Shakespeare's expression of human worth is typical of every humanist writer. Petrarch quoted Seneca's "Nothing is admirable besides the mind." Pico della Mirandola (1463–1494) wrote, "Who is there that does not wonder at man?" Human beings were placed at the center of God's creation, lords over nature, and in intellect like the angels and even like God himself. Optimism about a person's potential and faith in a person's powers separated the humanists from their medieval predecessors.

One might have thought that, in an age that glorified humans, there would have been an outpouring of psychological studies, but there was not. Authors wrote to exalt humanity, to establish humans' proper place in nature but not to study them. Even the most scientifically oriented of all Renaissance philosophers, Sir Francis Bacon, simply modified the faculty psychologies of the Middle Ages.

However, we should note three related harbingers of the post-Renaissance age. First was the tendency to see the body as a *machine,* for example, in the drawings of Leonardo da Vinci, an acute observer of human and animal anatomy. The Renaissance was also a time of renewed medical research and dissection. As physiological knowledge grew over the years, the mechanistic attitude increased until it became the basis for Descartes' conception of animal and human bodies.

Second was Renaissance *nature philosophy.* Nature philosophy was an ambitious attempt to explain happenings in the world without reference to supernatural beings, but tended to impute to matter the very magical powers previously granted to gods, demigods, angels, and demons. Magnetism, for example, is quite mysterious. Certain metallic substances have the power to attract or repel other metallic substances, and it had been easy to attribute the powers of magnets to enchantment by a wizard wielding supernatural powers. Nature philosophers rejected supernatural explanations of magnetism, however, and said that magnets naturally possess the power to attract and repel metals by themselves, without the intervention of magical powers. As Robert Fludd, a leading scientist of the era wrote, a magnet draws "iron to it by a secret virtue, inbred by nature, and not by any conjuration." His colleague Elias Ashmole concurred, venturing that, in light of the natural power of magnets, "there is no other mystery, celestial, elemental, or earthly, which can be too hard for our belief" (both quotations from Thomas, 1971, p. 266).

Nature philosophers were scientific to the extent that they sought to explain events by reference only to natural causes, but they failed to spell out mechanisms by which forces such as magnetism worked, leaving them somewhere between science and magic. During the Scientific Revolution, Newton faced a similar problem with regard to his proposed force of gravity, which, like magnetism, is an invisible force by which objects act on one another at a distance. Gravity was criticized by other scientists as mysterious, but Newton's mathematical brilliance allowed him to get away with leaving gravity unexplained. Descartes, on the other hand, worked with a more rigorously mechanical conception of the universe, rejecting the occult powers given matter by the nature philosophers.

In the works of Sir Francis Bacon (1561–1626) we find the third way the Renaissance foreshadows the modern world—the beginning of systematic *empirical research*. Bacon died, characteristically, of pneumonia caught while stuffing a chicken with snow to study the effects of refrigeration. He believed that philosophy should investigate nature in a wholly naturalistic and mechanistic way, eschewing theology and teleology equally. He was the first to deny that Aristotle's final cause was legitimate. He believed that scientific study should be wholly inductive, that one should carefully collect facts unguided by any biasing hypothesis, until one could cautiously draw some simple generalization. Bacon died for his belief.

Although the Reformation had nothing directly to do with psychology, its general impact on European life and thought was profound, and its consequences affected psychological thinking in the seventeenth century. The Reformation officially began in 1517 when Martin Luther nailed his 99 Theses to the door of Wittenberg Cathedral and challenged the Catholic hierarchy. The Reformation pitted Augustine against Aquinas. Luther wanted a personal, intensely introspective religion, an Augustinian religion that deemphasized ritual, priesthood, and hierarchy. Catholics responded with a Counter-Reformation built on Aquinas and a deeper emphasis on the personal side of religion.

The Reformation divided Europe into warring camps and encouraged intolerance. Bloody wars were fought in a futile attempt to extinguish the Protestants, who fought back successfully. Both sides felt that whoever was not wholeheartedly with them must be against them, and the victim was dispassionate thought. Philosophers were caught in the middle; in the seventeenth century, charges of heresy haunted Descartes and affected his psychology.

The End of the Renaissance

Tomorrow, and tomorrow, and tomorrow
Creeps in this petty pace from day to day,
To the last syllable of recorded time,
And all our yesterdays have lighted fools

PART I *BACKGROUND TO PSYCHOLOGY*

The way to dusty death. Out, out, brief candle!
Life's but a walking shadow, a poor player
That struts and frets his hour upon the stage
And then is heard no more. It is a tale
Told by an idiot, full of sound and fury,
Signifying nothing.

Shakespeare, *Macbeth,* V, v, 17–28

For all its creativity, the Renaissance was a time of tremendous social disloca-
tion, misery, anxiety, and superstition. Lynn White (1974, p. 131) has written that
the Renaissance was the "most psychically disturbed era in European history." The
Hundred Years' War and, later, the Thirty Years' War raged, bringing destruction to
much of France and Germany, as mercenary armies alternately fought each other and
pillaged the countryside when they were not paid. The Black Death that began in 1348
had by 1400 devastated the population of Europe. Famines and various diseases
struck year after year. The feudal order crumbled.

Everyday life reflected the anxiety engendered by stress. Europe was obsessed
with death. Picnics were held under the rotting corpses of the hanged. The image of the
Grim Reaper was born. Scapegoats were sought; mobs attacked Jews and "witches." At
a time when humanity was being glorified by the humanists, human mortality and suffering were reaching new levels of bestiality, and the dark side of human nature was
everywhere in evidence. Intellectuals practiced the magical arts of occultism.

The later sixteenth century was a time of doubt and skepticism. Ambiguity
about humanity is found dramatically in William Shakespeare (1564–1616). The passage from *Hamlet* quoted at the start of the Renaissance section of this chapter sums
up the optimistic humanist view of humans as noble, infinite, admirable, and godlike.
Yet Hamlet goes on immediately to say, "And yet to me what is this quintessence of
dust? Man delights not me. . . ." The quotation from *Macbeth* at the beginning of this
section is a powerful statement of disdain for humankind and life in the face of mortality, an existentialist expression of the seeming absurdity of life. Shakespeare's
dramatic genius saw both the positive side of humans stressed by the humanists and
the negative side evident in history.

A more philosophical thinker, Michel de Montaigne (1533–1592), also felt and
articulated the limits of humanity. In stark contrast to the earlier humanists, Montaigne (1580/1959, p. 194) wrote: "Of all creatures man is the most miserable and
frail, and therewithal the proudest and disdainfulest." The humanists made the
human the paragon of animals with a unique and godlike intellect; Montaigne denied
the uniqueness of humans. People are not the lords of creation, they are part of it; they
are not the highest of animals, they are on a par with them. Animals as well as humans have knowledge. Montaigne decried reason as a weak reed on which to base
knowledge and argued instead for experience. But he then went on to show how deceptive and untrustworthy are the senses. In short, Montaigne toppled humans from
the special place given them by medieval and Renaissance thinkers.

Montaigne pointed to the future, to a skeptical and naturalistic theory of humanity and the universe. Montaigne was, in fact, denying the worldview that held
sway in Europe from classical times. Polished and refined in the Middle Ages and Renaissance, it was ultimately to be shattered and replaced by science and an increasingly secular philosophy.

CONCLUSION: THE CLASSICAL-MEDIEVAL-RENAISSANCE OUTLOOK

> The World's a book in Folio, printed all
> With God's great works in letter Capital:
> Each creature is a Page, and each Effect
> A fair character, void of all defects.
>
> du Bartas, *Divine Weeks*

The Renaissance perfected a worldview implicit in classical culture and developed by the Middle Ages. Fundamental to this worldview was the idea that all things in the universe are linked in a grand order that we can decipher through resemblance. So, for example, the Renaissance physician thought skull and brain damage could be cured by the administration of walnuts, for the walnut shell resembles the skull and the nut resembles the brain.

As the poet du Bartas wrote, the world is like a book, and any being is like a page, in that it bears signs that indicate its secret meaning to others with which it shares linkage. Nature is to be understood by deciphering these signs, not through experiment but by close observation, seeking out similarities and relationships, a practice called *hermeneutics*. Hence the medieval-Renaissance scrutiny of the classic writers: Just as the world is a book revealing nature's symbolic order, so are books collections of words, signs that should reveal universal order. This order is not the scientific order of natural law, but an order built on sympathies and analogies between things, sympathies and analogies signified by resemblance, as between walnut and brain.

The human being occupied the central place in this orderly web of analogies. Annibale Romei's seventeenth-century *Courtier's Academy* states: "The body of man is no other than a little model of the sensible world, and his soul an image of the world intelligible [Plato's world of the Forms]." The human body is a summary analogy of the physical world, and the mind is a summary analogy of the invisible world. The human is a microcosm reflecting the natural and supernatural macrocosm. The human is at the exact midpoint of the universe. The human body is worldly flesh and the bodily passions tie humans to the animals. The human's rational soul is angelic, for angels are rational souls without bodies. In between, mediating between rational soul and worldly body, are human faculties, such as imagination and common sense. These faculties in the brain are subtle animal spirits, the purest of earthly substances, which link body and soul.

This worldview was shattered in the seventeenth century and brushed away in the eighteenth. Montaigne pointed the way: The human is not the center of creation, but one animal among many. So also did Sir Francis Bacon: Nature is to be investigated by experiment and explained mechanistically. Soon, Galileo would show that the world is to be understood not by the decipherment of signs, as in language, but by the application of mathematics, which transcends particular observation.

BIBLIOGRAPHY

There are several fine introductions to medieval life and history. The briefest, but still an excellent treatment, is Denys Hay, *The medieval centuries* (New York: Harper Torchbooks, 1964). Morris Bishop, *The middle ages* (New York: American Heritage Press, 1970) is an attractive, well-written book for the general reader; also for the general reader, but more detailed, is Heer

(1962). Norman Cantor, one of the outstanding students of the Middle Ages, has written two texts: *Medieval history* (New York: Macmillan, 1969), and *The meaning of the Middle Ages* (Boston: Allyn & Bacon, 1973). The classic scholarly work on medieval social structure is Marc Bloch, *Feudal society* (Chicago: University of Chicago Press, 1961). Finally, William Brandt, *The shape of medieval history* (New York: Schocken, 1973), provides a general intellectual history of the Middle Ages. The flavor of life in one place and one time during the Middle Ages is provided in David Howarth, *1066: The year of the conquest* (Harmondsworth, England: Penguin, 1977). Three general surveys of medieval philosophy are Frederick Artz, *The mind of the Middle Ages* (Chicago: Phoenix Books, 1980); David Knowles, *The evolution of medieval thought* (New York: Vintage Books, 1962); and J. Weinberg, *A short history of medieval philosophy* (Princeton, NJ: Princeton University Press, 1964). M. Fakhry, *A history of Islamic philosophy* (New York: Columbia University Press, 1970) describes the work of medieval Islamic thinkers.

For the early Middle Ages, see W. C. Bark, *Origins of the medieval world* (Stanford: Stanford University Press, 1958); Geoffrey Barraclough, *The crucible of Europe: The ninth and tenth centuries in European history* (Berkeley: University of California Press, 1976); Michael Grant, *Dawn of the Middle Ages* (New York: McGraw-Hill, 1981); H. St. L. B. Moss, *The birth of the Middle Ages 394–814* (New York: Oxford University Press, 1964), and R. W. Southern, *The making of the Middle Ages: Europe 972–1204* (New Haven, CT: Yale University Press, 1953). For philosophy in the period, see George Bosworth, *Early medieval philosophy* (Freeport, NY: Books for Libraries Press, 1971). For psychology, see Augustine, *Confessions* (Harmondsworth, England: Penguin, 1961); Marcia Colish, *The mirror of language* (New Haven, CT: Yale University Press, 1968), which discusses Augustine's psychology; George Mora, "Mind–body concepts in the Middle Ages: Part I. The classical background and its merging with the Judeo-Christian tradition in the early Middle Ages," *Journal of the History of the Behavioral Sciences* (1978, *14:* 344–61); and two works on medieval faculty psychology: E. Ruth Harvey, *The inward wits: Psychological theory in the Middle Ages and Renaissance* (London: The Warburg Institute, Survey VI, 1975), and Harry Austryn Wolfson, "The internal senses in Latin, Arabic, and Hebrew philosophical texts," *Harvard Theological Review* (1935, *28:* 69–133).

Many of the general works already cited discuss popular culture in the Middle Ages; here are some other sources. C. Erickson *The Medieval Vision* (New York: Oxford University Press, 1976); Georges Duby, *The knight, the lady, and the priest: The making of modern marriage in medieval France* (New York: Pantheon, 1983); Charles Homer Haskins, *The rise of the universities* (Ithaca, NY: Cornell University Press, 1923); Colin Morris, *The discovery of the individual 1050–1200* (New York: Harper & Row, 1972); and Jeffrey Burton Russell, *Witchcraft in the Middle Ages* (Ithaca, NY: Cornell University Press, 1972). For psychology in the high Middle Ages, see the works by Harvey and Wolfson already cited; Charles A. Hart, *The Thomistic conception of mental faculty* (Doctoral dissertation, Catholic University, Washington, DC, 1930); and George Mora, "Mind–body concepts in the Middle Ages: Part II. The Moslem influence, the great theological systems, and cultural attitudes toward the mentally ill in the late Middle Ages," *Journal of the History of the Behavioral Sciences* (1980, *16:* 58–72).

The late Middle Ages, grim as they were, are nevertheless fascinating. The pivotal century was the fourteenth, admirably captured by Barbara W. Tuchman, *A distant mirror: The calamitous fourteenth century* (New York: Knopf, 1978). The classic work on the period is J. Huizinga, *The waning of the Middle Ages* (Garden City, NY: Doubleday, 1954). The intellectual history of the period is told by Gordon Leff, *The dissolution of the medieval outlook* (New York: Harper & Row, 1976). The most important thinker of the late Middle Ages was William of Ockham, a selection of whose works is in *Philosophical writings: A selection* (Indianapolis: Library of Liberal Arts, 1964); his biographer is Gordon Leff, *William of Ockham* (Manchester, England: Manchester University Press, 1975). Ockham's skeptical follower was Nicholas of Autrecourt, *The universal treatise* (Milwaukee, WI: Marquette University Press,

1971). The folk thought of the late Middle Ages has received much attention from historians since the first edition of this book. The most important finding has been how little the Christian Neoplatonic outlook penetrated the thought of uneducated men and women. The best known of these revisionist works is Emmanuel Le Roy Ladurie, *Montaillou: The promised land of error* (New York: George Braziller, 1978), which examines the daily life of an unChristian village in southern France. A similar book on Italy is Carlo Ginzburg, *The cheese and the worms: The cosmos of a sixteenth century miller* (London: Routledge & Kegan Paul, 1980). A related and more general work, which tries to describe the characteristic mentality of the late Middle Ages, is Le Roy Ladurie's *Love, death, and money in the Pays d'Oc* (New York: George Braziller, 1982). A useful commentary on the mentality works is H. C. Erik Midelfort, "Madness and the problems of psychological history in the sixteenth century," *Sixteenth Century Journal* (1981, *12:* 5–12).

Important works on medieval science include R. Dales, *The scientific achievement of the Middle Ages* (Philadelphia: University of Pennsylvania Press, 1973); Edward Grant, "Scientific thought in fourteenth century Paris: Jean Buridan and Nicole Oresme," in M. P. Cosman and B. Chandler, eds., *Machaut's world: Science and art in the fourteenth century* (New York: New York Academy of Science, 1978); E. Moody, *Studies in medieval philosophy, science and logic* (Berkeley: University of California Press, 1975); Tina Stiefel, "The heresy of science: A twelfth century conceptual revolution," *Isis* (1977, *68:* 347–62); Nicholas H. Steneck, *Science and creation in the Middle Ages* (South Bend, IN: University of Notre Dame Press, 1975); K. Wallace, *Francis Bacon on the nature of man* (Urbana: University of Illinois Press, 1967); and Lynn White, *Medieval technology and social change* (London: Oxford University Press, 1962). Lindberg (1992) provides an excellent general history of science up to the eve of the scientific revolution. He carefully considers the degree to which modern science is a continuation of ancient and medieval science, concluding that although early scientists made important contributions, the Scientific Revolution was a genuine revolution, a break with the past. Continuity, however, is seen by Thomas Goldstein, *Dawn of modern science: From the ancient Greeks to the Renaissance* (New York: Da Capo Press, 1988).

On the Renaissance: The classic work is Jakob Burkhardt, *The civilization of the Renaissance in Italy* (New York: Mentor, 1862/1960); more recent works include J. R. Hale, *Renaissance Europe* (Berkeley: University of California Press, 1971); Denys Hay, *The Italian Renaissance in its historical background* (Cambridge, England: Cambridge University Press, 1961); Lacey Baldwin Smith, *The Elizabethan world* (Boston: Houghton Mifflin, 1972). For the Reformation, see Roland Bainton, *The Reformation of the sixteenth century* (Boston: Beacon Press, 1956). On Renaissance thought, see E. Cassirer, P. O. Kristeller, and J. H. Randall, eds., *Renaissance philosophy of man* (Chicago: University of Chicago Press, 1948); Paul Kristeller, *Renaissance thought* (New York: Harper & Row, 1961); D. Wilcox, *In search of God and self: Renaissance and Reformation thought* (Boston: Houghton Mifflin, 1975); and, for a work emphasizing the continuity rather than the break between the Middle Ages and the Renaissance, Walter Ullman, *Medieval foundations of Renaissance humanism* (Ithaca, NY: Cornell University Press, 1977).

For the medieval and Renaissance worldviews, see Erickson (1976), and E. M. W. Tillyard, *The Elizabethan world-picture* (New York: Vintage Books, n.d.).

REFERENCES

Clarke, E. C. and Dewhurst, K. (1972). *An illustrated history of brain function.* Berkeley: University of California Press.

Heer, F. (1962). *The medieval world.* New York: Mentor.

Jankowiak, W. (1995). *Romantic passion: A universal experience?* New York: Columbia University Press.

Lindberg, D. (1992). *The beginnings of western science.* Chicago: University of Chicago Press.

Montaigne, M. de (1580/1959). *Essays.* New York: Pocket Library.

Pagels, E. (1989). *Adam, Eve, and the serpent.* New York: Vintage Books.

Spencer, T. (1966). *Shakespeare and the nature of man.* New York: Collier Books.

Tennov, D. (1979). *Love and limerence: The experience of being in love.* New York: Stein & Day.

Thomas, K. (1971). *Religion and the decline of magic.* Harmondsworth, England: Penguin.

White, L. (1974). Death and the devil. In D. S. Kinsman, ed., *The darker vision of the Renaissance.* Berkeley: University of California Press.

4 The Mechanization of the World Picture (1600–1700)

Isaac Newton, the founder of modern science. While Newton's own work was confined to physics, his approach to science—the Newtonian style—ultimately revolutionized all the sciences and philosophy. He loomed almost like a god over the Enlightenment, when many thinkers endeavored to become "Newtons of the mind." His stature was captured in Alexander Pope's lines, "God said, 'Let Newton be!' And all was light."

The two centuries after 1600 were literally revolutionary. The period began with the Scientific Revolution of the seventeenth century and closed with political revolutions in colonial America and monarchical France. The Scientific Revolution and the revolutions in conceptions of human nature and society that followed in its wake laid the basis for political revolutions that implemented their ideas. The seventeenth century experienced a general crisis in which the old feudal order died away and began to be replaced by the modern, secular, capitalist, nation-states that survive today. The transformation was completed during the eighteenth century, the Enlightenment, in which traditional ideas were replaced by ideas that were scientific, or scientifically inspired.

To the medieval and Renaissance thinker, the cosmos was a somewhat mysterious place, organized in a grand continuous hierarchy from God to angels to human to material world, in which each event had a special meaning. This worldview was profoundly spiritual, as matter and soul were not sharply divided. In the seventeenth century, this view was attacked and replaced by one that was scientific, mathematical, and mechanical. Natural scientists demonstrated the mechanical nature of heavenly and earthly phenomena and then of the bodies of animals. Eventually, the mechanical approach was extended to humanity itself, and the study of humankind, from politics to psychology, was subjected to the scientific method. By 1800, both the universe and humanity were believed to be machines subject to natural law. In the process, the older view of the world and its relation to humankind as a pattern of mystically meaningful symbols disappeared.

THE SCIENTIFIC REVOLUTION

> The Scientific Revolution outshines everything since the rise of Christianity and reduces the Renaissance and Reformation to the rank of mere episodes, mere internal displacements, within the system of medieval Christendom. (Butterfield, 1965, p. 7)

The importance of science in the modern world cannot be doubted, and the Scientific Revolution cannot be passed over by any history of the West—especially a history of a science, even if that science (psychology, in this instance) was not part of the revolution. The outcome of the Scientific Revolution is unquestioned. It displaced the earth from the center of the universe and made of the universe a gigantic machine quite independent of human feelings and needs. It overthrew the bookish philosophy of scholasticism, substituting a public search for precise mathematical regularities confirmable by experiment. It also proposed that people could improve their lot by the application of reason and experiment rather than prayer and devotion (Rossi, 1975).

It used to be traditional to write the early history of science as if it were an unrelenting step-by-step progression to modern science, in which prototypical materialist scientists rejected superstition and alchemy for mathematics, experiment, and mechanism. However, this story is no longer tenable. Far from rejecting alchemy, Newton spent more time on it than on physics (Westfall, 1975). Some fathers of the Catholic Church saw mechanism as vindicating God, the creator of the perfect world-machine. Galileo was greatly influenced (as was Newton) by Renaissance Neoplatonism, and he drew on medieval philosophers for a number of his scientific ideas.

The Scientific Revolution took a long time, and drew from many sources, but it *was* a revolution, for it profoundly and permanently altered human life and human self understanding. The revolution may be said to have begun in 1543 with the publication of Nicholas Copernicus's *Revolution of the Heavenly Orbs,* which proposed that the sun, not the earth, was the center of the solar system. Sigmund Freud would later call Copernicus's hypothesis the first great blow to the human ego. No longer could humans pride themselves on living at the center of the universe and being those around whom everything else revolved.

However, Copernicus's physics was Aristotelian, and his system was no better supported by the data than the old Ptolemaic one, although some found its simplicity attractive. Galileo Galilei (1564–1642) was the most effective spokesman for the new system, supporting it with his new physics, which helped make sense of the sun-centered proposal, and producing telescopic evidence that the moon and other celestial bodies were no more "heavenly" than the earth. However, Galileo, like Copernicus, could not shake the old Greek assumption that the motion of the planets had to be circular, even though his friend Johann Kepler (1571–1630) showed planetary orbits to be elliptical. The final unity of celestial and earthly physics, and the ultimate victory of the new worldview of science, came from Isaac Newton's *Principia mathematica,* published in 1687.

Newton's laws of motion put the capstone on the idea that the universe was a machine, a celestial clockwork. The machine analogy was proposed by Galileo and René Descartes and quickly became a popular view of the universe. Originally, it was put forward as a support for religion against magic and alchemy: God the master engineer constructed a perfect machine and left it running. The only operative principles are, therefore, mechanical, not occult; magical machinations cannot affect machines. However, implicit in the mechanical view is the possibility that God is dead and has left behind a cold, impersonal universe. The view was deadly to the old medieval conception of God as an ever-present being manifested in signs and portents.

During the Scientific Revolution, an important epistemological distinction was made that ultimately helped create psychology itself. The distinction concerned the correspondence of the world as we experience it to the world as it is. Following Aristotle, medieval thinkers had believed that every conscious sensation corresponded to something real in nature. Thus, it was thought that if we see a bluebird, it is really blue; or, more importantly, if we see a person as beautiful, he or she is really beautiful; or if we see an act as just, it is really just. Beginning with Galileo, scientists argued that some sensory qualities, the *primary qualities,* are objective, while others, the *secondary properties,* are subjective. Subjective properties are those that depend on the state of the perceiver. For example, color is experienced only by people with the full complement of retinal cones. Those with less than a full complement experience partial or complete color blindness. Color, therefore, does not exist in nature itself, but in our natures as perceivers. Should all humans possess only retinal rods, there would be no color. On the other hand, some experienced properties can be quantitatively measured independently of individual consciousness. We can objectively count how many of some class of objects there are, how much each weighs, how much space each occupies, and so on. Scientists drew the distinction between primary and secondary properties as a way of guaranteeing that science—the study of the world machine—would be objective and independent of human bias.

In an important sense, the distinction of primary and secondary properties created psychology, or at least the psychology of consciousness. People were now compelled to ask how and why the secondary properties originate. If experience simply reflects the world as it is, then the problem of how it does so is a legitimate but uninteresting question. If, however, the world of experience is radically different from the world as it is, then the creation of that subjective world—our world as human beings—becomes a more interesting and important matter. Ultimately, the subjective world of experience proved intractable, and the psychology of consciousness gave way to the objective psychology of behavior.

At the same time, the Scientific Revolution began to alienate human beings from the world. Humans discovered that the world they experienced was not the real world, after all, but something created by their minds. Bluebirds are not really blue. And beautiful things are not really beautiful and just acts are not really just. All are subjective judgments of private human minds. E. A. Burtt (1954) contrasted the old worldview, when experience and reality were harmonious, with the new scientific one:

> The scholastic scientist looked out upon the world of nature, and it appeared to him a quite sociable and human world. It was finite in extent. It was made to serve his needs. It was clearly and fully intelligible, being immediately present to the rational powers of his mind; it was composed fundamentally of, and was intelligible through, those qualities which were most vivid and intense in his own immediate experience—colour, sound, beauty, joy, heat, cold, fragrance and its plasticity to purpose and ideal. Now the world is an infinite and monotonous mathematical machine. Not only is his high place in a cosmic teleology lost, but all these things which were the very substance of the physical world to the scholastic—the thing that made it alive and lovely and spiritual—are lumped together and crowded into the small fluctuating and temporary positions of extension which we call human nervous systems. It was simply an incalculable change in the viewpoint of the world held by intelligent opinion in Europe. (Burtt, 1954, pp. 123–4)

REMAKING PHILOSOPHY

The Scientific Revolution seemed to require that human nature and the human mind be rethought. Ancient science was discredited, and so, therefore, was ancient philosophy. It was time to set old psychologies aside and seek new ones. The two most important seekers were the Frenchman, René Descartes, and the Englishman, John Locke.

Consciousness Created: René Descartes (1596–1650)

Psychology as we know it began with Descartes. For good or ill, Descartes created a framework for thinking about mind and body within which virtually all philosophers and psychologists have worked since, even when they were busy attacking Descartes's ideas.

Descartes developed his radical new approach to psychology within a Christian worldview that had been profoundly altered by the Reformation and was being further reshaped by the Scientific Revolution. During the Middle Ages, the Catholic Church had permitted the persistence of a wide range of pagan beliefs and practices that it either tolerated or exploited (Thomas, 1971; Gaukroger, 1995). Although condemned (but meeting little practical interference), witches and cunning men, even werewolves and vampires continued to ply their trades (Ginzburg, 1991), and people danced around maypoles. Saints were often identified with old pagan gods, and churches were built on sites sacred to them. As the pagan churches had, the medieval Catholic Church stressed orthopraxy—correct religious practice—over orthodoxy—correct religious belief.

However, the new Protestant churches of the Reformation played down ritual and began to demand that their followers sincerely hold the right Christian beliefs. When the Catholic Church reformed itself during the Counter Reformation, it, too, compelled not just external behavioral submission to Christianity, but internal personal submission (Gaukroger, 1995). Magical practices such as the wearing of amulets to cure headaches were denounced; witches, Jews, and heretics were persecuted; and priests were forbidden to run taverns on the side. Despite official doctrinal differences among the sects, a single rather austere and puritanical religious sensibility appeared in seventeenth-century Europe. The Christian God became a forbidding and remote figure whose power could not be commanded by magic. Into the vacuum stepped science, a secular, material—and effective—way of gaining power over nature. Psychologically, the situation resembled the Hellenistic period, when traditional religions that demanded only that their followers practice cult rites, were challenged by philosophies and new religions that drew people into themselves, demanding faith. Descartes's philosophy, as we shall see, was based on a radical version of such withdrawal.

Descartes was closely connected with a circle of reforming Catholics, led by the scientist and theologian Marin Mersenne (1588–1648), which was particularly worried about the scientifically appealing but religiously dangerous ideas of Renaissance naturalism. Renaissance naturalism was scientific in that it explained the world without reference to supernatural powers, but it was suspect religiously because it seemed to grant supernatural powers to matter itself. Naturalism was especially dangerous to religious orthodoxy when applied to living things, particularly people. If a magnet had the natural power to attract metals, it seemed only a short step (taken in the eighteenth century) to saying that the brain has the power to think. Medieval and Renaissance physicians already attributed sensation, perception, common sense, imagination, memory, and other powers to the brain, so why not thought and knowledge, too? However, if all mental functions are functions of the body, as Aristotle had thought, then the existence of the Christian soul was placed in doubt.

To counter Renaissance nature philosophy, Mersenne and his followers, including Descartes, believed and taught a clockwork view of the universe. Matter was completely inert, possessing no magnetism, gravity, or any other active powers of any kind. Active power was reserved to God alone. Matter moved or changed only when physically pushed by another piece of matter. Newton's tolerance for unexplained forces—he proposed no hypothesis about how gravity worked—ultimately triumphed, but not without a struggle and with Descartes's followers on the other side.

Descartes's conception of mind and body was very carefully worked out within this religious-scientific framework, and it decisively shaped the scientific psychology that was yet to come. Descartes was committed to viewing animals as complex automata, machines whose operations could be fully explained as physical processes and without resort to vital forces of any kind. Thus, Descartes had to reject the idea that the heart was a spontaneously working pump circulating blood through the body, because its action seemed self-caused by an internal power, little different from attributing attractive power to magnets. However, the "mental" powers of the beast-machine were considerable. Everything Aristotle had attributed to the sensitive soul was included, and, to the extent people were animals, human "mental" powers had to have a purely mechanical explanation. The place of the immortal human soul in a mechanical world and a mechanical body had become a serious problem.

For our purposes, Descartes's life work may be divided into two phases. In the first phase, he focused on scientific and mathematical projects, including physics but with a growing interest in physiology. His main philosophical project during this period was working out methodological rules by which the mind ought to be governed in its search for truth. Descartes's scientific work culminated in the writing of two large books, *Le Monde* (The World), on physics, and the unfinished *L'Homme* (The Human), on physiology.

Then, in November 1633, on the eve of the publication of *Le Monde,* Descartes learned of the condemnation by the Roman Inquisition of Galileo's advocacy of the Copernican hypothesis. To Mersenne, Descartes wrote that he was so surprised by

Galileo's fate of house arrest for life that "I nearly decided to burn all my papers," because his own system of the world depended so much on Galileo's. Nevertheless, "I wouldn't want to publish a discourse which had a single word that the Church disapproved of; so I prefer to suppress it rather than publish it in mutilated form" (quoted by Gaukroger, 1995, pp. 290–1). Thus began the second, primarily philosophical, phase in Descartes's career. He decided that in order for his scientific views to win the acceptance that Galileo's had not, they needed careful and convincing philosophical justification, and he proceeded to develop the philosophy that made him famous and influential.

While working on his system of physics, Descartes took up the path to psychology through physiology that had begun with Empedocles and would ultimately lead to the founding of scientific psychology. In a letter to Mersenne in December 1629, Descartes described beginning to study anatomy by watching butchers slaughter cattle and taking parts back to his lodgings for his own dissections. These researches took him in a new and exciting direction. Three years later, he wrote to Mersenne that he would now "speak more about man than I had intended to before, because I shall try to explain all of his principal functions. I have already written about those that pertain to life such as . . . the five senses. Now I am dissecting the heads of different animals in order to explain what imagination, memory etc. consist of" (quoted by Gaukroger, 1995, p. 228). In 1890, William James will tell his readers to begin their study of psychology by getting a sheep's head from the butcher shop and dissecting its brain.

It is important to understand the goal Descartes set for himself in undertaking to give physiological accounts of mental processes, for it is a key to understanding the problems he later created for his own theory of human consciousness and to comprehending his complex, troubling, even contradictory, legacy to later psychology. As we have learned, from the time of Aristotle right through the religious Middle Ages, physicians, philosophers, and theologians had attributed most psychological functions to the animal soul, and therefore to the animal, and human, body. The Islamic physician-philosophers had even proposed specific locations in the brain in which imagination, memory, and so on took place. Within Descartes's renovated Christian framework, however, these older treatments of the faculties were unacceptable, precisely because they endowed matter with soul-like powers, the way Renaissance naturalism endowed matter with magical powers such as magnetic attraction. Saying that a given piece of brain tissue has "the power of memory" is not a scientific explanation at all, because it does not specify any mechanism by which memories are created and retrieved. "Descartes' aim was to show that a number of psychophysiological functions *that had always been recognized as being corporeal could be accounted for in a way which did not render matter sentient*" (Gaukroger, p. 278, italics in original).

In *Le Monde*, Descartes described a mechanistic universe that behaved exactly like ours, thus inviting us to believe that it *is* ours. In *L'Homme*, Descartes asks us to imagine "statues or earthen machines"—indeed, a "man-machine"—whose inner operations he described in detail, thus inviting us to believe that they *are* us, except that they lack a soul. His optimism that he could explain the behavior of animals (and much of that of humans) as the product of inner machinery was fed by the high artisanship of contemporary craftsmen who could build statues of animals and people that behaved in lifelike ways. Seeing mechanical statues move and respond to stimuli helped Descartes think that animals were sophisticated machines, too.

The novelty and daring of Descartes's undertaking are perhaps hard to appreciate today. We live with machines that perceive, remember, and, perhaps, think, and because we build and program computers we can explain how they work at whatever level of mechanical detail might be demanded. In this decade of the brain, we are learning how the brain's machinery works, down to the biophysics of single cells. Struggling to oust magical, occult powers from matter, Descartes set in motion the reduction of mental functions to mechanical processes that is only now coming to fruition. Although the details of Descartes's physiological psychology are not important for our purposes here (see Gaukroger, 1995, for a full treatment) the conceptual difficulties his approach created for his treatment of the human mind are.

The problems for Descartes's psychology, and therefore for all later psychologists, begin when we turn to the human soul, which Descartes as a Christian had to exempt from mechanistic explanation. Descartes's account is usually presented as clean and simple, but it is in fact slippery and elusive, a tortured attempt to preserve a Christian soul in a mechanistic universe. Descartes had to avoid two heretical temptations, each of which could be traced to the difficulty of assimilating Aristotle to Christianity. One was called *Averroism,* after the Latinized name of the Islamic physician-philosopher Ibn Rushd (1126–1198) who first proposed it. Averroism resulted from splitting Aristotle's human mind off from the body and then identifying it with the Christian or Muslim soul.

The heresy of Averroism derived from the fact that the Aristotelian *mind* contained only general knowledge and was therefore not the essence of one's personality, a possibly immortal, individual soul. In a religious context, *mind* was interpreted by Averroes and others, including Ibn Sīnā, as a divine inner light from God that illuminates general knowledge, but that remerges with God at death. In earlier phases of Christianity, Averroism could be resisted by emphasizing, as Aquinas did, the Resurrection, when the mind is reunited with its body, reconstituting the whole person. In Descartes's time, however, the idea of the Resurrection was fading, being replaced by the idea of immediate judgment of a soul that would live forever in Heaven or Hell. If the soul were impersonal, however, its reward or suffering became absurd. Thus, it was more important than ever that the soul be one's personal essence, not an inner light from God.

The other heretical temptation, called *Alexandrism* after Alexander of Aphrodisias (fl. 200), arose from dropping Aristotle's sharp distinction of form and matter and simply attributing to the matter of the brain the power not only to perceive and remember, but to think and have knowledge. Like Averroism, Alexandrism denied the immortality of a personal soul and was becoming increasingly tempting through the influence of Renaissance naturalism.

In *L'Homme,* the human soul is distinguished from the functions of the animal body it inhabits by the power to think, which had three important facets for Descartes. Defining the soul by the power of thought, or reason, is, of course, entirely traditional, stretching back to the ancient Greeks. What is new is Descartes's focus on how thinking separates humans from animals in *experience, behavior, and the possession of language.*

Thought makes *human experience* different from *animal experience.* Descartes never denied that animals have experience, that is, that they are aware of their surroundings. What they lack is reflective, thoughtful awareness of their own awareness. Descartes wrote (quoted by Gaukroger, pp. 282 and 325):

Animals do not see as we do when we are aware that we see, but only as we do when our mind is elsewhere. In such a case the images of external objects are depicted on our retinas, and perhaps the impressions that they make in the optic nerves cause our limbs to make various movements, although we are quite unaware of them. In such a case we too move just like automata.

As did William James centuries later, Descartes here drew a sharp dividing line between *simple awareness* and *self-awareness*. James pointed out that much of our behavior can be carried out by simple habit and without thought. In a contemporary example, a driver can respond to a traffic light's turning red, without interrupting an intense conversation with a friend. The impression of the red light on the retina causes the driver to carry out the foot movement of hitting the car's brakes. The driver experiences the light's becoming red, but does not think about it, because his or her mind is elsewhere, in conversation.

Thought makes human behavior more *flexible* than animal behavior. Animals, Descartes wrote, require some preset "disposition for every particular action" (quoted by Gaukroger, 1995, p. 276). Hitting the brakes when a traffic light turns red is a preset habit that is automatically and thoughtlessly activated by the stimulus of the red light. Descartes viewed animals as machines that always responded in such reflexive ways. Humans, on the other hand, can respond to entirely novel situations by thinking about them. Approaching an intersection where all the lights are out, a driver will drop the ongoing conversation and think carefully about what to do. An animal, lacking any stimulus to control its behavior, would be frozen into inaction or spurred by some other stimulus into inappropriate action. Behavioral flexibility became the hallmark of mind for James.

Concerning animal thought, Descartes was inconsistent. Sometimes, he denied that animals think at all. At other times, he regarded the question as empirical rather than philosophical, though, as with experience, he said that animal thinking, should it exist, would be quite different from human thinking (Gaukroger, 1995). After the acceptance of evolution made a sharp line between human and animal harder to draw, comparative psychologists tried, with controversial results, to investigate animal thought.

The third outcome of human thinking was *language,* which Descartes regarded as unique to human beings. In *L'Homme,* language played a crucial role in Descartes's understanding of the human mind, being critical to human self-awareness. Although engaged in conversation, a driver reflexively applies the brakes upon seeing a red traffic light. Seeing-eye dogs are trained to stop themselves and their master when they see a red light. At this level of reflexive response, there is no difference between the driver and the dog. However, according to Descartes's analysis, only the driver, as a human being, can think about traffic lights and think the thought that the red light means stop. The trained dog stops too, but it cannot formulate the proposition "Red means stop." Being able to think about red lights in this way gives humans the ability to think about experience reflectively, rather than simply having it.

Animals do not think as we do (if they think at all) because they cannot think with linguistically stated propositions. For Descartes, the ability of the human soul to formulate propositions did not, however, depend on acquiring any particular human language. He proposed that there is an innate human language of the mind of which actual human languages are outward translations. Thus, while our driver says, "Red means stop," and a German driver says, "*Rot bedeutet halten,*" at a deeper level each thinks the same thought linking the concept of "redness of traffic light" to "need to stop one's motor vehicle."

The role of language in thinking, and its presence or absence in animals, has proven enormously controversial in the centuries since Descartes. Some philosophers and psychologists have followed Descartes in closely linking language and thought, while others have strongly disagreed. In the 1960s, linguist Noam Chomsky proposed a *Cartesian linguistics* in which language was a unique, species-specific property of the human mind, and his student, Jerry Fodor, dubbed Descartes's universal inner language "mentalese." Cartesian linguistics played a large role in the downfall of behaviorism—which saw no essential dividing line between human and beast—and in the creation of the field of cognitive science, which aligns humans with language-using computers instead of non-language-using animals. In 1748, a French philosopher suggested teaching language to apes as a way of defeating Descartes's belief in the soul, a project carried out with uncertain results by behaviorists defending themselves from Chomsky's belief in the mind.

Unfortunately, Descartes never completed the part of *L'Homme* in which he planned to give a scientific treatment of the human soul. In 1633, as he suppressed publication of *Le Monde,* he abandoned the study of physiology and the writing of *L'Homme.* Faced with the possibility that his science might be condemned like Galileo's, he turned to providing it with an unshakable philosophical foundation (Gaukroger, 1995). For the development of psychology, Descartes's new direction was fateful. It created the concept of consciousness, the definition of psychology as the science that studies consciousness, and a set of deep, perhaps intractable problems with which psychology has struggled to the present day (Dennett, 1993; Searle, 1994).

Descartes had inconclusively worked on philosophical topics all along. Most important was his project of discovering or creating methodological rules by which the mind might reliably know the truth in science and philosophy. As Aristotle's physics crumbled before the research of the Scientific Revolution, it became widely believed that Aristotle had erred because he had relied on poor methods for theorizing about and investigating nature. Descartes wanted the new science to be guided by a better methodology, and for some years he worked on writing *Rules for the Direction of the Mind.* Eventually, he abandoned it, but it was published posthumously in 1684. In 1635, he returned to giving science its epistemological foundation in *Discourse on the Method of Rightly Conducting One's Reason and Seeking Truth in the Sciences,* published in 1637.

In this work, he described how he found his philosophy. Returning home after military service at the coronation of the Holy Roman Emperor Ferdinand II, he spent one day, possibly November 10, 1619, in a stove-heated room meditating on his own thoughts and formulating the basic principles of his philosophy. Descartes wanted to find a firm philosophical foundation for the apparently dangerous science he was developing, and to find his foundation he adopted a method of radical doubt. He resolved to systematically doubt every belief he had—even those no sane person would doubt—until he found something so self-evidently true that it could not be doubted. His aim was not to actually cast doubt on commonsense truths, but to force himself to find sound reasons for believing them. In a sense, Descartes was subjecting himself to Socrates' *elenchus,* seeking explicit reasons for holding intuitively obvious beliefs, and thereby providing a foundation for his scientific investigations.

Descartes found he could doubt the existence of God, the validity of his own sensations, and the existence of his body. He continued in this way until he found one thing he could not doubt: his own existence as a self-conscious, thinking being. One cannot doubt that one doubts, for in doing so, one makes real the very action supposedly in doubt. Doubting is an act of thinking, and Descartes expressed his first indubitable truth as the famous *"Cogito, ergo sum"* (I think, therefore I am). I am a thing that thinks, and that is all. The soul, the thinking thing, was a spiritual substance wholly without matter, not occupying space (unextended), and completely separate from the body. Descartes proposed a radical new *dualism* in which soul and body are utterly unalike, sharing neither matter nor form in common. Nor is the soul conceived as the form of the body. Instead, the soul dwells within the mechanical body as a sort of ghost, receiving sensations from it and commanding it by acts of will.

Descartes's dualism of soul and body was a way of explaining the dualism of secondary and primary sense properties. According to Descartes, the material world was made of *corpuscles,* or *atoms,* which possess only the properties of extension in space and physical location. In addition to that material world, which includes the body, there is a subjective world of *consciousness* and *mind.* Perhaps this second world is spiritual as well, for God and the soul are not material. In any case, as far as human knowledge is concerned, Descartes concluded there are two worlds: an objective, scientifically knowable, mechanical-material world—the world as it really is— and a subjective world of human consciousness known through introspection—the world of a person as a thinking being.

Descartes was not the first to prove his own existence from mental activity. St. Augustine had said, "If I am deceived, I exist," and Parmenides had said, "For it is the same thing to think and to be." What was new and carried profound implications was Descartes's radical reflexivity (Taylor, 1989), his focus on the self and his invention of consciousness as a thing that could be studied. Augustine had turned inward and found *God.* Descartes turned inward and found only *himself.* It is a momentous point in the history of psychology and philosophy, and we need to examine it and its implications carefully.

Descartes's argument of the *cogito* created consciousness as an object of scrutiny by radically dividing the self from conscious experience. Prior to the Scientific Revolution, people had assumed that the world was as it seemed to be, and had simply lived in and through experience. However, the division of the primary and secondary sense properties destroyed the traditional naive belief in the validity of experience. Descartes built on this distinction by claiming that we can step back from our experience and examine it as a collection of objects—sensations—that are not part of the self.

Imagine you are looking at a green leaf. Now I ask you to look at the green more closely. In the older naive view, you would simply take yourself to be carefully inspecting the green that the leaf really is. Descartes, however, asks you to do something different, to think about your sensation of *green,* how greenness appears in consciousness. Looked at this way, you are no longer inspecting the leaf, but are *introspecting a bit of consciousness, the sensation of green.*

A useful way to think of the model of experience Descartes is setting up has been suggested by Daniel Dennett (1993). He calls Descartes's model of mind the *Cartesian Theater.* A viewer, the inner self, the existence of which Descartes has (apparently) proved by the *cogito,* looks at a screen on which the visual stimuli from the retina are projected. Naively, when we see the image of a leaf, we believe we are seeing an actual leaf outside us. If, however, the Cartesian Theater is true, what the self actually sees is not a leaf but the projected *image* of a leaf. Introspection then consists of thinking of the image as an image and of then inspecting the image without reference to the object outside.

Consider a newspaper photograph. It may show a space shuttle on the launch pad, and you might say, "I see the shuttle." But in fact, you are seeing an image of the shuttle, not the shuttle itself, and closer examination will reveal the image to be much fuzzier than you first thought. Look even more closely, and you will see the picture is made up of gray and black dots that you didn't notice when first naively "seeing" the shuttle. Descartes says conscious experience is like a theater or a photograph, an image the self naively takes to be real, but which can be examined as a thing—consciousness itself—through a special kind of inward observation called introspection.

With the Cartesian Theater, the psychology of consciousness was born, although it was not yet a science. After Descartes, it was generally taken for granted that consciousness is a collection of sensations projected to the mind; the self can then reflectively examine them. Natural science continued to examine the world naively as a collection of objects to be carefully observed and about which theories might be propounded and tested. Psychological science became defined as the reflective, introspective study of sensations qua sensations. By submitting experience to experimental control, sensations could be carefully observed, and theories about them might be propounded and tested. Thinking of experience as an object, consciousness, apart from the things causing it, gave rise in the mid-nineteenth century to both scientific psychology and modern art. Modern art began when painters rebelled against the idea of art as representation and asked viewers to look at the surface of the canvas. Traditional art, like traditional theories of perception, focused on the thing represented. The goal of a landscape, for example, was to show how a mountain or lake really was. Modern artists, however, wanted viewers to look at the canvas, seeing not what the artist saw, but the subjective impression created in the artist by the mountain or lake.

Along with consciousness, the Cartesian Theater created the modern "point like" self (Taylor, 1989; Taylor actually uses the word "punctual," but I regard it as misleading). According to Descartes, the soul was like a *mathematical point* located in, but not actually occupying any, space, and doing but one thing, thinking. Thinking of the soul as a point was radically new. For the Greeks and others, including Christians such as Aquinas, a person had been taken to be the embodied soul, including the faculties of the animal soul, that was directly connected to the world outside by experience. According to the argument of the *cogito,* on the other hand, our essence is a small, self-aware point of pure thought, dwelling in the Cartesian Theater, detached from the body and even from experience, which it receives at second hand via projection on the screen of the Cartesian Theater.

Such a small self became easy to erase. The leading British philosopher of the next century, Hume, could not find it in himself. The leading German philosopher, Kant, could not find it either, but posited it as a logical necessity. In the psychology of consciousness, the pointlike self was called on to control, observe, and precisely report on experience. In the psychology of the unconscious, the pointlike self became the *ego,* only partly able to manage the ferocious desires of the animal *id.* In the psychology of adaptation, the soul began to disappear, merging with the screen of consciousness itself. In the twentieth century, behaviorism and cognitive science have done without consciousness and self altogether, content to study what we do rather than what we are.

By splitting off experience from the self and making it a thing, consciousness, to be studied, Descartes made psychology possible—and philosophically important. As a philosopher and scientist, Descartes wanted to know how the world really is. For traditional philosophies, this was not a problem; experience was thought to reveal the world directly to us. However, in Descartes's scheme, the thinking self is trapped in the Cartesian Theater, seeing only a projection of the world, not the world itself. Consciousness was indelibly subjective, a presentation of how the world is for us. For it to be the basis of science and of knowledge more generally, it had to be purged of its subjectivity. This made it imperative to study *us*—to practice psychology—so that the subjective contributions to experience might be subtracted, leaving only objective truth (Gaukroger, 1995). In the next century, during the Enlightenment, psychology became even more important, as philosophers moved to base ethics, politics, and the definition of a good society on the study of human nature.

Descartes's radically new conception of soul and body was in tune with the Scientific Revolution, which had begun to question the validity of perception and to think of the world as a machine. His psychology and his followers' variants of it quickly swept over the intellectual world of Europe, becoming the starting point from which virtually every psychologist began, even when disagreeing with Descartes. A host of difficulties arose, some of which we will find emerging later, but two of which Descartes himself recognized and tried to deal with.

The first problem was how mind, or soul, and body interact. Descartes attempted to create a physiological mechanism by which the interaction takes place. He proposed that a small gland at the base of the brain, the *pineal gland,* was the site of the Cartesian Theater. He believed that sensory nerves projected to the pineal gland and displayed on its smooth surface an image of the world for the soul to see. Being at the base of the brain, the pineal gland was, Descartes thought, at the site at which the nerve-tubes come together, and by causing it to tilt this way and that, the soul could direct the movements of the animal spirits in the nerves, thus commanding the motions of the body.

Descartes's theory of interaction was eventually rendered wildly implausible by advances in the study of the brain, but it always had a philosophical problem it never surmounted. The problem was perhaps first noticed by one of Descartes's most prolific correspondents and acute critics, Princess Elisabeth of Bohemia (1615–1680), to whom he later dedicated his *Principles of Philosophy.* In June 1643, Elisabeth wrote to Descartes that she could not comprehend "how the soul (nonextended and immaterial) can move the body;" how can "body be pushed by something immaterial . . . which cannot have any communication with it. And I admit it would be easier for me to concede matter and extension to the soul, than the capacity of moving a body and of being moved, to an immaterial being" (Blom, 1978, pp. 111–112). Descartes replied with a vague argument about the "unity" of mind and body, but in her letter of July 1, 1643, the Princess remained perplexed. "I too find that the senses show me that the soul moves the body; but they fail to teach me (any more than the understanding and the imagination) the manner in which she does it." Perhaps "there are unknown properties in the soul" that make interaction possible, but the matter remains mysterious; I will despair of finding certitude in any matter unless you provide me with it" (Blom, 1978, p. 117). In his next letter, Descartes became concerned about the Princess's health, and the correspondence left mind–body interaction unresolved.

The first patches to Descartes's psychology were sewn in an effort to answer Elisabeth's question of how an immaterial ghost can push the material pineal gland, or be affected by it. Eventually, as we will see, instead of dumping the Cartesian Theater, philosophers and psychologists kept the pointlike mind, but denied that mind and body interact, violating Elisabeth's natural intuition that "the soul moves the body."

The other difficulty with Descartes's position is called by philosophers "the problem of other minds." If my mind is a pointlike thinking substance locked up in the body, how do I know mine is not the only soul in the universe? I know I have a soul from the argument of the *cogito,* but how do I know that you or Bill Clinton has one? As he had in his scientific works, Descartes responded by pointing to language. From my own self-awareness, I know that I think and that I express my thoughts in language. Therefore, any creature that possesses language—all human beings and only human beings possess language—thinks, and so has a mind. As suggested earlier, the problems for Descartes's analysis were not long in coming. If soulless animals could learn language, perhaps people also lacked souls; evolution undermined Descartes's radical break between human and animals; and today, computers, mere machines, may soon speak as we do.

Along with his dualism and emphasis on reason, Descartes's nativism links him to Plato. Descartes found in himself ideas that derived from experience, such as of trees or rocks, and ideas that the mind invented, such as "sirens and hippogriffs," but he also found in himself ideas that could not be traced to any sensation, and which, being universal ideas, he did not think he could have invented. These included the "ideas of God, mind, body, triangle, and in general, all those things which represent true, immutable and eternal essences" (letter to Mersenne of June 23, 1641, quoted by Gaukroger, 1995, p. 342). Descartes proposed that these ideas come not from the senses but from "certain germs of truth which exist naturally in our souls," implanted by God. Thus, the indubitable, principal truths are innate. As for Plato, they are potential ideas only; they require activation by experience.

It is generally recognized today that Descartes's philosophy failed to negotiate its way between the heresies he wished to avoid. Specifically, by denying personal memory to the soul, he fell into Averroism, and his works were, in fact, placed on the Catholic Church's Index of prohibited books in 1663. At the popular level, Descartes was often identified with Faust, a scientist who sold his soul to the devil for knowledge. A story, entirely false, began to circulate in the eighteenth century that he had built a mechanical girl in the image of his own illegitimate daughter Francine, and it was said to be so lifelike that the two could not be told apart. There were intimations that he had sexual relations with the doll. By then, some thinkers had taken the controversial step that Descartes never took—proclaiming that humans were mere machines like the animals—and the story no doubt arose as a response to such a shocking idea (Gaukroger, 1995). Today, Descartes's psychology is under assault (e.g. Dennett, 1993; Searle, 1994). By reducing mind to a point; by making experience a mysterious, subjective, thing called consciousness; by assuming there is a point in the brain where experience happens; and by creating the problem of other minds and the issue of interaction, it appears that Descartes dug a hole from which psychology is only now escaping.

However, because the hole was deep, Descartes's influence cannot be denied. His framework created the idea of psychology as the study of consciousness and made the search for self-understanding an important one. Interestingly, a variation on Descartes's framework was more immediately influential. It was more commonsensical, more intuitive, less encumbered with metaphysics, and informed by Newton's *Principia,* published 37 years after Descartes's death. It was the attempt at scientific psychology made by the physician-philosopher John Locke.

Human Understanding: John Locke (1632–1704)

John Locke was a friend of the scientists Isaac Newton and Robert Boyle (in whose laboratory he assisted), a member of the Royal Society, adviser and tutor to noble politicians, and, at times, a practicing physician. As we might expect, therefore, Locke brought a practical and empirical bent to his philosophy. His major work in psychology was *An Essay Concerning Human Understanding* (1690), which he started writing in 1671. Like Descartes, Locke wanted to understand how the human mind works—the sources of its ideas, and the limitations of human knowledge. Locke, however, as befits a physician and practical politician, was less in the grip of a comprehensive metaphysical system than was Descartes. His picture of the mind was straightforward and, to English-speakers who follow after him, commonsensical.

Locke (1690/1975) asked what the human mind knows, and then answered, "Since the Mind, in all its thoughts and Reasonings, hath no other immediate Object but its own *Ideas* . . . it is evident, that our Knowledge is only conversant about them." Like Descartes, Locke revived the copy theory of cognition, holding that ideas are mental representations of objects. The mind does not know Forms or Essences, or even objects themselves, but its own ideas only. Where do our ideas come from? "To this I answer, in one word, From Experience: In that, all our knowledge is founded and derived. Our Observation employed either about *external, sensible objects; or about the internal Operations of our Minds . . . is that which supplies our Understandings with all the materials of thinking.* These two are the Fountains of Knowledge, from whence all the *Ideas* we have, or can naturally have, do spring" (1690/1975, pp. 104–5; italics in original). The first fountain of knowledge, or kind of experience, was *sensation,* resulting in ideas about the objects that cause sensations, including pleasures and pains. The second fountain of experience was *reflection,* observation of our own mental processes.

In positing the process of reflection, Locke tackled an important question about the mind that had been left open by Descartes. Descartes's radical reflexivity created the Cartesian Theater, which severed the self from its experience. According to Descartes, the self could separate itself from its experience of the world and critically scrutinize its sensations. However, the degree to which the self could scrutinize itself remained unaddressed. Descartes was certain that he thought, but he did not say that he knew *how* he thought. The two are not the same. Just as a high-wire walker knows that she can walk on a narrow wire without knowing how she does it, so it is possible that Descartes might know that he thinks without knowing how he thinks. Locke proposed that, in addition to observing its own experience of the outside world—sensation—the self can observe its own mental processes—reflection.

The existence and trustworthiness of reflection have become an enduring problem for psychology. Immanuel Kant later answered Descartes's implicit question about self-knowledge in the negative, denying that reflection is possible at all. David Hume, on the other hand, failing to find a self, simply denied it existed, concluding that the mind was simply the sum total of its ideas. From psychology's founding as a science, research and theory have continued to divide on when, if ever, the mind can accurately observe its own operations. If it can, as Locke thought, then the task of psychology is simplified, because hypotheses about mental processes may be directly tested by observation in the form of reflection. If it cannot, as most psychologists now believe, then hypotheses about mental processes can only be tested indirectly, raising the possibility that, as cognitive science says, extending Kant, the inner workings of the human mind can never be known with certainty, or that, as behaviorism says, extending Hume, there are no mental processes.

If Descartes is usually held to be the father of modern rationalist philosophy, Locke is said to be the father of empiricism because he stated the empiricist principle that knowledge derives from experience alone. He proposed the famous simile for the mind—the *tabula rasa*, or piece of white paper, on which experience writes ideas. Locke, however was not attacking Descartes's conception of innate ideas. Rather, he opposed a large number of English writers who believed in innate *moral principles,* seeing in them the foundations of Christian morality. Thus, these writers could say that it was God's law, implanted in the soul, that a person should believe in God; anyone who did not believe was depraved and as much a moral monster as a three-legged baby would be a physical monster. Indeed, Locke himself was widely denounced as a dangerous atheist for denying innate moral truths. Locke believed the idea of innate moral and metaphysical truths to be a pillar of dogmatism. The schools of his day used maxims as the basis of teaching. Students were to accept them and then prove them. Locke advocated a discovery principle. Students should keep open minds, discovering truth through experience and following their own talents, instead of being forced into the straitjacket of scholastic maxims.

The difference between Locke and Descartes on innate ideas is virtually nonexistent. Descartes maintained that he found in himself ideas that he could not trace to experience, and so he concluded they were innate. But he did not insist that they be innate as fully formed ideas. Instead, he thought it was also possible that people "are born with a certain disposition or faculty to contract them [innate ideas]" (quoted by Gaukroger, 1995, p. 408). This was certainly Locke's view. There is a great deal of innate active mental machinery in Locke's "empty mind." For example, with Descartes, Locke said that language is a human, species-specific trait. He wrote in his *Essay:* "God having designed Man for a sociable Creature . . . furnished him also with language. . . . Parrots, and general other Birds, may be taught to make articulate sounds distinct enough, which yet, by no means, are capable of Language." Only humans can use articulate sounds to represent ideas. In his work on education, Locke held that much of a child's personality and abilities is innate. Man's basic motives, to seek happiness and avoid misery, are likewise "innate practical principles," although of course they have nothing to do with truth.

For Locke, the mind was not merely an empty room to be furnished by experience; rather, it was a complex information-processing device prepared to convert the materials of experience into organized human knowledge. Direct experience provides us with simple ideas, which are then elaborated and combined by the mental machinery into complex ideas. Knowledge comes about as we inspect our ideas and see how they agree or disagree. The bedrock of knowledge for Locke, as for

Descartes, was intuitively self-evident propositions. For example, we know directly and intuitively, without possibility of error, that the colors black and white are not the same (they "disagree"). More complex forms of knowledge arise as we deduce consequences from self-evident propositions. Like Descartes, Locke believed that, in this way, all human knowledge, even ethics and aesthetics, could be systematized.

Locke also addressed a problem that was becoming pressing as the scientific view that the world, and possibly people, are machines became more plausible. Do we have free will? As we shall see in a moment, thinkers such as Hobbes and Spinoza denied that we do, saying we are unfree. Locke first proposed an answer that has been popular ever since. Locke said that asking if the *will* is free is asking a wrong question. The proper question is whether *we* are free. Seen this way, the answer is straightforward. We are free when we are able to do what we want, but we do not consciously will our desires. Locke offered a parable in explanation. Imagine you have gone to a room to talk to someone fascinating. While you are in conversation, someone locks the door from the outside. In a sense, you are not free to leave, but as long as you do not want to leave, you never feel unfree. What matters, then, is freedom of action, not freedom of the will. We simply want what we want, and we all want happiness. As long as we are happy, getting what we wish, we feel free, and do not worry about supposed "unfreedom of the will." The self, however, ought to control desire, for, in the long run, happiness will be determined by our lot in Heaven or Hell. The economist John Maynard Keynes repudiated Locke's long-range thinking when he said, "In the long run we are all dead."

Locke's version of the rational self radically separated from experience, which it can critically scrutinize as consciousness, proved enormously influential both in Britain, where later British philosophers built on it, and in France, where it was popularized by Voltaire as a less metaphysical, more straightforward, picture of the mind than Descartes's. Nevertheless, in their psychological essentials, these two modern philosophies were strikingly alike, possessing differences of nuance, not substance.

PHILOSOPHY, SCIENCE, AND HUMAN AFFAIRS

In the wake of the Scientific Revolution, it became clear that humanity's place in nature would have to be reevaluated. As religion began to lose its authority and science began to assume its own authority, new answers to the traditional questions of philosophy, psychology, politics, and values were demanded. The task of reworking human self-understanding and human life within the framework of science is an enterprise in which psychology is intimately involved, and it is one that continues in our own day. Science raises important questions about the springs of human conduct, about the place of values in a world of facts, about moral responsibility, about the proper forms of human government, and about the place of feelings in worldviews founded on scientific reason. In the seventeenth century, philosophers began to wrestle with these problems and to offer solutions that still inspire or infuriate us today.

The Laws of Social Life: Thomas Hobbes (1588–1679)

Hobbes's importance derives from being the first to comprehend and express the new scientific view of humans and their place in the universe. Hobbes wrote: "For seeing life is but a motion of limbs . . . why may we not say, that all *automata* . . . have an artificial life? For what is the *heart,* but a spring; and the *nerves,* but so many strings;

and the *joints,* but so many wheels, giving motion to the whole body" (Bronowski and Mazlish, 1960, p. 197, italics in original). Hobbes's contemporary, Descartes, believed animals, but not humans, were entirely machines. Hobbes went considerably further, claiming that spiritual substance is a meaningless idea. Only matter exists, and the actions of people, no less than those of animals, are fully determined by material, never spiritual, causes.

On one point Hobbes and Descartes agreed: Philosophy should be constructed after the model of geometry. Indeed, Hobbes's accidental exposure, at age forty, to the elegant proofs of Euclid led him to philosophize. Hobbes believed that all knowledge is ultimately rooted in sense-perception. He upheld extreme nominalism, seeing in universals no more than convenient names grouping remembered sense-perceptions. He dismissed arguments over metaphysics as scholastic wrangling about meaningless concepts. He rigidly separated philosophy, which is rational and meaningful, from theology, which is irrational and meaningless. His most interesting psychological doctrine is that language and thinking are closely related, perhaps even identical. In his major work, *Leviathan* (1651/1962), Hobbes wrote: "Understanding is nothing else but conception caused by speech." Further, he stated that "Children are not endowed with reason at all, till they have attained the use of speech." Hobbes was the first in the long, and still living, line of British philosophers who equate right thinking with right use of language. For psychology, this is an old and unresolved issue: whether thinking is overt or covert speech, or whether speech merely dresses up abstract concepts. Hobbes clearly argued the former.

However, Hobbes's real interest was political science, which he claimed to have invented. Hobbes believed that if human beings are deterministic machines like the stars and planets, then a science of human affairs ought to be as attainable as astronomy and physics.

Having endured the English civil war, he desired to put government on a sound rational footing that would avoid such horrors in the future. In *Leviathan,* Hobbes begins with a commonplace of modern liberalism, that persons are created roughly equal in physical and mental powers. However, were there no government, each person would seek his or her own interest against fellow humans. Outside of organized society, Hobbes wrote: "*There is always war of every one* against *every one* . . . and the life of man is solitary, nasty, brutish, and short" (italics in original). The solution is for people to recognize that their rational self-interest lies in a regulated state that will provide security, the fruits of industry, and other benefits. This means recognizing the existence of Laws of Nature—for example, that each person should give up the total liberty and equal right to all things that breed war, and "be contented with so much liberty against other men, as he would allow other men against himself." The best state for securing such liberties, Hobbes went on to argue, is an absolute despotism, in which all members of society contract their rights and powers to a sovereign, whether king or parliament, who will then rule and protect them, uniting their many wills into one will. Hobbes was not, however, the father of modern totalitarianism. For him, the authoritarian state would establish the peaceful conditions within which people could freely do what they like as long as it did not harm others. Later totalitarians such as Hitler and Stalin wanted the state to control every aspect of citizen's lives, including their thoughts.

Hobbes's idea that Natural Law would apply to people is of considerable importance to psychology. He said that there are regulations inherent in nature, existing apart from humanity's recognition of them, that govern everything from the planetary machine of the solar system to the biological machines of the animals, including humans. Hobbes's attitude, however, is not fully scientific, for he says that we rationally consent to follow Natural Laws. Only in times of security must we follow them; they may be broken should government or other persons try to compel anyone to personal ruin. The planets cannot choose to obey or not obey Newton's laws of motion, and in this respect Hobbes's Natural Laws are not like the laws of physics.

The Heart Has Its Reasons Which the Reason Does Not Understand: Blaise Pascal (1623-1662)

If Descartes prefigures the confident rationalist of the Enlightenment, Pascal prefigures the anguished existentialist of recent times. For Descartes, doubt led to the triumphant certainty of reason; for Pascal, doubt led to worse doubt. Wrote Pascal: I am "engulfed in the infinite immensity of spaces whereof I know nothing and which know nothing of me, I am terrified" (Bronowski and Mazlish, 1960). Pascal detested Descartes's excessive rationalism and derived solace and truth from his faith in God. For Pascal, what is essential in humans is not natural reason, but will and the capacity for faith—that is, the heart. Pascal thus resembles earlier Christian skeptics such as Montaigne. But Pascal is Cartesian in the value he places on self-consciousness, as shown by his statement in the *Pensées:* "Man knows that he is wretched. He is wretched, then, because he is wretched; but he is great, because he knows it. . . . Man is only a reed, the frailest thing in nature; but he is a thinking reed." Pascal doubted a person's capacity to fathom nature or to understand self—humanity is wretched. Yet a human's unique self-consciousness lifts her or him above nature and the animals, offering salvation through faith in the Christian God. Pascal's anguish and need for faith echo through all modern existentialists, not excepting atheists such as Sartre.

Pascal was also a scientist and mathematician who investigated the vacuum and helped found probability theory. As a mathematician, he was a child prodigy. At nineteen, he constructed the first mechanical calculator. Although its purpose was humble—to help his father, a tax official, do calculations—its implication was profound. Pascal wrote: "The arithmetical machine produces effects which approach nearer to thought than all the actions of animals" (Bronowski and Mazlish, 1960). Pascal was the first to sense that the human mind could be conceived as an information processor capable of being mimicked by a machine, a concept central to contemporary cognitive psychology. In Pascal's time, and to someone with his sensibilities, the implication was frightening, for it meant that reason—which Descartes exempted from his mechanical system—could not be so exempted. Perhaps animals, wholly mechanical creatures according to Descartes, *do* reason. Pascal then declared that a human's free will, not reason, is what distinguishes humans from animals. It is the heart, not the brain, that makes a human being human.

Determinism Extended: Baruch Spinoza (1632-1677)

Spinoza was a thinker out of step with his own time. Born a Jew, but excommunicated for his disbelief in Yahweh, he articulated a philosophy that identified God with nature and saw the state as merely a revocable social agreement. He was spurned by the people of his birth and denounced by Christians, and his works were suppressed even in the liberal state of Holland where he lived. In the Enlightenment, he was admired for his independence but rejected for his pantheistic philosophy. Later, the Romantics venerated his apparent mysticism, and scientists saw in him a naturalist.

Spinoza's philosophy begins with metaphysics and ends with a radical reconstruction of human nature. Spinoza argued that God is essentially nature. Without the existing natural world, nothing would exist, so that God (nature) is the supporter and creator of all things. But God is not a separate being apart from nature; all things are a part of God without exception, and God is no more than the totality of the universe. Hence, Spinoza was thought to be an atheist. Furthermore, nature (God) was held to be entirely deterministic. Spinoza argued that to understand anything means to unravel its efficient causes. Spinoza denied the existence of final causes, believing teleology to be a projection of humanity's feelings of purpose onto nature, applied only to events we cannot explain with efficient—that is, deterministic—causes.

Spinoza extended his deterministic analysis to human nature. Mind is not something separate from body but is produced by brain processes. Mind and body are one but may be viewed from two aspects, as physiological brain processes or as mental events—thoughts. Spinoza did not deny that mind exists, but he saw it as one aspect of a fundamentally material nature. Thus, for Spinoza, mental activity is as deterministic as bodily activity. Spinoza rejected Cartesian dualism, and so for him there is no problem of interaction. We feel we are free, but this is only an illusion. If we properly understood the causes of human behavior and thinking, we would see we are not free. Just as no blame may be attached to the river that floods and destroys a town, so no blame can be attached to a multiple murderer. Society may act to control the river or the killer, to prevent future devastation, but this is a pragmatic consideration rather than a moral one. Spinoza's account of responsibility thus calls for a psychological science to unravel the causes of human behavior, and it bears a striking resemblance to B. F. Skinner's.

Spinoza, however, went on to describe an ethics of self-control that transcended materialistic determinism and, to some degree, conflicted with the rest of his thought. He argued that right action and thinking depend on the control of bodily emotions by reason. The wise person is one who follows the dictates of reason rather than the dictates of the momentary and conflicting passions arising from the body. Reason will lead one to act out of enlightened self-interest—helping others as one would want to be helped. Spinoza's ethics and his view of humanity are quite Stoic. The physical universe is beyond our control, but our passions are not. Thus, wisdom is rational self-control, rather than a futile effort to control nature or God. Spinoza also argued that governments should allow freedom of thought, conscience, and speech, for each person should be free to order his or her mind as he or she sees fit.

Levels of Consciousness: Gottfried Wilhelm Leibniz (1646–1716)

Leibniz was a mathematician, logician, and metaphysician. He independently invented calculus and dreamed of a formal conceptual calculus that would do for verbal reasoning what mathematics had done for the sciences. His metaphysics is extremely difficult. Briefly, he conceived of the universe as composed of an infinity of geometrical-point entities called *monads,* each of which is to some extent living and possesses some degree of consciousness. Animals and people are made up of monads that subserve a most conscious, and hence most dominant, monad.

Leibniz's theory of monads led to a solution to the mind–body problem that became increasingly popular over the next two centuries. Descartes had said that mind and body interact. However, because it was unclear how spirit could act on matter and vice versa, a view called *occasionalism* emerged, in which God saw to it that when a bodily event occurred, so did a mental event and vice versa. This, too, has its difficulties, with God running around keeping mind and body coordinated. Leibniz proposed an answer that has since been called mind–body (or psychophysical) *parallelism*. Leibniz argued that God had created the universe (the infinitude of monads) such that there is a preestablished harmony among the monads. Leibniz used an analogy of two identical and perfect clocks, both set to the same time and started at the same moment. From then on, the clocks would always agree with, and mirror, one another, but they would not be causally connected. Each would run in an identical but parallel—not interacting—course of development. Just so mind and body. Consciousness (mind) mirrors exactly what happens in the body, but only because of God's preestablished harmony, not because of a causal connection. In fact, Leibniz extended this scheme to the whole universe, holding that monads never interact but stay coordinated in their pictures of the universe because of God's perfect harmony. Although the metaphysical basis of psychophysical parallelism was dropped later, the doctrine itself caught on as physiological knowledge of the body and the growth of physics rendered both interactionism and occasionalism implausible.

Leibniz upheld innate ideas. Like Descartes, Leibniz believed many ideas, such as God and mathematical truths, could not be derived from experience for they are too abstract. Such ideas must be innate. Leibniz expressed his conception by a statue metaphor. The mind at birth is likened to a block of marble. Marble is veined, and it may be that the veins outline the form of Hercules in the marble, for example. Certain activities are required to bring out the statue, but in a sense Hercules is "innate" in the marble. Similarly, an infant's innate dispositions to certain kinds of knowledge must be activated, either by experience or by the infant's own reflection on mental life.

For psychology, Leibniz's most important ideas concerned his account of perception, for here Leibniz laid the ground for both psychophysics and Wundt's founding psychology (McRae, 1976). First, Leibniz distinguished *petite perception* from *perception*. *Petite perception* is a stimulus event (to borrow a modern term) so weak it is not perceived. To use Leibniz's most usual metaphor, one does not hear the sound of a single drop of water hitting a beach; this is a *petite perception*. A wave crashing on the beach is thousands of drops hitting the beach, and this we do hear. Thus, our perception of the wave's crash is made up of many *petite perceptions;* each is too small to be heard, but together they make a conscious experience. This doctrine points the way to psychophysics, the systematic study of the quantitative relation between stimulus intensity and experience, which we will discuss in Chapter 6. Leibniz's account also implies the existence of the unconscious, or, as Leibniz writes, "changes in the soul itself of which we are not conscious." As modified in the nineteenth century and adopted by Freud, the concept of the unconscious had momentous impact on psychology.

Leibniz also distinguished perception from *sensation.* A perception is a raw, confused idea, not really conscious, which animals, as well as humans, may possess. However, a person can refine and sharpen perceptions and become reflectively aware of them in consciousness. They then become sensations.* This refining process is called *apperception.* Apperception also seems to be involved in uniting *petite perceptions* to become perceptions. This uniting process, stressed Leibniz, is not a process

---

* Leibniz's usage is roughly the opposite of modern psychological usage. Today, a sensation refers to a sensory receptor process, and a perception is a central brain or mental event.

of mere aggregation. Perceptions, rather, are emergent properties coming from masses of *petite perceptions*. If we combine blue and yellow lights, for example, we do not experience blue and yellow separately but instead green, an emergent experience not present in the simpler constituent lights.

Attention is the major component of apperception for Leibniz, and he distinguished two types, passive and active. If we are absorbed in some activity, we may not notice another stimulus, such as a friend speaking to us, until that stimulus grows so strong that it automatically draws our attention. Here, the shift in attention is passive, for the new stimulus captures attention. Attention may also be voluntary, as when we focus it on one person at a party to the exclusion of others. Sometimes, Leibniz tied apperception closely to voluntary attention, for he saw apperception as an act of will. Leibniz's doctrine of active mental apperception would be Wundt's central theoretical concept.

CONCLUSION: THE SEVENTEENTH CENTURY—SEEDS OF CHANGE

The seventeenth century laid the foundations for the Enlightenment of the eighteenth. The Newtonian-Cartesian mechanical universe had no room for miracles, oracles, visions, and Descartes's soul. In the eighteenth century, science and reason would further replace religion as the chief intellectual institution of modern society. Human beings would be proclaimed soulless machines, and societies would be overthrown in the name of material happiness.

The triumph of reason in the Age of Reason was at hand. Yet, a different undercurrent lurked just below the surface. The voyages of discovery had found strange primitive cultures. To Hobbes and Locke, these wild men represented humanity in an uncivilized and unhappy state of Nature. Locke wrote in his *Second Treatise on Government:* "In the beginning all the world was America." Yet were the Indians unhappy? Close to nature and unfettered by artifice, they lived according to natural instinct. Perhaps happiness lies in giving up reason, with its abstract, artificial ways, and returning to the instinct of the happy savage. A reaction against reason was about to set in. The poet Chaulieu wrote in 1708 that reason is an "inexhaustible source of errors, poison that corrupts the natural feelings" (Hazard, 1963, p. 396). Jean Rousseau wrote that reason "feeds our mad pride . . . continually masking us from ourselves." Asked Rousseau: "Which is the least barbarous . . . reason which leads you astray, or instinct which guides [the Indian] truly?" Chaulieu said he came "to destroy the altars which have been raised to thee [Reason]." Here the seed is sown for the Romantic Rebellion against reason and for the concept of the Noble Savage. The tension between the individual and society, so poignantly felt by Sigmund Freud, was increasing as reason demanded more and more of men and women.

BIBLIOGRAPHY

The seventeenth century is recognized by historians as critical in Western history because the modern world of science and nations was created during this century. It was a period of incredible ferment in philosophy, political thought, and religion. The most distinguished historian of the century is Christopher Hill, who aptly titles his text on the seventeenth century *The century of revolution: 1603–1714* (New York: Norton, 1966). As a Marxist, Hill has been concerned to show how deeply seventeenth-century thinkers challenged the shibboleths of their time. His main work along this line is *The world turned upside down: Radical ideas during the English revolution* (Harmondsworth, England: Pelican, 1972); regardless of whether one agrees with Hill's politics (I don't), his works amply repay reading, for they cast new and revealing light on our attempts to understand ourselves. Paul Hazard, *The European mind 1680–1715* (New York: New American Library, 1963), suggested that Europe experienced a "general crisis" during the seventeenth century, and his thesis has generated controversy ever since he proposed it in 1935. Theodore K. Rabb, *The struggle for stability in early modern Europe* (New York: Oxford University Press, 1975), updates Hazard's thesis; and G. Parker and L. M. Smith, eds., *The general crisis of the seventeenth century* (London: Routledge & Kegan Paul, 1978), present a symposium on the thesis. Basil Willey, *The seventeenth century background* (Garden City, NY: Doubleday, 1953), provides a general survey of society and politics in the century.

The most important event of the seventeenth century was, of course, the Scientific Revolution. Here are some general histories: Vern Bullough, ed., *The scientific revolution* (New York: Holt, Rinehart & Winston, 1970); Herbert Butterfield (1965), the standard history; I. Bernard Cohen, *The Newtonian revolution* (Cambridge, England: Cambridge University Press, 1980); A. Rupert Hall, *The scientific revolution 1500–1800: The formation of the modern scientific attitude,* 2nd ed. (Boston: Beacon Press, 1962), another standard history; Hugh Kearney, *Science and change 1500–1700* (New York: McGraw-Hill, 1971), a book that incorporates some of the occult-vs.-reason debate in the newest history of science; and Richard S. Westfall, *The construction of modern science: Mechanisms and mechanics* (Cambridge, England: Cambridge University Press, 1971). Thomas (1971) is an invaluable source for how the puritanizing tendencies in Reformation religion paved the way for the Scientific Revolution. An important question about the Scientific Revolution is why it occurred only in Europe, rather than in China or Islam, which were, in the Middle Ages, more scientifically advanced. Toby Huff (1993), *The rise of early modern science: Islam, China, and the West* (Cambridge, England: Cambridge University Press) provides one surprising answer: the development of law and the corporation.

Scientists have always fancied that science is a self-contained, rational enterprise, relatively free from philosophical and social influence. As we saw in Chapter 1, this assumption has come under sharp questioning and has set off historical debates on the roots of the Scientific Revolution. Burtt (1954) was the first to challenge science's philosophical purity and is, in consequence, much cited today. Richard Westfall, "Newton and the fudge factor," *Science* (1973, *179:* 751–58), showed how Newton's psychological commitment to his theory led him to bend data to suit it; see also Westfall's biography of Newton, *Never at rest* (Cambridge, England: Cambridge University Press, 1980). The most violent debates among historians of science have been over the degree to which the Scientific Revolution was influenced by the deep occultism of the Renaissance and seventeenth century. The claim that science was indebted to the occult is often known as "the Yates thesis" after historian Frances Yates—for example, her chapter on "The hermetic tradition in Renaissance science" in C. S. Singleton, ed., *Art, science, and history in the Renaissance* (Baltimore: Johns Hopkins University Press, 1968). A good collection favoring the occult connections of science is M. L. Righini Bonelli and W. R. Shea, eds., *Reason, experiment, and mysticism in the scientific revolution* (New York: Science History Publications, 1975). The sides of reason and occult influence are respectively upheld in a debate between Mary Hesse, "Reasons and evolutions in the history of science," and P. M. Rattansi, "Some evaluations of reason in sixteenth- and seventeenth-century natural philosophy," both in M. Teich and R. Young, eds., *Changing perspectives in the history of science* (London: Heinemann, 1973). The most recent symposium on the topic is B. Vickers, ed., *Occult and scientific mentalities in the Renaissance* (New York: Cambridge University Press, 1984); see also G. A. J. Rogers, "The basis of belief: Philosophy, science, and religion in seventeenth century England," *History of European Ideas* (1985, *6:* 19–39). For a case study on the influence of occult ideas on one scientist, see Betty Jo Teeter Dobbs, *The foundations of Newton's alchemy* (Cambridge, England: Cambridge University Press, 1983).

For seventeenth-century philosophy, see Bronowski and Mazlish (1960); and, with special reference to France, Edward John Kearns, *Ideas in seventeenth century France* (Manchester, England: Manchester University Press, 1983). For a comparative study of Descartes's and Locke's psychologies, see David E. Leary, "The intentions and heritage of Descartes and Locke: Toward a recognition of the moral basis of modern psychology," *Journal of General Psychology* (1980, *102:* 283–310). For the individual philosophers, see the following. An important general source is Taylor (1989), who focuses on the development of the punctate self. I have found much insight and inspiration in this source.

Descartes. The new biography by Stephen Gaukroger is first-rate; it illuminates many vexed and significant issues concerning Descartes's philosophy and psychology; my treatment of Descartes has been deeply reshaped by reading this book; Richard B. Carter, *Descartes' medical philosophy: The organic solution to the mind–body problem* (Baltimore: Johns Hopkins University Press, 1983); Desmond M. Clarke, *Descartes' philosophy of science* (University Park: Pennsylvania State University Press, 1984); Bernard Williams, *Descartes: The project of pure inquiry* (Harmondsworth, England: Pelican, 1978). Descartes's works have been recently retranslated. The important psychological works are contained in *The philosophical writings of Descartes,* R. Descartes (Cambridge, England: Cambridge University Press, 1985).

Locke. Locke (1690/1975); *The Locke reader,* J. W. Yolton, compiler (Cambridge, England: Cambridge University Press, 1977); I. C. Tipton, ed., *Locke on human understanding* (Oxford, England: Oxford University Press, 1977); J. W. Yolton, *Locke and the compass of human understanding* (Cambridge, England: Cambridge University Press, 1970). These works discuss a modern controversy on whether Locke meant ideas to be mental copies or direct acts by which the mind grasps objects in the world. As we learned, both views have their advocates in psychology, but whatever Locke meant, his successors took him to mean ideas are mental representations, not mental acts. The intimate connection between the thinking of Locke and Newton is detailed in G. A. J. Rogers, "The system of Locke and Newton," in Z. Bechler, ed., *Contemporary Newtonian research* (Dordrecht, The Netherlands: D. Reidel, 1982).

Hobbes. Hobbes (1651/1962).

Pascal. Blaise Pascal, *Pensées* (New York: Washington Square Press, 1965).

Spinoza. Baruch Spinoza, *The works of Spinoza,* 2 vols. (New York: Dover Books, 1955); Stuart Hampshire, *Spinoza* (Harmondsworth, England: Pelican, 1962).

Leibniz. G. W. Leibniz, *Leibniz: Selections* (New York: Scribner's, 1951); Robert D. Brandom, "Leibniz and degrees of perception," *Journal of the History of Philosophy* (1981, *19:* 447–79); McRae (1976).

REFERENCES

Blom, J. J. (1978). *Descartes: His moral philosophy and psychology.* New York: New York University Press.

Bronowski, J. and Mazlish, B. (1960). *The western intellectual tradition.* New York: Harper & Row.

Burtt, E. A. (1954). *The metaphysical foundations of modern science.* Garden City, NY: Doubleday.

Butterfield, H. (1965). *The origins of modern science 1300–1800.* New York: Free Press.

Dennett, D. (1993). *Consciousness explained.* Boston: Little, Brown.

Gaukroger, S. (1995). *Descartes: An intellectual biography.* Oxford, England: Clarendon Press.

Ginzburg, C. (1991). *Ecstasies: Deciphering the witches' sabbath.* New York: Pantheon.

Hazard, P. (1963). *The European mind 1680–1715.* New York: New American Library.

Hobbes, T. (1651/1962). *Leviathan.* New York: Collier Books.

Locke, J. (1690/1975). *An essay concerning human understanding* (Variorum edition), Peter Nidditch, ed. Oxford, England: Clarendon Press.

McRae, R. (1976). *Leibniz: Perception, apperception, and thought.* Toronto: University of Toronto Press.

Rattansi, R. (1972). The social interpretation of science in the seventeenth century. In P. Mathias, ed., *Science and society 1600–1900.* Cambridge, England: Cambridge University Press.

Rossi, P. (1975). Hermeticism, rationality, and the scientific revolution. In M. Bonelli and W. Shea, eds., *Reason, experiment and mysticism in the scientific revolution.* New York: Science History Publications.

Searle, J. (1994). *The rediscovery of the mind.* Los Angeles: University of California Press.

Taylor, C. (1989). *Sources of the self: The making of modern identity.* Cambridge, MA: Harvard University Press.

Thomas, K. (1971). *Religion and the decline of magic.* Harmondsworth, England: Penguin.

Westfall, R. (1975). The role of alchemy in Newton's career. In M. Bonelli and W. Shea, eds., *Reason, experiment and mysticism in the scientific revolution.* New York: Science History Publications.

5 Reason and Reaction
The Eighteenth-Century Enlightenment

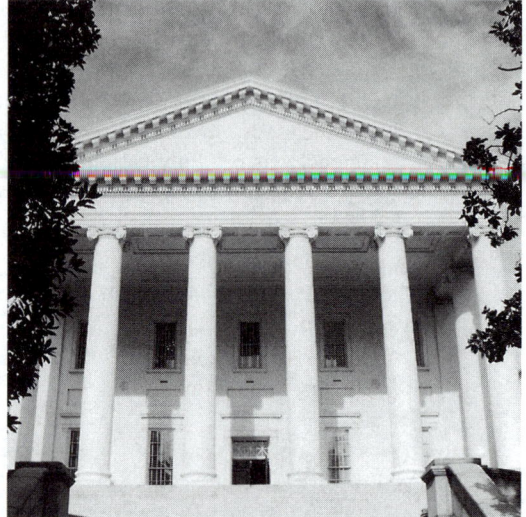

The State Capitol Building in Richmond, Virginia, designed by Thomas Jefferson. The American Founders were deeply influenced by the classical world, and this is an outstanding example of Greek Revival architecture. It recalls the Parthenon as an expression of self-confidence, in this time of a new society just making its way along a radically democratic path. It was in the eighteenth century that the idea of a science of human nature began, and it would be in America that it would flourish. The Classical revival poet Alexander Pope linked the eras in his *Essay on Man,* "Know then thyself/Presume not God to scan/The proper study of mankind, is man."

THE ENLIGHTENMENT PROJECT

The eighteenth century is known as the Age of Reason, or the Enlightenment. Unlike eras that are named by historians, the Enlightenment named itself. Its leaders were a collection of educated, reforming, and ultimately revolutionary thinkers and writers best called by the French term *philosophe* (Gay, 1966). Their project carried on, broadened, and deepened the enterprise begun by Descartes and Locke, the rethinking of old questions in the light of Newtonian science. Descartes and Locke had shown that philosophy and science depended on the workings of the human mind, and the philosophes took the study of human nature in directions only suggested by Descartes and Locke, carrying it into new areas, including ethics and politics.

The Enlightenment project changed Western civilization in profound and deep ways, some good and some bad. The philosophes sought to overthrow the authority of religion and tradition. Few philosophes were outright atheists, but their God was even more distant than the God of the seventeenth century. Most believed that God had created a good, indeed perfect, world, in which everything was carefully provided for human happiness. For example, according to the Abbé Pluche, domestic animals were created so "they naturally love us and come to us spontaneously to offer their various services" (quoted by Hampson, 1982, p. 82). However, having created the perfect world for the highest creatures, human beings, God had no need to intervene in human affairs. Organized religion was excoriated as superstition peddled by priests for their own benefit. As it had been for Socrates, tradition was suspect because it was not based on reasoned argument, but on unthinking habit. The philosophes, however, were not content to be skeptical of tradition, trusting with Plato that intuition was sometimes right. They tended to assume that tradition was always wrong, "the stupid veneration of the peoples for ancient laws and customs," as Claude Helvetius put it (quoted by Hampson, 1982, p. 126).

In short, the philosophes aimed to dispel the darkness of superstition and tradition with the Newtonian science. As Alexander Pope had written in eulogy of Newton, now carved over the fireplace in the room where Newton was born, "Nature and nature's laws lay hid in night/God said let NEWTON be, and there was light." Newton was the light of the Enlightenment, and the philosophes set out to do for human affairs what Newton had done for the affairs of the universe.

Unfortunately, wiping the slate clean of old beliefs and erecting new ones is fraught with danger, and the Enlightenment experienced two profound crises. The first crisis was the direct result of the inquiries of Descartes and Locke. They raised the question of how we know the world, given the actual operations of the human mind. However, as others developed this epistemological line of argument, it began to appear that human knowledge was, at the very least, terribly limited and perhaps nonexistent. This is the skeptical crisis. As David Hume wrote, "While Newton seemed to draw off the veil from some of the mysteries of nature . . . [by refusing to propose hypotheses he] restored her ultimate secrets to that obscurity to which they ever did and ever will remain" (quoted by Hampson, 1982, p. 75).

The other crisis is the moral crisis, set off by the effort to place morality, like everything else, on a scientific foundation. Moreover, as Plato had worried, if skepticism is correct, then not only is nature mysterious, so is morality. A contemporary, Bishop Butler, saw the practical danger in rethinking morality. "Foundations of morality are like all other foundations; if you dig too much about them the structure will come tumbling down" (quoted by Dworkin, 1980, p. 36).

The philosophes made it possible for a sophisticated young man to say to his father, "The point is, father, that in the last resort the wise man is subject to no laws . . . the wise man must judge for himself when to submit and when to free himself from them." Stripped of the certainties of religion and tradition, the father could only reply, "I should not be too worried if there were one or two people like you in the town, but if they all thought that way I should go and live somewhere else" (quoted by Hampson, 1982, p. 190). The young man's numbers would grow and their voices would become loud.

THE SKEPTICAL CRISIS

When the philosophers of the eighteenth century extended scientific reason to understanding the human mind, they ran into an old problem. With reliance only on the evidence of the senses and on human logic, is it possible to justify human knowledge at all? An irony of the Scientific Revolution is that it concluded as an apparent triumph of human reason, but ended by casting doubt on the very possibility of human knowledge. In Newton's wake came philosopher-psychologists who examined the human mind and human nature in the light of Newtonian reason and concluded that no human opinion was free from the possibility of error, and that the very existence of the physical world was open to doubt. These were the conclusions of the British philosophers George Berkeley and David Hume, and they were, unsurprisingly, stoutly resisted by philosophers loath to give up the possibility of secure human knowledge. Against the skepticism of Hume, the Scottish followers of Thomas Reid asserted commonsense faith in human cognition and religious faith in God, who made men and women so that they might know God's world. In Germany, Immanuel Kant responded to Hume's skepticism by asserting the old claim that metaphysics was science's true foundation, but he, too, left mysterious the deepest question of human existence.

Is There a World? Bishop George Berkeley (1685–1753)

As a philosopher, Berkeley, like Descartes and Locke, wanted to place philosophy on new, secure foundations; but as a religious man, he feared the Newtonian materialism that imperiled faith in God. He admired Locke and believed Locke had taken the correct road toward knowledge. However, Berkeley saw that Locke's copy theory of cognition opened the door to skepticism. Locke believed in the existence of "real" objects that cause our perceptions, but his belief was unjustified. The secondary sense properties cast doubt on the appealing assumption that the ideas of consciousness simply reflect objects in the world. The skeptic might ask how we know that ideas, supposed copies of objects, resemble their originals in any respect at all. Perhaps the world is completely, not partially, different from the world of consciousness. Berkeley took the bold step of asserting that ideas were not copies of anything at all. They, not things, were the ultimate reality.

Berkeley believed that the skeptic's challenge derived from another assumption we all make, that matter, things, exist apart from our perceptions of them. For example, as I am sitting here word processing, I know my computer exists because I see and feel it. But when I leave the room, what grounds have I for asserting that the computer still exists? All I can say is that if I went back I would see it, or if someone else looks for it, he or she will see it. Ultimately, then, I know the computer exists only when I see it. More strongly, Berkeley would assert that the computer exists only when it is perceived. Berkeley's famous motto was "Esse est percipi" (To exist is to be perceived). Berkeley thus refuted skepticism by an astoundingly simple assertion. Locke said that all we know are our ideas. Berkeley added that therefore, ideas are all that exist. The question of how ideas correspond to "real objects" does not arise if there are no "real objects" at all. Furthermore, Berkeley's philosophy refutes atheism, for God may now be introduced as the omniscient perceiver who sees all things and so continues their existence.

In a work on the history of psychology, we do not want to get embroiled in philosophical questions about what exists. It is best to view Berkeley as asking about the material world what Descartes asked about other minds. Descartes did not want us to give up our belief that other people have minds; Berkeley did not want us to give up our belief that the physical world exists. Thinking that only I have a mind and that everything else vanishes when I'm not around is impractical to the point of madness. Instead, as Descartes tried to figure out the psychological basis for our belief in other minds outside ours, Berkeley tried to figure out the psychological basis for our belief in a physical world outside our minds. Both engaged in radically reflexive introspection, and set agendas for later psychological research.

In this respect, Berkeley's analysis of depth perception is especially significant. An important ground for our belief in external objects is that we see objects in three dimensions, including a dimension of depth—distance away from us; yet the retinal image, the immediate (or "proper") object of vision, is only two-dimensional, lacking depth. So, for example, as a friend walks away from you, you see him or her getting farther and farther away, but if we were to examine your retinal image, we would find only that the image of the friend gets smaller and smaller. You may observe that indeed your friend looks smaller, but your subjective experience is that he or she is only going farther away, not shrinking. The problem arises: How does one perceive three dimensions when one can only see (on the retina) two dimensions?

Berkeley's answer was that other sensations are available which do give cues about distance. For example, as an object approaches, we move the pupils of the eyes close together as we follow it; as it recedes, we move them apart. Thus, there is a regular association between an object's distance from us and the degree to which we cross our eyes to focus on it. (Berkeley and others found many additional distance cues.) So far, Berkeley's analysis of how we see depth is the foundation of modern analyses of depth perception. However, Berkeley went on to make the empiricist claim that the association must be learned. According to Berkeley's reasoning, infants would not know that a person was receding as the person walked away; infants would simply see the figure shrink. Berkeley's claim that depth perception must be learned was countered later by Immanuel Kant, who asserted that depth perception is innate. The controversy between the nativist and empiricist views continued for decades; not until the 1960s did experiments with infants show that Kant was reasonably correct (Bower, 1974).

The real importance of Berkeley's argument becomes clear if we generalize the problem to all visual experience. If you hold a blue book at right angles to your eyes, what do you see? The naive answer is to say "A book," yet, as Berkeley would argue, all you really see is a rectangular patch of blue, the retinal image. If you rotate the book to a 45-degree angle, what do you see? Again, you want to say, "A book," and in fact you would still believe the book to be a rectangle. But Berkeley would say that what you are really seeing is a blue patch that now has the shape of a truncated pyramid. Berkeley's argument is that all anyone ever sees is a collection of colored patches on one's retina. One must learn to "see" them as books, people, cats, cars, and so on. One must learn to believe one is still seeing a rectangular book when in fact one is seeing a truncated-pyramid blue patch.

Berkeley's analysis of vision supports his idealism. One's sensory and ideational world is just a collection of sensations, and one believes in the permanence of objects only because certain collections of sensations are regularly associated. Belief in matter is therefore a learned inference only, for matter is not directly perceived.

Berkeley's philosophy of the mind became the basis for at least one important psychology of consciousness, E. B. Titchener's structuralism. Berkeley had said that we are born seeing the world as isolated sensations on a two-dimensional screen of consciousness. Titchener's research aimed to undo that learning. He taught students never to commit the "stimulus error," reporting as the object of introspection the thing that caused the stimuli they were to report. Instead, subjects were to describe pure consciousness as lines, curves, and color patches—pure sensations, the basic Berkeleyan building blocks of experience. Titchener also tried to show how we learn to associate stimuli together into complex ideas, such as a book or a person, in line with Berkeley's associative psychology.

Berkeley had established the ultimate in skepticism. He showed that belief in a physical world of permanent objects outside consciousness is not one that can be rationally justified, but is a psychological inference we learn to make. How, then, are we to get on with our lives, with philosophy, morality, and politics, if there are no certainties? An answer was found in human nature itself by the Scottish philosopher David Hume (Norton, 1982).

Living with Skepticism: David Hume (1711–1776)

> It is evident that all the sciences have a relation, greater or less, to human nature. . . . To explain the principles of human nature, we in effect propose a complete system of the sciences, built on a foundation almost entirely new, and the only one upon which they can stand with any security . . . and the only solid foundation we can give to this science itself must be laid on experience and observation. (Hume, 1739/1962/1974, p. 172)

So Hume wrote in his *Treatise of Human Nature*. Locke began the attempt to replace metaphysics with psychology as the foundation for the other sciences, and Hume carried out the task in a rigorously Newtonian manner. Hume analyzed human nature as he found it in himself and in the behavior of others. Hume's aim was to replace metaphysics with psychology, his "science of human nature." He wound up showing that reason alone—the Cartesian essence of the human mind—was powerless to construct usable knowledge of the world.

Hume has long been depicted as the great skeptic, the man who showed we can know nothing at all with certainty. It is better to regard him as the first postskeptical philosopher (Norton, 1993a). He believed that skepticism had been established by Berkeley and others, and wanted to move beyond skepticism to a practical philosophy that allowed us to live our lives without the certainties that Plato, Aristotle, and religion had pretended to give us. In essence, Hume taught that the philosophical quest for absolute certainty was a fool's errand, that human nature itself was enough on which to build fallible science and fallible morals.

Hume began his inquiry into human nature by categorizing the contents of our minds somewhat as Locke had. Locke had spoken of the contents of our minds as "ideas," for which Hume, following the Scottish moral philosopher Francis Hutcheson (1694–1746), substituted "perceptions." Perceptions are then divided into two types, impressions and ideas. Impressions are essentially what we today call sensations, and ideas were for Hume less vivid copies of impressions. Thus, you have an immediate impression of the book before you, an impression you may recall later on as an idea, a less vivid copy of the actual experience. Both impressions and ideas come either through sensation of external objects or through reflection, by which Hume meant our emotional experiences (or what Hume also called the passions). Passions are of two sorts: the violent passions, such as love, hate, and the other emotions we ordinarily

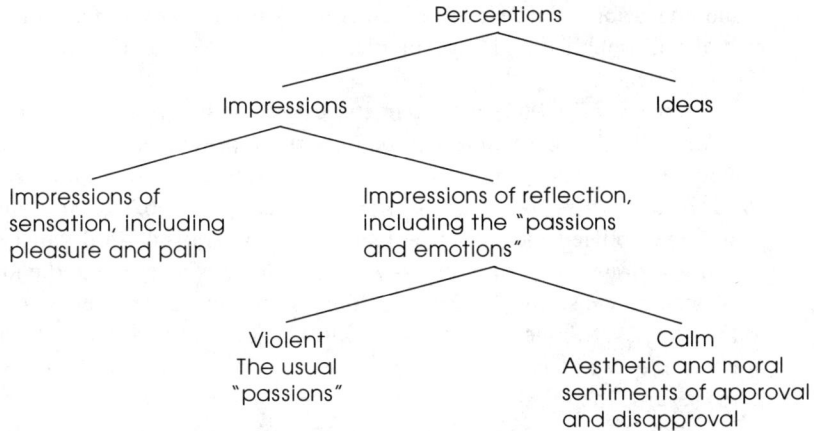

Perceptions
├── Impressions
│   ├── Impressions of sensation, including pleasure and pain
│   └── Impressions of reflection, including the "passions and emotions"
│   ├── Violent — The usual "passions"
│   └── Calm — Aesthetic and moral sentiments of approval and disapproval
└── Ideas

FIGURE 5-1 Hume's categorization of the contents of the human mind. (Adapted from Smith, 1941; reprinted by permission of Macmillan, London and Basingstoke).

call passions; and the calm passions, such as aesthetic and moral feelings. Figure 5–1 summarizes Hume's categories.

Finally, Hume distinguished *simple* and *complex* perceptions. A simple impression is a single, unanalyzable sensation, such as a blue spot of ink. Most impressions are complex, because our senses are usually exposed to many simple sensations at once. Simple ideas are copies of simple impressions, and complex ideas are aggregates of simple ideas. This means that complex ideas may not exactly correspond to some complex impression; you may imagine a unicorn, which of course you have never seen. However, complex ideas may always be broken down into simple ideas, which are copies of simple impressions. Your complex idea of a unicorn combines the impression or idea of a horse with the impression or idea of a horn, both of which you have experienced. Before considering how complex perceptions are formed, two important conclusions may already be drawn from Hume's category of mental content. First, Hume gave priority to impressions over ideas. Impressions bring us directly in touch with reality by perception, but ideas may be false, corresponding to nothing (such as the unicorn). The truth is to be determined by tracing ideas to impressions, and whatever ideas are found to have no empirical content, such as the ideas of metaphysics and theology, are to be expunged. Thus, Hume asserted a positivism—the claim that all meaningful ideas must be reducible to something observable. The second important conclusion is that Hume assigned priority to simple perceptions over complex ones. All complex perceptions are built up from our experiences of simple ones and may be completely analyzed into simple components. Hume was a psychological atomist, holding that complex ideas are built up out of simple sensations.

When we turn to how complex perceptions are built up out of elementary ones, we come to what Hume himself thought was his central contribution to the science of human nature: his doctrine of the association of ideas. The concept of association was not new with Hume. We have found it in Plato, Aristotle, Hobbes, and Berkeley; the phrase "association of ideas" was coined by Locke. However, they had used it in only a limited way—Locke, for example, saw in association an obstacle to clear thinking and sound education. What Hume prized was his use of association to inquire into fundamental philosophical and psychological questions. It was the chief theoretical tool of his new science.

Hume (1777/1962) wrote, in his essay *An Inquiry Concerning Human Understanding,* "To me there appear to be only three principles of connection among ideas, namely, Resemblance, Contiguity in time or place, and Cause [and] Effect." In his *Abstract of a Treatise of Human Nature* (Hume, 1777/1962, p. 38), Hume (1740/1962, p. 302) exemplified each: " 'resemblance'—a [portrait] naturally makes us think of the man it was drawn for; contiguity—when St. Denis is mentioned, the idea of Paris naturally occurs; 'causation'—when we think of the son we are likely to carry our attention to the father . . . [T]hese are the only links that bind the parts of the universe together or connect us with any person or object exterior to ourselves." At least, said Hume, "so far as regards the mind."

Hume's wording reveals the influence of Newton on eighteenth-century psychological thought. For Newton, gravity was the attractive force that binds the atomic parts of the universe together. For Hume, association "is a kind of attraction which in the mental world will be found to have as extraordinary effects as in the natural" (Hume, 1817), and the laws of association "are really to us the cement of the universe" (Hume, 1740/1962, p. 302) as experienced. Thus, for Hume, complex human experience (complex ideas) is at root simple ideas (derived from impressions) united together by the principle of association. As Newton did with gravity, Hume thus made association into an ultimate principle that could not be reduced further.

Hume then proceeded to investigate human knowledge in light of these three (soon to be two) laws. Cause and effect is the most important law underlying most everyday reasoning. You will to lift your arm; it rises. You knock one billiard ball into another; the second one moves. You turn off a light switch; the light goes out. Cause and effect even lies at the root of the inference that, contrary to Berkeley, a material world exists; for one assumes the world acts on the senses so as to cause one to perceive it. However, Hume asked, whence comes our knowledge of causation? Causes are never directly perceived. Rather, we perceive a regular conjoining of two events: the feeling of intention with the subsequent movement of the arm; the motion of one ball with the subsequent motion of the second; the flipping of the switch with the subsequent extinguishing of the light; the opening of the eyes with the appearance of things. Furthermore, no rational argument can be produced to prove causation. Hume argued that belief in causes is learned through experience. As a child experiences many regular conjunctions of events, a "propensity" of the child's mind leads to the firm conviction that the first event caused the second. This propensity also brings along a feeling of necessity. Causation is not simply correlation for Hume, it is a feeling of necessity between two events. This means, of course, that cause and effect is not a basic principle of association, because it is reducible to contiguity plus the feeling of necessity.

Hume generalized his argument to all generalizations. When one claims "All swans are white," it is on the basis of experiencing a number of swans, all of which were white. One then assumes that future swans in one's experience will also be white and one therefore draws the conclusion. It is quite like assuming—based on past experiences—the light will go out when one flips the switch. In neither case, however, can the generalizations be given a rational justification, for they are based on experience, not on reason. No principle of reason underlies empirical generalizations. But we do make them, and Hume wanted to explain how we do so, in order to have a complete theory of human nature.

The principle Hume employed is the principle of custom or habit. In *Inquiry,* Hume (1777/1962, p. 61) wrote: "For whenever the repetition of any particular act or operation produces a propensity to renew the same act or operation without being impelled by any reasoning or process of the understanding, we always say that this propensity is the effect of custom. . . . All inferences from experience . . . are effects of custom [habit], not of reasoning."

It was, and is, frequently assumed by Hume's readers that, by reducing causation and inductive generalization to habit, he is denying their validity, and that he must have been a total skeptic, surprised each morning to find that the sun had risen. This assumption is wrong (Smith, 1941). Hume was only trying to find out how we reach causal and inductive conclusions; he was not concerned with validity. He discovered that reason is not involved; but he did not therefore have to deny the validity of causation and induction. In fact, Hume (1777/1962, p. 72) wrote, "as this operation from the mind, by which we infer effects from causes, and vice versa is so essential to the subsistence of all human creatures, it is not probable that it could be trusted to the fallacious deductions of our reason, which is slow . . . appears not, in any degree, during . . . infancy, and, at best, is . . . extremely liable to error and mistake." Further, the "wisdom of nature" has implanted in us this "instinct or mechanical tendency" that is "infallible in its operation" and appears at birth. Thus, the ability to form general conclusions, or habits, is founded on association, on our propensity to generalize from limited instances, and on our propensity to feel causes necessarily linked to effects. This ability to generalize is innate and "infallible," and of its operations we are "ignorant." Habit is a surer guide to the world than reason.

In support of this conclusion, Hume noted that the same generalizing tendency is present in animals. Their practical knowledge of the world is nearly faultless, yet they do not possess reason. Animals learn habits, and, according to Hume (1777/1962, p. 111) "any theory by which we explain the operations of the understanding . . . in man will acquire additional authority if we find the same theory is requisite to explain the same phenomenon in other animals." Other philosophers had stressed humans' uniqueness, but Hume here stressed their similarity to animals, implying the value of a comparative approach to human and animal mind.

As a consequence of his views, Hume made a statement that seems startling coming from a philosopher in the Age of Reason. He writes, in *A Treatise of Human Nature* (1817): "Reason is, and ought only to be the slave of the passions, and can never pretend to any other office than to serve and obey them." This is quite natural, given Hume's position. Reason is helpless to know reality; it must serve experience and the instinct for generalization, which reflect the world as it is. For Hume, morality is a matter of feeling (passion). We approve and disapprove the actions of ourselves and others according to how we feel about them, and reason must thus serve our moral sentiments.

Hume resisted skepticism by relying on human nature. As he and others pointed out, the most extreme skeptic never behaves according to his beliefs; he always assumes there will be a tomorrow. Hume (1777/1962, p. 158) wrote in his *Inquiry:* "[N]o durable good can ever result from excessive skepticism," nor can it hope that "its influence will be beneficial to society." Hume preferred a moderate skepticism, one that accepts the limits of reason, properly values animal nature, and knows that general conclusions may be false (after all, there are black swans). Such a skepticism is practical (it does not doubt the accumulated wisdom of experience) and useful (it preaches toleration and provides a science of human nature for the proper founding of the other sciences).

In Hume's work, we see the first glimmerings of the psychology of adaptation. At bottom, human knowledge is habit, whether mental as with Hume, or behavioral, as with the behaviorists. Hume stressed the practical knowledge of the everyday world that lets us adapt to our environment, as would post-Darwinian American and British psychologists. Hume appealed to human continuity with animals, as would psychologists after Darwin, especially the behaviorists. Hume viewed feeling—the passions—as an essential part of human nature. A person is not pure rational soul locked in a material, passionate body. So, too, would Freud and the behaviorists stress the emotional, or motivational, side of humans. Finally, in preferring one theory to another because of its social and practical utility, Hume also anticipated those American psychologists for whom one defect of structuralism was its avowed practical inutility.

As had Socrates, the Sophists, and the atomists, Hume annoyed minds incapable of living without at least the possibility of knowing fixed and eternal truths. Although Hume simply taught how to live in a world without absolute certainties, his critics took him to be much more dangerous. For them, Hume was at worst an atheistical advocate of skepticism, reveling in the destruction of knowledge, or at best a dead end, demonstrating by his skepticism the necessary futility of empiricist philosophy. In reply, Hume's critics cited God-given common sense or alleged proofs of the necessary character of all experience.

The Reassertion of Common Sense: The Scottish School

Some of Hume's philosophers-countrymen regarded Hume as having falling victim to a sort of "metaphysical lunacy"—believing nothing—traceable to Locke's revival of the copy theory of cognition. These philosophers asserted the claims of the common person against the abstruse speculations of philosophy. "I despise philosophy, and renounce its guidance—let my soul dwell with Common Sense," wrote Thomas Reid, the founder of the movement. In addition to Reid (1710–1796), other members of the Scottish School included James Beattie (1735–1803), popularizer and polemicist against Hume, and Reid's student, Dugald Stewart (1753–1828).

Reid believed that philosophy had begun to go astray with the creation of the Cartesian Theater (though he did not use the term). According to the model of Descartes and Locke, the mind is not acquainted with objects themselves, but only with their copies, ideas, projected into consciousness. Here, Reid thought, was the first step toward skepticism, because if the mind works as Descartes and Locke say, then there is no way of ensuring that ideas are veridical copies of objects; we can never inspect objects themselves and compare them to their representations. In a contemporary parallel, we insert into a copying machine an original document that we have not seen, and are then allowed to look only at the copies. We assume that the copies resemble the original, but because we cannot look at the original itself, we cannot justify our assumption. Had Berkeley seen the same problem, he would have responded by saying there was no original document. For Berkeley, the "copy machine," the mind itself, made the "copies" out of bits and pieces of sensations, but the "copies" correspond to no original. As long as the machine of the mind produced stable and coherent experience, we could study it and build science on it.

Reid founded commonsense philosophy by eliminating the copier; he returned to the older, intuitively appealing Aristotelian view that perception simply records the world as it is. He maintained that there are three, not four, elements in perception: the perceiver, the act of perception, and the real object. There is no separate stage of representation as in the Cartesian Theater. Our perceptual acts make direct contact with objects, not only with their representative ideas. We know the world in a direct, unmediated way that is consistent with what each of us believes without the misleading tutoring of philosophy. This view is known to philosophers as direct realism, in contradistinction to Descartes's, Locke's, and Hume's representational realism and Berkeley's and Kant's idealism.

Reid also raised two issues that were important to later psychology. First, Reid rejected the idea, found in Berkeley, Locke, Hume, and Kant, that conscious experience is manufactured out of bits and pieces of sensations. Because we directly experience objects as they are, there is no need to posit a gravity of the mind or force of sensation that holds complex impressions and ideas together. Reid acknowledged that one can artificially analyze complex impressions into simple ones, but he denied that doing so returned one to the raw material of experience, pure sensations. For Reid, the raw material of experience is objects themselves. Most later psychologists would follow Hume or Kant in seeing experience as manufactured out of simpler bits, but Reid was followed by the Gestalt psychologists, and William James, both of whom refused to think of the mind as a "machine shop" manufacturing experience out of pieces of "mind stuff" (James, 1890). As a realist, Reid believed that perception is always meaningful. Concepts are mental symbols that stand for something real. Perception is thus like language. Like the medievals, Reid believed we get knowledge by reading the "book of the world," which tells us the meaning of reality as surely as reading a book tells us its meaning. Complex experience cannot be reduced to atomic sensations without robbing it of something vital—its meaning.

The second general point central to Reid's philosophy is his own brand of nativism. According to Reid, we are naturally endowed with certain innate faculties and principles of mind that allow us to know the world accurately and furnish us with essential truths as well. Reid (1764/1785/1975) wrote:

> Such original and natural judgments are, therefore, a part of that furniture which Nature had given to the human understanding. They are the inspiration of the Almighty . . . they serve to direct us in the common affairs of life, where our reasoning faculty would leave us in the dark . . . and all the discoveries of reason are grounded upon them. They make up what is called the common sense of mankind. . . . When a man suffers himself to be reasoned out of the principles of common sense, by metaphysical arguments, we may call this metaphysical lunacy.

Knowledge of the world is secure because of our innate constitution, which delivers it. We are so constructed as to know. Reid's claims for the existence of innate mental faculties sometimes cause his school to be called faculty psychology; but his followers clearly did not invent the concept, they only popularized it.

In his own way, Reid restated Hume's arguments, as Hume realized. We have seen how Hume, too, subordinated reason to human nature's innate powers of association and propensities to generalize. Reid exceeded Hume in the number of principles he believed are built into the human constitution, including such "first principles" as the worship of God.

The root difference between them was a religious one. A curious aspect of the nativism-empiricism debates of the eighteenth century often escapes the modern, secular, eye. Following Darwin, we now assume that native constitution is the product of natural selection. Our ability to see depth, for example, stems from our having descended from originally arboreal apes for whom binocular vision was adaptive. However, most philosophers before Darwin believed in God and assumed that, because God made human beings, whatever ideas or principles he implanted must be true, unless God is a deceiver. Thus, Locke, staunch opponent of innate truths, never used the best counterclaim to so-called innate principles—namely, to show that they may not be true—because Locke assumed that whatever God did implant must be true. Hume was an atheist, and his moderate skepticism was an inevitable result. Our faculties, not being God-given, may err. Reid, however, avoided skepticism by asserting that the Almighty implanted in us first principles, necessarily valid because of their source. Thomas Reid was a clergyman—perhaps a clergyman first and a philosopher second.

Among the Scots, an important step toward psychology was taken by Reid's student, Dugald Stewart. Stewart, who was more reconciled to Hume than was Reid, abandoned the term common sense and used association extensively. His basic work, *Philosophy of the Human Mind* (1792), reads like an introductory psychology text based on everyday experience instead of laboratory experiments. There are sections on attention, association (learning), memory, imagination, and dreaming. Stewart wrote charmingly about magicians, jugglers, and acrobats to illustrate his points. His discussions of attention and memory have a contemporary air about them, with Stewart making some distinctions found in modern information-processing psychology, and citing everyday experiences to support them. Stewart followed Reid in dissecting the mind into component faculties, each of which is assigned its role in mental life and knowledge. Stewart spent sixty-two pages showing the practical value of the study of psychology.

In all, Stewart's work is engaging and attractive. Through Stewart especially, Scottish philosophy became quite influential, especially in America. Some of America's earliest college founders were adherents of the Scottish School, as were some important college presidents in the nineteenth century. In the hands of later writers (beginning with Stewart), Scottish philosophy became a readily acceptable psychology, intuitively appealing and consistent with Christianity. Most American colleges were (and many still are) religious, and in the nineteenth century Scottish faculty psychology was part of the "moral sciences" taught to their students.

The Reassertion of Metaphysics: Immanuel Kant (1724–1804)

Kant said that Hume's skeptical arguments roused him from his "dogmatic slumbers." Before reading Hume, Kant had been a follower of Leibniz through his teacher, Christian Wolff (1679–1754). However, Hume upset Kant's Leibnizian "dogmatism" by his psychological analysis of human knowledge. Kant saw Hume's conclusions as undermining certain knowledge and as threatening the achievement of Newton's physics. Like Plato, Kant sought transcendent Truth, and was not content with merely useful truths. As a result, Kant tried to rescue metaphysics. He realized that the old speculative metaphysics about God and humankind's spiritual substance was dead, and, in fact, Kant proved that it had always been an illusion. However, Kant could not accept Hume's merely psychological analysis of knowledge, for it only said we have a tendency to form general conclusions based on association. Kant wanted to prove the validity of human knowledge quite apart from any empirical facts about human habit formation. He thus reasserted the claim of philosophical metaphysics, over psychology, to be the foundation of the other sciences.

Kant's answer to Hume bears a strong resemblance to Reid's. What we have knowledge of, in Kant's term, are phenomena. The objects of science, such as planets or balls rolling down inclined planes, are found in human experience. Kant argued that experience is organized by the inherent nature of human perception and thinking. For example, in our experience, every event has a cause. Why? According to Hume, belief in causation is something learned, primarily by association. For Kant, Hume's account undermined the absolute truth of causation; a mere habit cannot be absolutely True, as required by the Newtonian physics Kant took as his model of human knowledge. Belief in causation therefore cannot derive from habit, but from something inherent in human thinking. The world as we experience it, phenomena, must be such that every event has a cause, for this is the only way we can conceive the world. Our experience will never violate causality because we are so constructed that every experienced event has a cause. The Newtonian assumption of universal causality can never be falsified, and it is therefore absolutely and necessarily true—at least as regards phenomena.

Behind phenomena are what Kant called noumena, or things-as-they-are. In the noumenal world, there may be uncaused events—in fact, Kant assigned human moral freedom to the noumenal realm. However, as noumena affect us to produce phenomena, all events are perceived to be caused. Thus, according to science, all behavior is caused, for science rests on phenomena; but people may very well be noumenally free—in fact, they must be free if moral responsibility is to have any meaning. Kant built in many inherent principles of understanding that structure our phenomena—from time and space as preconditions of sensation, to concepts of causality and existence.

Previous empiricist philosophers assumed that humans have knowledge because objects impose themselves on understanding, which conforms itself to them. Hume's philosophy is the end point of this assumption. For Hume, events in the real world are regular because of the laws of nature, and these regularities register themselves in our mind as habits. But Hume's view leads to at least moderate, if not total, skepticism, which Kant (like so many others) found appalling. So Kant advanced the startling assumption that objects conform themselves to our understanding. The following example may help clarify Kant's view (Copleston, 1964). If a person wears red glasses, every object of his or her understanding will be red. The person will probably assume, if he or she has worn the glasses all his or her life, that all objects are red, that is, that understanding conforms itself to objects. However, it is possible (and in fact true, in this instance) that objects have many colors, but that something about the perceiver (the glasses) imposes redness on all objects of knowledge, and for the wearer it is phenomenally true to say, "Everything is red." Kant argued that something like this is true of human knowledge as it is. We are endowed with certain qualities of perception and thinking that impose themselves on experience to create the objects of knowledge about which science makes true statements. For the empiricist, the mind is passive in registering the qualities of objects; for Kant, the mind actively structures experience into an organized, knowable shape. Only thus can human knowledge be rescued from skepticism. Only phenomena, of course, are rescued from skepticism; noumena may or may not be always caused or always organized in time and space. Illusory metaphysics arises when human reason applies its inherent concepts to noumena, to which they do not apply. Thus, attempts to prove the existence of God are futile, for God is never known phenomenally, and so the empirical, if innate, concept of "existence" simply cannot apply to God. God cannot be proved *not* to exist either, however.

Kant's philosophy is extremely difficult, and its influence in pure philosophy has been very great. However, from the psychological standpoint, we may question whether Kant departs in any essential way from Hume or Reid. Hume gave a psychological analysis of knowledge as founded on our propensity to form habits. Reid proposed an involved nativism in which commonsense beliefs are implanted by God and therefore correspond to the material world. Kant also proposed that human innate principles so structure experience that knowledge is necessarily true of phenomena, though not of noumena. Kant thought he had proved the transcendental validity of his innate concepts, but, from a modern perspective, these concepts, if they exist, are evolutionary designs, and Kant's explanation is just as psychological as Hume's or as physiological as Reid's. In other words, what applied to Reid as against Hume applies to Kant as well. The major difference between Hume, on the one hand, and Reid and Kant, on the other, is the amount and nature of innate equipment humans come with. The verdict of history is mixed on this score. Kant has been supported by findings that perception of three-dimensional space is innate, but he has been undermined by modern quantum physics (in which not all events have causes) and the construction of non-Euclidean geometries (which Kant implied were inconceivable).

Kant's philosophy directly influenced the Swiss psychologist Jean Piaget. Kant taught a form of idealism, maintaining that the world of experience is constructed by the transcendental categories of perception. Piaget studied the process by which the categories and the construction of the world develop in growing children. Indeed, one of his works was entitled *The Construction of Reality by the Child,* and other works study each Kantian category in turn: *The Child's Conception of Space, The Child's Conception of Time, . . . of Number,* and so on.

Given his disdain for Hume's psychological account of knowledge, Kant cared little for psychology. Kant believed that psychology, defined as the introspective study of the mind, could not be a science, for two reasons. First, he did not think that enough aspects of consciousness could be measured quantitatively to make possible Newtonian equations about the mind. Second, according to Kant, any science has two parts—the empirical part, involving observation and research, and the rational or metaphysical part, comprising the philosophical foundations that justify the empirical science's claim to produce knowledge. Kant believed that he had provided the metaphysical grounding of physical science in his account of human experience, the *Critique of Pure Reason.* There he showed that the basic assumptions of physics, such as universal causality, were necessarily true of human experience. Hence, physics is a complete science.

Kant argued, however, that rational psychology is an illusion. The object of rational psychology is the thinking substance, or soul—Descartes's "I think." However, we do not experience the soul—or what Kant called the Transcendental Ego—directly; it has no content, being pure thought, and has only noumenal, not phenomenal, existence. In Lockean terms, Kant asserted that there is no introspective power of reflection, because the self cannot observe its own thought. There is an empirical ego, of course, the sum total of our sensations or mental content, and we can study it through introspection. However, this empirical psychology, unlike empirical physics, cannot be a science; because it lacked its rational counterpart, Kant thought little of it.

Nevertheless, Kant believed in a science, or at least a discipline, concerned with humanity; he called it anthropology, the study (*logos*) of humans (*anthropos*). Kant's anthropology was psychology, not modern anthropology, being the study of human intellectual faculties, human appetite, and human character, not the cross-cultural study of societies. Kant delivered a very popular series of lectures, published as *Anthropology from a Pragmatic Point of View* (1798/1974). If Kant's philosophy is similar to Reid's, his *Anthropology* is similar to Stewart's psychology, complete with an enumeration of faculties. Kant's lectures are accessible, full of shrewd observations of everyday behavior, charming and even funny anecdotes, and popular prejudice. In short, *Anthropology* is Kant's commonsense psychology and bears some attention.

Kant distinguished physiological anthropology, concerned with the body and its effect on mind, and pragmatic anthropology, concerned with the person as a morally free agent and citizen of the world. Wundt's later division of psychology into physiological and social branches was like Kant's division of anthropology. The goal of pragmatic anthropology was to improve human behavior and so was grounded not in the metaphysics of experience, but in the metaphysics of morals. Pragmatic anthropology's methods were many. First, we have some introspective knowledge of our own minds and, by extension, of others' minds. Kant was aware of the pitfalls of introspection, however. When we introspect, we change the state of our minds, so what we find is unnatural and of limited value; the same holds for trying to observe our own behavior. Kant even went so far as to say that excessive reflection on one's own mind may drive one insane. Similarly, when we observe others, they will act unnaturally if they know we are watching. Anthropology must be an interdisciplinary study embracing these methods—but using them with care—and also calling on history, biography, and literature for information about human nature.

Anthropology is a rich work. Kant discusses everything from insanity (which he felt was innate) to the nature of women (they are weaker but more civilized than men), and to how to give a dinner party for philosophers. Just one of Kant's many topics will be presented here, however, for it occurs in Wundt's psychology in much the same form.

Kant discussed "ideas that we have without being aware of them." If we examine our awareness, we will find that some perceptions are clear—the ones we are attending to—while others are obscure. As Kant put it, "Our mind is like an immense map, with only a few places illuminated." This view of consciousness as a field with clear and obscure areas is identical to Wundt's. The obscure ideas are those we are not clearly aware of, so obviously Kant's doctrine is not Freud's view of repression into the unconscious. However, Kant does say we can be subtly affected by obscure ideas. He observes that we often unthinkingly judge persons by the clothes they wear, without being conscious of the connection between the clothes and our feelings for the wearer. Kant also offers pragmatic advice to writers: Make your ideas a little obscure so that when a reader clarifies them you will make him feel clever.

In addition to his conception of consciousness, many of Kant's other ideas influenced Wundt, the founder of the psychology of consciousness. By Wundt's time, ways to experiment on and quantify mind had become available, and so Wundt was able to show that a scientific empirical psychology was possible without a rational companion.

Wundt thus could abandon the Transcendental Ego altogether. However, it still lived in Wundt's system in modified form. Wundt emphasized how apperception gives unity to conscious experience, a role Kant assigned to the Transcendental Ego. In addition, Wundt put thinking beyond the reach of introspection, as did Kant, holding that it could be investigated only indirectly through a study of people in society, similar to Kant's *Anthropology*. Wundt's psychology had two parts: the laboratory study of experience via introspection (Kant's empirical psychology made into a science despite him), and the study of the higher mental processes via the comparative study of culture, similar to Kant's *Anthropology* (although Wundt did not use the label). Wundt also modified Kant's view of introspection. Wundt said good scientific introspection was not the intense scrutiny of the soul, which Kant found dangerous, but only the self-observations of one's experience, which even Kant said was possible.

We have noted here only some of Kant's influence on Wundt, but Kant's overall influence on Western thinking was profound. He is frequently viewed as the greatest thinker since Plato, and all philosophy after him was shaped by his philosophy—either through elaboration on his system or by provoking alternative answers to the problems he raised. His thought thus influences psychology directly (as in Wundt's case) and indirectly (as in behaviorism, which discarded the ego altogether), for it emerged out of philosophy. His most direct intellectual successors were the German speculative idealists Johann Fichte (1762–1814), Friedrich Schelling (1775–1854), Arthur Schopenhauer (1788–1860), and G. W. F. Hegel (1770–1831), who all, in one way or another, dispensed with the things-in-themselves so that the Transcendental Ego—or, alternatively, the World-Spirit—constitutes the world via its own ideas. The value of Kant's influence on psychology is controversial. Some historians of psychology claim that Kant's influence on psychology was a disaster, because of its exclusive emphasis on introspection and its radical dualism between self and world (Wolman, 1968). It may be replied, however, that Kant did not invent introspection, and indeed warned against it, and that the dualism of self and world has been part of Western thought at least since Plato. The categories of human understanding he thought necessarily true have proven unnecessary, but Kant was trying to reconcile human nature—including morality and the concept of freedom that it requires—to the mechanical Newtonian–Cartesian worldview that seemed about to engulf and alienate humanity.

THE MORAL CRISIS

"It has seemed to me that one must treat ethics like all the other sciences and construct experimental ethics in the same way as experimental physics," wrote the philosophe Claude Helvetius in *De l'esprit* (1758; quoted by Hampson, 1982, p. 124). Here is the heart of the Enlightenment project: finding the ideal human way of life by scientific research, and constructing it by applied scientific technology. However, constructing experimental ethics proved more daunting and much more perilous than experimental physics. Hobbes had approached human nature in a scientific spirit and found that humans were vicious and dangerous creatures, apt to be at each other's throats without the stern control of an authoritarian government. Thinkers of the French Enlightenment undertook their project in an optimistic spirit of improving everyone's life through science, but ended up in their Revolution apparently confirming Hobbes's pessimism. As scientific epistemology eventually resulted in a skeptical crisis, so scientific ethics resulted in a moral crisis. In Scotland, the commonsense philosophers resisted the moral crisis in ways that were especially important to American thought. Moreover, a reaction against the Enlightenment began to set in at the very time Helvetius wrote *De l'esprit.*

Experimental Ethics: French Naturalism

In France, the Enlightenment project was pursued more radically and ruthlessly than in Britain. There were two major sources for the philosophes' naturalism (Vartanian, 1953). One was John Locke's empirical psychology. In eighteenth-century France, there was a mania for things English, especially Newton's science and Locke's psychology. The supreme philosophe, Voltaire, wrote in his philosophical letters: "So many philosophers having written the romance of the soul, a sage has arrived who has modestly written its history. Locke sets forth human reason just as an excellent anatomist explains the parts of the human body. He everywhere takes the light of Newton's physics for his guide" (Knight, 1968, p. 25). The other source of naturalism was native to France, Descartes's mechanistic physiology.

Immediately after Descartes proposed that animals are simply machines but humans are not machines (and so escape science, by virtue of having souls), many of his religious opponents saw the trap he had unwittingly set. For if animals, which behave in such diverse and often sophisticated ways, are but machines, is not the next logical step to say that a person, too, is but a machine? They believed that Descartes was a secret materialist who only intimated what he hoped others might later say openly. Defenders of religion said these things to ridicule Descartes's system as subversive of faith; but in the irreligious eighteenth century, there were those who said them in earnest, proclaiming materialism.

Although there have been materialists since at least Hellenistic times, they were few and silent during the middle ages. However, in the Age of Reason, their number multiplied in the eighteenth century and they became more open and vocal. They spoke up first in anonymous pamphlets, fearing persecution, but they soon grew bolder. The most outspoken and complete extension of Descartes's beast-machine into the human-machine was made by the physician-philosopher Julien Offray de La Mettrie (1709–1751), whose major work was *L'Homme Machine* (The Man-Machine) (1748/ 1961). Interestingly, La Mettrie, too, thought Descartes was a secret materialist, but he praised Descartes for it. La Mettrie wrote: "He was the first to prove completely animals are pure machines," a discovery of such importance that one must "pardon all his errors." La Mettrie took the step feared by religionists: "Let us boldly conclude that man is a machine," that the soul is but an empty word.

As a physician, La Mettrie held that only a physician may speak on human nature, for only a physician knows the mechanism of the body. La Mettrie went into some detail to show how the state of the body affects the mind—for example, in the effects of drugs, disease, and fatigue. Against Descartes's insistence on the uniqueness of human language, La Mettrie suggested that apes might be made into "little gentlemen" by teaching them language the way the deaf are taught. La Mettrie remained a Cartesian, however, in asserting that language is what makes a person human. He only denied that language is innate, claiming that we can make the ape human, too, via language.

In general, La Mettrie gives the impression not of lowering humans to the level of animals, but of raising animals to near-human status. This intent emerges most clearly in his discussion of natural moral law. La Mettrie argued that animals share with humans moral sentiments such as grief and regret, so that morality is inherent in the natural biological order. Having said this, however, La Mettrie left the door open to sheer hedonism by stating that the point of living is to be happy.

La Mettrie adopted an uncompromisingly scientific, anti-Aristotelian attitude to his subject. He denied finalism or any Godly act of intentional creation. For example, the animal eye was not created by God to make seeing possible, but arose by evolution because seeing was important to creatures' biological survival. La Mettrie here stated a doctrine called *transformism,* which was increasingly popular in the later eighteenth century and which marks the beginning of evolutionary thought. According to transformism, the universe was not created by God but emerged from primordial matter as a result of the action of natural law. The development of the physical and, La Mettrie implied, biological universe is a necessary consequence of the way nature is organized. Voltaire's Creator is no more necessary than the Christian God.

When it came to discussing living creatures, La Mettrie returned to the view of the Renaissance nature philosophers Descartes had rejected, and attributed special powers to living matter. He thought biological tissue to be capable, at least, of self-generation and motion. La Mettrie cited recent physiological research to prove his point. Polyps cut in two regenerate their missing halves; muscles of a dead animal still move when stimulated; the heart may beat after removal from the body. Matter is alive; it is vital, not dead; and it is precisely this natural vitality that made La Mettrie's human-machine plausible. In the twentieth century, vitalism became the great enemy of scientific biologists, but it was an important step in the founding of biology as a coherent field apart from physics. La Mettrie's vitalism again attests that his materialism was not meant to degrade humanity, to make of a human being a cold, metallic machine (the image we have today of the machine), but rather to make of a human a vital, living, dynamic machine, an integral part of a living nature. Descartes's human being—like Plato's and Christianity's, was torn between nature and heaven. La Mettrie's was simply part of nature.

We should conclude this summary as La Mettrie did his book. Like a good philosopher, and like B. F. Skinner, La Mettrie urged the progressive nature and moral goodness of accepting materialism, of giving up vain speculation and religious superstition to live pleasurable lives. Recognizing ourselves to be part of nature, we can then revere, honor, and never destroy nature. Our behavior toward others will improve. Wrote La Mettrie (1748/1961):

> Full of humanity we will love human character even in our enemies . . . in our eyes they will be but mismade men . . . we will not mistreat our kind. . . . Following the natural law given to all animals we will not wish to do to others what we would not wish them to do to us. . . . Such is my system, or rather the truth, unless I am much deceived. It is short and simple. Dispute it now who will. (pp. 148–9)

With this passage, La Mettrie closed *L'Homme Machine.* Although his "truth" was not acceptable to all philosophes in its extreme form, and Christians hotly disputed it, materialism was a growing doctrine. It was reluctantly and partially accepted by Voltaire himself and by Denis Diderot, conceiver of the Encyclopedia, and espoused in extreme form by Baron Paul d'Holbach (1723–1789), who worked out its deterministic and atheistic implications. Its link to the moral crisis we will see shortly.

The other route to naturalism was through Locke's empiricism, which inspired France's *soi-disant* "Newtons of the mind." The general tendency of their thought was toward sensationism, deriving the mind entirely from sensations, denying the existence of autonomous mental faculties and the power of reflection found in Locke's psychology. The French commentators thought they were purifying and improving Locke's philosophy.

The first important French Lockean was Etienne Bonnot de Condillac (1715–1780). Condillac dismissed everyone but Locke ("Immediately after Aristotle comes Locke") and to his first book, *An Essay on the Origin of Human Knowledge* (1746/1974), he gave the subtitle *Being a Supplement to Mr. Locke's Essay on the Human Understanding*. Like Berkeley, Condillac believed Locke had not pursued his own empiricism far enough, but in his *Essay* he followed Locke closely. Only in a later work, *Treatise on Sensations* (1754/1987), did Condillac really fulfill his earlier promise to "reduce to a single principle whatever relates to the human understanding." That principle is sensation.

Locke had allowed the mind certain autonomous powers: the power of reflection on itself, and mental faculties or acts, such as attention and memory. Condillac strove to see the mind in a more purely empiricist way. He denied the existence of reflection and tried to derive all mental faculties from simple sensation. His motto might have been, "I sense, therefore I am." Condillac asked his readers to imagine a statue that is endowed with each sense in turn, starting with smell. Condillac then endeavored to build up complex mental activity from these senses. For example, memory arises when a sensation is experienced for a second time and recognized. We should observe that here Condillac cheated, for he assumed an inner power or faculty to store the first sensation, an innate power indistinguishable from memory. Attention is reduced to the strength of one sensation to dominate, in the mind, other weaker sensations. In his *Essay,* Condillac had followed Locke and said attention was a mental act (as will Wundt a century later); but in the *Treatise,* his sensationism is consistent, and he anticipates Titchener's identical sensationist revision of Wundt's theory.

In short, Condillac attempted to work out an empiricist theory of mind. However, on one point, he remained a good Cartesian. At the end of Condillac's thought experiment about the statue, although it had acquired every mental faculty and every human sense, the statue still lacked the essential Cartesian human trait: It could not speak. Condillac said, with Descartes, that it could not speak because it lacked reason. Its mind was passive, not active; it lacked the power of thought. In Condillac's scheme, as in Descartes's, the statue and animals are set off from human beings. Condillac simplified the emerging picture of the animal soul, showing how it might be built up without the innate faculties that had been attributed to it since the time of Aristotle. The human soul he left as Descartes had left it, as the power to think. Condillac, a Christian, left the stripping of human beings of their soul, the seat of reason, to more radical men who were more willing to embrace La Mettrie's materialism and to work out its consequences.

One of these more radical thinkers was Claude Helvetius (1715–1771), who accepted Condillac's empiricism and a mechanical version of La Mettrie's materialism. Helvetius consequently proclaimed a complete environmentalism, in which humans have neither a divine soul nor a complex biological structure. The human possesses only senses, a passive mind able to receive sensations, and a body capable of certain actions. This mind is passively built up through watching the effects of a person's own and others' actions and observing the ways of the world. For Helvetius, then, the mind at birth is both blank and powerless; everything a person becomes is the result of the environment. Helvetius found cause for optimism in the malleability of the mind, holding out the hope that improved education would lead to improved people. In this tenet, he presaged the radical behaviorists, who believe human behavior is similarly malleable. Such beliefs, however, have a negative potential as well—an effective dictatorship can be founded on brainwashing.

We now come to the moral crisis created by the Enlightenment project. Is it possible to have a scientific ethics as Helvetius hoped? With few exceptions in the history of the West up to this time, including Descartes, Locke, and Kant, reason had been assigned the job of imposing moral behavior on humans' natural tendencies toward pleasure. Ironically, however, in the Age of Reason the scope of reason had been reduced and belief in a transcendent moral order, whether Platonic, Stoic, or Christian, had been shattered. All that remained was human nature as a guide to right and wrong.

The problem was finding good in human nature. La Mettrie said pleasure is the natural cause for our existence; nature made us to pursue pleasure. Condillac, too, reduced reason to desire, or need. If each sensation produces pleasure or pain, then our thinking, built up out of our sensations by association, is determined by their affective quality and directed by our momentary, animal needs. Hence, empiricism undercuts the autonomy of reason. For the rationalist, reason is prior to, and independent of, sensation, so hedonism is only a temptation to be overcome. The empiricist, however, constructing reason out of affectively charged sensations, makes hedonism the directing force behind all thought. Seeing happiness entirely as physical pleasure, not eudaemonia (living well), La Mettrie turns Socrates on his head. Socrates had always said that the moral life is the happy life. But La Mettrie wrote, in his *Anti-Seneque* (1750; quoted by Hampson, 1982, p. 123):

> Since the pleasures of the mind are the real source of happiness, it is perfectly clear that, from the point of view of happiness, good and evil are things quite indifferent in themselves and he who obtains greater satisfaction from doing evil will be happier than the man who obtains less satisfaction from doing good. This explains why so many scoundrels are happy in this life and shows that there is a kind of individual felicity which is to be found, not merely without virtue, but even in crime itself.

Here we see the fundamental crisis of naturalism, which was first confronted by the philosophes and which became acute after Darwin. If we are only machines, destined to pursue pleasure and avoid pain, what can be the ground of moral value and of meaning in our lives? The early philosophes assumed, as humanists, that the world was made for humans by a beneficent, if non-Christian, Creator. As the century progressed, however, it became evident that this optimism was unjustified. The great Lisbon earthquake of mid-century, for example, blotted out thousands of lives. Newton's universe seemed to be a machine indifferent to human life, which was a mere speck of no consequence. Moreover, the extension of materialism, determinism, and hedonism to human beings, while intellectually persuasive, was hard to accept emotionally. Diderot, for example, wrote in a letter, "I am maddened at being entangled in a devilish philosophy that my mind can't help approving and my heart refuting" (Knight, 1968, p. 115). The whole dilemma thus comes down to a question of feelings—feelings of freedom and dignity versus a natural desire to seek pleasure and avoid pain.

There is a remarkably existentialist sentence in La Mettrie's *L'Homme Machine:* "Who can be sure that the reason for man's existence is not simply the fact that he exists?" He continued: "Perhaps he was thrown by chance on some spot on the earth's surface, nobody knows how or why, but simply that he must live and die, like the mushrooms which appear from day to day." La Mettrie stated the possibility of a meaningless world, the abyss of moral nihilism that every philosophe saw and tried to avoid.

However, one man cheerfully jumped into that abyss, proclaiming the autonomy of pleasure, the illusion of morals, the rule of the strong, and a pleasurable life of crime. The Marquis de Sade (1740–1814) wrote, in *History of Juliette,* this description of why the strong, in the pursuit of happiness, should dominate the weak:

> [T]he strong, . . . in despoiling the weak, that is to say in enjoying all the rights he has received from nature, in giving them the greatest possible extension, finds pleasure in proportion to this extension. The more atrociously he harms the weak, the more voluptuously he is thrilled; injustice is his delectation, he enjoys the tears that his oppression snatches from the unfortunate wretch; the more he grieves him, the more he oppresses him, the happier he is. . . . . this truly delicious gratification never establishes itself better for the fortunate man than when the misery he produces is complete. . . . Let him pillage then, let him burn, let him ravage, let him not leave the wretch more than the breath to prolong a life whose existence is necessary for the oppressor . . . whatever he does will be in nature, whatever he invents will be only the active use of the forces which he has received from her, and the more he exercises his forces, the more he will experience pleasure, the better he will use his faculties, and the better, consequently, he will have served nature.*

If the only goal in life that naturalism can find is pleasure, then we should each seek it uninhibited by morals or the opinions of society, according to Sade. In doing so, we will be fulfilling natural law. The strong must triumph over the weak. Sade extended comparative psychology to morals. Animals prey on one another without compunction; they have no moral law. We are animals, so we should act in the same way. Moral law is a metaphysical illusion. The philosophes first struggled with the problem of a world ruled only by efficient causes and hedonism, and tried to avoid Sade's logical extrapolation of naturalism. In the twentieth century, the problem has remained unsolved, and in our own time we have seen moral nihilism proclaimed again, while modern existential humanists seek to restore humanity's dignity. The problem became acute in the nineteenth century when Darwin cut away all reason for believing that humans transcend nature. In Darwin's universe, too, the strong destroy the weak. Sade was a harbinger of the moral nihilism that stared Victorians in the face and posed for their therapist, Freud, his deepest problem.

Moral Sense: The Scottish School

The apocalyptic vision of Hobbes and the fevered prose of Sade seem to set humans in a fetid swamp of violence and immorality from which there is no rescue save the

---

* Quoted and translated by Lester Crocker, *An age of crisis* (Baltimore: Johns Hopkins University Press, 1959), 212–3.

arbitrary power of a police state. However, if we move to the cooler climate of Scotland, we find its commonsense philosophers reminding us that people are not as bad as Hobbes, Sade, and their alarmed readers fear (or like) to think. Although crime and war exist, most of the time most people act decently toward one another, and when they do not, they feel guilty or ashamed. Animal mothers care for their young; animal fights rarely result in death; and many animal species love in cooperative groups, all without society or government of any kind. Surely, the Scots (including Hume [Norton, 1993b]) argue, human nature, while not necessarily moral, tends to be moral. Scottish philosophers maintained the Enlightenment project of constructing a science of human nature, but they found in human nature a new foundation for the explanation of morality.

Thomas Reid's own teacher, George Turnbull, concisely set out the Scottish position. Turnbull aimed to do for morals what Newton did for nature, inquiring "into moral phenomena, in the same manner as we do into physical ones" (quoted by Norton, 1982, p. 156). Nature is orderly and ruled by natural laws, observes Turnbull, and the existence of Newton's physics demonstrates that God furnished human nature with mental faculties capable of knowing nature's order and discovering nature's laws. By analogy, Turnbull reasoned, human behavior is orderly and ruled by moral laws, and God has furnished us with a moral sense by which we may discover moral laws: "I am apt to think, that everyone shall immediately perceive, that he has a moral sense inherent in him, and really inseparable from him. . . . If we experience approbation and disapprobation, then we must have an approving and disapproving faculty" (Norton, 1982, p. 162). That is, we are equipped by nature so as to see that some actions are right—we approve of them—and others are wrong—we disapprove of them.

Scottish moral sense theory is important in three respects. First, it coolly rejects the extreme claims of Hobbes and the French naturalists. People are made to be sociable and to behave decently, not to be utterly vicious and selfish. People spontaneously and without coercion care for each other and try to do what is right. La Mettrie's happy criminals and Sade's sadists are exceptions, not images of what we would all be without Hobbes's authoritarian state. Second, it helps establish the science of human nature, psychology. There are principles that govern human behavior other than those imposed by governmental *nomos,* and it is possible for us to learn and use them. Finally, the Scottish school exerted great influence in psychology's modern home, the United States. Along with many Americans, Thomas Jefferson read the great Scottish philosophers. When he wrote, "We hold these truths to be self-evident, that all men are created equal . . . ," he built on Reid: "Moral truths may be divided into two classes, [the first of which are] such as are self-evident to every man whose understanding and moral faculty are ripe . . ." (quoted by Wills, 1978, p. 181).

The only point that stymied the Scots was where human nature came from. Reid and his followers thought it came from God, which would place it beyond science. Hume, the atheist, placed it beyond science by taking it for granted. "It is needless to push our researches so far as to ask why we have humanity or fellow-feeling with others. It is sufficient, that this is experienced to be a principle in human nature" (quoted by Norton, 1993b, p. 158). Hume asked only how human nature worked and refrained from asking why it is what it is. In the next century, Darwin began to create a science that only today, as the field of evolutionary psychology, could answer Hume's unasked question (Dennett, 1995).

The Counter-Enlightenment

Newton had applied human reason, logic, and mathematics to nature, and he had shown that the human mind could encompass nature's laws and bend nature to human will. The vision of the philosophes of the Enlightenment was that Newtonian reason could be applied to human affairs—to psychology, ethics, and politics. In the Newtonian scheme of the philosophes, scientific reason would banish superstition, religious revelation, and historical tradition, setting in their place laws of human conduct whose use by enlightened despots could create the perfect human society. The philosophes were intolerant of cultural diversity, because cultural traditions are not products of reason, so that all existing cultures fall short of the rational ideal. The philosophes were scornful of history, regarding it as no more than gossip from the past, entirely irrelevant to understanding contemporary society and to the task of reconstructing society in the light of reason.

The philosophes' imperialism of reason and science provoked a reaction from diverse thinkers who found it horrifyingly unhuman. Against the imperialism of natural science they set the autonomy of culture, and against the excesses of reason they set the feelings of the heart. Their horror at the mechanistic universe of the philosophes was expressed by the English poet William Blake (1757–1827; quoted by Hampson, 1982, p. 127):

> I turn my eyes to the Schools and Universities of Europe
> And there behold the Loom of Locke, whose woof rages dire,
> Wash'd by the Water-wheels of Newton: black the cloth
> In heavy wreathes folds over every nation: cruel Works
> Of many Wheels I view, wheel without wheel, with cogs tyrannic
> Moving by compulsion each other.

The Criterion and Rule of Truth Is to Have Made It: Giambattista Vico (1668–1744)

One current of the Counter-Enlightenment began with this obscure Italian philosopher who formed his ideas even before the Enlightenment began. Neoplatonic Christian theology and Cartesian philosophy had placed the human mind in a spiritual realm beyond the reach of science. The philosophes denied that human beings stood in any respect outside Newtonian science, and looked toward a universal experimental ethics based on the idea that human nature is everywhere the same and is unchanging. If such a nature exists, it follows that science may know it and technology may construct around it a perfect society. Vico began a tradition in philosophy that respects the old Platonic and Christian intuition that human beings are radically different from the other animals, but does so without invoking an immaterial soul. Instead, followers of Vico hold that what makes humans unique is culture, and that therefore there can be no Newtonian science of human mind and behavior.

Vico began with the astonishing assertion that knowledge of nature is inferior, secondhand knowledge compared to knowledge of society and history. Vico's criterion of knowledge derived from the scholastics of the Middle Ages, who held that one cannot really know something unless one has made it. In the case of nature, only God can really know the natural world, because he made it. To us humans, nature is a given, a brute fact, something we can observe only from the outside, never from the inside. People, however, make their societies in the historical process of creation. We can see our own lives from the inside and, through sympathetic understanding, we can understand the lives of men and women in other cultures and other historical times.

For Vico, then, history is the greatest science; through history, we come to know how our society, or any society we choose to study, was created. History is not gossip, said Vico, but the process of human self-creation. The Enlightenment philosophes claimed there was a universal, timeless human nature that could be known to science, and on which we could build a perfect society. But according to Vico, human beings make themselves through history, so there is no eternal human nature, and each culture must be respected for the human creation it is. We understand cultures by studying what they create, especially their myths and language. Myths express the soul of a culture at a certain point of development, and language shapes and expresses the thoughts of its members. To understand another time's or place's myths and language is thus to understand how men and women thought and felt then and there.

Vico anticipated a distinction that is clearer in Herder, and clearer still in nineteenth-century German historians: the distinction between *Naturwissenschaft* and *Geisteswissenschaft*. *Naturwissenschaft* is Newtonian natural science, built on the observation of nature from the outside, noting regularities in events and summarizing them in scientific laws. *Geisteswissenschaft* is much harder to translate, meaning literally "spiritual science," but more often rendered today as "human science." Human science studies the human creations of history and society. Its method is not observation from without, but sympathetic understanding from within.

It is apparent that psychology straddles the divide between the two sciences. People are part of nature—things—and as such are subject in part to natural science. But people live in human cultures and as such are subject to human science. Wundt's division of psychology between experimental, "physiological" psychology of human conscious experience on the one hand, and *Völkerpsychologie*—the study, as Vico recommended, of human myth, custom, and language, on the other hand—reflected Vico as well as Kant. Within Germany, however, the distinction was challenged by Wundt's young pupils, who wanted psychology to be a science on a par with physics. Outside Germany, the division was largely unknown, and psychology was assimilated, as the philosophes would have wished, to natural science and the search for universal laws of human behavior.

We Live in a World We Ourselves Create: Johann Gottfried Herder (1744–1803)

Vico was little read outside his own circle in Italy. However, his ideas reappeared, independently asserted, in the works of Herder, who rejected the Enlightenment's worship of reason and universal truth in favor of romanticism's trust in the human heart, and a historical reverence for many human truths. Herder's views are remarkably similar to Vico's, although they were formed in ignorance of Vico's works. His motto, "We live in a world we ourselves create," could have been said by Vico. Herder, too, stressed the absolute uniqueness of each living or historical culture. We should strive to fulfill ourselves and our own culture, not slavishly follow classical styles and attitudes of a bygone age. Herder is modern in his belief that each person should try to fulfill his or her potential as a total person instead of being an alienated collection of roles. Herder opposed faculty psychology for its fragmentation of the human personality. For both the individual and the individual's culture, Herder stressed organic development.

Because each culture is unique, Herder opposed any attempt to impose one culture's values on any other. He detested the tendency of the philosophes to caricature the past and hold out their own times as a universal model for humanity. Herder even went so far as to imply the degeneracy of the Age of Reason. It was artificial; it aped the Greeks and Romans; it was too reasonable and insufficiently spiritual.

Herder's views were highly influential, especially in Germany. Although Kant had written one of the great manifestos of the Enlightenment, *What is Enlightenment,* and although Prussia's Frederick the Great was the prototypical "Enlightened Despot," the ahistorical and aggressively rationalist attitudes of the philosophes did not take root in Germany, which found Herder's emphasis on historical development and profound feeling more attractive. German philosophy rejected the exaltation of individual consciousness found in the Enlightenment. Fichte wrote, "The individual life has no existence, since it has no value in itself, but must and should sink to nothing, while on the contrary the race alone exists" (quoted by Hampson, 1982, p. 278). Although Herder and Fichte defined race in terms of common language rather than the fanciful biology of the later Nazis, they helped create an environment in which Germans regarded themselves as special. As Fichte wrote, "We appear to be the elect of a universal divine plan" (quoted by Hampson, 1982, p. 281). German psychology would be deeply shaped by German philosophy's alienation from the Enlightenment. German thinkers, including Wundt and even the proud Jew Freud, saw themselves as apart from and better than the supposedly shallower thinkers to their west, and English-speaking psychologists would have little use for the impractical alleged profundities of German *Geisteswissenschaft.*

More generally, Herder helped lay the foundation for romanticism. He passionately opposed the mock-classical art of his time, calling modern critics "masters of dead learning." Instead, he advocated "Heart! Warmth! Blood! Humanity! Life!" Descartes had said, "I think, therefore I am." Condillac implied, "I sense, therefore I am." Herder wrote "I feel! I am!" Thus ended, for many people, the rule of abstract reason, the geometric spirit, and reasonable emotion. Instead, organic development led by emphatic emotion was the base of the new romanticism.

Nature versus Civilization: Jean-Jacques Rousseau (1712–1778)

In France, the Counter-Enlightenment began in 1749. In that year, the Dijon Academy of arts and sciences set an essay contest on the question "Whether the restoration of the arts and sciences has contributed to the refinement of morals." Rousseau's essay began his career as an influential writer. He argued, against the tide of Enlightened opinion, that the answer was no, that human beings had been corrupted rather than improved by Newtonian science and philosophy. In many ways, Rousseau's complaints about the Enlightenment paralleled Herder's, although Rousseau was less conscious of history than was Herder. Rousseau said, "To exist is to feel" and "the first impulses of the heart are always right"—sentiments that recall Herder and point to romanticism. Like Herder, Rousseau rejected mechanism because it could not explain human free will.

Rousseau argued with Hobbes's conceptions of human nature and of society. Hobbes had found in the English Civil War an impression of what people without government were like: violent and warlike. In Rousseau's time, travelers from the South Pacific brought different tales of what people were like without government. They drew an idyllic picture of life unencumbered by the demands of European society. People lived without clothes, ate the food freely available on the trees, and took sexual pleasure where they found it. In the Pacific islands, it appeared, the life of humans was the opposite of being solitary, nasty, brutish, and short. These island peoples became Rousseau's famous Noble Savages. Rousseau argued that the present state of society corrupted and degraded human nature. Instead of a return to primitivism, Rousseau advocated building a new, less alienating society, and the makers of the French Revolution followed him.

Rousseau was a friend of Condillac and was similarly empiricistic and interested in education. Rousseau described his ideal educational program in *Emile* (1762/1974), in which a child and his tutor retire from corrupt civilization and return to nature for education. After his education is complete, Emile returns to society. Rousseau advocated a kind of nondirectional education, believing that a child should be allowed to express his or her native talents, and described a good education as one that cultivates the natural growth of these talents. The tutor should not impose views on the student. Nevertheless, behind the apparent freedom is firm control. At one point, Rousseau described what we would call open education: "It is rarely your business to suggest what he ought to learn; it is for him to want to learn." However, earlier, he had written: "Let him always think he is master while you are really master. There is no subjection so complete as that which preserves the forms of freedom." For Rousseau the empiricist, the corrupt state of civilization may be overcome by a proper education, which perfects the potentialities of each person. Herder believed in self-fulfillment, but he was less individualistic, seeing fulfillment in the larger context of the person's culture, which the person helped perfect while perfecting self.

Rousseau's influence has been wide. His affinities with romanticism and political revolutionaries have been alluded to. In education, he inspires those who support open education of the "whole child" against those who prefer highly structured teaching of separate basic skills. He is also behind those who want to reform society through education. In his belief in human malleability and perfectibility, he foreshadowed B. F. Skinner, who advocated a carefully controlled society whose goal is human happiness, although Skinner openly disbelieved in human freedom.

CONCLUSION: REASON AND ITS DISCONTENTS

The major theme of the period between 1600 and 1800 was the triumph of science—in particular, Newtonian science—over the old medieval theological worldview. In the seventeenth century, Galileo, Kepler, Descartes, and Newton demonstrated the power of a new kind of understanding of nature. The new scientific view substituted the idea of universal mathematical order for the older idea of universal meaning in nature. Humanity's view of nature changed greatly. Nature had been a book of signs revealing the invisible world beyond. Now it became an indifferent machine that could be known only in a limited way, via mathematics. Nature lost its meaningfulness, but humanity gained power over it from mathematically precise predictions.

The viewpoint of science was something fundamentally new in human history. Heretofore, thinkers had merely speculated about the nature of reality, and their speculations were comprehensive in scope but lacking in detail. Newtonian science substituted detailed analysis of concrete cases for vast speculations about cosmic order. Since Newton's time, of course, science has grown in comprehensiveness until for many it has entirely supplanted religion as a world picture.

No sooner had Newton propounded the new antimetaphysical science of physics, than philosophers began to see the possibility of extending it to human nature. The enterprise began with Locke and occupied almost every eighteenth-century thinker. The keynote was sounded by Hume in his call for a science of human nature to be as fundamental to science as metaphysics had been thought to be. It has emerged that natural science can get along quite well without psychology, and the average physicist would laugh at Hume's proposal. Still, the eighteenth century did move significantly toward creating a science of human nature. The philosophes believed in Hume's science, but they showed no more unanimity on the nature of human nature than psychologists show today.

Alexander Pope (1688–1744), the English poet, caught the spirit of the Enlightenment view of human nature before the French Revolution:

> Know then thyself, presume not God to scan;
> The proper study of Mankind is Man.
> Placed on this isthmus of a middle state,
> A being darkly wise, and rudely great:
> With too much knowledge for the Sceptic side,
> With too much weakness for the Stoic's pride,
> He hangs between; in doubt to act, or rest,
> In doubt to deem himself a God, or Beast,
> In doubt his Mind or Body to prefer,
> Born but to die, and reas'ning but to err;
> Alike in ignorance, his reason such,
> Whether he thinks too little, or too much:
> Chaos of Thought and Passion, all confused;
> Still by himself abused, or disabused;
> Created half to rise, and half to fall;
> Great lord of all things, yet a prey to all;
> Sole judge of Truth, in endless Error hurled:
> The glory, jest, and riddle of the world!
>
> Go, wondrous creature! mount where Science guides,
> Go, measure earth, weigh air, and state the tides;
> Instruct the planets in what orbs to run,
> Correct old Time, and regulate the Sun;
> Go, soar with Plato to th' empyreal sphere,
> To the first good, first perfect, and first fair;
> Or tread the maze round his follow'rs trod,
> And quitting sense call imitating God;
> As Eastern priests in giddy circles run,
> And turn their heads to imitate the Sun.
> Go, teach Eternal Wisdom how to rule—
> Then drop into thyself, and be a fool!*

* Alexander Pope (1733), *An essay on man.* Epistle II, l. 1–30.

There is no doubt that the Enlightenment finally marks the beginning of modern times. The philosophes wrestled with the problem of understanding human nature apart from God and faith. They generally agreed that humanity could be improved, but they did not agree on what was beneath the social veneer. Their optimistic hopes seemed upheld by the American Revolution, which apparently put the new worldview into motion in the New World. But the French Revolution cast doubt on the providential hopes of the philosophes. They aimed to reform humanity, but were not prepared for the violence of the Reign of Terror or its suppression by a new Emperor, Napoleon.

The French Revolution began in an unstable stew of ancient grievances, the Enlightenment's calls for scientific reform, and the Counter-Enlightenment's reverence of emotion and action. The reforming philosophes did not realize with what social dynamite they were playing. The French people had accumulated centuries of vaguely understood but powerfully felt resentments, as the growth of the monarchical state began to weigh heavily on them. In the United States, reason guided the passions that led to Revolution. In France, reason failed, and passion gained the upper hand.

Nevertheless, the ideas of the Enlightenment did not die; they were put to the service of building a new society and a new humanity to inhabit it. The revolutionary Fabre d'Eglantine looked to Lockean empiricism to construct the propaganda—the new "empire of images"—by which the Revolution might erase loyalty to the old regime and build affection for the new. "We conceive of nothing except by images: even the most abstract analysis or the most metaphysical formulations can only take effect through images" (quoted by Schama, 1989). Rousseau had wanted to take children away from their parents, to be raised by the state. A revolutionary leader, Louis de Saint-Just (1767–1794), sought to make the scheme a reality. With Helvetius, Saint-Just looked forward to the possibility of scientific control of human behavior, which depended on denying free will, "We must form men so they can only will what we wish them to will" (quoted by Hampson, 1982, p. 281). But Saint-Just also warned that an empire of virtue was bought at a terrible price: "Those who want to do good in this world must sleep only in the tomb" (quoted by Schama, 1989, p. 767).

BIBLIOGRAPHY

A general history of the centuries culminating in the eighteenth is Fernand Braudel's three-volume history, *Civilization and capitalism 15th–18th century* (New York: Harper & Row): vol. 1, *The structures of everyday life: The limits of the possible* (1981); vol. 2, *The wheels of commerce* (1982); and vol. 3, *The perspective of the world* (1984). Braudel aims to write "total history" reaching from everyday life at the base of society to the total world economy. Braudel is very difficult, but widely influential. On the Enlightenment itself, a fine two-volume treatment is given by Peter Gay (1966, 1969). Of special interest to the history of psychology is the second volume, subtitled *The science of freedom,* which covers the Newtons of the mind. A selection of the philosophes' major writings has been assembled by Gay in *The Enlightenment: A comprehensive anthology* (New York: Simon & Schuster, 1973). A somewhat older book that stresses the darker side of the Enlightenment is Crocker (1959). A recent book that does for the eighteenth century what Christopher Hill did for the seventeenth in his *The world turned upside down* (see Chapter 4 bibliography) is Margaret C. Jacob, *The radical enlightenment: Pantheists, Freemasons and Republicans* (London: Allen & Unwin, 1981). The revolutionary consequences of the Enlightenment are discussed by Norman Hampson, *The first European revolution 1776–1815* (New York: Norton, 1969), who gives a broader picture of the Enlightenment in his 1982 work; in this connection, see also James H. Billington, *Fire in the minds of men: Origins of the revolutionary faith* (New York: Basic Books, 1980). For science in the period, see Thomas L. Hankins, *Science and the Enlightenment* (Cambridge, England: Cambridge University Press, 1985). Finally, for social histories of the period, see Richard Sennett, *The fall of public man* (New York: Vintage Books, 1978); Lawrence Stone, *The family, sex, and marriage in England 1500–1800* (New York: Harper & Row, 1982); and Neil McKendrick, John Brewer, and J. H. Plumb, *The birth of a consumer society: The commercialization of eighteenth century England* (New Haven, CT: Yale University Press, 1982), especially the last chapter, by Plumb, on how people responded to modernity.

In discussing the philosophy of the eighteenth century, a paper by David Fate Norton, "The myth of 'British empiricism,' " *History of European Ideas* (1981, *1:* 331–44), caused me to reorganize the present and preceding chapters. Norton shows that neither rationalism nor empiricism is the fixed tradition it is taken to be; Thomas Reid started the idea of empiricism vs. rationalism, and his myth has been enshrined by teachers ever since. A survey of the philosophy of the period is in S. C. Brown, ed., *Philosophers of the Enlightenment* (Sussex, England: Harvester Press, 1985). Two books by John Yolton discuss the central psychological ideas of the eighteenth-century philosophers: *Thinking matter,* on materialism, and *Perceptual acquaintance from Descartes to Locke,* on perception (both Minneapolis: University of Minnesota Press, 1983 and 1984, respectively).

Works on the specific philosophers follow, omitting works cited in the text.

Berkeley.   Berkeley's major philosophical works are *Three dialogues between Hylas and Philonus* and *A treatise concerning the principles of human knowledge* (Indianapolis: Hackett, 1979 and 1982, respectively). His analysis of perception is in *Works on vision* (Indianapolis: Bobbs-Merrill, 1963). For commentary on Berkeley, see Ian C. Tipton, *Berkeley: The philosophy of immaterialism* (London: Methuen, 1974); J. O. Urmson, *Berkeley* (Oxford, England: Oxford University Press, 1982); or G. J. Stock, *Berkeley's analysis of perception* (The Hague, The Netherlands: Mouton, 1972).

Hume.   David Hume, *An inquiry concerning the principles of morals* (Indianapolis: Hackett, 1983). For commentary, David Fate Norton, *David Hume: Common sense moralist, sceptical metaphysician* (Princeton, NJ: Princeton University Press, 1982), John Passmore, *Hume's intentions* (New York: Basic Books, 1968), John P. Wright, *The skeptical realism of David Hume* (Manchester, England: Manchester University Press, 1980), or D. F. Norton, ed., *The Cambridge Companion to Hume.* (Cambridge, England: Cambridge University Press, 1993).

The Scots.   Dugald Stewart, *Elements of the philosophy of the human mind* (London: A. Strahan & T. Caddell, 1792). For a broad view of the Scottish Enlightenment, see R. H. Campbell, ed., *The origins and nature of the Scottish Enlightenment* (Edinburgh: John Donald, 1982).

Kant.   Kant's most important book is *Critique of pure reason* (New York: St. Martin's Press, 1929), but it is extraordinarily difficult; more accessible, and deliberately so, is *Prolegomena to any future metaphysics that will be able to come forward as science* (Indianapolis: Hackett, 1977). There is also a large amount of Kant commentary. A useful short introduction is S. Körner, *Kant* (Harmondsworth, England: Pelican, 1955). Karl Ameriks discusses *Kant's theory of mind* (Oxford, England: Clarendon Press, 1982).

French Naturalism.   The account of French naturalism is based largely on the cited works and on the general treatments of the period listed above, especially Gay (1966, 1969). See also Robert J. Richards, "Influence of sensationalist tradition on early theories of the evolution of behavior," *Journal of History of Ideas* (1979, *40:* 85–105). That Condillac has long been misrepresented has been demonstrated by Hans Aarslef, *From Locke to Saussure: Essays on the study of language and intellectual history* (Minneapolis: University of Minnesota Press, 1982).

Enlightenment in Germany. Again, see the general sources. Also Robert J. Richards, "Christian Wolff's prolegomena to empirical and rational psychology: Translation and commentary," *Proceedings of the American Philosophical Society* (1980, *124:* 227–39).

The Counter-Enlightenment. Without doubt, the outstanding modern student of the Counter-Enlightenment is Isaiah Berlin. For Vico and Herder, see his *Vico and Herder: Two studies in the history of ideas* (New York: Vintage Books, 1977). Several essays in his *Against the current* (Harmondsworth, England: Penguin, 1982) touch on the Counter-Enlightenment, especially "The Counter Enlightenment," which briefly but insightfully reviews the major spokesmen of the movement. Vico, in particular, has experienced a revival in interest; see G. Tagliacozzo and D. P. Verene, eds., *Giambattista Vico's science of humanity* (Baltimore: Johns Hopkins University Press, 1976).

REFERENCES

Bower, T. G. R. (1974). *Development in infancy.* San Francisco: Freeman.

Condillac, E. B. de (1746/1974). *An essay on the origin of human knowledge.* New York: AMS Press.

Condillac, E. B. de (1754/1982). *Philosophical writings.* Hillsdale, NJ: LEA.

Copleston, F. (1964). *A history of philosophy* (Vol. 5). Garden City, NY: Image Books.

Crocker, L. (1959). *An age of crisis.* Baltimore: Johns Hopkins University Press.

Dennett, D. D. (1995). *Darwin's dangerous ideas.* New York: Simon & Schuster.

Dworkin, G. (1980). Commentary: Ethics, foundations, and science: Response to Alaisdair MacIntyre. In H. T. Englehardt and D. Callahan (Eds.) *Knowing and valuing: The search for common roots.* Hastings-on-Hudson, NY: The Hastings Center.

Gay, P. (1966, 1969). *The enlightment: An interpretation,* 2 vols. New York: Knopf.

Hampson, N. (1982). *The enlightment: An evaluation.* Harmondsworth, England: Penguin.

Hume, D. (1817). *A treatise of human nature.* London: Thomas and Joseph Allman.

Hume, D. (1739/1962/1974). *David Hume on human nature and the understanding,* Anthony Flew, ed. New York: Collier Books.

James, W. (1890). *Principles of psychology,* 2 vols. New York: Henry Holt.

Kant, I. (1798/1974). *Anthropology from a pragmatic point of view,* trans. M. J. Gregor. The Hague, The Netherlands: Martinus Nijhoff.

Knight, I. F. (1968). *The geometric spirit: The Abbé Condillac and the French enlightenment.* New Haven, CT: Yale University Press.

La Mettrie, J. O. de (1748/1961). *Man a machine.* La Salle, IL: Open Court.

Norton, D. F. (1982). *David Hume: Commonsense moralist, sceptic, metaphysician.* Princeton, NJ: Princeton University Press.

Norton, D. F. (1993a). An introduction to Hume's thought. In D. F. Norton, ed., *The Cambridge companion to Hume.* Cambridge, England: Cambridge University Press.

Norton, D. F. (1993b). Hume, human nature, and the foundations of morality. In D. F. Norton, ed., *The Cambridge companion to Hume.* Cambridge, England: Cambridge University Press.

Reid, T. (1764/1785/1975). *Thomas Reid's inquiry and essays,* K. Lehrer and R. Beanblossom, eds. Indianapolis: Bobbs-Merrill.

Rousseau, J. (1762/1974). *Emile.* New York: Dutton.

Schama, S. (1989). *Citizens: A chronicle of the French Revolution.* New York: Knopf.

Smith, N. K. (1941). *The philosophy of David Hume.* London: Macmillan.

Stewart, D. (1792). *Elements of the philosophy of the human mind.* Facsimile reprint, 1971, New York: Garland Press.

Vartanian, A. (1953). *Diderot and Descartes: A study of naturalism in the enlightenment.* Princeton, NJ: Princeton University Press.

Wills, G. (1978). *Inventing America: Jefferson's Declaration of Independence.* Garden City, NY: Doubleday.

Wolman, B. (1968). Immanuel Kant and his impact on psychology. In B. Wolman, ed., *Historical roots of contemporary psychology.* New York: Harper & Row.

6 *To the Threshold of Psychology*
The Nineteenth Century

Charles Darwin, Newton's equal as a scientific thinker. Publication of his *Origin of Species* in 1859 was the most important intellectual event of the nineteenth century. Darwin's theory of how and why evolution happens continues to revolutionize the life sciences, including psychology.

The Enlightenment consensus ended with the French Revolution, which at first appeared to be the political fruit of the Age of Reason. The fruit, it emerged, was poisoned, for the Revolution drowned in the blood of guillotined aristocrats and ferociously exterminated peasant counter-revolutionaries. At the peak of the Reign of Terror, one revolutionary leader proclaimed that the Revolution consisted in the murder of its enemies. The upshot of the Revolution was Napoleon's new military empire and his failed wars of conquest. The disturbing implications of the geometric spirit became clear, and nineteenth-century thinkers were forced to come to grips with the implications of naturalism. This task was made more pressing by Darwin's theory of evolution, which not only made man into an ape but also took all purpose and progress out of natural history. Throughout this period, the problems of human nature were considered by many philosophers, physiologists, writers, and revolutionaries. Out of this ferment grew the triple founding of psychology in the last quarter of the century.

THE WORLDS OF THE NINETEENTH CENTURY

In discussing the general intellectual background of the founding of psychology, we will follow Baumer's (1977) division of social and intellectual history into four intellectual "worlds":

1. The Romantic world, which reacted strongly against the naturalism of the philosophes, asserting the claims of feeling against the claims of reason.
2. The New Enlightenment, which continued to develop the Enlightenment project.
3. The world of Darwinism, the central intellectual event of the nineteenth century.
4. The *fin de siècle* (end of the century), a world of anxiety born of the loss of faith in traditional religion and searches for alternative sources of solace.

The Reassertion of Emotion and Intuition: The Romantic Revolt

Although we usually think of romanticism as a movement in the arts, it was much more; it carried on the protests of the Counter-Enlightenment against the Cartesian-Newtonian worldview. As romantic poet and artist William Blake (1757–1827) prayed, "May God us keep/From Single vision and Newton's sleep." The romantics regarded Cartesian claims for the supremacy of reason as overweening, and combated them with paeans to strong feeling and nonrational intuition. Whereas some Enlightenment writers, notably Hume, had valued mild and moral "passions," the romantics were inclined to worship all strong emotions—even violent and destructive ones. Above all, the romantics fervently believed there was more in the universe than atoms and the void, and, by unleashing passion and intuition, one might reach a world beyond the material. To this end, many romantics took psychoactive drugs, hoping to escape the bonds of ordinary rational consciousness in search of higher, almost Platonic, Truth.

Unsurprisingly, the romantics' conception of the mind differed from that of the Enlightenment's Newtons of the mind. Most Enlightenment writers concerned themselves with conscious experience; the romantics adumbrated ideas of the unconscious, the primal and chaotic home of feeling and intuition. The German philosopher Arthur Schopenhauer (1788–1860) posited Will as the noumenal reality behind appearances. Schopenhauer's Will, specifically the will to live, pushes humanity on to endless, futile striving for something better. This description of the Will foreshadows Freud's id. Schopenhauer wrote, in *Parerga,* "In the heart of every man there lives a wild beast." Intelligence tries to control the Will, but its raging inflicts pain on the self and others. Also prefiguring Freud were those writers who saw in dreams the language of the unconscious needing only to be decoded to reveal the secrets of the infinite.

In contrast to the rather bloodless and mechanical picture of the mind advanced by most philosophers, especially in Britain, the romantics depicted the mind as free and spontaneously active. The Will is a wild beast, but while that wildness implies pain, it also implies freedom of choice. Schopenhauer's philosophy thus was voluntaristic, a romantic reaction against the Enlightenment's materialistic determinism. Generally, this led the romantics to worship heroes, geniuses, and artists—those who asserted their Wills and did not bow to the way of the world. Thomas Carlyle, for instance, revered heroes who ranged from Odin to Shakespeare to Napoleon. The romantic emphasis on the mind's independent activity can be found even in the study of perception. Most philosophers followed Hume in seeing perception as a process of making "impressions" on a passive mind. Influenced by Kant, Leibniz, and the European Idealist tradition, Samuel Taylor Coleridge (1772–1834), for instance, likened the mind to a lamp. Instead of merely registering impressions, the mind casts intellectual light, actively reaching out to the world and shaping the resulting experience.

Romantics rejected the mechanical conception of society that had led to the French Enlightenment, whose beginning they applauded but whose bloody ending they lamented. If society, like physical nature, is just a machine, then, like nature, it may be rationally and scientifically controlled. Against this view, romantics such as Edmund Burke (1729–1797) held that societies were grown, not made. The customs of civil society grew slowly into a rich, interconnected set of customs, norms, and beliefs often only marginally present to consciousness. Thinking some social practice is irrational was akin to thinking the shape of a tree is irrational. Moreover, just as too much pruning and shaping may kill a tree, so scientific planning may kill a culture. As a member of Parliament, a lonely Burke applauded the American Revolution because it asserted the time-honored rights of English people against a tyrannical King. Later, however, Burke denounced the French Revolution for overturning the natural, evolved, French way of life in the name of abstract reason.

Although the Romantic movement was short-lived, its legacy was a great split in psychology. Although not necessarily elevating passion and intuition, the founding psychologists all viewed the mind in the spirit of romanticism. Wundt called his psychology voluntaristic, stressing the independence of mental principles of development from physical ones. James, too, was a voluntarist, deeply committed to the reality and freedom of will. Freud, of course, picked up the notion of the unconscious, and elevated its passions over the still, small voice of reason as the causes of human thought and behavior. Nevertheless, in the English-speaking world with which we are primarily concerned, the conception of mind, and later behavior, as essentially mechanistic and driven from outside soon replaced the romantic one, despite James's protestations. Likewise, in the twentieth century, psychologists would be deeply involved in the kinds of scientific social engineering that horrified the conservative heirs to Burke. At least in psychology, romanticism was defeated by the New Enlightenment.

The New Enlightenment

Not everyone was disenchanted by the Newtonian spirit. Many important thinkers carried on the Enlightenment project, especially in England and France. Indeed, out of the New Enlightenment came the central concepts of twentieth-century American psychology.

Utilitarianism

Utilitarianism in one form or another has been powerfully influential in all the social sciences. It proposes a simple and potentially quantifiable theory of human motivation, *hedonism*. First advanced by Greeks such as Democritus, hedonism proposes that people are moved solely by the pursuit of pleasure and the avoidance of pain. Part of the appeal of utilitarianism is its flexibility. Although the principle of utility is simple, it respects individual differences and the quite varied kinds of pleasures and pains that people pursue or avoid. The principle of utility is fundamental to most theories in economics. In psychology, it provided the motivational doctrines of behaviorism, and continues to influence theories of decision making and choice.

Turning hedonism into a practical, quantitative, scientific theory was an enterprise of an English reformer and Newton of the mind, Jeremy Bentham (1748–1832). He opened his *Introduction to the Principles of Morals and Legislation* (1789/1973, p. 1) with a forceful statement of utilitarian hedonism: "Nature has placed mankind under the governance of two sovereign masters, pain and pleasure. It is for them alone to point out what we ought to do, as well as to determine what we shall do. . . . They govern us in all we do, in all we say, in all we think." Typical of an Enlightenment philosophe, Bentham's claim fuses a scientific hypothesis about human nature with an ethical canon about how people ought to live. Not only do pleasure and pain "govern us in all we do" (the scientific hypothesis), they "ought" to do so as well (the moral canon). Previous thinkers had certainly recognized the temptation of hedonism, but they had hoped that it might be controlled by some other motive—for example, by the Scottish philosophers' moral sense. What made Bentham daring were his rejection of motives other than utility as superstitious nonsense and his attempt to erect an ethics on that rejection. Bentham's definition of utility was, however, not limited to mere sensual pleasures and pains. In addition to them, Bentham recognized the pleasures of wealth, power, piety, and benevolence, to name only a few.

Bentham's Newtonian proposal that pleasure and pain might be quantified made his principle of utility scientifically important. The strength of Newtonian physics was its mathematical precision, and Bentham hoped to bring similar precision to the human sciences. His "felicific calculus" attempted to measure units of pleasure and pain so that they might be entered into equations that would predict behavior or could be used by decision makers to make correct—that is, most happiness-maximizing—choices. In economics, prices are a convenient stand-in for Bentham's calculus of happiness. Economists may readily determine how much people will pay for pleasures—whether cookies, concerts, cannabis, or cars—and how much they will pay to avoid pain—buying security systems, health insurance, or aspirin—and they have developed a highly mathematical science based on the principle of utility. In psychology, attempts to directly measure units of pleasure and pain have proved controversial, but nevertheless continue. For example, in the emerging field of behavioral economics, equations have been developed based on how much rats or pigeons will "pay" in terms of operant responses for various economic "goods" such as food, water, or electrical stimulation.

As a social reformer, Bentham wanted legislators—the audience Bentham aimed at in his *Principles*—to employ the felicific calculus in making the laws. Their goal should be "the greatest happiness for the greatest number." That is, legislators should try to figure out how many happiness units and how many pleasure units would be generated in the country as a whole by any given action, and always act to maximize the net amount of pleasure. Because he believed with the Sophists that what is pleasurable and painful varies from person to person, Bentham generally advocated minimal government. In the utilitarian view, people ought to be left alone to do what makes them happy, not dictated to by a meddling government pursuing its own utility function.

Associationism

Utilitarianism provided a simple, potentially scientific, yet flexible theory of human motivation. Associationism, as developed by Locke, Berkeley, and Hume, provided a simple, potentially scientific, yet flexible theory of the human cognitive processes. In the early nineteenth century, the two theories were combined to provide a powerful general account of the human mind. Associationism described the *how* of thought and behavior—the mechanics of perception and thinking—and utilitarianism described the *why* of thought and behavior—the motives and goals that drove thought and behavior. Meshing of the two theories was encouraged by Bentham's discussion of the principles governing pleasure and pain, because they resembled the principles that associationists had already said governed the formation of associations. For example, Bentham said that the overall value of any pleasure or pain is determined by the intensity, duration, certainty, and propinquity of the corresponding sensation.

Associationism was developed as a psychological doctrine by David Hartley's (1705–1757) *Observations on Man* (1749), which proposed a complete associationistic account of human mind and behavior. Although Hartley's ideas often resemble Hume's, Hartley developed them from the work of John Gay (1699–1745). Like so many protopsychologists, Hartley was a physician, and one of his aims was to establish the physiological basis of association. Hartley's greatest influence, however, as with the other Newtons of the mind, was naturally Isaac Newton. Not only did Hartley strive to see the mind through Newtonian eyes, he adopted Newton's own speculations about the operations of the nerves.

Hartley believed in a close correspondence between mind and brain, and he proposed parallel laws of association for both. He was not a strict parallelist like Leibniz, however, for he believed that mental events causally depend on neural events. Beginning with the mental sphere, Hartley built up the mind from simple atomic units of sensation, as did Hume. Our sensory contact with a perceivable quality (what Hartley called an impression) causes a sensation (similar to Hume's impression) to arise in the mind. If the mind copies the sensation, this constitutes a simple idea of sensation (comparable to Hume's simple ideas) which may be compounded via association to form complex intellectual ideas (comparable to Hume's complex ideas). Turning to the physiological substrate of association formation, Hartley adopted Newton's theory of nervous vibrations, which said that the nerves contain submicroscopic particles whose vibrations pass along through the nerves and constitute neural activity. An impression started the sensory nerve-substance vibrating, and this vibration passed to the lower brain where it brought a sensation to the mind. Repeated occurrence created a tendency in the cortex to permanently copy this vibration as a smaller vibration, or vibratiuncle, corresponding to an idea.

Hartley's associationism was quite popular. It was propounded to the public and defended against critics by Joseph Priestley (1733–1804), a great chemist and the codiscoverer of oxygen. It was also quite influential in artistic and literary circles, for it deeply affected the critical sensibility of turn-of-the-century artists, especially the romantics. (Coleridge named his eldest son David Hartley.) In the long run, associationism eventually gave rise to analysis of behavior in terms of associated habits. Because Hartley said pleasure and pain accompanied sensations and so affected thought and action, associationism linked up with utilitarianism.

The fusing of the principle of utility with associationism seriously began with James Mill (1773–1836), a politician turned philosopher. His associationism, a simple, almost building-toy theory of mind, was the frequent target of later, more holistic psychologists such as Wundt, James, and the Gestalt psychologists. In Mill's view, the mind is a passive, blank slate that is receptive to simple sensations (the building-toy nodes) out of which complex sensations or ideas are compounded by forming associative links (the sticks linking the nodes) between atomic units.

With Condillac, Mill (1829/1964) dispensed with the mental faculties retained by Hume, Hartley, and other previous associationists. Combined with utilitarian hedonism, the result was a completely mechanical picture of mind in which idea follows idea automatically, with no room left for voluntary control. The exercise of will is an illusion, Mill maintained. Reasoning is no more than the associative compounding of the ideas contained in syllogisms. Attention is no more than the fact that the mind is preoccupied with whichever ideas are particularly pleasurable or painful. The mind does not direct attention; its attention is mechanically directed by the principle of utility.

Like Bentham and many others who wrote on the mind, Mill expounded his psychology for purposes of reform. Influenced by Helvetius, as Bentham also was, Mill was especially interested in education. If the person is entirely passive at birth, it is the duty of education to correctly mold the person's mind. Mill put his ideas into practice by the rigorous education he gave his son, teaching him ancient Greek at age three and Latin at age eight. This son wrote a history of Roman law when he was ten years old.

The son, John Stuart Mill (1806–1873), did not become the perfect utilitarian his father had expected, however. Although an early adherent of Benthamism, he experienced a nervous breakdown during which he came to find Benthamism sterile, narrow, and excessively calculating. He even went so far as to call Bentham's program "evil." He eventually tempered Bentham's hedonistic principles with Wordsworth's romantic vision of nature and human feeling. He endorsed the romantic preference for the grown or natural over the manufactured, and he denied that the human being is a machine. He saw people as living things whose autonomous development and growth should be nurtured, a vision most fully expressed in his *On liberty* (1859/1978), the founding document of modern political liberal Harian thought.

J. S. Mill's version of associationism was called mental chemistry. Earlier associationists, including his father, had recognized that certain associative links became so strong that the linked ideas appeared inseparable. J. S. Mill went further, maintaining that elementary ideas could fuse into a whole idea not reducible to its elements. The elements generate the new idea, they do not merely compose it. He offered colors as an example of such a process. Spin a wheel divided into wedges, each colored with a primary color, and at a certain speed the experience will be of whiteness, not of spinning colors. The atomic colors on the wheel are generating a new color, a different kind of experience. Mill was influenced by the romantics' concept of coalescence, the idea that active imagination may synthesize atomic elements into a creation that is more than the sum of the atomic units themselves, as when elementary colors are mixed to make a qualitatively different one. Wundt made much of the power of the mind to synthesize mental elements, and the Gestalt psychologists became even more holistic.

We must emphasize, however, that although Mill tempered his father's associationistic Benthamism with the broader conceptions of romanticism, he still sought to improve utilitarianism and empiricism, not to refute them. He always detested the mystic intuitionism of Coleridge, Carlyle, and the other romantics. Nor did Mill accept romantic voluntarism. His mental chemistry, although it recognized the possible coalescence of sensations and ideas, remained a passive description of mind. It is not the mind's autonomous activity that brings about the qualitative chemical change, but the way the sensations are associated in experience. One does not choose to see the white spinning disk; the experience is forced on one's perception by the conditions of the experiment.

John Stuart Mill was the last great philosophical associationist. His associationism arose in the context of logical and metaphysical—not purely psychological—discussions. Mill believed in the possibility of Hume's science of human nature and, in fact, tried to contribute to its methodology. Later associationists became more distinctly psychological; therefore, we will postpone a discussion of them to a later section.

Positivism

As we saw in the previous chapter, the Enlightenment philosophes venerated Newtonian science and began to apply the Newtonian spirit to the study of human nature and human affairs. These tendencies deepened in the nineteenth century, and were given clear and forceful expression in the "positive philosophy" of Auguste Comte (1798–1857). Like the philosophes to whom he was heir, Comte was not a formal philosopher, scientist, or academician, but a public writer and lecturer aiming at political and social change rather than abstract knowledge. Unlike the philosophes, who talked among themselves in their glittering aristocratic salons and who cultivated "enlightened" despots, Comte (1975) addressed the working classes and the women excluded from politics by the restored French aristocracy.

Comte described human history as passing through three stages, culminating, like most revolutionary ideologies, in a final, perfect stage of government. Comte's stages were defined by the characteristic way people explained events in the world around them.

The first stage was the *theological stage*. In this stage, people explained phenomena by positing unseen supernatural entities—gods, angels, demons, souls—behind them. Traditional religious dualism or Plato's rational soul represents theological thinking in psychology, because the soul is seen as a nonmaterial and immortal being that guides the behavior of the body. Similarly, the Egyptians conceived the sun as a god, Ra, and worshipped him to ensure his arising each morning.

The second stage was the *metaphysical stage*. Things were still explained by unseen entities and forces, but they were no longer anthropomorphized as gods or elevated to the supernatural. In psychology, Aristotle's concept of form is at Comte's metaphysical stage. The soul of a living being is not conceived as supernatural or immortal, but as an unseen "essence" that defines and governs it. Indeed, Aristotelian thinking was a favorite target of the positivists. With its essences and entelechies, and seeing hidden purposes in all things, it committed the positivist crime of metaphysics on a grand scale.

The third stage was the *scientific stage*. In this last stage, explanations drop all references to unseen entities or forces of any type. Following Newton, positivist science feigns no hypotheses about any hidden causal structure of nature, but provides precise mathematical principles by which to gain power over nature. This stage represented the triumph of the philosophy of positivism, described in Chapter 1.

Each stage is also ruled by a characteristic form of government, depending on the reigning mode of explanation. During the theological stage, the government is run, as it was in Egypt, by priests, those who possess knowledge of the gods and so can communicate with them, propitiate them, and, to a degree, control them. The metaphysical stage is ruled by refined aristocrats such as Plato's Guardians or a philosophe elite who are in touch with the "higher" things of art and philosophy. Finally, in the scientific stage, scientists will rule. In particular, a new science—sociology—would come into being. Sociologists, armed with a Newtonian science of society, would have the same precise and accurate power over society that natural scientists had over nature. With the triumph of science, superstition and religion would disappear, Comte thought, and would be replaced by a rational, naturalistic Religion of Humanity that would worship the only real creative power in the universe, *Homo sapiens.*

Comte disdained psychology as it was then defined. Its very name, *psyche-logos,* proclaimed its dependence on an unseen construct, the soul, that was at least metaphysical, and at worst, religious. A genuine positive science of individuals—one that discarded all reference to the unseen—would have to be neurophysiological. Comte described a hierarchy of sciences, from most basic (and first developed) to most comprehensive (and last to develop), that became the logical positivists' Unity of Science thesis. In this hierarchy are mathematics, astronomy, physics, chemistry, physiology and biology, and sociology. Phrenology—the first thoroughly material view of the mind/brain—was sometimes inserted between biology and sociology. For Comte, as for J. S. Mill, all science used a single set of methods and aimed at a single Newtonian ideal. The view of Vico and Herder that the social sciences were fundamentally different from the natural sciences, thus exerted little influence in France or the English-speaking world.

Some features of Comte's comprehensive scheme seem a bit bizarre. He designed a new flag for the coming scientific France, along with special uniforms for the sociologist-rulers. He proposed a new "rational" calendar of 13 28-day months (plus a set of festival days to use up the remaining days). The new calendar would do away with Christmas, Easter, and the Saints' Days, replacing them with Newton Day, Galileo Day, and the like. His Religion of Humanity never took off; it failed to appeal even to other rationalists such as Mill. Later, less flamboyant thinkers narrowed positivism down to a philosophy of science. The most important of these sober positivists was Ernst Mach (1838–1916).

Mach was a great German physicist who elaborated positivism as a foundational philosophy for science. He admired Berkeley, and, like Berkeley, saw human consciousness as a collection of sensations, making the goal of science no more than the economical ordering of sensations. Mach stood by his austere antirealistic philosophy during the great debate on the reality and scientific legitimacy of atoms, asking of their defenders, "Have you ever seen one?" For Mach, knowledge, including scientific theory, served only pragmatic functions, allowing us to adaptively predict and control nature. Theory should never commit the crime of metaphysics by aspiring to Truth. Mach also introduced a critical, historical method to the study of science. He believed that many scientific concepts had incorporated metaphysical accretions in the course of their development, and that the best way to strip off the accretions and reduce the concepts to their sensory base was to study their historical development. Echoing Comte, Mach noted that early science had grown up in the theological atmosphere of the seventeenth century, and, consequently, concepts such as force had acquired "divine" attributes as something transcending mere experience.

Though positivism was controversial, its influence on psychology was substantial. Although Wundt was very critical of positivism and postulated unperceived mental processes to explain conscious experience, many of his students, including Külpe and Titchener, were much friendlier to it. On the other hand, Freud's unconscious, with its lush but unseen mental apparatus, committed the crime of metaphysics on a large scale.

In America, however, the influence of positivism was more pervasive. William James was a great admirer of Mach, whose concept of knowledge as a practical adaptation to life is quite consistent with James's Darwinianly inspired pragmatism. Mach was a source of inspiration to the twentieth-century logical positivists, who had considerable influence on behaviorism. In the twentieth century, B. F. Skinner's radical behaviorism constituted a thoroughgoing positivist account of behavior. Although Mach's psychology was introspective, that is, a psychology of the subject, once behaviorists decided to treat human beings as objects of observation, Mach's philosophy, fused with a revised Scottish realism, led directly to radical behaviorism. Skinner maintained that the single goal of science is to find lawful relations between independent and dependent variables, leading to prediction and control. Reference to unobservable "mental" processes was as much illegitimate metaphysics to Skinner as it was to Mach. Furthermore, Skinner's call for a scientifically managed, nondemocratic utopia was Comtism without the Religion of Humanity. Both believed in the perfectibility of human beings through scientific control.

More generally, the New Enlightenment set the agenda for twentieth-century American psychology. Reinforcement theory in behaviorism was an extension of utilitarianism, theories of association of ideas became theories of associations between stimulus and response, and psychologists were eager to use their achievements in the interests of social control, to "give society a new weapon for controlling the individual" as John B. Watson, the founder of behaviorism, put it.

Heraclitus Triumphant: The Darwinian Revolution

Background

The Newtonian-Cartesian mechanical world was as changeless as the ancient one. God, or some Creator, had constructed a marvelous machine perfect in conception and endless in time. Each object, each biological species, was fixed for eternity, changelessly perfect in obedience to fixed natural laws. Such a worldview was equally consistent with Plato's Forms, Aristotle's essences, and Christian theology. On this view, change was something unusual in nature. In biology, the Aristotelian belief that species were fixed and immutable was a dogma supported by the highest scientific authorities right up until Darwin's time. Given the Cartesian-Newtonian concept that matter is inert, incapable of acting, and passive only, and that spontaneous change is the origin of new species, the mutation of old seemed impossible. Once the supreme Intelligence had acted creatively, dead matter could effect nothing new.

In the atmosphere of progress characteristic of the Enlightenment, however, this static view of nature began to change. One old Aristotelian-theological concept that helped evolution along was the Great Chain of Being, or Aristotle's *scala naturae*. The Chain was viewed by medievals as a measure of a creature's nearness to God and consequently its degree of spiritual perfection. To later Lamarckian thinkers, on the other hand, it became a record of the ascent of living things toward nature's crowning perfection, humankind.

The idea that living forms might change over time was aided by the vitalistic conception of living things that had survived the pure mechanism of Mersenne and Descartes. If living things spontaneously changed in the course of their own development from life to death, and if they could give rise to new life through reproduction, then it became more plausible to think that living forms might alter themselves over great reaches of time. The vitalist, Romantic concept of evolution was not mechanical, however, for it endowed matter with godlike attributes. For the Newtonian, stupid matter was set in mechanical motion by an intelligent, purposeful Creator. For the vitalist, matter itself is intelligent and purposeful. Vitalism was thus a Romantic view of Nature—self-perfecting and self-directing, progressively unfolding itself throughout time.

The conclusion that living things had changed was becoming hard to resist by about 1800. As the entrepreneurs of the Industrial Revolution cut roads and railways through hills and mountains, they uncovered layers of rock that told a story of life unfolding. In different strata were to be found fossils of living things, and as the strata got deeper, and therefore older, the fossils became stranger and stranger. It seemed that life was not fixed forever, like the Newtonian heavens, but changed and grew, as vitalists maintained.

Charles Darwin's contribution to the concept of evolution was to mechanize it, to deromanticize nature and capture evolution for the Newtonian worldview. However, the first important theory of evolution was proposed by Jean-Baptiste Lamarck (1744–1829). Lamarck, a naturalist well known for his work in taxonomy, was the most scientific exponent of the romantic-progressive view of evolution. There were two important aspects of Lamarck's theory. The first said that organic matter is fundamentally different from inorganic, that each living species possesses an innate drive to perfect itself. Each organism strives to adapt itself to its surroundings and changes itself as it does so, developing various muscles, acquiring various habits. The second part of his theory claimed that these acquired characteristics could be passed on to an animal's offspring. Thus, the results of each individual's striving for perfection were preserved and passed on, and, over generations, species of plants and animals would improve themselves, fulfilling their drives for perfection. Modern genetics has destroyed the romantic–vitalist vision of nature. Organic matter is now known to be merely complexly arranged inorganic molecules; DNA is a collection of amino acids. The DNA chain is unchanged by modifications to an individual's body. (Certain external influences, such as drugs or radiation, can affect genetic information, but that is not what Lamarck meant.) In the absence of genetics, however, the inheritance of acquired characteristics was plausible and even Darwin from time to time accepted it, although he never accepted the vitalist view of matter. Later, both Wundt and Freud believed that acquired habits and experiences were capable of being passed through heredity.

So, by Darwin's time, evolution was a widespread concept, disbelieved only by firm religionists and a few in the biological establishment who still accepted the fixity of species. A naturalistic but romantic conception of evolution was in place. The phrase "survival of the fittest" had already been coined in 1852 by Herbert Spencer, an English Lamarckian. And in 1849, a decade before the publication of Darwin's *Origin of Species* (1859/1959), Alfred, Lord Tennyson wrote in his greatest poem, *In Memoriam,* lines that foreshadowed the new view of evolution, in the struggle for survival—a view of which Tennyson disapproved (Canto 55, 1.5–8):

> Are God and Nature then at strife,
> That Nature lends such evil dreams?
> So careful of the type [species] she seems,
> So careless of the single life.

Later in the poem, in a widely quoted line, Tennyson calls nature "red in tooth and claw" (Canto 56, l. 15).

The Victorian Revolutionary: Charles Darwin (1809–1882)

Evolution could not long remain a poetic effusion, although Darwin's own grandfather, Erasmus Darwin, anticipated his grandson's theory in a scientific poem, *Zoonomia.* Nor could it remain a romantic fancy, inspiring but finally implausible. Darwin's achievement was to make evolution into a scientific theory by providing a mechanism—natural selection. Then a campaign to convince scientists and the public of the fact of evolution was needed. Darwin never campaigned himself. He was something of a hypochondriac—one biographer (Irvine, 1959) called him "the perfect patient"—and after his trip on the *H.M.S. Beagle,* he became a recluse, rarely leaving his country home. The struggle for the survival of natural selection was carried on by others, most spectacularly by Thomas Henry Huxley (1825–1895), "Darwin's bulldog."

Darwin was a young naturalist who had the good fortune to be included on a round-the-world scientific voyage aboard the *Beagle* from 1831 to 1836. Darwin was impressed, especially in South America, by the tremendous variation within and between species. Darwin noted that there are innumerable distinct natural forms, each of which is peculiarly suited to its particular habitat. It was easy to imagine that each subspecies had descended from a common ancestor, and that each subspecies had been selected to fit some part of the environment.

Then, sometime after his return to England, Darwin began to collect data on species—their variation and origin. In his *Autobiography* (1888–1958), he said that he collected facts "on a wholesale scale," on "true Baconian principles." Part of his investigation centered on artificial selection, that is, on how breeders of plants and animals improve their stocks. Darwin talked with pigeon fanciers and horticulturalists and read their pamphlets. One pamphlet he read, "The Art of Improving the Breeds of Domestic Animals," written in 1809 by John Sebright, indicated that nature, too, selected some traits and rejected others, just as breeders did: "A severe winter, or a scarcity of food, by destroying the weak and unhealthful, has all the good effects of the most skillful selection" (Ruse, 1975, p. 347). So, by the 1830s, Darwin already had a rudimentary theory of natural selection: Nature produces innumerable variations among living things, and some of these variations are selected for perpetuation. Over time, isolated populations become adapted to their surroundings. What was entirely unclear was what maintained the system of selection. Why should there be improvement in species? In the case of artificial selection, the answer is clear. Selection is made by the breeder to produce a desirable kind of plant or animal. But what force in nature parallels the breeder's ideal? Darwin could not accept Lamarck's innate drive to perfection. The cause of selection must reside outside the organism, he insisted, but where?

Darwin got his answer in 1838 while reading Thomas Malthus's (1766–1834) *Essay on the Principle of Population as It Affects the Future Improvement of Society* (1798). Malthus addressed a problem that troubled the late Enlightenment: If science and technology had progressed, why did poverty, crime, and war still exist? Malthus proposed that although human productivity had improved, population growth always outstrips growth in the supply of goods, so that life is necessarily a struggle of too many people for too few resources. In his *Autobiography,* Darwin stated he had at last "got a theory on which he could work." It was the struggle for survival that caused natural selection. Creatures struggled over scarce resources, and those who were "weak and unhealthful" could not support themselves and died without offspring. The strong and healthy survived and procreated. In this way, favorable variations were preserved and unfavorable ones were eliminated. Struggle for survival was the engine of evolution, in which only successful competitors had heirs.

Darwin need not have gone to Malthus for the concept of individual struggle for survival. As William Irvine (1959) points out, nature, in her evolutionary aspects, is almost tritely mid-Victorian. Darwin's theory "delighted mid-century optimists" who learned that "nature moved forward on the sound business principles of laissez-faire" (p. 346). Natural selection may have offended the pious, but not the Victorian businessman of the Industrial Revolution, who knew that life was a constant struggle that rewarded failure with poverty and disgrace. The improvement of the species from the struggle of individuals was Adam Smith's "invisible hand" all over again. It was also consonant with Edmund Burke's conservative vision of societies as collections of successful practices and values.

Darwin had formulated the essentials of his theory by 1842, at which time he first set them on paper with no thought of publication. His theory may be summarized as a logical argument (Vorzimmer, 1970). First, from Malthus, Darwin holds that there is a constant struggle for existence because of the tendency of animals to outgrow their food sources. Second, nature constantly produces variant forms within and between species. Some variants are better adapted to the struggle for survival than others. Consequently, organisms possessing unfavorable traits will not reproduce, causing their traits to disappear. Finally, as small adaptive change follows small adaptive change over eons, species will differentiate from a common stock as each form adapts to its peculiar environment. Furthermore, environments will change, selecting new traits for perpetuation, and as environment succeeds environment, species will diverge ever more from their parent forms. Thus, the observed diversity of nature can be explained as the result of a few mechanical principles operating over millions of years, as species evolve from species.

The theory as it stood was deficient. Without today's knowledge of genetics, the origin of variations and the nature of their transmission could not be explained. Darwin was never able to overcome these difficulties and was in fact pushed closer and closer to Lamarckism as he defended his theories against critics. It is an irony of history that while Darwin was writing and defending his *Origin of Species,* an obscure Polish monk, Gregor Mendel (1822–1884), was doing the work on heredity that eventually supplied the answer to Darwin's difficulties. Mendel's work, published and ignored in 1865, was rediscovered in 1900 and became the foundation of modern genetics. By the time Darwin died, he had earned burial in Westminster Abbey, and his thought had revolutionized the Western worldview, but not until the synthesis of genetics and natural selection into modern neo-Darwinian theory in the 1930s did evolution seriously affect biology.

Darwin set his ideas down in 1842, but it is not clear why he did not then seek to publish them. Some historians suggest Darwin, who had once considered becoming a minister, was made neurotic by the idea of evolution. Others suggest he wanted to gather more facts to support his ideas before a probably disbelieving world. In any event, Darwin continued to investigate nature, spending eight years, for example, studying barnacles. Then, on June 18, 1858, Darwin was shocked to discover that someone else had discovered his theory. He received a letter from Alfred Russel Wallace (1823–1913), a fellow naturalist, but younger and bolder than Darwin. Wallace had also been to South America and had been impressed by the natural variation of life there. In southeast Asia, trapped in his tent by rain, he had read Malthus and had Darwin's insight. Although he did not know Darwin, he attached a paper outlining his theory to his letter and asked Darwin to get it published.

Darwin's hand was forced. He wanted to be known as the discoverer of natural selection, but it would be unseemly to deny Wallace credit, too. So, it was arranged by Darwin and some friends that Wallace's paper and one by Darwin be read on July 1, 1858, in their absence, to the Linnean Society of London, thus establishing Darwin and Wallace as codiscoverers of natural selection. Darwin rushed through a short version of his projected work on evolution, which appeared in 1859 as *The Origin of Species by Means of Natural Selection or the Preservation of Favored Races in the Struggle for Life*. It presented his theory backed by a mass of supporting detail. It was revised until its sixth edition in 1872, as Darwin tried to answer his scientific critics—unsuccessfully, as it turned out—in ignorance of genetics. Darwin wrote numerous other works, including two on the descent of humans and the expression of emotion in humans and the animals. The latter two works form part of the founding of the psychology of adaptation and therefore will be considered in Chapter 9.

Reception and Influence

The world was well prepared for Darwin's theory. The idea of evolution was already around well before 1859, and when the *Origin* was published, it was taken seriously by learned men in all quarters. Biologists and naturalists greeted the work with varying degrees of criticism. Part of Darwin's thesis, that all living things descend from one common ancestor in the remote past, was scarcely novel and was widely accepted. Great difficulties were seen with the theory of natural selection, however, and it was still easy for scientists to hang on to some form of Lamarckism, to see the hand of God in progressive evolution, or to exempt humans from natural selection, as Darwin had, as yet, said nothing about them. Nevertheless, the implication that humans were part of nature was now hanging in the air, and Freud called Darwinism the second great blow to the human ego.

In many respects, Darwinism was not a revolution but part of the fulfillment of Enlightenment naturalism. Darwin cared only for his theory of natural selection, but others wove it into the emerging tapestry of a scientific image of humankind. Herbert Spencer, who had believed in the survival of the fittest before Darwin and applied it ruthlessly to humans and society, was one forceful proponent of metaphysical

Darwinism. Another was T. H. Huxley (1825–1895), who used evolution to batter the Bible, miracles, and the church generally.

Huxley did much to popularize Darwinism as a naturalistic, even scientistic metaphysics. Darwin's theory did not begin the modern crisis of conscience. Profound doubts about the existence of God and about the meaning of life go back to the eighteenth century. Darwinism was not the beginning of the scientific challenge to the old medieval–Renaissance worldview. It was the culmination of this challenge, making it most difficult to exempt human beings from immutable, determinate natural law. In *Man's Place in Nature* (1863/1954), Huxley carefully related mankind to the living apes, lower animals, and fossil ancestors, showing that we did indeed evolve from lower forms of life, that no Creation was needed. In the hands of people like Huxley, science then became not just the destroyer of illusions, but also a new metaphysics offering a new kind of salvation through science itself. Huxley wrote that:

> This new nature begotten by science upon fact . . . [constitutes] the foundation of our wealth and the condition of our safety . . . it is the bond which unites into a solid whole, regions larger than any empire of antiquity; it secures us from the recurrence of pestilences and famines of former times; it is the source of endless comforts and conveniences, which are not mere luxuries, but conduce to physical and moral well being.

More effusively, Winwood Reade wrote, in *The Martyrdom of Man:* "The God of Light, the Spirit of Knowledge, the Divine Intellect is gradually spreading over the planet. . . . Hunger and starvation will then be unknown. . . . Disease will be extirpated . . . immortality will be invented . . . Man will then be perfect . . . he will therefore be what the vulgar worship as a God" (quoted in Houghton, 1957, p. 152). This hope is similar to Comte's positivism, which Huxley called "Catholicism minus Christianity." For some, the new religion of scientific humanity was clearly at hand. Huxley (1863/1954) also boasted of science's practical fruits: "Every chemically pure substance employed in manufacture, every abnormally fertile race of plants, or rapidly growing and fattening breed of animals . . . ." This immediately brings to mind today's cancerous chemicals, tasteless tomatoes, and steroid-stuffed steers.

Darwinism did not instigate Victorian doubt, but it did intensify it. Darwin effected a Newtonian revolution in biology, robbing nature of her Romantic capital N, reducing evolution to random variation and happenstance victory in the struggle for survival. The beginning of the reduction of biological nature to chemical nature that was completed with the discovery of DNA had begun. In psychology, Darwinism led to the psychology of adaptation. Assuming evolution, one may ask how mind and behavior, as distinct from bodily organs, help each creature adapt to its surroundings. Skinner carefully modeled his radical behaviorism on Darwinian variation, selection, and retention. Skinner, however, tended to underestimate the degree to which each species, including *Homo sapiens,* has a nature shaped by its evolutionary heritage. Today, evolutionary psychology (Barkow, Cosmides, and Tooby, 1992; Dennett, 1996) is developing a more complete picture of human nature.

Many, however, could not accept naturalism or were depressed by it. Huxley himself, in his last writings, said that man was unique among animals, for by his intelligence he could lift himself out of the natural Cosmic Process and transcend organic evolution. Similar sentiments, not at all uncommon among both scientists and laypeople, help account for the popularity both before and after Darwin's time of various semi- or pseudoscientific trends based on the uniqueness of humanity. Beginning with Bishop Wilberforce and continuing with William Jennings Bryan, defenders of the Bible attacked evolution, only to be crushed by such powerful personalities as T. H. Huxley and Clarence Darrow. As the authority of science increased and the authority of religion declined, many people were attracted by movements that blended science and faith.

The Fringes of Science and the *Fin de Siècle*

As religious doubt deepened in the nineteenth century and the authority of science rose, many people began to turn to science to explain traditionally religious beliefs or to find support for them (Webb, 1974). Two movements resulting from these impulses bear on psychology. The first was mesmerism, which gave a Newtonian scientific explanation of personal healing. The second was psychical research, which purported to give scientific evidence for the existence of a personal, immortal soul. The two are united by their being scientific versions of religious ideas. As the parapsychologist J. B. Rhine said later, they wanted to "naturalize the supernatural."

Mesmerism: The First Popular Science

The term *mesmerism* comes from the name of the movement's founder, Franz Anton Mesmer (1734–1815), a Viennese physician who attributed numerous bodily diseases to an impalpable fluid penetrating the entire universe. Mesmer believed that this fluid was vital to the nervous activity of the body and that physicians could cure various diseases by manipulating the fluid in a patient's body. Mesmer began by using magnets to draw the fluid away from the afflicted areas, but he soon decided that the fluid was really susceptible to animal magnetism rather than to mineral magnetism. Mesmer devised a complicated and outre therapy for his patients, involving, among other things, striking the diseased parts of the body with his hands or a magic wand, tubs of water with iron rods focused on a patient's symptoms, and a "crisis room" lined with mattresses in which Mesmer's cures were effected during a kind of seizure. He specialized in what we now call "functional" illnesses, those that come from purely psychological causes. Although it was suggested at the time that at least some of the cures were a result of the patient's suggestibility, Mesmer firmly resisted any such hypothesis, insisting on his theory of animal fluids.

No single element of mesmerism was new. The curing of apparently physical diseases by inspired individuals is ancient in religions. It was also practiced by such contemporaries of Mesmer as Valentine Greatraks in England and Johann Gassner in Germany. Greatraks's specialty was scrofula, or the King's Evil, so-called because the touch of the monarch was said to cure it. If Mesmer's practice was not new, neither was the hypothesis of an ineffable universal fluid. Central to Newton's universe was the ether, a subtle fluid that carried electromagnetic waves and defined absolute space. A whole line of alchemical doctors had believed in a universal fluid essential to health, and even such a modern chemist as Robert Boyle attributed Greatraks's cures to invisible particles passing from doctor to patient. Gassner was a German priest who allegedly cast out demons. Mesmer himself investigated Gassner, concluding that Gassner's cures resulted from the natural use of animal magnetism, not religious exorcism.

Mesmer's novel approach was to try to put such cures and theorizing on a scientific basis. He attempted to convince medical establishments, first in Vienna and later in Paris, that his cures were genuine and that animal magnetism was real. Over and over again, physicians admitted that Mesmer had seemingly effected great cures, but they found his methods too bizarre, his theory unscientific. Some even intimated that he was a fraud. Mesmerism was too close to the occult—using trances, magical passes, and the trappings of the seance—to satisfy any Newtonian doctors. Mesmer was eventually worn down by these repeated rebuffs and by what he felt were betrayals by some of his followers. In 1784, he left Paris to live the rest of his life detached from the movement he had started.

That movement was enormously popular. In the years before the French Revolution, it garnered far more attention from the French public than the issues of the Revolution. Mesmeric lodges sprang up all over France in the 1780s. Mesmer enlisted the Marquis de Lafayette as a patron, and corresponded briefly with George Washington. Mesmer and mesmerism seemed to fill perfectly a gap left by religion's receding influence. Science was all the rage in the late eighteenth century, and its influence grew in the nineteenth. People were hungry for a new set of certainties to replace the old. Mesmer offered at least the trappings of science—a reasoned theory about why his cures worked, an explanation that also covered the ancient miracle workers. Yet, at the same time, Mesmer's practice, served up in mystical and magical dress, was more interesting than the austere rationalism of Newton's science. In short, Mesmer offered exactly the right pseudoscience for the times. It was scientific enough to appeal to the new rationalism, but spiritual enough to appeal to latent religious needs as well.

Whether Mesmer himself was a charlatan is an extremely difficult question to answer. He demanded absolute obedience from his followers, lest they betray his invention (but so did Freud). His treatment sessions were lurid seances, with Mesmer attired in mystic robes and wielding an iron wand. Moreover, Mesmer drifted into genuine occultism, using animal magnetism to explain clairvoyance, telepathy, and precognition. Yet Mesmer always tried to convince the medical establishment, even when it brought him nothing but ridicule. Mesmer was at once a magician and a pioneer in abnormal psychology.

There was at the center of mesmerism a useful tool for the treatment of neuroses. Mesmer did cure many people of a great range of hysterical symptoms, from hysterical blindness to mysterious pains. He obscured the sources of his cures with the trappings of the seance and the theory of the universal fluid. What was central to Mesmer's cures, however, was the trance he could induce in his patients. In this trance, he could command their actions and effect a cure. Although Mesmer attributed the trance to animal magnetism, it became apparent to his critics and even to some of his followers that something simpler was involved. The trance was due to the psychological control of one person over another rather than the passing of an invisible fluid from one body to another.

Once this insight was obtained, it became possible to extract the mesmeric trance from the mystical context Mesmer had given it and make it into a tool for the ordinary physician. Mesmerism was transformed into hypnotism.

This transformation began in France, the locale of Mesmer's greatest successes and greatest denunciations. In 1825, the French Royal Academy of Sciences decided to look into animal magnetism again, and its report, delivered in 1831, was far more favorable than any Mesmer had received in his lifetime. Without Mesmer's abrasive personality and occult theory, the magnetic trance could be viewed more objectively as an unusual but real mental state that was of possible use to doctors and merited further investigation.

In the late 1830s, animal magnetism was brought to England by the Baron Dupotet de Sennevoy, who conducted a series of magnetic demonstrations. They caught the attention of a young, radical, and innovative physician named John Elliotson (1791–1868). He began to use magnetism both as a cure for various diseases and as an anesthetic drug during surgery. Like Mesmer, Elliotson was eventually drummed out of established medicine for his beliefs. He founded a journal devoted to animal magnetism and phrenology, and encouraged other physicians to use magnetism in their practices. James Esdaile (1808–1859) was another persecuted English physician who tried to use mesmerism, especially as an anesthetic (1852). Despite his popularity with the natives of India, where he worked, the government denied support for his mesmeric hospital.

The transformation of mesmerism was completed by James Braid (1795–1860), who named it neuro-hypnotism, or more briefly hypnotism, derived from the Greek *hypnos,* meaning sleep. Braid considered the hypnotic state to be "nervous sleep." He began as a skeptic of mesmerism, but his own investigations convinced him that the phenomena were real enough; it was the theory of animal magnetism that was incorrect. In *Neurypnology,* Braid (1843, pp. 19–20) wrote: "The phenomena of mesmerism were to be accounted for on the principle of a derangement of the state of the cerebrospinal center . . . induced by a fixed state, absolute repose of the body, [and] fixed attention. . . ." The hypnotic state, Braid wrote, depends "on the physical and psychical [mental] condition of the patient . . . not at all on the volition or passes of the operator, throwing out a magnetic fluid, or exciting into activity some mystical universal fluid or medium." Braid rescued hypnotism from the occult surroundings of mesmerism and gave it to scientific medicine. But Braid himself encountered resistance from the medical establishment. The development of chemical anesthetics rendered the use of hypnosis in surgery unnecessary. Even today, hypnotism has not completely shed its occult image.

In France, hypnotism advanced as a treatment for hysteria. In this connection, two theories arose as to the nature of the hypnotic trance. A. A. Liebeault (1823–1904) began one school of thought in Nancy, France, which was carried on by his student Hippolyte Bernheim (1837–1919). The Nancy school held that the hypnotic state was an intensification of certain tendencies in ordinary sleep or wakefulness. Some actions, even sophisticated ones, are automatic: We all respond impulsively to some suggestions; we all hallucinate in dreams. According to the Nancy school, in hypnosis the conscious will loses its usual close control over perception and action, and the orders of the hypnotist pass immediately and unconsciously into action or hallucinatory perception. The rival school of the Salpêtrière Hospital in Paris maintained that, because hypnotic suggestion could be used to remove hysteric symptoms, the hypnotic state must be a completely abnormal one, found in hysteric patients only. Hypnosis and hysteria were both seen as evidence of a pathological nervous system. The leading spokesman for the Salpêtrière school was Jean Martin Charcot (1825–1893), under whom Freud studied for several months. With Freud, the study of hypnotism became part of the psychology of the unconscious, for Freud used hypnosis in his early activities as a psychotherapist. Subsequent developments have supported the Nancy school's concept of hypnosis, but today the exact nature of the hypnotic state, including its proposed existence as a distinct state of consciousness, still remains unclear.

Revolt against Materialism: Spiritualism and Psychic Research

The doctrine of materialism and the religion of positivism may have inspired enthusiasts of scientism, but many people were unsettled and even repelled by them. The crisis of naturalism got worse after Huxley proclaimed humans to be only well-developed apes. Traditional religion seemed to many people to be moribund; blind faith in an immortal soul had been annihilated. So, especially after 1859, many thoughtful people, including well-known scientists, turned to science itself for assurance that there was more to human life than the bodily machine.

"The discovery that there was a life in man independent of blood and brain would be a cardinal, a dominating fact in all science and in all philosophy." So wrote Frederic Myers (1843–1901), the leading psychical researcher of the nineteenth century. Myers was horrified even as a child with the thought of not living forever. This fear was intensified when, like many Victorians, he lost his religious faith during his education. He met the philosopher Henry Sidgwick, who encouraged Myers to search scientifically for evidence of immortality. Sidgwick, too, had lost his faith, but he deeply believed that ethics required personal immortality for the rectification of evil on earth. Myers took up Sidgwick's challenge and gathered an enormous amount of relevant data. Sidgwick and Myers founded the Society for Psychical Research, and in 1882 their journal published Myers's findings. These were also published posthumously in two volumes in 1903.

Simply as a catalog of unusual psychological phenomena, Myers's *Human Personality and Its Survival of Bodily Death* (1903) won the respect of no less a psychologist than William James, himself once president of the Society for Psychical Research. Although from its title one might expect a collection of ghost stories, Myers in fact surveyed the realm of abnormal psychology, from sleep and hysteria to messages from departed spirits. Myers's approach to his problem was psychological. He was the first English writer to disseminate Freud's early studies of hysteria. Hysteria was an important phenomenon for Myers, for it demonstrated the power of purely mental activity over the body when physical symptoms are caused by psychological disturbances.

Indeed, Myers fixed on exactly what Freud found most instructive in his early cases, that a hysteric's symptoms express unconscious desires that the patient does not want to admit to consciousness. Like Freud, Myers formulated a theory of the unconscious, which Myers called the subliminal self. In Freud's hands, the unconscious was an affront to human pride, revealing the irrational, impulsive, frightening depths that underlie rational, discursive conscious thought. Myers's conception of the subliminal self, however, was romantic, Platonic, optimistic, and progressive. True, the subliminal self is irrational, said Myers, but it enables us to communicate with a spiritual world that transcends the material one. The existence of the subliminal self demonstrated for Myers the separability of soul and matter. It opened up the prospect of more than material evolution, in which the individual plays only a brief part; in spiritual, cosmic evolution, each soul perfects itself forever, actualizing mental powers hindered by our animal bodies. Although Myers scientifically investigated spiritualistic phenomena—and he was as skeptical of mediums as anyone could wish—his scientific searching was really guided by a Neoplatonic and occult view of the cosmos.

On occasion, Myers could sound like a Huxleyan naturalist, as when he wrote: "The authority of creeds and Churches will be replaced by the authority of observation and experiment," but psychical research was not well received in Huxley's circle. Huxley (1871) himself sarcastically denounced spiritualism, likening "the talk in the spiritual world" to "the chatter of old women and curates," and saying of both, "They do not interest me." Despite this hostility, the intellectuals of the Society for Psychical Research carried on, and, at the popular level, spiritualism approached a mania around the turn of the century. As quickly as debunkers (magicians Harry Houdini and John Maskelyne, for example) exposed fake mediums, new ones sprang up. The dialectic of paranormal claim and skeptical counterclaim continues today, as illustrated by the controversy over persons such as Uri Geller. Psychical research, now called parapsychology, persists in scholarly journals and research programs, and college courses in the subject proliferate. Nevertheless, it is an even more suspect subject than hypnotism, and its very mention makes most psychologists uncomfortable.

TOWARD THE SCIENCE OF PSYCHOLOGY

Within the general intellectual climate of the nineteenth century, developments in various areas made important contributions to the nascent science of psychology.

Understanding the Brain and Nervous System

The Brain

So far, in treating the history of psychology, we have found it to be primarily part of philosophy. Even the occasional physician-psychologists generally founded their psychologies on philosophical, not physiological, principles. Hartley is a case in point. He erected his psychology on the principles of associationist philosophy and only buttressed it with Newton's speculative account of nerve function. The separation of the physiological and philosophical portions of Hartley's psychology was so complete that his follower, Priestley, could issue an edition of Hartley's *Observations on Man* that omitted all the physiology. Hartley wanted to create a psychology that combined philosophy and physiology, but philosophy clearly came first.

Franz Joseph Gall (1758–1828) reversed this relationship. Gall may fairly be regarded as the founder of neuropsychology because he was the first to take seriously the idea that the brain is the seat of the soul. The idea was hardly new: Plato believed it; the Hellenistic scientists of Alexandria demonstrated it; the medieval faculty psychologists located each faculty in a different portion of the brain. However, beyond encouraging materialism, the concept had little effect on psychological thought. The locations assigned to the medieval faculties were based on prior analysis of mind, not brain, and philosophical psychology had done nothing to change this. Gall, however, stated that the brain was the specific organ of mental activity, in the same way that the stomach is the organ of digestion and the lungs the organs of respiration. Therefore, the study of human nature should begin with those functions of the brain that give rise to thought and action, rather than with abstract and introspective inquiries into mind.

The philosophical background against which Gall reacted was French empiricism and associationism, especially Condillac's sensationism. Gall offered several reproaches to that philosophical approach to psychology (Young, 1970). To begin with, the empiricists claimed that experience was the proper basis of science, yet their own psychology, Hume's science of human nature, was wholly speculative, having no reference to objective behavior or to the brain that controls it. Furthermore, the categories of analysis used by the philosophes were "mere abstractions." None of the faculties proposed by philosophers—such as memory, attention, and imagination—was specific enough to explain actual human behavior and concrete individual differences. In *On the Functions of the Brain,* Gall wrote: "How are we to explain, by sensation in general, by attention [etc.] . . . the origin and exercise of the principle of propagation; that of the love of offspring, of the instinct of attachment? How explain by all these generalities, the talents for music, for mechanics, for a sense of the relations of space, for painting, poetry, etc." The philosophers' faculties exist but "they are not applicable to the detailed study of a species, or an individual. Every man, except an idiot, enjoys all these faculties. Yet all men have not the same intellectual or moral character. We need faculties, the different distribution of which shall determine the different species of animals, and the different proportions of which explain the differences in individuals" (quoted in Young, 1970, p. 18). In short, the philosophers' concepts are useless for the specific empirical investigations that science requires.

Gall's ideas brought him into conflict with empiricist philosophers in a final way. Condillac had attempted to derive every faculty of mind from sensation and association. Gall, however, believing the brain to be the organ of the mind, concluded that each of his proposed faculties was innate, based in a particular region of the brain. Gall's approach also implies a comparative psychology. Given that the brains of species differ up and down the Great Chain of Being (Gall wrote before Darwin), so should the corresponding faculties differ. In fact, Gall carried out comparative anatomical studies to support this argument.

The problem for Gall, then, was to correlate specific behavioral functions with particular regions of the brain. Although he carried out detailed anatomical studies of the brain and nervous system, he found the techniques of his time too crude to answer the questions he posed, and he had moral scruples about experimenting on living but "martyrized" animals. Gall's method, therefore, was different. He assumed that well-developed faculties would correspond to well-developed parts of the brain. Those "organs" corresponding to the well-developed faculties in the brain would be larger than those organs corresponding to less developed faculties, and their relative size would be registered on the skull as bumps overlying the developed organ. Empirically, then, Gall's method was to show that people possessing certain striking traits would possess skulls with bumps over the corresponding organs of the brain, and that weak traits would go with undeveloped brain organs and skull regions. Although Gall's specific hypothesis was new, the idea that personality traits reveal themselves in physique and face was as old as antiquity. Gall's theory has been schematized by Young (1970), as shown in Figure 6–1.

Thus, Gall could observe an individual's unique behaviors and correlate them with cranial prominences. On the basis of such observations, Gall drew up a long list of faculties—destructiveness, friendship, and language, for example—and located each in a particular region of the brain. Destructiveness, for example, was located just above the ear. Later followers of Gall expanded his list to include such faculties as veneration, whose presence was believed to show that God must exist to be the object of veneration.

Certain conceptual features of Gall's approach have been mentioned: It was nativistic; it compared humans with other animals; it was materialistic, although Gall

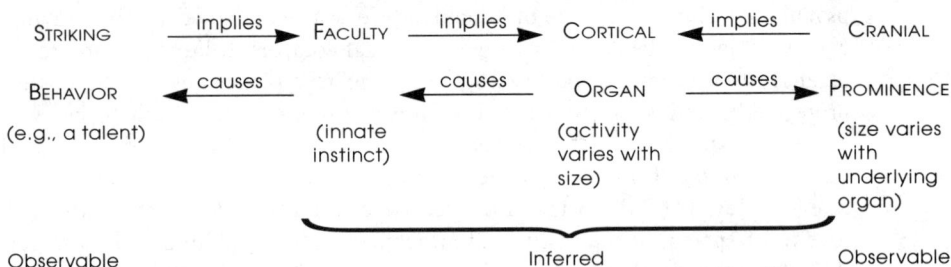

STRIKING	→implies→	FACULTY	→implies→	CORTICAL	←implies←	CRANIAL
BEHAVIOR	←causes←		←causes←	ORGAN	→causes→	PROMINENCE
(e.g., a talent)		(innate instinct)		(activity varies with size)		(size varies with underlying organ)
Observable			Inferred			Observable

FIGURE 6-1   Gall's theory of mind, brain, and behavior. (Adapted from Young, 1970)

himself struggled against this tendency. Gall's psychology was also behavioristic rather than introspectionistic. His system rested on the observation of behaviors and of bumps on the skull rather than on the introspection of his own mind. Gall's psychology was therefore the first *objective*, rather than *subjective, psychology.* More broadly, Gall's was a functional psychology concerned with how the mind and its organ, the brain, actually adapt a person or animal to everyday demands. Philosophical psychology was more concerned with grand problems of epistemology. Finally, Gall's psychology was a psychology of individual differences. He explicitly rejected the study of the generalized adult mind in favor of a study of how people differ.

Gall's conception pointed in two directions, one scientific and one occult. Scientifically, it inspired more experimentally minded physiologists to investigate the localization of behavioral functions in particular parts of the brain. At the hands of these men, Gall's system suffered badly. His specific locations were found to be faulty. Worse, the basic assumptions that size of brain corresponds to strength of faculty and that bumps on the skull conform to the shape of the brain, were found to be without foundation. The entire system was violently rejected as a pseudoscience, appealing, like astrology, only to the credulous lay society.

The appeal to the lay society was the other direction—the occult direction—taken by Gall's ideas. His close associate, Johann Caspar Spurzheim (1776–1832), who coined the term phrenology (which Gall refused to accept), popularized the concept by turning it into a general and optimistic philosophy of life. In Spurzheim's hands, phrenology became the new popular psychology, and Spurzheim aimed to reform education, religion, and penology. His missionary activities carried him to the United States, where the ground was most fertile for phrenology. He died shortly after arriving, but his work was carried on by the English phrenologist George Combe. The story of phrenology in the United States belongs to Chapter 9, on the psychology of adaptation, where we will find that precisely those features in phrenology that appealed to ordinary Americans were also those that ensured the success of evolutionary psychology in America.

Gall's major critic was a leading French physiologist, Jean-Pierre-Marie Flourens (1794–1867), a pioneer in experimental brain research. Flourens discovered the functions of the various lower parts of the brain, but, regarding the cerebral hemispheres, he parted company with Gall. Flourens ridiculed phrenology and argued on the basis of his own research—which involved lesioning or ablating parts of the brain—that the cerebral hemispheres act as a unit, containing no specialized organs for special mental faculties. In his conclusions, Flourens was more dominated by philosophical ideas than Gall was. Flourens was a Cartesian dualist who viewed the soul as residing in the cerebral hemispheres, and, said Flourens, since the soul is unitary, the action of the hemispheres must be so too. He believed there was no organic connection between the sensory and motor functions of the lower parts of the brain and the cerebrum. Flourens's stature assured the success of his attack on Gall, and his view of the unitary action of the cerebrum remained orthodox dogma for decades.

The Nervous System

In 1822, a discovery of momentous long-term implications (Cranefield, 1974) was announced by François Magendie (1783–1855). Earlier, on the basis of post-mortem dissections, the English physiologist Charles Bell (1774–1842) had distinguished two sets of nerves at the base of the spinal column. Bell suggested that one set carried information to the brain (sensory nerves), while the other carried information from the brain to the muscles (motor nerves). Previously, it had been thought that nerves work in both directions. Magendie discovered the same thing independently and more conclusively, because he demonstrated the different functions of the nerves in the spinal column by direct experiment on living animals. The next decade in brain physiology brought the extension of the sensorimotor distinctions up the spinal column and into the cerebrum. Magendie, however, did not take this step. Like Flourens, his views on the functions of the cerebral hemispheres were controlled by a philosophy—in Magendie's case, by a modified sensationism. For Magendie, all faculties were just modifications of perception, and he saw no role for the hemispheres in the direct control of behavior. The empiricist philosophy traces sensations and their associations as concepts are formed by the understanding, but it says little or nothing about human action. Magendie, therefore, went no further in his physiology.

Another breakthrough in the study of the functions of the cerebrum suggested that Gall was at least correct in asserting that different parts of the brain have specific behavioral functions. This discovery was made by Pierre Paul Broca (1824–1880), who observed that patients with speech disorders showed, when autopsied, damage to the same area of the left frontal lobe of the brain. Broca, who rejected the study of bumps on the head, viewed his finding as limited support for Gall, although the faculty of language had not been found where Gall had predicted.

Meanwhile, other researchers had been extending the distinction between sensory and motor nerves up the spine and into the cranium. Young (1970, p. 204) reports that, in 1845, one English physician wrote, "The brain . . . is subject to the laws of reflex action, and that, in this respect it does not differ from the other ganglia of the nervous system . . . [and] must necessarily be regulated . . . by laws identical with those governing the spinal ganglia and their analogues in the lower animals." That is, it was known that the involuntary reflexes of the lower nervous system work by sensorimotor reflex, and it is suggested here that the cerebrum works the same way.

Against this view was the observation that the cerebral hemispheres seemed insensitive. They had been poked, prodded, pressed, and pricked, but no movement resulted in living animals. This supported Flourens's view that the hemispheres were not involved in action. However, in 1870, two German researchers, Gustav Fritsch and Eduard Hitzig, announced that electrical excitation of the cerebrum can elicit movement, and that different parts of the brain, when stimulated, seem to regulate different movements.

This finding encouraged others to map out the brain, locating each sensory and motor function. Today, brain maps are remarkably precise and allow tumors to be located with great accuracy. A "new phrenology" was thus born, in which each part of the brain was assigned a discrete sensory or behavioral function. But the new localizations were different from Gall's, for they resulted from an extension of the sensorimotor nerve distinction to the cerebrum. Some parts of the brain receive sensations, others govern specific actions, and the association of sensation and action produces behavior. In this view, the brain is a complex reflex machine. It should be pointed out here that not all neurophysiologists accepted then, or accept now, the localization of brain functions. Some maintain that the brain acts at least in some respects as a unit, and that information present in one part of the brain is at least potentially present in others.

The formulation of the brain as a reflex device associating sensory input with motor action made possible the integration of associationism with scientific rather than speculative physiology, and the extension of associationism and empiricism to action as well as understanding.

Inventing Experimental Methods

Mental Chronometry

An important function of astronomy is to precisely map the stars. Until the advent of modern mechanical and photographic methods in which an astronomer rarely looks through a telescope, accurately locating stars depended on the ability of an astronomer to note the exact moment when a star passed a point directly overhead, marked by a single cross-hair in the telescope's field of vision. In one common early method, the astronomer noted the exact time on a clock when a star entered the field of vision and then counted as the clock beat seconds until the star crossed the cross-hair. Accurate notation of the exact moment of transit was critical; slight errors would be translated into immense interstellar distances in calculating the exact positions of stars in the galaxy.

In 1795, an assistant astronomer at Greenwich Observatory lost his job when his superior discovered that his own transit-times were about 0.5 second faster than his assistant's. The head astronomer naturally assumed his own times to be correct and his assistant's in error. Years later, this event came to the attention of the German astronomer F. W. Bessel (1784–1846), who began systematically to compare the transit-times of different astronomers. Bessel discovered that all astronomers differed in the speed with which they reported transits. To correct this grave situation, Bessel constructed "personal equations" so that the differences among astronomers could be canceled out in astronomical calculations. For example, the "personal equation" of the two Greenwich astronomers would be Junior − Superior = 0.5 sec. The observations of any pair of astronomers could be compared in these equations reflecting their personal reaction times, and calculations of star positions could be corrected accordingly. Unfortunately for astronomers, use of the personal equations assumed that individual differences were stable, which proved to be false. Indeed, experiments with artificial stars, which had known transit-times, showed that sometimes observers "saw" the star intersect the cross-hair before it occurred. Only the increasing automation of observation was able to eliminate these problems.

Meanwhile, the reaction-time experiment had been independently devised by the great German physicist Hermann von Helmholtz, to answer the question of the speed of nerve conduction. In 1850, Helmholtz stimulated the motor nerve of a frog's leg at points near and far from the muscle itself, measuring the time it took for the muscle to respond. Before Helmholtz's investigation, it had been widely assumed that nerve impulses traveled at infinite or at least immeasurably fast speeds. Helmholtz estimated the speed to be only 26 meters per second.

These two lines of research on reaction time came together in the work of F. C. Donders (1818–1889), a Dutch physiologist. Donders saw that the time between a stimulus and its response could be used to objectively quantify the speed of mental processes. Helmholtz had measured the simplest sort of stimulus–response (S–R) reaction, and astronomers had, for another purpose, investigated mental processes such as judgment. It was Donders's special contribution to use reaction time to infer the action of complex mental processes. So, for example, one could measure a person's simple key-press response to a single stimulus—a mild shock to the foot. This is simple reaction time. However, one might ask the subject to press a key with the left hand when the left foot is shocked and with the right hand when the right foot is shocked. A simple reaction is still involved, but the subject must discriminate which foot is shocked and choose which response to make. If simple reaction takes, for example, 150 msec to complete, and the discrimination-and-choice experiment takes 230 msec to complete, then, Donders reasoned, the mental actions of choice and discrimination inserted into the simple reaction must take 230 msec − 150 msec, or 80 msec. This method, which seemed to offer an objective way of measuring physiological and mental processes, was called *mental chronometry*.

The method was taken up early by Wundt and extensively used by the early mentalistic psychologists. Precisely because it was a quantitative method, it helped to ensure the scientific stature of experimental psychology as apart from qualitative philosophical psychology. It took the mind out of the armchair and into the laboratory. The use of reaction times has had its ups and downs in the subsequent history of psychology, but it remains an important technique today.

Psychophysics: Psychology's First Research Program

The dean of historians of psychology, E. G. Boring, dates the founding of experimental psychology to the publication, in 1860, of *Elements of Psychophysics,* written by a retired physicist, Gustav Theodore Fechner (1801–1887). Boring's claim rests on the fact that Fechner conceived and carried out the first systematic research in experimental psychology—research, moreover, that produced mathematical laws. Before Fechner, philosophers had widely assumed, following Kant, that the mind can neither be experimented on nor subjected to mathematical scrutiny. Fechner showed these assumptions to be false. The difficulties do at first seem to be immense. In physics, we can manipulate objects and observe what they do, and we can measure their position and momentum, writing mathematical laws interrelating these variables (such as Newton's inverse-square law of gravitation). However, minds are private, and no instruments can be applied to conscious experiences.

Fechner's greatness was to overcome these problems. He saw that the content of consciousness can be manipulated by controlling the stimuli to which a person is exposed. This control makes mental experiment possible. We can have a person lift objects of known weight, listen to tones of known pitch and volume, and so on. Even so, how do we measure the resulting conscious experiences, or sensations? We can assign no number to a tone or weight sensation. Fechner perceived the difficulty and got around it by quantifying sensations indirectly. We can ask a subject to say which of two weights is heavier, which of two tones is louder. By systematically varying both the absolute values of the pairs of stimuli and the differences between them, and by observing when subjects can and cannot distinguish the pairs, sensation can be indirectly quantified. Hence, we can mathematically relate stimulus magnitude (R) with the resulting strength of sensation (S). One might expect that sensation would vary directly with stimulus, but Fechner found it did not. Instead, he found that $S = k \log R$ (where k is a constant). That is, stimulus differences are easier to detect when both stimuli are of moderate absolute intensity than when they are of high absolute intensity (for example, it would be easier to distinguish a 10-ounce weight from an 11-ounce weight than a 10-pound weight from a 10-pound, 1-ounce weight).

Fechner's approach was not without antecedents. The basic method of asking subjects to distinguish stimulus differences had been pioneered by a physiologist, E. H. Weber (1795–1878). The concept of treating sensations as quantitatively varying conscious states goes back to Leibniz's monads and his doctrines of petite perception and apperception. The immediate motivation of Fechner's work was the mind–body problem. Fechner held a dual aspect position, believing that mind and brain were simply two aspects of the same underlying reality, and therefore that physical stimuli and subjective sensations ought to be functionally related. Fechner hoped his psychophysics would solve the mind–body problem.

Fechner is not the founder of the science of psychology because, unlike Wundt, he carved out no societally recognized role for psychologists to take. Nevertheless, Fechner founded experimental psychology, for his methods, broadened to encompass more than sensations, were basic to Wundt's experimental psychology of consciousness. In Wundt's experiments, antecedent stimulus conditions were controlled, as in Fechner's, and data were provided as subjects reported the resulting conscious content. It was not Wundt's only method, but it was an important one, and it was the one most of his students carried away with them from his laboratory.

Philosophy to the Threshold of Psychology

In 1851, Alexander Bain wrote to his friend and colleague, John Stuart Mill, "There is nothing I wish more than so to unite psychology and physiology that physiologists may be made to appreciate the true ends and drift of their researches into the nervous system." Bain fulfilled his desire in two massive volumes, *The Senses and the Intellect* (1855) and *The Emotions and the Will* (1859). Bain's comprehensive survey of psychology from the standpoints of associationism and physiology embraced every psychological topic from simple sensation to aesthetics and ethics.

Bain's importance lies in his synthesis of material borrowed from others. The idea of uniting physiology and philosophical psychology was ancient. His associationism derived from Hartley and the Mills. His physiology was drawn from the sensorimotor physiology of the German physiologist, Johannes Müller (1801–1858). In his *Elements of Physiology* (1842), Müller had already proposed that the role of the brain is to associate incoming sensory information with appropriate motor responses. Bain knew the *Elements* and incorporated Müller's conception of the role of the brain into his psychology. Thus, Bain united the philosophy of associationism with sensorimotor physiology to give a unified human psychology. Even today, most general psychology texts are organized like Bain's, beginning with simple nerve function in sensation and working up to thinking and social relations. Bain's integration was quite influential. He wrote before the functions of the cerebrum were known, and his uncompromising associative view of physiology guided later English investigators to press their studies into the mysterious cerebral hemispheres.

Bain had a considerable lasting effect on psychology. The journal *Mind,* which he founded in 1874, is still in existence as an organ of philosophical psychology. He was, however, too philosophical in his outlook; his conception of mind was soon out of date. Despite his use of physiological data, he did no experiments, and although he recognized the importance of Darwin's work, his associationism remained preevolutionary. In the long run, it was his practical attitude toward psychology that mattered. Like the phrenology that had once excited him, Bain wanted to explain human action, not just consciousness. His ideas about behavior would be developed by American pragmatists.

The last notable French philosophical psychologist was Hippolyte-Adolphe Taine (1828–1893). Although most of his works were on history and literature, he was most proud of his psychological book, *On Intelligence* (1870, 1875), which William James used as his text when he first taught psychology at Harvard. In *On Intelligence,* Taine presents an integration of association psychology similar to Bain's, arguing that all ideas, no matter how apparently abstract, may be reduced to a collection of sensations associated with each idea's name. The business of psychology is thus similar to chemistry's—"to decompose [compounds] into their elements to show the different groupings these elements are capable of, and to construct different compounds with them" (Taine, 1875). Following Leibniz, Taine proposed that conscious sensations are simply aggregates of weaker, more fleeting sensations that are only marginally conscious at best.

Taine also discussed the physiological substrate of sensation. He maintained a dual-aspect psychophysical parallelism, holding that every event in consciousness has a corresponding neural event. According to Taine, the reverse is not true because some neural events give rise only to unconscious sensations. Taine's neurophysiology presents the brain as an unspecialized organ associating stimulus and response: "The brain, then, is the repeater of the sensory centers." That is, the brain simply copies incoming neural information, as mental images copy sensations. Mind and brain are both seen in terms similar to Hume's or Hartley's.

In Germany, philosophical psychology struggled with the mixed legacy of Kantian idealism. Certain concepts of the idealists found a place in early German psychology. Wundt studied individual consciousness; proposed a historical, genetic approach to the investigation of the higher mental processes; and stressed human will as the unifying force in mental life. All of these ideas are part of idealist philosophy. Freud, too, was influenced by Schopenhauer's concept of unconscious primitive forces lurking in the personality. Nevertheless, the German idealists, following Kant, took a dim view of psychology as a would-be science. Psychology studies only a concrete individual, or a set of individuals, whereas the idealists sought transcendent Platonic knowledge of a godlike Absolute Spirit, which they took to be the noumenal reality behind physical appearances and the individual mind. Empirical research seems trivial in the idealist context, and the idealists—most forcefully Hegel—actively opposed the development of empirical psychology (Leary, 1978, 1980).

The leading German philosophical psychologist was Hermann Lotze (1817–1881). Before he turned to philosophy, Lotze received his M.D., and he was Fechner's friend and physician. In one respect, Lotze appears to be German psychology's Bain or Taine. In his *Outlines of Psychology* (1881), Lotze proposed an empiricist view of consciousness, saying that depth perception is learned, not innate, and experience is compounded out of simple ideas. This empiricism he integrated with the growing sensorimotor concept of brain function.

However, Lotze was not wholly dedicated to empiricism and naturalism. He insisted that, although physiology offered a valid approach to the material aspects of mind and behavior, human beings and animals each possessed divinely given souls. As was typical of German philosophers, Lotze emphatically rejected materialism in favor of Cartesian dualism. By insisting on the spiritual side of humans, Lotze earned the admiration of English-speaking psychologists who were dissatisfied with the associationistic and reductive psychologies they found around them. Among them were James Ward, the English psychologist who bitterly attacked naturalism, and William James, the tender-minded psychologist who took part in psychical research.

A more consistent exponent of naturalism and empiricism was Hermann von Helmholtz (1821–1894), probably the greatest natural scientist of the nineteenth century. For much of his career, he was occupied with physiology. We have already learned of his measurement of the speed of nerve conduction; he also conducted definitive studies of physiological optics and acoustics. But he was also a leading physicist: he formulated the law of conservation of energy when he was only twenty-six.

Helmholtz's approach to the mind was essentially that of a Lockean empiricism in which ideas are interpreted as mental content. Helmholtz argued that all we know for certain are our ideas, or images of the world gathered by experience. He struck a pragmatic note by acknowledging that we cannot know whether our ideas are true, but argued that this does not matter as long as they lead to effective action in the real world. Science was an example of such effective action. Although he followed Kant in holding causality to be an innate principle, Helmholtz, like the empiricists, maintained that the other Kantian categories of knowledge are acquired.

Of particular importance to psychology is Helmholtz's theory of unconscious inference. If, for example, visual perception of space is not an innate intuition, then, in the course of development, we must learn to calculate the distance of objects from us, as Berkeley proposed. Yet we are not aware of performing such calculations. Helmholtz theorized that these kinds of calculations, or inferences, must be unconscious and moreover must be unconsciously learned, as happens in language acquisition. Like words, ideas (including sensations) are mental contents that represent reality. Just as children learn language spontaneously and with no direct instruction, so too they spontaneously and unconsciously learn the meanings of ideas.

As we would expect of a physicist and physiologist, Helmholtz was a forceful advocate of the natural sciences. He welcomed their growth in the German universities and heaped scorn on the idealist philosophers for whom natural science was the trivial study of physical reality, which was of no consequence compared to the spirit behind physical reality. Furthermore, Helmholtz's own researches supported materialism. His physiological studies of sensation established the dependence of perception on mere fleshly matter. His theory of conservation of energy inspired some young physiologists to swear, as Helmholtz's friend Emil du Bois-Reymond put it in a letter, "a solemn oath to put in effect this truth: no other forces than the common physical-chemical ones are active within the organism" (Kahl, 1971). This attitude encouraged the young Freud to compose his unfinished "Psychology for neurologists."

Helmholtz, however, was aware of the dangers of too much materialism when he wrote, in "Thought in Medicine" (1877/1971, pp. 355–6): "Our generation has had to suffer under the tyranny of spiritualistic metaphysics; the younger generation will probably have to guard against materialistic metaphysics." He continues, "Please do not forget that materialism is a metaphysical hypothesis. . . . If one forgets this, materialism becomes a dogma [compare this to the "solemn oath" above] which hinders the progress of science and, like all dogmas, leads to violent intolerance." Helmholtz could not accept spiritualism or vitalism, but neither could he accept aggressive materialism.

CONCLUSION

The Nineteenth-Century Crisis

The nineteenth century was a century of conflicts and its conflicts are our conflicts. The Industrial Revolution brought unparalleled material progress and tremendous urban poverty. Religious revival was widespread, even as the foundations of belief were steadily eroded by science. People were inculcated with acute and ferocious sexual morality, while allowing—or causing—prostitution and crime to be endemic. The sciences and humanities flourished as never before, but the practical businessman sneered at the ivory tower intellectual. Pessimism and optimism mixed in the same mind. Wrote Carlyle: "Deep and sad as is our feeling that we stand yet in the bodeful night; equally deep, indestructible is our assurance that the morning also will not fail" (quoted in Houghton, 1957, p. 27).

Central to the nineteenth century was the conflict between the new scientific naturalism and the older beliefs in a transcendent spiritual reality. Naturalism, product of the Enlightenment, occasioned both hope and despair. It held out the hope of perpetual progress, of the perfectibility of humanity, of useful and profound knowledge of the universe. Yet it challenged the traditional beliefs people had accumulated and lived by for centuries. Science also threatened to dehumanize humans, reducing the individual to a collection of chemicals laboring in a vast industrial machine. It seemed to strip the world of meaning—and each person, of freedom and dignity.

Proponents of naturalism did not see the conflicts. They believed that technical, scientific solutions could be found for every human problem. Their problem was to convince society of their sincerity and efficacy. Science became scientism, a new religion, most clearly seen in Comte's positivism but also present in popularizing scientists such as Huxley. The naturalists benefited from being united in a single Newtonian conception of nature, differing among themselves only in detail. Forceful, optimistic, successful, natural science came to dominate the intellectual world.

Founding Psychology

Out of the nineteenth century emerged the three founding forms of psychology. Wundt founded the *psychology of consciousness*. Freud founded the *psychology of the unconscious*. And various evolutionary psychologists founded the *psychology of adaptation*. All the concepts for each were in place, awaiting only the creative minds and forceful personalities needed to weld them into coherent psychological programs.

BIBLIOGRAPHY

The literature on the nineteenth century is understandably vast. For social history, at least in Victorian England, see Houghton (1957); W. J. Reader, *Life in Victorian England* (New York: Capricorn, 1964); or G. M. Young, *Victorian England: Portrait of an age* (New York: Oxford University Press, 1953); and, for the late nineteenth and early twentieth centuries, Samuel Hynes, *The Edwardian turn of mind* (Princeton, NJ: Princeton University Press, 1968). For intellectual history, see Owen Chadwick, *The secularization of the European mind in the nineteenth century* (Cambridge, England: Cambridge University Press, 1975); Elie Halevy, *The growth of philosophical radicalism* (Boston: Beacon Press, 1955); Maurice Mandlebaum, *History, man, and reason: A study in nineteenth-century thought* (Baltimore: Johns Hopkins University Press, 1971); John Passmore, *A hundred years of philosophy,* rev. ed. (New York: Basic Books, 1966); W. M. Simon, *European positivism in the nineteenth century* (Ithaca, NY: Cornell University Press, 1963); and D. C. Somerville, *English thought in the nineteenth century* (New York: David McKay, 1929). Patrick L. Gardiner, ed., *Nineteenth century philosophy* (New York: Free Press, 1969), collects important writings by the major philosophers.

The worlds of the nineteenth century are well covered in the general sources and the references. Some additional useful sources are worth noting. As a spokesman for romanticism, Edmund Burke resembles Vico and Herder; see L. Bredvold and G. Ross, eds., *The philosophy of Edmund Burke* (Ann Arbor: University of Michigan Press, 1960). For a biography of the Mills, see Bruce Mazlish, *James and John Stuart Mill* (New York: Basic Books, 1975). Auguste Comte's own *A general view of positivism* (New York: Robert Speller & Sons, 1975) provides a starting point for understanding the movement. Ernst Mach's most important philosophical-psychological work is *The analysis of sensations* (New York: Dover Books, 1959); a biography of him is John Blackmore's *Ernst Mach* (Berkeley: University of California Press, 1972). For the occult movements of the nineteenth century, see Thomas H. Leahey and Grace Evans Leahey, *Psychology's occult doubles: Psychology and the problem of pseudoscience* (Chicago: Nelson-Hall, 1983); the references and bibliography therein are fairly exhaustive. An important work subsequently published is Roger Cooter, *The cultural meaning of popular science: Phrenology and the organization of consent in the nineteenth century* (Cambridge, England: Cambridge University Press, 1984). Deserving special mention is Robert Darnton, *Mesmerism and the end of the Enlightenment in France* (New York: Schocken, 1968), a model of intellectual and social history.

Works on Darwin flourish. To read the first formulations of the theory by Darwin and Wallace, see their *Evolution by natural selection* (Cambridge, England: Cambridge University Press, 1958). For the background in biology, see William Coleman, *Biology in the nineteenth century: Problems of form, function, and transformation* (Cambridge, England: Cambridge University Press, 1977); or Ernst Mayr's authoritative *The growth of biological thought* (Cambridge, MA: Harvard University Press, 1984). For the specific background to Darwin's work, see Loren Eiseley, *Darwin's century* (Garden City, NY: Doubleday, 1958), a beautifully written standard introduction to evolution. Eiseley has also drawn attention to a previously unknown forerunner and influence on Darwin in his *Darwin and the mysterious Mr. X: New light on the evolutionists* (New York: Dutton, 1979). Another very readable account of the rise of evolutionary theory is John C. Greene, *The death of Adam: Evolution and its impact on Western thought* (Ames: Iowa State University Press, 1959). Two interesting but more technical works are B. Glass, O. Temkin, and W. Straus, eds., *Forerunners of Darwin: 1745–1859* (Baltimore: Johns Hopkins University Press, 1959), and Peter J. Bowler, *Fossils and progress: Paleontology and the idea of progressive evolution in the nineteenth century* (New York: Science History Publications, 1976). Works focusing on Darwin's thinking include P. Bamler, "Malthus, Darwin, and the concept of struggle," *Journal of the History of Ideas* (1976, *37:* 631–50); Michael Ghiselin, *The triumph of the Darwinian method* (Berkeley: University of California Press, 1969); and Dov Ospovat, *The development of Darwin's theory: Natural history, natural theology, and natural selection 1838–59* (New York: Cambridge University Press, 1981). Works concentrating on the reception of evolution include Tess Cosslett, ed., *Science and religion in the nineteenth century* (Cambridge, England: Cambridge University Press, 1984), which reprints major works by nineteenth-century debaters of the subject, including Darwin himself; Gertrude Himmelfarb, *Darwin and the Darwinian revolution* (New York: Norton, 1959); D. R. Oldroyd, *Darwinian impacts: An introduction to the Darwinian revolution* (Milton Keynes, England: The Open University Press, 1980); Michael Ruse, *The Darwinian revolution: Science red in tooth and claw* (Chicago: University of Chicago Press, 1979), who, with Himmelfarb and Oldroyd, set the Darwinian revolution in broad perspective. Peter J. Bowler, *The eclipse of Darwinism* (Baltimore: Johns Hopkins University Press, 1983); David Hull, *Darwin and his critics* (Cambridge, MA: Harvard University Press, 1973); and Cynthia Eagle Russett, *Darwin in America: The intellectual response 1865–1912* (San Francisco: Freeman, 1976), focus on the more scientific aspects of Darwin's reception. J. W. Burrow, *Evolution and society: A study in Victorian social theory* (Cambridge, England: Cambridge University Press, 1966), discusses the effect of evolution on social thought and on the nascent sciences of anthropology and sociology. In a short but far-ranging paper, D. P. Crook considers "Darwinism—The political implications," *History of European Ideas* (1981, *2:* 19–34). An excellent work on Darwin and the broad implications of Darwinism is Dennett (1995), which also includes discussion of contemporary rivals to Darwin's account of adaptation by natural selection.

Works by some of the important transitional figures to psychology include A. Bain, *Mental science* (New York: D. Appleton, 1868); F. C. Donders, "On the speed of mental processes: Attention and performance II," *Acta Psychologica* (1969, *30:* 412–31). G. T. Fechner, *Elements of psychophysics,* vol. 1 (New York: Holt, Rinehart & Winston, 1966); H. Helmholtz, *A treatise on physiological optics,* partially reprinted in T. Shipley, ed., *Classics in psychology* (New York: Philosophical Library, 1961); and H. Lotze, *Outlines of psychology* (Boston: Ginn & Co., 1886). Young (1970) is the standard history of neuroscience in the nineteenth century. For a broader history, see S. Finger, *Origins of neuroscience* (Oxford, England: Oxford University Press, 1994). L. Hearnshaw, *A short history of British psychology 1840–1940* (New York: Barnes & Noble, 1964), covers nineteenth-century British philosophical psychology. Two papers by David Leary (1978, 1980) discuss the situation in Germany. See also several papers in the Woodword and Ash collection, in the bibliography of Chapter 7.

REFERENCES

Barkow, J., Cosmides, L., and Tooby, J. (1994). *The adapted mind.* Oxford, England: Oxford University Press.

Baumer, F. (1977). *Modern European thought.* New York: Macmillan.

Bentham, J. (1789/1973). Introduction to the principles of morals and legislation. Reprinted in *The utilitarians.* Garden City, NY: Doubleday.

Braid, J. (1843). *Neurhypnology.* London: John Churchill.

Comte, A. (1975). *Comte and positivism: The essential writings.* New York: Harper & Row.

Cranefield, P. F. (1974). *The way in and the way out: François Magendie, Charles Bell and the roots of the spinal nerve.* Mt. Kisco, NY: Futura.

Darwin, C. (1888/1958). *The autobiography of Charles Darwin and selected letters,* F. Darwin, ed. New York: Dover Books.

Darwin, C. (1859/1959). *The origin of species.* New York: Mentor.

Dennett, D. C. (1995). *Darwin's dangerous idea: Evolution and the meaning of life.* New York: Simon & Schuster.

Esdaile, J. (1852). *Natural and mesmeric clairvoyance.* London: Hippolyte Bailliere.

Hartley, D. (1749/1971). *Observations on man, his frame, his duty, and his expectations.* Facsimile reprint, New York: Garland Press.

Helmholtz, H. (1877/1971). Thought in medicine. Reprinted in R. Kahl, ed., *Selected writings of Hermann von Helmholtz.* Middletown; CT: Wesleyan University Press.

Houghton, W. E. (1957). *The Victorian frame of mind.* New Haven, CT: Yale University Press.

Huxley, T. H. (1871). Letter. In London Dialectical Society, eds., *Report on spiritualism.* London: Longmans, Green, Reader & Dyer.

Huxley, T. H. (1863/1954). *Man's place in nature.* Ann Arbor: University of Michigan Press.

Irvine, W. (1959). *Apes, angels, and Victorians.* Cleveland, OH: Meridian Books.

Kahl, R. K., ed. (1971). *Selected writings of Hermann von Helmholtz.* Middletown, CT: Wesleyan University Press.

Leary, D. E. (1978). The philosophical development of the conception of psychology in Germany, 1750–1850. *Journal of the History of the Behavioral Sciences 14:* 113–21.

Leary, D. E. (1980). German idealism and the development of psychology in the nineteenth century. *Journal of the History of Philosophy 18:* 299–317.

Malthus, T. R. (1798/1993). *An essay on the principle of population.* Oxford, England: Oxford University Press.

Mill, J. (1829/1964). Analysis of the phenomena of the human mind. Partially reprinted in J. M. Mandler and G. Mandler, eds., *Thinking: From association to gestalt.* New York: John Wiley.

Mill, J. S. (1859/1978). *On liberty.* Indianapolis: Hackett.

Myers, F. (1903). *Human personality and its survival of bodily death,* 2 vols. London: Longmans, Green & Co.

Ruse, M. (1975). Charles Darwin and artificial selection. *Journal of the History of Ideas 36:* 339–50.

Taine, H. (1875). *On intelligence.* New York: Holt. (French edition 1870)

Vorzimmer, P. (1970). *Charles Darwin: The years of controversy.* Philadelphia: Temple University Press.

Webb, J. (1974). *The occult underground.* LaSalle, IL: Open Court.

Young, D. (1970). *Mind, brain, and adaptation in the nineteenth century.* Oxford, England: Clarendon Press.

PART II

FOUNDING PSYCHOLOGY

Although psychologists traditionally revere one man, Wilhelm Wundt, as the founder of psychology, and one date, 1879, as the founding year of psychology, their faith is misleadingly simple. Wundt's long-term importance for psychology has proven to be institutional, for he created a socially recognized and independent science and a new social role for its practitioners. Conceptually, psychology was founded three times, and each founding gave rise to a distinctive way of thinking about psychology's problems.

The most traditional founding psychology was the psychology of consciousness, the introspective study of the normal mind of the adult human. This psychology directly continued traditional philosophical psychology and made it more rigorous. Wundt stands at the head of this tradition, although many others took part. The psychology of consciousness proved to be the least durable form of psychology, notwithstanding Wundt's unique and momentous creation of institutional psychology.

The most famous—and in its own time, notorious—founding psychology was Sigmund Freud's psychology of the unconscious. Freud attempted to plumb the hidden and threatening dark side of human nature, and what he found there offended some and inspired others. Freud's psychology of the unconscious is less a rival to Wundt's psychology than it is its complement. Freud's ideas have profoundly affected Western thought in the twentieth century, and Freud's psychotherapy—psychoanalysis—has spawned innumerable variants into our own time.

Among academic psychologists, the most important founding psychology has been the psychology of adaptation. Its founding was the work of many, first among them being William James. The psychology of adaptation does not see the problem of psychology to be the philosophically motivated dissection of consciousness or the therapeutic exploration of the unconscious, but, instead, the biological study of the evolutionary utility of mind and behavior. The psychology of adaptation began as an introspective study of mental activity, but it soon became the study of activity itself, that is, the study of behavior.

In the next three chapters, we will describe each founding psychology in turn.

7   *The Psychology of Consciousness*

Although his psychological system died with him, Wilhelm Wundt is still revered as the founder of experimental psychology as an officially recognized science.

INTRODUCTION: THE FOUNDING OF PSYCHOLOGY

By the last quarter of the nineteenth century, conditions were ripe for psychology to emerge as an autonomous science. As we have seen, scientific psychology was fated to be born as the hybrid offspring of physiology and philosophy of mind—called *psychology* by the middle of the century. Wilhelm Wundt (1832–1920) was the philosopher-physician who established psychology as an academic discipline. Like Moses, he did not follow his people—the future generations of psychologists—entirely into the land of science, but he made possible psychology's recognition as a science.

The Path through Physiology

In the work that first defined scientific psychology, *Principles of Physiological Psychology,* Wundt (1873) proclaimed "an alliance between two sciences." The first was physiology, which "informs us about those life phenomena that we perceive by our external senses," and the second was psychology, in which "the person looks upon himself from within." The result of the alliance was to be a new science, physiological psychology, whose tasks were:

> [F]irst, to investigate those life processes [consciousness] that, standing midway between external and internal experience, require the simultaneous application of both methods of observation, the external and the internal; and second, to throw light upon the totality of life processes from the points of view gained by investigations of this area and in this way perhaps to mediate a total comprehension of human existence. [This new science] begins with physiological processes and seeks to demonstrate how these influence the domain of internal observation. . . . The name physiological psychology . . . points to psychology as the real subject of our science. . . . If one wishes to place emphasis on methodological characteristics, our sciences might be called experimental psychology in distinction from the usual science of mind based purely on introspection. (Wundt, 1873, pp. 157–8)

Besides being a culmination of the ideas of centuries of philosopher-physicians, the alliance of physiology and psychology served several important functions for the fledgling science of psychology. The first functions concerned methodology, both broadly and narrowly defined. Although in Wundt's time the word *physiology* was acquiring the biological meaning it has today, it still possessed a broader and different meaning. Physiology and physics have the same Greek root, *physis,* and in the nineteenth century the word was often used simply to designate taking an experimental approach to a subject. More specifically, in the case of psychology, apparatus and techniques such as reaction time measurement were taken over from physiology and put to use in psychology laboratories. Because of the important methodological aspect of the alliance, Wundt also called physiological psychology *experimental psychology.*

A second set of functions of the alliance between physiology and psychology is only alluded to by Wundt in the quoted passage and concerned the content of the new science. At a philosophical level, the alliance helped psychology become part of the aggressively emerging naturalistic worldview of science. Traditionally, psychology meant *psyche-logos,* the study of the soul. But the supernatural soul had no place in naturalistic science, so to continue pursuing psychology along traditional lines would bar it from science on the grounds of unscientific dualism. However, by insisting that the nervous system is the basis of all mentality, and by defining psychology as the investigation of the physiological conditions of conscious events, the new field of physiological psychology could establish itself as a science. For example, the most important mental process in Wundt's psychology was apperception, and Wundt proposed the existence of an "apperception center" in the brain. In addition, psychologists could borrow established physiological concepts such as neural excitation and inhibition and use them in psychological theories.

One theoretical possibility that was opened up by the creation of physiological psychology was reductionism: not simply borrowing physiological concepts for psychological usage, but explaining mental and behavioral events in terms of physiological causes. To take a familiar modern example, it appears that the cause of long-term depression is depletion of catecholamines in the brain rather than repressed psychological conflicts. All three of the main founders of psychology—Wundt, Freud, and James—were initially attracted by the idea of jettisoning psychological theories altogether in favor of explaining consciousness as the outcome of neural causes, without positing a level of unconscious mediating psychological processes. Ultimately, all three rejected this eliminativist vision. At the very least, if physiology could explain mind and behavior, psychology's status as a discipline was threatened: physiological psychology would become simply physiology. Wundt and Freud moved away from reductionism, and James struggled mightily with it and eventually gave up psychology altogether for philosophy. Nevertheless, the idea of reduction lived on in the succeeding generations of psychologists, sometimes hidden but never dying, and today it is reasserting itself with new vigor (see Chapter 15).

The last function of the alliance between physiological psychology and psychology was a tactical move in the academic politics of nineteenth-century Germany. Physiology was the most recently established scientific discipline. Its practitioners, such as Hermann von Helmholtz, with whom Wundt studied, were among the leading scientists, and its rapid progress soon gave it enormous prestige. For an ambitious academic like Wundt, the champion of a new field seeking funds, space, and students, alliance with physiology was a way to gain respectability (Ben-David and Collins, 1966).

Cultural and Intellectual Setting: The German Mandarins

Ancient Confucian China was largely ruled by an intellectual elite called the Mandarins. Theoretically, the Mandarin class was open to all who received a classical education and could pass the civil service examinations, but in practice, few besides the established Mandarin families could afford the private tutoring needed to enter the ruling elite. The Mandarins made up the bureaucracy that governed China through the rise and fall of emperors and imperial dynasties. They ruled by controlling the life of the emperor, establishing endless and exacting rounds of rituals and duties for the emperor to perform according to carefully prepared rules. Often, it was difficult if not impossible for the emperor to leave the Forbidden City or do anything on his own. The historian Fritz Ringer (1969) has described German intellectuals as comprising a Mandarin class of their own, based on classical education of the personality—*Bildung*—and governmental control through bureaucracy and education. Wilhelm Wundt was the very model of a modern German Mandarin, and his career reveals the Mandarin mind that shaped German psychology before the rise of Nazism.

Wilhelm Maximilian Wundt was born on August 16, 1832, in Neckarau, Baden, Germany—the fourth child of a minister, Maximilian Wundt, and his wife, Marie Frederike. Many ancestors on both sides of Wundt's family were intellectuals, scientists, professors, government officials, and physicians. At the age of thirteen, Wundt began his formal education at a Catholic gymnasium.* He disliked school and failed, but he transferred to a school in Heidelberg from which he graduated in 1851. Wundt decided to go into medicine, and after an initially poor start, he applied himself and excelled in his studies. His scientific interests emerged in physiological research. He got

---

* The German gymnasium was a college-preparatory high school; entrance was generally restricted to the sons of middle-class intellectuals.

his M.D. summa cum laude in 1855, and after some study with the physiologist Johannes Müller, Wundt received in 1857 the second doctorate that German universities required of lecturers. He immediately gave his first course in experimental physiology—to four students, in his mother's apartment in Heidelberg.* These courses were interrupted by an acute illness from which he almost died.

During his convalescence, Wundt applied for and received an assistantship with Hermann von Helmholtz. Although Wundt admired Helmholtz, they were never close, and Wundt rejected Helmholtz's materialism. While with Helmholtz, Wundt gave his first course in "Psychology as a Natural Science" in 1862, and his first important writings began to appear. He worked his way up the academic ladder at Heidelberg while dabbling in politics, for the first and last time, as an idealistic socialist. He got married in 1872. His publications continued, including the first edition of his fundamental work, *Grundzuge der Physiologischen Psychologie,* in 1873 and 1874. This work, in its many editions, propounded the central tenets of his experimental psychology.

After a year in a "waiting room" position in Zurich, Wundt received a chair in philosophy at Leipzig, where he taught from 1875 to 1917. At Leipzig, Wundt won a degree of independence for psychology by founding his Psychological Institute. Beginning as a purely private institute in 1879, it was supported out of his own pocket until 1881. Finally, in 1885, it was officially recognized by the university and listed in the catalog. It began as a primitive, one-room affair and expanded over the years; in 1897, it moved to its own specially designed building, later destroyed during World War II.

During the years at Leipzig, Wundt continued his extraordinary output—supervising at least 200 dissertations, teaching over 24,000 students, and writing or revising volume after volume, as well as overseeing and writing for the psychological journal he founded, *Philosophische Studien.* He trained the first generation of psychologists, many of them Americans.

In 1900, he began a massive undertaking, the publication of his *Völkerpsychologie,* which was completed only in 1920, the year of his death. In this work, Wundt developed what he believed was the other half of psychology, the study of the individual in society as opposed to the individual in the laboratory. Wundt's work continued to the last. His final undertaking was his reminiscences, *Erlebtes und Erkanntes,* which he completed only a few days before he died on August 31, 1920, at the age of eighty-eight.

During World War I, Wundt, like almost all German intellectuals, was fervently nationalistic. He, like many other "patriots of the lectern," wrote violently anti-English and anti-American tracts that can be read only with embarrassment today. They are interesting, however, for their revelation of the gulf between the German and the Anglo-French-American worldviews. For Wundt and other German intellectuals, the English were, in the words of Werner Sombart, mere "traders" who regarded "the whole existence of man on earth as a sum of commercial transactions which everyone makes as favorably as possible for himself" (Ringer, 1969).

---

* The German university system in the nineteenth century was very different from the modern American system. One had to obtain the usual doctorate and then a second, higher-level doctorate before one could teach—and even then, one had no regular salary and could only give private, fee-supported courses. Only after years of private teaching and a life of relative poverty could one obtain a salaried professorship.

The English were excoriated by Wundt for their "egotistic utilitarianism," "materialism," "positivism," and "pragmatism" (Ringer, 1969). The German ideal, on the other hand, was "the hero," a warrior whose ideals were "sacrifice, faithfulness, openness, respect, courage, religiosity, charity and willingness to obey" (Ringer, 1969). The goal of the Englishman was seen as personal comfort while that of the German was seen as sacrifice and service. Germans also had a long-standing contempt for French "civilization," which they considered a superficial veneer of manners as opposed to the true German organic "culture."

Such polemics illustrate the German intellectual climate in the nineteenth century. The Germans as a whole, and despite Kant, followed Herder in openly rejecting the Enlightenment. They were romantic intellectuals who valued things of the heart, spirit, and soil rather than things of the cold intellect. They saw Germany as midway between the intellectualism of the countries west of the Rhine, and the anti-intellectual, religious culture of Holy Mother Russia to the east. They rejected the atomism and utilitarianism of British philosophy and were anti-individualistic. In place of atomism, the German intellectuals constantly sought synthesis, to reconcile opposites into a higher truth. Wundt and the other elitist intellectuals of the German "Mandarin" tradition perceived, maintained, and strengthened an immense intellectual gulf between themselves and the West (Ringer, 1969). Wundt held himself to be the heir of Kant, Fichte, and Hegel, and he rejected the philosophies of Locke, the Mills, Spencer, and William James.

Underneath all this, we can once more detect the division between rationalism and empiricism. The West was empiricist: associationistic, atomistic, utilitarian, and concerned with individual rights and happiness. Germany was nationalistic and romantic, rejecting the narrow utilitarian rationalism of the West in favor of a spiritual romantic rationalism. Since Plato, there has always been a mystic, anti-individualistic aspect to rationalism. Ascent to the Forms is a sort of mystical union. People existed to serve Plato's republic, not vice versa; rationalism easily tends toward totalitarianism. Hence, German thinkers were rationalists: antiassociationistic, searching for synthesis, avowedly impractical (the universities cultivated unworldly fields like philosophy and refused to recognize such practical fields as engineering), and statist (the individual is seen as the servant of the state).

Wundt's psychology shared this Mandarin tradition. It rejected association of static ideas and the building-toy theory of mind. It rejected atomism and reductionism in favor of psychological synthesis and an analysis of consciousness. It sought no practical results, although it did not exclude them. Finally, it rejected the study of individual differences in favor of an almost Platonic investigation of the human mind.

Institutional Setting: The German Research Universities

Throughout the nineteenth century, German universities were unique both in quality and organization, especially with regard to science. In Britain and France, for different reasons, scientists worked outside the educational system, and British universities were moribund backwaters of no distinction. The United States had colleges devoted to undergraduate learning rather than universities offering graduate training. Higher education in the United States was largely a private, rather than a government-supported enterprise as was the case in Europe. Most colleges were established by religious denominations to educate and build character among their members and to train their clergy. Faculty were generalists whose primary vocation was teaching; they were not specialists in research who were teaching in those specialized fields. German universities, however, combined research and teaching functions and established the world's leading programs of graduate education. Moreover, the governments of the separate German principalities, and the Central Imperial German government, after the unification of Germany in 1870, strongly supported German universities with money and resources.

This setting affected the establishment of psychology as a science. Germany was then at the forefront of the Industrial Revolution, and Richard Littman (1979, p. 51) argues that, in their universities, "Germany had industrialized the process of acquiring and applying knowledge." Thus, says Littman, Germany was uniquely open to the creation of new scientific disciplines promising more production of world-leading research. If the German system was well suited to give birth to psychology, however, it also possessed features that would slow its growth and shape its form (Ash, 1980, 1981). First, although German universities valued research, their primary function remained the *Bildung* of the Mandarin elite, and the bureaucrats who ran the education ministry never lost sight of that fact. After its establishment by Wundt as a research specialty, psychology had a hard time making a case that aspiring lawyers, doctors, and teachers—the Mandarin elite—needed physiological psychology to build their character.

Related to this primary educational mission of the university was the concept of *Wissenschaft,* which guided *Bildung.* Today, *Wissenschaft* is translated as "science," suggesting natural experimental science. However, in the nineteenth century, *Wissenschaft* meant knowledge systematically organized along philosophical lines, and philosophy and other humanistic studies were the controlling models of organized thought. Natural science was gaining prestige, but experimentation was still, to many intellectuals, an untested, unreliable, unorganized way to procure truth. When Wundt was called to Leipzig, he was called as a philosopher, and he never sought autonomous status for psychology outside philosophy. From his arrival at Leipzig onward, Wundt regarded physiological psychology as a continuation of traditional philosophical psychology with new means and with new concepts taken over from physiology. Philosophers came to resent the intrusion of rude experiments into their hallowed field, and they did much to slow the growth of psychology in Germany.

WILHELM WUNDT'S PSYCHOLOGY OF CONSCIOUSNESS

Will to System

Instead of the narrow expertise expected of most modern professors, the Mandarins of the nineteenth century strove to coordinate the ideas of different disciplines and to subsume them into a single comprehensive scheme of human life. James (1875) called them "heaven-scaling Titans," and we see just a hint of Wundt as a "heaven-scaling Titan" in the opening of the 1873 edition of *Principles of Physiological Psychology,* when he offered the hope that physiological psychology might "mediate a total comprehension of human existence."

As a good Mandarin, Wundt was thoroughly in the grasp of the "Will to System" (Woodward, 1982) and conceived of psychology as but one component in a grand scheme of human knowledge. Although the personalities of Wundt and Freud are, in other respects, as different as night and day, they shared a trait necessary to a founder of a general system of thought: They were both ambitious hedgehogs (see Preface). Freud, as we shall see, called himself a conquistador; William James observed that Wundt "aims at being a sort of Napoleon of the mind." Freud, in large measure, succeeded in conquering the world in the name of a few salient ideas. Wundt, however, seemed to have no central theme; James called him "a Napoleon without genius and with no central idea which, if defeated, brings down the whole fabric in ruins. . . . Cut him up like a worm and each fragment crawls; there is no *noeud vital* [vital node] in his medulla oblongata, so you can't kill him all at once" (quoted by van Hoorn and Verhave, 1980, p. 72).

Wundt offered to the world two different systems of psychology. He formulated the first at Heidelberg but came to repudiate it later as a "sin of my youthful days" (quoted by van Hoorn and Verhave, 1980, p. 78), as Freud later repudiated his early "Project for a scientific psychology." Wundt's second program, propounded in Leipzig, changed significantly over the years (Diamond, 1980; Graumann, 1980; Richards, 1980; van Hoorn and Verhave, 1980; but see Blumenthal, 1980a, 1980b, 1986a; Danziger, 1980a, 1980b).

What remained constant was Wundt's traditional definition of psychology as the study of the mind and the search for the laws that govern it, but Wundt's assumptions about the mind and the methods used to investigate it changed dramatically. Wundt's Heidelberg program conceived of psychology as a natural science. Echoing John Stuart Mill's sentiments, Wundt wrote that the mind could be brought within the ambit of natural science by experimental method: "It has been the experiment only that has made progress in the natural sciences possible; let us then apply the experiment to the nature of the mind" (quoted by van Hoorn and Verhave, 1980, p. 86). In his early definition of psychology, Wundt did not identify the mind with consciousness, as he was to do later. Rather, the goal of experimentation was to gather data permitting inferences about unconscious processes: "The experiment in psychology is the major means which guides us from the facts of consciousness to those processes which in the dark background of our mind prepare conscious life" (quoted by Graumann, 1980, p. 37).

Wundt was called to Leipzig, however, as a philosopher, to lecture in philosophy, to build a philosophical system, and to conduct psychology as part of philosophy. In the Mandarin German university system, philosophy held sway, and Wundt had to find a new place for psychology in the Mandarin scheme of knowledge. In the spirit of Herder and Vico, German intellectuals typically distinguished between *Naturwissenschaft* and *Geisteswissenschaft*. *Naturwissenschaft* translates straightforwardly as "natural science," the study of the physical world and the search for the laws that govern it. *Geisteswissenschaft* is a more difficult concept. A literal translation is "spiritual (*Geist* means spirit) science," but what was meant was a study of the human world created by human history, and the search for laws governing human life, human development, and human history.

In the medieval Neoplatonic conception of the universe, human beings stood betwixt the material and spiritual worlds, half bodily animal and half divine soul. In the scheme of Vico, Herder, and their followers, human beings occupied a similar position, betwixt the material world and the social world. In each case, the human body and the elementary mental functions humans share with animals belong to the world of matter and natural science, and the higher reaches of the human mind—the soul, for Christians; the higher mental processes, for scientific psychology—belong to the world of *Geist* and the *Geisteswissenschaften.* Thus "psychology forms . . . the transition from the *Natur-* to the *Geisteswissenschaften.*" The experimental methods of physiological psychology, which study those aspects of consciousness close to sensation and motor response, lead to an approach that "is related to the methodology of the physical sciences." On the other hand, above these elementary phenomena "rise the higher mental processes, which are the ruling forces in history as well as in society. Thus, they, on their side, require a scientific analysis, which approaches those of the special *Geisteswissenschaften*" (Wundt, quoted by van Hoorn and Verhave, 1980, p. 93).

Over the years, the Leipzig program also changed. Solomon Diamond has translated the introductory argument of Wundt's *Principles of Physiological Psychology* from its first edition in 1873 to its last edition in 1908–1911. As edition supplanted edition, Wundt declared the alliance between physiology and psychology was weakened. In the earliest versions, psychology was linked, as we have seen, substantively as well as methodologically, to physiology. The study of the nervous system was expected to shed light on the nature of human consciousness. However, by the fourth edition, in 1893, only the methodological link remained, and physiological psychology had come to mean only experimental psychology (Wundt, 1873–1908). Like Freud and James, Wundt moved away from seeing psychology as a simple extension of physiology.

Methods

Wundt's conceptions of the methods to be used by psychology changed, too. However, in one fundamental respect, Wundt's conception of psychology's central method, introspection, did not change. Old-fashioned philosophical psychology had used armchair introspection to reveal the contents and workings of the mind, but it had fallen into bad odor among some scientists and philosophers as unreliable and subjective. Wundt agreed with these critiques of introspection, recognizing that a science of consciousness could be erected only on objective, replicable results based on standardized conditions capable of duplication and systematic variation (Wundt, 1907–1908). Precisely in order to achieve these aims, he introduced physiological techniques into the hitherto philosophical realm of psychology.

Wundt distinguished between two means of psychological observation whose German names are unfortunately, rendered into English as "introspection," giving rise to passages in which Wundt both condemns introspection and commends it as the fundamental method of psychology (Blumenthal, 1980a, 1980b, 1986a). *Innere Wahrnehmung,* or "internal perception," referred to the prescientific method of armchair subjective introspection, as practiced, for example, by Descartes or Locke. This kind of introspection is carried out in a haphazard, uncontrolled way and cannot hope to yield results useful to a scientific psychology. On the other hand, *Experimentelle Selbstbeobachtung,* experimental self-observation, designates a scientifically valid form of introspection in which subjects are exposed to standard, repeatable situations and are asked to respond with simple, quantifiable responses. Conducting armchair introspection, philosophers contemplate the depths of their mental processes; in experimental introspection, experimental subjects do not reflect on their minds at all, but simply respond to stimuli.

The rationale and limits of experimental introspection changed as Wundt's systematic definition of psychology changed. In the Heidelberg years, when Wundt believed in unconscious psychological processes, traditional introspection was rejected because it was limited to observation of consciousness and could not, by definition, reveal the workings of the unconscious. Careful experimentation, Wundt held, might reveal phenomena from which the workings of unconscious mental processes might be deduced. During this period, Wundt assigned introspective method a wider scope of application than he would later. In his Heidelberg years, Wundt stated that it is mere "prejudice" to regard as "futile to attempt to penetrate into the realm of the higher mental processes by means of experimental methods" (quoted by van Hoorn and Verhave, 1980). Later, when Wundt rejected the existence of the unconscious, experimentation was valued as making it possible to recreate the same experience in different subjects or in the same subjects at different times. This emphasis on exact duplication of experiences severely limited the realm of experimental introspection to the simplest mental processes, and Wundt duly excluded the study of the higher mental processes from physiological psychology, completely reversing his Heidelberg stance.

Alongside experimental introspection, Wundt recognized other methods of psychological investigation. The method of experimental introspection was, by its nature, limited to the study of normal minds of human adults, that is, the minds of experimental subjects. In addition to experimental introspection, then Wundt recognized *vergleichend-psychologische* (comparative-psychological) and *historisch-psychologische* (historical-psychological) methods (van Hoorn and Verhave, 1980). Both methods involved the study of mental differences. The comparative method applied to the study of consciousness in animals, children, and the "disturbed." The historical method applied to "mental differences as determined by race and nationality" (quoted by van Hoorn and Verhave, 1980, p. 92). The relations among the study of normal adult, animal, disturbed, and historically conditioned consciousness shifted over the years (van Hoorn and Verhave, 1980), but the most general change was in the importance Wundt assigned to the historical method, or *Völkerpsychologie*.

Wundt always believed, as would Freud, in the biogenetic law, that the development of the individual recapitulated the evolution of the species. In keeping with this notion, Wundt held that the best way to construct a theory of psychological development in individuals was to study the historical development of the human race. In his earliest program of psychology, the historical method was put forward as an adjunct to the main method of psychology, experimental introspection. However, when Wundt repositioned psychology as the crucial discipline lying between *Naturwissenschaft* and *Geisteswissenschaft*, the historical method was elevated to parity with the experimental method. The experimental method faced toward *Naturwissenschaft*, applying to the more strictly physiological aspects of the mind; the historical method faced toward *Geisteswissenschaft*, applying to the inner processes of mental creativity revealed in history, especially through language, myth, and custom. Thus, when Wundt withdrew experimental introspection from the study of the higher mental processes, he replaced it with the historical method of *Völkerpsychologie*.

Theory and Research

To illustrate the nature of Wundt's psychology, we shall consider two topics taken up in the two branches of his psychology. The first applies the experimental method of physiological psychology to an old question in philosophical psychology: How many ideas can consciousness contain at a given moment? The second applies the method of the Völkerpsychologie to the question of how human beings create and understand sentences.

Physiological Psychology

How many ideas can the mind hold at once? Traditional philosophical introspection, Wundt held, could provide no reliable answers. Without experimental control, attempting to introspect the number of ideas in one's mind is futile, because their content varies from time to time, and we must rely on fallible memories to give us the facts that introspection reports.

An experiment was called for, one that would complement and perfect introspection and would yield quantitative results. The following is an updated and simplified version of Wundt's experiment. Imagine sitting in a darkened room and facing a projection screen. For an instant, about 0.09 second, a stimulus is flashed on the screen. This stimulus is a four-column by four-row array of randomly chosen letters, and your task is to recall as many letters as possible. What is recalled provides a measure of how many simple ideas can be grasped in an instant of time and so may give an answer to the original question. Wundt found that unpracticed subjects could recall about four letters; subjects who had practiced could recall up to six but no more. These figures agree remarkably well with modern results on the capacity of short-term memory.

Two further important phenomena can be observed in this experiment. First, imagine an experiment in which each line of four letters forms a word, for example, work, many, room, idea. Under these conditions, one could probably recall all four words, or at least three, for a total of twelve to sixteen letters. Similarly, one could quickly read and recall the word "miscellaneousness," which contains seventeen letters. Letters as isolated elements quickly fill up consciousness so that only four to six can be perceived in a given moment, but many more can be grasped if these elements are organized. In Wundt's term, the *letter-elements* are synthesized by apperception into a greater whole, which is understood as a single complex idea and grasped as one new element.

Second, the subjects notice that some letters—the ones they then name—are perceived clearly and distinctly, but other letters are only dimly and hazily perceived. Consciousness seems to be a large field populated with ideational elements. One area of this field is in the focus of attention, and the ideas within it are clearly perceived. The elements lying outside the focal area are only faintly felt as present and cannot be identified. The focus of consciousness is where apperception works, sharpening stimuli into those seen clearly and distinctly. Items outside apperception's focus are apprehended only; they are not seen clearly.

Apperception was especially important in Wundt's system. Not only was it responsible for the active synthesis of elements into wholes, but it also accounted for the higher mental activities of analysis (revealing the parts of a whole) and of judgment. It was responsible for the activities of relating and comparing, which are simpler forms of synthesis and analysis. Synthesis itself took two forms: imagination and understanding. Apperception was the basis for all higher forms of thought, such as reasoning and use of language, and was central to Wundt's psychology in both its individual and social divisions.

Wundt's emphasis on apperception displays the voluntaristic nature of his system. When neither mind nor self referred to a special substance for Wundt, to what did he attribute our sense of self and the feeling that we have a mind? It is this feeling that provides the answer. Apperception is a voluntary act of the will by which we control and give synthetic unity to our mind. The feeling of activity, control, and unity defined the self. Wundt wrote (1896, p. 234): "What we call our 'self' is simply the unity of volition plus the universal control of our mental life which it renders possible."

Wundt did not neglect feelings and emotions, for they are an obvious part of our conscious experience. He often used introspectively reported feelings as clues to what processes were going on in the mind at a given moment. Apperception, for instance, he thought to be marked by a feeling of mental effort. He also studied feelings and emotions in their own right, and his tridimensional theory of feeling became a source of controversy, especially with Titchener. Wundt proposed that feelings could be defined along three dimensions: pleasant vs. unpleasant, high vs. low arousal, and concentrated vs. relaxed attention. He conducted a long series of studies designed to establish a physiological basis for each dimension, but the results were inconclusive, and other laboratories produced conflicting findings. Recent factor-analyses of affect, however, have arrived at similar three-dimensional systems (Blumenthal, 1975). Wundt emphasized the active, synthesizing power of apperception, but he recognized the existence of passive processes as well, which he classified as various forms of association or "passive" apperception. There were, for example, assimilations, in which a current sensation is associated to an older element. When one looks at a chair, one knows immediately what it is by assimilation, for the current image of the perceived chair is immediately associated with the older universal element, *chair*. Recognition is a form of assimilation, stretched out into two steps—a vague feeling of familiarity followed by the act of recognition proper. Recollection, on the other hand, was, for Wundt, as for some contemporary psychologists, an act of reconstruction rather than reactivation of old elements. One cannot reexperience an earlier event, for ideas are not permanent. Rather, one reconstructs it from current cues and certain general rules.

Finally, Wundt considered abnormal states of consciousness. He discussed hallucinations, depressions, hypnosis, and dreams. Of particular interest was his discussion of what we now call schizophrenia. He observed that this disease involves a breakdown in attentional processes. The schizophrenic loses the apperceptive control of thoughts characteristic of normal consciousness and surrenders instead to passive associative processes, so that thought becomes a simple train of associations rather than coordinated processes directed by volition. This theory was developed by Wundt's student and friend, the great psychiatrist Emil Kraepelin, and it has been revived by modern students of schizophrenia and autism.

Völkerpsychologie

Wundt believed that experimental individual psychology could not be a complete psychology. The minds of living individuals are the products of a long course of species development of which each person is ignorant. Therefore, to understand the development of the mind, we must have recourse to history. The study of animals and children is limited by their inability to introspect. History expands the range of the individual consciousness. In particular, the range of existing human cultures represents the various stages in cultural and mental evolution, from primitive tribes to civilized nation-states. Völkerpsychologie is thus the study of the products of collective life—especially of language, myth, and custom—that provide clues to the higher operations of mind. Wundt said the experimental psychology penetrates only the "outworks" of the mind; Völkerpsychologie reaches deeper.

Emphasis on historical development, a legacy from Vico and Herder, was typical of German intellectuals in the nineteenth century. In the German view, every individual springs from, and has an organic relationship with, his or her natal culture. Further, cultures have complex histories that determine their forms and contents. Thus, it was generally believed that history could be used as a method for arriving at an intuitive understanding of human psychology.

Wundt's remarks on myth and custom were typical of his time. He saw history as going through a series of stages from primitive tribes to an age of heroes and then to the formation of states, culminating in a world state based on the concept of humanity as a whole. It was, however, in the study of language (which, early in his career, Wundt almost pursued instead of psychology) that he made his most substantial contribution, articulating a theory of psycholinguistics that reached conclusions being rediscovered today. Language was a part of *Völkerpsychologie* for Wundt because, like myth and custom, it is a product of collective life.

Wundt divided language into two aspects: outer phenomena, consisting of actually produced or perceived utterances, and inner phenomena, the cognitive processes that underlie the outer string of words. This division of psychological phenomena into inner and outer aspects is central to *Ganzheit* psychology and has come up before in the contrast between the "outworks" of the mind, which can be reached by experimentation, and the deeper processes, which cannot. The distinction between inner and outer phenomena is easiest to understand with regard to language. It is possible to describe language as an organized, associated system of sounds that we speak or hear; this constitutes the outer form of language. However, this outer form is the surface expression of deeper cognitive processes that organize a speaker's thoughts, preparing them for utterance, and enable the listener to extract meaning from what she or he hears. These cognitive processes constitute the inner mental form of speech.

Sentence production, according to Wundt, begins with a unified idea that one wishes to express, the *Gesamtvorstellung,* or whole mental configuration.* The analytic function of apperception prepares the unified idea for speech, for it must be analyzed into component parts and a given structure that retains the relationship between the parts and the whole. Consider the simple sentence, "The cat is orange." The basic structural division in such a sentence is between the subject and predicate and can be represented with the tree-diagram introduced by Wundt. If we let G = *Gesamtvorstellung,* S = subject, and P = predicate, then we have

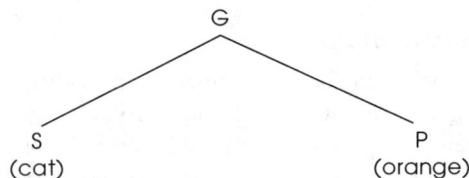

```
              G
           /     \
         /         \
       S             P
     (cat)        (orange)
```

---

* *Gesamtvorstellung* was misleadingly translated by Titchener, Wundt's leading translator, as "aggregate idea" but Blumenthal (1970) has shown Titchener's error and proposed the phrase used here: "whole mental configuration." The mistranslation reveals Titchener's misperception of *Ganzheit* psychology.

The idea of an orange cat has now been divided into its two fundamental ideas and can be expressed verbally as "the cat is orange" with the addition of the function words (the, is) required in our particular language. More complex ideas require more analysis and must be represented by more complex diagrams. The entire process, in all cases, can be described as the transformation of an inexpressible, organized, whole thought into an expressible sequential structure of words organized in a sentence.

The process is reversed in comprehension of speech. Here, the synthesizing rather than the analytic function of apperception is called on. The words and grammatical structure in a heard sentence must be used by the hearer to reconstruct in his or her own mind the whole mental configuration that the speaker is attempting to communicate. Wundt supported his view of comprehension by pointing out that we remember the gist of what we hear, but only rarely the surface (outer) form, which tends to disappear in the process of constructing the *Gesamtvorstellung*.

We have touched on only a small portion of Wundt's discussion of language. He also wrote on gesture-language; the origin of language from involuntary, expressive sounds; primitive language (based more on association than on apperception); phonology; and meaning-change. Wundt has a fair claim to be the founder of psycholinguistics as well as psychology.

Nevertheless, there remains a puzzle about Wundt's *Völkerpsychologie*. Although he seemed in his writings to value it highly, and lectured on it to over 600 people, he never trained anyone in its practice (Kusch, 1995).

AFTER LEIPZIG: NEW METHODS, NEW MOVEMENTS

The Next Generation

Wundt established psychology as a discipline, but he could not and did not retain a monopoly on it, as new psychologists founded new laboratories and new movements in Germany and around the world. Indeed, Wundt had surprisingly little effect on the next generation of psychologists. The younger German generation established new journals and the Society for Experimental Psychology, but Wundt was conspicuous by his absence and lack of participation (Ash, 1981). At the founding of the society in 1904, Wundt was honored in a telegram, but he was called the "Nestor of experimental psychology" (Ash, 1981, p. 266). In the Iliad, Nestor was an allegedly wise but pompous old windbag whose advice was usually ignored.

Foremost among the Wundtian strictures ignored by the new generation of psychologists was Wundt's limitation on the introspective method. The generation after Wundt was much influenced by positivism (Danziger, 1979) and believed that if psychology was going to be a science erected on positive facts, the higher mental processes would have to be observed directly. So, Wundt's simple and rigorously controlled method of introspection was replaced by "systematic introspection," a looser, more retrospective probing of consciousness that in some respects resembled psychoanalysis more than experimental psychology. In both, mental events were analyzed in detail after the fact, by subjects responding to questions posed by another person. The accuracy of the introspective reports of both thus suffered from the limitations of memory and the human tendency to invent memories upon suggestion.

At the same time, theories in psychology moved away from Wundt. Structural psychology recast the psychology of consciousness in terms defined by British associationism. Gestalt psychology redefined the study of experience, rejecting the analysis of experience into theoretically defined atoms of experience, and replacing it with the study of meaningful objects given directly in consciousness. Act psychology proposed a system of mind built around mental acts rather than the contents of experience.

Systematic Introspection: The Würzburg School (1901–1909)

One of Wundt's most outstanding and successful students was Oswald Külpe (1862–1915). Although his early psychology was even more conservative than Wundt's, during his brief professorial tenure at the University of Würzburg, he helped develop a new approach to psychological experiment, one that claimed that thinking could be studied experimentally. Two important sets of results emerged from this research. The first indicated, contrary to Wundt, that some thoughts are imageless; the second undermined associationism as an account of thinking.

As early as 1879, Hermann Ebbinghaus undertook to study the higher mental process of memory; his results appeared in 1885. Shortly after leaving Wundt, Külpe seems to have decided that the highest mental process of all, thinking, could be experimentally studied and could be introspected—if only Wundt's methods were changed. Wundt's experiments were quite simple, involving little more than reaction to, or a brief description of, a stimulus. Fechner's psychophysics, Donder's mental chronometry, and Wundt's apperception experiments are examples of this procedure. Under Külpe (who never published an experiment from his Würzburg days but participated in others' experiments), the tasks were made more difficult and the job of introspection was more elaborate.

During the years of the Würzburg school, the complexity of the experimental tasks increased from giving free associations to single stimulus words to agreeing or disagreeing with difficult metaphysical theses or Nietzsche's aphorisms. These tasks, whether simple or difficult, required thinking, whereas Wundtian tasks did not. Subjects had to respond to the problem and then describe the thought processes leading to the response. As the method developed, the subjects would be asked to concentrate introspective attention on different parts of the subjective experience—that is, the subjects would focus on their mental state while awaiting the stimulus word, or on the appearance of the answer in consciousness. In these experiments, the Würzburgers hoped to directly observe thinking as it happened.

The first results were a shock to almost all psychologists: Thoughts can be imageless. This finding emerged in the first Würzburg paper by A. M. Mayer and J. Orth, published in 1901. In this experiment, the subject was instructed to respond with the first word that came to mind after hearing a stimulus word. The experimenter gave a ready signal, called out the stimulus word, and started a stopwatch; the subject gave a response and the experimenter stopped the watch. The subject then described the thinking process. Mayer and Orth reported that most thinking involved definite images or feelings associated with acts of will. However, wrote Mayer and Orth (1901), "apart from these two classes of conscious processes, we must introduce a third group. . . . The subjects very frequently reported that they experienced certain conscious processes which they could describe neither as definite images nor as acts of will." For example, while serving as a subject, Mayer "made the observation that following the stimulus word 'meter' there occurred a peculiar conscious process, not further definable, which was followed by the spoken word 'trochee.' " So Wundt was wrong, according to Mayer and Orth; nonimaginal events in consciousness had been found.

The Würzburgers refined their methods over the years, but the results remained: There are imageless thoughts. Moreover, the finding was made independently in Paris by Alfred Binet in his studies of children's thinking, and in New York by Robert Woodworth. Both studies were reported in 1903, but the investigators did not know the Würzburg work. In fact, Binet later claimed that the new method should be called the "method of Paris." In any event, the finding of imageless thought was a challenge to psychological orthodoxy and provoked a controversy that aided and abetted the birth of behaviorism.

What was to be made of imageless thought? The Würzburgers' own interpretation changed during the life of the school. Mayer and Orth did no more than discover imageless thoughts—vague, impalpable, almost indescribable "conscious states." Later on, they were identified simply as "thoughts" themselves. The final interpretation was that thought is actually an unconscious process, reducing the imageless thought elements to conscious indicators of thinking rather than thinking itself. However, on both sides of the Atlantic, many psychologists found the Würzburg methods, results, and interpretations to be unacceptable or at least suspect.

Writing in 1907, Wundt tried to falsify the Würzburg results by attacking the method. He argued that the Würzburg experiments were sham experiments, merely reversions to unreliable armchair introspection that happened to be conducted in a laboratory. According to Wundt, experimental control was entirely lacking in the thought experiments. The subject did not know exactly what task would be set. The ensuing mental process would vary from subject to subject and from trial to trial, so the results could not be replicated. Finally, said Wundt, it is difficult if not impossible for a subject to both think about the set problem and watch that process at the same time. Consequently, Wundt said, the so-called findings of imageless thought are invalid. Properly conducted experiments would show that, when properly analyzed, "imageless" content was imaginal after all.

Titchener undertook the experimental refutation of the Würzburg findings. Methodologically, Titchener echoed Wundt by claiming that subjects' reports of "imageless" thought were not descriptions of consciousness at all, but fabrications based on beliefs about how one would solve the problems set in the experiments. Experimentally, Titchener's students performed thought experiments and reported that they could find no evidence of imageless thought elements; they successfully traced all conscious content to sensations or feelings (Clark, 1911). Titchener concluded that the Würzburgers had failed as introspectors by declining to analyze a mental content and then calling it "imageless thought."

Other commentators offered alternative interpretations of the Würzburg results. It was suggested by some that certain types of minds possess imageless thought while others do not, reducing the Titchener–Külpe controversy to one of individual differences. This hypothesis was criticized as unparsimonious: Why should nature create two types of mind to attain the same end—accurate thinking? The hypothesis of unconscious thinking was rejected on the grounds that what is not conscious is not mental but physiological, and therefore not a part of psychology. A similar criticism greeted Freud's hypothesis of the unconscious.

Perhaps the most important consequence of the debate about imageless thought was the suspicion that introspection was a fragile and unreliable tool, easily prejudiced by theoretical expectations. The Würzburg subjects believed in imageless thought, and they found it. Titchener's subjects believed only in sensations and feelings, and they found only those. R. M. Ogden, an American supporter of imageless thought, wrote that if Wundt's and Titchener's criticisms of the Würzburg methods were valid, "may we not carry the point a step farther and deny the value of all introspection. Indeed, in a recent discussion among psychologists, this position was vigorously maintained by two among those present" (1911a). Ogden himself suggested that the differential results from Titchener's laboratory at Cornell and Külpe's in Würzburg betray "unconscious bias" based on different training (Ogden, 1911b, p. 193). The imageless thought controversy revealed difficulties with the introspective method and, by 1911, the year of Ogden's papers, we find some psychologists ready to discard it altogether. Two years later, Watson, the founder of behaviorism, included this controversy in his indictment of mentalism.

The imageless thought results represented a budding anomaly for certain forms of mentalism. Woodworth wrote as late as 1938 that "the whole question may well be shelved as permanently debatable and insoluble" (p. 788). This is one fate of anomalies, according to Kuhn. The debate over imageless thought showed signs of developing into a Kuhnian paradigm clash. In 1911, J. R. Angell wrote: "One feels that the differences which divide certain of the writers are largely those of mutual misunderstanding as to the precise phenomenon under discussion" (p. 306). Angell was disturbed that the combatants in the dispute had been "largely reduced to mere assertion and denial . . . 'It is!' or 'It isn't!' (p. 305). However, the anomaly and paradigm clash were incipient only; their development was cut short by the advent of behaviorism. Woodworth found the topic being shelved in 1938 not because the problem had been exhausted, but because no one cared anymore. By the second (1954) edition of Woodworth's *Experimental Psychology,* this controversy, which had occupied many pages in the 1938 edition, had shriveled to four paragraphs.

The Würzburgers' second shock for the psychological establishment arose when they studied the process of thinking. Their results led them to reject traditional associationism as an adequate account of mind. Their problem was this: What makes one idea rather than another follow a given idea? For free association, as in Mayer and Orth's experiment, associationism has a plausible answer. If the stimulus word is "bird," the subject may respond "canary." The associationist can then say simply that the bird–canary bond was the strongest in the subject's associative network. However, this situation is complicated if we use a method of constrained association, as Henry J. Watt did in 1905. In this method, we set a specific task for the subject to carry out, such as "give a subordinate category" or "give a superordinate category." To the former task, the subject may still reply "canary." To the second task, the correct response cannot be "canary" but instead should be "animal." However, these tasks are no longer free associations, but rather acts of directed thinking that produce propositions that may be true or false—unlike free association. So the simple associative bond, bird–canary, is overridden in directed thinking.

The Würzburgers argued that associationism fails to explain thinking, for something must direct thought along the proper lines in the associative network in order for a subject to respond correctly to such tasks as Watt's. The Würzburgers proposed that the task itself directed thinking. In their later terminology, they said that the task establishes a mental set—or a determining tendency—in the mind that properly directs the subject's use of his or her associative network. These experiments suggested unconscious thinking, for subjects found that given the task "Give superordinate to canary," the response "bird" popped into their heads with little experienced mental activity. The Würzburgers concluded that the mental set accomplishes thinking even before the problem is given; the subject is so prepared to give a superordinate that the actual response occurs automatically.

Their investigations of the process of thinking took the Würzburg psychologists toward a psychology of function instead of content. They found that laboratory work could reveal something about how the mind functions, in addition to what it contains. We will find that American psychology was predominantly functional, and the reception of the idea of the mental set was much more favorable in America than the reception given imageless thought. Although the discussion of imageless thought in Woodworth's authoritative *Experimental Psychology* shrank between 1938 and 1954, index references to "set" increased from nineteen to thirty-five, with more extended discussions. The concept of set made sense to American functional psychologists interested in mental operations, and the behaviorists found that they could reinterpret set as establishing determining tendencies in behavior instead of in mind.

Although Würzburg-inspired work continued after 1909 (especially by Otto Selz, who had worked there), the school essentially dissolved when Külpe left for the University of Bonn. No systematic theory based on the Würzburg studies was ever published, although there is evidence that Külpe was working on such a theory when he died. It is puzzling that, from 1909 until his death, Külpe said almost nothing about the dramatic Würzburg results. Therefore, no alternative psychology arose from the Würzburg school. Their methods were innovative, their findings stimulating and anomalous, and, in the concept of the mental set, they made a permanent contribution. But the Würzburg school remained a school, a research program cut off prematurely.

Structural Psychology

Edward Bradford Titchener (1867–1927) was an Englishman who brought German psychology to America. He thus played an important role in the founding of American psychology, for he was the foe of both functionalism and behaviorism, while on the European front he was the enemy of act psychology and of imageless thought. In this section, we will examine his system, *structuralism,* especially in its relation to Wundt's psychology, with which it is often confused.

E. B. Titchener was born in 1867 at Chichester, England, and went to Oxford from 1885 to 1890. While at Oxford, his interests shifted from classics and philosophy to physiology. The conjunction of interests in philosophy and physiology naturally predisposed Titchener to psychology, and while at Oxford he translated the third edition of Wundt's massive *Principles of Physiological Psychology.* Titchener could find no one in England to train him in psychology, so in 1890 he went to Leipzig, taking his doctorate in 1892.

As an Englishman, Titchener arrived in Leipzig from the other side of the intellectual gulf separating Germany from the West. He was thoroughly versed in philosophy and was much impressed by James Mill, remarking that Mill's speculations could be empirically demonstrated. In his first systematic book, *An Outline of Psychology* (1897), he wrote: "The general standpoint of [my] book is that of the traditional English psychology." It is reasonable to expect, therefore, that Titchener may well have assimilated Wundt's German psychology into the "traditional English psychology" that Wundt rejected.

After a short stint as a lecturer in biology in England—a country long unreceptive to psychology—Titchener left for America to teach at Cornell, where he remained until his death in 1927. He transformed Cornell into a bastion of mentalistic psychology, even as America's focus went first functionalist and then, after 1913, behaviorist. Titchener never compromised with these movements, despite his friendships with the functionalist J. R. Angell and with Watson, the founder of behaviorism. He did not participate actively in the American Psychological Association, even when it met at Cornell, preferring instead his own group, the Experimental Psychologists, which he kept true to his version of psychology and which eventually became central to the movement of cognitive psychology in the 1950s and 1960s.

Titchener apparently possessed a mind in which everything had imaginal-sensational character. His mind even had an image for such an abstract word as *meaning*. Titchener (1904, p. 19) wrote: "I see meaning as the blue-grey tip of a kind of scoop, which has a bit of yellow above it . . . and which is just digging into a dank mass of . . . plastic material." Even though he recognized that not everyone had an imaginal mind as he called it, he built his psychology on the premise that the mind was made up of sensations or images of sensation and nothing else. This led to his rejection of various Wundtian concepts such as apperception, which is inferred rather than observed directly. Titchener's psychology conformed to the Humean view of the mind as a collection of sensations rather than the Kantian or Cartesian view that mind was separate from its experience.

The first experimental task of Titchener's psychology was the discovery of the basic sensation-elements to which all complex processes could be reduced. As early as 1897, he drew up a catalog of elements found in the different sense-departments. There were, for instance, 30,500 visual elements, four taste elements, and three sensations in the alimentary canal.

Elements were defined by Titchener as the simplest sensations to be found in experience. They were to be discovered through the systematic dissection by introspection of the contents of consciousness; when an experience could not be dissected into parts, it was declared elemental. Titchener's method of introspection was much more elaborate than Wundt's, for it was not a simple report of an experience, but a complicated retrospective analysis of that experience. Wrote Titchener (1901–1905): "Be as attentive as possible to the object or process which gives rise to the sensation, and, when the object is removed or the process completed, recall the sensation by an act of memory as vividly and completely as you can." Persistent application of this method would, in Titchener's view, eventually produce a complete description of the elements of human experience. The task was unfinished (and, as many thought, unfinishable) when Titchener died.

The second task of Titchener's psychology was to determine how the elementary sensations are connected together to form complex perceptions, ideas, and images. These connections were not all associations, because, for Titchener, an association was a connection of elements that persisted even when the original conditions for the connection could no longer be obtained. Titchener rejected the label of associationism, not only for this reason but also because the associationists spoke of association of meaningful ideas, not of simple meaningless sensations, which was all that concerned Titchener.

The third task of Titchener's psychology was to explain the workings of mind. Introspection, according to Titchener, could yield only a description of mind. At least until about 1925, he (Titchener, 1929/1972) believed that a scientific psychology required more than mere description. Explanation for Titchener was to be sought in physiology, which would explain why the sensory elements arise and become connected. Titchener rejected Wundt's attempt to psychologically explain the operation of the mind. According to Titchener's system, all that can be found in experience are sensory elements rather than processes such as attention. Appeal to such an unobservable entity as apperception was illegitimate in Titchener's eyes—a view that betrays his positivism. He therefore sought to explain mind by reference to observable nerve-physiology.

Titchener rejected as wholly unnecessary the term *apperception,* which in Wundt's psychology gave rise to attention. Attention itself Titchener reduced to sensation. One obvious attribute of any sensation is clarity, and Titchener said that "attended" sensations are simply the clearest ones. Attention was not for him a mental process, but simply an attribute of sensation—clearness—produced by certain nerve processes. What of the mental effort that Wundt says goes along with attention? This, too, Titchener reduced to sensations. Wrote Titchener (1908, p. 4): "When I am trying to attend I . . . find myself frowning, wrinkling my forehead etc. All such . . . bodily sets and movements give rise to characteristic . . . sensations. Why should not these sensations be what we call 'attention?' "

Titchener's psychology represented an attempt to turn a narrowly conceived version not so much of British philosophical psychology as Condillac's version of it into a complete science of the mind. It was never very popular or influential beyond Titchener's own circle, and is in many respects important only as a significant dead end in psychology and for misleading English-speaking psychologists about Wundt's voluntaristic ideas. Structuralism died with Titchener and has seldom been mourned since.

Gestalt Psychology

Atomism is a useful dimension on which to classify psychologists. The most atomistic psychology was James Mill's building-toy theory, and Titchener's catalog of sensory atoms is not much different. Moving toward holism, we find John Stuart Mill's mental chemistry and Wundt's theory of apperceptive synthesis. Both recognized the emergence of new properties as mental elements combine, but both still believed psychology should analyze complexes into elements, just as chemists do. More holistic still was Thomas Reid, who maintained that complex ideas are not built up out of elements by any process, but are immediately given in experience as meaningful wholes. Introspection can break them down into elements, but this is artificial and does not imply that the mind starts with atoms and forms wholes; according to Reid, the wholes are there from the beginning.

The Gestalt psychologists went even further, arguing that decomposing wholes into parts is not only artificial, but pointless and scientifically sterile, revealing nothing about the mind whatsoever. The philosophical root of their protest was phenomenology, whose proponents argued that experience should be simply described as given, never analyzed. Presented with a triangle, a good Titchenerian introspector would report, "I see three lines"; the report would contain only meaningless sensory atoms. The phenomenologist would say, "I see a triangle," reporting a meaningful mental whole transcending the atomic elements.

Some elementalists were moving in this direction. Christian von Ehrenfels (1859–1932) discussed "Gestalt qualities" in 1890. Ehrenfels wanted to know how certain experiences maintain their character despite sensory changes. This is most apparent in hearing tunes. Despite transposition of keys, and thus its sensory elements, we always hear the same tune as the same. Ehrenfels was dealing with the problem of organized perceptions, not elements, and arguing for a new mental element. A tune is made up of sensory elements—its specific notes—but it possesses in addition a Gestalt (or form) quality that represents the organization. Similarly, a triangle is made up of three sensory elements, the lines, plus a form-quality element of triangularity. Ehrenfels's former teacher, the philosopher Alexius Meinong (1853–1920), tried to specify the source of the form-quality. Sensory elements are given by experience, and then the mind, in a mental act, adds the structuring form-quality. This theory of an additional mental act derived from the act psychology of Franz Brentano, whom we shall consider next. Both Ehrenfels's and Meinong's theories remained elementalistic, merely adding a mental element of organization to the accepted list of sensory elements.

Both atomistic elementalism and the act interpretation of form-qualities were rejected by the phenomenologically oriented Gestalt psychologists, as is shown by the following Gestalt experiment. A subject is seated in a darkened room and two spots of light are flashed off and on alternately. When the interval between flashes is more than 0.2 second, the subject sees two flashing lights; but when the interval is less than 0.2 second the subject sees one light in continuous motion. The subject perceives apparent motion where in fact there is none. This phenomenon underlies our experience of movies, which are actually a rapidly displayed series of still photographs. Such experiments indicated that more than a mental element was needed. The apparent motion undermines the atomistic account of consciousness, for sensational "atoms" given on the retina are not perceived, but instead give rise to a qualitatively different experience. Apparent motion is an experience that emerges from simple sensations but cannot plausibly be reduced to them. It is, in short, a perceptual whole (*Gestalt,* in German), given immediately to consciousness and deserving direct study. The Gestalt psychologists advocated a holistic psychology based on the mind's perception of complete forms.

This experimental demonstration (called the *phi* phenomenon), which shows that conscious experience is not usefully reducible to bundles of discrete sensations, was the starting point of the Gestalt movement. Its inspiration, however, had deeper and more general sources. We have already seen how German culture rejected the tide of associationism, atomism, and mechanism that flowed from traditional British and French philosophies. Wundt's psychology was a partial reaction to this tide, but the young men of the next generation reacted even more strongly. Even more than Wundt, they looked for wholeness and transcendence as a way out of the post-World War I crisis of German culture. They fought against all philosophies or sciences that saw creatures or cultures as machines, as no more than collections of simpler parts.

The leader of this movement in psychology was Max Wertheimer (1880–1943), who carried out the phi phenomenon research in 1912 using the other two great Gestalt psychologists, Wolfgang Köhler (1887–1967) and Kurt Koffka (1887–1941), as the main subjects. Wertheimer was by nature a prophet for whom the idea of the Gestalt was "not only a theory of perception or of thinking, or a theory of psychology, or even an entire philosophy; it was, rather, a *Weltanschauung,* indeed an all-encompassing religion. The core of this religion is the hope that the world is a sensible coherent whole, that reality is organized into meaningful parts, that natural units have their own structure" (Wertheimer, 1978).

The phi phenomenon demonstrated a faith that Wertheimer had held before 1912. Despite being a Jew, he received an education "typical of the elite of his day" including studies with von Ehrenfels at Prague and Külpe at Würzburg (Wertheimer, 1978). In all his studies, he was immersed in the reaction against traditional atomism and traditional psychology, but Wertheimer moved in a more holistic direction than either of his teachers. His Gestalt ideas appeared first in a 1910 paper on the primitive music of a Ceylonese tribe, in which he concluded that their compositions were organized by "Gestalten that are rhythmically and melodically strict" (Wertheimer, 1978).

Central to the Gestalt movement was the "Gestalt vision," Wertheimer's holistic *Weltanschauung.* In 1924, Wertheimer declared that "Gestalt theory is neither more nor less" than the belief that "there are wholes, the behavior of which is not determined by that of their individual elements, but where the part processes are themselves determined by the intrinsic nature of the whole. It is the hope of Gestalt theory to determine the nature of such wholes." Wundt's halfway holism, in which wholes are constructed by the mind, was unacceptable. Wertheimer condemned traditional— Wundtian—psychology for containing what he called an abundance of "things arid, poor and inessential" and for having "alien, wooden, monstrous" implications (1925). He argued that traditional psychology rested on two erroneous assumptions. The first is the mosaic or bundle hypothesis, which is Wertheimer's term for sensationism. The second is the association hypothesis, by which Wertheimer means the building-toy theory. Nor could Wertheimer accept Wundt's idea that the mind's power of apperception unites elements into greater wholes, for this still concedes the fundamental status of sensational elements. Wrote Wertheimer (1922): "Gestalten" are not "the sums of aggregated contents erected subjectively upon primarily given pieces. . . . Instead, we are dealing with wholes and whole-processes possessed of inner intrinsic laws. 'Elements' are determined as parts by the intrinsic conditions of their wholes and are to be understood 'as parts' relative to such wholes." This is the central formula of Gestalt psychology.

Two important new concepts were used by the Gestalt psychologists to put their formula into practice. The first is the concept of the *psychological field,* consciously borrowed from field theory in physics. Gestaltists deny that experience is like a mosaic, a collection of inert, noninteracting, discrete units or sensations. Instead, they see experience as a field of dynamically interacting parts. In the phi phenomenon, the "parts" of the field, the two flashing lights, interact to give rise to the perception of motion. Thus, a visual illusion such as the Muller–Lyer is produced by interactions among the visual elements. The central lines are the same size, but, because of the context in which they are viewed (the arrowheads), they seem to be different lengths.

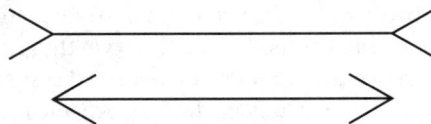

The Gestalt psychologists extended the field concept to refer not only to the phenomenal field of immediate experience involved in the phi phenomenon or illusions, but also to the behavioral field in which our actions take place. For the Gestalt psychologists, a problem to be solved defined a behavioral field in stress. An animal or child, for example, might be prevented from reaching visible food by a barrier. The "stress" in such a field is obvious. The problem is resolved when the field is reorganized by "insight," that is, when the subject sees that the barrier may be walked around. The solution allows access to the food and relieves the stress in the behavioral field; the problem no longer exists. An important implication is that the subject must be aware of all elements in a problem situation before a real psychological problem exists. Should the subject not be able to see the food, no problem would exist, for no psychological field-stress would exist, even if the subject were hungry. For this reason, the Gestalt psychologists criticized animal learning experiments, such as E. L. Thorndike's, in which the animal could not perceive all elements of the situation. How can an animal exhibit its intelligence unless the relevant factors are available for intelligence to consider? According to Gestaltists, animals are reduced to trial-and-error conditioning if this is the only kind of behavior allowed in an experiment.

The field concept proved capable of indefinite extension to psychological problems. Not only could it be applied to simple visual experiences and problem solving, but also to creativity (by Wertheimer himself) and social psychology (by Kurt Lewin, 1890–1947). However, the concept of the experiential field was insufficient. The two flashing lights do not by themselves create apparent motion; it is a psychological phenomenon. Problems do not solve themselves, they only pose themselves. The Gestalt psychologists, however, were unwilling to posit an active mind "which is able to grasp intrinsic relations and utilize such understanding," just as they did not recognize active apperception as a unifying force behind the creation of whole ideas. In their view, this alternative would lead to "vitalistic or spiritualistic dualism which we . . . have refused to accept." (Koffka, 1935/1963, p. 63). Instead, he said, "the dynamics of the process (of perceiving or thinking) are determined by the intrinsic properties of the data."

These "intrinsic properties" must act on the organism to produce experience or behavior. If there is no mind to act on, the action must be directly on the nervous system. This leads us to the second important concept of Gestalt psychology, the principle of *isomorphism*. This principle has given rise to numerous misconceptions. The Gestalt psychologists held that the brain is not the sensorimotor association machine that most believed it to be; instead, it is a complex electrical field. The idea of isomorphism is that the structural relationships in the behavioral field create in the individual who experiences them a pattern of brain-fields isomorphic to themselves. So, in the phi phenomenon, the flashing lights create two brain-fields that overlap and create the experience of motion. In a problem situation, the stresses in the behavioral field are represented in the brain as stresses in its electrical field. Insight is the resolution of the brain-field stresses that leads to resolution of the real problem.

The concept of isomorphism is difficult to grasp. A good analogy was suggested by Woodworth (1938). Functional isomorphism exists between the United States and a map of the United States. The two things are not the same, but structural relations in the former are directly related to structural relations in the latter. So, the problem of driving from Chicago to Los Angeles can be experienced and solved through the map. The "stresses" of the trip can be seen and resolved on the map. But Woodworth's analogy is simplified. The Gestalt psychologists did not maintain that a picture of the behavioral-field exists in the brain. Exactly what they did mean remains obscure; it is only certain that they maintained a functional isomorphism between behavioral- and brain-fields. Only through isomorphism and the electric field picture of the brain could the Gestalt psychologists uphold their holistic dynamic-field explanations of experience and behavior without falling into dualism.

The Gestalt movement thus attempted to avoid both atomism and dualism by considering people as perceiving organisms that respond to whole perceptual fields. The Gestalt experiments uncovered several interesting quirks of perception, such as the phi phenomenon, that had to be included in any later perceptual psychology. The Gestalt psychologists' almost mystical theory, however, did not travel well. It was far too German to do well in England and America, where psychology has been most studied since World War II.

Act Psychology

By and large, all the psychologies we have considered so far may be regarded primarily as psychologies of content; that is, they are concerned with discovering and describing the contents of consciousness. The imageless thought debate, for example, is a controversy about mental content: Do sensations, feelings, and images exhaustively describe all possible mental contents, or must we add "conscious states" to the list?

Franz Brentano (1878–1917), however, insisted that what is most important and characteristic of the mind is that it acts. Mental acts are directed at contents, Brentano said, but more important than the content is the act. Brentano divided mental acts into three classes: ideating (I see, I hear, I imagine), judging (I reject, I believe, I recall), and loving-hating (I wish, I intend, I desire). Acts are always directed at mental contents, and here arises Brentano's most significant concept, *intentionality*, as the criterion of mind. Rather than advocating a Cartesian dualism of substances, Brentano argued that only mental states—his "acts"—possess intentionality. Mental states are always directed at, or represent, something. So my idea of my cat Freya is directed at, is about, Freya; I possess a mental representation of her. The direction of thought on object Brentano called intentionality, and it should not be confused with the idea of purpose, for it is much broader. Purposes possess intentionality, for they are directed at something, a goal. However, Brentano said that all mental states are directed, even those that are purely cognitive. Intentionality separates mind from brain because only mental states are intentional. A neuron can never refer to, be about, or intend anything, because it is mere matter and can no more refer to something outside itself than can a rock.

In his own time, Brentano's influence on psychology was limited. He was sympathetic to experimental psychology and tried, but failed, to establish an experimental laboratory at the University of Vienna. Psychologists, among them Titchener, tended to regard him as an armchair functional psychologist and paid little heed to his doctrine of intentionality. His influence was much greater in philosophy, especially through his student Edward Husserl's phenomenology. Today, however, his impact on psychology is greater than in his own time. For today, Brentano's separation of mind and brain via intentionality as the criterion of the mental looms as a serious challenge to cognitive science's goal of creating intelligence in a computer.

THE FATE OF THE PSYCHOLOGY OF CONSCIOUSNESS

Unlike psychoanalysis and the psychology of adaptation, the psychology of consciousness is no longer with us. Some of its methods (such as reaction time measurement) and ideas (such as mental set) endure, but the enterprise of the psychology of consciousness is dead. In its home, the psychology of consciousness met heavy weather attempting to establish itself as an autonomous discipline, while in the United

States—psychology's future home—it was an alien Mandarin presence in a distinctly practical country.

Slow Growth in Germany

In Germany, the growth of psychology was greatly inhibited by the Mandarin culture of philosophical *Bildung*. As long as psychology remained where Wundt left it, in philosophy, psychologists had to compete with philosophers for professorships and resources. Especially as psychology became more completely experimental, it seemed to philosophers to be a rude intrusion on their traditional concerns, and they banded together to oppose its growth within psychology. However, efforts to move it elsewhere—to medicine, for example, as Külpe proposed—were unsuccessful.

The coming of the Nazis to power in 1933 complicated matters. They destroyed the old Mandarin system and drove from Germany its best minds. Jews and others sickened by Nazi oppression left Germany in a remarkable emigration that included outstanding intellectuals of every type, from writers such as Thomas Mann to physicists such as Einstein. Important psychologists were among their number, most notably the Gestalt psychologists, who moved to the United States, and Sigmund Freud, who spent his last months in England. Appallingly, many psychologists who remained in Germany turned with rapidity in the Nazi direction, in some cases providing "scientific" justification for Nazi racial policies.

On the other hand, psychology won its autonomy under the Nazi regime. One route to independence for psychology had been rejected by the Mandarins—that of making psychology a practical, applied discipline, which, for example, the mayor of Berlin had asked for as early as 1912 (Ash, 1981). Applied psychology was called "psychotechnics" in Germany, and, in 1941, German psychotechnic psychology won bureaucratic recognition as an independent field of study "because the *Wehrmacht* required trained psychologists to assist in the selection of officers" (Ash, 1981, p. 286). This proved a Faustian bargain, of course, when the Nazi regime brought upon Germany the destruction of World War II and the subsequent division of Germany into East and West. Not until the 1950s did psychology in Germany get on its feet again (Ash, 1981), and then it was in an entirely new environment, dominated by American ideas.

Transplantation to America

In one respect, German psychology flourished in America. As we shall see in Chapters 9 and 10, growth of psychology in America quickly outpaced growth in Germany. For example, the American Psychological Association was founded a decade before the German Society for Experimental Psychology. In other respects, however, the psychology of consciousness in its German form could not be carried beyond the borders of Mandarin Germany. G. Stanley Hall wrote, in 1912, "We need a psychology that is usable, that is dietetic, efficient for thinking, living, and working, and although Wundtian thoughts are now so successfully cultivated in academic gardens, they can never be acclimated here, as they are antipathetic to the American spirit and temper" (quoted by Blumenthal, 1986b).

Of all the early psychologies of consciousness, Wundt's was the most Mandarin and the most liable to rejection by practical-minded Americans. But the other psychologies of consciousness did not fare much better. Although Titchener created a psychology of consciousness along the lines of English-speaking philosophy, his adamant rejection of applied psychology, his prickly personality, and his cultivation of arcane research problems left him decisively outside the mainstream of psychology in America. The Würzburg movement was too short-lived to create a systematic approach to psychology. Brentano's act psychology possessed similarities to the functional psychology that came to dominate psychological theorizing after 1900, but his direct influence in psychology was limited by obscurity and by the lack of a psychological laboratory. Ironically, Brentano's significance lay in the future, when his concept of intentionality posed a fundamental challenge to the computer model of the mind.

The influence of Gestalt psychology in the United States is the hardest to evaluate. There is no question that the Gestalt psychologists were well received and honored in America. Wertheimer, Koffka, Köhler, and Lewin all settled in the United States either before or during the German intellectual migration. All of them were listened to respectfully, and Köhler was eventually elected president of the American Psychological Association. Some of their findings, such as those on insight learning, and some of their ideas, such as the principles of object perception, are found in textbooks to the present day. Nevertheless, the depth of their influence remains unclear.

Their greatest contribution, perhaps, lay in reformulating the study of perception so that it "carved nature at the joints," as philosophers today put it. The image is unpleasant, but vividly meaningful. When we buy precut chicken parts at the supermarket, they are often not carved at the joints: The chicken is divided into pieces by a saw that imposes arbitrary divisions on the chicken skeleton. When we carve a chicken at home, however, the parts into which we cut it conform to the structure of the skeleton: We carve the chicken at the joints, and the pieces we create respect the lineaments of nature. If they could have used this metaphor, the Gestalt psychologists would have maintained that traditional, atomistic psychology did not carve perception at the joints, but imposed on experience an arbitrary atomism of simple sensations, the way the saw imposes arbitrary sectioning on the chicken carcass. They objected not to analyzing experience into parts (Henle, 1985) but to analyzing it into arbitrary parts. In place of analysis of experience into meaningless sensations, they proposed it be analyzed into meaningful phenomenal objects (Henle, 1985), and in fact perceptual psychology no longer insists on a Titchenerian analysis of experience into theoretical atoms of basic sensations.

Gestalt psychologists may be said, therefore, to have reoriented the study of experience, but the influence of their own theories on psychology seems to have remained limited. Perhaps the most balanced summary of Gestalt psychology's impact is offered by one of the last surviving Gestalt psychologists, A. S. Luchins. Luchins (1975) acknowledges that Gestalt terminology is often used in contemporary—especially American—psychology but denies that the concepts to which the terms refer have been assimilated. With its emphasis on wholes, on synthesis, and on placing psychology within a larger "total comprehension of human existence," the Gestalt psychology, like Wundt's, may have been too Mandarin for export.

BIBLIOGRAPHY

Largely because of psychology's centennial celebration in 1979, a great deal has been written about psychology's founding, the psychology of consciousness, and Wundt and his psychology, in particular. In this bibliography, I will indicate only some of the literature on Wundt and the founding of psychology, and will try to highlight the more important and accessible new work.

First, there are several edited volumes on psychology's beginnings: Wolfgang Bringmann and Ryan D. Tweney, eds., *Wundt studies* (Toronto: 1980); Josef Brozek and Ludwig Pongratz, eds., *Historiography of modern psychology* (Toronto: Hogrefe, 1980); C. Buxton, ed., *Points of view in the history of psychology* (New York: Academic Press, 1986); Eliot Hearst, ed., *The first century of experimental psychology* (Hillsdale, NJ: Erlbaum, 1979); Sigmund Koch and David Leary, eds., *A century of psychology as science* (New York: McGraw-Hill, 1985); R. W. Rieber, ed., *Wilhelm Wundt and the making of a scientific psychology* (New York: Plenum, 1980); and William W. Woodward and Mitchell G. Ash, eds., *The problematic science: Psychology in nineteenth century thought* (New York: Praeger, 1982).

An excellent introduction to the intellectual climate in nineteenth-century Germany is provided by Ringer (1969). Three papers discuss the conditions of psychology's founding. Richard Littman (1979) provides a general account of psychology's emergence as a discipline. Ash (1981) describes Germany in 1879–1941. Kurt Danziger, in "Historical construction of social roles in the psychological experiment," a paper presented at the annual meeting of the American Psychological Association, 1981, uses sociological techniques to analyze the emergence of the human psychology experiment. Finally, an older but still useful account of psychology's beginnings, written just after it happened, is found in J. Mark Baldwin, "Sketch of the history of psychology," *Psychological Review* (1905, *12:* 144–165).

A great deal of work has been done on Wundt and his psychology. Besides Wundt (1896), the following works of his are available in English: *Outlines of psychology* (1897; reprinted, St. Clair Shores, Michigan Scholarly Press, 1969); *Principles of physiological psychology,* Vol. 1, 5th ed. (New York: Macmillan, 1910); *An introduction to psychology* (1912; reprinted, New York: Arno, 1973); *Elements of folk psychology* (London: Allen & Unwin, 1916); and *The language of gestures,* an excerpt from his *Völkerpsychologie* of 1900–1920 (The Hague, The Netherlands: Mouton, 1973). For Wundt's biography, see Wolfgang Bringmann, William Balance, and Rand Evans, "Wilhelm Wundt, 1832–1920: A brief biographical sketch," *Journal of the History of the Behavioral Sciences* (1975, *11:* 287–97; Wolfgang Bringmann, Norma J. Bringmann, and William Balance, "Wilhelm Maximilian Wundt 1832–74: The formative years," in Bringmann and Tweney (1980, cited above), and Solomon Diamond (1980).

Other sources on Wundt include Joseph Jastrow, "Experimental psychology in Leipzig," *Science* (1886, *7* [198, Supplement]: 459–62), which describes in detail a few of Wundt's experiments, some of which are startlingly similar to current work in cognitive psychology. These parallels are discussed in my own "Something old, something new: Attention in Wundt and modern cognitive psychology," *Journal of the History of the Behavioral Sciences* (1979, *15:* 242–52). Theodore Mischel discusses "Wundt and the conceptual foundations of psychology," *Philosophical and Phenomenological Research* (1970, *31:* 1–26). William R. Woodward, "Wundt's program for the new psychology: Vicissitudes of experiment, theory, and system" (in Woodward and Ash, 1982, cited above), presents Wundt as a typical German intellectual with a Will to System. Two papers by Kurt Danziger (1979, 1980a) correct errors in the older picture of Wundt and examine his fate in Germany. Arthur Blumenthal (1986a) provides a good general orientation to Wundt's psychology.

Titchener was a prolific writer. Important works, in addition to those cited in the chapter include "The past decade in experimental psychology," *American Journal of Psychology* (1910, *21:* 404–21); "The scheme of introspection," *American Journal of Psychology* (1912, *23:* 485–508; "Experimental psychology: A retrospect," *American Journal of Psychology* (1925, *36:* 313–23); and *A text-book of psychology* (New York: Macmillan, 1913). In my article, "The mistaken mirror: On Wundt's and Titchener's psychologies," *Journal of the History of the Behavioral Sciences* (1981, *17:* 273–82), I show that Titchener was not, as is usually assumed, a simple follower of Wundt who faithfully reflected the master's views.

Some of the Würzburg school's papers are translated and excerpted in George and Jean Mandler, eds., *The psychology of thinking: From association to Gestalt* (New York: John Wiley, 1964). Besides the references in the text, there were two important contemporary discussions of imageless thought: Angell (1911), and Robert S. Woodworth, "Imageless thought," *Journal of Philosophy, Psychology, and Scientific Methods* (1906, *3:* 701–8). A recent discussion is David Lindenfield, "Oswald Külpe and the Würzburg school," *Journal of the History of the Behavioral Sciences* (1978, *14:* 132–41). George Humphrey, in part of his *Thinking* (New York: Science Editions, 1963), discusses the Würzburg findings, although he overestimates their damage to Wundt's psychology. The imageless thought controversy is addressed from a sociology of science perspective by Kusch (1995).

Köhler's important works include *The mentality of apes* (New York: Liveright, 1938); *The place of value in a world of facts* (New York: Liveright, 1938); *Dynamics in psychology* (New York: Liveright, 1940); *Gestalt psychology* (New York: Mentor, 1947); and *Selected papers of Wolfgang Köhler* (New York: Liveright, 1971). Wertheimer's, *Productive thinking* (New York: Harper & Row, 1959) is recommended. Mary Henle has edited a selection of papers by the Gestaltists, *Documents of Gestalt psychology* (Berkeley: University of California Press, 1961). The most influential Gestalt psychologist in the United States was Kurt Lewin, who for some time affected social, personality, and, to a lesser extent, learning, psychology; see, for example, his *Principles of topological psychology* (New York: McGraw-Hill, 1936). Julian Hochberg, "Organization and the Gestalt tradition," in E. Carterette and M. Friedman, eds., *Handbook of perception, vol. 1: Historical and philosophical roots of perception* (New York: Academic Press, 1974) discusses the Gestalt influence on perception. Mary Henle tries to explain isomorphism in "Isomorphism: Setting the record straight," *Psychological Research* (1984, *46:* 317–27). The roots of Wertheimer's ideas are discussed in Abraham S. and Edith H. Luchins, "An introduction to the origins of Wertheimer's Gestalt Psychologie," *Gestalt Theory* (1982, *4:* 145–71). In a massive doctoral dissertation, Mitchell Graham Ash thoroughly documents and discusses the origin and development of Gestalt psychology in Germany in *The emergence of Gestalt theory: Experimental psychology in Germany 1890–1920,* unpublished doctoral dissertation (Cambridge, MA: Harvard University, 1982). The reception of Gestalt psychology in the United States is discussed by Michael Sokal, "The Gestalt psychologists in behaviorist America," *American Historical Review* (1984, *89:* 1240–63).

Brentano's basic work is *Psychology from an empirical standpoint* (New York: Humanities Press, 1973). For discussions of Brentano, see L. McAlister, ed., *The philosophy of Brentano* (Atlantic Highlands, NJ: Humanities Press, 1976).

The review containing James's "heaven-scaling Titans" description is reprinted in Bringmann and Tweney, eds. (1980) and Rieber, ed. (1980), both cited above.

Two other books which contain good information on Gestalt psychology include W. D. Ellis, ed., *A sourcebook of Gestalt psychology* (London: Routledge & Kegan Paul, 1938) and M. Henle, "The influence of Gestalt psychology in America" (*Annals of the New York Academy of Sciences 291:* 3–12).

REFERENCES

Angell, J. R. (1911). On the imageless thought controversy. *Psychological Review 18:* 295–323.

Ash, M. G. (1980). Wilhelm Wundt and Oswald Külpe on the institutional status of psychology: An academic controversy in historical context. In W. Bringmann and R. D. Tweney, eds., *Wundt studies.* Toronto: Hogrefe.

———. (1981). Academic politics in the history of science: Experimental psychology in Germany, 1879–1941. *Central European History 13:* 255–86.

Ben-David, J. and Collins, R. (1966). Social factors in the origins of a new science: The case of psychology. *American Sociological Review 31:* 451–65.

Blumenthal, A. L. (1970). *Language and psychology: Historical aspects of psycholinguistics.* New York: John Wiley.

_____ . (1975). A reappraisal of Wilhelm Wundt. *American Psychologist 30:* 1081–88.

_____ . (1980a). Wilhelm Wundt and early American psychology: A clash of cultures. In R. W. Rieber, ed., *Wilhelm Wundt and the making of a scientific psychology.* New York: Plenum.

_____ . (1980b). Wilhelm Wundt—Problems of interpretation. In W. Bringmann and R. D. Tweney, eds., *Wundt studies.* Toronto: Hogrefe.

_____ . (1986a). Wilhelm Wundt: Psychology as the propadeutic science. In C. Buxton, ed., *Points of view in the history of psychology.* New York: Academic Press.

_____ . (1986b). Shaping a tradition: Experimentalism begins. In C. Buxton, ed., *Points of view in the history of psychology.* New York: Academic Press.

Clark, H. M. (1911). Conscious attitudes, *American Journal of Psychology 22:* 214–49.

Danziger, K. (1979). The positivist repudiation of Wundt. *Journal of the History of the Behavioral Sciences 15:* 205–30.

_____ . (1980a). The history of introspection reconsidered. *Journal of the History of the Behavioral Sciences 16:* 241–62.

_____ . (1980b). Wundt and the two traditions of psychology. In R. W. Rieber, ed., *Wilhelm Wundt and the making of a scientific psychology.* New York: Plenum.

Diamond, S. (1980). Wundt before Leipzig. In R. W. Rieber, ed., *Wilhelm Wundt and the making of a scientific psychology.* New York: Plenum.

Graumann, C. (1980). Experiment, statistics, history: Wundt's first program of psychology. In W. Bringmann and R. D. Tweney, eds., *Wundt studies.* Toronto: Hogrefe.

Henle, M. (1985). Rediscovering Gestalt psychology. In S. Koch and D. Leary, eds., *A century of psychology as science.* New York: McGraw-Hill.

James, W. (1875). Review of *Grundzuge der physiologischen psychologie. North American Review 121:* 195–201.

Koffka, K. (1935/1963). *Principles of Gestalt psychology.* San Diego, CA: Harcourt Brace Jovanovich.

Kusch, M. (1995). Recluse, interlocutor, interrogator: Natural and social order in turn-of-the-century research schools. *Isis, 86,* 419–39.

Littman, R. (1979). Social and intellectual origins of experimental psychology. In E. Hearst, ed., *The first century of experimental psychology.* Hillsdale, NJ: Erlbaum.

Luchins, A. S. (1975). The place of Gestalt theory in American psychology. In S. Ertel, L. Kemmler, and M. Sadler, eds., *Geltalt-theorie in der medernen psychologie.* Darmstadt, Germany: Dietrich Steinkopf Verlag.

Mayer, A. M. and Orth, J. (1901). Experimental studies of association. Partially reprinted in G. Mandler and J. Mandler, eds. (1964) *The psychology of thinking: From associationism to Gestalt.* New York: John Wiley.

Ogden, R. M. (1911a). Imageless thought. *Psychological Bulletin 8:* 183–97.

_____ . (1911b). The unconscious bias of laboratories. *Psychological Bulletin 8:* 330–1.

Richards, R. J. (1980). Wundt's early theories of unconscious inference and cognitive evolution in their relation to Darwinian biopsychology. In W. Bringmann and R. D. Tweney, eds., *Wundt studies.* Toronto: Hogrefe.

Ringer, F. K. (1969). *The decline of German Mandarins: The German academic community 1890–1933.* Cambridge, MA: Harvard University Press.

Titchener, E. B. (1897). *An outline of psychology.* New York: Macmillan.

_____ . (1901–1905). *Experimental psychology: A manual of laboratory practice,* 4 vols. New York: Macmillan.

_____ . (1904). *Lectures on the experimental psychology of the thought processes.* New York: Macmillan.

_____ . (1908). *Lectures on the elementary psychology of feeling and attention.* New York: Macmillan.

_____ . (1929/1972). *Systematic psychology: Prolegomena.* Ithaca, NY: Cornell University Press.

van Hoorn, W. and Verhave, T. (1980). Wundt's changing conception of a general and theoretical psychology. In W. Bringmann and R. D. Tweney, eds., *Wundt studies.* Toronto: Hogrefe.

Wertheimer, Max. (1922/1938). The general theoretical situation. In W. D. Ellis, ed., *A sourcebook of Gestalt psychology.* London: Routledge & Kegan Paul.

_____ . (1925/1938). Gestalt theory. In W. D. Ellis, ed., *A sourcebook of Gestalt psychology.* London: Routledge & Kegan Paul.

Wertheimer, Michael. (1978, Aug. 31). *Max Wertheimer: Gestalt prophet.* Presidential Address to Division 26 (History), annual meeting of the American Psychological Association, Toronto.

Woodward, W. W. (1982). Wundt's program for the new psychology: Vicissitudes of experiment, theory, and system. In W. Woodward and M. Ash, eds., *The problematic science: Psychology in nineteenth century thought.* New York: Praeger.

Woodworth, R. S. (1938). *Experimental psychology.* New York: Holt, Rinehart & Winston.

Woodworth, R. S. and Schlosberg, H. (1954). *Experimental psychology,* 2nd ed. New York: Holt, Rinehart & Winston.

Wundt, W. M. (1896). *Lectures on human and animal psychology.* New York: Macmillan.

_____ . (1873). *Principles of physiological psychology.* Portions of translation by S. Diamond reprinted in R. W. Rieber, ed. (1980), *Wilhelm Wundtand the waking of a scientific psychology.* New York: Plenum.

_____ . (1907–1908). Uber Ausfrageexperimenten und über die Methoden zur Psychologie des Denkens. *Psychologischen Studien 3:* 301–60.

8 *The Psychology of the Unconscious Mind*

Without doubt the most famous and influential of the founders of scientific psychology, Sigmund Freud's ideas were controversial in his own day and remain so in ours. While some revere him as an heroic explorer of the hidden springs of human motives, others censure him as the founder of a pseudoscience.

INTRODUCTION

The Significance of Psychoanalysis

The psychology of the unconscious was markedly different from the psychology of consciousness. Wundt and the other psychologists of consciousness focused on the normal, human, adult mind known through introspection, attempting to make an experimental science out of philosophers' traditional questions and theories. Sensation/perception and cognitive psychology largely defined the field, although some attention was given to social, developmental, and animal psychology. Freud's psychology, in contrast, focused on abnormal minds and claimed to unmask consciousness—including normal consciousness—as a self-deceiving puppet of disgusting primal impulses it dared not acknowledge. Instead of conducting experiments, Freud investigated the mind by clinically probing it, looking for the concealed springs of human conduct in unconscious, primitive residues of childhood and evolution. Freud and psychoanalysis rounded out what psychology was to be, adding the fields of personality, motivation, and psychopathology, and strengthening interest in developmental and social psychology.

Freud's character, too, was different from the other German founders of psychology. Wundt, his students, and the Gestalt psychologists were, for all their differences, products of Mandarin Germany, cautious and circumspect scholars and scientists. Freud, however, rejected the Mandarin outlook, "scorn[ing] to distinguish culture and civilization" (Freud, 1930/1961). He was born a Jew—but was an atheist proud of his Jewish heritage—and lived in the shadow of centuries of oppression by the Mandarin class. Freud created psychoanalysis in part as a political challenge to the rulers of Austria-Hungary (Schorske, 1980; McGrath, 1986).

Freud wanted to be a conquering hero in the mold of Moses, bringer of disagreeable commandments to a disbelieving people. Possibly under the influence of cocaine—he used it regularly in the late 1880s and 1890s (Crews, 1986)—Freud (1960, p. 202, letter 94) described himself to his fiancée, Martha Bernays (February 2, 1886):

> Breuer [sometime friend and collaborator] told me he had discovered that hidden under the surface of timidity there lay in me an extremely daring and fearless human being. I had always thought so, but never dared tell anyone. I have often felt as though I had inherited all the defiance and all the passions with which our ancestors defended their temple and could gladly sacrifice my life for one great moment in history.

On February 1, 1899, awaiting the reception of *The Interpretation of Dreams*, Freud wrote to his intimate friend Wilhelm Fliess:

> For I am actually not at all a man of science, not an observer, not an experimenter, not a thinker. I am by temperament nothing but a conquistador—an adventurer, if you want it translated—with all the curiosity, daring, and tenacity characteristic of a man of this sort. Such people are customarily esteemed only if they have been successful, have really discovered something; otherwise they are dropped by the wayside. And that is not altogether unjust. (Freud, 1985, p. 398*)

To the world he aimed to conquer, Freud presented psychoanalysis as a revolution. Psychoanalysis, he often said (Gay, 1989), represented the third great blow to human self-esteem. The first blow was Copernicus's demonstration that human beings did not live at the center of the universe. The second blow was Darwin's demonstration that human beings were part of nature—being animals like any other. The third blow, Freud claimed, was his own demonstration that the human ego is not master in its own house.

---

* Source note: Excerpts from thirteen letters have been reprinted in this chapter, by permission of the publishers, from *The Complete Letters of Sigmund Freud to Wilhelm Fliess, 1887–1904*, J. M. Masson, ed., Cambridge, MA: Harvard University Press, Copyright © 1985 and under the Bern Convention Sigmund Freud Copyrights, Ltd.; translation and editorial matter © 1985 by J. M. Masson.

Freud and Scientific Psychology

Freud and Academic Psychology

"Freud is inescapable": Peter Gay (1989) thus summarizes the conquistador's achievement. There can be no doubt that "we all speak Freud whether we know it or not." Freud's terminology and his essential ideas "pervade contemporary ways of thinking about human feelings and conduct" (Gay, 1989, p. xii). Nevertheless, it is both ironic and inevitable that Freud's influence should have been less in academic psychology than in any other field concerned with human affairs save perhaps economics. Psychologists of consciousness rejected the existence of the unconscious, Freud's indispensable hypothesis. Behaviorists rejected the existence of mind altogether. So it is unsurprising that, apart from occasional recognition of Freud's somewhat literary insights into human motives, academic psychology has largely ignored or rejected psychoanalysis. Rapprochements between academic psychology and psychoanalysis have sometimes been sought (Erdelyi, 1985; Sears, 1985) but never achieved.

Moreover, the isolation of psychoanalysis from academic psychology has been abetted by the development—over Freud's own objections—of psychoanalysis as a branch of medicine. Especially in the United States, an M.D. degree with specialization in psychiatry became the prerequisite for undertaking training as a psychoanalyst. Isolation became enmity with the professional rivalry that arose between psychiatry and clinical psychology. Psychiatrists have always tended to look on clinical psychologists as poorly trained interlopers in the business of medicine, and in the case of psychoanalysis, this resulted in exclusion of Ph.D. psychologists from training in schools of psychoanalysis, a policy that remains bitterly contentious to the present day.

Freud and Experimental Method

Freud may have regarded himself as a conquistador rather than a scientist, but there is no doubt that Freud shared the goal of the other founders of psychology—to create a psychology that was a science like any other. Freud rejected the suggestion that psychoanalysis offered anything other than a scientific view of the world: "Psychoanalysis, in my opinion, is incapable of creating a *Weltanschauung* of its own. It does not need one; it is a part of science" (Freud, 1932 in Gay, 1989, p. 796). Yet Freud did not undertake to construct an experimental psychology of the unconscious, nor did he welcome attempts to experimentally verify his ideas. In the 1930s, an American psychologist, Saul Rosenzweig, wrote to Freud about his attempts at experimental testing of psychoanalysis. Freud replied very briefly (February 28, 1934): "I have examined your experimental studies for the verification of psychoanalytic propositions with interest. I cannot put much value on such confirmation because the abundance of reliable observations on which these propositions rest makes them independent of experimental verification. Still, it can do no harm" (quoted by Rosenzweig, 1985, pp. 171–2).

The "abundance of reliable observations" on which Freud erected psychoanalysis consisted of his clinical cases. We are apt to think today of psychoanalysis as primarily a therapy; but even though Freud certainly valued therapeutic success, he intended psychoanalytic psychology to be a science. He therefore regarded the talk of his patients as scientific data and the analytic session as a scientifically valid method of investigation. Indeed, his remarks to Rosenzweig suggest that he regarded analysis as more than the equal of experimentation as a scientific method.

For Freud, successful therapy was not an end in itself, but constituted evidence that psychoanalytic theory was true.

Such dismissal of experimental methodology served to further isolate psychoanalysis from mainstream psychology. Psychoanalysts said that only someone who had been through psychoanalysis was fit to criticize it, leading academic psychologists to regard psychoanalysis more as a cult with an initiation rite than as a science open to all (Sulloway, 1991). Furthermore, reliance on clinical evidence raised more than political difficulties for psychoanalysis as a science. Fechner, Donders, Wundt, and others had introduced experiment to psychology in order to rid it of unscientific subjectivity, replacing armchair introspection with experimental rigor. Psychoanalysis sought to replace armchair introspection with couch introspection, and it could be reasonably asked whether Freud had replaced a bad method with a worse one. After all, the introspective observer in psychoanalysis is a patient: a sick individual wishing to be cured of neurosis, rather than a trained observer committed to the advancement of science. These were not and are not idle concerns, and, as we shall see, they may have played a subterranean role in Freud's greatest challenge, his seduction mistake.

Freud and the Path through Physiology

Like the other founding psychologists, Freud was attracted to the idea of approaching psychology through physiology, but he struggled with it as well. In the previous chapter, we reviewed why, for Wundt and other founding psychologists, the path through physiology was attractive. Freud's situation and ambition as a founder were in large degree the same as the other founders'. He had a medical degree and carried out important work in anatomy and physiology. Ernst Brücke, a distinguished physiologist of a reductive temper had taught Freud and influenced him considerably. Thus, Freud's psychology was likely to be physiological for the same reasons as Wundt's, but once Freud took up clinical practice and began to create psychoanalysis as both science and therapy, the path through physiology also exerted two special attractions for him.

First, one charge that could reasonably be leveled against a science built on the talk of neurotic patients was cultural parochialism. Science is supposed to discover universal truths—laws of nature that hold good across time and space. In the case of psychology, this means finding laws of human behavior that transcend any particular culture or historical era. Living up to this standard of science was vexing enough for experimental psychologists, who could at least point to the rigor and simplicity of their experiments as warrant of their universal character, but such a claim could not be made for psychoanalytic therapy. However, if therapeutic findings were used to elaborate a neurophysiological theory of mind and behavior, then charges of cultural parochialism might be deflected (Sulloway, 1979). After all, human nervous systems exist apart from culture, so that a theory pitched at the neural level could stake a claim to universal truth.

For Freud, however, the most unique attraction of the path to science through physiology lay in his situation as a clinical neurologist. Today, the term "neurosis" is virtually synonymous with a disorder that is entirely mental ("all in your head"), but in Freud's time, neuroses were viewed as primarily neural disorders. By far the most common neurosis of the time was hysteria. In our post-Freudian world, hysteria is called dissociative disorder, defined as a physical symptom having a psychological cause; but in Freud's time, the physical symptoms of hysteria—such things as paralyses and failures of sense perception—were thought to stem from an unknown disorder of the nervous system (Macmillan, 1991).

Before the advent of scientific medicine, hysteria had been viewed as a moral failing, whether a weakness of will or a possession by evil spirits. William James, who suffered from "nervous" diseases himself, spoke for enlightened medical opinion and long-suffering patients when he said, in his 1896 Lowell Lectures on abnormal mental states, "Poor hysterics! First treated as victims of sexual trouble . . . then of moral perversity and mendacity . . . then of imagination . . . honest disease not thought of" (quoted by Myers, 1986, ellipses in original, p. 5). Ironically, in the same year, 1896, Freud gave a paper on hysteria before the Society for Psychiatry and Neurology in which he broached for the first time his view that hysteria had a psychological—specifically sexual—etiology. Chairing the session was the greatest student of sexual psychopathology of the day, Richard von Krafft-Ebing, who pronounced it a "scientific fairytale." With James, Krafft-Ebing and the rest of the medical establishment—Freud called them "donkeys"—regarded the strictly medical view of hysteria as a great advance (Sulloway, 1979).

Patients treated for hysteria would probably have disagreed. A physical etiology for hysteria prescribed physical treatments, no matter how mysterious the malady. The nosological term "hysteria," derived from the Greek word *hyster,* meaning womb, reflected the prevailing belief that hysteria was almost always suffered only by women. Because physicians were always male, the doctor–patient relationship was defined by the norms of a patriarchal social order. Doctors expected all patients to be quietly submissive, an expectation doubled for women. Moreover, there could be a hidden sexual element in male doctor–female patient relationships. Freud had trouble handling his own feelings for at least one patient (Decker, 1981, 1991). These factors made the physical treatments for hysteria especially unpleasant for women.

Treatments for hysteria were often "heroic" in the extreme, bordering on torture. The leading treatment was "electrotherapy." Its milder form was "faradization," for which Freud bought the needed equipment in 1886. The patient, naked or lightly covered, was seated in water with her feet on a negative electrode, while the physician probed her body from head to foot with a positive electrode or (for "sensitive" patients) with his "electrical hand," the current passing through his own body. Treatment sessions lasted ten to twenty minutes and were frequently repeated. Many patients had severe adverse reactions, ranging from burns to dizziness or defecation.

Other therapies included suffocation, beating with wet towels, ridicule, hard icy showers, insertion of tubes in the rectum, application of hot irons to the spine, and, in "intractable" cases, ovariectomies and cauterization of the clitoris. Such treatments may fairly be regarded as abuse of women by powerful men, but it should also be noted that treatment for some male disorders was equally "heroic," involving, for example, cauterization of parts of the genitalia (Decker, 1991). Whether or not psychoanalysis worked, it could not have worked worse than such "heroic" treatments and must have been regarded with relief by experienced hysterics.

In Freud's case, the physiological path to scientific psychology found fullest expression in a manuscript he never completed, the "Project for a Scientific Psychology" (1950). It was written in a white heat of Newtonian passion (Solomon, 1974) in the fall of 1894 and the spring of 1895. On April 27, 1895, Freud wrote to Fliess, "Scientifically, I am in a bad way; namely caught up in the 'Psychology for neurologists' [Freud's working title], which regularly consumes me totally" (p. 127). On May 25:

". . . a man like me cannot live without a hobbyhorse, without a consuming passion, without—in Schiller's words—a tyrant. I have found one. In its service I know no limits. It is psychology" (p. 129).

Freud was "tormented by two aims: to examine what shape the theory of mental functioning takes if one introduces quantitative considerations, a sort of economics of nerve forces; and second to peel off from psychopathology a gain for normal psychology" (letter to Fliess of May 25, 1895, p. 129). In the "Project" itself, Freud defined his Newtonian "intention . . . to furnish a psychology that shall be a natural science: that is, to represent psychical processes as quantitatively determinate states of specifiable material particles." He went on to develop a general theory of mind and behavior in entirely physiological and quantitative terms. For example, motivation is described as resulting from the buildup of tension at "barriers"—today called synapses—between neurons. This buildup is felt as unpleasure, and its eventual discharge across the barrier is felt as pleasure. Memory is explained (as it is in most neural models today) as changes to the permeability of neuronal barriers (changes in synaptic strength) resulting from repeated firing of connected neurons. In similarly quantitative-neurological ways, Freud explained the full range of "mental" functions from hallucinations to cognition.

Freud's "Project" remains one of the most fascinating but troublesome documents in the history of psychoanalysis. It is fascinating because so much of Freud's psychological theory is introduced in the "Project" in neurological guise, but it is troublesome because it is hard to evaluate Freud's final attitude toward it, or properly place it in the history of psychoanalytic thought. Because he abandoned writing it and later resisted its publication, it is fair to conclude that Freud regarded the "Project" as fatally flawed, but the question remains: Why? The standard account accepted by later Freudians is that, shortly after working on the "Project," Freud undertook a "heroic" self-analysis in which he discovered that the causes of behavior are psychological events occurring in a psychological unconscious, and he consequently abandoned the "Project" as a young man's foolishness. He remained driven by his "tyrant," psychology, but his later theories, like Wundt's, became more psychological. In his clinical work, he came to distinguish between "actual neuroses" and "psychoneuroses." The actual neuroses were true physical diseases, caused by "excess or deficiency of certain nerve-poisons" (Freud, 1908/1953, p. 81); the psychoneuroses, including hysteria, have causes that "are psychogenic, and depend upon the operation of unconscious (repressed) ideational complexes" (Freud, 1908/1953, p. 81).

On the other hand, Sulloway (1979) has persuasively argued that regarding Freud's self-analysis as the critical event in the history of psychoanalysis was a myth put out by Freud and his followers to turn Freud into a heroic conqueror of pure psychology and to obscure Freud's continued reliance on biology as the secret foundation of psychoanalytic theory. Freud gave up the "Project" because he could not construct a mechanism compatible with his main guiding thesis about the origin of neurosis. Whether in the seduction theory or later, Freud always held that adult neurotic symptoms find their ultimate cause in a childhood trauma or disgusting thought. At the time, this event or thought has no pathological effect, but it lies dormant and is unconsciously reawakened, expressed as a symptom, years later.

This view of the etiology of symptoms was so dear to Freud that he gave up neurologizing, but he did not give up biology. According to Sulloway (1979, 1982), Freud turned from mechanistic physiological biology to Lamarckian evolutionary biology to explain human development. For example, most scientists of the day (including Wundt) accepted the "biogenetic law" of Ernst Haeckel (1834–1919), Germany's leading Darwinian. According to the biogenetic law—which we now know to be false—"ontogeny recapitulates phylogeny," that is, the embryological development of any creature repeats its species' evolutionary path. Thus, to casual inspection, a human fetus passes through an amphibian stage, a reptile stage, a simple mammal stage, and so on, until it resembles a miniature human being. Freud simply extended the biogenetic law to include psychological development. The stages of psychosexual development he regarded as recapitulations of the sex life of our predecessor species, including latency as a recapitulation of the ice ages! Lamarckian inheritance became a convenient way out of many difficulties. Thus, in order for a child to develop castration anxiety, he or she did not have to see that opposite-sexed people have different genitals; the knowledge was written in the genes. In Sulloway's view, then, Freud ceased to seek the cause of psychoneuroses in the physiochemical mechanics of the nervous system, but he never gave up the search for an organic basis for neurotic and normal psychological development.

Central to Freud's new biological conception of human development and behavior was the sex instinct. Sex provided a basis for constructing a truly universal and naturalistic scientific psychology because it was neither species- nor culture-specific. Following the path of the Enlightenment and going against the German Mandarins, Freud wanted a psychology shorn of scientifically irrelevant cultural factors. The ubiquity of the sex drive provided its foundation. Freud always supposed that the list of biological needs was short: hunger, thirst, self-preservation, and sex (and later, aggression). If one accepts this list as exhaustive, then one has a problem explaining much of human behavior. It is clear that animal behavior always seems to serve one of these needs, but it is equally clear that human behavior does not. Humans build cathedrals, paint pictures, write novels, think of philosophies, and conduct science, none of which immediately meets any biological need. Earlier writers on human motivation, from Plato to Franz Joseph Gall, to the Scottish realists, were not faced with this problem, because they supposed that human beings have special motives that lead to religion, art, philosophy, and science.

Freud, however, by taking a biologically reductive and simplifying view of motivation, accepted a short list of drives and needed to show that behavior not directly caused by them was in reality indirectly caused by them. It had to be the case that instincts could be redirected from their innately determined channels into other, less biological ones. Hunger, thirst, and self-preservation are poor candidates for rechanneling, because satisfying them is necessary for the survival of the organism. Sexuality, on the other hand, is a powerful motive whose satisfaction can be postponed or even abandoned; the animal may be unhappy, but it lives. Sexuality, then, is the biological motive most capable of displacement from sexual satisfaction into more socially acceptable and creative activity, or into neurosis. Freud was not the first to find in sex the hidden cause of human achievement; romantic poets and philosophers such as Schopenhauer talked about the sublimation of sexuality into higher things, as did Freud's friend Fliess (Sulloway, 1979). Only Freud, however, made sublimation part of a general theory of human mind and behavior.

Moreover, the sexual drive is the one human societies take the greatest interest in regulating. Societies universally regulate the sort of person one may take as a sex partner and marry, while taking no interest in one's dining companions. It appeared to Freud, then, that society actively seeks to rechannel sex away from its native goal toward more civilized ones, but often has succeeded in making neuroses instead.

Sex played the key role in the formation of neuroses, giving Freud's science a biological foundation (Sulloway, 1979). In the case of the actual neuroses, "the sexual factor is the essential one in [their] causation" (Freud, 1908/1953), since the "nerve poisons" that cause actual neuroses are generated by wrong sexual practices such as adult masturbation or sexual abstinence (Sulloway, 1979). The situation with regard to psychoneuroses was different, with sexuality playing a more psychological role. The most purely biological factor in psychoneurosis was the prior state of the nervous system, because "hereditary influence is more marked" than in the actual neuroses (Freud, 1908/1953). Sexuality came into play as the factor working on the nervous system to cause the symptoms of hysteria. In Freud's early theorizing, sexual seduction as a child provided the trauma that would later blossom into neurosis. In his later theory, childhood sexual fantasies provided the kernels of adult neuroses.

By 1905, Freud had written the founding works of psychoanalysis, *Interpretation of Dreams* and *Three Essays on the Theory of Sexuality,* and had sorted out what was biological and what was psychological in psychoanalysis:

> Some of my medical colleagues have looked upon my theory of hysteria as a purely psychological one, and have for that reason pronounced it ipso facto incapable of solving a pathological problem. . . . [But] it is the therapeutic technique alone which is purely psychological; the theory does not by any means fail to point out that neuroses have an organic basis—though it is true that it does not look for that basis in any pathological anatomical changes. . . . No one, probably, will be inclined to deny the sexual function the character of an organic factor, and it is the sexual function that I look upon as the foundation of hysteria and of the psychoneuroses in general. (1905b, quoted in Gay, 1989, p. 372)

Issues and Concepts

Freud always regarded two concepts as fundamental to psychoanalysis. One was the concept of the psychological unconscious. To give a psychological explanation of hysteria, Freud was led to posit the existence of a willfully hidden part of the mind. This unconscious contained ancient wishes and thoughts from the racial or personal past, thoughts too terrible to allow into consciousness Although hidden, these thoughts still found expression as symptoms in hysterics, and in dreams and slips of the tongue in allegedly "normal" people. The other cornerstone of psychoanalysis was Freud's insistence that what was repressed into the unconscious was primarily sexual in nature, so that sexual wishes—most importantly, childhood sexual wishes—lay at the root of neurotic symptoms and modern nervousness as well as much of the rest of human behavior. Yet, both concepts were and remain controversial in scientific psychology. Not all psychologists have believed in the unconscious—nor do all value sex so highly, or agree with Freud's interpretation of childhood sexuality.

THE UNCONSCIOUS

Issue: Does the Unconscious Exist?

Positing the existence of unconscious mental states was not new with Freud. Leibniz's petite perceptions are unconscious. Like Freud, Herbart divided the mind into conscious and unconscious areas and viewed mental life as a competition among ideas seeking access to consciousness. Helmholtz believed that the construction of the experienced world from the atoms of sensation required the existence of unconscious inferences. The hypnotic trance and the power of posthypnotic suggestion, with which Freud was familiar from his studies with Charcot and his own use of hypnosis in therapy, seemed to point to a realm of mind apart from consciousness. Schopenhauer spoke of the "wild beast" within the human soul, and Nietzsche said "Consciousness is a surface" (Kaufmann, 1985). Freud acknowledged Nietzsche's grasp of unconscious dynamics in *Psychopathology of Everyday Life* (1914/1966) when he quoted Nietzsche's pithy aphorism: " *'I have done that,'* says my memory. *'I could not have done that,'* says my pride and remains inexorable. Finally, my memory yields" (Kaufmann, 1985; italics in Kaufmann). By the turn of the century, students of human affairs were increasingly regarding human behavior as being caused by processes and motives lying outside awareness (Hughes, 1958; Ellenberger, 1970).

Nevertheless, the hypothesis of unconscious mental states was not the dominant one among academic psychologists, who viewed mind as coextensive with consciousness. For them, the science of mind—psychology—was the science of consciousness. Freud's most important instructor in philosophy, Franz Brentano, rejected the unconscious (Krantz, 1990), and he was joined in his views by the preeminent American psychologist, William James (1890). Brentano and James were united in holding the doctrine called, by Brentano, the infallibility of inner perception and, by James, *esse est sentiri.* According to this view, ideas in consciousness were (*esse est*) exactly what they appeared to be (*sentiri*). That is, ideas in consciousness were not compounded, by what James called "the Kantian machine shop of the unconscious," out of simpler mental elements. The Gestalt view was similar, arguing that complex wholes were given directly in consciousness without hidden mental machinery behind the stage of experience.

It is important to realize that neither Brentano nor James denied the validity of a purely descriptive use of the term "unconscious." They fully recognized that behavior or experience may be determined by factors of which humans are not aware, but they believed that the existence of unconscious causes of experience and behavior did not require the positing of unconscious mental states. They proposed a number of alternative mechanisms by which mind and behavior might be unconsciously shaped. James fully treated the problem in his *Principles of Psychology* (1890).

As James points out, consciousness is a brain process, and we are not aware of the states of our brain. Our cerebellum keeps us balanced upright, for example, but to explain upright posture we need not suppose that the cerebellum is unconsciously computing the laws of physics. So memories not now recalled need not be supposed to exist psychologically at all, but to exist as traces in the brain, dispositions toward consciousness awaiting activation (James, 1890). Other apparently unconscious mental states may be explained as lapses in attention and memory. Apprehended stimuli, to use Wundt's terms, are conscious but, because they are not apperceived, they may not be remembered. If we are influenced by them, we might be disposed to think they influenced us "unconsciously," when in fact their presence in consciousness was merely no longer recollected. In 1960, George Sperling would show that, in Wundt's letter perception experiment, apprehended letters were perceived briefly but forgotten during the time it took the subjects to pronounce the letters they had seen. A dream or memory we cannot recover need not be thought to be unconscious because repressed, but "unconscious" because forgotten (James, 1890). Finally, phenomena such as hypnotism and the existence of multiple personalities may be explained by dissociation of consciousness rather than the existence of an unconscious. That is, within the brain of a single individual, two distinct consciousnesses may be present, unknown to each other, rather than a single consciousness beset by unconscious forces.

Positing an unconscious seemed to James and other psychologists to be scientifically dangerous. Because the unconscious, by definition, lies outside inspection, it can easily become a convenient vehicle by which to construct untestable theories. As James (1890, p. 163) wrote, the unconscious "is the sovereign means for believing what one likes in psychology, and of turning what might become a science into a tumbling-ground for whimsies."

Nevertheless, Freud cast his lot with the party of the unconscious, and it is the one truly indispensable shibboleth of psychoanalysis (Gay, 1989), the "consummation of psychoanalytic research" (Freud, 1915b). Unconscious causes of hysterical symptoms make their first psychoanalytic appearance in *Studies in Hysteria,* published by Freud and Joseph Breuer (1842–1925) in 1895. Breuer was a distinguished general physician and physiologist who, in 1880, first treated the patient whose case starts the story of psychoanalytic therapy. Called Anna O. in *Studies,* Bertha von Pappenheim was a young middle-class woman who, like many others, had to nurse a sick father (as Anna Freud later nursed Sigmund). She fell prey to hysteria, primarily minor paralyses and difficulties speaking and hearing. Treating her over a period of time, Breuer found that she gained some symptomatic relief by falling into autohypnosis and talking about her symptoms, recovering, while doing so, forgotten events that had caused them. For example, her inability to drink water from a glass was traced to having seen a dog licking water from a glass, and when she recovered this memory she immediately drank from a glass again. Despite continued treatment, Anna O. showed no continued improvement and, in fact, had to be hospitalized at one point. The statement in *Studies* that she got well was false, nor did she experience a hysterical pregnancy naming Breuer as the father, as analytic legend has it.

In some respects, Anna invented psychotherapy, for she was one of a number of reported cases in the nineteenth century in which hysterical patients guided doctors to their cures (Macmillan, 1991). In Anna's case, she set her own timetable for therapy, placed herself in hypnosis, and led herself to the precipitating causes of her symptoms, a procedure she named the talking cure. She was an intelligent and forceful woman who went on to an important, influential, and successful career as the founder of social work in Germany. Despite being present at the creation, however, she never had kind words for psychoanalysis.

Freud had nothing to do with the case of Anna O., but later collaborated with Breuer in applying the talking cure to hysterics and formulating a general theory of hysteria. The case of Anna O. was tidied up, and Freud contributed the rest of the case histories which, together with a theoretical chapter, comprise *Studies in Hysteria.* In the theoretical chapter, Breuer and Freud argued that hysterics fall ill because they "suffer mainly from reminiscences"; that is, they experience an emotional trauma that is repressed. Instead of working through the negative emotions aroused by the event, the affect is "strangulated"—repressed—along with the memory itself, but the affect survives in the unconscious and manifests itself as a symptom. Under hypnosis, the experience is relived fully: The affect is unstrangulated, or "abreacted," and the symptom connected with the event disappears. Macmillan (1991) points out that, in Anna O.'s case, the abreaction described in the book never took place. Breuer's rediscovered clinical notes showed that Anna got relief from simply remembering events, not reliving them.

In *Studies in Hysteria,* Breuer and Freud began to move away from a purely medical-physiological view of hysteria, and toward a psychological view involving unconscious processes. Freud soon found that hypnosis was not the only way to tap unconscious wishes and ideas. Patients could slowly plumb their unconscious during sessions of uninhibited talk guided by the interpretations of the therapist. In 1896, Freud first used the term "psychoanalysis" to describe his new, nonhypnotic technique (Sulloway, 1979). In the same year, Freud's rejection of Breuer began. Breuer the scientist was too cautious for Freud the conquistador. Freud rejected Breuer because Freud was a hedgehog and Breuer a fox; he confided in a letter to Fliess on March 1, 1896 (p. 175):

> According to him [Breuer] I should have to ask myself every day whether I am suffering from moral insanity or paranoia scientifica. Yet, I regard myself as the more normal one. I believe that he will never forgive that in the *Studies* I dragged him along and involved him in something where he unfailingly knows three candidates for the position of one truth and abhors all generalizations, regarding them as presumptuous. . . . Will the two of us experience the same thing with each other?

For his part, Breuer agreed: "Freud is a man given to absolute and exclusive formulations; this is a psychical need which, in my opinion, leads to excessive generalization" (quoted by Crews, 1986). Breuer was the first of several friend-collaborators used and then discarded by Freud. Years later, when Breuer was an old man hobbling along the street with his daughter, they saw Freud; Breuer threw his arms out in greeting, but Freud hurried past giving no sign of recognition (Roazen, 1974). An even more bitter estrangement awaited Wilhelm Fliess.

Changing Conceptions of the Unconscious

Freud spelled out his conception of the unconscious mind in detail in *The Unconscious* (1915b). To counter arguments such as James's, Freud began by justifying his positing of unconscious mind. Part of the dispute over the unconscious seemed to Freud merely verbal. To say that memories are brain traces, not unconscious mental states, simply restates the definition of psychology as the study of consciousness and defines unconscious states out of existence rather than disproving their existence. As Freud saw it, equating mind and consciousness was "inexpedient," primarily because physiological explanations of experience were not available (a likely reason for giving up the "Project") and represented an abandoning of psychology altogether.

Beyond his claim that psychological theorizing in terms of unconscious processes is thus more satisfying than theorizing in terms of physiology, Freud offered two main arguments for the unconscious. The first "incontrovertible proof" was the therapeutic success of psychoanalysis: Only therapy based on true theory can cure. Opponents of the unconscious might have reasoned as Mesmer had, in rejecting the proffering of cures as evidence for the validity of the fluidic theory of medicine. Mesmer had pointed out the problem later discovered in therapy outcome studies: Cures may be spontaneous, having nothing to do with the physician's treatments. Moreover, critics could continue, even if the therapy works, the theory may not be true. Effective action may be based on wrong theory, as when ancient mariners sailed the seas by the principles of Ptolemaic astronomy. Modern critics may challenge the efficacy of psychoanalysis, as we will see later in the chapter.

The second argument in defense of the unconscious is based on the philosophical issue of other minds, raised by Descartes. Freud built from Descartes's argument that we infer consciousness in others to the conclusion of an inferred unconscious within us. Freud argued that just as we infer the presence of mind in other people, and perhaps animals, from "observable utterances and actions," so we should in our own individual case as well. "[A]ll the acts and manifestations which I notice in myself must be judged as if they belonged to someone else," another mind within me. Freud acknowledged that this argument "leads logically to the assumption of another, second consciousness" within oneself, but notwithstanding James's espousal of this very hypothesis, Freud thought it unlikely to win approval from psychologists of consciousness. Moreover, Freud asserted, this other consciousness possesses characteristics "which seem alien to us, even incredible," to the point that it is preferable to regard them as possessed not by a second consciousness but by unconscious mental processes (Gay, 1989, pp. 576–7).

Freud proceeded to distinguish several senses of the term "unconscious." We have already recognized a descriptive usage on which Freud and psychologists of consciousness agreed—namely, that we are not always fully conscious of the causes of our behavior. Disagreement began with Freud's topographical conception of an unconscious mental space—the unconscious—where ideas and wishes live when they are not present to consciousness. Freud's scheme is like Nietzsche's: Consciousness is a surface lying over a vast and unknown realm sensed dimly, if at all. In Freud's description of the mind, all mental events begin in the unconscious, where they are tested for acceptability to consciousness. Thoughts that pass the censorship test may become conscious; if they fail, they will not be allowed into consciousness. Applied to perception, this analysis provided the foundation for the important "New Look in Perception" movement of the 1950s. Passing the test of censorship does not directly lead to consciousness but only makes an idea "capable of becoming conscious." Ideas that are available to consciousness in this way reside in the preconscious, which Freud did not regard as importantly different from consciousness.

More important and psychoanalytically interesting was the fate of ideas or wishes that did not pass muster with the mental censor. These ideas and wishes are often very powerful, constantly seeking expression. Because they are repugnant, however, they must continually be forced to remain unconscious. This dynamic unconscious is created by repression, the act of actively and forcefully opposing the entrance to consciousness of unacceptable thoughts. When, as is sometimes the case in modern textbooks, the dynamic unconscious is presented as a mental dungeon, its dynamic character is lost, and one of Freud's crucial theses is ignored. Repression is a dynamic act, not a locking-away. Repressed thoughts and wishes live on and, blocked by censorship and repression, find indirect expression in neurotic symptoms, dreams, mental errors, and rechanneling—sublimation—into more acceptable forms of thought and behavior.

To the descriptive, topographical, and dynamic usages of the unconscious, Freud added a systematic usage. The unconscious is not simply a place in space (topographical use) containing readily available thoughts (the preconscious) and repressed thoughts (the dynamic unconscious). It is also a separate system of mind from consciousness, and it follows its own fantastical principles. In contrast to consciousness, it is exempt from logic, emotionally unstable, lives as much in the past as the present, and is wholly out of touch with external reality.

The systematic conception of the unconscious became increasingly important to Freud and was central to the later restructuring of his picture of the mind (Freud, 1923/1960). The topographical model of the mind as a collection of spaces (conscious, preconscious, dynamic unconscious) was replaced by a structural model in which the mind was comprised of three distinct mental systems: (a) the innate, irrational, and gratification-oriented id (the old systematic conception of the unconscious); (b) the learned, rational, reality-oriented ego (consciousness plus the preconscious); and (c) the moralistically irrational superego (the censor), composed of moral imperatives inherited by Lamarckian evolution. The old dichotomy of consciousness and unconsciousness, Freud said, "begins to lose significance" with the adoption of the systematic viewpoint.

The id represents the biological basis of the mind, the source of all motives, and thus is the ultimate engine of behavior. The desires of the id usually lie hidden behind all that is best and worst in human history, behind tragedy and achievement, war and art, religion and science, health and neurosis, and all of human civilization. The study of the instincts of the id is the heart of Freudian psychoanalysis.

THE INSTINCTS

Unlike earlier philosophers such as the Scots, and earlier neuropsychologists such as Franz Joseph Gall (1758–1828), Freud took a narrow view of animal and human motivation. Gall had postulated a wide range of animal motives differing from species to species, and he and the Scottish faculty psychologists believed that human beings possessed motives unique to their species. Freud's view of the forces in the id was much simpler and more reductive. Animals had only a few instincts, and humans had none they did not share with the animals. In the original formulation of psychoanalysis, the most important instinct by far was sex. After World War I, it was joined, in Freud's estimation, by death.

In his time and our own, Freud is best known—even notorious—for tracing every symptom, every dream, every apparently noble act back to sex. Some of Freud's readers have always regarded psychoanalysis as a sewer, and psychoanalytic writings as "pornography gone to seed" (Cioffi, 1973). Others found Freud's explicit treatment of sexuality refreshing in an antisexual age—an important recognition of a major human drive. The founder of behaviorism, John B. Watson, had no use for Freud's hypothesized mental apparatus, but he applauded Freud's attention to the biological side of the mind, so neglected by traditional psychologists of consciousness. It should be remembered that Freud, while sometimes shocking, was not a lone voice in a sexually repressive wilderness. Just as he did not invent the concept of the unconscious, so he was not the only thinker to draw attention to sexuality and attack sexual hypocrisy. In Britain, for example, the path of sexual openness was blazed by Havelock Ellis (1859–1939), whose works were sometimes banned but always read. In Germany, Richard von Krafft-Ebing may have branded one of Freud's early ideas a "fairytale," but his *Psychopathia Sexualis* was a best-selling compendium of abnormal sexual practices whose decorous use of Latin was transparent to his educated readers. Nevertheless, although Ellis and Krafft-Ebing may have prophesied its coming, ours is truly a post-Freudian age, because it was he who not only brought sex into the open but built on it a theory of human nature.

Issue: Why Sex? Historical Factors

Freud, for several reasons, came to find in sex the main motive in human life. As we have seen, sex furnished an organic basis for neurosis and a universal biological basis for his theoretical psychology. Another reason was his "discovery" of childhood sexuality as the root cause of neuroses (see later discussion). A third is found in social history: Men and women of Freud's day really did find sexuality hard to cope with.

Freud and other physicians found themselves presented with problems rooted in the nineteenth century's struggles with sexuality. The cause of the problem is straightforward. As societies develop economically, they experience an important demographic transition from large families to small ones. In rural and village societies, children are economic resources—hands to be put to work as soon as possible, and the main support in their parents' old age. In industrially developed societies, children turn into economic liabilities. Costly to raise and educate before they can join the workforce, they become drains on parents' income. As standards of living rise, children become increasingly less attractive economically, and parents begin to have fewer children.

The middle classes of Victorian Europe felt most acutely the problem of controlling reproduction without modern contraceptives. To succeed economically, they had to work hard and exert enormous self-control, including control of potentially costly reproduction. They looked on the large families of rural and laboring classes, for whom children were still exploitable resources, with a mixture of horror and, sometimes, salacious envy. The middle class abhorred the squalor and misery of lower-class lives, but was envious of their sexual freedom. Poet George Meredith expressed both attitudes: "You burly lovers on the village green/Yours is a lower and a happier star!" (quoted by Gay, 1986). Freud, too, saw greater sexual happiness among the poor without wishing to join them. Describing for a lecture audience two imagined case histories, he said, "Sexual activity appeared to the caretaker's daughter just as natural and unproblematic in later life as it had in childhood" and is "free from neurosis," while the landlord's daughter "experienced the impact of education and acknowledged its claims," turned from sex with "distaste," and became neurotic (quoted by Gay, 1986). Yet Freud, like most educated and agnostic or atheist Victorians, continued to live on nerve, never prescribing sex. He wrote to his fiancée, Martha Bernays (August 29, 1883; Freud, 1960, letter 18, p. 50), "The rabble live without constraint while we deprive ourselves." We bourgeois do so "to maintain our integrity. . . . We keep ourselves for something, we know not what, and this habit of constantly suppressing our natural drives gives us the character of refinement" (quoted by Gay, 1986, p. 400).

There is abundant evidence that the struggle for integrity among the middle classes—from which Freud drew most of his patients—was intense and was fought in an environment that we today would find shocking.

> Where should we find that reverence for the female sex, that tenderness towards their feelings, that deep devotion of the heart to them, which is the beautiful and purifying part of love? Is it not certain that all of the delicate, the chivalric which still pervades

our sentiments, may be traced to the repressed, and therefore hallowed and elevated passion?

So wrote W. R. Greg in 1850 (quoted by Houghton, 1957, p. 380). The Victorians did not accept the animal part of their nature, whether sexual or simply sensual. Wrote the anonymous author of an antismoking pamphlet: "Smoking . . . is liked because it gives agreeable sensations. Now it is a positive objection to a thing that it gives agreeable sensations. An earnest man will expressly avoid what gives agreeable sensations" (Houghton, 1957, p. 236). (Earnestness was a cardinal virtue to Victorians.) Victorian culture and religion thundered against pleasure, especially sexual pleasure, and Victorians were burdened by an oppressive sense of guilt. Like a medieval saint, British Liberal Prime Minister William Gladstone recorded his least sin and grieved over it. Guilt was heightened by constant temptation. Prostitution was rampant; men and women, boys and girls—all could be had for a price. The anonymous author of *My Secret Life*, a sexual autobiography, claimed to have seduced over two thousand people of all ages and sexual orientations, and engaged in every vice. Boys at the finest private schools were sexually abused. The Victorians were caught between stern conscience and compelling temptation.

Freud (1912/1953) named as the most common cause of impotence the inability of men to love where they lusted and lust where they loved, and not only because sleeping with one's wife might beget children. Physicians often taught, and men came to believe, that women, at least middle-class women, had no sexual feelings, and men felt guilty about thrusting brutish sexuality on their wives. The results were impotence at worst and greatly inhibited sex at best. Men could fully lust after prostitutes, but these women were degraded by their very sexuality, made unworthy of love. Middle-class women, for their part, were trapped and inhibited by being idealized and idolized. Writing to his fiancée on November 15, 1883, Freud (1960, letter 28, p. 76) wrote against feminism: "Am I to think of my delicate, sweet girl as a competitor? . . . Women's delicate natures . . . are so much in need of protection. [Emancipation would take away] the most lovely thing the world has to offer us: our ideal of womanhood." Perhaps Freud was typical of many men of his day. On October 3, 1897, at age 41, Freud wrote Fliess, "Sexual excitement, too, is no longer of use for someone like me." From about 1900, the year *Interpretation of Dreams* came out, Freud ceased having sex with his wife (Decker, 1981), but there is little evidence he took up with anyone else (Gay, 1988).

Notwithstanding, or perhaps because of, his own situation, Freud sided with the movement of sexual reform led by people such as Havelock Ellis. In 1905, Freud gave a deposition before a commission looking into liberalization of Austria's laws on marriage and sexuality. Freud testified in favor of "legalization of relations between the sexes outside of marriage, according a greater measure of sexual freedom and curtailing restrictions on that freedom" (Boyer, 1978, p. 100, original German; p. 92, English translation). Ten years later, Freud repeated this sentiment in a letter to one of his leading American supporters, the neurologist J. J. Putnam: "Sexual morality—as society, in its most extreme form, the American, defines it—seems to me very contemptible. I advocate an incomparably freer sexual life" (quoted by Gay, 1988, p. 143). In *"Civilized" sexual morality and modern nervousness* (1908/1953), Freud paints a devastating portrait of the effects of civilized marriage. Men become impotent, as we've seen, or "undesirably immoral" by finding sex outside marriage, but women, suffering from a double standard, are made ill.

> [Can] sexual intercourse in legitimate marriage offer full compensation for the restraint before marriage[?] The abundance of material supporting a reply in the negative is . . . overwhelming. We must above all keep in mind that our civilized sexual morality restricts sexual intercourse in marriage itself. . . and all the contraceptives available hitherto impair sexual enjoyment. . . . [The "physical tenderness" and "mental affection" between husband and wife disappear] and under the disappointments of matrimony women succumb to severe, lifelong neurosis. . . . Marital unfaithfulness would . . . be a . . . probable cure for the neurosis resulting from marriage. . . . [But] the more earnestly [a wife] has submitted to the demands of civilization, the more does she fear this way of escape, and in conflict between her desires and her sense of duty she again will seek refuge in neurosis. Nothing protects her virtue so securely as illness. (pp. 89–90)

Freud the clinician identified sex as the root of his patients' problems because, at that time and place, his patients had a hard time fitting in sex alongside their economic and moral aspirations. If Freud's emphasis on sexuality sometimes seems outrageously alien and implausible today, it may be because the sexual reforms he championed (but did not gain from) came about and because technology has improved contraception. Sex is still a problem for us, but not in the way it was for Freud's civilized sufferers.

Issue: Why Sex? The "Discovery" of Childhood Sexuality

It was not just sexuality but *childhood sexuality* that Freud claimed to find as the root of neuroses. If some of Freud's contemporaries found his emphasis on sex shocking, many more found shocking his postulation of childhood sexuality. Asserting the existence of sexual feelings in childhood was central to the psychoanalytic strategy for explaining human behavior. Without childhood sexual drives, there could be no Oedipus complex, whose happy or unhappy resolution held the key to later normality or neurosis. Childhood sexuality and the Oedipus complex are also crucial to the whole idea of depth psychology. Freud located the causes of neurosis—and, by implication, happiness—entirely in the minds of his patients. Their personal situations were not the ultimate cause of sufferers' problems, Freud said. The feelings they had had as children were. Consequently, therapy consisted of adjusting a patient's inner life, not changing the circumstances in which she or he lived. Health would come when one resolved the difficulties one had when one was five years old, not the difficulties one faced today.

The central episode in the history of psychoanalysis is Freud's abandonment of his seduction theory of hysteria—in which he had asserted that hysteria was caused by childhood sexual seductions—and its replacement by the Oedipus complex. In recent years, especially following the publication of the complete and unexpurgated letters of Freud to Fliess, the seduction mistake has occupied center stage in Freud scholarship, and the ensuing controversies have generated, at times, more heat than light. I will first recount "The Official Story"—Freud's own account of the seduction mistake, the account followed by loyal Freudians unto the present day—and will then present several alternative accounts of the same events.

We begin with the Official Story. As he was writing the "Project," Freud was equally excited by making apparent progress on the cause and cure of hysteria. Writing to Fliess on October 15, 1895, "in the throes of writing fever," he asked, "Have I revealed the great clinical secret to you . . . ? Hysteria is the consequence of a presexual sexual shock. . . . The shock is . . . later transformed into [self-]reproach . . . hidden in the unconscious, . . . effective only as memories" (p. 144). Five days later, Freud exclaimed, "Other confirmations concerning the neuroses are pouring in on me. The thing is really true and genuine" (p. 147). On October 31, he told Fliess that "I perpetrated three lectures on hysteria in which I was very imprudent. I am now inclined to be arrogant" (p. 148).

So, in April 1986, Freud delivered the paper that Krafft-Ebing (1840–1902) called a "scientific fairytale," containing his seduction theory of hysteria. As we have seen, in *Studies in Hysteria,* Freud and Breuer had proposed that the kernel of every hysterical symptom is a repressed traumatic event. Freud now claimed, based on the psychoanalytic recollections of his patients, that there was a single traumatic event at the heart of hysteria, seduction of sexually innocent children by their fathers. Krafft-Ebing and the other "donkeys" of the medical establishment hooted at the theory for being a reversion to the prescientific conceptions of hysteria they had worked so hard to escape.

However, Freud's enthusiasm for the seduction theory turned to ashes. On September 21, 1897, Freud confessed to his friend Fliess that perhaps the seduction theory was a fairytale after all: "I want to confide in you immediately the great secret that has been slowly dawning on me in the last few months. I no longer believe my neurotica [theory of the neuroses]." The stories of seduction told by his patients were untrue; they had not been seduced after all. Freud advanced four reasons for giving up the seduction theory. The first was therapeutic failure: "disappointment in my efforts to bring a single analysis to a real conclusion; the running away [of previously successful patients]; the absence of the complete successes on which I had counted." The second was "the surprise that in all cases, the father, not excluding my own, had to be accused of being perverse" when "surely such widespread perversions are not very probable." Third, there was "the certain insight that there are no indications of reality in the unconscious, so that one cannot distinguish between truth and [emotionally believed] fiction. . . . (Accordingly there would remain the solution that the sexual fantasy invariably seizes upon the theme of the parents)." Fourth and finally, such stories are not found in delirium, when all mental defenses break down. Freud was so shaken that "I was ready to give up two things: the complete resolution of neurosis and the certain knowledge of its etiology in childhood." Nevertheless, the conquistador felt no sense of "weakness" or "shame." Instead, Freud wrote, "I have more the feeling of a victory than a defeat" and he hoped that "this doubt merely represents an episode in the advance toward further insight. . . . In spite of all this I am in very good spirits." (pp. 264–6).

At this point, Freud's self-analysis plays its dramatic role in the tale of psychoanalysis. The critical revelation, the discovery of his own childhood sexuality, is reported by Freud to Fliess on October 3, 1897. Freud claimed to have remembered an event on a train trip when he was 2½ years old: "[M]y libido towards matrem was awakened . . . we must have spent the night together and there must have been an opportunity of seeing her nudam (p. 268)." On October 15, Freud announces, "My self analysis is the most essential thing I have at present and promises to become of the greatest value to me if it reaches its end" (p. 270). Further, he declared his own experience to be universal. In his "own case," Freud had learned of "being in love with my mother and jealous of my father, and I now consider it a universal event in early childhood" (p. 272). Now, Freud concluded, we can understand the power of *Oedipus Rex* and *Hamlet*. As he suggested in his letter to Fliess, Freud now regarded the seduction stories as Oedipal fantasies from childhood, falsely recalled as memories. This resolution allowed Freud to retain his treasured view that neuroses result from the unconscious reawakening of childhood events. In the old theory, the events were real childhood sexual seductions; in the new theory, the events were real childhood sexual fantasies.

The Official Story concludes by saying that Freud heroically discovered the existence of childhood sexuality and the Oedipus complex by giving up his old theory and constructing the new one out of his own unsparingly honest self-interrogation.

Before evaluating the Official Story, it is important to observe that the very foundations of psychoanalysis are at stake. Anna Freud, daughter and loyal disciple, wrote to Jeffrey Masson, controversial critic of the seduction episode: "Keeping up the seduction theory would mean to abandon the Oedipus complex, and with it the whole importance of phantasy life, conscious or unconscious phantasy. In fact, I think there would have been no psychoanalysis afterwards" (quoted by Masson, 1984a, p. 59).

Every claim of the Official Story has been disputed, often bitterly, by Freud's critics, and important Unofficial Stories abound. I shall discuss three. One is Sulloway's (1979) contention that the Official Story has served to obscure the influence of Fliess on Freud, and that Freud's insistence on having heroically "discovered" childhood sexuality all by himself led to the breakup of their deep friendship. Fliess is, in retrospect, a man with odd ideas from which later psychoanalysis wanted to distance itself. He believed in a theory of biorhythms, based on twenty-three-day male and twenty-eight-day female cycles whose combination in complex permutations could explain events such as births and deaths. Freud, for a time, believed Fliess's theory wholeheartedly; his letters to Fliess often contain calculations concerning himself, and calculations concerning the birth of Anna (under a pseudonym) were used in a publication by Fliess. Fliess believed that the nose plays an important role in the regulation of human sexual life, and that surgery on the nose could cure sexual problems like masturbation. Freud himself submitted at least once to Fliess's knife.

The critical issue for understanding the development of psychoanalysis is Fliess's influence on Freud's thinking after the abandonment of the "Project." Sulloway argues that, in the aftermath of the failure of the "Project," Freud adopted almost in toto Fliess's theories of sexuality and human development, while systematically concealing that he had done so. In Sulloway's account, Fliess conceived of the id and Freud took it over without acknowledgment. Fliess's influence on Freud was so thoroughgoing that it cannot be briefly summarized, but in the present context the most important borrowing is the concept of childhood sexuality. Fliess campaigned for the view that children had sexual feelings—advancing, for example, observations of his own children in support. Moreover, Fliess believed in the innate bisexuality of human beings, an important component of the biorhythm theory and, later, a central thesis in the psychoanalytic theory of libidinal development. At what proved to be their last personal meeting, Freud boasted of his discovery of the innate childhood bisexual nature of human beings, and Fliess tried to remind him who had the idea first. Freud persisted in claiming personal credit for the discovery, and Fliess, fearing his ideas were being stolen, withdrew from the relationship. The

Official Story of Freud the hero claims Freud was little influenced by Fliess and himself withdrew from the relationship when he saw through Fliess's crazy ideas.

The second Unofficial Story persuasively argues that Freud either bullied his patients into reporting childhood seductions or foisted upon them such stories, and that he later lied about the whole seduction episode (Cioffi, 1972, 1974, 1984; Schatzman, 1992; Esterson, 1993).

Freud's critics have demonstrated that, from early in his career, Freud believed in sexual causes of neurotic disorders. It has also been shown that, although Freud's later therapeutic technique may have been nondirective and noninterpretive as is the current ideal, at least in his early cases Freud was highly directive and interpretive, showering his patients with sexual interpretations of their condition, and wearing them down until they agreed with his view of their behavior (Rieff, 1979; Crews, 1986; Decker, 1991). As befits a conquistador, Freud was supremely confident of his ability to discern secrets hidden even from a patient's own consciousness: "[N]o mortal can keep a secret. If his lips are silent, he chatters with his fingertips; betrayal oozes out of him at every pore" (Freud, 1905b). Freud wrote of finding facts that "I did not hesitate to use against her [the patient Dora]" (Freud, 1905b). In the paper he gave to the Vienna Society, Freud described "boldly demand[ing] confirmation of our suspicions from the patient. We must not be led astray by initial denials" (Esterson, 1993, p. 17), and he reported having at least once "laboriously forced some piece of knowledge" on a patient (p. 18). His patients certainly resisted. "The fact is, that these patients never repeat these stories spontaneously, nor do they ever . . . present the physician with the complete recollection of a scene of this kind' (Schatzman, 1992, p. 34). Before conquering the world, Freud first conquered his patients.

Freud enjoyed forcing his patients to accept what he, Freud, regarded as the truth, and every resistance he interpreted as a sign that he was getting near a great secret. Given Freud's therapeutic technique, then, if he were on the path of childhood sexuality, as his critics show he was, surely his patients would produce stories to support it. Cioffi (1972, 1973, 1974, 1984) claims that Freud's patients invented the stories of their seductions in order to placate their conqueror, who was, no doubt, pleased to find verification of his hypotheses. Esterson (1993) and Schatzman (1992) think he deduced the seduction stories and forced them on his patients. In either case, it is no wonder patients ran away.

Cioffi, Esterson, and Schatzman argue that, at some point, Freud came to believe that the seduction stories were false, and he was put in the position of explaining how that could be so while at the same time maintaining psychoanalytic therapy as a means for revealing scientific truth. He did so, they aver, by inventing the Oedipus complex and childhood sexuality. In the new formulation, the seduction stories about patients' outer lives as children are admitted to be false but are wonderfully revealing about their inner lives, their sexual fantasies about mother or father. Psychoanalysis became a doctrine concerned only with the inner life of human beings, and psychoanalytic method was said to reveal that inner life even to the earliest days of childhood. In making this move, however, Freud later had to falsify what he had believed during the original seduction episode. In his later writings, Freud depicted himself as a naive, nondirective therapist, "intentionally keeping my critical faculty in abeyance" (Esterson, 1993, p. 23), when earlier he had prided himself on discovering the seduction by "search[ing] for it single-mindedly" (p. 13). He said that he had been stunned to hear patient after patient describe being seduced by their fathers, when, in the paper of 1896, the seducers were adult strangers, older boys having sex with slightly younger sisters, or adults in whose care the child had been placed—never fathers. He even later retracted the blame he directed at his own father (Schatzman, 1992; Esterson, 1993).

The last and most flamboyantly controversial student of the seduction episode is Jeffrey Moussaieff Masson (1984a, 1984b), who says Freud was right to begin with: His patients suffered from sexual abuse. Today, we have become increasingly aware of the extent of sexual abuse of children, and Masson argues that Freud discovered the reality of child abuse and then walked away from it, constructing a theory that not only denied the existence of seductions but provided a means for disbelieving children when they complained of abuse. Masson alleges two motives for Freud's abandoning the seduction theory. The first was a desire to curry favor with the medical establishment by agreeing that the seduction theory was the fairytale they had pronounced it to be in 1896.

The second motive involves a dramatic episode that was deleted from the official publication of the Freud–Fliess letters (Masson, 1984a, 1984b). Freud had a patient named Emma Eckstein, who suffered from stomach pains and menstrual irregularities. We have already seen that Freud regarded masturbation as pathogenic, and he apparently agreed with Fliess that masturbation caused menstrual problems. Moreover, Fliess taught that nasal surgery could eliminate masturbation and hence the problems it caused. Freud brought Fliess to Vienna to perform surgery on Emma Eckstein's nose. The operation may have been Fliess's first; in any event, postoperative recovery did not go well. Eckstein suffered pain, bleeding, and discharge of pus. Freud eventually called in a Viennese doctor, who removed from Eckstein's nose a half-meter of gauze that had been incompetently left behind by Fliess. At this point, Eckstein hemorrhaged, turned pale, and very nearly died. Freud was so shattered by the sight of Emma Eckstein seemingly dying that he fled, revived by brandy brought by the doctor's wife.

Remarkably, I think, Eckstein stayed in therapy with Freud. She continued to suffer pain and occasional, sometimes violent, bleeding from the nose. For Masson, the critical moments in the story concern Freud's attitude to Eckstein's suffering. Following Fliess's operation, Freud had come to regard her nasal problems as hysterical symptoms. The dramatic events following the removal of the gauze made Freud admit otherwise. He wrote to Fliess, "So we had done her an injustice; she was not abnormal" but suffered from Fliess's mistake, and, by extension, Freud's mistake in subjecting her to Fliess.

Masson shows that Freud returned to his psychological interpretation of Eckstein's bleeding. Just over a year after her brush with death, on June 4, 1896, Freud wrote that Eckstein's continued bleeding was "due to wishes." In this way, Masson says, Freud absolved both Fliess and himself of guilt. They had not by bungled surgery nearly killed Emma Eckstein; her hysterical wishes had. Having let himself off the hook about Eckstein, Freud was "free to abandon the seduction hypothesis" (Masson, 1984a). In both cases, Freud moved from locating the causes of hysterical symptoms in real events to locating them in unconscious wishes.

Even Freud's most outspoken detractors have found Masson's arguments as tendentious as Freud's own (Cioffi, 1984; Crews, 1986). Masson claims that Freud gave up the seduction theory in order to regain the favor of the "donkeys" of established medicine who had called it a fairytale, but the even more complex theory of childhood sexual fantasies seems ill-calculated to recoup his standing. Moreover,

Freud's problem was not to explain why his patients were miserable, but why they were hysterical. By extensively canvassing the evidence for child abuse in the nineteenth century, Masson himself shows that Freud should have been aware of the extent of child abuse and should have believed his patients' stories. However, most child abuse then—and now—is not sexual. As Cioffi (p. 743) writes, "Children [in the analytic view] may be starved, beaten, or tortured but providing they have not simultaneously been sexually stimulated the experience can have no neurotic aftermath." Thus, psychoanalysts could concede that child abuse is a genuine problem yet deny that it has anything to do with the etiology of the neuroses with which they were concerned. Moreover, the big problem with Masson's theory is that, as we have seen, Freud never heard tales of parental sexual abuse to begin with (Schatzman, 1992).

Although Masson's criticisms of Freud's abandonment of the seduction theory are flawed, they may be regarded as part of a broader critique, often made by psychoanalysts themselves, of Freud as insensitive—sometimes brutally so—to the life problems faced by his patients (Decker, 1981, 1991; Holt, 1982; Klein and Tribich, 1982). As Freud constructed his depth psychology, he came to locate the causes of neurosis entirely in his patients' fantasies, blinding himself to how people can suffer from circumstances.

The most important document in this indictment of Freud is *Fragment of an Analysis of a Case of Hysteria* (1905b), describing Freud's admittedly unsuccessful treatment of an eighteen-year-old woman known as "Dora" (Ida Bauer). Shortly after the publication of *Interpretation of Dreams,* Dora was brought in for therapy by her father, a successful businessman and former patient of Freud's. Dora was suffering from symptoms Freud thought were neurotic—primarily, shortness of breath and a cough. As therapeutic sessions proceeded day by day (Freud saw his patients six days a week), Freud discovered that Dora came from a family whose tangled intrigues would do justice to a soap opera today. Dora's father's real reason for seeking Dora's treatment was to make her less unhappy about his affair with Frau K. The Ks were close friends of the Bauers, seeing each other regularly and vacationing together; on a vacation, Dora deduced the affair from her father's rearranging hotel rooms in order to have convenient access to Frau K. Dora's mother suffered, Freud opined, from "housewife's psychosis"—obsessive neatness—and had long since ceased having sexual relations with her husband. Dora objected most of all to the advances of Herr K.—whose wife had stopped sleeping with him—who had twice attempted to force himself on her, the first attempt coming when Dora was thirteen. Herr K. arranged to be alone in his place of business with Dora, ostensibly to watch a parade, but he suddenly grabbed her, pressed himself against her, and kissed her. Dora fled in disgust, tried to avoid Herr K., but nevertheless had to turn down a proposition from him two years later.

Freud's (1905b) reaction to the scene is remarkable: "This was surely just the situation to call up a distinct feeling of sexual excitement in a girl of fourteen [Freud miscalculated the age; Decker, 1991, p. 124] who had never before been approached. . . . [T]he behavior of this child of fourteen was already entirely and completely hysterical. I should without question consider a person hysterical in whom an occasion for sexual excitement elicited feelings that were preponderantly or exclusively unpleasurable." Instead of the genital sensation that would certainly have been felt by a healthy girl in such circumstances, Dora was overcome by the "unpleasurable feeling" of disgust. Freud was especially puzzled since "I happen to know Herr K."—he came with Dora and Dora's father to Freud's office—"and he was still quite young and of prepossessing appearance" (Gay, 1989, p. 184). At this point in his career, Freud was an aggressive therapist, and he quickly used against Dora every interpretation he could. Playing with her purse during therapy represented desire to masturbate; her cough represented hidden thoughts of Frau K. performing fellatio on her father and, therefore, Dora's secret wish to do the same. Unsurprisingly, Dora was a patient who ran away. Freud ascribed his therapeutic failure to unanalyzed transference: Dora had transferred her sexual desires from Herr K., whom Freud was certain Dora secretly desired, to himself, and he had not taken due notice of it at the time. Freud said nothing about possible countertransference—from a middle-aged man no longer sleeping with his wife—to Dora, an attractive adolescent girl (Decker, 1981, 1991).

In Dora's case, we find Freud pushing all responsibility for hysteria onto his patient. Dora should have been sexually excited by Herr K.'s attentions; the disgust she felt was a symptom of her hysteria, not the cause of her distaste for the handsome Herr K. In 1895, when Freud still believed in the seduction theory, Freud had treated another young woman on whom sexual advances had been made, and he wrote of "the horror by which a virginal mind is overcome when it is faced for the first time with the world of sexuality" (quoted by Decker, 1991). In sum, the Dora case is typical of Freud's dismissal of family dynamics and other current influences on patient's troubles. Depth psychology imputed to the unconscious full sovereignty over mental health and mental illness, making patients solely responsible for their health.

Changing Conceptions of the Instincts

By 1905, when he wrote *Three Essays on the Theory of Sexuality,* Freud had concluded that one's becoming healthy, neurotic, or sexually "perverse" depended on childhood sexual thoughts, and, most importantly, on the resolution of the Oedipus complex. Central to his concept of the dynamic unconscious, which contained the wishes lying behind symptoms, dreams, and slips of the tongue, was repression. Yet, because repression was a continuing act of denying unacceptable sexual wishes access to consciousness, there remained a problem of explaining the source of the mental energy used to carry out repression of libido. Freud (1915a) proposed, as a "working hypothesis," that there exist two groups of "primal instincts": "the ego or self-preservative, instincts and the sexual instincts." The ego uses its ego-instinct energy to defend itself from—that is, repress—wishes driven by the sexual instincts. With this formulation, the mind as depicted by psychoanalysis became an arena of struggle, the compromised results of which were conscious thoughts and behavior.

Freud did not remain satisfied with his working hypothesis. In 1920, he published *Beyond the Pleasure Principle,* the first of two major revisions of his theory, culminating in the structural model of personality in *The Ego and the Id* (1923/1960). Perhaps because of his own suffering from intractable cancer of the jaw—he endured numerous operations and had to painfully replace a prosthesis in his jaw every day— and perhaps because of the carnage of World War I, Freud became increasingly pessimistic. In *Beyond the Pleasure Principle,* Freud proposed that "The aim of all life is death." Freud here gave psychoanalytic expression to an older truth, that we are born in order to die. In a sermon from 1630, John Donne had said, "Wee have a winding sheete in our Mother's wombe, which growes with us from our conception, and wee come into the world, wound up in that winding sheet, for we come to seek a grave" (quoted by Macmillan, 1991, p. 429).

Freud's argument is based on his conceptions of instincts as drives and behavior as motivated by drive reduction. Unsatisfied instincts give rise to states of arousal, which the organism seeks to reduce by engaging in behavior that satisfies the instinct. Satisfaction is only temporary, so, in time, the instinct must be gratified anew, causing a cyclical process of arousal and satisfaction Freud called the *repetition compulsion*. It appears, then, that the optimum state sought by every living thing is complete oblivion—freedom from arousal. The wheel of the repetition compulsion is broken by death, when the aim of living—tension reduction—is permanently reached. There lies within us, Freud concluded, a drive toward death along with drives toward life. The ego instincts preserve the life of the individual, and the sexual instincts preserve the life of the species, so Freud bundled them together as the life instincts, named Eros, after the Greek word for love. Opposed to the life instincts is the death instinct, or Thanatos, Greek for death. Eros and Thanatos are mutually repressing. Thanatos provides the energy by which the ego, at the behest of the moralizing superego, represses sexual wishes, and Eros provides the energy to repress the death instinct from immediately fulfilling its lethal wish.

Postulation of the death wish provided a new solution for the problem of aggression. In Freud's earlier theory, aggressive acts were deemed to occur out of frustrated ego or sexual needs. Thus, animals fought out of self-defense or over food, water, territory, or reproductive opportunities. In the new theory, aggression was an autonomous drive in itself. Just as sexual instincts could be rechanneled from their proper biological object, so too could the death instinct be redirected away from bringing about the death of the organism. Eros could for a time repress Thanatos's suicidal aggression, but the necessary result was aggression displaced onto others. Freud's new theory did not win universal acclaim among later analysts, many of whom preferred to accept Freud's earlier, less pessimistic, view of human nature, but both theories of aggression appear in later nonpsychoanalytic psychology. The first conception of aggression as caused by frustration surfaced in social learning theory's frustration–aggression hypothesis (Dollard et al., 1939), and the second conception of aggression as a necessary part of nature was reasserted by the ethologists, who stressed the adaptive value of an aggressive drive (Lorenz, 1966), if not a suicide drive.

THREE MASTERPIECES

To convey the flavor of Freud's arguments, I will discuss three of his works that are generally reckoned to be his most important and influential. The first two, *The Interpretation of Dreams* and *Three Essays on the Theory of Sexuality,* were the only books Freud continued to revise as psychoanalysis developed; thus, they constitute the defining documents of psychoanalysis. The third work, *Civilization and Its Discontents,* written late in Freud's life, represented the summing up of a lifetime's work and proved to be the most widely influential of Freud's books (Gay, 1989). In it, Freud took up the Enlightenment problem of reconciling human happiness with the advance of civilization, and reached a deeply pessimistic Hobbesian conclusion.

The Interpretation of Dreams (1900)

Of all his works, Freud himself believed *The Interpretation of Dreams* to be his greatest. In a letter to Fliess (Freud, 1960), he hoped that a plaque would be erected some day saying, "In this House on July 24, 1895 the Secret of Dreams was revealed to Dr. Sigmund Freud." The insight Freud valued so highly was that a dream is not the meaningless collection of images it appears to be, but is "the royal road to the unconscious": a clue to the innermost recesses of the personality. That dreams have meaning was not a new idea, as Freud acknowledged, but it was out of step with the received academic opinion of his times. Most thinkers, including Wundt, assigned little importance to dreams, believing them to be only confused nighttime versions of waking mental processes. Freud sided instead with supposedly disreputable philosophers and ancient religions in valuing dreams as symbolic statements of a reality unavailable to waking experience.

Freud's basic idea is simple, but its details and ramifications are complex and far-ranging: All of us, whether neurotic or not, carry within us desires that we cannot accept consciously. In fact, we deliberately keep these desires unconscious, or repress them. Nevertheless, they remain active, precisely because they are repressed and not subject to conscious scrutiny and memory-decay. They constantly press for access to awareness, and hence the control of behavior. In our waking life, our ego, or conscious self, represses these wishes; but during sleep, consciousness lapses and repression weakens. If our repressed desires ever completely eluded repression, we would awaken and reassert control. Dreaming is a compromise that protects sleep, for dreams are hallucinatory, disguised expressions of repressed ideas. They give partial satisfaction of unacceptable wishes, but in such a way that consciousness and sleep are rarely disturbed.

Freud summarized his view by saying that every dream is a wish-fulfillment, that is, a disguised expression (fulfillment) of some unconscious desire or wish. This characteristic of dreams makes them the royal road to the unconscious: If we can decipher a dream and retrieve its hidden meaning, we will have recovered a piece of our unconscious mental life and be able to subject it to the light of reason. Dreams and hysteria thus have the same origin, for both are symbolic representations of unconscious needs, and both can be understood by tracing them back to their sources. The existence of dreams shows that no sharp line can be drawn between neurotic and normal mental lives. All individuals have needs of which they are unaware and whose realization they would find disturbing. In neurotics, however, the usual means of defense have broken down, and symptoms have taken their place.

The method of decoding is the same in both hysteria and dreams—the method of free association. Just as hysterical patients were asked to freely talk about their symptoms, so we may understand dreams by free associating to each element of the dream. Freud's assumption was that free association would reverse the process that produced the dream and bring one at last to the unconscious idea embodied in it. In symptom analysis and dream analysis, the goal is the same: to reach rational self-understanding of the irrational unconscious, a step toward mental health.

The major change in later editions of *The Interpretation of Dreams* was in the means by which dreams may be decoded. In the early editions of the book, the only method was free association; but because of the work of a follower, Wilhelm Stekel, Freud came to believe that dreams could also be interpreted according to a more or less uniform set of symbols. That is, in most cases, certain objects or experiences could be shown to stand for the same unconscious ideas in everyone's dreams. So, for example, walking up a flight of stairs symbolizes sexual intercourse, a suitcase stands for the vagina, and a hat for the penis.

Such an approach, of course, simplified the process of dream interpretation. It also made possible a wider application of Freud's insight, namely, in the interpretation of myths, legends, and works of art. Freud had already engaged in such an analysis in the early versions of the work, treating Sophocles' *Oedipus Rex* and Shakespeare's *Hamlet* as Oedipal stories, and he and other psychoanalysts would go on to do many such analyses. Psychoanalysis was never limited to a mere psychotherapy, but it was increasingly used as a general tool for understanding all of human culture. Myth, legend, and religion were seen as disguised expressions of hidden cultural conflicts; art was seen as the expression of the artist's personal conflicts—all shared the same mechanism with dreams. The symbol system helped justify and make possible this extension of psychoanalysis. We cannot put Sophocles, Shakespeare, or a whole culture on the analytic couch and ask them to free associate, but we can search their products for universal clues to the universal human unconscious.

The Interpretation of Dreams was more than an analysis of dreams as expressions of repressed wishes and thoughts, because it provided Freud with his general model of the mind as a multilayered system in which the unconscious shapes thought and behavior according to a peculiar set of rules (Sulloway, 1979). Moreover, the dream theory provided the foundation for the unmasking function of psychoanalysis, so important to its hermeneutical employment by later social and literary critics. For, according to psychoanalysis, dreams—and, by extension, neurotic symptoms, slips of the tongue, and indeed all behavior—are never what they appear to be. They all are caused by motives of which we are unaware because we find them reprehensible, and they serve by hiding us from unpleasant mental realities. In the hands of the literary critic, psychoanalysis could be used to show that works of art are never what they seem, expressing yet hiding the artist's—and, if the work was popular or controversial, the audience's—deepest needs and conflicts. To social critics, psychoanalysis suggested that social practices, institutions, and values existed to enforce and at the same time hide rule by reprehensible value systems (usually capitalism) and reprehensible elites (usually white males). In therapy, art, and politics, the psychoanalytic line of argument placed the therapist and critic in a privileged position, beyond the subterfuges of the unconscious, uniquely capable of revealing the truth to deluded clients, audiences, and citizens.

Three Essays on the Theory of Sexuality (1905)

There is no denying that Freud's most revolutionary impact has been on our willingness, in contrast to the Victorians, to accept sexuality as an essential part of being human. The influence and impact of Freud's discussion stem not from the details of his theory, which are anachronistic and culture-bound, but from his lack of shocked hypocrisy. By drawing attention to sexuality, he provoked the research and the culture change that transcended his own concepts.

As the title of the book says, the text consists of three short essays on different aspects of sex: "The Sexual Aberrations," "Infantile Sexuality," and "The Transformations of Puberty." Far more than *The Interpretations of Dreams,* his three essays—especially the last two—were revised after 1905 as Freud developed his later libido theory.

Freud made two important general points in the first essay on sexual aberrations. First: "There is indeed something innate lying behind the perversions but . . . it is something innate in everyone" (p. 64). What society calls "perverse" is only a development of one component of the sexual instinct, an activity centering on an erotogenic zone other than the genitals, a zone that plays its part in "normal" sexual activity in foreplay. The second point was that "neuroses are, so to say, the negative of perversions" (p. 57). That is, all neuroses have a sexual basis and arise out of the patient's inability to deal with some aspect of his or her sexuality. Freud went so far as to say that a neurotic's symptoms are his or her sex life. The neurotic has symptoms rather than perversions or healthy sexuality.

Freud's second essay, on infantile sexuality, finally introduced the world at large to the ideas about childhood sexuality and the Oedipus concept that he had developed during the episode of the seduction mistake.

In the last essay, Freud turned to adult sexuality, which begins in puberty when maturational changes reawaken and transmute the dormant sexual instincts. At this time in the healthy person, sexual desire is directed to a person of the opposite sex, and reproductive genital intercourse becomes the goal; the instincts of childhood sexuality now serve, through the kissing and caressing of foreplay, genital drives that create the arousal necessary to actual coitus. In perverse individuals, the pleasure associated with some infantile instinct is great enough to replace genital activity altogether. The neurotic is overcome by adult sexual demands and converts his or her sexual needs into symptoms.

At various places in *Three Essays*, but especially in the conclusion, Freud introduced a concept that was central to the analysis of culture that occupied his later years. This was the concept of sublimation, the most important form of displacement. We may express our sexual desires directly; we may repress them, in which case they may find expression in dreams or neurotic symptoms; or we may employ sexual energy to motivate higher cultural activities, such as art, science, and philosophy. This last process is sublimation, and it diverts animalistic drives to the service of civilization. In *Three Essays*, Freud only discussed sublimation as an option for a person with a constitutionally strong sexual disposition; in his later works, the alternatives of satisfying direct sexual expression, on the one hand, and repression, sublimation, and consequent residual tension on the other, were to pose a dilemma for Freud and—as he saw it—for civilization itself.

Civilization and Its Discontents (1930)

Sublimation, the conversion of sexual libido into neutral mental energy, is carried out by the child's narcissism. This unbound energy allows the ego to function, but it is an energy that serves both eros and the death instincts. On the one hand, the ego is adaptive and hence enables the person to live; on the other hand, it opposes the id's pleasure principle, as do the death instincts. Thus, a dilemma is raised for civilization. Civilized life makes increasing demands on the ego to control the immoral id and to pursue civilized activities rather than simple animal pleasures. Yet such demands aid death and oppose pleasures, making happiness harder to achieve. The problem of civilization occupied Freud more and more as the years went by and he no longer had to establish psychoanalysis as a movement.

In *Future of an Illusion* (1927/1961), the simple precursor to the complexities to come in *Civilization and Its Discontents* (1930/1961), Freud used psychoanalysis as a scalpel to dissect religion, the social institution that many people cherished but the object of hatred among the Enlightenment philosophes. The war between science and religion was well under way, and Freud hoped to strike a decisive blow for science by unmasking the infantile motives behind religious feelings. The nineteenth century appears to us to be a religiously secure age. In public, people professed strong belief in religion, holding it to be the bulwark of civilization. However, in private, these same believers were often tormented by grave doubts about the validity of what they professed. They wanted to believe, they tried to believe, they yearned for the simple untroubled faith of their childhoods—but the doubts remained. Doubt was especially frightening precisely because it appeared to be a crack in the bulwark of civilization.

Freud, however, had no doubts; *Future of an Illusion* is Freud's most polemical and assured work. He said simply that religion is an illusion, a massive attempt at wish-fulfillment. Religion is based on nothing more than our infantile feelings of helplessness and the consequent desire to be protected by an all-powerful parent who becomes God. Moreover, to Freud, religion is a dangerous illusion, for its dogmatic teachings stunt the intellect, keeping humankind in a childish state. Religion is something to be outgrown as humans develop scientific resources and can stand on their own. The secret religious doubters are people who have outgrown religion but do not know it, and it was to them Freud addressed his work. His goal was, as ever, to assert the "primacy of the intellect" over infantile wishes and emotional needs.

In *Future of an Illusion,* Freud made some startlingly pessimistic statements that he took up in *Civilization and Its Discontents.* He wrote: "Every individual is virtually an enemy of civilization . . . and people . . . feel as a heavy burden the sacrifices which civilization expects of them to make a communal life possible." In a phrase, the topic of *Civilization and Its Discontents* is the necessary unhappiness of civilized people.

At the beginning of *Civilization and Its Discontents* (p. 81), Freud wrote, "The sense of guilt [is] the most important problem in the development of civilization and . . . the price we pay for our advance in civilization is a loss of happiness through the heightening of a sense of guilt." Each person seeks happiness, and, according to Freud, the strongest feelings of happiness come from direct satisfaction of our instinctual, especially sexual, desires. Civilization, however, demands that we renounce to a large degree such direct gratification and substitute cultural activities in their stead. Such sublimated drives provide us less pleasure than direct gratification. To add to our discontents, we also internalize the demands of civilization as harsh super-egos, burdening us with guilt for immoral thoughts as well as deeds. Civilized people are consequently less happy than their primitive counterparts; as civilization grows, happiness diminishes.

On the other hand, civilization has its rewards and is necessary to human social life. Along with Hobbes, Freud feared that without a means of restraining aggression, society would dissolve into a war of all against all. Civilization is therefore necessary for the survival of all but the strongest, and at least partly serves eros. Moreover, in return for repression, civilization gives us not only security but also art, science, philosophy, and a more comfortable life through technology.

Civilization thus presents a dilemma from which Freud saw no way out. On the one hand, civilization is the protector and benefactor of humanity. On the other hand, it demands unhappiness and even neurosis as payment for its benefactions. Near the end of the book, Freud hinted that civilizations may vary in the degree of unhappiness they produce—a question he left for others to consider.

This question has been taken up by many thinkers, for *Civilization and Its Discontents* has proven to be one of Freud's most provocative works. Some writers have argued that Western civilization is neurotic and they anoint some utopia as savior, as

Fromm does socialism. Others believe the only way out of Freud's dilemma is renunciation of civilization itself and a return to the simple physical pleasures of childhood. Whatever the validity of these claims, Freud's dilemma remains and is acutely felt today when the rebellion against inhibition and guilt that Freud saw beginning in his own time has achieved such large dimensions, challenged, if at all, not by repression and morality but by practical worries about death and disease.

THE FATE OF PSYCHOANALYSIS

Unlike the psychology of consciousness, psychoanalysis survives, though as so-called mental disorders get traced to malfunctions of the nervous system, their numbers dwindle. The young Freud alienated his friends and mentors, and the older Freud, founder and keeper of psychoanalysis, alienated independent-minded followers. Otto Rank, Alfred Adler, and Carl Jung—at one time Freud's Crown Prince—were expelled from the psychoanalytic movement for disagreeing too sharply with the founder. Schism followed schism in post-Freudian psychoanalysis, too, until the field became what it remains, a Babel of competing sects. If Freud's influence on academic psychology was limited, that of his former followers was virtually nonexistent. But, as Peter Gay reminds us, Freud himself is inescapable. Is Freud the great hero of legend? Is psychoanalysis "the most stupendous confidence trick of the twentieth century" as biologist Peter Medawar (quoted by Sulloway, 1979) insists? Or could Freud be a tyrant-lizard—Tyrannosaurus—whose time has past?

Psychoanalysis and Science

The claim of psychoanalysis to be a science like any other has been contested since the beginning. Positivists find Freudian hypotheses vague and difficult to test (Nagel, 1959). The most influential attack on the scientific status of psychoanalysis was mounted by Karl Popper, who regarded psychoanalysis as a pseudoscience. As we learned in Chapter 1, Popper formulated the falsifiability principle as the demarcation criterion separating genuine scientific viewpoints from those that merely pretended to be scientific. According to the falsifiability principle, to be worthy of science a theory must make predictions that may be proven unequivocally wrong. Popper, however, found that psychoanalysts were always able to explain any behavior, no matter how apparently inconsistent with psychoanalysis. Somewhere in the complex topography, structures, and dynamics of the mind could be found an explanation for anything at all from a woman's fiddling with her purse (symbolic masturbation) to the space race (phallic competition to build the biggest missile). In this Popperian spirit, the late philosopher Sidney Hook (1959) asked numerous psychoanalysts over a span of decades to describe what a person without an Oedipus complex would be like. He never received a satisfactory reply. Indeed, in more than one instance, he was regarded with hostility and his question met with screaming.

Although Popper's argument has been widely accepted, most analysts unsurprisingly reject it. Philosopher Adolf Grünbaum (1984, 1986) has agreed with them and proceeded to take Freud at his word that psychoanalysis was a science. Grünbaum argues that Freud did after all propose tests by which psychoanalysis might be falsified, the most important of which Grünbaum calls the Tally Argument. When he offered the therapeutic success of psychoanalysis as "incontrovertible proof" of psychoanalysis, Freud said that psychoanalysis and only psychoanalysis could provide real cures for neuroses, because only psychoanalysis found the inner wishes and thoughts that "tallied" with the symptoms. As therapy recovered and eliminated the unconscious wishes, symptoms would disappear until the neurosis was completely dissolved. Other therapies, Freud argued, could achieve only partial and temporary success, since they did not go to the causes of neuroses, effecting by suggestion alone what little relief they provided.

Grünbaum accepts the Tally Argument in refutation of Popper's claim that psychoanalysis is not a science, for the Tally Argument is falsifiable. Therefore, psychoanalysis is a science, and the question becomes one of determining whether its claims are true or false. To be accepted as true on its own grounds, psychoanalysis must demonstrate unique therapeutic success. Unique success is vital to the Tally Argument, for if other therapeutic systems work at least as well as psychoanalysis, there is no reason to prefer the complexities of psychoanalysis to simpler theories. Behavior therapy, for example, rests on the simple principles of conditioning, and should it prove to be the equal of psychoanalysis, then by Ockham's razor, it is scientifically preferable to psychoanalysis.

When we look into the therapeutic success of psychoanalysis, we find that although Freud boasted of success after success, he provided remarkably little data to support his claim. Freud reported only six cases in detail, one of which he did not treat and only two of which he claimed to be successes (Sulloway, 1991). The two allegedly successful cases were those of the Rat Man and the Wolf Man. The Rat Man was so-called because of his morbid fears and fantasies about rats, and the Wolf Man was named for a dream about seeing wolves. Freud's descriptions of both cases fail to stand up to scrutiny. Numerous distortions of the truth mark both reports, and neither patient seems to have been cured. After claiming success with the Rat Man in print, Freud confessed to Jung that the Rat Man was far from cured, and, like Dora, the Rat Man broke off therapy. The case of the Wolf Man is better known, since he outlived Freud by many years and, near the end of life, told his story to a journalist. He stayed in analysis (for free) years after Freud's death. He told the reporter that he wrote a memoir about his case at the behest of one of his later analysts "[t]o show the world how Freud cured a seriously ill person," but "it's all false." He felt just as ill as when he went to Freud. In fact, he said, "The whole thing looks like a catastrophe" (quoted by Sulloway, 1991). Fisher and Greenberg (1977) wrote a largely sympathetic review of the status of psychoanalysis as science but concluded that Freud's own cases were "largely unsuccessful."

Later therapy outcome studies provide no evidence that psychoanalysis is a uniquely effective therapy. Gains from all forms of therapy are modest, and most forms of therapy have about equal success (see Chapter 15). Although Freud thought little of experimental attempts to verify psychoanalysis, many psychologists and analysts have carried out experiments, with highly variable results (for reviews of therapy and experimental studies, see Eysenck and Wilson, 1973; Fisher and Greenberg, 1977; Farrell, 1981; Kline, 1981; Grünbaum, 1984, 1986; Eysenck, 1986; Macmillan, 1991). Psychoanalysis seems to be caught on the horns of a dilemma. Either psychoanalysis cannot be tested, in which case it is a pseudoscience, or it can be tested, in which case it is at best a very poor science.

As a consequence, some partisans of psychoanalysis try to dissolve the dilemma by claiming that psychoanalysis is not a science at all, but a means of interpretation (Lacan, 1968; Ricoeur, 1970). This hermeneutical version of psychoanalysis maintains that the activity of psychoanalysis is more like literary criticism than science. A literary critic closely reads a text in order to discern its meaning, a meaning that may even have been hidden from the author who created it. Similarly, a psychoanalyst works with a patient to closely read the text of the patient's life, looking for or constructing the hidden meaning it holds. According to this version of psychoanalysis, the goal of therapy is to reach an interpretation with which the patient agrees and which can form the basis of a fuller life. Hermeneutics was originally the art of Bible interpretation, and hermeneutical psychoanalysis constitutes in part a return to the medieval conception of the world as a book containing meanings to be decoded, not causes to be discovered.

The plausibility of hermeneutic psychoanalysis is debatable (see commentary to Grünbaum, 1986). For us now, the main objection to it is that Freud clearly meant psychology to be a science (Grünbaum, 1984, 1986) even if his conception of science is now out of date (Breger, 1981). Notwithstanding Freud's intention, the hermeneutical Freud has had the greatest impact on society.

Psychoanalysis and Society

Jacques Lacan (1968), one of the most influential leaders of hermeneutical psychoanalysis, places Freud among the three leaders of the Party of Suspicion—the others are Marx and Nietzsche—whose impact on twentieth-century thought has been immense. The common enemy of the Party of Suspicion is the middle class. Breuer said that Freud's emphasis on sex was motivated in part by "a desire to d'epater [skewer] le bourgeois" (quoted by Sulloway, 1979). Marx worked for the proletarian revolution that would destroy capitalism and the bourgeoisie. Nietzsche denounced middle-class morals as unfit for the *Übermensch* (literally, "Over-man," a Superman, Nietzche's idealized man of the future). The common weapon of the Party of Suspicion was unmasking. Freud revealed depths of sexual depravity behind the seemingly innocent screen of middle-class respectability. Marx revealed self-centered greed in the aspirations of entrepreneurial capitalists. Nietzsche revealed craven cowards behind Christian martyrs.

To the Party of Suspicion, nothing is as it seems to be; in Freudian psychology, this means that no utterance, no action, is what it seems to be—everything requires interpretation. As Alasdair MacIntyre (1985) observes, the social sciences, especially psychology, are unique among the sciences because their theories may influence the subjects about which they write. As a result, psychology shapes the reality it describes, and the overinterpretative mode of life, as MacIntyre calls it, plays an important role in modern life.

"Freud made available the thought of the unacknowledged motive as an all-pervasive presence, so that each of us is encouraged to try and look behind the overt simplicities of the behavior of others to what is actually moving them and equally encouraged to respond to that hidden reality rather than to the surface appearance of the other" (MacIntyre, 1985, p. 899). Working within the overinterpretative mode of life, nothing can be believed; every statement, every action, requires an interpretative gloss. The interpretations no longer need be traditionally Freudian. To see the effects of overinterpretation, one need only consider the oddity of modern television news in which reporters, quoting experts and anonymous "insiders," tell us, the people, how a presidential speech will "play" to the people. No longer do government officials say things, they "send messages" to be decoded by pundits. Authority and sincerity have been dissolved. What Freud and the Party of Suspicion have bequeathed us is paranoia.

Two fellow Viennese were never fooled by Freud. The philosopher Ludwig Wittgenstein wrote to a friend, "He is full of fishy thinking and his charm and the charm of his subject is so great that you may be easily fooled . . . . So hang on to your brains" (Schatzman, 1992, p. 34). The witty journalist Karl Kraus said, "Psychoanalysis is itself that mental illness of which it purports to be the cure" (Gay, 1988, p. 449).

BIBLIOGRAPHY

Trying to master the scholarly literature on Freud is like trying to drink from a fire hose: One is more likely to be blasted away and drowned than to be refreshed. I have listed here only a *very* tiny portion of the literature. Readers can find much more, browsing in any library.

General Works. The standard biography of Freud is Ernest Jones's three-volume *Life and work of Sigmund Freud,* available in a one-volume abridgment (New York: Basic Books, 1961). Jones was a member of Freud's inner circle, and his biography enjoys both the benefits—privileged information—and the defects—hagiographical character—of close friendly association with its subject. Moreover, it is now out of date. An up-to-date biography is Peter Gay (1988). It is well written and incorporates access to some (but not all) documents hidden from the general public (some of the Freud materials held in the Library of Congress and elsewhere cannot be published until after 2100!). Gay is a historian who underwent psychoanalysis, and he writes as something of a convert; although he criticizes Freud, Freud remains a hero for Gay. Moreover, the text hides scholarly controversies about Freud, although they are discussed in the excellent and combative bibliography.

My two favorite general works on Freud are Sulloway's (1979; his 1982 contribution may be regarded as a summary, and his 1991 article, a sequel) for the elegant arguments about Freud the cryptobiologist, and the dissection of the myth of Freud the hero, and Rieff's (1979) for sympathetic consideration of Freud not as a doctor or a scientist or a hero, but as a moral philosopher of enormous influence. Two other biographies are philosopher Richard Wollheim's *Sigmund Freud* (New York: Viking, 1971), and professional biographer Ronald Clark's *Freud: The man and the cause* (New York: Meridian, 1980). A more critical survey, in which the cultlike nature of psychoanalysis (see also Sulloway, 1991) emerges, is Roazen (1974); one old analyst interviewed by Roazen shrieked at him, "You will never learn our secrets!" For later history of psychoanalysis, see Ellenberger (1970) and Reuben Fine, *A history of psychoanalysis* (New York: Columbia University Press, 1979). There are three collections of essays on Freud. The first two are general: S. G. M. Lee and M. Herbert, eds., *Freud and psychology* (Harmondsworth, England: Penguin, 1970), and R. Wollheim, ed., *Freud: A collection of critical essays* (Garden City, NY: Doubleday). The third, edited by Wollheim and J. Hopkins, *Philosophical essays on Freud* (Cambridge, England: Cambridge University Press, 1982) focuses on Freud as philosopher. A charmingly wicked, and even vicious, summary of recent scholarly research on Freud's character is Frederick Crews, "The unknown Freud," *New York Review of Books* (November 18, 1993, 55–66). Crews writes from the same perspective as mine, that of a deeply disenchanted former believer.

Various collections of Freud's letters have been published. However, because of the extraordinarily secretive nature of the keepers of the Freud archives, only two complete and unexpurgated sets of letters have been published: W. McGuire, ed., *The Freud–Jung letters* (Princeton, NJ: Princeton University Press, 1974), and Freud (1985), the Freud–Fliess correspondence. Freud began the tradition of a cultlike secrecy surrounding psychoanalysis, twice destroying collections of letters and manuscripts so his biographers could not get at them and tarnish his heroic image. The Freud–Fliess letters are extraordinarily revealing. Fliess was Freud's most intimate friend, and in the letters we find revealed the early development of Freud's thought and insights into Freud's character (the first letter was written while Freud had a woman hypnotized before him). Freud attempted to get hold of the Fliess letters when he discovered late in his life that they existed (he had destroyed Fliess's letters to him). The letters were published in a highly laundered edition together with the "Project" in 1954 (*The origins of psychoanalysis.* [New York: Basic Books]). Masson was hired to prepare Freud's complete letters for publication, but despite having been psychoanalyzed, he turned out not to be a safe choice. When he developed his version of the seduction mistake, he was fired by the Freud archives, and only the Freud–Fliess volume was published; I fear I shall not live to see the rest. The uproar in the analytic community was considerable: see Janet Malcolm, *In the Freud archives* (New York: Random House, 1985). Masson brought a libel suit against Malcolm, a procedural motion from which was decided by the U.S. Supreme Court in 1991. In its spring session, the Court ruled that Masson's case could go to trial, and at press time for this book Masson had lost his suit.

The best general work of Freud's is the pair of lectures, *A general introduction to psychoanalysis* (New York: Washington Square Press, 1924/1952), and its sequel, *New introductory lectures on psychoanalysis* (New York: Norton, 1933/1965). The "bible" of psychoanalysis is J. Strachey, ed., *The standard edition of the complete psychological works of Sigmund Freud,* 24 vols. (London: Hogarth Press, 1966–74). Peter Gay (1989) has assembled a useful one-volume compilation of Freud's works based on the *Standard edition.* Complaints have often surrounded James and Alix Strachey's translations of Freud, especially by Bruno Bettleheim, *Freud and man's soul* (New York: Vintage, 1984). Light is thrown on the difficulties of translating Freud in a delightful collection of letters by the two Freudian Bloomsburians themselves, *Bloomsbury/Freud: The letters of James and Alix Strachey 1924–1925,* P. Meisel and W. Kendrick, eds. (New York: Norton, 1990).

Background.   The general works listed above provide various perspectives on the background against which to view Freud. Useful for the Viennese cultural setting are Schorske (1980), a wonderful book on the whole Viennese scene, and his student McGrath (1986), who develops Freud's situation more fully. Decker (1991) also discusses Freud in Vienna, with special attention to the history and status of the Austrian Jewish community. David Bakan, *Sigmund Freud and the Jewish mystical tradition* (Princeton, NJ: D. van Nostrand, 1958), connects Freud's thought to Jewish theology.

For the medical background, two books on the development of the concept of neurosis are available, José M. Lopez Pinero, *Historical origins of the concept of neurosis* (Cambridge, England: Cambridge University Press, 1983), and George Frederick Drinka, *The birth of neurosis: Myth, malady and the Victorians* (New York: Touchstone, 1984). For no obvious reason, the scholarly study of hysteria has proliferated in just the past few years. Mark Micale has provided guides to the literature: "Hysteria and its historiography: A review of past and present writings," *History of Science* (1989, *27:* I: 223–61, II: 319–56), and "Hysteria and its historiography: The future perspective," *History of Psychiatry* (1990, *1:* 33–124).

One of the most important of Freud's self-perpetuated myths is that his ideas met with a hostile reception; like so many other Freud stories, it isn't true (Sulloway, 1979). See the following studies of Freud's reception and influence: Hannah S. Decker, "The interpretation of dreams: Early reception by the educated German public," *Journal of the History of the Behavioral Sciences* (1975, *11:* 129–41); Hannah S. Decker, *Freud in Germany: Revolution and reaction in science, 1893–1907* (New York: International Universities Press, 1977); Psychological Issues Monographs *11* (31), Monograph 41; Nathan Hale, *Freud and the Americans* (New York: Oxford University Press, 1971); and David Shakow, *The influence of Freud on American psychology* (New York: International Universities Press, 1964).

The Path through Physiology.   In addition to the cited works, especially Solomon's (1974), see Karl H. Pribram and Merton Gill, *Freud's "Project" re-assessed: Preface to contemporary cognitive theory and neuropsychology* (New York: Basic Books, 1976).

Pribram is a leading neuropsychologist, and he and Gill view the "Project" as pioneering and prescient.

Dora and Other Cases.   Decker (1991) provides a full account of what is now probably Freud's most studied case. For brief accounts and critical treatments of Freud's few published case studies, see Sulloway (1991).

The Unconscious.   The standard, massive history of the unconscious is Ellenberger (1970). Also useful are D. B. Klein, *The unconscious: Invention or discovery?* (Santa Monica, CA: Goodyear, 1977); and Lancelot Law Whyte, *The unconscious before Freud* (New York: Basic Books, 1960). Hughes (1958) shows how the concept of the unconscious came to grip social thought more generally. The view from continental hermeneutics is given in David Archard, *Consciousness and the unconscious* (La Salle, IL: Open Court, 1984). The concept of the unconscious is still controversial: see John R. Searle, "Consciousness, explanatory inversion, and cognitive science," *Behavioral and Brain Sciences* (1990, *13*: 585–642, with commentary), and Erdelyi (1985).

Victorian Sexuality.   How prudish and repressed the Victorians were has become a matter of controversy between a traditional picture of uptight Victorians and Peter Gay's, *The bourgeois experience: Victoria to Freud, Vol 1: Education of the senses* (New York: Oxford University Press, 1984) picture of almost hedonistic Victorians (although in Gay, 1986, they seem more conservative). In the text, I try to steer a middle course, focusing on the problem as Freud saw it. Herewith is a brief introduction to the enormous literature. The traditional view is that Victorians—especially women—were intensely repressed and deeply ashamed about sex. Standard sources here include Stephen Marcus, *The other Victorians* (New York: Meridian, 1964), a work I relied on; Vern and Bonnie Bullough, *Sin, sickness, and sanity: A history of sexual attitudes* (New York: Meridian, 1977), which covers periods before and after the Victorian; G. J. Barker-Benfield, *The horrors of the half-known life: Male attitudes toward women and sexuality in nineteenth-century America* (New York: Harper Colophon, 1976), which takes a feminist perspective; Ronald Pearsall, *The worm in the bud: The world of Victorian sexuality* (Harmondsworth, England: Penguin, 1983), a social history of Victorian sexuality; John S. and Robin M. Haller, *The physician and sexuality in Victorian America* (Champaign: University of Illinois Press, 1974), a fascinating study of physicians' ideas about sex, and how they were translated into popular and professional "cures" for alleged sexual disorder; and Jeffrey Weeks, *Sex, politics and society: The regulation of sexuality since 1800* (New York: Longman, 1981). Victorians were especially alarmed by masturbation: see Arthur N. Gilbert, "Masturbation and insanity: Henry Maudsley and the ideology of sexual repression," *Albion* (1980, *12:* 268–82). However, revisionist historians have begun to assert that the traditional view of repressed Victorian sexuality is seriously mistaken. For example, a recently discovered unpublished sex survey—the first ever—of women who had grown up in the Victorian period suggests that they may have had orgasms with the same frequency as today's "liberated" women: Clelia Duel Mosher, *The Mosher survey: Sexual attitudes of Victorian women* (New York: Arno, 1980). Peter Gay (see *The bourgeois experience: Victoria to Freud, Vol. 1: Education of the senses.* New York: Oxford University Press, 1984) has used the Mosher survey, a diary by a sexually active young American woman, and other sources to try to debunk the "myth" of the asexual Victorian; see also Cyril Pearl, *The girl with the Swansdown seat: An informal report on some aspects of mid-Victorian morality* (London: Robin Clark, 1980), and Edmund Leites, *The Puritan conscience and human sexuality* (New Haven, CT: Yale University Press, 1986). How much of the revisionist picture is accurate, however, is still open to question. For an evaluation, see Carol Zisowitz Sterns, "Victorian sexuality: Can historians do it better?" *Journal of Social History* (1985, *18:* 625–34). Freud himself was an advocate of sexual reform. See Boyer (1978), which contains a transcript with translation of

Freud's reply to a query from a commission looking into the laws regulating marriage in Austria in 1905; and Timothy McCarthy, "Freud and the problem of sexuality," *Journal of the History of the Behavioral and Social Sciences* (1981, *17:* 332–39). Other important rebels against Victorian sexual repression, assuming it existed, are described by Paul Robinson, *The modernization of sex: Havelock Ellis, Alfred Kinsey, William Masters and Virginia Johnson* (New York: Harper Colophon, 1977), and Phyllis Grosskurth, *Havelock Ellis* (New York: Knopf, 1980). For general background, see Bernard Murstein, *Love, sex, and marriage through the ages* (New York: Springer, 1974), and Lawrence Stone, *The family, sex, and marriage in England 1500–1800* (New York: Harper & Row, 1977). Although Stone's history stops before the Victorian period, Stone shows that a cycle of sexual repression alternating with sexual freedom was a regular feature of English history.

There are many works on the seduction error. Schatzman (1992) is a succinct but penetrating account. More lengthy, and leading into the broader issue of Freud's scientific standing, is Esterson (1993). See also Crew's *The unknown Freud,* cited above. David Livingston Smith, *Hidden conversations: An introduction to communicative psychoanalysis* (London: Tavistock/Routledge, 1991), provides a useful perspective from within modern psychoanalysis.

The Standing of Psychoanalysis. The text cites the most important books evaluating psychoanalysis. Freud's luster has tarnished over the years for myself and others. I came to psychology by reading Isaac Asimov's *Foundation* trilogy, and then Freud, and Freud was long one of my heroes. However, between becoming a fox and writing this revised chapter, I must confess I no longer regard Freud with much affection. For similar disenchantments, see Crews (1986) and Sulloway (1991). An interesting assessment of Freud is provided by leading literary critic Harold Bloom, "Freud, Greatest modern writer," *New York Review of Books* (March 23, 1986, 1, 26–27). Bloom makes his point by canvassing rival views of Freud, concluding that what Freud gave the world was great mythology; art, not science.

While putting this new edition through the press, three important works on Freud and psychoanalysis appeared that deserve mention. The first is Richard Webster, *Why Freud was wrong: Sin, science, and psychoanalysis* (New York: Basic Books, 1995). Webster's book is up-to-date and gives useful summaries of all of Freud's critics while also mentioning his defenders. More importantly, Webster carefully places Freud in the context of nineteenth-century psychiatry. Webster shows how Freud remained primarily a medical man all his life, always focusing on organic symptoms and ignoring his patients' mental distress. Webster critically describes Charcot's ideas about hysteria and demonstrates its deep influence on Freud, and argues persuasively that hysteria never existed, but was a category physicians found convenient for disposing of ill-understood disorders of the brain. That criticism of Freud still generates bitter controversy is amply demonstrated by Frederick Crews, *The memory wars: Freud's legacy in dispute* (New York: New York Review of Books, 1995). The book reprints three articles by Crews that are highly critical of Freud's character and that link him to the controversial "repressed memory" movement, together with passionate and even vituperative defenses of Freud, the "repressed memory" movement, and Crews's response. At the very least, *Memory wars* makes lively reading. Webster argues that psychoanalysis became popular because it repackaged Christian religion in scientific guise while pretending to be radically new. Richard Noll, *The Jung cult: Origins of a charismatic movement* (Princeton, NJ: Princeton University Press, 1994) makes a similar argument about Freud but then concentrates on Jung. The book is excellent on the odd religious-political situation in pre-Hitler Germany and on showing how Jung thought of himself as a religious figure.

Hermeneutics. Key books are Lacan (1968) and Ricoeur (1970) works cited in the text. For a remarkably readable survey of a notoriously difficult and slippery subject, see Roy J. Howard, *Three faces of hermeneutics: An introduction to current theories of understanding* (Berkeley: University of California Press, 1982). See also Charles D. Axelrod,

Studies in intellectual breakthrough: Freud, Simmel, Buber (Amherst: University of Massachusetts Press, 1970); and Richard Lichtman, *The production of desire: The integration of psychoanalysis into Marxist theory* (New York: Free Press, 1982). Freud is connected to the founder of deconstructionism, Jacques Derrida, in Samuel Weber, *The legend of Freud* (Minneapolis: University of Minnesota Press, 1982). For critical views of the Party of Suspicion, I recommend R. Geuss, *The idea of a critical theory: Habermas and the Frankfurt School* (Cambridge, England: Cambridge University Press, 1971), and D. Lehman, *Signs of the Times* (New York: Poseidon, 1991).

General Influence. Freud's influence has been very great in fields other than psychiatry and psychology. A collection that is especially useful for a beginner is Jonathan Miller, ed., *Freud: The man, his world, his influence* (Boston: Little, Brown, 1972); it contains essays on Freud and his time, and then a set on Freud's influence in various fields. Books on specific areas of influence follow. Art: Ellen H. Spitz, *Art and psyche: A study in psychoanalysis and aesthetics* (New Haven, CT: Yale University Press, 1985). The social sciences, including anthropology, sociology, and political science: Paul Roazen, *Freud: Political and social thought* (New York: Da Capo Press, 1986); Arthur Berliner, *Psychoanalysis and society* (Washington, DC: University Press of America, 1982); Peter Bocock, *Freud and modern society: An outline of Freud's sociology* (Sunbury-on-Thames, England: Nelson, 1976); H. M. Ruitenbeek, ed., *Psychoanalysis and social science* (New York: Dutton, 1962); Melford Spiro, *Oedipus in the Trobriands* (Chicago: University of Chicago Press, 1983); and Edwin R. Wallace, *Freud and anthropology* (New York: International Universities Press, 1983). One controversial offspring of psychoanalysis is psychohistory, which is discussed and critically examined in David E. Stannard, *Shrinking history: On Freud and the failure of psychohistory* (New York: Oxford University Press, 1980).

REFERENCES

Boyer, J. W. (1978). Freud, marriage, and late Viennese liberalism: A commentary from 1905. *Journal of Modern History 50:* 72–102.

Breger, L. (1981). How psychoanalysis is a science—and how it is not. *Journal of the American Academy of Psychoanalysis 9:* 261–75.

Cioffi, F. (1972). Wollheim on Freud. *Inquiry 15:* 172–86.

———. (1973). Introduction. In F. Cioffi, ed., *Freud: Modern judgements.* London: Macmillan.

———. (1974). Was Freud a liar? *The Listener 91:* 172–4.

———. (1984, July 6). The cradle of neurosis. *Times Literary Supplement:* 743–4.

Crews, F. (1986). *Skeptical engagements.* New York: Oxford University Press.

Decker, H. S. (1981). Freud and Dora: Constraints on medical progress. *Journal of Social History 14:* 445–64.

———. (1991). *Freud, Dora, and Vienna 1900.* New York: Free Press.

Dollard, J., Doob, L., Miller, N., Mowrer, O., and Sears, R. (1939). *Frustration and aggression.* New Haven, CT: Yale University Press.

Ellenberger, H. F. (1970). *The discovery of the unconscious.* New York: Basic Books.

Erdelyi, M. H. (1985). *Psychoanalysis: Freud's cognitive psychology.* San Francisco: Freeman.

Esterson, A. (1993). *Seductive mirage: An exploration of the work of Sigmund Freud.* Chicago: Open Court.

Eysenck, H. J. (1986). *The decline and fall of the Freudian Empire.* Harmondsworth, England: Penguin.

Eysenck, H. J. and Wilson, G. D., eds. (1973). *The experimental study of Freudian theories.* London: Methuen.

Farrell, B. A. (1981). *The standing of psychoanalysis.* Oxford, England: Oxford University Press.

Fisher, S. and Greenberg, R. P. (1977). *The scientific credibility of Freud's theories and therapy.* New York: Basic Books.

Freud, S. (1900/1968). *The interpretation of dreams.* New York: Avon.

_____ . (1905a/1962). *Three essays on the theory of sexuality.* New York: Avon.

_____ . (1905b). Fragments of an analysis of a case of hysteria. Partially reprinted in P. Gay, ed., *The Freud reader* (New York: Norton, 1989).

_____ . (1908/1953). "Civilized" sexual morality and modern nervousness. In *Collected papers,* Vol. 2. London: Hogarth Press.

_____ . (1912/1953). Contributions to the psychology of love: The most prevalent form of degradation in erotic life. In *Collected papers,* Vol. 4. London: Hogarth Press.

_____ . (1914/1966). *The psychopathology of everyday life.* New York: Norton.

_____ . (1915a). Instincts and their vicissitudes. Partially reprinted in P. Gay, ed., *The Freud reader* (New York, Norton, 1989).

_____ . (1915b). The unconscious. Partially reprinted in P. Gay, ed., *The Freud reader* (New York, Norton, 1989).

_____ . (1920/1961). *Beyond the pleasure principle.* New York: Norton.

_____ . (1923/1960). *The ego and the id.* New York: Norton.

_____ . (1927/1961). *Future of an illusion.* New York: Norton.

_____ . (1930/1961). *Civilization and its discontents.* New York: Norton.

_____ . (1932). The question of a *Weltanschauung.* Partially reprinted in P. Gay, ed., *The Freud reader* (New York, Norton, 1989).

_____ . (1950). Project for a scientific psychology. *The standard edition of the complete psychological works of Sigmund Freud,* Vol. 1. J. Strachey, trans. London: Hogarth Press.

_____ . (1960). *The letters of Sigmund Freud.* New York: Basic Books.

_____ . (1985). The complete letters of Sigmund Freud to Wilhelm Fliess 1887–1904. J. M. Masson, trans. and ed. Cambridge, MA: Harvard University Press.

Freud, S. and Breuer, J. (1895/1966). *Studies in hysteria.* New York: Avon.

Gay, P. (1986). *The bourgeois experience: Victoria to Freud, Vol. 2: The tender passion.* New York: Oxford University Press.

_____ . (1988). *Freud: A life for our time.* New York: Norton.

_____ . ed. (1989). *The Freud reader.* New York: Norton.

Grünbaum, A. (1984). *The foundations of psychoanalysis: A philosophical critique.* Berkeley: University of California Press.

_____ . (1986). Precis of The foundations of psychoanalysis: A philosophical critique, with commentary. *Behavioral and Brain Sciences 9:* 217–84.

Holt, R. R. (1982, November). Family secrets. *The Sciences 22:* 26–28.

Hook, S. (1959). *Psychoanalysis, scientific method, and philosophy.* New York: New York University Press.

Houghton, W. E. (1957). *The Victorian frame of mind.* New Haven, CT: Yale University Press.

Hughes, H. S. (1958). *Consciousness and society: The reorientation of European social thought 1890–1930.* New York: Vintage Books.

James, W. (1890). *Principles of psychology,* 2 vols. New York: Holt.

Kaufmann, W. (1985). Nietzsche as the first great (depth) psychologist. In S. Koch and D. Leary, *A century of psychology as science.* New York: McGraw-Hill.

Klein, M. I. and Tribich, D. (1982, November). Blame the child. *The Sciences 22:* 14–20.

Kline, P. (1981). *Fact and fantasy in Freudian theory,* 2nd ed. London: Methuen.

Krantz, S. (1990). Brentano on "Unconscious consciousness." *Philosophy and Phenomenological Research 1:* 745–53.

Lacan, J. (1968). *The language of the self.* A. Wilden, trans. Baltimore: Johns Hopkins University Press.

Lorenz, K. (1966). *On aggression.* San Diego, CA: Harcourt Brace Jovanovich.

MacIntyre, A. (1985). How psychology makes itself true—or false. In S. Koch and D. Leary, *A century of psychology as science.* New York: McGraw-Hill.

Macmillan, M. (1991). *Freud evaluated. The completed arc.* Amsterdam, The Netherlands: North-Holland.

Masson, J. M. (1984a, February). Freud and the seduction theory. *Atlantic Monthly:* 33–60.

_____ . (1984b). *The assault on truth: Freud's suppression of the seduction theory.* New York: Farrar, Straus, & Giroux.

McGrath, W. J. (1986). *Freud's discovery of psychoanalysis: The politics of hysteria.* Ithaca, NY: Cornell University Press.

Myers, G. E. (1986). *William James: His life and thought.* New Haven, CT: Yale University Press.

Nagel, E. (1959). Methodological issues in psychoanalytic theory. In S. Hook, *Psychoanalysis, scientific method, and philosophy.* New York: New York University Press.

Ricoeur, P. (1970). *Freud and philosophy,* B. Savage, trans. New Haven, CT: Yale University Press.

Rieff, P. (1979). *Freud: The mind of the moralist,* 3rd ed. Chicago: University of Chicago Press.

Roazen, P. (1974). *Freud and his followers.* New York: New American Library.

Rosenzweig, S. (1985). Freud and experimental psychology: The emergence of idiodynamics. In S. Koch and D. Leary, *A century of psychology as science.* New York: McGraw-Hill.

Schatzman, M. (1992, March 21). Freud: Who seduced whom? *New Scientist,* 34–7.

Schorske, C. E. (1980). Fin-de-siècle *Vienna: Politics and culture.* New York: Knopf.

Sears, R. R. (1985). Psychoanalysis and behavior theory: 1907–65. In S. Koch and D. Leary, *A century of psychology as science.* New York: McGraw-Hill.

Solomon, R. C. (1974). Freud's neurological theory of the mind. In R. Wollheim, ed., *Freud: A collection of critical essays.* Garden City, NY: Doubleday.

Sperling, G. A. (1960). The information available in brief visual presentations. *Psychological Monographs 74:* entire no. 498.

Sulloway, F. J. (1979). *Freud: Biologist of the mind.* New York: Basic Books.

_____ . (1982). Freud and biology: The hidden legacy. In W. R. Woodward and M. J. Ash, eds., *The problematic science: Psychology in nineteenth-century thought.* New York: Praeger.

_____ . (1991). Reassessing Freud's case histories: The social construction of psychoanalysis. *Isis 82:* 245–75.

9 The Psychology of Adaptation (1855-1891)

William James, self-portrait. As a young man, William James wanted to be an artist but was dissuaded by his parents and got an MD instead. Almost Wundt's equal as a founder of the first laboratory, James's ideas did not and have not died. His *Principles of Psychology* (1890) marks a watershed in the history of psychology, looking at the mind in all its aspects through an evolutionary lens. It set the agenda for American psychology in the twentieth century. Ironically, James soon tired of psychology and turned to philosophy, becoming the great first spokesman for America's native philosophy, pragmatism.

The last founding psychology we will examine has proved the most durable and influential in academic psychology. In the twentieth century, Wundt's psychology of consciousness quickly became an anachronistic product of nineteenth-century German thought, and it survived neither transplantation to other countries nor the destruction of its intellectual ecology by the Nazis and World War II. The same is largely true of Gestalt psychology. Psychoanalysis is a living tradition, having adapted to conditions outside nineteenth-century Vienna, and its influence on modern culture has been greater than that of any other psychology. Nevertheless, psychoanalysis remains primarily a branch of medical psychiatry, and its relations with academic psychology have been ambivalent from Freud's time to our own.

The approach that academic psychologists, first in England and later in America, have found most attractive and useful is a psychology based on evolution—Lamarckian or Darwinian. With the ascendance of American psychology in the twentieth century, the psychology of adaptation in one form or another has dominated academic psychology.

Any theory of evolution raises two questions that can engender psychological research programs. The first we may call the *species question*. If the body and brain are products of organic evolution, then we may ask in what ways this inheritance shapes the thought and behavior of organisms. Hume erected his philosophical system on his science of human nature, but he did not inquire into why we have the nature we have. Darwinian evolution makes feasible asking and answering Hume's unasked question, because we can ask how each aspect of human nature is adaptive in the struggle for existence. This question leads to comparative psychology, ethology, and evolutionary psychology, which study species differences in mental and behavioral capacities—differences presumably created by evolution. However, in the context of the psychology of consciousness, the first Darwinian question to be asked will be: Why are we conscious at all? The second psychological question raised by evolution we may call the *individual question*. As the individual creature grows up, it can be seen as adapting psychologically to the environment in a way analogous to organic evolution. This question leads to the study of learning, research designed to uncover how the individual adjusts to the environment.

The species question and the individual question are interrelated. If species differences are great, then different psychologies of individual adaptation will be needed for different species. If, on the other hand, species differences are small, then the same laws of individual learning will apply to all individuals, regardless of species. In this chapter, we will trace the development of the psychology of adaptation and will soon discover that its proponents adopt the latter line of thought. Gall's phrenology had implied a comparative psychology that looked for species differences in the possession of mental faculties. To a phrenologist, structural differences in the brain meant structural differences in mind. However, by the middle of the nineteenth century, the sensorimotor concept of the brain had vanquished phrenology among scientists, and associationism was displacing faculty psychology among philosopher-psychologists. The view of the brain as an initially formless associative machine and the view of the mind as a tabula rasa awaiting associations combined to cause psychologists to focus on the individual question and minimize species differences.

THE BEGINNINGS OF THE PSYCHOLOGY OF ADAPTATION IN BRITAIN

Lamarckian Psychology: Herbert Spencer (1820–1903)

In the summer of 1854, Herbert Spencer began to write a psychology whose "lines of thought had scarcely anything in common with lines of thought previously pursued" (Spencer, 1904). His work appeared the following year, 1855, as *Principles of Psychology*. This book gives Spencer a good claim to be the founder of the psychology of adaptation. Bain had integrated associationism and the sensorimotor conception of brain function; but, although he acknowledged the validity of Darwinian evolution, his psychology remained part of classical, pre-evolutionary associationism. Writing before Darwin, Spencer integrated associationism and sensorimotor physiology with Lamarckian evolution. Consequently, he anticipated the psychology of adaptation. Furthermore, not only did he raise the two evolutionary questions, but he also answered them in the ways that have been basic to Anglo-American psychology ever since.

Spencer's *Principles of Psychology* was just one part of his all-embracing synthetic philosophy. Spencer was the greatest systematizer since Aquinas, although Spencer thought of himself as the new Newton. Another part of his system was the *Principles of Sociology,* and Spencer is regarded as a founder of that field, too. Aquinas organized all philosophy around the Christian God. Spencer organized it around Lamarckian evolution, in which he believed as early as 1852. He referred all questions, metaphysical or otherwise, to the principle of evolution and presented it as a cosmic process, embracing not only organic evolution but also the evolution of mind and societies.

In 1854, Spencer wrote, "If the doctrine of Evolution is true, the inevitable implication is that Mind can be understood only by observing how Mind is evolved." Here is the starting point of the psychology of adaptation. Spencer proceeded to discuss both evolutionary psychological questions. Considering the individual, Spencer viewed development as a process by which the connections between ideas come to mirror accurately the connections between events prevailing in the environment. The connections between ideas are built up by contiguity. Wrote Spencer (1897): "The growth of intelligence at large depends upon the law, that when any two psychical states occur in immediate succession, an effect is produced such that if the first subsequently recurs there is a certain tendency for the second to follow it." This tendency is strengthened as ideas are more frequently associated together. Like Bain, Spencer attempted to "deduce" the laws of mental association from the sensorimotor constitution of the nervous system and brain. In general, then, Spencer's analysis of the individual mind is that of atomistic associationism. He broke down the more complex phenomena of intelligence into basic elements (Spencer, 1897). What Spencer adds to Bain is the evolutionary conception, viewing the development of the mind as an adaptive adjustment to environmental conditions.

Spencer pictured the brain as a sensorimotor associational device, stating (1897) that "the human brain is an organized register of infinitely numerous experiences." His view has two important consequences. Given the Lamarckian idea of the heritability of acquired characteristics, instinct can be made acceptable to associationists and empiricists. Following the passage just quoted, Spencer described how the brain accumulates experiences "during the evolution of that series of organisms through which the human organism has been reached." Thus, innate reflexes and instincts are simply associative habits so well learned that they have become part of a species' genetic legacy. Such habits may not be acquired during an individual's life, but they are still acquired, following the laws of association, in the life of the species. Innate ideas need no longer terrify the empiricist.

The second consequence of Spencer's integration of evolution and the sensorimotor concept of nervous function is more portentous: Differences in the mental processes of different species reduce to the number of associations the brains are able to make. All brains work the same way, by association, and they differ only quantitatively in the richness of their associations. As Spencer (1897) put it, "The impressions received by inferior intelligences, even down to the very lowest, are dealt with after a like model." Thus, his answer to the species question is to deny qualitative differences among species and admit only quantitative, associational differences. This idea extends to differences within, as well as between, species; the "European inherits from twenty to thirty cubic inches more brain than the Papuan," he said. This implies that the "civilized man has also a more complex or heterogeneous nervous system than the uncivilized man," as he wrote in *First Principles* (1880).

Spencer's conclusions are of tremendous importance for the development of the psychology of adaptation. Given his framework, comparative psychology would be directed toward studying species differences in simple associative learning, studies aimed at quantifying a single dimension of "intelligence" along which species can be arranged. Moreover, such studies could be performed in the laboratory, ignoring an organism's native environment. If the brain is no more than an initially empty stimulus–response associating mechanism, then it is irrelevant whether the associations are natural or contrived; in fact, the laboratory offers greater control of the process than does naturalistic observation.

It also follows that if all organisms learn the same way, then the results of studies of simple animal learning, with their precision, replicability, and rigor, can be extended without serious modification to human learning. We will find that all of these conclusions are of fundamental importance to behaviorism, the twentieth-century psychology of adaptation. Behaviorists seek laws of learning that are valid for at least all mammals, and they assume the extension of animal findings to human psychology—often without supporting data.

Finally, the quantitative conception of associative mental function would help develop intelligence testing, which purports to assign a number to a person's intelligence. Although it is not demanded by the theory, the connection of associational ability with brain mass and complexity of association would push mental testing in a racist direction. We have already seen Spencer denigrate "uncivilized" people for having low brain mass and a simple nervous system, and, in *First Principles,* he implies that the "lower human races" are children: "In the infant European we see sundry resemblances to the lower human races."

One application of the theory of evolution to human society is to see it as an arena for the struggle for existence. This attitude is called social Darwinism, although it began before Darwin with Herbert Spencer. Spencer argued that natural selection should be allowed to take its course on the human species. Government should do nothing to save the poor, weak, and helpless. In nature, poor, weak, helpless animals, and their poor hereditary traits, are weeded out by natural selection. This should be the way in human society as well, said Spencer. Government should leave the cosmic process alone, for it will perfect humanity by the selection of the fittest. To help human failures would only serve to degrade the species by allowing them to have children and thus pass on their hereditary tendency to fail.

When Spencer toured America in 1882, he was lionized. Social Darwinism had great appeal in a laissez-faire capitalist society where it could justify even cutthroat competition on the grounds that such competition perfected humanity. Although it promised eventual perfection of the species, social Darwinism was profoundly conservative, for all reform was seen as tampering with nature's laws. The American social Darwinist Edward Youmans complained bitterly about the evils of the robber barons, but when asked what he proposed to do about them, he replied, "Nothing" (Hofstadter, 1955). Only centuries of evolution could relieve human problems.

Darwinian Psychology

Spencer's evolutionary principles, while inspired by Lamarck, are not inconsistent with Darwin's theory of natural selection. The only new assumption needed is that natural selection has produced the sensorimotor nervous system believed to exist in all animals, which justifies an associationist theory of mind or, later, of behavior. Many naturalistic thinkers, including Darwin himself, consciously or unconsciously adhered to the Lamarckian view of progressive evolution, however, and sometimes even accepted the heritability of acquired characteristics. Thus, Spencer's Lamarckian psychology shades insensibly into a Darwinian psychology.

Darwin on Humans

The central challenge of Darwin's *Origin of Species* concerned what Huxley called man's place in nature. In the comprehensive, naturalistic scheme of evolution, humanity was made part of nature, no longer a being who transcended it. This implication was immediately seen by all, whether they agreed with it or not. Yet *Origin* itself contains very little on human psychology. We know that, in his early notebooks, dating back to the 1830s, Darwin was concerned with these topics, but he seems to have set them aside from his initial publication as too troublesome. All his life, Darwin projected, but never completed, a master work on evolution in all its facets. In any event, it was not until 1871 that he finally published *The Descent of Man,* which brings human nature within the scope of natural selection.

Darwin's aim in *The Descent of Man* was to show that "man is descended from some lowly organized form," a conclusion that he regretted would "be highly distasteful to many." He broadly compared human and animal behavior and concluded:

> The difference in mind between man and the higher animals, great as it is, is certainly one of degree and not of kind. We have seen that the senses and intuitions, the various emotions and faculties, such as love, memory, attention, curiosity, imitation, reason, etc., of which man boasts may be found in an incipient, or even sometimes in a well-developed condition, in lower animals. [Even the] ennobling belief in God is not universal with man. (Darwin, 1896)

Descent was not primarily a work of psychology; it mainly attempted to incorporate humans fully into nature. Darwin felt that Spencer had already laid the foundations for an evolutionary psychology. Yet Darwin's work contrasts importantly with Spencer's *Principles.* Darwin followed philosophical faculty psychology, relegating association to a secondary factor in thought. Partly as a consequence, Darwin was concerned almost exclusively with the species question, for he assumed that evolution shaped the faculties. He also allowed great scope to the effects of heredity, sounding at times like an extreme nativist. For Darwin, both virtue and crime were heritable tendencies; woman is genetically inferior to man in "whatever he takes up." On the other hand, Darwin agreed with Spencer that the nature of species differences is quantitative rather than qualitative and that well-learned habits can become innate reflexes. Lamarckian psychology and Darwinian psychology differ only in emphasis, not in content. The major difference is that Darwin's psychology is only a part of a materialistic, evolutionary biology. Spencer's psychology, in contrast, was part of a grand metaphysics that tended toward dualism and postulated an "Unknowable" forever beyond the reach of science. Darwin sheared off this metaphysical growth from the psychology of adaptation.

The Spirit of Darwinian Psychology: Sir Francis Galton (1822–1911)

Galton was an outstanding example of that distinct Victorian type, the gentleman dilettante. Independently wealthy, he was able to turn his inventive mind to whatever he chose. He traveled over most of Africa and wrote a manual for travelers in wild lands. He empirically investigated the efficacy of prayer. He pioneered the use of fingerprints for personal identification. He invented composite photographic portraiture. Many of his wide-ranging investigations were psychological or sociological. He once tried to understand paranoia by suspecting everyone he met of evil intentions. He canvassed the female beauties of Great Britain trying to ascertain which county had the most beautiful women in it. He measured boredom at scientific lectures. He applied anthropomorphic tests to thousands of individuals visiting a fair in Kensington. However, Galton's researches were so eclectic that they do not add up to a research program. Consequently, Galton cannot be considered a psychologist in the same sense as Wundt, Titchener, or Freud.

Nevertheless, Galton made important contributions to the growing psychology of adaptation. He broadened psychology to encompass topics excluded by Wundt. In his *Inquiries into the Human Faculty* (1883/1907, p. 47), he wrote: "No professor of . . . psychology . . . can claim to know the elements of what he teaches, unless he is acquainted with the ordinary phenomena of idiocy, madness, and epilepsy. He must study the manifestations of disease and congenital folly, as well as those of high intellect." Wundt wanted to understand only the normal, adult mind. Galton inquired into any human mind.

Galton devised a number of important methods used by the psychology of adaptation. He was the first to systematically apply statistics to psychological data, and he invented the correlation coefficient. He studied twins to sort out the contributions of nature and nurture to human character, intellect, and behavior. He tried to use indirect behavioral measures (rate of fidgeting) to measure a mental state (boredom). He invented the free-association technique of interrogating memory. He used questionnaires to collect data on mental processes such as mental imagery. He tried to use a psychophysical method (lifting weights) to measure acuteness of perception, and thus—he thought—intelligence. He tried to directly introspect his higher mental processes, which Wundt had said was impossible. All these techniques found a place in English and American psychology.

Spencer began the psychology of adaptation, but Galton epitomized it. His eclectic attitude concerning both method and subject matter, and his use of statistics, would strongly characterize Darwinian psychology from this point on. Above all, his interest in individual differences points to the future: In German rationalist fashion, Wundt had wanted to describe the transcendent human mind; he quite literally found the study of individual differences to be foreign and the existence of individual differences to be a nuisance. Guided by evolution—especially the concept of variation—Galton, however, was interested in all those factors that make people different. The study of individual differences is an essential part of Darwinian science, for without variation there can be no differential selection and no evolutionary improvement of the species.

Improvement of the human species was precisely Galton's aim. Underlying his various investigations was not a research program, but rather a "religious duty." He was convinced that the most important individual differences, including those of morals, character, and intellect, are not acquired. His great aim was to demonstrate that these characteristics are innate and then to measure them so that they could inform the procreative behavior of humanity. Eugenics is the selective breeding of human beings to improve the species.

In his *Hereditary Genius* (1869), Galton

> propose[d] to show that a man's natural abilities are derived by inheritance, under exactly the same limitations as are the form and physical features of the whole organic world. Consequently, as it is easy, not withstanding these limitations, to obtain by careful selection of permanent breed of dogs or horses gifted with peculiar powers of running, or of doing anything else, so it would be quite practicable to produce a highly gifted race of men by judicious marriages during several consecutive generations.

In this work, Galton endeavored to show that abilities as different as those required to be a good judge or a good wrestler are innate and heritable, which would make a eugenics program feasible. Galton's main interest was in the improvement of individuals, and he thought selective breeding would improve humanity faster than improved education. Galton's program for selective human breeding was a form of positive eugenics, attempting to get especially "fit" individuals to marry one another. Galton proposed that examinations be used to discover the ten most talented men and women in Great Britain. At a public ceremony recognizing their talent, each would be offered £ 5,000—a staggering sum in days when a moderately frugal person might live on a pound or so a week—as a wedding present should they choose to marry one another.

Galton's proposals gained few adherents when he first set them in 1869. Just after the turn of the century, however, Britons were more disposed to listen. In the wake of their near defeat in the Boer War in South Africa, and the gradual recession of their empire, Britons began to worry that they were degenerating as a nation. In 1902, the Army reported that 60 percent of Englishmen were unfit for military service, setting off a furious public debate on the physical deterioration (after the name of the Army report) of the British people. In this atmosphere, worriers of all political stripes were excited by Galton's eugenic program for race improvement.

In 1901, Karl Pearson (1857–1936), an intimate of Galton's who had extended and perfected Galton's statistical approach to biology, pressed Galton to reenter the fray for eugenics. Pearson was a socialist who opposed conservative, laissez-faire social Darwinism and hoped to replace it with planned, politically enforced programs of eugenics. Galton agreed, despite his advanced age, to take up the cause again, and in that year he gave a public lecture on eugenics and began to work for the establishment of eugenics policies. In 1904, he gave £ 1,500 to establish a research fellowship in eugenics and a eugenics record office at the University of London. In 1907, he helped found the Eugenics Education Society, which began to publish a journal, *Eugenics Review*. Eugenics appealed to people all across the political spectrum. Conservative, establishment leaders used alleged "laws of heredity and development" to support their crusade for moral, especially sexual, reform. Social radicals could press eugenics into service as part of their programs for political and social reform. Eugenics was much talked about in the first decade of the twentieth century in Britain.

Despite the attention it received, British eugenics, in contrast to American eugenics, enjoyed only limited success in affecting public policy. Galton's program of rewards was never seriously considered. Some attention was given to laws enforcing negative eugenics—attempts to regulate the reproduction of the alleged "unfit"—but these were relatively mild measures that placed the socially incapacitated in institutions where they could receive care. British eugenicists were themselves divided on the need for government eugenics programs, the social radical eugenicists in particular urging education and voluntary control instead of legal compulsion. British eugenics was never fueled, as American eugenics was, by racism and race hysteria. British eugenicists were more concerned to encourage the reproduction of the middle and upper classes, whose birthrate had long been in decline, than to restrict spitefully the reproduction of allegedly inferior races. Although eugenics began in Britain, in the English-speaking world it was practiced mostly in America, as we shall see.

The Rise of Comparative Psychology

A psychology based on evolution should call forth research aimed at comparing the various abilities of different species of animals. Simple comparison of human and animal abilities goes back to Aristotle, and both Descartes and Hume buttressed their philosophies with such considerations. The Scottish faculty psychologists argued that humans' moral faculty distinguished them from animals. Galton studied animals and people to discover the special mental faculties of each species. The theory of evolution, however, gave comparative psychology a powerful impetus, placing it in a wider biological context and giving it a specific rationale. In the later nineteenth century, comparative psychology grew in strength until, in the twentieth century, learning theorists studied animals in preference to humans.

Modern comparative psychology may be said to have begun in 1872 with the publication of Darwin's *The Expression of the Emotions in Man and Animals* (Darwin, 1872/1965, p. 12). The new approach is heralded by Darwin's statement early in the book: "No doubt as long as man and all other animals are viewed as independent creations, an effectual stop is put to our natural desire to investigate as far as possible the causes of Expression." However, he who admits "that the structure and habits of all animals have been gradually evolved, will look at the whole subject in a new and interesting light." In the rest of his book, Darwin surveyed the means of emotional expression possessed by humans and animals, noting the continuity between them and demonstrating their universality among the races of humanity. Darwin's theory is very Lamarckian: "Actions, which were at first voluntary, soon become habitual, and at last hereditary, and may then be performed even in opposition to the will." Darwin's theory was that our involuntary emotive expressions have gone through this development.

Darwin's early work in comparative psychology was systematically carried on by his friend George John Romanes (1848–1894). In *Animal Intelligence* (1883), Romanes surveyed the mental abilities of animals from protozoa to apes. In later works, such as *Mental Evolution in Man* (1889), Romanes attempted to trace the gradual evolution of mind down the millennia. Romanes died before he could complete his comparative psychology. His literary executor was C. Lloyd Morgan (1852–1936), who, in his own *Introduction to Comparative Psychology* (1894), objected to Romanes's overestimation of animal intelligence. Romanes had quite freely attributed complex thinking to animals from analogy to his own thinking. Morgan, in formulating what has since been called Morgan's canon, argued that inferences of animal thinking should be no more than absolutely necessary to explain some observed behavior. The last of the early founding British comparative psychologists was the philosopher Leonard T. Hobhouse (1864–1928), who used the data of comparative psychology to construct a general evolutionary metaphysics. He also carried out some experiments on animal behavior that, in some respects, anticipated Gestalt work on animal insight and were designed to undermine the artificiality of behaviorist animal experiments.

These comparative psychologists combined faculty psychology with associationism in their theories of development and collected some interesting facts. What proved important and controversial about their work, however, were their method and goal. What Romanes consciously introduced to psychology was an objective, behavioral method in contrast to the subjective method of introspection. We cannot observe the minds of animals, only their behavior; nevertheless, the theoretical goal of the British animal psychologists was never merely to describe behavior. Rather, they wanted to explain the workings of animal minds, and therefore they attempted to infer mental processes from behavior. The problems involved in this research program importantly affected the development of behavioralism, which was founded by American comparative psychologists.

Methodologically, comparative psychology began with Romanes's anecdotal method. He collected vignettes of animal behavior from many correspondents and sifted through them for plausible and reliable information from which to reconstruct the animal mind. The anecdotal method became an object of derision among the experimentally oriented Americans, especially E. L. Thorndike. The method lacked the control available in the laboratory and was felt to overestimate animal intelligence. The anecdotal method did have the virtue, largely unappreciated at the time, of observing animals in natural, uncontrived situations. We will find that animal psychology ran into real difficulties in the 1960s because of its exclusive reliance on controlled laboratory methods that overlooked the animals' ecological histories.

Theoretically, inferring mental processes from behavior presented difficulties. It is altogether too easy to attribute to animals complex mental processes they may not possess—any simple behavior can be explained (incorrectly) as the result of complex reasoning. Anyone who today reads Romanes's *Animal Intelligence* will feel that he frequently committed this error. Morgan's canon was an attempt to deal with this problem by requiring conservative inferences.

In his own treatment of animal mind, Morgan (1886) contributed a distinction that unfortunately was less known and less influential than his famous canon of simplicity. Morgan distinguished objective inferences from projective—or, as he called them in the philosophical jargon of his time, ejective—inferences from animal behavior to animal mind. Imagine watching a dog sitting at a street corner at 3:30 one afternoon. As a school bus approaches, the dog gets up, wags its tail, and watches the bus slow down and then stop. The dog looks at the children getting off the bus and, when one boy gets off, it jumps on him, licks his face, and together the boy and the dog walk off down the street. Objectively, Morgan would say, we may infer certain mental powers possessed by the dog. It must possess sufficient perceptual skills to pick out one child from the crowd getting off the bus, and it must possess at least recognition memory, for it responds differently to one child among all the others. Such inferences are objective, because they posit certain internal cognitive processes that may be further investigated by, for example, testing dogs' discriminative learning capacities. On the other hand, we are tempted to attribute a subjective mental state, happiness, to the dog on analogy with our own happiness when we greet a loved one who has been absent. Such inferences by analogy to our own subjective mental states are Morgan's projective inferences, because in making them we project our own feelings onto the animal. Objective inferences are legitimate in science, Morgan held, because they do not depend on analogy, are not emotional, and are susceptible to later verification by experiment. Projective inferences are not scientifically legitimate because they result from attributing our own feelings to animals and may not be more objectively assessed. Morgan did not claim that animals do not have feelings, only that their feelings, whatever they may be, fall outside the domain of scientific psychology.

Morgan's distinction is important, but it was neglected by later comparative psychologists. When Romanes's methods of anecdote and inference were challenged by American animal psychologists in the 1890s, the absurdities of subjective inference—calling rats "happy" and "carefree"—led to wholesale rejection of any discussion of animal mind. Had Morgan's distinction between objective and projective inference been heeded, however, it might have been seen that, although projective inferences are scientifically worthless, objective inferences are perfectly respectable.

However, no matter how conservatively and carefully mind might be reconstructed from behavior, it remained possible for the skeptic to doubt. As Romanes (1883, pp. 5–6) put it: "Skepticism of this kind is logically bound to deny evidence of mind, not only in the case of lower animals, but also in that of the higher, and even in that of men other than the skeptic himself. For all objections which could apply to the use of [inference] . . . would apply with equal force to the evidence of any mind other than that of the individual objector." Such skepticism constitutes the essence of the behaviorist revolution. The behaviorist may admit that she or he possesses consciousness, if not mind, but refuses to use mental activity to explain the behavior of animals, or of other human beings.

The psychology of adaptation began in England, where the modern theory of evolution was born. However, it found more fertile ground in one of Britain's former colonies: the United States. There it became the only psychology; and, as the United States came to dominate psychology, so did the psychology of adaptation.

PSYCHOLOGY IN THE NEW WORLD

Background

General Intellectual and Social Environment

America was new. Its original inhabitants were seen as savages, noble or brutish, who revealed original human nature untouched by civilization. The first settlers confidently expected to displace the Indians, replacing their primitive state with farms, villages, and churches. The wilderness found by the settlers opened up possibilities of erecting a new civilization in the new world. The Puritans came to establish a "city on a hill," a perfect Christian society, an example to be looked up to by the rest of the world. In America, there was no feudal hierarchy, no established church, no ancient universities. Instead, each person could make his or her own way in the wilderness.

This is not to say that the European settlers brought no intellectual baggage. They did, and two traditions are particularly important: evangelical religion and Enlightenment philosophy. America was initially settled by Protestants, not Catholics. In fact, when Catholics first came to America in large numbers, they were forced to remain outside the mainstream of American life. Catholics were seen as agents of a dangerous foreign power, the pope, and anti-Catholic riots and the burning of Catholic churches were not unknown in nineteenth-century America. What emerged most strongly from the dominant American Protestantism was evangelical Christianity. This form of Christianity has little or no theological content, looking instead to the salvation of the individual soul in an emotional conversion experience when the person accepts the will of God.

An important part of the European reaction to the excessive geometric spirit of the Enlightenment was romanticism. In America, however, the reaction against the Age of Reason was a religious one. America experienced revivals in the colonial period, and another took place shortly after the French Revolution. Romanticism touched America only briefly, in the transcendental movement. Henry David Thoreau, for example, decried industry's encroachment on romantic nature. However, more important for most people was evangelical Christianity, which rejected the antireligious skepticism of the Enlightenment.

It is no accident that many early American psychologists, including John B. Watson, the founder of behaviorism, were early intended for the church. The stock in trade of the evangelical preacher is conversion, playing on an audience's emotions to change people from sinners to saints, modifying both soul and behavior. The goal of many American psychologists in both the functional and behavioral periods has been to modify behavior, to make the person of today into the new person of tomorrow. The evangelical preachers wrote about the ways to change souls through preaching; the psychologists wrote about the ways to change behavior through conditioning.

Early America did possess some genuine philosophes. There was Benjamin Franklin, whose experiments on electricity were admired in Europe, who charmed France as the "natural man" of the new world, and who was enshrined as one of the leading figures of the Enlightenment, ranking even with Voltaire. Thomas Jefferson, another philosophe, is perhaps the best example of the geometric spirit in America. Jefferson attempted to apply numerical calculation to every subject from crop rotation to human happiness. His Newtonian mechanism even blinded him to biological facts: Arguing against the possibility of Noah's flood, he "proved" from physical calculations that, in any flood, the waters cannot rise more than about fifty feet above sea level, and that consequently the fossil sea shells found in America's Appalachian Mountains were just unusual rock growths (Wills, 1978).

The more radical ideas of French naturalism, however, were offensive to America's religious temperament, and only certain moderate elements of Enlightenment thought became important in America. Foremost among these acceptable ideas were those of the Scottish Enlightenment, which in fact exerted more influence on Jefferson than is commonly supposed. As we have seen, Reid's commonsense philosophy was perfectly compatible with religion. In America's religious colleges, which were the vast majority of American colleges, Scottish philosophy became the established curriculum, dominating every aspect of higher education from ethics to psychology. Scottish philosophy was American orthodoxy.

In considering the intellectual climate of the United States, to the influences of evangelical Christianity and a moderate Enlightenment must be added a third element, business, which interacted with the other two in important ways. America came to be a nation of business unlike any other nation on earth. There was no feudal aristocracy, no established church, and only a distant king. What remained were individual enterprise and the individual's struggle to survive in confrontation with the wilderness and in competition with other businessmen. The business of America was indeed business.

Out of this unique American mix of ideas, combined with a growing national chauvinism, several important ideas emerged. One was the supreme value placed on useful knowledge. The Enlightenment certainly held that knowledge should serve human needs and should be practical rather than metaphysical. American Protestants came to think of inventions as glorifying the ingenuity of God in creating the clever human mind. Technology was an American word. An unfortunate consequence of this attitude was anti-intellectualism. Abstract science was scorned as something European and degenerate. What counted was practical accomplishment that at once enriched the businessman, revealed God's principles, and advanced the American dream. The businessman valued the same hardheaded "common sense" taught in the colleges. Commonsense philosophy told the ordinary person that his or her untutored ideas were basically right, which tended to increase American anti-intellectualism.

In the use of the term "businessman," the syllable *man* ought to be stressed. It was the men who struggled for survival in the world of business and who valued clearheaded common sense and practical achievement. Feeling and sentiment were the special province of women, who in the nineteenth century were increasingly removed from the world of work, as such formerly domestic activities as baking, brewing, cheese making, spinning, and weaving became industrialized. This change stripped women of their earlier economic importance, leaving only the realm of the emotions to female rule. In America, emotions were not romantically inspiring, but were instead taken to be feminine and weak.

Americans also tended to be radical environmentalists, greatly preferring to believe that peoples' circumstances, not their genes, were the primary cause of human characteristics and achievements. They believed that, contrary to the prejudices of Europeans, the American environment was the best in the world and would produce geniuses to surpass Newton. This belief reflects the empiricism of the Enlightenment and the flexible beliefs of the businessman. There would be no bounds on the perfectibility of humans in the new world, no bounds on the achievement of the free individual. Progress was the order of the day. A cult of self-improvement dated back to the early days of the American republic. In the 1830s, there was a monthly magazine called *The Cultivator*, "designed to improve the soil and the mind." Not only could a man improve his farm business, but he could improve his mind as well. In fact, it was expected that the good Christian would be a successful businessman or farmer.

One observer of the early American scene recognized these American trends. Alexis de Tocqueville wrote in *Democracy in America*, following his visit to America during 1831 and 1832: "The longer a nation is democratic, enlightened and free, the greater will be the number of these interested promoters of scientific genius, and the more will discoveries immediately applicable to productive industry confer gain, fame and even power." However, Tocqueville worried that "in a community thus organized . . . the human mind may be led insensibly to the neglect of theory." Aristocracies, on the other hand, "facilitate the natural impulse of the highest regions of thought." Tocqueville foresaw well. American psychology since its founding has neglected theory, even being openly hostile to theory at times. While Europeans such as Jean Piaget constructed grand, almost metaphysical theories, B. F. Skinner argued that theories of learning are unnecessary.

Pre-Darwinian Background in Philosophical Psychology

The Puritans brought medieval faculty psychology with them to America. It perished in the early eighteenth century, however, when America's first great philosopher, Jonathan Edwards (1703–1758), read Locke. His enthusiasm for empiricism was such that his genius carried him independently in the direction of Berkeley and Hume. Like Berkeley, he denied the distinction between primary and secondary qualities and concluded that the mind knows only its perceptions, not the external world. Like Hume, he expanded the role of associations in the operation of the mind, finding, as Hume had, that contiguity, resemblance, and cause and effect are the laws of association (Jones, 1958). Finally, like Hume, he was driven toward skepticism through his recognition that generalizations about cause cannot be rationally justified, and that emotion, not reason, is the true spring of human action (Blight, 1978). Edwards, however, remained a Christian (Hume did not) and he may be regarded as more medieval than modern in this respect (Gay, 1969).

Edwards's stress on emotion as the basis of religious conversion helped pave the way for the American form of romanticism and idealism: transcendentalism. Transcendentalism was a New England revolt against what had become a comfortable, stuffy, and dry form of Puritanism. The transcendentalists wanted to return to the lively, emotional religion of Edwards's time, and to the direct, passionate encounter with God that Edwards had believed in. Such an attitude was compatible with both romanticism and post-Kantian idealism. The former prized individual feeling and communion with nature, similar to Thoreau's report of an extended, solitary sojourn in the wilderness in Walden. The latter believed Kant's transcendent noumena were knowable; similarly, George Ripley, a leading transcendentalist, wrote in *A Letter Addressed to the Congregational Church in Purchase Street* that they "believe in an order of truths which transcend the sphere of the external senses" (White, 1972). Thus, in some respects, transcendentalism was in tune with European romanticism and idealism.

In other respects, however, transcendentalism appears very American. It supported, for example, an evangelical, emotional Christianity that put the individual's feelings and conscience above hierarchical authority. Ralph Waldo Emerson (1950) preached "self-reliance," always an American ideal. He derided the radical empiricists as "negative and poisonous." Whether European or American in tone, however, transcendentalism's effect on mainstream American thought was limited. Like romanticism, its chief products were artistic rather than philosophical, and even its great art, such as Melville's *Moby Dick,* was much less popular than other works totally forgotten today. The American intellectual establishment of the colleges viewed transcendentalism, Kant, and idealism with horror, so that budding scientists and philosophers had little contact with the movement.

A bulwark against any romantic revolt, Scottish commonsense philosophy maintained its grip on American thought. Americans, too, began to produce faculty psychology texts at an accelerating rate as the nineteenth century progressed. American texts on psychology repeated the arguments of the Scottish moral sense theorists. For example, Thomas Upham's *Elements of Mental Philosophy* (1831) taught that moral character could be built through the "thorough acquaintance with the emotions and passions" (p. 25) that psychology provided. Moral sense, which Upham called conscience, was given by God to "excite in us emotions of approval . . . [or] emotions of disapprobation" (p. 304) occasioned by seeing the actions of others. To the question, "Why should I do right?" Upham says that "the true source of moral obligation is in the natural impulses of the human breast" (p. 306).

One of the most revealing episodes in the history of prescientific American psychology is the remarkable career of phrenology. Early in the nineteenth century, Gall's colleague, Johann Spurzheim, started on a triumphal tour of the United States; the rigors of the trip took his life after only a few weeks. Spurzheim was followed by the British phrenologist George Combe, who was well received by educators and college presidents. The lectures were too theoretical for American audiences, however, and phrenology fell into the hands of two industrious and businesslike brothers, Orson and Lorenzo Fowler. They minimized the scientific content of phrenology, maximized the practical applications, and set up an office in New York where clients could have their characters read for a fee. They wrote endlessly of the benefits of phrenology and published a phrenological journal that endured from the 1840s to 1911. They traveled around the country, especially the frontier areas, giving lectures and challenging skeptics. Like the great magician Houdini, they accepted any kind of test of their abilities, including blindfolded examinations of volunteers' skulls.

What made the Fowlers' phrenology so popular was its appeal to the American character. It eschewed metaphysics for practical application. It pretended to tell employers what people to hire and to advise men which wives to take. This first mental testing movement in America was Galtonian in its scrutiny of individual differences. Furthermore, it was progressive and reformist. Gall had believed the brain's faculties to be set by heredity. The Fowlers, however, said that weak faculties could be improved by practice and overly strong ones could be controlled by efforts of will. Many people sought out the Fowlers for advice on how to lead their lives; the Fowlers were the first guidance counselors. They also held out the hope that the nation and the world could be improved if only every person would be "phrenologized." Finally, the Fowlers believed they served religion and morality. They encouraged their clients to improve their moral faculties and believed that the existence of the faculty of veneration demonstrated the existence of God, because the existence of the faculty implied the existence of its object.

America's Native Philosophy: Pragmatism

In 1871 and 1872, a group of young, Harvard-educated, well-to-do Bostonians—"the very topmost cream of Boston manhood," William James called them—met as the Metaphysical Club to discuss philosophy in the age of Darwin. Among the members of the club were Oliver Wendell Holmes (1809–1894), destined to become perhaps the United States' most distinguished jurist; and, more important for the history of psychology, Chauncey Wright (1830–1875), Charles S. Peirce (1839–1914), and William James (1842–1910). All three were important to the founding of psychology in America. Wright articulated an early stimulus–response theory of behavior, Peirce carried out the first psychological experiments in the new world, and James laid the foundations of American psychology with his book *Principles of Psychology* (1890). The immediate fruit of the Metaphysical Club was America's only homegrown philosophy, pragmatism, a hybrid of Bain, Darwin, and Kant. The club opposed the regnant Scottish philosophy, which was dualistic and closely connected to religion and creationism, and proposed a new naturalistic theory of mind.

From Bain, they took the idea that beliefs were dispositions to behave; Bain defined belief as "that upon which a man is prepared to act." From Darwin, they, like most intellectuals of the day, learned to treat mind as part of nature, not a gift from God. More important—this was Wright's contribution—they took the survival of the fittest as a model by which to understand mind. Wright combined Bain's definition with Darwin's theory of natural selection and proposed that a person's beliefs evolve just as species do. As one matures, one's beliefs compete for acceptance, so that adequate beliefs emerge "from the survival of the fittest among our original . . . beliefs." This is the essential idea of the individual approach to the psychology of adaptation— and, if we substitute "behaviors" for "beliefs," it states the central thesis of B. F. Skinner's radical behaviorism. Wright also tried to show how self-consciousness, far from being a mystery to naturalism, evolved from sensorimotor habits. A habit, Wright held, was a relation between a class of stimuli and some response or responses. The cognition needed to link stimulus and response was rudimentary, involving recalled images of past experiences. Self-consciousness arose when one—or people, as compared with the animals—became aware of the connection between stimulus and response. Wright's ideas go a long way to making mind part of nature, and they point to the behavioral emphasis of American psychology, in which beliefs are important only insofar as they produce behavior.

In summing up the conclusions of the Metaphysical Club, Charles S. Peirce invented pragmatism. Kant had, as a foundational philosopher, sought the foundation of certain knowledge. Nevertheless, he recognized that men and women must act on beliefs that are not certain; a physician, for example, may not be absolutely certain of a diagnosis but must nevertheless proceed believing the diagnosis is correct. Kant called "such contingent belief which still forms the basis of the actual use of means for the attainment of certain ends, pragmatic belief." The upshot of the meditations of the Metaphysical Club was that beliefs could never be certain. The best that humans could hope for were beliefs that led to successful action in the world, natural selection operating to strengthen certain beliefs and weaken others as beliefs struggled for acceptance. Darwin had shown that species were not fixed, and the Metaphysical Club concluded that truth, contrary to Kant, could not be fixed either. All that remained to epistemology, then, was Kant's pragmatic belief, which Peirce refined into "the pragmatic maxim," reflecting the conclusions of the club.

In 1878, Peirce published these conclusions in a paper, "How to Make Our Ideas Clear," first read to the Metaphysical Club at the end of its life. Peirce (1878/1966) wrote that "the whole function of thought is to produce habits of action," and that what we call beliefs are "a rule of action, or, say for short, a habit." "The essence of belief," Peirce argued, "is the establishment of a habit, and different beliefs are distinguished by the different modes of action to which they give rise." Habits must have a practical significance if they are to be meaningful, Peirce went on. "Now the identity of a habit depends on how it might lead us to act. . . . Thus we come down to what is tangible and conceivably practical as the root of every real distinction of thought . . . there is no distinction so fine as to consist in anything but a possible difference in practice." In conclusion, "the rule for attaining [clear ideas] is as follows: consider what effects, which might conceivably have practical bearings, we conceive the object of our conceptions to have. Then, our conception of these effects is the whole of our conception of the object." Or, as Peirce put it more succinctly in 1905, the truth of a belief "lies exclusively in its conceivable bearing upon the conduct of life."

Peirce's pragmatic maxim is revolutionary because it abandons the old Platonic aim of a foundational philosophy. It admits with Heraclitus that nothing can ever be certain and draws from Darwin the idea that the best beliefs are those that work in adapting us to our changing environment. The pragmatic maxim is also consistent with scientific practice. Peirce had been a working physicist and had learned that a scientific concept was useless and meaningless if it could not be translated into some observable phenomenon; thus, Peirce's pragmatic maxim anticipates the positivist concept of operational definition. Later, when William James allowed emotional and ethical considerations to weigh in deciding whether a belief works, Peirce, the hardheaded physicist, refused to go along. In psychology, pragmatism represents a clear articulation of the individual-question approach to the psychology of adaptation. It takes, as B. F. Skinner later would, Darwin's account of species' evolution as a model by which to understand individual learning. The pragmatic maxim also anticipates the behavioral turn in American psychology, because it says that beliefs are always (if meaningful) manifested in behavior, so that reflection on consciousness for its own sake is idle.

Peirce never became a psychologist, but he did aid psychology's development in the United States. He read some of Wundt's researches in 1862 and campaigned against the continued reign of Scottish commonsense psychology and for the establishment of experimental psychology in U.S. universities. In 1877, he published a psychophysical study of color, the first experimental work to come from America. A student of his, Joseph Jastrow, became one of the leading American psychologists in the first part of the twentieth century, and a president of the American Psychological Association. In 1887, Peirce asked the central question of modern cognitive science: Can a machine think like a human being? Despite these accomplishments, his influence remained remarkably limited. He was an extraordinarily difficult man to get along with. Despite the best efforts of William James, he never could hold a permanent position at Harvard and lived most of his life as a nearly penniless recluse. He wrote badly, and most of his papers were not published during his lifetime. Pragmatism's great influence on philosophy and psychology came from his associate, William James.

America's Psychologist: William James

James began to work out his own version of pragmatism in the 1870s and 1880s. At first, he advanced his philosophy timidly, as psychology rather than philosophy. In 1878, he contracted with the publisher Henry Holt to write a textbook on psychology; and during the 1880s, James published a series of articles that formed the core of his new psychology and philosophy and were incorporated into the book, *Principles of Psychology*. Its publication in 1890 marks a watershed in the history of American psychology, for it inspired American students as neither the Scots nor Wundt could, and it set the tone for American psychology from 1890 to 1913 and beyond. James combined the usual interests of a founding psychologist: physiology and philosophy.

He began his academic career with an M.D. and held a variety of posts at Harvard. Beginning as an instructor of physiology, he next saw to the establishment for himself of a Chair in Psychology; he spent his last years as a professor of philosophy. In *Principles,* James began to develop his pragmatic philosophy.

"Psychology is the Science of Mental Life," James told his readers (*Principles,* vol. I, p. 1). Its primary method is ordinary introspection, accompanied by the "diabolical cunning" of German experimentalism and by comparative studies of men, animals, and savages. James rejected sensationistic atomism, the billiard-ball theory also rejected by Wundt. According to James, this theory takes the discernible parts of objects to be enduring objects of experience, falsely chopping up the flow of experience. Wrote James:

> Consciousness . . . does not appear to itself chopped up in bits. Such words as "chain" or "train" do not describe it fitly, as it presents itself in the first instance. It is nothing jointed; it flows. A "river" or a "stream" are the metaphors by which it is most naturally described. In talking of it hereafter let us call it the stream of thought, of consciousness, or of subjective life. (*Principles,* vol. I, p. 239)

In Darwinian fashion, James found that what consciousness contains is less important than what it does; it is function, not content, that counts. The primary function of consciousness is to choose. He wrote (1890): "It is always interested more in one part of its object than in another, and welcomes and rejects, or chooses, all the while it thinks" (*Principles,* vol. I, p. 284). Consciousness creates and serves the ends of the organism, the first of which is survival through adaptation to the environment. For James, however, adaptation is never passive. Consciousness chooses, acting always toward some end. The ceaseless flow of choices affects perception as well as conduct: "The mind, in short, works on the data it receives very much as a sculptor works on his block of stone" (*Principles,* vol. I, p. 288). James's mind is not the passive blank slate of the sensationists. It is a "fighter for ends," actively engaged with a practical world of experience.

Although James said psychology is the Science of Mental Life, it must simultaneously be "cerebralist." It is a fundamental assumption that "the brain is the one immediate bodily condition of the mental operation," and the *Principles,* all 1,377 pages of it, is "more or less of a proof that the postulate is correct" (vol. I, p. 4). He applauded Hartley's attempt to show that the laws of association are cerebral laws, "and so far as association stands for a cause, it is between processes in the brain" (vol. I, p. 554).

This seemed to involve James in a contradiction; the brain-machine must make choices. He had said that consciousness plays a positive role in human and animal life, and explicitly rejected mechanism, or what he called the "automaton theory." For James, evolutionary naturalism demanded that consciousness exist, because it fulfilled a vital adaptive function. A dumb machine knows no direction, it is like "dice thrown forever on a table . . . what chance is there that the highest number will turn up oftener than the lowest?" James argued that consciousness increases the efficiency of the cerebral machine by "loading its dice." Wrote James (*Principles of Psychology,* vol. I, p. 140): "Loading its dice would bring constant pressure to bear in favor of those of its performances" that serve the "interests of the brain's owner." Consciousness transforms survival from "mere hypothesis" into an "imperative decree. Survival shall occur and therefore organs must so work. . . . Every actually existing consciousness seems to itself at any rate to be a fighter for ends. . . ." Consciousness thus possesses survival value. Association may depend on cerebral laws, but our will can, through emphasis and reinforcement, direct chains of association to serve our interests, and their direction is "all that the most eager advocate of free will need demand," for by directing association it directs thinking, and hence action (*Principles,* vol. I, p. 141).

Although James has here proclaimed the efficacy of consciousness and will, the central doctrine of the *Principles,* on which American psychologists built for thirty years, was the "motor theory of consciousness." James's famous theory of emotion, the James–Lange theory, aptly illustrates the motor theory. On common understanding, if I see a bear in the woods, I feel afraid, and as a consequence I run away. On James's motor account of consciousness, however, I see the bear, begin to run away, and then, finding myself fleeing, feel scared. More generally, James said that mental states have two sorts of bodily effects. First, unless some inhibition is present, the thought of an act automatically leads to the execution of the act. Second, mental states cause internal bodily changes, including covert motor responses, changes in heart rate, glandular secretions, and perhaps "processes more subtle still." Therefore, James argued, "it will be safe to lay down the general law that no mental modification ever occurs which is not accompanied or followed by a bodily change" (*Principles,* vol. I, p. 5). The contents of consciousness are thus determined not only by sensations coming in from outside, but by kinesthetic feedback (as we call it today) from the body's motor activity. "Our psychology must therefore take account not only of the conditions antecedent to mental states, but of their resultant consequences as well. . . . The whole neural organism [is] . . . but a machine for converting stimuli into reactions; and the intellectual part of our life is knit up with but the middle or 'central' part of the machine's operations" (*Principles,* vol. II, p. 372).

James found himself caught in the same dilemma felt by Diderot and other philosophes, between the heart's feeling of freedom and the intellect's scientific declaration of determinism. James was deeply committed to free will from personal experience. As a young man, he had pulled himself out of a black depression by literally willing himself to live again, and, dogged by depression his whole life, he made human will the center of his philosophy. However, in his psychology, committed to cerebralism, he found himself almost forced to accept determinism as the only scientifically acceptable view of behavior. He stoutly resisted the conclusion, denouncing mechanistic conceptions of human conduct and, as we have seen, proclaiming that consciousness decreed survival and commanded the body. After writing *Principles,* James abandoned psychology for philosophy and developed his own brand of pragmatism. There he tried to resolve the struggle between the head and the heart by setting the feelings of the heart on an equal footing with the cognitions of the head. Nevertheless, the conflict remained, and the influence of *Principles* was to lead American psychologists away from consciousness and toward behavior, and so away from James's own definition of psychology as the science of mental life.

The New Psychology

In the United States, experimental psychology was called the "new psychology," to distinguish it from the "old psychology" of the Scottish commonsense realists. The great majority of American colleges were controlled by Protestant denominations, and, in the 1820s, the Scottish system was installed as a safeguard against what religious leaders took to be the skeptical and atheistic tendencies of British empiricism as described by Reid. The works of Locke, Berkeley, and Hume—and, later, the German idealists—were banished from the classroom and replaced with texts by Reid, Dugald Stewart, or their American followers. Commonsense psychology was taught as a pillar of religion and Christian behavior. For the American followers of the Scots, psychology "is the science of the soul," and its method, ordinary introspection, reveals "the soul as an emanation from the Divine, and as made in the image of God" (Dunton, 1895). "Mental science, or psychology, will therefore, be [foundational] for moral science. . . . The province of psychology will . . . be to show what the faculties are; that of moral philosophy to show how they should be used for the attainment of their end" (Hopkins, 1870, quoted by Evans, 1984). Unsurprisingly, with few exceptions, adherents of the old psychology looked askance at the new psychology, which brought the mind into a laboratory and investigated the connection of mental states to nervous processes.

Nevertheless, as higher education became more secular after the Civil War, the intellectual tide turned in favor of the naturalism of the new psychology. In 1875, William James established an informal psychological laboratory at Harvard in connection with a graduate course, "The Relations between Physiology and Psychology," in the department of natural history. In 1887, he began to offer a course called "Psychology" in the philosophy department; in 1885, he had obtained recognition and funds from Harvard and had established the first official psychology laboratory in America (Cadwallader, 1980). At Yale, the old psychology of the president, Noah Porter, yielded to George Trumball Ladd (1842–1921), who, though a Congregationalist minister and a psychological conservative, respected Wundt's experimental psychology and incorporated it into an influential text, *Elements of Physiological Psychology* (1887). At Princeton, the president, James McCosh, was a staunch Scot but recognized that "the tendency of the day is certainly towards physiology" (Evans, 1984) and taught Wundt's psychology to his students.

Harvard minted its first Ph.D. philosopher, G. Stanley Hall (1844–1924), in 1878. A student of James, Hall was really a psychologist. He went to Johns Hopkins University—the United States' first graduate university—where he established a laboratory and a series of courses in the new psychology. Hall's psychology went well beyond Wundt, however, including, in typically American eclectic fashion, experimental studies of the higher mental processes, anthropology, and abnormal psychology, or "morbid phenomena." Hall also vigorously pursued developmental psychology, launched the child study movement, and coined the term "adolescence." Hall led the institutionalization of American psychology; he started the *American Journal of Psychology* in 1887, and organized the founding of the American Psychological Association in 1892. One of Hall's students was James McKeen Cattell (1860–1944), who later studied with Wundt and then returned to the United States to establish laboratories at the University of Pennsylvania (1887) and Columbia University (1891).

As historians have often pointed out, Americans got the methods of experimental psychology from Wundt, but their ideas and theories came from elsewhere. When Cattell was in Leipzig, he proposed to study individual differences in reaction time, but Wundt disapprovingly called the subject *"ganz Amerikanisch"* (completely American). After Leipzig, Cattell studied with Francis Galton, and E. G. Boring (1950) explains American psychologists' departure from Wundtian ideals by saying that "the apparatus was Wundt's, but the inspiration was Galton's." Rand Evans (1984) locates the source of American inspiration in the continuing influence of

Scottish psychology. The Scots had always emphasized mind in use—mental activity—more than mental content. Their faculty psychology was, like Aristotle's, implicitly a psychology of function. And, as Aristotle's was a biological psychology, the Scots' psychology of mental function, despite its religious connection, was ultimately compatible with modern Darwinian biology, as McCosh himself saw. Experiment was new in American psychology, but American psychologists have retained to the present day the Scots' concern with mental activity and with making psychology serviceable to society and the individual.

CONCLUSION: PERCEPTION AND THINKING ARE ONLY THERE FOR BEHAVIOR'S SAKE

By 1892, psychology in America was well launched. In Europe, scientific psychology was making slow headway even in Germany, the country of its birth. In the United States, by contrast, psychology expanded rapidly. In 1892, there were fourteen laboratories, including one as far west as Kansas. Half of them had been founded independently of philosophy or any other discipline. Psychology would soon be what it largely remains, an American science.

But psychology in America would not be the traditional psychology of consciousness. Once psychology met evolution, the tendency to study behavior instead of consciousness became overwhelming. Traditionally, philosophers had been concerned with human knowledge, with how we form ideas and how we know they are true or false. Action resulting from ideas formed only a tiny part of their concern. However, in a biological, evolutionary context, ideas matter only if they lead to effective action. The Metaphysical Club realized this and created the pragmatic maxim. The struggle for existence is won by successful action, and any organism "sicklied o'er with the pale cast of thought," no matter how profound, is doomed to failure. The essence of the psychology of adaptation was the idea that mind matters to evolution because it leads to successful action, and so is adaptive. As James said, "If it ever should happen that [thought] led to no active measures, it would fail of its essential function, and would have to be considered either pathological or abortive. The current of life which runs in at our eyes or ears is meant to run out at our hands, feet, or lips. . . . perception and thinking are only for behavior's sake" (Kuklick, 1977, p. 169).

The psychology of adaptation, from Spencer to James, remained nevertheless the science of mental life, not the science of behavior. However, much consciousness was tied up with behavior. No matter that it was merely a way station between stimulus and response; it was real and deserved serious study because it was a vital way station. James said consciousness decreed survival, it commanded the body to behave adaptively. Underneath the main current of mentalism, however, ran an undercurrent that headed toward the study of behavior instead of the study of consciousness, and, in time, the undercurrent became the main current, and finally a flood tide, virtually erasing the Science of Mental Life.

BIBLIOGRAPHY

Samuel Hynes, *The Edwardian turn of mind* (Princeton, NJ: Princeton University Press, 1968), provides a social history of turn-of-the-century Britain; he describes the impact of the Army's

Physical Deterioration Report, treating it as the dividing point between the Victorian and post-Victorian eras. The changes in psychology during these years are discussed by Reba N. Soffer, *Ethics and society in England: The revolution in the social sciences 1870–1914* (Berkeley: University of California Press, 1978). Spencer's biographer is J. Peel Herbert, *Spencer* (New York: Basic Books, 1971). Howard Gruber insightfully discusses *Darwin on man: A psychological study of scientific creativity,* 2nd ed. (Chicago: University of Chicago Press, 1981). On Galton, see F. Forest, *Francis Galton* (New York: Taplinger, 1974). For Galton and British eugenics, see Ruth Schwartz Cowan, "Nature and nurture: The interplay of biology and politics in the work of Francis Galton," in W. Coleman and C. Limoges, eds., *Studies in the history of biology,* vol. 1, 133–208 (Baltimore: Johns Hopkins University Press, 1977); Robert C. Bannister, *Social Darwinism: Science and myth in Anglo-American social thought* (Philadelphia: Temple University Press, 1979); and Daniel Kevles, *In the name of eugenics: Genetics and the uses of human heredity* (New York: Knopf, 1985). Greta Jones, *Social Darwinism in English thought: The interaction between biological and social theory* (Sussex, England: Harvester Press, 1980), discusses both social Darwinism and eugenics during the period. In addition to the cited work, an important book by Romanes is *Mental evolution in man* (New York: D. Appleton, 1889); the only biography of Romanes is Ethel Romanes, *The life and letters of George John Romanes* (New York: Longmans, Green & Co., 1898), but Frank Miller Turner, "George John Romanes, From faith to faith," in F.M. Turner, *Between science and religion: The reaction to scientific naturalism in late Victorian England* (New Haven, CT: Yale University Press, 1974), provides a fine short discussion of Romanes, focusing on his part in the Victorian crisis of conscience. Morgan's major work is *An introduction to comparative psychology* (London: Walter Scott, 1894).

For a comprehensive treatment of American life in the years before 1890, see Bernard Bailyn, "Shaping the Republic to 1760," Gordon S. Wood, "Framing the Republic 1760–1820," David Brion Davis, "Expanding the Republic 1820–1860," and David Herbert Donald, "Uniting the Republic 1860–1890," in B. Bailyn, D. B. Davis, D. H. Donald, J. L. Thomas, R. H. Wiebe, and G. S. Wood, *The great Republic: A history of the American people* (Boston: Little, Brown, 1977). Daniel Boorstin concentrates on intellectual and social history during the same years in *The Americans: The colonial experience* (New York: Vintage Books, 1958) and *The Americans: The national experience* (New York: Vintage Books, 1965); both are wonderfully readable and exciting books. The best book on the American character is still de Tocqueville (1850/1969); reporter Richard Reeves, *In search of America* (New York: Simon & Schuster, 1982), retraced de Tocqueville's itinerary, and his insights do not surpass de Tocqueville's. An important and fascinating survey of American colonial life is David Hackett Fischer, *Albion's seed: Four British folkways in America* (New York: Oxford University Press, 1989), first in a series comprising a cultural history of the United States. A valuable general intellectual history of thought in the United States is Morton White, *Science and sentiment in America: Philosophical thought from Jonathan Edwards to John Dewey* (New York: Oxford University Press, 1972). Intellectual life in the early colonial and postrevolutionary periods is discussed by Henry Steele Commager, *The empire of reason: How Europe imagined and America realized the Enlightenment* (Garden City, NY: Doubleday, 1978); Henry May, *The Enlightenment in America* (New York: Oxford University Press, 1976); and Perry Miller, *Errand into the wilderness* (New York: Harper & Row, 1956).

For specific relevant movements of the nineteenth century, see A. Douglas, *The feminization of American culture* (New York: Knopf, 1977); Richard Hofstadter, *Anti-intellectualism in American life* (New York: Vintage Books, 1962); and R. B. Nye, *Society and culture in America 1830–1860* (New York: Harper & Row, 1974); and for American phrenology, see Thomas H. and Grace E. Leahey, *Psychology's occult doubles* (Chicago: Nelson-Hall, 1983). For American philosophy, see A. L. Jones, *Early American philosophers* (New York: Ungar, 1958); Herbert W. Schneider, *History of American philosophy* (New York: Columbia University Press, 1963); and, especially for the post-Civil War period, Kuklick (1977), from which all quotes in the Metaphysical Club section are drawn, unless otherwise indicated. The standard biography of Jonathan Edwards is Perry Miller, *Jonathan Edwards* (New York: Meridian, 1959). On Wright, see Edward H. Madden, "Chauncy Wright's functionalism," *Journal of the History of the Behavioral Sciences* (1974, *10:* 281–90). For the early philosophy of pragmatism and its influences, see Philip P. Wiener, *Evolution and the founders of pragmatism* (Cambridge, MA: Harvard University Press, 1949); J. K. Feibleman, *An introduction to the philosophy of Charles S. Peirce* (Cambridge, MA: MIT Press, 1946); and Thomas S. Knight, *Charles Peirce* (New York: Twayne, 1965). For Peirce as psychologist, see Thomas Cadwallader, "Charles S. Peirce: The first American experimental psychologist," *Journal of the History of the Behavioral Sciences* (1974, *10:* 191–8). The standard biography of William James is Ralph Barton Perry, *The thought and character of William James,* 2 vols. (Boston: Little, Brown, 1935); Perry's biography, while still the standard, suffers somewhat from Perry's attempt to make James into a realist like himself. A recent biography is Gay Wilson Allen, *William James* (Minneapolis: University of Minnesota Press, 1970). For James's lasting influence, see Don S. Browning, *Pluralism and personality: William James and some contemporary cultures of psychology* (Lewisburg, PA: Bucknell University Press, 1980). The most important recent biography of James is G. Myers, *William James: His life and thought* (New Haven, CT: Yale University Press, 1987), for a full-scale evaluation of his thought see T. H. Leahey, "Heroic metaphysician," *Contemporary Psychology* (1988, *33:* 199–201).

The only comprehensive source for the establishment of American psychology is Evans (1984); related is R. Dolby, "The transmission of two new scientific disciplines from Europe to North America in the late nineteenth century," *Annals of Science* (1977, *34:* 287–310). For psychology before the new psychology, see J. W. Fay, *American psychology before William James* (New York: Octagon Books, 1966); J. R. Fulcher, "Puritans and the passions: The faculty psychology in American Puritanism," *Journal of the History of the Behavioral Sciences* (1973, *9:* 123–39); and E. Harms, "America's first major psychologist: Laurens Perseus Hickock," *Journal of the History of the Behavioral Sciences* (1972, *8:* 120–3). Two overlapping collections edited by Robert W. Rieber and Kurt Salzinger treat American psychology primarily in the old and new periods, but also after: *The roots of American psychology: Historical influences and implications for the future* (New York: New York Academy of Sciences, Annals of the New York Academy of Sciences vol. 291, 1977), and *Psychology: Theoretical-historical perspectives* (New York: Academic Press, 1980). Josef Brozek, ed., *Explorations in the history of psychology in the United States* (Lewisburg, PA: Bucknell University Press, 1984), contains articles on both the old and the new psychologies. On the early psychologists mentioned in the text: Eugene S. Miller, *G. T. Ladd: Pioneer American psychologist* (Cleveland: Case Western Reserve University Press, 1969); Dorothy Ross, *G. Stanley Hall: Psychologist as prophet* (Chicago: University of Chicago Press, 1972). Michael Sokal has spent his career writing about James McKeen Cattell, for example: "The unpublished autobiography of James McKeen Cattell," *American Psychologist* (1971, *26:* 626–35), and *An education in psychology: James McKeen Cattell's journal and letters from Germany and England, 1880–1888* (Cambridge, MA: MIT Press, 1980).

One of the landmark articles in the introduction of the new psychology to the United States is John Dewey, "The new psychology," *Andover Review* (1884, *2:* 278–89); the background and influence of the piece is discussed in Morton White, *The origin of Dewey's instrumentalism* (New York: Octagon Books, 1964). Two other contemporary or near-contemporary articles are useful for the history of the early laboratories in the United States: Anonymous, "Psychology in American universities," *American Journal of Psychology* (1892, *3:* 275–86); and Christian A. Ruckmich, "The history and status of psychology in the United States," *American Journal of Psychology* (1912, *23:* 517–31). J. Mark Baldwin provides a more general account, with more background, in his "Sketch of the history of psychology," *Psychological Review* (1905, *12:* 144–65).

REFERENCES

Blight, J. G. (1978, September). *The position of Jonathan Edwards in the history of psychology.* Paper presented at the annual meeting of the American Psychological Association, Toronto.

Boring, E. G. (1950). *A history of experimental psychology.* Englewood Cliffs, NJ: Prentice-Hall.

Cadwallader, T. C. (1980, September). *William James' Harvard psychology laboratory reconsidered.* Paper presented at the annual meeting of the American Psychological Association, Montreal.

Darwin, C. (1896). *The descent of man and selection in relation to sex* (rev. ed). New York: Appleton & Co.

_____ . (1872/1965). *The expression of emotion in man and animals.* Chicago: University of Chicago Press.

Dunton, L. (1895). The old psychology and the new. In L. Dunton, H. Münsterberg, W. T. Harris, and G. Stanley Hall, *The old psychology and the new: Addresses before the Massachusetts Schoolmaster's Club, April 27, 1895.* Boston: New England Publishing Co.

Emerson, R. W. (1950). *Selected prose and poetry.* New York: Holt, Rinehart & Winston.

Evans, R. (1984). The origins of American academic psychology. In J. Brozek, ed. *Explorations in the history of psychology in the United States.* Lewisburg, PA: Bucknell University Press.

Galton, F. (1883/1907). *Inquiries into the human faculty and its development.* London: J. M. Dent.

_____ . (1869/1925). *Hereditary genius.* London: Macmillian.

Gay, P. (1969). The obsolete Puritanism of Jonathan Edwards. Reprinted in J. Opie, ed., *Jonathan Edwards and the Enlightenment.* Lexington, MA: Heath.

Hofstadter, R. (1955). *Social Darwinism in American thought,* rev. ed. Boston: Beacon Press.

Hopkins, M. (1870). *Lectures on moral science.* Boston: Gould & Lincoln.

James, W. (1890). *Principles of psychology,* 2 vols. New York: Dover Books.

Jones, A. L. (1958). *Early American philosophers.* New York: Ungar.

Kuklick, B. (1977). *The rise of American philosophy: Cambridge, Massachusetts 1860–1930,* New Haven, CT: Yale University Press.

Morgan, C. L. (1886). On the study of animal intelligence. *Mind 11:* 174–85.

Peirce, C. S. (1878/1966). How to make our ideas clear. Partially reprinted in A. Rorty, ed., *Pragmatic philosophy.* Garden City, NY: Anchor Books.

_____ . (1887). Logical machines. *American Journal of Psychology 1:* 165–70.

_____ . (1905/1970). What pragmatism is. In H. S. Thayer (Ed.) *Pragmatism: The classic writings.* New York: Mentor.

Romanes, G. (1883). *Animal intelligence.* New York: Appleton & Co.

Spencer, H. (1897). *The principles of psychology,* 3rd ed. New York: Appleton & Co.

_____ . (1904). *An autobiography,* 2 vols. London: Williams & Norgate.

_____ . (1880/1945). *First principles.* London: Watts & Co.

Tocqueville, A. de (1850/1969). *Democracy in America.* New York: Anchor.

Upham, T. G. (1831). *Elements of mental philosophy.* Boston: Hilliard, Gray & Co.

White, L. (1972). *Science and sentiment in America.* London: Oxford University Press.

Wills, G. (1978). *Inventing America: Jefferson's Declaration of Independence.* Garden City, NY: Doubleday.

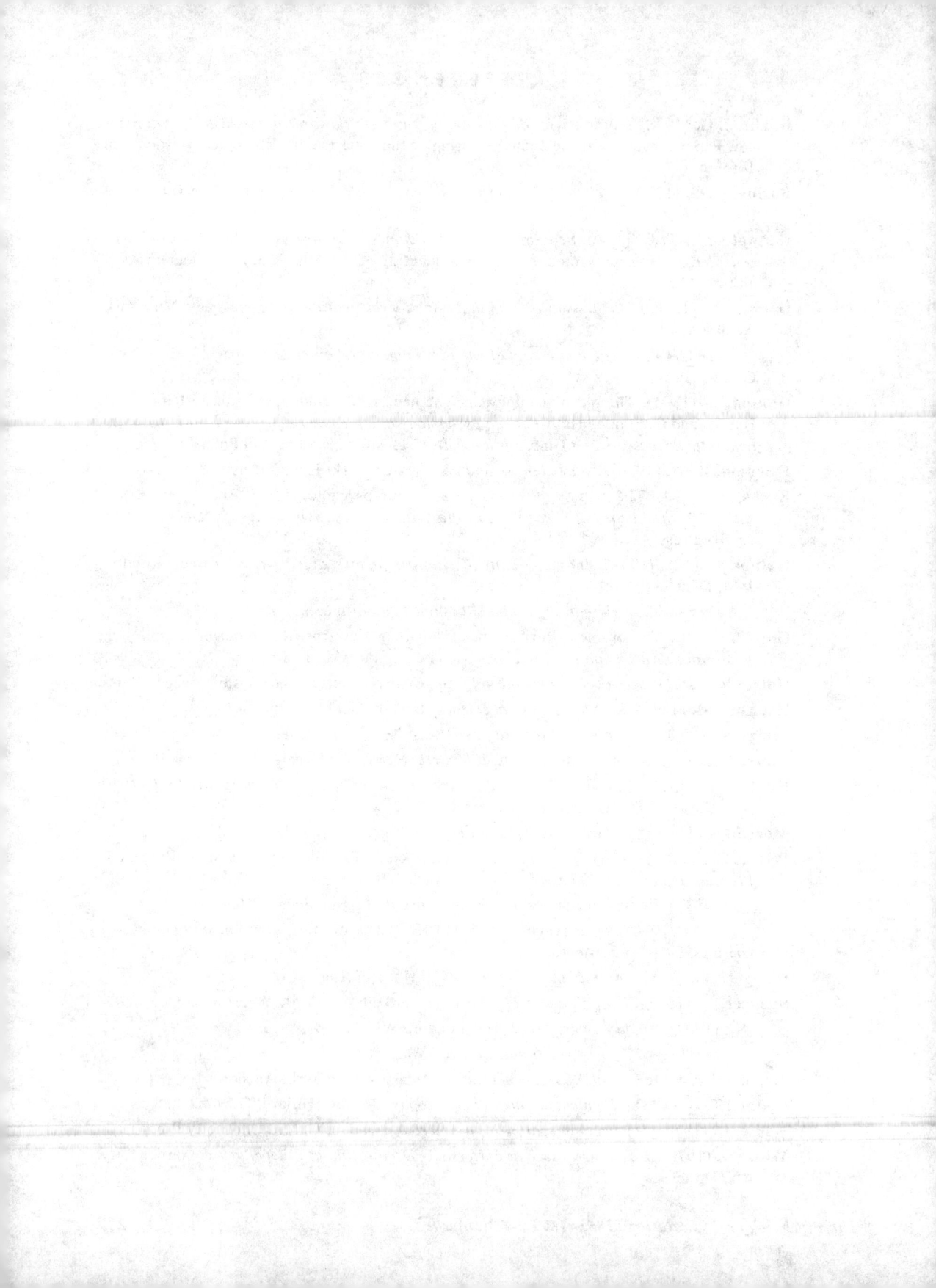

PART III

THE RISE *OF BEHAVIORALISM*

The founders of psychology took psychology to be the science of mental life. For Wundt and James, psychology was the study of consciousness; for Freud, it was the study of both consciousness and the unconscious. Scientific psychologists in the twentieth century, however, have had little use for conscious experience and little tolerance for Freud's cauldron of the id; instead, they have taken psychology to be the study of behavior. How psychology was transformed from mentalism to behavioralism, and how behavioralism became entrenched, will occupy us here and in the next two chapters.

Part of the reason for psychologists' increasing interest in behavior and flagging interest in introspection was their desire to be practical, to succeed in business, industry, and government, and to move as equals among other professional providers of services, such as physicians and lawyers. During World War I, psychologists established their social usefulness; after the war, psychologists became involved in applied activities and in such social issues as eugenics and remaking the family. The trend toward applied psychology nearly tore institutional psychology apart, but the demands of World War II reunited psychologists at least temporarily. In the chapters to come, we will see how social forces helped shape psychology into a behavioral science and how psychologists in turn helped shape society.

On the scientific side, the major development of the years just before and then between the world wars was the articulation and development of *behaviorism*. Behaviorism is a movement that has been much misunderstood by historians of psychology, primarily because their thinking has been controlled by behaviorism's own myths of origin. Behaviorism is usually seen as a dramatic break with the past, largely created by one man, John B. Watson; in fact, behaviorism was part of the larger trend toward *behavioralism*—defining psychology as the science of behavior—with roots in the 1890s. Behaviorism is similarly seen as a reasonably coherent movement—marked by theoretical disagreements, to be sure, but held together by shared assumptions about the nature of science and psychology; in fact, the disagreements among behaviorists are so profound that, in some cases, they were invisible to the behaviorists themselves and have remained so to many historians.

10 *The Conspiracy of Naturalism*
From Consciousness to Behavior (1892–1912)

This busy street in Chicago around 1900 shows that America was rapidly becoming an urban, industrial power, during psychology's first years of explosive growth. American's traditional rural ways of life were being destroyed, and the pace of change created social problems that seemed to demand rational, scientific solutions. Psychology soon gave up being a pure science of consciousness and became the practical study of behavior.

INTRODUCTION

In April 1913, the philosopher Warner Fite reviewed—anonymously, as was the custom at *The Nation*—three books on "The Science of Man." One was a text on genetics, but the other two were by psychologists: Hugo Münsterberg's *Psychology and Industrial Efficiency* and Maurice Parmellee's *The Science of Human Behavior*. Fite observed that psychology in 1913 seemed little concerned with consciousness; Münsterberg explicitly stated that the psychological "way of ordinary life, in which we try to understand our neighbor by entering into his mental functions . . . is not psychological analysis." Fite went on to conclude:

> Precisely. True "psychological analysis" ignores all personal experience of mentality. The science of psychology is, then, the finished result of what we may call the conspiracy of naturalism, in which each investigator has bound himself by a strange oath to obtain all his knowledge from observation of the actions of his fellows—"as a naturalist studies the chemical elements or the stars" [Münsterberg]—and never under any circumstances to conceive them in the light of his own experience of his living. Even the psychologist's "mental states" or "objects of consciousness" are only so many hypothetical entities read from without. . . . [W]hat is to be expected from a science of humanity which ignores all that is most distinctive of man? (p. 370)

Psychology had clearly changed since we left it in 1897. Wundt and James had created a science of mental life, the study of consciousness as such; Freud used introspection and inference to enter his patients' minds, both conscious and unconscious. But by 1913, Fite found a psychology aimed at behavior, not consciousness, and based on treating people as things, not as conscious agents.

In twenty years, a new kind of psychology had arisen, which we will call *behavioralism.* One might imagine that a scientific revolution had occurred, but there was instead an inevitable, steady—if rapid—evolution of psychology from the science of consciousness to the science of behavior. The traditional term "behaviorism" is too narrow for psychology defined as the study of behavior because many psychologists, as we shall see, define psychology as the study of behavior, but resist the label "behaviorist." "Behaviorism" is thus a subset of "behavioralism." In what follows, "behavioralism" will designate anyone for whom the subject matter of psychology is behavior rather than consciousness. Some behavioralists propose theories that invoke mental processes to explain behavior, but it is behavior they seek to explain, not conscious experience. The term "behaviorist" will be used to designate only those behavioralists who accepted that label.

Psychology and Society

It is appropriate to begin the history of modern psychology in 1892 because, in that year, the American Psychological Association (APA) was founded, largely due to the activities of G. Stanley Hall. Our attention from now on will be fixed on American psychology, for although Germany granted the earliest degrees in psychology, it was in America that psychology became a profession; the German equivalent of the APA (see Chapter 7) was not founded until 1904 (Danziger, 1979). For better or worse, and for sometimes extraneous reasons, modern psychology is essentially American psychology. American movements and theories have been adopted overseas—so much so that, in 1980, a German text in social psychology was filled with American references and made no mention of Wundt or *Völkerpsychologie.*

Society today is so professionalized—even beauticians need a license in many states—that we may overlook the impact of professionalization on the content and shape of a discipline. Until now, we have happily called "psychologists" people whose aims, ideas, and circumstances were quite different: Plato and Freud; Aristotle and Descartes; Leibniz and Galton. But professionalization brings self consciousness about the definition of a field, and control over who may call himself or herself a member of it. To establish an organization such as the APA means to establish criteria for membership, to allow some to call themselves "psychologists," to forbid the name to others. Government is then induced to enforce the rules, issuing licenses to applicants who meet the criteria for "psychologist," and prosecuting those who falsely practice psychology.

The founding of the APA took place early in a period of important change in American life, in which the professionalization of academic and practical disciplines played an important part. The years between 1890 and World War I are generally recognized as critical in U.S. history. America in the 1880s was, in Robert Wiebe's phrase, a nation of "island communities" scattered across the immense ocean of rural America. In these small, isolated communities, peoples' lives were enclosed in a web of family relations and familiar neighbors; the world outside was psychologically distant and did not—indeed, could not—intrude very often. By 1920, all this had changed. The United States had become a nation-state, united by technology and forming a common culture.

Part of the change was urbanization. In 1880, only 25 percent of the population lived in cities; by 1900, 40 percent did so. The trend has continued apace until the past few years. A city is not an island community—it is a huge collection of strangers, especially when immigration, from farm communities and from foreign countries, brings hundreds to the metropolis every day. Changing from farm- or village-dweller to urban citizen effects psychological changes and demands new psychological skills.

Changing from island community to nation-state has, as Daniel Boorstin (1974) argues, deeply affected daily lives, widening personal horizons, narrowing the range of immediate experience, and introducing a constant flow of change with which people must keep up. The railroad could take the rural immigrant to the big city. It could also bring to farmers and villagers the products of the city: frozen meat and vegetables, canned food, and, above all, the wonders of the Ward's and Sears-Roebuck catalogs. Previously, most men and women lived out their lives in the small radius of a few hours' walking. Now, the train took them immense distances occasionally, and the trolley took them downtown every day to work and to shop at the new department stores. Mobility freed people from what could be the stultifying confines of small-town life. It also homogenized experience. Today, we can all watch the same television programs and news broadcasts—even when a report is originating from a hotel room in Baghdad; we can buy the same brands of foods and clothes, and travel from coast to coast, staying in standardized Holiday Inn motel rooms and eating the same recipe of McDonald's hamburgers.

The years 1892 to 1896, now generally agreed to mark the beginning of the modern era, were especially chaotic and disquieting. The Panic of 1893 started a four-year depression of major proportions; in its wake came not only unemployment but riots and insurrection. The *"Année terrible"* of 1894 to 1895 witnessed 1,394 strikes and a march on Washington by Coxey's Army of unemployed, dispersed by troops amid rumors of revolution. The turmoil culminated in the crisis and election of 1896. One candidate, William Jennings Bryan, was the voice of Populism—and, to established leaders, a leftist revolutionary and a leader of "hideous and repulsive vipers." His opponent was William McKinley, a dull, solid Republican. Far from being a Marxist, Bryan was really the voice of the rural, small-town, pietistic past, a preacher of religious morality. McKinley represented the immediate future: urban, pragmatic, the voice of big business and big labor. McKinley narrowly won and revolution was averted; reform, efficiency, and progress became the watchwords of the day. After 1896, psychology would participate strongly in all three noble goals.

Against this background of chaos and crisis, professional discussions in the APA's early years appear parochial. Nevertheless, one important theme of the times does emerge—the last defense of the old psychology against the new.

Ladd—who had done much to introduce the new psychology to America—rejected what it was becoming. He rejected the physiological, natural-science conception of psychology he found in James, and he defended spiritualistic dualism (Ladd, 1892). In his APA presidential address, he decried as "absurd" the replacement of introspection by experiment and objective measurement, and pointed out that objective experimentation was incompetent to say anything about important parts of human psychology, including the religious sentiments. Other adherents of the old psychology, such as Larkin Dunton (before the Massachusetts School Masters' Club in 1895), defended the old psychology as "the science of the soul," "an emanation of the Divine," furnishing the key "to moral education."

Like Bryan and his oratory, Ladd, Dunton, and the old psychology represented the passing world of rural, village America, which had been based on traditional religious truths. The Scottish commonsense psychology had been created to defend religion and would continue to do so as fundamentalists clung to it against the tide of modernism. The old psychology had a soul and taught the old moral values of an American culture that was being overtaken by progress.

The decade of the 1890s was the "age of the news"—the new education, the new ethics, the new woman, and the new psychology. The future belonged to aggressive new psychologists, professionalizers of psychology who looked to its future. Chief among them was Wundt's *ganz Amerikanisch* student, Cattell, fourth president of the APA. Cattell (1896) described the new psychology as a rapidly advancing quantitative science. Moreover—and this would be a key part of professional psychology in the years to come—he claimed for experimental psychology "wide reaching practical applications . . . in education, medicine, the fine arts, political economy, and, indeed, in the whole conduct of life." The new psychology, not the old, was in step with the times: self-confident, self-consciously new and scientific, and ready to face the challenges of urbanization, industrialization, and the unceasing, ever-changing flow of American life.

Reform, efficiency, and progress were the actuating values of the major social and political movement following the crisis of 1896, Progressivism. Progressives were middle-class professionals—including the new psychologists—who aimed to rein in the rapacious American aristocracy (the "Robber Barons") and the disorderly masses of urban immigrants. Not only did the Robber Barons prey on Americans through business, but they were turning their riches to the control of politics and the living of opulent but empty lives, captured by F. Scott Fitzgerald in *The Great Gatsby*. Progressives saw the urban masses as victims exploited by corrupt political machines, which traded votes for favors and controlled indispensable services to hopeful immigrants.

In place of what they defined as the greedy self-interest of the moneyed class, and the opportunistic self-interest of the political bosses, the Progressives sought to establish disinterested, expert, professional government, that is, government by themselves. There can be no doubt that, especially in the urban areas, living conditions were often appalling as the waves of immigrants stretched American cities beyond their old bounds and beyond their ability to cope. Urban political machines were an organic, adaptive response to urban ills; for bewildered immigrants, the machines provided a helpful intermediary between them and their new society. But because the machines' help was bought with votes, rational, middle-class Progressives, led by academics, saw only corruption and manipulation of helpless victims by self-serving politicians. The Progressives replaced corruption with the scientific management principles of the great corporations.

John Dewey (1859–1952)

The philosopher of Progressivism and the prophet of twentieth-century liberalism was John Dewey, elected president of the APA for the last year of the old century. In his presidential address, "Psychology and Social Practice," Dewey examined psychology's role in modern society by focusing on the reform of education.

Educational reform was one of the central concerns of Progressivism, and John Dewey was the founder of Progressive education. According to Dewey, education as it stood was ill-suited to the needs of urban, industrial America. G. Stanley Hall had begun the reform of education with his child study movement and the idea that schools should be child-centered institutions. Nevertheless, more reforms were urgently needed, as Dewey and others recognized. Immigrants were perforce bringing with them alien customs and alien tongues; they, and especially their children, needed to be Americanized. Immigrants from rural communities also needed to be educated in the habits appropriate to industrial work and in new skills unknown on the farm. Above all, the schools had to become the child's new community. America's island communities were disappearing, and immigrants had left their home communities. The school had to be a community for children now, so that the American community could later be reformed through the adults the school produced.

"The school is an especially favorable place in which to study the availability of psychology for social practice," Dewey told the assembled psychologists. Sounding the themes of the psychology of adaptation, Dewey argued that "mind [is] fundamentally an instrument of adaptation" to be improved by school experience, and that "[for] psychology to become a working hypothesis"—that is, to meet the pragmatic test—it would have to involve itself with the education of America's young minds.

Once we involve ourselves with education, Dewey continued, psychologists would inevitably be led to society at large. Above all, schools must teach values, and these values must be the values of social growth and community solidarity, the values of pragmatism and urban life. Finally, these values are not just the school's values but must become the values of every social institution; and so psychologists must naturally become engaged in the great enterprise of Progressive social reform.

Progressivism was the American New Enlightenment and, as such, condemned custom and replaced it with rational calculation. Dewey recognized that the island communities' values were maintained through custom, but that once values "are in any way divorced from habit and tradition," they must be "consciously proclaimed" and must find "some substitute for custom as an organ of their execution." Consequently, psychology, the study of mental adaptation, plays a special role in the reconstruction of society:

> The fact that conscious, as distinct from customary, morality and psychology have a historic parallel march, is just the concrete recognition of the necessary equivalence

between ends consciously conceived, and interest in the means upon which the ends depend. . . . So long as custom reigns, as tradition prevails, so long as social values are determined by instinct and habit, there is no conscious question . . . and hence no need of psychology. . . . But when once the values come to consciousness . . . then the machinery by which ethical ideals are projected and manifested, comes to consciousness also. Psychology must needs be born as soon as morality becomes reflective. (Dewey, 1900/1978 pp. 77–8)

Psychology, then, is a social analog to consciousness. According to James, as we shall see, consciousness arises in an individual when adaptation to new circumstances is imperative. American society faced imperative changes, Dewey said, and psychology was arising to meet them. Only psychology offers an "alternative to an arbitrary and class view of society, to an aristocratic view" that would deny to some their full realization as human beings. Echoing the philosophes of the French Enlightenment, Dewey said that "we are ceasing to take existing social forms as final and unquestioned. The application of psychology to social institutions is . . . just the recognition of the principle of sufficient reason in the large matters of social life." The arrangements that exist among people are the results of the working of scientific laws of human behavior, and once psychologists understand these laws, they will be able to construct a more perfect society by substituting rational planning for haphazard growth.

Individual personality would be blended into the social whole. "To save personality in all, we must all serve alike" by reducing personality to lawful scientific mechanism. "To affirm personality independent of mechanism is to restrict its full meaning to a few [the lucky aristocracy]. . . . The entire problem," Dewey concluded, "is one of the development of science, and of its applications to life." For relief from the capricious freedom of aristocratic society, we should look forward to a scientific society, anticipating "no other outcome than increasing control in the ethical sphere." In the new society, psychology will "enable human effort to expend itself sanely, rationally, and with assurance."

In his address, Dewey touched all the themes of Progressivism, and he deepened and developed them over the course of a long career as a public philosopher. He gave Progressivism its voice; as one Progressive said, "We were all Deweyites before we read Dewey." For not only was Progressivism the politics of the moment and of the future, it also reflected America's deepest traditions: distrust of aristocrats—hereditary, moneyed, or elected—and a commitment to equal treatment of all.

Progressivism and Dewey broke new ground in their conceptions of the ends to be reached by society and the means to be used to reach those ends. As de Tocqueville had observed earlier, Americans distrusted intellect, which they associated with aristocracy; that distrust still remained nearly a century later. *The Saturday Evening Post,* in 1912, attacked colleges for encouraging "that most un-American thing called class and culture. . . . There should be no such thing [in America] as a superior mind." Yet Progressivism called for government rule by a scientifically trained managerial elite. In a Progressively reformed city, the political authority of the mayor was replaced by the expertise of a university-trained city manager, whose job description was taken from big business. Progressives were obsessed by social control, the imposing of order on the disordered mass of turn-of-the-century American citizens. Progressivism's permanent legacy is government bureaucracy. The "corrupt" politicians of the urban machine knew their constituents as individuals who were to be helped or harmed according to how they supported the machine. Bureaucracy, in contrast, is rational and impersonal rule by experts. Questing for fairness, it imposes anonymity; people become numbers; the poor become case files, to be scientifically managed and manipulated to ensure the good of the whole.

The goal of society in the Progressive vision was the cultivation of the individual within a supportive and nurturing community. Permanent achievements were replaced by growth. As Dewey later wrote, "The process of growth, of improvement and progress, rather than . . . the result, becomes the significant thing. . . . Not perfection as a final goal, but the ever-enduring process of perfecting, maturing, refining is the aim in living. . . . Growth itself is the only moral end" (Dewey, 1920/1948/1957). Progressivism's novel goal is Darwinian. Because there is no end to evolution, there should be no end to personal growth. Darwin had abolished God, but Dewey defined a new sin; as a Progressive enthusiast wrote: "The long disputed sin against the holy ghost has been found . . . the refusal to cooperate with the vital principle of betterment."

Were the goals of individual self-cultivation and the attainment of scientific social control at odds? By no means. In Dewey's view, individuals acquire their personality and thought from society. There is, in reality, no individual who preexists society, nor is society a collection of atomic individuals. Although the island communities were vanishing, Americans still craved community, and Progressives offered a new kind of rationally planned community. A leading Progressive, Randolph Bourne, argued that, in the new order of things, nothing was as important as a "glowing personality"; self-cultivation "becomes almost a duty if one wants to be effective toward the great end" of reforming society. Hence, deliberate social planning would bring about individual fulfillment.

So, despite its resonance with certain American values, Progressivism was at odds with America's individualistic, libertarian past. The scientific view of people and the scientific management of society on psychological principles had no room for individual freedom, for, to a scientific, there is no freedom. The individual should be cultivated but in the interests of the whole state. As Saint-Just had said during the French Revolution, it was necessary to form people to want what their expert rulers wanted them to want.

> Social control cannot be individually determined, but must proceed from a controlled environment which provides the individual with a uniform and constant source of stimuli. . . . The counter plea of "interference with individual liberty" should have no weight in court, for individuals have no liberties in opposition to a scientifically controlled society but find all their legitimate freedom in conformity to and furtherance of such social function. (Bernard, 1911)

The Progressive vision was not, of course, confined to psychology; it was remaking all the social sciences along similar lines. The inevitable direction was behavioral, because, ultimately, social control is control of behavior. To achieve social control, psychologists would have to give up the arcane procedure of introspection for the study of how behavior is controlled by its circumstances, and, finally, how control of the environment gives managers control of behavior. As the twentieth century went on, psychologists would fulfill Dewey's hopes. Psychologists would increasingly move out into society and remake its misfits, its children, its schools, its government, its businesses, its very psyche. Psychology in the twentieth century would profoundly alter our conceptions of ourselves, our needs, our loved ones, and our neighbors. John Dewey, philosopher and psychologist, more than any other single person drew the blueprint of the twentieth-century American mind.

James and Pragmatism

For all its influence on psychology, James's *Principles* turned out to be for him just a diversion. In 1892, he brought out a one-volume *Briefer Course,* more suitable as a classroom text, but pronounced himself weary of psychology. In that same year, he secured a successor to himself as Harvard's experimental psychologist and resumed his career as a philosopher, making 1892 a doubly significant year for psychology.

In response to Ladd's attack on psychology—that is, on the new psychology—as a natural science, James (1892) agreed that psychology was not then a science, but "is a mass of phenomenal description, gossip and myth." He wrote the *Principles,* he said, wishing "by treating Psychology like a natural science to help her become one" (p. 146).

James correctly set out the new psychology's theme as a natural science. The cerebralist, reflex-action theory is invaluable because, by treating behavior as the outcome of physiologically rooted motor habits and impulses, it works toward the "practical prediction and control" that is the aim of all natural sciences. Psychology should no longer be regarded as part of philosophy but as "a branch of biology." Finally, what is needed, said James, is a practical psychology that tells people how to act, that makes a difference to life. "The kind of psychology which could cure a case of melancholy, or charm a chronic insane delusion away, ought certainly to be preferred to the most seraphic insight into the nature of the soul" (1892, p. 153).

Psychology should be practical, should make a difference. James not only voiced the growing desire of American psychologists as they organized and professionalized, but he announced his own touchstone of truth: True ideas make a real difference to life. James's next task was, then, the full development of the characteristically American philosophy, pragmatism.

By the mid-1890s, the outlines of a new psychology, distinctively American in character, were emerging. The interest of American psychologists was shifting away from what consciousness contains and toward what consciousness does and how it aids an organism, human or animal, in its adaptation to a changing environment. In short, mental content was becoming less important than mental function. This new functional psychology was a natural offspring of Darwinism and the new American experience. Mind, consciousness, would not exist, James had said in the *Principles,* unless it served the adaptive needs of its host; in the America of the 1890s, it was clear that consciousness's prime function was to guide adjustment to the rapid flow of change engulfing immigrant and farmer, worker and professional. In a world of constant change, ancient truths—mental content, fixed doctrines—became uncouth every day. Heraclitus's universe had at last become true, and people no longer believed in Plato's eternal Forms. In the Heraclitean flux, the only eternal constant was change, and therefore the only reality of experience—psychology's subject matter—was adjustment to change.

In both philosophy and psychology, America was ready to produce new doctrines to meet the challenge of the modern American experience. In philosophy, William James expanded Peirce's narrow scientific pragmatism into a broad method capable of guiding one in the flux of modern experience: pragmatism. In psychology, a new generation of young American psychologists, inspired by James's *Principles,* built a psychology of mental adjustment: functionalism.

Pragmatism had begun with the practical, scientific attitude of C. S. Peirce as a way of determining whether concepts had any empirical reality. But Peirce's conception was too narrow and dry to meet fully the demands of a post-Darwinian, Heraclitean world. Virtually every nineteenth-century philosophy—romanticism, Darwinism, Hegelian idealism, Marxism—pictured a universe of change. It had become clear that there were no Platonic permanent truths; yet people will not live without some certainty, some fixed star to steer by. James found in Peirce's pragmatism a fixed star of a new sort. James offered a method for making, rather than finding, truths.

In a series of works beginning in 1895 and culminating in *Pragmatism* (1907/1955), James developed a comprehensive pragmatic approach to the problems of science, philosophy, and life. James argued that ideas were worthless or, more precisely, meaningless, unless they mattered to our lives. An idea with no consequences was pointless and meaningless. As he wrote in *Pragmatism:*

> True ideas are those that we can assimilate, validate, corroborate and verify. False ideas are those that we can not. That is the practical difference it makes for us to have true ideas. . . . The truth of an idea is not a stagnant property inherent in it. Truth happens to an idea. It becomes true, is made true by events. Its verity is in fact an event, a process. (p. 133, italics not duplicated)

So far, this sounds like Peirce: a hardheaded, Darwinian approach to truth. James went beyond Peirce, however, when he said that the truth of an idea should be tested against its agreement with all of one's experience, "nothing being omitted." When Peirce had said we weigh ideas against experience, he meant experience in a narrow, cognitive sense: the scientist's apprehension of the physical world. James, however, with the romantics, saw no reason to value one kind of experience above another. Noncognitive experience—hopes, fears, loves, ambitions—were just as much part of a person's living reality as sensations of number, hardness, or mass. "Ideas," James said, "(which themselves are but parts of our experience) become true just in so far as they help us get into satisfactory relations with other parts of our experience" (1907/1955, p. 49, italics not duplicated). James's criterion of truth was thus much broader than Peirce's and could apply to any concept, no matter how seemingly fanciful or metaphysical. To the tough-minded empiricist, the ideas of God or of free will were empty and meaningless because they were devoid of sensory content. To James, these ideas could make a difference in the way we conduct our lives. If the idea of free will and its corollary, moral responsibility, leads men and women to live better, happier lives than if they believed in the automaton theory, then free will was true; or, more exactly, it was made true in the lives and experience of the people who accepted it.

James's pragmatism held no metaphysical prejudices, unlike traditional rationalism and empiricism. "Rationalism sticks to logic and the empyrean. Empiricism sticks to the external senses. Pragmatism is willing to take anything, to follow either logic or the senses and to count the humblest and most personal experiences. She will count mystical experiences if they have practical consequences" (1907/1955, p. 61). Against the cold intellectual positivism of Peirce's pragmatism, James asserted the claims of the heart, so congenial to Americans since the time of Jonathan Edwards. As James recognized, his pragmatism was anti-intellectual in setting heart and head as equals in the search for truth. Compared to the rationalist and the search for perfect Truth, James wrote (p. 168), "A radical pragmatist is a happy-go-lucky anarchist sort of creature." Functional psychologists and their heirs, the behaviorists, would likewise depreciate the intellect. Learning and problem solving, as we shall see, would soon be explained in terms of blind trial and error and resulting reward and punishment, not in terms of directed cognitive activity.

Pragmatism was a functional philosophy—a method, not a doctrine. It provided a way of coping with the Heraclitean flux of experience no matter what the challenge or the topic. In the fields of theology and physics, politics and ethics, philosophy and psychology, it offered a star to navigate by. Although one could not hope to find a fixed, final truth about God or matter, society or morality, metaphysics or the mind, one could at least know what questions to ask: Does this concept matter, does it make a difference to me, to my society, to my science? Pragmatism promised that even though there were no final solutions to any problem, at least there was a method of concretely resolving problems here and now.

Heretofore, philosophers had searched for first principles, indubitable ideas on which to erect a philosophical system and a philosophy of science. James's pragmatism gives up the quest for first principles, recognizing that, after Darwin, no truth could be fixed. Instead, James offered a philosophy that worked by turning away from content (fixed truths) and toward function (what ideas do for us). As James did this, psychologists were quietly developing a psychology of function, studying not the ideas a mind contained but how the mind worked in adapting its organism to a changing environment. At the same time, they hoped that psychological science would work in the modern world, meeting the challenges of immigration and education, madness and feeblemindedness, business and politics.

BUILDING ON THE PRINCIPLES: THE MOTOR THEORY OF CONSCIOUSNESS (1892–1896)

The spirit of the new psychology in America was that of James's *Principles of Psychology:* Cattell said it "has breathed the breath of life into the dust of psychology." James himself detested the professional, even commercial, attitudes overcoming academia and harbored doubts about the validity of scientific psychology. Nevertheless, on his text, American psychology built itself for years to come.

Hugo Münsterberg and Action Theory

By 1892, James was weary of psychology and eager to move on to philosophy. He looked for someone to replace him as Harvard's experimental psychologist, and his attention was drawn to Hugo Münsterberg, a student of Wundt's, who nevertheless disagreed with his teacher in a way that attracted James to him.

We have already discussed in Chapter 9 James's ideo-motor theory of voluntary behavior and contrasted it to Wundt's. Münsterberg's "action theory" developed a more thoroughgoing motor theory of consciousness that did away with will altogether (a step James could never take) and reduced consciousness to sensation and behavior.

Anyone who, like Wundt, was a voluntarist and assigned to will an active, determining role in mind and behavior must see consciousness as deciding on actions.

Information, or stimuli, are attended to, a decision is made, and behavior follows, roughly:

$$S \longleftrightarrow \text{Consciousness} \longrightarrow R$$

(the double arrow following S reflects the role of active apperception in determining what we experience).

As we have seen, will is a tricky concept for psychology as a natural science: If humans have free will, their behavior is not predictable and there can be no science of human nature. Moreover, by the turn of the century, will was especially imperiled, because reflex theory seemed now to be a tenable conception of how behavior is produced. As Münsterberg wrote, "For the preservation of the individual, it is obviously irrelevant whether a purposeful motion is accompanied by contents of consciousness or not" (Hale, 1980, p. 41).

However, there *are* conscious contents (the traditional subject matter of psychology) to explain: Why do we believe we have an effective will? With James, but more consistently, Münsterberg located the source in behavior—"our ideas are the product of our readiness to act, . . . our actions shape our knowledge" (quoted by Kuklick, 1977). Our feeling of will, the motor theory explains, comes about because we are aware of our behavior and our incipient tendencies to behave. Thus, I might announce that I'm going to stand up from my chair, not because I've reached a decision to stand but because the motor processes of standing have just begun and have entered consciousness. I feel my "will" to be effective because generally the incipient tendencies to act are followed by real action, and the former trigger memories of the latter. Because the covert tendencies have usually in fact preceded overt behavior, I believe my "will" is usually carried out.

We may summarize the motor theory of consciousness this way:

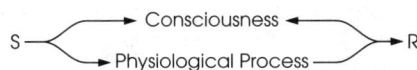

$$S \underset{\longrightarrow \text{Physiological Process} \longrightarrow}{\overset{\longrightarrow \text{Consciousness} \longleftarrow}{\Big\langle}} \quad \rightarrow R$$

The contents of consciousness are determined by stimuli impinging on us, by our overt behaviors, and by peripheral changes in muscles and glands produced by the physiological processes linking stimulus and response. As Münsterberg argued, in this account, consciousness is no more than an epiphenomenon; it plays no role in causing behavior. Psychology, moreover, had to be physiological in a reductive sense, explaining consciousness in terms of underlying physiological processes, especially at the periphery. Practical, applied psychology, a field in which Münsterberg was quite active, would perforce be behavioral, explaining human action as the outcome of human circumstances.

The motor theory of consciousness was not confined to James or Münsterberg. In one form or another, it grew in influence. We have before us now the central philosophical-psychological theme of these two decades: What, if anything, does consciousness do? Why are we conscious at all? Is consciousness Darwinianly adaptive? These questions surface over and over in place after place. In the motor theory of consciousness, we see a good reason for the rise of behavioralism. If the theory is true, consciousness in fact does nothing. So why, except from faith in the old definition of psychology as the study of consciousness, should we study it?

John Dewey and the Reflex Arc

After 1890, following James's *Principles,* John Dewey moved away from his earlier Hegelian idealism and began to develop what he later called instrumentalism, becoming the most influential of all American philosophers. In the mid-1890s, he wrote a series of important but tediously phrased papers that, taking the *Principles* as the footings, laid the foundations of his lifelong attempt to bring together philosophy, psychology, and ethics in a harmonious whole. These papers also furnished the central conceptions of America's native psychology, functionalism.

The most influential of these papers was "The Reflex Arc Concept in Psychology" (1896). He criticized the traditional associationist reflex arc concept for artificially breaking up behavior into disjointed parts. He did not deny that stimulus, sensation (idea), and response exist. He did, however, deny that they were separately occurring events arranged in time like beads on a string. Instead, Dewey considered stimulus, idea, and response to be divisions of labor in an overall coordination of action—as the organism adjusts to its environment.

Developing his own motor theory of mind, Dewey regarded perception not as the passive registration of an impression but as itself a behavior conditioned by other behaviors occurring at the same time. So, to a soldier anxiously awaiting contact with the enemy, the sound of a twig snapping has one significance; to a hiker in a peaceful woods, it has quite another. Indeed, the hiker may not even notice the snapping sound at all.

Dewey made here a decisive move whose significance, buried in his dry, abstract prose, is not immediately apparent. We might, with Wundt and even James, naively attribute the differences in apperception of the twig's snapping to willfully focused attention. The soldier is actively listening for sounds of approach, the hiker is attending to the songs of birds. But Dewey's motor theory, like Münsterberg's, dispensed with the individual ego and its will. It is the current behavior, claimed Dewey, that gives a sensation its significance, or even determines whether a stimulus enters consciousness at all. A stimulus counts as a sensation, and takes on value, only if it has a relationship with our current behavior.

James had advanced a cerebralist approach to mind but had not fully drawn out the implications of this view. Dewey saw that behavior often runs off by itself, occasioning no sensations or ideas in any significant sense of the term. Only when behavior needs to be newly coordinated to reality—that is, needs to be adjusted—do sensation and emotion arise. The hiker's behavior need not be adjusted to the snap of a twig, and his walking continues uninterrupted. The soldier urgently needs to coordinate his behavior to the snap of a twig and its sound thus looms large in consciousness. Moreover, the soldier's emotions, fear, apprehension, and perhaps anger at the enemy are felt, Dewey argued, only because his behavior is in check; his emotions arise from feedback from his thwarted action tendencies. Emotion, said Dewey, is a sign of conflicting dispositions to act; in the soldier's case, to fight or flee. Could he do either immediately and wholeheartedly, he would feel nothing, Dewey said.

Dewey's formulation was centrally important for later American psychology; in 1943, the reflex arc paper was chosen as one of the most important articles ever published in *Psychological Review.* Dewey showed that psychology could do away with the central willing self of Wundt and James, a mysterious and unscientific being. Rather than assigning the control of perception and decision to an inaccessible ego, it became possible to account for them in terms of coordinated, ever-changing, adaptive behaviors. So hearing was one sort of behavior, attending another, and responding a third. All were coordinated toward the end of survival in a constant, fluid stream of behavior ever in motion, not unlike the daily lives of contemporary Americans. Dewey's ideas became the commonplaces of functionalism.

The new psychology had eliminated the soul; Dewey and Münsterberg eliminated the willing self, but a self, and ego, remained. What remained for psychological study were consciousness and behavior. Soon, the existence of consciousness, too, would become problematic.

FROM PHILOSOPHY TO BIOLOGY: FUNCTIONAL PSYCHOLOGY (1896–1910)

Experiments Become Functional

In keeping with epistemological aims, traditional philosophy had been concerned with the ideas the mind contains and whether they are true. Philosophers did not ignore or even neglect mental processes, of course; nevertheless, their first concern was with mental content, that is, putative knowledge. Traditional psychology of consciousness, while naturally investigating mental processes such as apperception, retained an emphasis on conscious content as the subject matter of psychology; its primary novelty was subjecting consciousness to experimental control in order to capture psychology for science. However, as we saw in the previous chapter, James, in his *Principles of Psychology,* shifted the interest of psychology from content to process. As he pictured the mind, mental contents were evanescent, fleeting things, seen once, never to return; what endured in the mind was function, especially the function of choosing. James's new emphasis was reinforced by the new American experience of the 1890s—old truths replaced by new ones, familiar scenes by strange ones. What remained constant was the process of adjusting to the new.

The development of the motor theory of consciousness continued the process of depreciating mental content and, by implication, the method used to access it, introspection. In the motor theory, conscious content was a result of sensation and incipient motor response and seemed to play little, if any, role in actually producing behavior. It remained possible to introspect and report conscious content—as Münsterberg continued to do in his laboratory—but it could easily be seen as pointless, even irresponsible. American psychologists agreed with James: What was needed was a psychology that met the pragmatic test by being effective. Awash in change, Americans needed a psychology that did something to cope with the new. Introspection only revealed what was; Americans needed to prepare for what is to be. James, Münsterberg, and Dewey were preparing for the new functional psychology by turning their attention from content to adaptive process.

At the same time, experimental psychologists were shifting their interest from introspective report of conscious content to objective determination of the correlation between stimulus and response. As developed by Wundt, the experimental method had two aspects. A standardized, controlled stimulus was presented to a subject, who responded to it in some way, reporting at the same time the contents of his experience. Wundt, as a mentalist, was interested in the experience produced by given conditions and used objective results as clues to the processes that produced conscious content.

However, in the hands of American psychologists, emphasis shifted from conscious experience to the determination of responses by stimulus conditions.

As an example, we may take an experiment on how people locate an object in space on the basis of sound, described by Angell, (1903a). In his experiment, a blindfolded observer—in this case, one of them was John B. Watson, the founder of behaviorism—was seated in a chair at the center of a circular device that could present a sound at any point around the observer. After setting the sound generator at a given point, the experimenter made it produce a tone, and the observer pointed to where he or she believed the sound was coming from. Then the observer provided an introspective report of the conscious experience concomitant with the experimental procedure. Watson reported seeing a mental image of the apparatus surrounding him, with the sound generator located where he pointed. Now one could, as a true mentalist would, focus on the introspective report as the data of interest, aiming to describe and explain this bit of mental content. On the other hand, one could focus on the accuracy of the pointing response, correlating the position of the sound generator with the observer's indicated position.

In the present case, although both objective data—the correlation of stimulus position with the observer's response—and introspective reports were discussed, the latter were given secondary importance. The objective findings were highlighted and extensively discussed; the introspective findings were briefly mentioned at the end of the article. In the motor theory of consciousness, introspection was becoming less important, for consciousness played no causal role in determining behavior. The same attitude is found in the experiments of the time, such as Angell's. For him, too, introspective report was less important than the determination of behavior by the environment, and in the experiments of this entire period one finds, with the exception of reports from Titchener's laboratory, introspective reports being first isolated from the primary objective results and then shortened or removed altogether.

In addressing how behavior is adjusted to stimulus, American psychologists were turning from the study of mental content to the study of adaptive mental functions. Another experiment, by Bryan and Harter (1897), reveals a second sense in which American psychology was becoming functional—*socially* functional. Bryan, an experimental psychologist, and Harter, a former railroad telegrapher turned graduate student in psychology, investigated the acquisition of telegraphic skills by new railroad telegraphers. Their report contained no introspective reports at all but instead charted the students' gradual improvement over months of practice and telegraphic work. This completely objective study was socially significant because Bryan and Harter were studying an important skill learned by people who were assuming an important role in industrialized America. As the railroads expanded and knit together the island communities of formerly rural America, railroad telegraphers were vital: They kept track of what goods were sent where, and what trains were going to what places; in short, they were the communication links that made the whole railroad system function. Their significance may be judged from the fact that Sears began his mail-order business as a railroad telegrapher. He picked up unwanted merchandise shipped west and then sold it by advertising up and down the railroad telegraph line. Bryan and Harter, then, were bringing psychological research to bear on a topic of real social value.

Their study is significant in another respect as well. It foreshadowed the central problem of experimental psychology in the twentieth century: learning. The traditional psychology of consciousness, mentalism, had primarily investigated perception and its allied functions, because these were the producers of introspectional mental contents available for introspection. But in the post-Darwinian psychology of James and his followers, consciousness was important for what it does, especially in the adjustment of the organism to its environment. Gradual adjustment over time is learning—finding out about the environment and then behaving in accord with it. Bryan and Harter plotted learning curves and discussed how the novice telegraphers gradually adjusted to the demands of their jobs. In its objectivism, in its concern with a socially useful problem, and in its choice of learning as subject matter, Bryan and Harter's paper was a sign of things to come. It is no wonder, therefore, that, in 1943, it was voted by leading American psychologists as the most important experimental study yet published in the *Psychological Review* and one of the five most important papers of any kind. Even today, it is cited in important texts in introductory psychology.

By 1904, it was clear that the "objective" method, in which responses were correlated with stimuli, was at least as important as the introspective analysis of consciousness. Speaking before the International Congress of Arts and Science, Cattell, the American pioneer in psychology, said, "I am not convinced that psychology should be limited to the study of consciousness as such," which of course had been the definition of psychology for James and Wundt. His own work, Cattell said, "is nearly as independent of introspection as work in physics or in zoology." Introspection and experiment should "continually cooperate," but it was obvious from "the brute argument of accomplished fact" that much of psychology now existed "apart from introspection." Although Cattell seemed to place introspection and objective measurement on an equal footing, it is clear from his tone, and from his later call for applied psychology, that the objective, behavioral approach to psychology was on the rise.

Functional Psychology Defined

In both theory and research, then, American psychology was moving away from the traditional psychology of conscious content and toward a psychology of mental adjustment inspired by evolutionary theory. Interestingly, it was not an American psychologist who spotted and identified this new trend but the staunchest defender of a pure psychology of content, E. B. Titchener. In his "Postulates of a Structural Psychology" (1898), Titchener cogently distinguished several kinds of psychology; and while others may have disagreed about which kind of psychology was best, his terminology endured.

Titchener drew a broad analogy among three kinds of biology and three kinds of psychology:

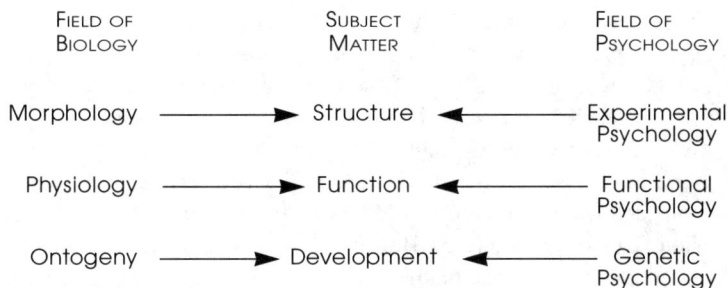

FIELD OF BIOLOGY		SUBJECT MATTER		FIELD OF PSYCHOLOGY
Morphology	⟶	Structure	⟵	Experimental Psychology
Physiology	⟶	Function	⟵	Functional Psychology
Ontogeny	⟶	Development	⟵	Genetic Psychology

In biology, the anatomist, the student of morphology, carefully dissects the body to discover the organs that compose it, revealing the body's structure. Once an organ is isolated and described, it is the job of the physiologist to figure out its function, what it does. Finally, one might study how an organ develops in the course of embryogenesis and postnatal development and how the organ came into being in the course of evolution; these studies constitute developmental biology, the study of the origin and path of change of an organ in the history of the species and of the individual.

Similarly, in psychology, the experimental psychologist—by which Titchener meant himself—dissects consciousness into its component parts; this anatomy of the mind defines structural psychology. What the revealed structures do is the province of the psychological physiologist—functional psychology. The development of mental structures and functions is the subject matter of genetic psychology, which investigates the course of individual and phylogenetic development.

In Titchener's estimation, structural psychology logically preceded functional psychology, because only after mental structures had been isolated and described could their functions be ascertained. At the same time, Titchener noted the appeal of functional psychology. Its roots were ancient; its analysis of mind hewed close to common sense, as it employed faculty concepts such as "memory," "imagination," and "judgment"; and it seemed to promise immediate practical application. Citing Dewey's reflex arc paper, Titchener also acknowledged that functional psychology was growing in influence. Nevertheless, Titchener urged psychologists to avoid the comfortable spaces of functional psychology and to stick to the tough scientific job of experimental introspective psychology. Genetic psychology, although logically possible and indeed already on the scene (Baldwin, 1895; Wozniak, 1982), remained a yet more distant prospect for Titchener.

From Undercurrent to Main Current

In the decade following Titchener's "Postulates," it became apparent that other psychologists found his analysis basically correct but his priorities reversed. In December 1900, in his presidential address to the American Psychological Association, Peirce's one-time collaborator, Joseph Jastrow, explored "Some Currents and Undercurrents in Psychology" (1901). He declared that, for him, psychology is "the science of mental function," not content. The functional approach arose out of evolution; it "at once cast a blinding light" upon dark areas of psychology long held by "dogmatism, misconception and neglect" and "breathed a new life" into "the dry bones" of psychology. Jastrow correctly observed that, although concern with mental function pervaded current research, it was not the central subject of investigation but rather gave a distinctive "color tone" to American psychology. Jastrow saw functional psychology as an accepted undercurrent, which he wanted to bring forward as a "main current." Functional psychology, said Jastrow, is more catholic than structural psychology. It welcomes to psychology the previously excluded topics of comparative psychology, abnormal psychology, mental testing, the study of the average person, and even psychical research, although this last clearly troubled him. Jastrow predicted that functional psychology would prove of more value to practical affairs than structural psychology. Finally, he noted (as we have) that all these trends are characteristically American, and he correctly prophesied that the future would belong to functional, not structural, psychology.

Various functionalists (e.g., Bolton, 1902; Bawden, 1903, 1904, 1910) advanced James's conception of consciousness toward behavioralism. Conscious content, as such, is not very important in their functional theory of mind. For them, mind is a process whose biological value lies in its ability to be summoned forth genielike when its organism finds itself faced with a new situation. It is not needed when instincts are adequate to the stimuli at hand, or when previously learned habits are functioning smoothly. Consciousness is a sometime thing, needed only occasionally, and it would not be long before psychologists were able to dispense with mind altogether. As Frank Thilly (1905) pointed out, the functional view of consciousness retained James's fatal flaw. Along with just about everyone else, James and the functional psychologists following him held to mind–body parallelism while at the same time arguing that consciousness actively intervenes in the adjustive activities of the organism. Why not claim more simply that behavior adjusts itself to the environment without dragging mind into the picture?

By 1905, it was clear to contemporary psychologists that the functional tide was in. Edward Franklin Buchner, who for some years wrote for *Psychological Bulletin* an annual history of the year's "Psychological Progress," observed "the widespread acceptance and defense of the 'functional' as over against the 'structural' view" of psychology. The replacement of the older system by a new one did have the unfortunate effect, Buchner noted, of starting the development of the field all over again, undoing cumulative progress. In the same volume, Felix Arnold raised "the great cry" of current psychologists: "WHAT IS IT GOOD FOR?" He praised functionalists for giving up the old view of perception, which Bolton had attacked, and replacing it with perception conceived "as a motor process . . . determining serial reactions toward [an] object."

In the same year, Mary Calkins (1863–1930) took the opportunity of her APA presidential address to advance her self psychology as a way to reconcile structural and functional psychologies. If psychology is conceived as the study of a real psychological self possessing both conscious content and mental functions, each system could be viewed as contributing part of the total psychological picture. Although Calkins aggressively pushed her self psychology over the years in every forum she could find, it seems to have found few followers. For the time of compromise had passed. In 1907, Buchner wrote that in 1906 "the functional point of view seem[ed] to have almost completely won out"—so much so that psychology's " 'older' (and almost consecrated) terms" were about finished. Buchner awaited the framing "of a new vocabulary of psychology for the new twentieth century."

The most important spokesman for the ascendant functional psychology was James Rowland Angell (1869–1949), who ultimately became President of Yale. He published an introductory psychology textbook written from the functional standpoint (*Psychology,* 1904). As President of the APA in 1906, Angell used his presidential address to reply to Titchener's "Postulates of a Structural Psychology with his own "The Province of Functional Psychology." Angell's address (published in 1907) was a milestone on the road to behavioralism. In it, we can see that functionalism was mainly a bridge between mentalism and behavioralism, a way station rather than an enduring movement in its own right. As Angell conceded at the outset, functional psychology was "little more than a program" and a "protest" against the sterilities of structural psychology. Functional psychology was also not new, being found in Aristotle, in Spencer, in Darwin, and in pragmatism.

Angell repeated the already familiar distinction: Structural psychology was concerned with mental "contents," functionalism with mental "operations." Functionalism studies mental process as it is in the actual life of an organism; structuralism studies how mind "appears" in a "merely postmortem analysis." To this end, "modern investigations . . . dispense with the usual direct form of introspection and concern themselves . . . with a determination of what work is accomplished and what the conditions are under which it is achieved." Angell here acknowledged the trend we earlier found in his and others' research and defined the point of view of behavioralist experimentation. Repeating his earlier argument (1903b), Angell justified this new research emphasis by quite correctly asserting that, unlike physical organs dissected by the anatomist, "mental contents are evanescent and fleeting." What endures over time are mental functions: Contents come and go, but attention, memory, judgment—the mental faculties of the old psychology rehabilitated—"persist."

Functional psychology also brings with it a change in psychology's institutional relationships. Structural, mentalistic psychology grew out of philosophy and remained closely allied to it. In contrast, functional psychology "brings the psychologist cheek by jowl with the general biologist," because both study the "sum total" of an organism's "organic activities," the psychologist concentrating on the "accommodatory service" of consciousness. This new biological orientation will bring with it practical benefits as well, Angell averred. "Pedagogy and mental hygiene . . . await the quickening and guiding counsel" of functional psychology. Animal psychology—"the most pregnant" movement of "our generation"—finds its "rejuvenation" in the new movement, because it is becoming "experimental . . . wherever possible" and "conservatively . . . non-anthropomorphic,"—trends we will examine in the next section. Genetic psychology and abnormal psychology—the former barely mentioned and the latter completely ignored by Titchener (1898)—will likewise be inspired by a functional approach.

Angell endorsed the view that consciousness "supervenes on certain occasions" in the life of an organism; he described the adjustment theory as "the position now held by all psychologists of repute." But he went further down the road to eliminating the mind altogether by claiming that consciousness "is no indispensable feature of the accommodatory process." Although, in a footnote, Angell held that accommodation to "the novel" is "the field of conscious activity," we may still sense here a further step toward behavioralism in its suggestion that learning may take place without conscious intervention.

In conclusion, functional psychology is "functional" in a triple sense. First, it considers mind to have a distinct biological function selected by Darwinian evolution: It adapts its organism to novel circumstances. Second, it describes consciousness as itself a result of the physiological functioning of the organism: Mind, in its view, is itself a biological function. Third, functional psychology promises to be socially useful in improving education, mental hygiene, and abnormal states: Psychology will become functional in twentieth-century life. In 1906, Angell stood at a hinge in the development of modern psychology. His continued concern with consciousness, however interpreted, still linked functional psychology with the mentalism of the past. At the same time, his emphasis on biology, on adaptation, and on applied psychology link functional psychology as a "new-old movement" whose time will someday pass with "some worthier successor [to] fill its place."

By 1907, then, functional psychology had by and large replaced structural psychology as the dominant approach to the field. However, it never became more than a program and a protest. It was finally too inconsistent to survive: It clung to a definition of psychology as the study of consciousness, while at the same time putting forth theories of perception and learning that made consciousness less and less necessary as a concept for scientific psychology. Functional theory embodied very clearly the historical forces of the time pushing psychology toward the study of behavior, and it helped psychologists change their fundamental conceptions of their profession without quite realizing that they were doing anything extraordinary.

Although functional psychology was strongest in America, psychologies that could be identified with functionalism also arose in Europe. Brentano's psychology, because it was labeled an "act" psychology, was often assimilated into the functional viewpoint. Similarly, the Würzburg school could be called "functional" because of its concern with and investigations of mental processes, and its discovery of contentless (imageless) thought.

In Britain, home of modern evolutionism, functional psychology found its William James in James Ward (1843–1975), sometimes called the "father of modern British psychology" (Turner, 1974). He was for a time a minister, but, after a crisis of faith, turned first to physiology, then psychology, and finally philosophy, exactly as James had done. His tremendous influence in British psychology comes from his article on psychology in the Encyclopaedia Brittanica's ninth edition, in 1886. It was the first article by that name in the Encyclopaedia, and Ward reworked it later into a text. Ward settled at Cambridge University, where he was active in attempts to establish a psychological laboratory.

Like James, Ward rejected atomistic analysis of the continuum of consciousness. Instead of a sensationistic atomism, Ward advocated a functional view of consciousness, the brain, and the whole organism: "Functionally regarded, the organism is from first to last a continuous whole . . . the growing complexity of psychical life is only parodied by treating it as mental chemistry" (1904, p. 615). To Ward, perception is not the passive reception of sensation, but active grasping of the environment. In a passage that resembles James, Ward wrote that "not mere receptivity but creative or selective activity is the essence of subjective reality" (p. 615). He struck a Darwinian note when he said: "Psychologically regarded, then, the sole function of perception and intellection is, it is contended, to guide action and subserve volition—more generally to promote self-conservation and betterment" (1920, p. 607).

Ward expounded the same kind of pragmatic, or functional, psychology that James did. For both men, consciousness was an active, choosing entity that adjusts the organism to the environment and so serves the struggle for survival. Ward resembled James in one more way—his *fin de siècle* concern with defending religion against the rising tide of Huxlean naturalism. Ward devoted his last great works to the refutation of naturalism and the support of Christianity.

Of greater influence on later psychology was Hermann Ebbinghaus's (1850–1909) study of memory. Ebbinghaus was a young doctor of philosophy unattached to any university when he came across a copy of Fechner's *Elements of Psychophysics* in a secondhand bookstore. He admired the scientific precision of Fechner's work on perception and resolved to tackle the "higher mental processes" that Wundt had excluded from experimental treatment. Using himself as his only subject, Ebbinghaus set out in 1879 to demonstrate Wundt's error; the result was his *On Memory* (1885). In the paper in which he criticized the methods of Würzburg (Chapter 7), Wundt praised Ebbinghaus for his more rigorous investigation of a higher mental process. It helped win him a professorship at the prestigious University of Berlin.

Memory represented a necessarily small-scale but well-thought-out research program. Ebbinghaus decided to investigate the formation of associations by learning serial lists of nonsense syllables, meaningless combinations of three letters he invented for the purpose. In electing to memorize nonsense syllables, Ebbinghaus revealed the functionalist cast of his thought. He chose nonsense syllables because they are meaningless, because the sameness of their content would not differentially affect the process of learning. He wanted to isolate and study memory as the pure function of learning, abstracting away any effects of content.

Ebbinghaus remained an eclectic rather than a systematic thinker, and his influence derives from his work on memory rather than from any theoretical views. But that influence was wide. In Germany, memory studies were carried on by G. E. Muller and his associates, whose distinctions, new procedures, and theories anticipated modern cognitive psychology. In America, James praised Ebbinghaus's work in *Principles,* and, in 1896, Mary Calkins augmented Ebbinghaus's serial learning method with a paired-associate procedure in which the subject learns specific pairs of words or nonsense syllables. More broadly, Ebbinghaus's *Memory* prefigured the style of twentieth-century psychology. Its subject was *learning,* the favorite topic of functionalists, behaviorists, and cognitive psychologists. The book minimized theory while multiplying facts and looking for systematic effects on behavior of independent variables, such as list length. Ebbinghaus strove to quantify his data and apply statistical methods. In short, Ebbinghaus represents the empirical, atheoretical, research-oriented, eclectic modern psychologist.

NEW DIRECTIONS IN ANIMAL PSYCHOLOGY (1898–1909)

Animal psychology, as it had been begun by Romanes, used two methods: the anecdotal method to collect data, and the method of inference to interpret it. Although both methods had been challenged, discussed, and defended from their inception, they came under special scrutiny and criticism among American psychologists in the late nineteenth and early twentieth centuries. Anecdote was replaced by experiment, particularly by the techniques of E. L. Thorndike and I. P. Pavlov. Inference was gradually given up, at least by some animal psychologists, as it became clear that Descartes's problem of other minds had no empirical solution.

From Anecdote to Experiment

Beginning in 1898, animal psychology experienced a surge in activity and a quickening of interest. But in the new animal psychology laboratory, experiment replaced anecdotes and informal, naturalistic experiments, as psychologists investigated the behavior of species ranging from protozoa to monkeys. The aim of animal psychology, as of psychology in general, was to produce a natural science, and the young men in the field felt that gentlemanly anecdote was not the path to science; as E. L. Thorndike (1898) wrote: "Salvation does not come from such a source." Although many psychologists were experimenting on animal mind and behavior, two research programs deserve special attention because their methods became enduring ones and their theoretical conceptions embraced the whole of psychology. These programs arose at almost the same time, but in very different places and circumstances: in William James's Cambridge basement, where a young graduate student employed his mentor's children as his research assistants, and in the sophisticated laboratories of a distinguished Russian physiologist already on his way to a Nobel Prize.

The Connectionism of Edward Lee Thorndike (1874–1949)

Thorndike was attracted to psychology when he read James's *Principles* for a prize competition at his undergraduate school, Wesleyan University (Connecticut). When Thorndike went to Harvard for graduate study, he eagerly signed up for courses with James and eventually majored in psychology. His first research interest was children and pedagogy, but, no child subjects being available, Thorndike took up the study of learning in animals. James gave him a place to work in his basement after Thorndike failed to secure official research space from Harvard. Before completing his work at Harvard, Thorndike was invited to go to Columbia by Cattell; at Columbia, he pursued his animal research. Upon graduation, Thorndike returned to his first love, educational psychology, which—along with psychometrics—he made his field of study. Thorndike's importance for us is in his methodological and theoretical approach to animal learning and in his formulation of an S–R psychology he called connectionism.

Thorndike's animal researches are summarized in *Animal Intelligence,* which appeared in 1911. It includes his most important work, the report on his graduate studies, "Animal Intelligence: An Experimental Study of the Associative Processes in Animals," originally published in 1898. In the introduction, Thorndike defined the usual problem of animal psychology: "to learn the development of mental life down through the phylum, to trace in particular the origin of the human faculty" (1911, p. 22). However, he deprecated the value of previous research, for it relied on the anecdotal method, which Thorndike argued focused only on unusual animal performances, not on the typical. As a substitute Thorndike argued that the experimental approach is the only way to completely control the animal's situation. Thorndike's goal was, by experiment, to catch animals "using their minds."

Thorndike placed an animal in one of many "puzzle boxes," each of which could be opened by the animal in a different way. When the animal escaped, it was fed. Thorndike's subjects included cats, chicks, and dogs. Thorndike's setup is an example of what would later be called operant conditioning or learning: An animal makes some response, and if it is rewarded—in Thorndike's case, with escape and food—the response is learned. If the response is not rewarded, it gradually disappears.

Thorndike's results led him to heap scorn on the older view of the anecdotal psychologists that animals reason; animals learn, he said, solely by trial and error, reward and punishment. In a passage that foreshadowed the future, Thorndike wrote that animals may have no ideas at all, no ideas to associate. There is association, but (maybe) not of ideas. Wrote Thorndike: "The effective part of the association [is] a direct bond between the situation and the impulse" (1911, p. 98). In 1898, Thorndike could not quite accept this radical thesis, although he acknowledged its plausibility.

Thorndike's scorn for the old animal psychology did not escape sharp replies. Wesley Mills (1847–1915), America's senior animal psychologist, attacked Thorndike for having swept away "almost the entire fabric of comparative psychology" and for regarding his predecessors as "insane." Mills argued that animals could only be properly investigated in their natural settings, not in the artificial confines of the laboratory. Directly addressing Thorndike's studies, Mills turned sarcastic: Thorndike "placed cats in boxes only $20 \times 15 \times 12$ inches, and then expected them to act naturally. As well enclose a living man in a coffin, lower him, against his will, into the earth, and attempt to deduce normal psychology from his behavior" (Mills, 1899, p. 266). By 1904, however, Mills had to concede the ascendancy of "the laboratory school," led by Thorndike, "the chief agnostic of this school." They denied that animals reason, or plan, or imitate. But Mills, and Wolfgang Köhler, maintained that animals seemed not to reason in the laboratory because their situations did not permit it. Köhler (1925) said that animals were forced into blind trial and error by the construction of Thorndike's puzzle boxes. Because the penned-up subject could not see how the escape mechanism worked, it simply could not reason its way out; without all the relevant information, insight cannot be achieved. So, instead, the poor animal is thrown back on the primitive strategy of trial and error. The method, as Flourens had said of his ablation technique, gives the results. Thorndike's method only permitted random trial and error, so that is what he found. But to go on to claim that all an animal is capable of is mere association is entirely unjustified.

Such considerations did not deter Thorndike from developing his radically simplified theory of learning. In 1911, he wrote, in the introduction to *Animal Intelligence:* Any "of the lower animals is . . . obviously a bundle of original and acquired connections between situation and response" (p. 4). He argued that we should try to study animal behavior, not animal consciousness, because the former problem is easier. He contended that this objective method could be extended to human beings, for we can study mental states as behavior. He criticized the structuralists for fabricating a wholly artificial and imaginary picture of human consciousness. He argued that the purpose of psychology should be the control of behavior: "There can be no moral warrant for studying man's nature unless the study will enable us to control his acts" (p. 15). He concluded his introduction by prophesying that psychology would become the study of behavior.

Thorndike proposed two laws of human and animal behavior. The first was the law of effect: "Of several responses made to the same situation, those which are accompanied or closely followed by satisfaction to the animal will, other things being equal, be more firmly connected with the situation, so that, when it recurs, they will be more likely to recur" (p. 244). Punishment, on the other hand, reduces the strength of the connection. Further, the greater the reward or punishment, the greater the change in the connection. Later, Thorndike abandoned the punishment part of the law of effect, retaining only reward. The law of effect is the basic law of operant conditioning, accepted in some form by most learning theorists. Thorndike's second law is the law of exercise: "Any response to a situation will, all other things being equal, be more strongly connected with the situation in proportion to the number of times it has been connected with that situation, and to the average vigor and duration of the connections" (p. 244).

Thorndike contended that these two laws could account for all behavior, no matter how complex: It would be possible to reduce "the processes of abstraction, association by similarity and selective thinking to mere secondary consequences of the laws of exercise and effect" (p. 263). He analyzed language as a set of vocal responses learned because parents reward some of a child's sounds but not others. The rewarded ones are acquired and the nonrewarded ones are unlearned, following the law of effect.

Thorndike applied his connectionism to human behavior in *Human Learning,* a series of lectures delivered at Cornell in 1928 and 1929. He presented an elaborate

S–R psychology in which many stimuli are connected to many responses in hierarchies of S–R associations. Thorndike asserted that each S–R link could be assigned a probability that S will elicit R. For example, the probability that food will elicit salivation is very near 1.00, while before conditioning the probability that a tone will elicit salivation is near 0. Learning is increasing S–R probabilities; forgetting is lowering them. Just as animal learning is automatic, unmediated by an awareness of the contingency between response and reward, so, Thorndike argues, is human learning also unconscious. A person may learn an operant response without being aware that he or she is doing so. As he did for animals, Thorndike reduced human reasoning to automatism, custom, and habit. Thorndike held out the promise of scientific utopia, founded on eugenics and scientifically managed education.

Thorndike recognized a number of difficulties with his S–R theory; they were exploited by later critics of behaviorism. For example, he admitted that the objective psychologist, who stresses how the environment determines behavior, has a difficult time defining the situation in which an animal acts. Are all stimuli equally relevant to an act? When I am asked, for example, "What is the cube root of sixty-four?" many other stimuli are acting on me at the same time as this question. Defining the response is equally difficult. I may respond, "Four," but many other behaviors (such as breathing) are also occurring. How do we know what S is connected with what R without recourse to subjective, nonphysical meaning? Thorndike admitted that such questions were reasonable and that answers would have to be given eventually. About reading and listening, Thorndike (1911) wrote: "In the hearing or reading of a paragraph, the connections from the words somehow cooperate to give certain total meanings." That "somehow" concealed a mystery only partially acknowledged. He realized the complexity of language when he said that the number of connections necessary to understand a simple sentence may be well over 100,000, and he conceded that organized language is "far beyond any description given by associationist psychology." In his effective attack on B. F. Skinner's theory of language, Noam Chumsky would later echo Thorndike's worries (Chapter 14).

Was Thorndike a behaviorist? His biographer (Joncich, 1968) says he was, and she can cite in support such statements as this: "Our reasons for believing in the existence of other people's minds are our experiences of their physical actions." He did formulate the basic law of operant learning, the law of effect, and the doctrine that consciousness is unnecessary for learning. Unlike Pavlov, he practiced a purely behavioral psychology without reference to physiology. On the other hand, he proposed a principle of "belongingness" that violates a basic principle of classical conditioning, that those elements most closely associated in space and time will be connected in learning. The sentences "John is a butcher. Harry is a carpenter. Jim is a doctor." presented in a list like this, would make butcher–Harry a stronger bond than butcher–John if the classical conditioning contiguity theory were correct. However, this is clearly not the case. John and butcher "belong" together (because of the structure of the sentences) and so will be associated, and recalled, together. This principle of belongingness resembled Gestalt psychology rather than behaviorism.

Historically, Thorndike is hard to place. He did not found behaviorism, though he practiced it in his animal researches. His devotion to educational psychology quickly took him outside of the mainstream of academic experimental psychology in which behaviorism developed. It might best be concluded that Thorndike was a behavioralist but not a wholehearted behaviorist.

The Neuroscience of I. P. Pavlov (1849–1936)

The other most important new experimental approach to animal psychology grew from Russian objective psychology, an uncompromisingly materialistic and mechanistic conception of biology. The founder of modern Russian physiology was Ivan Michailovich Sechenov (1829–1905), who studied in some of the best physiological laboratories in Europe, including Helmholtz's, and who brought back their methods and ideas to Russia. Sechenov believed that psychology, which was known to him only as a branch of philosophy, could be scientific only if it were completely taken over by physiology and adopted physiology's objective methods. Introspective psychology he dismissed as akin to primitive superstition. Sechenov (1973, pp. 350–1, translation anonymous) wrote:

> Physiology will begin by separating psychological reality from the mass of psychological fiction which even now fills the human mind. Strictly adhering to the principle of induction, physiology will begin with a detailed study of the more simple aspects of psychical life and will not rush at once into the sphere of the highest psychological phenomena. Its progress will therefore lose in rapidity, but it will gain in reliability. As an experimental science, physiology will not raise to the rank of incontrovertible truth anything that cannot be confirmed by exact experiments; this will draw a sharp boundary-line between hypotheses and positive knowledge. Psychology will thereby lose its brilliant universal theories; there will appear tremendous gaps in its supply of scientific data; many explanations will give place to a laconic "we do not know"; the essence of the psychical phenomena manifested in consciousness (and, for the matter of that, the essence of all other phenomena of nature) will remain an inexplicable enigma in all cases without exception. And yet, psychology will gain enormously, for it will be based on scientifically verifiable facts instead of the deceptive suggestions of the voice of our consciousness. Its generalizations and conclusions will be limited to actually existing analogies, they will not be subject to the influence of the personal preferences of the investigator which have so often led psychology to absurd transcendentalism, and they still thereby become really objective scientific hypotheses. The subjective, the arbitrary and the fantastic will give way to a nearer or more remote approach to truth. In a word, psychology will become a positive science. Only physiology can do all this, for only physiology holds the key to the scientific analysis of psychical phenomena.

Sechenov, like American functionalists, abandoned mentalism. Psychology is to be positive, concerned with objective, public facts. Starting with the simple, it will proceed to the more complex while being cautious and unspeculative. It will ignore consciousness.

Sechenov's great work was *Reflexes of the Brain* (1863/1965), in which he wrote: "All the external manifestations of brain activity can be attributed to muscular movement. . . . Billions of diverse phenomena, having seemingly no relationship to each other, can be reduced to the activity of several dozen muscles" (p. 308). Watson's peripheralism is found in Sechenov: "Thought is generally believed to be the cause of behavior . . . [but this is] the greatest of falsehoods: [for] the initial cause of all behavior always lies, not in thought, but in external sensory stimulation" (p. 321). He also stated that all conscious, voluntary movements are reflexes. Elsewhere, he too adopted the model of language as a chain of vocal responses.

Sechenov's objectivism was popularized by Vladimir Michailovitch Bechterev (1867–1927), who called his system reflexology, a name that accurately describes its character. However, the greatest of Sechenov's followers, though not his student, was Ivan Petrovich Pavlov (1849–1936), one of psychology's few household names. Pavlov was a physiologist whose studies of digestion won him the Nobel Prize in 1904. In the course of this work, he discovered that stimuli other than food may produce salivation, and this led him to the study of psychology, especially to the concept of the conditioned reflex and its exhaustive investigation.

Pavlov's general attitude was uncompromisingly objective and materialistic. He had the positivists' faith in objective method as the touchstone of natural science, and consequently he rejected reference to mind. In 1903, Pavlov wrote: "For the naturalist everything lies in the method, in the chance of obtaining an unshakable, lasting truth; and solely from this point of view . . . the soul . . . is not only unnecessary but even harmful to his work" (1903/1957, p. 168). Pavlov rejected any appeal to an active inner agency, or mind, in favor of an analysis of the environment: It should be possible to explain behavior without reference to a "fantastic internal world," referring only to "the influence of external stimuli, their summation, etc." His analysis of thinking was atomistic and reflexive. "The entire mechanism of thinking consists in the elaboration of elementary associations and in the subsequent formation of chains of associations." His criticism of nonatomistic psychology was unremitting. He carried out replications of Köhler's ape experiments in order to show that "association is knowledge, . . . thinking . . . [and] insight" (p. 586, from Wednesday Discussion Group statements, c. 1934–5), and he devoted many meetings of his weekly Wednesday discussion group to unfriendly analyses of Gestalt concepts. He viewed the Gestaltists as dualists who "did not understand anything" of their own experiments.

Pavlov's technical contribution to the psychology of learning was considerable. He discovered classical conditioning and inaugurated a systematic research program to discover all its mechanisms and situational determinants. In the course of his Nobel Prize-winning investigation of canine salivation, Pavlov observed that salivation could later be elicited by stimuli present at the time food was presented to an animal. He originally called these learned reactions psychical secretions because they were elicited by noninnate stimuli, but later he substituted the term conditioned response.*

Following the fully refined paradigm of classical conditioning, one begins with a reflex elicited by some innate stimulus, as salivation is elicited by presentation of food. This connection is between an unconditioned stimulus (US) and an unconditioned response (UR). Then, while presenting the US, one presents some other stimulus that does not elicit the reflex, such as the sound of a metronome. This stimulus is called the conditioned stimulus (CS), for, after several pairings with the US, it will come to elicit the same response (UR), now called the conditioned response (CR). It is also possible, although more difficult, to establish a new CS–CR relationship starting with a previously learned CS–CR relationship (for example, pairing a tone with the metronome sound to get the tone to elicit salivation). Such a procedure is known as higher-order conditioning.

Pavlov systematically investigated conditioned reflexes. He found that conditioned responses will occur to stimuli similar to the original CS; this is called *generalization*. Further, Pavlov found that one could require that an animal make a CR to one stimulus but not another; this is called *discrimination*. If too-fine discriminations

---

* This is the English term. However, a more accurate rendering of ooslovny would have been conditional response.

are required of an animal, it displays neurotic-like symptoms. Pavlov also studied how to inhibit conditioned reflexes. If one repeatedly presents the CS without the US, eventually the CR will disappear; this is called *extinction*. However, if one leaves the animal alone for a while, the CS will again elicit the CR; this is called *spontaneous recovery*. There is also *conditioned inhibition,* in which one presents the CS and some new CS together without the US, although the old CS is still occasionally paired with the US. After a while, the new combination will fail to elicit the CR. Pavlov's researches were meticulous and detailed, one of the best examples in psychology of a research program in Lakatos's sense.

Between them, Thorndike and Pavlov contributed important methods to psychology, especially the psychology of learning. At the same time, each questioned the need for psychologists and biologists to talk about animal mind. Thorndike found only blind association forming in his animals, denying that animals reason or even imitate. Pavlov, following Sechenov, proposed to substitute physiology for psychology, eliminating talk about the mind for talk about the brain. La Mettrie's vision seemed about to be fulfilled.

The Problem of Animal Mind

The trouble with animal psychology, said E. C. Sanford in his 1902 presidential address to the APA, is that it "tempts us beyond the bounds of introspection," as do the other growing elements of comparative psychology, the studies of children, the retarded, and the abnormal. But, Sanford asked, should we be "content with a purely objective science of animal or child or idiot behavior?" Sanford thought not and spelled out why, recognizing, with Romanes, the logical conclusion of an objective psychology:

> I doubt if anyone has ever seriously contemplated [a purely objective psychology] in the case of the higher animals, or could carry it to fruitful results if he should undertake it. Nor would anyone seriously propose to treat the behavior of his fellow men in the same way, i.e., to refuse to credit them with conscious experience in the main like his own, though this would seem to be required logically. (1903, p. 105)

However, comparative psychologists still faced Descartes's problem: If they were going to infer mental processes in animals, they had to come up with some criterion of the mental. Just which behaviors could be explained as due to mechanism alone, and which ones reflected mental processes? Descartes had had a simple answer, suited to the Age of Reason: The soul, not the body, thinks; so language—the expression of thought—is the mark of the mental. Things were not so simple for comparative psychologists, though. Accepting phylogenetic continuity and having disposed of the soul, Descartes's criterion was no longer plausible. It seemed clear that the higher animals possess minds and that paramecia do not (although a few animal psychologists thought they did possess very low-grade intelligence), but exactly where to draw the line was intensely problematic.

Comparative psychologists wrestled with the problem and proposed numerous criteria, thoughtfully reviewed (1905a) by Robert Yerkes (1876–1956), a leading animal psychologist. Like Sanford, Romanes, and others, Yerkes knew the problem was important for human psychology, too, for we know other human minds just as much by inference as we know animal minds. Indeed, "human psychology stands or falls with comparative psychology. If the study of the mental life of lower animals is not legitimate, no more is the study of human consciousness" (Yerkes, 1905b).

As Yerkes saw it, proposed "criteria of the psychic" could be divided into two broad categories. First, there were the structural criteria: An animal might be said to have a mind if it had a sufficiently sophisticated nervous system. More important were the functional criteria, behaviors that indicated presence of mind. Among the possible functional criteria, Yerkes found that most workers took learning to be the mark of the mind and arranged their experiments to see whether a given species could learn. Such a criterion was consistent with James's Darwinian psychology and with contemporary developments in functional psychology. As we have seen, functionalists, following James, viewed consciousness as, above all, an adjustive agency, so naturally they looked for signs of adjustment in their subjects. An animal that could not learn would be regarded as a mere automaton.

Yerkes thought the search for a single criterion simplistic, and he proposed three grades, or levels, of consciousness, corresponding to three classes of behavior. At the lowest level was discriminative consciousness, indicated by the ability to discriminate one stimulus from another; even a sea anemone had this grade of consciousness. Next, Yerkes proposed a grade of intelligent consciousness, whose sign was learning. Finally, there was rational consciousness, which initiates behaviors rather than just responding, however flexibly, to environmental challenges.

At least one young psychologist was coming to find the whole problem a hopeless tangle. John B. Watson was a graduate student of Angell's at the University of Chicago, stronghold of Dewey's instrumentalism and psychological functionalism. Watson disliked introspection and took up animal psychology. His dissertation, "Animal Education," which was cowritten by Angell, had very little mentalism in it and was mostly an attempt to find a physiological basis for learning. As a promising animal psychologist, Watson was one of the main reviewers of the literature in animal psychology for *Psychological Bulletin,* and there we find him becoming bored by the controversy over the criterion of the mental. In 1907, he called it "the *bête noir* of the student of behavior," and asserted, "The whole contention is tedious." However, he was still at Chicago under Angell's eye, and he defended a psychology of animal mind. Mind could not be eliminated from psychology, as long as mind–body parallelism was its working hypothesis.

In the fall of 1908, Watson obtained a position at Johns Hopkins University; away from Angell and on his own, he became bolder. At a talk before the Scientific Association of Johns Hopkins, the newly arrived professor said that the study of animal behavior could be carried out purely objectively, producing facts on a par with the other natural sciences; no reference to animal mind was made (Swartz, 1908).

On December 31 of that same year, Watson (1909) spelled out "A Point of View in Comparative Psychology" for the Southern Society for Philosophy and Psychology, then meeting at John Hopkins. Watson reviewed the controversy surrounding the criteria of consciousness in animals, and stated (quoting E. F. Buchner, the society's secretary) "that these criteria are impossible of application and . . . have been valueless to the science" of animal behavior. Watson argued that the "facts of behavior" are valuable in themselves and do not have to be "grounded in any criteria of the psychic." Human psychology, too, Watson said, is coming to be more objective, seeming to abandon the use of introspection and "the speech reaction." These trends away from introspection will lead psychology toward "the perfection of technique of the physical sciences." As "criteria of the psychic . . . disappear" from psychology, it will study the whole "process of adjustment" in "all of its broad biological aspects" rather than focusing narrowly on a few elements caught in a moment of introspection. Although Watson would not proclaim behaviorism as such until 1913, it is clear that the "viewpoint" he described that afternoon in McCoy Hall was behaviorism in all but name. For Watson, criteria of the mental were useless in animal psychology. Grasping the nettle of the logic of his argument, he had concluded that criteria of the mental were useless in human psychology, too.

RETHINKING MIND: THE CONSCIOUSNESS DEBATE (1904–1912)

Mind's place in nature was being fundamentally revised by functional psychologists and by their colleagues in animal psychology. Mind was becoming problematic, reduced to a problem-solving genie in later functional psychology, and slowly disappearing altogether in animal psychology. In 1904, philosophers, too, began to reexamine consciousness.

Does Consciousness Exist? Radical Empiricism

Pragmatism was a method for finding the truth, not a substantive philosophical position. James, nearing the end of his life, turned to the problems of metaphysics and worked out a system he called "radical empiricism," beginning in 1904 with a paper called "Does 'Consciousness' Exist?" As always, James was provocative, setting off a debate among philosophers and psychologists that reshaped their conceptions of mind.

James argued that consciousness did not exist as a distinct, separate thing apart from experience. There simply is experience: hardness, redness, tones, tastes, smells. There is nothing above and beyond it called "consciousness" that possesses it and knows it. Pure experience is the stuff of which the world is made, James held. Rather than being a thing, consciousness is a function, a certain kind of relationship among portions of pure experience.

James's position is complex and difficult to grasp, for it involves a novel form of idealism (experience is the stuff of reality) and panpsychism (everything in the world, even a desk, is conscious). For psychology, what was important was the debate James began, because out of it arose two new conceptions of consciousness that supported behavioralism: the relational theory of consciousness and the functional theory of consciousness.

The Relational Theory of Consciousness: Neorealism

To some extent, the important place of consciousness in psychology and philosophy derived from the copy theory of knowledge. The copy theory asserts, as James put it, a "radical dualism" of object and knower. For the copy theory, consciousness contains representations of the world and knows the world only through the representations. It follows, then, that consciousness is a mental world of representations separate from the physical world of things. In this traditional definition of psychology, the science of psychology studied the world of representations with the special method of introspection, and natural sciences such as physics studied the world of objects constructed by observation. James's challenge to the copy theory inspired a group of young American philosophers to propose a form of realism that owed nothing to the old Scottish realists.

They called themselves neorealists and asserted what they took to be a scientific theory of mind: There is a world of physical objects that we know directly, without the mediation of internal representations. Although this theory is epistemological in aim—asserting the knowability of a real external physical world—it carries interesting implications for psychology. For, in this realist view, consciousness is not a special inner world to be reported on by introspection. Rather, consciousness is a relationship between self and world, the relationship of knowing. This was the basic idea of the relational theory of consciousness, and it was developed in these years by Ralph Barton Perry (1876–1957), James's biographer and a teacher of E. C. Tolman; by Edwin Bissel Holt (1873–1946), with Perry at Harvard, and Münsterberg's successor as Harvard's experimental psychologist; and by Edgar Singer (1873–1954), whose papers on mind would later be regarded by some as the first and best statements of behaviorism.

The development of the neorealist theory of mind began with Perry's analysis of the allegedly privileged nature of introspection. Since Descartes, philosophers had supposed that consciousness was a private, inward possession of representations, known only to itself; on this idea, much of Descartes's radical dualism of world and mind rested. In the traditional view, introspection was a special sort of observation of a special place, quite different from the usual sort of observation of external objects. Traditional mentalistic psychology accepted the radical dualism of mind and object and enshrined introspection as the observational technique peculiar to the study of consciousness. Perry argued that introspection was special only in trivial ways, and that the "mind within" of introspection was in no essential way different from the "mind without" exhibited in everyday behavior.

Asking me to introspect is certainly an easy way to enter my mind, Perry conceded. Only I have my memories, and only I know to what I am attending at any given moment. But in these instances introspection is not specially privileged, nor is mind a private place. What I experienced in the past could in principle be determined by other observers present when memories were laid down; careful observation of my current behavior will reveal to what I am paying attention. In short, contents of consciousness are not exclusively my own: Anyone else may discover them. Indeed, such is the method of animal psychology, said Perry: We discover animal mind by attending to animal behavior, reading an animal's intentions and mental content by observing the way it behaves toward the objects in its environment. As Bolton had argued, an object perceived is an object acted toward, so an animal's percepts are revealed by its conduct.

Another kind of knowledge that seems to make self-consciousness and introspection special sources of knowledge is knowledge of the states of one's own body. No one else has my headache, and, in this sense, introspection is privileged. But Perry refused to see that any momentous conclusion was to be drawn from this circumstance. In the first place, although one does not have direct awareness of another's inner bodily states, one can easily know about them from one's own analogous states: you do not have my headache, but you know what a headache is. Second, inner bodily processes could be better known by a properly equipped outsider. "Who is so familiar with farming as the farmer?" Perry asked. No one, obviously; nonetheless, an expert who is scientifically trained may be able to tell the farmer how to grow more efficiently. Similarly, inner bodily processes are not one's exclusive possession; they are open to physiological study. Finally, to assert special introspective access to bodily states is a very trivial defense of introspective psychology, because such contents are hardly the essence of mind.

If we follow Perry, we must conclude that mentalistic psychology is misguided. Consciousness is not a private thing known only to myself and shareable only through introspection. Rather, my consciousness is a collection of sensations derived from the external world or from my own body; with James, Perry maintained there is no entity of "consciousness" apart from experienced sensations. But because these sensations may be known by anyone else, my mind is, in fact, an open book, a public object open to scientific study. Introspection remains pragmatically useful, of course, because no one has as convenient access to my sensations, past and present, as I have; so the psychologist who wishes to open my mind should simply ask me to look within and report what I find. In Perry's view, however, introspection alone is not the road to the mind, because mind is always on view as behavior. In principle, then, psychology can be conducted as a purely behavioral enterprise, engaging its subjects' self-awareness when expedient, but otherwise attending only to behavior. Perry's philosophical analysis of mind coincides ultimately with the view being developed in animal psychology: Mind and behavior are, functionally, the same, and both animal and human psychology rest on the same basis—the study of behavior.

Perry claimed anyone's consciousness could be known by a sufficiently well-informed outside observer. E. B. Holt, with his theory of specific response, took consciousness out of a person's head and put it in the environment. Holt argued that the contents of consciousness were just a cross section of the objects of the universe, past or present, distant or near, to which a person is responding. To clarify his proposal, Holt offered an analogy: Consciousness is like a flashlight's beam in a darkened room, revealing the things we see and leaving others in the dark. Similarly, at any given moment, we are reacting only to some of the objects in the universe, and these are the ones of which we are conscious. So consciousness is not inside a person at all but is "out there wherever the things specifically responded to are." Even memory was treated the same way: Memory is not the recovery of some past idea stored away and recalled, but it is simply the presentation before consciousness of an absent object.

Holt's view, like Perry's, rejected the alleged privacy of mind. If consciousness is no more than specific response, and its contents no more than an inventory of the objects controlling my current behavior, then anyone who turns the flashlight of consciousness on the same objects as mine will know my mind. Behavior, Holt argued, is always controlled by or directed toward some real object—that is, a goal—and behavior is to be explained by discovering the acted-toward objects. To do psychology, we need not—though, of course, we may—ask our subjects to introspect. We may understand their minds by examining their behavior and the circumstances in which it occurs, abandoning mentalistic for behavioralistic psychology. Objects to which an organism reacts are those of which it is conscious, said Holt; hence, the study of consciousness and the study of behavior were essentially the same.

Although he was not formally a neorealist, E. A. Singer proposed a behavioral concept of mind consistent with Perry's or Holt's. Singer applied the pragmatic test of truth to the problem of other minds: Does it matter, does it make a difference to our conduct whether other people have conscious experience or not? Singer argued that, pragmatically, the "other minds" problem is meaningless, because it cannot be resolved. It had been debated by philosophers and psychologists since Descartes with no sign of progress. So we should conclude that it is only a pseudoproblem incapable of solution: It doesn't matter.

Singer then considered a possible pragmatic objection that consciousness in others does deeply matter to our everyday behavior. James (1907/1955) once asked us to consider the "automatic sweetheart." Suppose you are deeply in love: Every adoring glance, every gentle caress, every tender sigh you will take as signs of your sweetheart's love for you; everything she does will bespeak a love for you like yours for her. Then, one day, you discover she is only a machine, cleverly constructed to exhibit tokens of love for you; she is not conscious, being but a machine, a simulacrum of a sweetheart. Do you love her still? James thought one could not; that vital to love is not just the glances, caresses, and sighs but the conviction that behind them is a mental state called love, a subjective condition of fondness, affection, and commitment like one's own. In short, belief in other minds passes the pragmatic test, James concluded, for we will feel very differently about—and, of course, act very differently toward—a creature depending on whether we think it possesses a mind.

Singer tried to refute James's argument. He asked how terms such as "mind" or "soul" or "soulless" are used in practice. They are inferences from behaviors, constructions we erect out of another's conduct. These constructions may be wrong, of course, and we discover our error when our expectations about a person's behavior are not fulfilled. In the case of the automatic sweetheart, Singer argued, discovering that she is "soulless" only means that you now fear that her behavior in the future will not be like her behavior in the past; that is, you have just misunderstood her, and falling out of love with her is not due to her not having a mind, but because you no longer can predict how she will act.

Singer went on to argue that mind is an observable object. "Consciousness is not something inferred from behavior, it is behavior. Or, more accurately, our belief in consciousness is an expectation of probable behavior based on observation of actual behavior, a belief to be confirmed or refuted by more observation" (1911, p. 183). We believe in a separate entity called consciousness only because of deeply ingrained habits of thought—most importantly, reification, the tendency to think that if we can name something it exists. So, for example, before the advent of the atomic theory of matter, heat was thought to be a fluid, called *caloric,* that flowed into an object, making it hot, or out of an object, making it cool. Thus, a hot poker was matter (the steel of the poker) plus a fluid, caloric. Similarly, Singer argued, traditionally people thought of a living creature as matter (the physical body) plus a soul. In these cases, people had reified into a separate entity something that merely describes behavior. Heat is not caused by a hidden thing, caloric, but a certain behavior caused by the state of movement in the atoms that compose it. Life is similarly not a thing added to a body (for example, the Greek *psyche*), but the behavior of the body caused by biological states within it. Just as the soul is not a separate substance from the body, Singer maintained, "mind" is not something separate from behavior, it is behavior, falsely reified by us. In Singer's view, then, there is no mind for anyone to investigate: Mentalistic psychology, like the theory of caloric, was a delusion from the start. Psychology should abandon mind, then, and study what is real: behavior.

Whether or not you find Singer's position plausible, his debate with James raised an issue probably more important today than then. For we can now build machines that appear to think, as James's automatic sweetheart appeared to love. Do they really think? And James's own creation has been brought to life in the writings of science-fiction novelists. Can a machine, an android, love? In our age of computers and genetic engineering, these are not idle questions, and we shall meet them again in the new field of cognitive science.

Neorealism did not last long as a philosophical movement. Its primary failing was epistemological, accounting for the problem of error. If we know objects directly and without mediation by ideas, how is it that we have mistaken perceptions? With the copy theory, error is easy to explain by saying that copies may not be accurate. Realism finds error difficult to account for. Realists did, however, have lasting influence. They made philosophy technical and so professionalized it. In psychology, their relational theory of consciousness aided the development of behavioralism and behaviorism, by reworking the mentalistic concept of consciousness into something knowable from behavior, and perhaps even something identical with behavior, in which case the concept of mind need play no role in scientific psychology, however important it might remain outside the profession.

The Functional Theory of Consciousness: Instrumentalism

The neorealists developed the relational conception of mind suggested by James (1904). Dewey and his followers developed the functional conception. Dewey's emerging philosophy was called instrumentalism, because of his emphasis on mind as an effective actor in the world, and on knowledge as an instrument for first understanding and then changing the world. Dewey's conception of mind was thus more active than that of the neorealists, who still adhered to what Dewey called the "spectator theory of mind." Copy theories are spectator theories because the world impresses itself (to use Hume's term) on a passive mind, which then simply copies the impression over into an idea. Although the neorealists rejected the copy theory, they had not, in Dewey's view, gotten away from the spectator theory because, in the relational theory, consciousness is still fully determined by the objects to which one is responding. So mind is still a spectator passively viewing the world, only directly rather than through the spectacles of ideas.

Dewey (1939) got rid of the spectator theory but retained a representational theory of mind. He described mind as a function of the biological organism adapting actively to the environment, a view going back to his 1896 reflex arc paper. As he developed his instrumentalism, Dewey became more specific about what mind actually does. Mind, he proposed, is the presence and operations of meanings, ideas; or, more specifically, mind is the ability to anticipate future consequences and to respond to them as stimuli to present behavior. So, mind is a set of representations of the world that function instrumentally to adaptively guide the organism in its dealings with its environment. Echoing Brentano, Dewey claimed that what makes something mental rather than physical is that it points to something else; that is, it has meaning. Postulation of meanings does not require postulation of a separate realm of mind, for ideas are to be conceived as neurophysiological functions whose total functioning we conveniently designate "mind."

Dewey also stressed the social nature of mind, even coming at times to deny that animals had minds—a change from his 1896 paper. Dewey was impressed by Watson's claim (to be described later) that thinking is just speech, or, more strongly, that vocalization is all thinking consists in, whether such vocalization is out loud or covert. Interestingly, this returns Dewey to Descartes's old view, seemingly rejected by functional psychologists, that animals do not think because they do not talk. Dewey has reversed Descartes's priorities, though. For Descartes, thinking comes first and is only expressed in speech; for Dewey, learning to speak creates the ability to think. Descartes was an individualist, endowing each human with an innately given self-consciousness endowed with thought, but forever isolated from other consciousnesses.

Dewey was, generally speaking, a socialist. Humans do not possess some a priori consciousness; because language—speech—is acquired through social interaction, it follows that thinking, perhaps all of mind, is a social construction rather than a private possession. When we think inwardly, we just "talk" to ourselves rather than out loud, adjustively using our socially given speech-reactions. Dewey, the philosopher of Progressivism, always aimed at reconstructing philosophy and society on a social basis, breaking down individualism and substituting for it group-consciousness and a submerging of the individual into the greater whole. By conceiving of mind as a social construction, the Cartesian privacy of the individual mind was erased. Instead, the truly mindful entity was society itself, the larger organism of which each person was a cooperative part.

CONCLUSION: BEHAVIORALISM DISCOVERED (1910–1912)

By 1910, all the forces moving psychology from mentalism to behavioralism were well engaged. Philosophical idealism, which made the study of consciousness so important, had been replaced by pragmatism, realism, and instrumentalism, all of which denied consciousness a special, privileged place in the universe. The concept of consciousness had been reworked, becoming successively motor response, relation, and function, and could no longer be clearly differentiated from behavior. Animal psychologists were finding mind to be a problematic, even an unnecessary concept in their field. Psychology as a whole, especially in America, was shifting its concern from the structural study of mental content to the functional study of mental processes, at the same time shifting the focus of experimental technique from the introspective ascertaining of mental states to the objective determination of the influence of stimulus on behavior. Lurking behind all these changes was the desire of psychologists to be socially useful, implying the study of behavior—what people do in society—rather than the socially useless study of sensory contents. The shift from mentalism to behavioralism was inevitable, and it only needed to be discovered to be a fait accompli.

Change was in the air. Surveying the year 1910, E. F. Buchner confessed that "some of us are still struggling at initial clearness as to what psychology was about." A signal event of the year was Yerkes's discovery of the "low esteem" in which psychology was held by biologists, whom most psychologists now considered their closest disciplinary colleagues. Surveying leading biologists, Yerkes found that most of them were simply ignorant of psychology, or convinced it would soon disappear into biology. Yerkes concluded that "few, if any, sciences are in worse plight than psychology," attributing its "sad plight" to a lack of self-confidence, an absence of agreed-on principles, poor training of psychologists in physical science, and a failure to teach psychology as anything more than a set of bizarre facts or as a branch of philosophy, instead of as a natural science. Yerkes's survey was widely discussed and clearly troubled psychologists, who had labored long and hard to make of psychology a dignified scientific profession.

Psychologists were casting about for a new central concept around which to organize their science, perhaps rendering it more securely a natural science. Bawden, who was continuing to push his own program of interpreting mind "in terms of hands and feet," observed that recently psychologists, without "being clearly conscious of what was happening," had begun to look at mind afresh, in terms of muscle movement, physiology, and "behavior." In any case, psychology needed a general shift in methods and attitudes away from philosophical conceptions and toward biological ones.

The APA convention of 1911 was dominated by discussion of the place of consciousness in psychology, according to an observer, M. E. Haggerty (1911). He noted with some surprise that no one at the convention defended the traditional definition of psychology as the study of self-consciousness. Speaking in a symposium on "Philosophical and Psychological Uses of the Terms Mind, Consciousness, and Soul," Angell (1911) put his finger on the change from mentalism to behavioralism. Soul, of course, had ceased as a psychological concept when the new psychology replaced the old. But mind, too, Angell noted, was now in "a highly precarious position," and consciousness "is likewise in danger of extinction." Angell defined behavioralism as we did at the beginning of the chapter:

> There is unquestionably a movement on foot in which interest is centered in the results of conscious process, rather than in the processes themselves. This is peculiarly true in animal psychology; it is only less true in human psychology. In these cases interest is in what may for lack of a better term be called "behavior"; and the analysis of consciousness is primarily justified by the light it throws on behavior, rather than vice-versa. (p. 47)

If this movement should go forward, Angell concluded, psychology would become "a general science of behavior," exactly the definition of the field being offered in the latest textbooks of psychology, Parmelee's (1913), C. H. Judd's (1910), and McDougall's (1912).

The year 1912 proved to be pivotal. Buchner observed further confusion about the definition of mind and noted the philosophers and their psychological allies who wanted to identify mind with behavior. Knight Dunlap, Watson's older colleague at Johns Hopkins, used the new relational theory of consciousness to make "the case against introspection." Introspection had value only under a copy theory of mind, Dunlap said, because introspection describes the privileged contents of consciousness. But on a relational view of mind, introspection loses its special character, becoming no more than a description of a real object under special conditions of attention. Introspection is thus not the reporting of an internal object, but merely the reporting of the stimulus currently controlling behavior. The term "introspection," Dunlap concluded, should be restricted to the reporting of internal stimuli, which can be gotten at no other way. Introspection was not the central method of psychology.

Elliot Frost (1912) reported on European physiologists who were taking a radical new view of consciousness. These physiologists, who included Jacques Loeb, an influence on Watson at Chicago, pronounced psychological concepts "superstitions" and found no room for animal consciousness in the explanation of animal behavior. Frost tried to refute these challenges with a functional view of mind as adaptive "consciousizing" behavior.

More important for us are the reductionistic claims of these European physiologists and certain psychologists then and soon to come. Mind may be eliminated from psychology in two ways that are distinct and should be kept separate. The program of the physiologists Frost reviewed, including Pavlov, and of psychologists such as Max Meyer, another influence on Watson, called for the reduction of mental concepts to underlying neurophysiological processes thought to cause them. Mental concepts could be eliminated from science as we learn the material causes the mentalistic terms designate. The other program for eliminating mind was inchoate as yet, and it would be often mixed up with reductionism for years to come. It claims that mental concepts are to be replaced by behavioral ones, which themselves may not be reducible to mechanical underlying physiological laws. We can see something of this view, perfected later by B. F. Skinner, in the relational theories of mind, especially Singer's; but it was not in 1912 a distinct psychological system. The historical importance of the reductionists reviewed by Frost remains—the validity of consciousness and mind as central concepts in psychology was under increasing assault from every quarter.

The December 1912 meeting of the APA in Cleveland marked the final transition of psychology, with only a few holdouts, from mentalism to behavioralism. Angell (1913) identified the behavioral view in "Behavior as a Category of Psychology." Angell began by recalling his own prophecy, made at the 1910 APA meeting, that the study of behavior was overshadowing the study of consciousness. Just two years later, consciousness had become a "victim marked for slaughter," as behavior was poised to completely replace mental life as the subject matter of psychology. In philosophy, the consciousness debate questioned consciousness's very existence. In animal psychology, researchers wanted to give up reference to mind and just study behavior, matched by a "general drift" in the same direction in human psychology. This drift, Angell pointed out, is "not deliberate" and is thus likely to be "substantial and enduring."

Moreover, there were many flourishing fields concerned with human beings in which introspection offered "no adequate approach": social psychology, racial psychology, sociology, economics, development, individual differences, and others. The tendency to eliminate introspection is not just a product of new topics like those mentioned, but it is aided by functional psychology, which studies response more than conscious content.

Angell was not willing to completely abandon introspection. While it could no longer be psychology's premier method, it retained an important role in providing data not otherwise obtainable. It would be a "crowning absurdity," Angell said, for the new behavioral psychology to deny any significance to the "chief distinction" of human nature—mind. There was another danger in a behavioral psychology, Angell warned. By concentrating on behavior, psychologists would trespass on the territory of another science, biology; and thus there was a risk that psychology might be "swallowed up" by biology, or might become a mere vassal to biology as its "overlord."

Still, there was no mistaking Angell's message. Psychology was now the study of behavior. It was a natural science closely allied to biology, forsaking its philosophical roots. Its methods were now objective, introspection serving pragmatically when needed, but no longer at the center of the field. Concern with consciousness as such had been replaced by concern with the explanation, prediction, and control of behavior. The psychology viewed with such horror by Warner Fite had arrived.

BIBLIOGRAPHY

A general overview of the period is given by John L. Thomas in "Nationalizing the republic," his contribution to Bailyn et al., *The great republic* (Boston: Little, Brown, 1977). The standard history of the transformation of America at the turn of the century is Robert Wiebe, *The search for order 1877–1920* (New York: Hill and Wang, 1967). Daniel Boorstin concludes his history of the United States in *The Americans: The democratic experience* (New York: Vintage Books, 1974), which provides a wonderfully readable, even entertaining, account of twentieth-century America, entirely dispensing with political and military history. There are several good histories of Progressivism: Richard Hofstadter, *The age of reform* (New York: Vintage Books, 1975); Eric Goldman, *Rendezvous with destiny,* rev. ed. (New York: Vintage Books, 1975); and two books by David Noble, *The paradox of Progressive thought* (Minneapolis: University of Minnesota Press), and *The Progressive mind,* rev. ed. (Minneapolis: Burgess, 1981). Works that concentrate on intellectual and social aspects of the period include Henry F. May, *The end of American innocence* (Chicago: Quadrangle, 1964); and Morton White, *Social thought in America* (London: Oxford University Press, 1976); and *Science and sentiment in America* (London: Oxford University Press, 1972).

Dewey's philosophy is central to the thought of the first part of the twentieth century. Two useful accounts of his intellectual development are Morton G. White, *The origin of Dewey's instrumentalism* (New York: Octagon, 1964), and the chapter on Dewey in E. Flower and M. Murphey, *A history of philosophy in America* (New York: Capricorn, 1977). Dewey was the leading educational philosopher in this period, which witnessed far-ranging debate about the nature and aims of education, as schools were refashioned to meet the needs of a mass, industrialized society. Merle Curti, *The social ideas of American educators,* rev. ed. (Paterson, NJ: Littlefield, Adams, 1965), summarizes the views not only of Dewey, but of James and Thorndike, to mention only the psychologists. Curti's book was originally published in 1931 and reflects an apparently socialist point of view that leads to much criticism of everyone but Dewey for putting too much emphasis on the individual. For Dewey's life, see R. B. Westbrook, *John Dewey and American democracy* (Ithaca, NY: Cornell University Press, 1991). John Patrick Diggins, *The promise of pragmatism: Modernism and the crisis of knowledge and authority* (Chicago: University of Chicago Press, 1994), sets the pragmatists in their larger intellectual and social context, focusing on Dewey, but including James and the links of pragmatism to Progressivism.

There are three important book-length studies of psychology in this period. Brian Mackenzie, *Behaviorism and the limits of scientific method* (London: Routledge and Kegan Paul, 1977), ties behaviorism closely to positivism (as did the first edition of the present text) and to the problem of animal mind. John M. O'Donnell's *The origins of behaviorism: American psychology 1870–1920* (New York: New York University Press, 1985), argues that behaviorism emerged gradually and inevitably out of American realist, new, and functional psychology. Reba N. Soffer's *Ethics and society in England: The revolution in the social sciences 1870–1914* (Berkeley: University of California Press, 1978), covers England for the same period we've covered America and relates similar developments there to the British intellectual climate, claiming, contrary to the thesis I have argued, that a "revolution" took place during these years.

A valuable source for the history of psychology from its founding days onward is the continuing series called *A history of psychology in autobiography.* The first three volumes, which cover the period here, were edited by Carl Murchison and published by Clark University Press. Subsequent volumes have been published under varying editorship and by different publishers, but always under the same title.

Perhaps because of their tenuous status as scientists, psychologists were acutely conscious of the history of their discipline in its early years and often wrote historical summaries of even recent developments. Edward Franklin Buchner wrote several such reviews, including an annual piece in *Psychological Bulletin,* from 1904 to 1912, called "Progress in psychology," and two general accounts, "Ten years of American psychology," *Science* (1903, *18:* 193–204) and "A quarter century of psychology in America," *American Journal of Psychology* (1903, *13:* 666–80). Another general summary from the same period is James Mark Baldwin, "A sketch of the history of psychology," *Psychological Review* (1905, *12:* 144–5). Christian Ruckmich, "The history and status of psychology in the United States," *American Journal of Psychology* (1912, *23:* 517–31), is a valuable institutional history, including not only accounts of the founding of laboratories and so on, but a comparative economic analysis of the status within universities of psychology compared with other disciplines. Another institutional history, by a participant, is J. M. Cattell, "Early psychological laboratories," *Science* (1928, *67:* 543–8).

Perhaps the final confrontation between the old psychology and the new occurred on April 27, 1895, at the Massachusetts Schoolmaster's Club, when Larkin Dunton and W. T. Harris, educators in the old mold, confronted Hugo Münsterberg and G. Stanley Hall, new psychologists. The encounter was published as *The old psychology and the new* (Boston: New England Publishing Co., 1895).

The writings of, and some contemporary comments on, the pragmatist philosophers Peirce, James, and Dewey have been collected by Amelie Rorty, *Pragmatic philosophy* (Garden City, NY: Doubleday), and H. Standish Thayer, *Pragmatism: The classic writings* (New York: Mentor, 1970). Bruce Kuklick's *Rise of American philosophy* (New Haven, CT: Yale University Press, 1977), traces the development of pragmatism and sets it against a larger framework. Dewey's major psychological papers have been gathered up by Joseph Ratner, *John Dewey: Philosophy, psychology, and social practice* (New York: Capricorn, 1965).

The presidential addresses of the presidents of the APA have been summarized, and the more important ones reprinted, in Ernest R. Hilgard, *American psychology in historical perspective* (Washington, DC: American Psychological Association, 1978).

In addition to the referenced works, students interested in animal psychology, Thorndike, and Pavlov may wish to consult the following. B. P. Babkin has written a biography, *Pavlov* (Chicago: University of Chicago Press, 1949); his experimental research program is detailed in *Conditioned reflexes,* available as a reprint paperback (New York: Dover Books, 1960). Thorndike's application of his learning theory may be found in his *Educational psychology* (New York: Arno, 1964), the brief edition of which appeared almost simultaneously with Watson's *Behaviorism* (1914). Watson wrote two popular articles for *Harper's Magazine* (1909, *120:* 346–53, and 1912, *124:* 376–82), which, although they offer few clues to his incipient behaviorism, are good accounts of early twentieth-century animal psychology. A fine history of animal psychology is given by Robert Boakes, *From Darwin to behaviorism: Psychology and the minds of animals* (New York: Cambridge University Press, 1984). Thomas Cadwallader, "Neglected aspects of the evolution of American comparative and animal psychology," in G. Greenberg and E. Tobach, eds., *Behavioral evolution and integrative levels* (Hillsdale, NJ: Erlbaum, 1984), concentrates on the American scene.

There are two good places to enter the consciousness debate. The debate grew so important that the American Philosophical Association decided to devote its 1912 convention to the problem. To prepare for the meeting, the Association appointed a committee to summarize the main points of the debate and to draw up a bibliography. The committee's report appears in *Journal of Philosophy* (1911, *8:* 701–8). The debate continued in philosophy past 1912 and eventually inspired an excellent treatment of the problem of consciousness, including views and issues not treated in the text, by Charles Morris, *Six theories of mind* (Chicago: University of Chicago Press, 1932). Between these two, every aspect of the debate is covered, and all the relevant literature is cited, with the exception (for some unknown reason) of the papers of Edgar Singer. His key paper was "Mind as an observable object," *Journal of*

Philosophy (1911, *8:* 180–6), followed up in the same publication with two replies the next year, "Consciousness and behavior," *Journal of Philosophy* (1912, *9:* 15–9), and "On mind as observable object," *Journal of Philosophy* (1912, *9:* 206–14).

In "The Mythical of revolutions of American psychology," *American Psychologist* (1992, *47:* 308–318), I provide a more detailed argument that behaviorism did not effect a revolution in psychology.

REFERENCES

Angell, J. R. (1903a). A preliminary study of the localization of sound. *Psychological Review 10:* 1–18.

_____ . (1903b). The relation of structural and functional psychology to philosophy. *Philosophical Review 12:* 243–71.

_____ . (1907). The province of functional psychology. *Psychological Review 14:* 61–91.

_____ , (1911), Usages of the terms mind, consciousness, and soul. *Psychological Bulletin 8:* 46–7.

_____ . (1913). Behavior as a category of psychology. *Psychological Review 20:* 255–70.

Arnold, F. (1905). Psychological standpoints. *Psychological Bulletin 2:* 369–73.

Baldwin, J. M. (1895). *Mental development in the child and the race.* New York: Macmillan.

Bawden, H. H. (1903). The functional theory of parallelism. *Philosophical Review 12:* 299–319.

_____ . (1904). The meaning of the psychical in functional psychology. *Philosophical Review 13:* 298–319.

_____ . (1910). Mind as a category of psychology. *Psychological Bulletin 7:* 221–5.

Bernard, L. L. (1911). *The transition to an objective standard of social control.* Chicago: University of Chicago Press.

Bolton, T. (1902). A biological view of perception. *Psychological Review 9:* 537–48.

Boorstin, D. J. (1974). *The Americans: The democratic experience.* New York: Vintage Books.

Bryan, W. L. and Harter, N. (1897). Studies in the psychology of the telegraphic language. *Psychological Review 4:* 27–53.

Calkins, M. W. (1906). A reconciliation between structural and functional psychology. *Psychological Review 13:* 61–81.

Cattell, J. M. (1896). Address of the president. *Psychological Review 3:* 134–48.

_____ . (1904). The conceptions and methods of psychology. *Popular Science Monthly 66:* 176–86

Danziger, K. (1979). The social origins of modern psychology. In A. Buss, ed., *Psychology in social context.* New York: Irvington.

Dewey, J. (1896). The reflex arc concept in psychology. *Psychological Review 3:* 357–70.

_____ . (1900/1978). Psychology and social practice. *Psychological Review 7:* 105–24. Reprinted in E. R. Hilgard, ed., *American psychology in historical perspective: Addresses of the Presidents of the American Psychological Association 1892–1977.* Washington, DC: APA.

_____ . (1939). *Intelligence in the modern world: The philosophy of John Dewey.* J. Ratner, ed. New York. Modern Library.

_____ . (1920/1948/1957). *Reconstruction in philosophy.* Boston: Beacon Press.

Ebbinghaus, H. (1885/1964). *Memory.* New York: Dover Books.

Fite, W. (1913, April 10). The science of man. *The Nation 96:* 368–70.

Frost, E. P. (1912). Can biology and physiology dispense with consciousness? *Psychological Review 3:* 246–52.

Haggerty, M. E. (1911). The nineteenth annual meeting of the A.P.A. *Journal of Philosophy 8:* 204–17.

Hale, M. (1980). *Human science and social order.* Philadelphia: Temple University Press.

James, W. (1892). A plea for psychology as a natural science. *Philosophical Review 1:* 146–53.

_____ . (1904). Does "consciousness" exist? *Journal of Philosophy 1:* 477–91.

_____ . (1907/1955). *Pragmatism.* New York: Meridian.

Jastrow, J. (1901). Some currents and undercurrents in psychology. *Psychological Review 8:* 1–26.

Joncich, G. (1968). *The sane positivist: A biography of E. L. Thorndike.* Middletown, CT: Wesleyan University Press.

Judd, C. H. (1910). *Psychology: General introduction.* New York: Scribner's.

Köhler, W. (1925). *The mentality of apes.* New York: Harcourt Brace.

Kuklick, B. (1977). *The rise of American philosophy.* New Haven, CT: Yale University Press.

Ladd, G. T. (1892). Psychology as a so-called "natural science." *Philosophical Review 1:* 24–53.

McDougall, W. (1912). *Psychology: The study of behaviour.* New York: Holt.

Mills, W. (1899). The nature of animal intelligence. *Psychological Review 6:* 262–74.

_____ . (1904). Some aspects of the development of comparative psychology. *Science 19:* 745–57.

Parmelee, M. (1913). *The science of human behavior.* New York: Macmillan.

Pavlov, I. P. (1903/1957). *Experimental psychology and other essays.* New York: Philosophical Library.

Sanford, E. C. (1903). Psychology and physics. *Psychological Review 10:* 105–19.

Sechenov, I. M. (1863/1965). Reflexes of the brain. Reprinted in R. Herrnstein and E. Boring, eds., *A source book in the history of psychology* (Cambridge, MA: Harvard University Press, 1965).

_____ . (1973). *Biographical sketch and essays.* New York: Arno.

Singer, E. A. (1911). Mind as observable object. *Journal of Philosophy 8:* 180–6.

Swartz, C. K. (1908). The scientific association of Johns Hopkins University. *Science 28:* 814–5.

Thilly, F. (1905). Review of Angell's psychology. *Philosophical Review 14:* 481–7.

Thorndike, E. L. (1898). Review of Evans' "Evolution, ethics and animal psychology." *Psychological Review 5:* 229–30.

_____ . (1911/1965). *Animal intelligence* (reprinted.). New York: Hafner.

_____ . (1929/1968). *Human learning.* New York: Johnson Reprint Corporation.

Titchener, E. B. (1898). Postulates of a structural psychology. *Philosophical Review 7:* 449–65.

Turner, F. M. (1974). *Between science and religion.* New Haven, CT: Yale University Press.

Ward, J. (1904). The present problems of general psychology. *Philosophical Review 13:* 603–21.

_____ . (1920). *Psychological principles.* Cambridge, England: Cambridge University Press.

Watson, J. B. (1907). Comparative psychology. *Psychological Bulletin 4:* 288–302.

_____ . (1909). A point of view in comparative psychology. *Psychological Bulletin 6:* 57–58.

Wozniak, R. (1982). Metaphysics and science, reason and reality: The intellectual origins of genetic epistemology. In J. Broughton and D. Freeman Noir, eds., *The cognitive developmental psychology of James Mark Baldwin*. Hillsdale, NJ: ABLEX.

Yerkes, R. (1905a). Animal psychology and the criterion of the psychic. *Journal of Philosophy 2:* 141–9.

_____ . (1905b). Review of Claparede, "Is comparative psychology legitimate?" *Journal of Philosophy 2:* 527–8.

_____ . (1910). Psychology in its relation to biology. *Journal of Philosophy 7:* 113–125.

11 *Psychology Takes Off*
The Behaviorist Era (1913–1950)

*DEVELOPING BEHAVIORALISM
(1913-1930)*
  Behaviorism Proclaimed
  The Initial Response (1913-1918)
  Behaviorism Defined (1919-1930)
  Watson's Behaviorism in Action
*MAJOR FORMULATIONS OF
BEHAVIORALISM (1930-1950)*
  Psychology and the Science of Science
  Edward Chace Tolman's Purposive
    Behaviorism
  Clark Leonard Hull's Mechanistic
    Behaviorism
  Conclusion: Tolman versus Hull
*CONCLUSION: WE'RE ALL
BEHAVIORISTS NOW*

While John Broadus Watson did not create behaviorism, he named it, gave it a creed, and advertised it aggressively. While they disagreed on much else, behaviorists rejected the old definitions of psychology as the science of the soul, of the mind, or of consciousness. In the 1930s and 1940s, leading psychologists emulated physics and proposed grand and ambitious theories of animal and human behavior.

In the years encompassing World War I and leading up to World War II, psychology experienced tremendous growth. The numbers of psychologists grew dramatically, their work took them increasingly into applied areas little known to the academic founders of psychology, and psychology enjoyed popularity with ordinary people, even if it did not always command their respect. Within the field, the chief developments are the rise of applied psychology, especially mental testing, and the triumph of behavioralism as the psychology of the twentieth century.

DEVELOPING BEHAVIORALISM (1913–1930)

Behaviorism Proclaimed

John Broadus Watson (1878–1958) was a young, ambitious animal psychologist who, as we saw in the previous chapter, had, by 1908, defined a purely objective, nonmentalistic approach to animal psychology, shortly after graduating from the University of Chicago and taking a position at Johns Hopkins University. In his autobiography, he says that he had broached the idea of a purely objective human psychology to his teachers during his days as a graduate student at Chicago, but his proposals were greeted with such horror that he kept his own counsel. After establishing himself as a leading animal psychologist in his own right, he felt emboldened to expand publicly the scope of his objective psychology. On February 13, 1913, he began a series of lectures on animal psychology at Columbia University with a lecture on "Psychology as the Behaviorist Views It." Encouraged by the editor of *Psychological Review,* Howard Warren (who for some time had been trying to get Watson to publish his new view of psychology [Warren, 1938]), Watson published his lecture. In 1943, a group of eminent psychologists rated this paper as the most important one ever published in the *Review* (Langfeld, 1943).

From the paper's aggressive tone, it was clear that Watson was issuing a manifesto for a new kind of psychology: behaviorism. In those years, manifestos were rather more common than they are today. For example, in 1913, modern art came to America in the notorious Armory Show, a kind of manifesto in paint for modernism. Modern artists also issued written manifestos for various modernist movements, such as futurism and dadaism. Watson's manifesto for behaviorism shared the goals of these modernist manifestos: to repudiate the past and set out, however incoherently, a vision of life as it might be. Watson began with a ringing definition of psychology as it might be:

> Psychology as the behaviorist views it is a purely objective branch of natural science. Its theoretical goal is the prediction and control of behavior. Introspection forms no essential part of its methods, nor is the scientific value of its data dependent on the readiness with which they lend themselves to interpretation in terms of consciousness. The behaviorist, in his efforts to get a unitary scheme of animal response, recognizes no dividing line between man and brute. The behavior of man, with all of its refinement and complexity, forms only a part of the behaviorist's total scheme of investigation. (1913a, p. 158)

In the tradition of modernist manifestos, Watson went on to repudiate psychology as it had been. Watson refused to see any difference between structuralism and functionalism. Both of them adopted the traditional definition of psychology as "the science of the phenomena of consciousness," and both of them used the traditional "esoteric" method of introspection. However, psychology so conceived had "failed to make its place in the world as an undisputed natural science."

As an animal psychologist, Watson felt especially constrained by mentalism. There seemed to be little room for animal work, as animals were unable to introspect, forcing psychologists to "construct" conscious contents for them on analogy to the psychologists' own minds. Moreover, traditional psychology was anthropocentric, respecting the findings of animal psychology only insofar as they bore on questions of human psychology. Watson found this situation intolerable and aimed at reversing the traditional priorities. In 1908, he had declared the autonomy of animal psychology as the study of animal behavior; now he proposed to use "human beings as subjects and to employ methods of investigation which are exactly comparable to those now employed in animal work." Earlier comparative psychologists had warned that we should not anthropomorphize about animals; Watson urged psychologists not to anthropomorphize about human beings.

Watson faulted introspection on empirical, philosophical, and practical grounds. Empirically, it simply failed to define questions it could convincingly answer. There was as yet no answer even to the most basic question of the psychology of consciousness—how many sensations there are and the number of their attributes. Watson saw no end to a sterile discussion (1913a, p. 164): "I firmly believe that, unless the introspective method is discarded, psychology will still be divided on the question as to whether auditory sensations have the quality of 'extension' and upon many hundreds of other [questions] of like character."

Watson's second ground for rejecting introspection was philosophical: It was not like the methods of natural science, and therefore it was not a scientific method at all. In the natural sciences, good techniques provide "reproducible results," and then, when these are not forthcoming, "the attack is made upon the experimental conditions" until reliable results are obtained. In mentalistic psychology, however, we must study the private world of an observer's consciousness. Watson's point seemed to be that the results of introspective psychology possess a personal element not found in the natural sciences; this contention forms the basis for methodological behaviorism.

Finally, introspection failed practical tests. In the laboratory, it demanded that animal psychologists find some behavioral criterion of consciousness. He now argued that consciousness was irrelevant to animal work: "One can assume either the presence or absence of consciousness anywhere in the phylogenetic scale without affecting the problems of behavior one jot or one tittle." Experiments are in fact designed to find out what an animal will do in some novel circumstance, and its behavior is then observed; only later must the researcher attempt the "absurd," reconstructing the animal's mind as it behaved. But Watson pointed out that reconstructing the animal's consciousness added nothing at all to what had already been accomplished in the observation of behavior.

To society, introspective psychology was likewise irrelevant, offering no solutions to the problems facing people in modern life. Indeed, Watson reports that it was his feeling that mentalistic psychology had "no realm of application" that early made him "dissatisfied" with it. So it is not surprising to find that the one area of existing psychology Watson praised was applied psychology: educational psychology, psychopharmacology, mental testing, psychopathology, and legal and advertising psychology. These fields were "most flourishing" because they were "less dependent on introspection." Sounding a key theme of Progressivism and of behavioralism to come, Watson lauded these "truly scientific" psychologies because they "are in search of broad generalizations which will lead to the control of human behavior."

On Watson's account, then, introspective psychology had nothing to recommend it and much to condemn it. "[P]sychology must discard all reference to consciousness" and "never use the terms consciousness, mental states, mind, content, introspectively verifiable, imagery and the like . . . . It can be done in terms of stimulus and response, in terms of habit formation, habit integrations and the like. Furthermore, I believe that it is really worthwhile to make this attempt now" (pp. 166–7).

The "starting point" of Watson's new psychology would be the "fact that organisms, man and animal alike, do adjust themselves to their environment"; that is, psychology would be the study of adjustive behavior, not conscious content. Description of behavior would lead to the prediction of behavior in terms of stimulus and response (p. 167): "In a system of psychology completely worked out, given the response the stimuli can be predicted [Watson meant retrodicted]; given the stimuli the response can be predicted." Ultimately, Watson aimed to "learn general and particular methods by which I may control behavior." Once control techniques become available, the leaders of society will be able to "utilize our data in a practical way." Watson did not cite Auguste Comte, but his program for behaviorism—describe, predict, and control observable behavior—was clearly in the positivist tradition. The only acceptable form of explanation for both Comte and Watson was "explanation in physico-chemical terms."

The methods by which we are to achieve psychology's new goals were left rather vague, as Watson was later to admit (Watson, 1916a). The only thing made really clear about behavioral methodology in the manifesto is that, under behaviorism, work "on the human being will be comparable directly with the work upon animals," because behaviorists "care as little about [a human subject's] 'conscious processes' during the conduct of the experiment as we care about such processes in the rat." He gives a few examples of how sensation and memory might be behavioristically investigated, but they are not very convincing and would soon be replaced by Pavlov's conditioned reflex method.

Watson does say some startling things about human thinking. He asserts that thinking does not involve the brain—there are no "centrally initiated processes"—but consists in "faint reinstatement of . . . muscular acts," specifically "motor habits in the larynx." "In other words, wherever there are thought processes there are faint contractions of the systems of musculature involved in the overt exercise of the customary act, and especially in the still finer systems of musculature involved in speech. . . . [I]magery becomes a mental luxury (even if it really exists) without any functional significance whatever" (p. 174) While Watson's claims may outrage the lay reader, we should see that his conclusions are the logical outcome of the motor theory of consciousness (McComas, 1916). On the motor theory, conscious content simply reflects without affecting stimulus–response connections; Watson is simply pointing out that because mental content has "no functional significance," there's no point in studying it save accumulated prejudice: "[O]ur minds have been warped by fifty odd years which have been devoted to the study of states of consciousness." Peripheralism had been gaining force as a doctrine in psychology since at least the time of Sechenov, and Watson's version of it would be found in the most influential and important forms of behavioralism until the coming of cognitive science in the 1960s.

In another Columbia lecture, "Image and Affection in Behavior" (1913b), Watson continued his assault on mental content. He considers, and rejects, the formula of what became methodological behaviorism, the view that "I care not what goes on in [a person's] so called mind" as long as his or her behavior is predictable. Methodological behaviorism was a "partial defeat" that Watson found unacceptable, preferring instead "to attack." He reiterated his view that "there are no centrally initiated processes." Instead, thinking is just "implicit behavior" that sometimes occurs between a stimulus and the resulting "explicit behavior." Most implicit behavior, he hypothesized, occurs in the larynx and is open to observation, though the technique of such observation had not been developed.

The important point for Watson is that there are no functional mental processes playing causal roles in determining behavior. There are only chains of behavior, some of which are difficult to observe. Should this be true—and Watson applied his thesis to both mental images and experienced emotions, as the title states—no part of psychology could escape the behaviorist's scheme, for mind would be shown to be behavior; the behaviorist would concede no subject to the mentalist.

Finally, Watson suggested a theme that would emerge more vividly in his later writings, and that shows how his behaviorism was part of a larger revolt against the cultural past, not simply a revolt against a failed introspective psychology. Watson claimed that allegiance to mentalistic psychology was at root clinging to religion in a scientific age that has made religion obsolete. Those who believe that there are centrally initiated processes—that is, behaviors begun by the brain and not by some outside stimulus—really believe in the soul. Watson said that because we know nothing about the cortex, it is easy to attribute the functions of the soul to the cortex: Both are unknown mysteries. Watson's position was extremely radical: Not only did the soul not exist, neither did the cortex as anything other than a relay station connecting stimulus and response; both soul and brain could be ignored in the description, prediction, and control of behavior.

The Initial Response (1913–1918)

How did psychologists receive Watson's manifesto? One might expect that behaviorism would become the rallying cry of younger psychologists and the object of denunciation by their elders. In fact, when Watson's manifesto later took its revered place as the starting point of behaviorism, it was thought to have been received in just such fashion. However, as Samelson (1981) has shown, published responses to "Psychology as the Behaviorist Views It" were both remarkably few and remarkably restrained.

In general, psychologists who said anything about Watson's paper agreed with many of its ideas, but felt that Watson went too far in rejecting introspection outright and in his intemperate tone of voice. For example, Mary Calkins (1913), who had earlier proposed her self psychology as a compromise between structural and functional psychology, now proposed it as a mediator between behaviorism and mentalism. Like most commentators, she agreed with much of Watson's critique of structuralism and applauded the study of behavior; but she nevertheless found introspection to be the indispensable, if sometimes troublesome, method of psychology.

Some critics said that Watson's proposed behaviorism was a worthy science, it just wasn't psychology. The study of behavior was biology; psychology, to retain its identity, had to remain introspective. A. H. Jones (1915) spoke for many when he wrote, "We may rest assured then, that whatever else psychology may be, it is at least a doctrine of awareness. To deny this . . . is to pour out the baby with the bath." Titchener (1914) also saw behavior study as biology rather than psychology. Because the facts of consciousness exist, he said, they can be studied, and such is the task of psychology. Behaviorism might accomplish much, since it was not psychology at all, but it posed no threat to introspective psychology. One of the few substantive (as opposed to methodological) criticisms of Watson's behaviorism was offered by H. C. McComas (1916), who correctly saw it as a natural extension of the motor theory of consciousness. McComas showed that Watson's identification of thinking with laryngeal movements stood falsified: Some people had already lost their larynxes due to disease, without thereby losing the ability to think.

The problem with Watson's critics was that they seemed not to notice that Watson might succeed in fundamentally redefining psychology altogether. As we have seen, Watson was riding the crest of behavioralism, and if enough psychologists adopted his definition of their field, it would as a matter of historical fact cease to be the study of the mind, and would become the study of behavior. Although his radical peripheralism might not be accepted, behavioralism would be, and behaviorism would be its name.

Watson, of course, did not remain silent while his views were debated. He was chosen by a nominating committee and ratified by the members of the APA to be the president for 1916. In his presidential address, he tried to fill the most conspicuous gap in behaviorism: the method and theory by which it would study and explain behavior. Watson had tried for some years to show that thinking was just implicit speech, but he had failed. So Watson turned to the work of Karl Lashley, a student in his laboratory, who had been replicating and extending Pavlov's conditioning techniques. Watson now presented the conditioned reflex work as the substance of behaviorism: Pavlov's method applied to humans would be behaviorism's tool of investigation, and the conditioned reflex theory would provide the basis for the prediction and control of behavior in animals and people. Watson's address set out in detail how the conditioned reflex method could be applied to both humans and animals, providing an objective substitute for introspection.

Nor was Watson reluctant to apply the theory outside the laboratory. In another paper published that year, Watson (1916b) argued that neuroses were just "habit disturbances," most usually "disturbances of speech functions." We see again that Watson's program was not merely scientific but social; even as he was first learning about and investigating conditioned reflexes, he was prepared to assert that speech, and thus neurotic symptoms, were just conditioned reflexes—poor behavior adjustments that could, in turn, be corrected by the application of behavior principles.

Watson was not an original thinker, but, as he proved in his later career in advertising, he was an effective spokesman. When we separate Watson's rhetoric from his substantive proposals, we find that he said little that was new, but said it powerfully. The behavioral approach had overcome psychology slowly and almost unnoticed in the years after 1892. Watson made psychologists notice the fact and gave it a name that stuck—"behaviorism"—however misleading that name has since become. So no one was either outraged or inspired by Watson's manifesto of psychological modernism, for they had learned to live with modernism or were already practicing it. Watson created no revolution, but he did make clear that psychology was no longer the science of consciousness. "Psychology as the Behaviorist Views It" simply marks the moment when behavioralism became ascendant and self-conscious, creating for later behavioralists a useful "myth of origin." It provided for them a secure anchoring point in the history of psychology, and a justification for the abandonment of an introspective method they found boring and sterile. But all of these things would have happened had Watson never become a psychologist.

Behaviorism Defined (1919–1930)

Along with the rest of psychology, the discussion of behaviorism was interrupted by World War I. As we shall see, psychology was much changed by its involvement with the war; when psychologists resumed their consideration of behaviorism, the grounds of the discussion were quite different from what they had been before the war. The value of objective psychology had been proved by the tests psychologists had devised to classify soldiers, and that success had brought psychology before a wider audience. After the war, the question was no longer whether behaviorism was legitimate, but what form behaviorism should take. In the 1920s, psychologists attempted to define behaviorism; but, as we shall see, they failed to make of it a coherent movement, much less a Kuhnian paradigm.

As early as 1922, it was clear that psychologists were having trouble understanding behaviorism, or formulating it in any widely agreeable way. Walter Hunter, a sympathizer of Watson's, wrote "An Open Letter to the Anti-Behaviorists." He thought behaviorism was exactly what Watson preached, the definition of psychology as the study of "stimulus and response relations." He viewed the various "new formulas" for behaviorism, which by then had been offered as "illegitimate offspring" making it difficult for psychologists to see what behaviorism was. Later, Hunter (1925) would try to finesse the issue by defining a new science, "anthroponomy," the science of human behavior. But Hunter's new science never caught on, leaving psychologists to redefine psychology in some new "behavioristic" way.

Some psychologists defined behaviorism in the spirit of La Mettrie, as seeking the physiological bases of mind and behavior. The most important spokesman for this view was Karl Lashley (1890–1958), Watson's student and the foremost neuropsychologist of the first half of the twentieth century. Lashley (1923) wrote that behaviorism had become "an accredited system of psychology," but, in its emphasis on "experimental method," it had failed to give any satisfactory "systematic formulation" of its views. In light of behaviorism's being "so great a departure from tradition in psychology," a clearer formulation of behaviorism was needed. Heretofore, Lashley claimed, three forms of behaviorism had been advanced.

The first two were scarcely distinguishable as forms of "methodological behaviorism." They allowed that "facts of conscious experience exist but are unsuited to any form of scientific treatment." It had been, according to Lashley, the beginning point of Watson's own behaviorism, but it ultimately proved unsatisfying because it conceded too much to introspective psychology. Precisely because it acknowledged the "facts of consciousness," methodological behaviorism admitted that it could never be a complete psychology and had to concede a science, or at least a study, of mind alongside the science of behavior. Opposed to methodological behaviorism was "strict behaviorism" (or, as Calkins [1921] and Wheeler [1923] named it, radical behaviorism [Schneider and Morris, 1987]), whose "extreme" view was that "the supposedly unique facts of consciousness do not exist." Such a view seems at first sight implausible, and Lashley conceded that it had not been put forward with any convincing arguments. Lashley made his own view plain:

> Let me cast off the lion's skin. My quarrel with behaviorism is not that it has gone too far, but that it has hesitated . . . that it has failed to develop its premises to their logical conclusion. To me the essence of behaviorism is the belief that the study of man will reveal nothing except what is adequately describable in the concepts of mechanics and chemistry. . . . I believe that it is possible to construct a physiological psychology which will meet the dualist on his own ground . . . and show that [his] data can be embodied in a mechanistic system. . . . Its physiological account of behavior will also be a complete and adequate account of all the phenomena of consciousness . . . demanding that all psychological data, however obtained, shall be subjected to physical or physiological interpretation. (pp. 243–4)

Ultimately, Lashley said, the choice between behaviorism and traditional psychology comes down to a choice between two "incompatible" worldviews, "scientific versus humanistic." It had been demanded of psychology heretofore that "it must leave room for human ideals and aspirations." But "other sciences have escaped this thralldom," and so must psychology escape from "metaphysics and values" and "mystical obscurantism" by turning to physiology. In physiology, it can find principles of explanation that will make of psychology a natural science, value-free, capable of addressing its "most important problems," its "most interesting and vital questions, the problems of human conduct." It would then be able to recapture the "problems of everyday life" from "sociology, education, and psychiatry," the applied fields ignored by introspective psychology. Lashley's formula for psychology was clearly La Mettrie's: the mechanistic, physiological explanation of behavior and consciousness. It was also clearly in the tradition of Comte's positivism. It preached a scientific imperialism against the humanities and questions of value, setting up instead a value-free technology claiming to solve human problems.

Lashley and his sympathizers attempted to define behaviorism quite narrowly, following a behavioral version of the path through physiology, and almost dismantling psychology as an independent discipline. Other psychologists and philosophical observers of psychology thought the physiologically reductive definition of behaviorism too narrow and defined a more inclusive behavioristic psychology.

The neorealist philosopher Ralph Barton Perry (1921) saw behaviorism as nothing new, but "simply a return to the original Aristotelian view that mind and body are related as activity and organ." Adopting behaviorism did not mean denying that mind has a role in behavior. On the contrary, "If you are a behaviorist you regard the mind as something that intervenes" in determining behavior, and behaviorism rescues mind from the parallelistic impotence imposed on it by introspective psychology. On the other hand, the neorealist Stephen Pepper (1923), who had studied with Perry at Harvard, while similarly refusing to identify Watson's behaviorism as *the* behaviorism, nonetheless flatly contradicted Perry. For Pepper, the central contention of behaviorism was that consciousness plays no causal role in determining behavior, and that behaviorism's destiny was to bring psychology into "connection with the rest of the natural sciences." Jastrow (1927), who had been around since the beginning of psychology in America, saw nothing new in behaviorism, calling James, Peirce, and Hall "behaviorists." Psychology as the study of behavior was part of the "reconstruction" of psychology that had been taking place for the previous fifty years. It was a mistake, Jastrow argued, to confuse Watson's "radical" behaviorism with the more general and moderate behaviorism held by most American psychologists.

When we set side by side the views of Lashley, Perry, Pepper, and Jastrow, it becomes clear that "behaviorism" was a term of nearly infinite elasticity. It might signify physiological reductionism, or just the study of behavior by objective means; it might mean a significant break with the past, or it might be very old; it might mean seeing mind as a causal actor in determining behavior, or it might mean the denial of mind as causal agent. Woodworth (1924) was correct when he wrote that there is no "one great inclusive enterprise" binding together the various claimants to the title "behaviorism." Woodworth saw behaviorism's "essential program" as "behavior study, behavior concepts, laws of behavior, control of behavior," not the "neuromechanistic interpretation" of psychology associated with Watson. Woodworth observed that psychology had begun as the nonintrospective study of reaction times, memory, and psychophysics, but had been sidetracked in its development as a science by Titchener, Külpe, and others, around 1900. Behaviorism—or, as we have defined it here, behavioralism—was a program for psychology, not a new method. Scientific psychology was bound to become behavioralistic; Watson had wrought nothing new.

One point of note arose in several of the papers advocating behaviorism, connecting behavioralism with its past in functionalism and its future in cognitive science: James's "automatic sweetheart." In contrasting behaviorism with humanism, Lashley noted that "the final objection to behaviorism is that it just fails to express the vital, personal quality of experience," an objection quite evident in James's arguments concerning the "automatic sweetheart." Hunter (1923) likewise considered James's possible objection to behaviorism: It claims one's beloved is an automaton, and can one truly love a machine? With Lashley, who said descriptions of experience "belong to art, not science," Hunter dismissed worries about whether one could love, or be loved by, a machine as concerned only with the "aesthetic satisfaction" of the belief, not its scientific truth. B. H. Bode (1918) treated the problem more fully, defending the behaviorist point of view. Bode argued that, upon reflection, there is no meaningful difference between a human sweetheart and a mechanical one, because no behavioral difference between them could be discerned:

> If there is no [objectively observable] difference, then the consciousness of the spiritually animated maiden plainly makes no difference in the behavior; it is a mere concomitant or epiphenomenon . . . [Therefore,] mechanism becomes the last word of explanation, and the mystery of the eternally feminine takes on much the same quality as the mystery of higher mathematics. (p. 451)

Finally, a critic of behaviorism, William MacDougall, put the issue in the most up-to-date terms. The term "robot" had just been coined by Carel Capek in his science fiction play, *R. U. R., Rossum's Universal Robots.* MacDougall (1925) saw the critical question framed by behaviorism as "Men or robots?" Behaviorism rested on the claim that human beings are just machines—robots—but that claim was unproved. In Woodworth's opinion, it remained to be determined that robots could do anything human beings can do.

The concern over James's automatic, or robot, sweetheart raises the central problem of scientific psychology in the twentieth century: Can human beings be consistently conceived of as machines? This question transcends all the systems of psychology since James's (or even La Mettrie's) time, for it ties together functionalism, realism, behaviorism, and cognitive psychology. Following the development of computers in World War II, one of their creators would pose James's question in more intellectual terms: Can a machine be said to think if you can talk to it and be fooled into believing you are talking to another person? And A. M. Turing, followed by many cognitive psychologists, would give Bode's answer: If you can't tell it's just a machine, then we're just machines, too. The prospect of the automatic sweetheart filled some psychologists with excitement, but others, such as James, with revulsion. Lashley was very likely right when he saw the battle over behaviorism not just as a battle between different ways of doing psychology, but as a much deeper battle between "mechanistic explanation and finalistic valuation," between a view of human beings as robots, or as actors with purposes, values, hopes, fears, and loves.

Watson's Behaviorism in Action

Following World War II, in which he served unhappily in the army, working up tests for aviators, Watson moved his research and his advocacy for behaviorism in a new direction. He now intensively pursued a human psychology based on the conditioned reflex by investigating the acquisition of reflexes in infants. Watson believed that nature endowed human beings with very few unconditioned reflexes, so that the complex behavior of adults might be explained as simply the acquisition of conditioned reflexes over years of Pavlovian conditioning. Contrary to eugenicists and their followers, who believed that people inherit a great deal of their intellect, personality, and morality, Watson (1930, p. 94) asserted that "there is no such thing as inheritance of capacity, talent, temperament, mental constitution and characteristics."

For example, Watson denied that human hand preference was innate. He could find no structural differences between babies' left and right hands and arms, nor were the different hands endowed with different strengths. So although he remained puzzled by the fact that most people were right-handed, he put the cause down to social training, and he said there would be no harm in trying to turn apparently left-handed children into right-handers. Nothing could better demonstrate Watson's radical peripheralism: Because he could find no peripheral differences between the hands' strength and structure, there could be, he concluded, no biological basis to handedness. He completely ignored the "mysterious" (Watson, 1913b) cerebral cortex, seeing it as no more than a relay station for neural impulses. We now know that the left and right hemispheres of the human brain have very different functions, and that differences between right- and left-handers are determined there. To attempt to change a natural left-hander into a right-hander is to impose a very trying task, one well calculated to make the left-handed child feel unhappy and inferior.

In any event, to establish the truth of his equally radical environmentalism— "Give me a dozen healthy infants . . . and my own specified world to bring them up in and I'll guarantee to take any one at random and train him to become any type of specialist I might select—doctor, lawyer, artist, merchant-chief, and, yes, even beggarman and thief" (Watson, 1930, p. 104)—Watson turned to the nursery to show that humans are so much plastic material waiting to be molded by society.

The most famous of his studies with infants is "Conditioned Emotional Reactions" (Watson and Rayner, 1920). Watson carried out, on an infant known as "Albert B.," an experiment designed to show that people are born with only a few "instincts"— fear, rage, and sexual response—and all other emotions are conditioned versions of these unconditioned ones. As his US to produce fear (UR), Watson chose a loud noise, the sound of a large metal bar being struck by a hammer; this stimulus had been determined to be one of the few that would scare little Albert. He paired the noise with a CS, a rat whom Albert had liked to pet. Now, however, when Albert touched the rat, Watson struck the bar; after seven such pairings, the child showed fear of the rat alone. Watson claimed to have established a "conditioned emotional reaction," and he asserted that his experimental arrangement was the prototype of emotional learning by a normal human in the normal human environment. Watson thought he had thus demonstrated that the rich emotional life of the adult human being was at bottom no more than a large number of conditioned responses built up over years of human development.

Watson's claims are dubious and his ethics in this experiment are questionable (Samelson, 1980); furthermore, the experiment is often misdescribed by secondary sources (Harris, 1979). Watson was, at least, consistent. He fell in love with graduate student and collaborator Rosalie Rayner–creating a scandal that cost him his job at Johns Hopkins in 1920–and wrote to her that "every cell I have is yours singly and collectively," and that all his emotional responses "are positive and towards you, . . . likewise each and every heart response" (Cohen, 1979).

Watson had always been willing to write about psychology for a popular audience. After 1920, following his expulsion from academia, he became the first modern popular psychologist (Buckley, 1984), writing, for example, a series of articles on human psychology from the behaviorist perspective in *Harper's* from 1926 to 1928. There, Watson began by laying out behaviorism as the scientific replacement for mentalistic psychology and for psychoanalysis, which had earlier captured the popular mind. According to Watson, psychoanalysis had "too little science—real science" to long command serious attention, and the traditional psychology of consciousness "never had any right to be called a science." As he often did in his popular writings, Watson connected mentalistic psychology with religion, asserting that "mind and consciousness" were but "carryovers from the church dogma of the middle ages." The mind, or soul, was, according to Watson, one of the mysteries by whose invocation "churchmen—all medicine men in fact—have kept the public under control." Psychoanalysis was just "a substitution of demonology for science," and through such "solid walls of religious protection" science was "blasting" a new path.

Watson defied the mentalist to "prove" that "there is such a thing as consciousness." To the assertion by a mentalist that he had a mental life, Watson simply replied, "I have only your unverified and unsupported word that you have" images and sensations. So the concepts of mentalism remained "mythological, the figments of the psychologist's terminology." In place of the fantastic, secretly religious, traditional mentalistic psychology, behaviorism substituted a positivistic, scientific psychology of description, prediction, and control of behavior. Watson said that behavioral psychology began with the observation of the behavior of our fellows, and, suitably codified by science, issued in "a new weapon for controlling the individual." The social use of behavioral science was made clear by Watson: "[We] can build any man, starting at birth, into any kind of social or a-social being upon order." Elsewhere, Watson (1930) said, "It is a part of the behaviorist's scientific job to be able to state what the human machine is good for and to render serviceable predictions about its future capacities whenever society needs such information."

Very much in the tradition of Comte's positivism, Watson's behaviorism rejected religion and the moral control of behavior and aimed to replace these with science and the technological control of behavior through behavioral psychology. Behaviorism was well prepared to mesh with Progressivism. Because of Progressivism's interest in establishing rational control over society through scientific means, Progressive politicians and apologists found an ally in behaviorism, which seemed to promise exactly the technology Progressivism needed to replace the outworn authority of tradition.

MAJOR FORMULATIONS OF BEHAVIORALISM (1930–1950)

By 1930, behavioralism was well established as the dominant viewpoint in experimental psychology. Watson's usage had triumphed, and psychologists called the new viewpoint "behaviorism," while recognizing that behaviorism took many forms (Williams,

1931). The stage was set for psychologists to create specific theories for predicting and explaining behavior within the new viewpoint of behavioralism. The central problem they would address in the coming decades would be learning (McGeoch, 1931). Functionalism had taken the ability to learn to be the criterion of animal mind, and the development of behavioralism had only magnified its importance. Learning was the process by which animals and humans adjusted to the environment, by which they were educated, and by which they might be changed in the interest of social control or therapy. So it is not surprising that what would later be regarded as the Golden Age of Theory in psychology—the years 1930 to 1950—would be golden only for theories of learning, rather than perception, thinking, group dynamics, or anything else.

The other major development of these decades in experimental psychology was psychologists' increasing self-consciousness about proper scientific method. Psychologists, as we have often noted, have always felt uncertain about the scientific status of their *soi-disant* "natural science" and have consequently been eager to find some methodological recipe to follow by which they could infallibly make psychology a science. Watson had, in denouncing mentalism, seen its irredeemable flaw to be the "unscientific" method of introspecting, and he had proclaimed psychology's scientific salvation to be objective method, taken over from animal study. Watson's message struck home, but his own recipe was too vague and confused to provide anything more than an attitude. In the 1930s, psychologists became aware of a very specific, prestigious recipe, *logical positivism,* for making science. Because the positivist's philosophy of science codified what psychologists already wanted to do, they accepted the recipe, which determined the goals and language of psychology for decades to come. At the same time, their own original ideas were molded so subtly by logical positivism that only today can we see the molding process at work.

Psychology and the Science of Science

Behavioralism reflected the image of science drawn by Comtean positivism: Its goal was the description, prediction, and control of behavior, and its techniques were to be put to use as tools of social control in a rationally managed society. The early, simple positivism of Comte and Mach had changed, however. By the early twentieth century, it was clear that positivism's extreme emphasis on talking about only what could be directly observed, excluding from science concepts such as "atom" and "electron," could not be sustained. Physicists and chemists found that their theories could not dispense with such terms, and their research results confirmed for them, albeit indirectly, the reality of atoms and electrons (Holton, 1978). So positivism changed, and its adherents found a way to admit into science terms apparently referring to unobserved entities, without giving up the basic positivist desire to expunge metaphysics from human, or at least scientific, discourse.

This new positivism came to be called logical positivism because it wedded the positivist's commitment to empiricism and the logical apparatus of modern formal logic. Logical positivism was a complex and changing movement directed by many hands, but its basic idea was simple: Science had proven to be humankind's most powerful means of understanding reality, of producing knowledge, so that the task of epistemology should be to explicate and formalize the scientific method, making it available to new disciplines and improving its practice among working scientists. Thus, the logical positivists purported to provide a formal recipe for doing science, offering exactly what psychologists thought they needed.

Logical positivism began with a small circle of philosophers in Vienna just after World War I, but it soon became a worldwide movement aimed at the unification of science in one grand scheme of investigation orchestrated by the positivists themselves. Logical positivism had many aspects, but two have proved especially important to psychologists looking for the "scientific way," and they were adopted as talismans of scientific virtue in the 1930s: formal axiomatization of theories, and the operational definition of theoretical terms.

Scientific language, the logical positivists explained, contained two kinds of terms. Most basic were observation terms, which referred to directly observable properties of nature: redness, length, weight, time durations, and so on. The older positivism had stressed observation and had insisted that science should contain only observation terms. Logical positivists agreed that observations provided the bedrock of science, but they recognized that theoretical terms were necessary parts of scientific vocabulary, providing explanations in addition to descriptions of natural phenomena. Science simply could not do without terms such as "force," "mass," "field," and "electron." The problem, though, was how to admit science's theoretical vocabulary as legitimate, while excluding metaphysical and religious nonsense. The solution the logical positivists arrived at was to closely tie theoretical terms to bedrock observation terms, thereby guaranteeing their meaningfulness.

The logical positivists argued that the meaning of a theoretical term should be understood to consist in procedures linking it to observation terms. So, for example, "mass" would be defined as an object's weight at sea level. A term that could not be so defined could be dismissed as metaphysical nonsense. Such definitions were called "operational definitions," following the usage of Percy Bridgman, a physicist who had independently proposed the same idea in 1927.

The logical positivists also claimed that scientific theories consisted of theoretical axioms relating theoretical terms to one another. For example, a central axiom of Newtonian physics was "force equals mass times acceleration," or "$F = M \times A$." This theoretical sentence expresses a putative scientific law and may be tested by deriving predictions from it. Because each term has an operational definition, it is possible to take an operational measure of the mass of an object, accelerate it to a measurable speed, and then measure the resulting force generated by the object. Should the predicted force correspond to the measured force in the experiment, the axiom would be confirmed; should the values disagree, the axiom would be disconfirmed and would need to be revised.

On the logical positivist account of theories, theories explained because they could predict. To explain an event was to show that it could have been predicted from the preceding circumstances combined with some scientific "covering law." So to explain why a vase broke when it was dropped on the floor, one would show that given the weight of the vase (operationally defined mass) and the height it was dropped from (operationally defined acceleration in earth gravity), the resulting force would be sufficient to crack the vase's porcelain structure.

Logical positivism was exciting to psychologists because it seemed to offer a specific recipe for turning their beloved but maligned field into a real science. First, operationally define one's theoretical terms, be they "mass" or "hunger"; second, state one's theory as a set of theoretical axioms from which predictions could be drawn; third, carry out experiments to test the predictions, using operational definitions to link theory and observations; and finally, revise one's theory as observations warrant.

Because the logical positivists had studied science and set out their findings in explicit logical form, S. S. Stevens (1939), the psychologist who brought operational definition to psychology (Stevens, 1935a, 1935b), called it "the Science of Science," which promised to at last make of psychology "an undisputed natural science" (as Watson had wished), and to unify it with the other sciences in the logical positivists' scheme for the "unity of science." Operationism promised to settle once and for all fruitless disputes about psychological terminology: What does "mind" mean? "Imageless thought"? "Id"? As Stevens (1935a) put it, operationism was "the revolution that will put an end to the possibility of revolution."

Operationism claimed that terms that could not be operationally defined were scientifically meaningless, and that scientific terms could be given operational definitions everyone could agree on. Moreover, operationism's revolution ratified behaviorism's claim to be the only scientific psychology, because only behaviorism was compatible with operationism's demand that theoretical terms be defined by linking them to observation terms (Stevens, 1939). In psychology this meant that theoretical terms could not refer to mental entities, but only to classes of behavior. Hence, mentalistic psychology was unscientific and had to be replaced by behaviorism.

By the end of the 1930s, operationism was entrenched dogma in psychology. Sigmund Koch—by 1950, an apostate from the operationist faith—wrote in his 1939 doctoral dissertation that "almost every psychology sophomore knows it is bad form if reference to 'definition' is not qualified by the adjective 'operational.' " In operationism lay psychology's scientific salvation: "Hitch the constructs appearing in your postulates to a field of scientific fact [via operational definition], and only then do you get a scientific theory" (Koch, 1941, p. 127).

At a loftier professional level, the president of the APA agreed with Koch. John F. Dashiell (1939) observed that philosophy and psychology were coming together again, not to have philosophers set psychologists' agenda—from that tyranny, psychology had won "emancipation"—but to work out science's proper methods. Foremost in the "rapprochement" of philosophy and psychology were two ideas of the logical positivists. The first was operationism; the other was the demand that scientific theories be collections of mathematically stated axioms. Dashiell commended one psychologist for meeting the second requirement: In "the same positivistic vein [as operationism] Hull is urging us to look to the systematic character of our thinking" by producing a rigorous, axiomatic theory. Dashiell's admiration of Clark L. Hull as the foremost logical positivist among psychologists was, as we will see, wrong. Hull was a mechanist and a realist, believing in the physiological reality of his theoretical terms. However, Dashiell's opinion became later psychologists' myth, a comforting belief that although the specifics of their theories were mistaken, Hull and E. C. Tolman had set psychology firmly on the path toward science as the logical positivists had defined it. The true natures of their theories of learning were obscured for decades, not only from the understanding of psychologists generally, but even from the understanding of Hull and Tolman themselves. Regardless of its flaws and its distorting effect on the independent ideas of Hull and Tolman, there can be no doubt that logical positivism became psychology's official philosophy of science until at least the 1960s.

Edward Chace Tolman's Purposive Behaviorism

Although it was seldom acknowledged, behaviorism's central problem was to account for mental phenomena without invoking the mind. More liberal behavioralists might—

and eventually would—leave mind in psychology as an unseen, but nevertheless causal, agent that determines behavior. But at least in its early days, and in its continuing radical strain, behaviorism has aimed to oust mind from psychology. Watson, Lashley, and the other reductive, or physiological, behaviorists tried to do so by claiming that consciousness, purpose, and cognition were myths, so that the task of psychology was to describe experience and behavior as products of the mechanistic operation of the nervous system. The motor theory of consciousness could be used to good effect in such arguments, as showing that conscious contents were just sensations of bodily movements, reporting, but not causing, behavior. Different approaches to explaining behavior without invoking the mind were taken by E. C. Tolman and C. L. Hull.

Bearing a B. S. in electrochemistry, E. C. Tolman (1886–1959) arrived at Harvard in 1911 to undertake graduate study in philosophy and psychology, settling on the latter as more in tune with his capacities and interests. There he studied with the leading philosophers and psychologists of the day, Perry and Holt, Münsterberg and Yerkes. For a time, reading E. B. Titchener "almost sold [him] on structuralistic introspection," but he noticed in his courses with Münsterberg that although Münsterberg "made little opening speeches to the effect that the method in psychology was introspection," the work in his laboratory was "primarily objective in nature" and that little use could be made of introspective results in writing up experimental papers. So reading Watson's *Behavior* in Yerkes's comparative psychology course came "as a tremendous stimulus and relief" for showing that "objective measurement of behavior, not introspection, was the true method of psychology." Tolman's years at Harvard were also the great years of neorealism, just then being promulgated by Perry and Holt.

Neorealism provided the foundation for Tolman's approach to the problem of mind as he developed it after taking a position at the University of California at Berkeley in 1918. Traditionally, the evidence offered to support the existence of mind was of two sorts: introspective awareness of consciousness, and the apparent intelligence and purposefulness of behavior. Following Perry, Tolman found Watson's "muscle-twitchism" (Tolman, 1959) too simple and crude to account for either kind of evidence. Neorealism implied that there was no such thing as introspection, because there were no mental objects to observe; in the neorealist view, "introspection" was only an artificially close scrutiny of an object in one's environment, in which one reported the object's attributes in great detail. Tolman allied this analysis with the motor theory of consciousness, arguing that introspection of internal states such as emotions was just the "back action" of behavior on awareness (Tolman, 1923). In either event, introspection was of no special importance to scientific psychology; in saying this, Tolman's (1922) "A New Formula for Behaviorism" was a methodological behaviorism, conceding that awareness existed, but ruling its study out of the domain of science.

Similarly, evidence of intelligent purpose in behavior could be handled from the neorealist perspective. The leading purposive psychology of the day was William McDougall's "hormic" psychology. In "Behaviorism and Purpose," Tolman (1925) criticized McDougall for handling purpose in the traditional Cartesian way: McDougall, "being a mentalist, merely infers purpose from [the persistence of] behavior, while we, being behaviorists, identify purpose with" persistence toward a goal. Following Perry and Holt, Tolman held that "purpose" is an "objective aspect of behavior" that an observer directly perceives; it is not an inference from observed behavior. Tolman subjected memory to the same analysis, at once recalling the Scottish realists and anticipating B. F. Skinner: "Memory, like purpose, may be conceived . . . as a purely empirical aspect of behavior." To say that one "remembers" a nonpresent object, X, is just to say that one's current behavior is "causally dependent" on X.

In summary, then, Tolman proposed a behaviorism that excised mind and consciousness from psychology, as Watson wanted to do, but retained purpose and cognition, not as powers of a mysterious "mind" inferred from behavior, but as objective, observable aspects of behavior itself. In another contrast to Watson, Tolman's behaviorism was "molar" rather than "molecular" (Tolman, 1926, 1935). In Watson's molecular view, behavior was defined as muscular responses caused by triggering stimuli, so that the appropriate strategy to adopt in predicting and controlling behavior was to analyze complex behaviors into their smallest muscular components, which in turn could be understood physiologically. Tolman, viewing behavior as ineliminably purposive, studied whole, integrated, molar acts.

For example, according to a molecularist, a subject who has learned to withdraw her finger from an electrode when a warning signal precedes shock has learned a specific conditioned muscular reflex; according to a molar behaviorist, she has learned a global avoidance response. Now turn the subject's hand over, so that the same reflex would drive her finger into the electrode; the Watsonian predicts just that—a new molecular reflex will have to be learned, while Tolman predicts that the subject will immediately avoid the shock with an untrained withdrawal movement based on having learned a molar response of shock-avoidance (Wickens, 1938; the results supported Tolman, unsurprisingly).

At the same time that he was treating purpose and cognition from a neorealist perspective, Tolman hinted at a different, more traditionally mentalistic approach to the problem they presented; this approach served Tolman well following the demise of neorealism in the 1920s and is fundamental to cognitive science today. In an early paper, Tolman (1920) wrote that thoughts "can be conceived from an objective point of view as consisting in internal presentations to the organism" of stimuli not now present. Later, right alongside arguments that cognitions are "immanent" in behavior and not inferred, Tolman (1926) wrote of consciousness as providing "representations" that guide behavior. To speak of cognitions and thoughts as internal representations of the world, which play a causal role in determining behavior, breaks with both neorealism and behaviorism: with neorealism because representations are inferred like Lockean ideas; with behaviorism because something mental is given a place among the causes of behavior. As Tolman developed his system, he relied more and more on the concept of representation, resurrecting the copy theory of cognition and believing in mind as something apart from observable behavior.

In 1934, Tolman traveled to Vienna, where he came under the influence of the logical positivists, particularly Rudolf Carnap, the leader of the Vienna Circle. In Carnap's treatment of psychology, the traditional terms of mentalistic folk psychology should be understood as referring not to mental objects, but to physicochemical processes in the body. So the real referent of the expression "My tooth hurts" is to the damage of neurons by decay in a tooth. However, since at present (in 1934 and now) scientists cannot specify how pain is caused, we must define pain operationally in terms of pain behaviors such as moaning and holding one's cheek. In the long run, such behavioral definitions will be eliminated by the advance of neuroscience, and psychologists will be able to translate mentalistic language into purely physiological, rather than behavioral, terms. Carnap did recognize that in addition to its referential function, language may serve an expressive function; if I say "I feel pain," I am not just referring to some physical process within my body, I am expressing anguish. According to Carnap, the expressive function of language lies outside scientific explication and is the subject of poetry, fiction, and, more generally, art.

Carnap's psychology was not incompatible with Tolman's independently developed views, but it did give Tolman a new way to articulate his behaviorism within a philosophy of science daily growing in prestige and influence. Soon after his return to the United States, Tolman reformulated his purposive behaviorism in logical positivist language. Scientific psychology, Tolman (1935) wrote, "seeks . . . the objectively statable laws and processes governing behavior." Descriptions of "immediate experience . . . may be left to the arts and to metaphysics."

Tolman was now able to be quite precise about behaviorism's research program. Behavior was to be regarded as a dependent variable, caused by environmental and internal (but not mental) independent variables. The ultimate goal of behaviorism, then, is "to write the form of the function which connects the dependent variable [behavior] . . . to the independent variables—stimulus, heredity, training, and physiological" states such as hunger. Because this goal was too ambitious to be reached all at once, behaviorists introduced intervening variables that connected independent and dependent variables, providing equations that ought to allow them to predict behavior when given values of the independent variables.

Tolman (1936) expanded these remarks and redefined his behaviorism as "operational behaviorism." Operational behaviorism was cast in the mold of "the general positivistic attitude now being taken by many modern physicists and philosophers." The adjective "operational" reflects two features of his behaviorism, Tolman explained. First, it defined its intervening variables "operationally" as demanded by modern logical positivism; second, it emphasized the fact that behavior is "essentially an activity whereby the organism . . . operates on its environment."

In these 1935 and 1936 papers, Tolman set out clearly and forcefully the classical program of methodological behaviorism as defined under the influence of logical positivism. However, Tolman did not get his conception of psychology from the logical positivists. Their philosophy of science meshed with what Tolman already thought and practiced, providing at most a sophisticated and prestigious justification for his own conceptions; his terms "independent," "dependent," and "intervening variable" are enduring contributions to psychological language. More importantly, Tolman seems quickly to have shed operationism for psychological realism, thinking of his theoretical terms as real mental states, not useful fictions. So, "cognitive maps," for example (Tolman, 1948), were conceived as representations of the environment that a rat or person consults to guide intelligent behavior toward a goal. In the years after his return from Vienna, Tolman did not teach or even especially discuss logical positivism (Smith, 1986). It is therefore possible that his 1935 and 1936 papers, although widely read expositions of methodological behaviorism, never represented Tolman's real conception of psychology.

Sometimes, Tolman seemed to be fumbling for a conception of psychology that was not quite available—namely, the computational conception of cognitive science. In 1920, Tolman had rejected the "slot machine" view of organisms associated with Watson. In this view, the organism was a machine in which a given stimulus elicited a predefined reflexive response, just as putting a coin in the slot of a vending machine produces a fixed product. Rather, Tolman suggested thinking of an organism as "a complex machine capable of various adjustments such that, when one adjustment was in force," a given stimulus would produce one response, while under a different internal adjustment, the same stimulus would call out a different response. Internal adjustments would be caused either by external stimuli or by "automatic changes within the organism." The model Tolman wished for in 1920 was the computer, whose responses to input depend on its programming and its internal state. Similarly, Tolman anticipated the information-processing account of mind when in 1948 he described the mind as "a central control room" in which "incoming impulses are usually worked over and elaborated . . . into a cognitivelike map of the environment."

Clark Leonard Hull's Mechanistic Behaviorism

Clark Leonard Hull (1884–1952), like so many people born in the nineteenth century, lost his religious faith as a teenager and struggled ever afterward to find a substitute faith. Hull found his substitute in mathematics and science. Just as Thomas Hobbes had been inspired by reading the book of Euclid, so Hull could say that "the study of geometry proved to be the most important event of my intellectual life." Hull also concluded, as had Hobbes, that one should conceive of thinking, reasoning, and other cognitive powers, including learning, as quite mechanical in nature, and capable of being described and understood through the elegant precision of mathematics. His infatuation with mathematics led him first to seek a career as a mining engineer, but an attack of polio forced him to make new plans. He toyed with the idea of being a minister in the Unitarian church—"a free, godless religion"—but "the prospect of attending an endless succession of ladies' teas" led him to abandon that calling. He sought "a field allied to philosophy in the sense of involving theory," which was so new that he might quickly "find recognition," and that would engage his penchant for machinery by allowing him "to design and work with automatic apparatus." Psychology met "this unique set of requirements," and Hull set out to "deliberately make a bid for a certain place in the history of science." He began by studying James's *Principles,* at first by having his mother read to him during his convalescence. Hull spent his undergraduate years at the University of Michigan, where for a course in logic he built a machine for displaying the logic of syllogisms. Turned down for graduate study by Yale—where he eventually spent most of his professional career—and Cornell, Hull took his Ph.D. from the University of Wisconsin.

Hull eventually made his mark in psychology by his theory and research on learning, and his first investigations presage the influential Hull of the 1930s. As an undergraduate, he studied learning in the insane, and he attempted to formulate mathematically precise laws to account for how they form associations (Hull, 1917). His doctoral dissertation concerned concept formation and again was very quantitative (Hull, 1920). However, circumstances led Hull to spend the next few years doing research in unrelated areas: hypnosis (an "unscientific" field, which Hull tried to improve using "quantitative methodology"); the effects of tobacco on behavior; and aptitude testing, for which Hull designed a machine for calculating the correlations between the scores of the various tests in a test battery. Doing so confirmed for him the idea that thinking was a mechanical process that might be simulated by an actual machine; Pascal had been horrified by the same insight, but Hull found in it a hypothesis on which to work.

Like every psychologist, Hull had to grapple with Watson's behaviorism. At first, although he sympathized with Watson's attacks on introspection and call for objectivity, Hull was put off by Watson's dogmatism, and by "the semi-fanatical ardor with which some young people would espouse the Watsonian cause with . . . a fanaticism more characteristic of religion than of science" (Hull, 1952b, pp. 153–4). Flirting with Gestalt psychology instead, Hull managed to get Kurt Koffka to visit the University of Wisconsin for a year. However, Koffka's "strikingly negative" attitude toward Watson paradoxically convinced Hull "not that the Gestalt view was sound" but that Watson's behaviorism needed improvement along the mathematical lines Hull was already inclined to follow: "Instead of converting me to *Gestalttheorie,* [I experienced] a belated conversion to a kind of neobehaviorism . . . concerned with the determination of the quantitative laws of behavior and their deductive systematization" (Hull, 1952b, p. 154). In 1929, Hull moved to Yale University, where he embarked on a career as the preeminent experimental psychologist of his day.

Hull's program had two components. First, as we have seen, Hull was fascinated by machinery and became convinced that machines could think, so he attempted to build machines capable of learning and thinking. In 1929, he described such a machine representing, as he put it (echoing La Mettrie and anticipating artificial intelligence), "a direct implication of the mechanistic tendency of modern psychology. Learning and thought are here conceived as by no means necessarily a function of living protoplasm than is serial locomotion" (Hull and Baernstein, 1929). The other component of Hull's theoretical ambition continued the geometric spirit of Hobbes and the associationism of Hume, whom Hull thought of as the first behaviorist. Around 1930, Hull says, "I came to the definite conclusion . . . that psychology is a true natural science" whose task is the discovery of "laws expressible quantitatively by means of a moderate number of ordinary equations" from which individual and group behaviors might be deduced as consequences (Hull, 1952b, p. 155). Given Hull's mechanistic and mathematical interests, it is unsurprising to learn that he contracted a bad case of physics envy and fancied himself the Newton of behavior. In the mid-1920s, he read Newton's *Principia,* and it became a sort of bible for him (Smith, 1986). He assigned portions of it to his seminars and placed it on his desk between himself and visitors; it represented for him the very pinnacle of scientific achievement, and he strove to emulate his hero.

During the early 1930s, Hull pursued both formal theory and learning machines in tandem, publishing increasingly mathematical treatments of complex behaviors such as the acquisition and assembling of simple S–R habits, and promising the production of "psychic machines" capable of thought and useful as industrial robots (Hull 1930a, 1930b, 1931, 1934, 1935). However, as the 1930s wore on, Hull's psychic machines played a decreasing role in his work. It appears that he feared that his preoccupation with intelligent machines would appear "grotesque" to outsiders, and that his work on them would be suppressed, as university authorities had suppressed his earlier work on hypnosis (Smith, 1986). At the same time, Hull came under the influence of logical positivism. Its insistence on formalism and the reduction of the mental to the physical was quite consistent with Hull's own philosophy of science, so that he found increased emphasis on formal, mathematical theory to be most useful as "propaganda" by which to advance his cause (Smith, 1986).

Hull's turn from the pursuit of psychic machines and formal theories to the exclusive pursuit of the latter may be conveniently dated to 1936, the year in which he was president of the APA. In his presidential address, he described his ambitions for theoretical psychology and tackled the central problem of behaviorism: accounting for mind (1937). He noted the same outward signs of mind as Tolman did: purposive, persistent behavior in the striving for goals. However, he proposed to account for them in a completely different way, as the outcome of mechanistic, lawful, principles of behavior: "The complex forms of purposive behavior [will] be found to derive from . . . the basic entities of theoretical physics, such as electrons and protons." Hull recognized that traditionally such a mechanistic position had been only philosophical, and he proposed to make it scientific by applying what he took to be scientific procedure. Science, Hull stated, consisted of a set of "explicitly stated postulates" (as did Euclid's geometry) from which, "by the most rigorous logic," predictions about actual behaviors would be deduced. Just as Newton had derived the motions of the planets from a small set of physical laws, so Hull proposed to predict the motions of organisms from a (rather larger) set of behavioral laws set forth in his paper. The virtue of the scientific method, Hull claimed, was that its predictions could be precisely tested against observations, while the nebulous claims of philosophy, whether idealistic or materialistic, could not be.

Using his set of proposed postulates, Hull tried to show that purposive behavior could be accounted for mechanistically. Finally, he asked, "But what of consciousness?" and in answering this question articulated his own version of methodological behaviorism. Psychology could dispense with consciousness, Hull said, "for the simple reason that no theorem has been found as yet whose deduction would be facilitated in any way by including" a postulate referring to consciousness. "Moreover, we have been quite unable to find any other scientific system of behavior which . . . has found consciousness necessary" (1937, p. 31) to deduce behavior. As did Tolman, Hull set conscious experience, the original subject matter of psychology, outside the bounds of psychology as behaviorists viewed it. Hull, like Watson, attributed continued interest in consciousness among psychologists to "the perseverative influences of medieval theology," claiming that "psychology in its basic principles is to a considerable degree in the thrall of the Middle Ages, and that, in particular, our prevailing systematic outlook in the matter of consciousness is largely medieval." But, concluded Hull, "fortunately the means of our salvation is clear and obvious. As ever, it lies in the application of scientific procedures . . . . For us to apply the methodology, it is necessary only to throw off the shackles of a lifeless tradition" (p. 32).

Reference to purposive robots was relegated to a footnote in which Hull mentioned "a kind of experimental shortcut to the determination of the ultimate nature of adaptive behavior." If one could build "from inorganic materials . . . a mechanism which would display" the adaptive behaviors derived from his postulates, then "it would be possible to say with assurance and a clear conscience that such adaptive behavior may be 'reached' by purely physical means" (p. 31). During his actual presentation to the APA, Hull demonstrated for the audience one of his learning machines, and they were deeply impressed by its performance (Chapanis, 1961). Because Hull rarely mentioned his "psychic machines" again, his statement of the central thesis of cognitive science has gone unnoticed or has been dismissed as peripheral to Hull's thinking. In fact, it is obvious that mechanical simulation of thought was central to Hull's thinking, and it gave rise to the formal theory for which he became famous and through which he became influential.

Along with Tolman, Hull began to adopt the language of logical positivism in the mid-1930s. After 1937, he identified his system with "logical empiricism" and applauded the "uniting" of American behavior theory with Viennese logical positivism, which was producing "in America a behavioral discipline which will be a full-blown natural science" (Hull, 1943a). From then on, Hull bent his efforts to the creation of a formal, deductive, quantitative theory of learning and largely left his psychic machines behind, though they continued to play a heuristic, unpublished role in Hull's thinking (Smith, 1986). Adoption of positivist language obscured Hull's realism, as it did Tolman's. Hull, of course, did not believe in purposes and cognitions, as Tolman did, but he was a realist in believing that the postulates of his theories described actual neurophysiological states and processes in the nervous systems of living organisms, human or animal.

He set forth his postulate systems in a series of books. The first was *Mathematico-Deductive Theory of Rote Learning* (Hull et al., 1940), which offered a mathematical treatment of human verbal learning. The book was praised as "giving a foretaste of what psychology will be like when it reaches systematic, quantitative, precision" (Hilgard, 1940). The rote learning theory was a "dress rehearsal" for his major work, *Principles of Behavior* (Hull, 1943b), the expression of "the behavior system . . . which I had gradually been developing throughout my academic life," and which had formed the basis of his APA presidential address. Upon publication, the *Psychological Bulletin* accorded it a "special review" in which *Principles of Behavior* was praised as "one of the most important books published in psychology in the twentieth century" (Koch, 1944). The book promised to unify all of psychology under the S–R formulation, and to perform needed "radical surgery" on the "withering corpus of social science," saving it for real science. Hull revised his system twice more (Hull, 1951, 1952a), but it was *Principles* that fulfilled his ambition of making a permanent name for himself in the history of psychology.

Conclusion: Tolman versus Hull

Tolman's purposive behaviorism inevitably came into conflict with Hull's mechanistic behaviorism. Tolman always believed that purpose and cognition were real, although his conception of their reality changed over time. Hull, on the other hand, sought to explain purpose and cognition as the result of mindless mechanical processes describable in logico-mathematical equations. During the 1930s and 1940s, Tolman and Hull engaged in a sort of intellectual tennis match: Tolman would attempt to demonstrate that purpose and cognition were real, while Hull and his followers patched up the theory or tried to show that Tolman's demonstrations were flawed.

Let us consider an example of an experiment that contrasts the cognitive and S–R views. It was actually reported in 1930 (Tolman, 1932), well before the Hull–Tolman debates really got under way, but it is a simpler version of more complex experiments described in Tolman's (1948) "Cognitive Maps in Rats and Men," meant to differentially support Tolman's theory. The maze is shown in Figure 11–1. Rats were familiarized with the entire maze by forcing them to run each path in early training. Having learned the maze, a rat coming out of the start box into the choice point must pick one of the paths. How does the rat do this?

A Hullian analysis may be sketched. The choice point presents stimuli (S) to which three responses (Rs), corresponding to each path, have been conditioned during initial training. For a variety of reasons, most obviously the different amounts of running that must be done in each alley, Path 1 is preferred to Path 2, which is

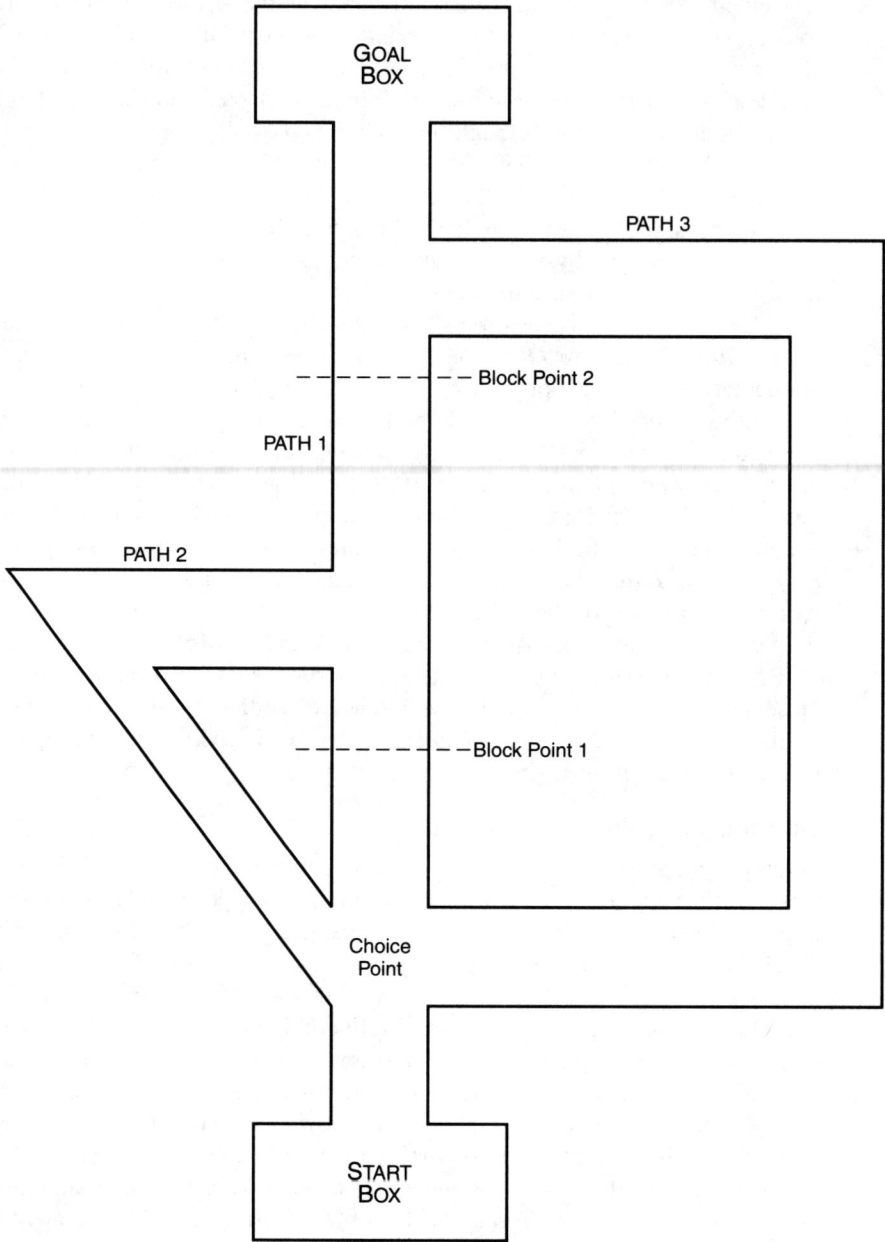

FIGURE 11-1   Tolman–Honzik Maze

preferred to Path 3. That is, connection $S \rightarrow R_1$ is stronger than $S \rightarrow R_2$, which is stronger than $S \rightarrow R_3$. Such a state of affairs may be notated:

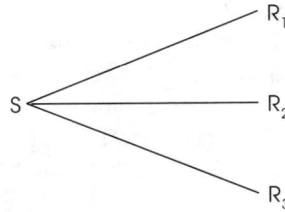

$$S \begin{array}{c} \nearrow R_1 \\ \longleftarrow R_2 \\ \searrow R_3 \end{array}$$

This is called a *divergent habit family hierarchy*. Now, should a block be placed at Point 1, the rat will run into it, back up, and choose Path 2. The connection $S \rightarrow R_1$ is weakened by the block, so that $S \rightarrow R_2$ becomes stronger and is acted on. On the other hand, if the second block is placed, the rat will retreat to the choice point and again choose Path 2 as $S \rightarrow R_1$ is again blocked, and $S \rightarrow R_2$ becomes stronger. However, the block will be met again, $S \rightarrow R_2$ will weaken, and finally $S \rightarrow R_3$ will be strongest and Path 3 will be chosen. This is the Hullian prediction.

Tolman denied that what is learned is a set of responses triggered to differing degrees by the stimuli at the choice point. Instead, he held that the rat learns a mental map of the maze that guides its behavior. According to this view, the rat encountering the first block will turn around and choose Path 2, as in the S–R account, because Path 2 is shorter than Path 3. However, if it encounters Block 2, the rat will know that the same block will cut off Path 2 as well as Path 1. Therefore, the rat will show "insight": It will return and choose Path 3, ignoring Path 2 altogether. A map displays all aspects of the environment and is more informative than a set of S–R connections. The results of the experiment supported Tolman's cognitive theory of learning over Hull's S–R account.

Although Hull and Tolman differed sharply on their specific accounts of behavior, we should not forget that they shared important assumptions and goals. Both Tolman and Hull wanted to write scientific theories of learning and behavior applying to at least all mammals, including human beings. They pursued their mutual goal by experimenting on and theorizing about rats, assuming that any difference between rat and human was trivial, and that results from laboratories represented naturalistic behavior as well; they followed Herbert Spencer's formula for psychology. Both Tolman and Hull rejected consciousness as the subject matter of psychology and took the description, prediction, and control of behavior as psychology's task; they were behavioralists—specifically, methodological behaviorists. Finally, both were influenced by, and seemed to endorse, logical positivism.

Psychologists have tended to assume that Tolman and Hull were slavish adherents of logical positivism, and that they personally set the positivist style of modern psychology. However, such a judgment does them a disservice, obscures their independence, and depreciates their creativity. Tolman and Hull reached their conceptions of science, psychology, and behavior quite independently of logical positivism. When they encountered logical positivism in the 1930s, each found he could use this prestigious philosophy to more powerfully state his own ideas; but we must not forget that their ideas were their own. Unfortunately, because they did adopt positivist language and because positivism quickly came to be psychologists' philosophy of science, the real programs of Tolman and Hull were obscured or forgotten, resulting in some fruitless controversies in the 1950s, as we shall see in Chapter 13.

Although both Tolman and Hull were honored and influential, there is no doubt that Hull was very much more influential than Tolman. At Berkeley, Tolman filled students with enthusiasm for psychology and a healthy disrespect for scientific pomposity. He wrote lively papers and took a zestful approach to science, saying that "in the end, the only sure criterion is to have fun. And I have had fun" (Tolman, 1959). He was never a systematic theorist and had finally to confess to being a "crypto-phenomenologist" who designed his experiments by imagining what he would do if he were a rat, being gratified to find that rats were as clever and commonsensical as he was, being no machines. Unfortunately, this all meant that while Tolman could inspire students, he could not teach them a systematic viewpoint with which to evangelize psychology. Tolman had no disciples.

Hull, however, did. Instead of valuing having fun, Hull valued the long, arduous labor of constructing postulates and deriving theorems from them. Though tedious, this gave Hull an explicit set of ideas with which to infect his students for spreading throughout the discipline. Moreover, Hull's institutional situation was ideal for building discipleship. Besides the department of psychology at Yale, Hull was strategically placed at Yale's Institute of Human Relations (IHR), which attracted bright minds from many disciplines eager to learn the rigors of science for application to their fields and to the problems of the world. We will later see how social learning theory emerged from Hull's seminars at the IHR. Hull found someone to continue his program in Kenneth Spence (1907–1967). Spence collaborated on Hull's great books, continued his rigorous theorizing into the 1950s, created a truly positivist version of neobehaviorism, and trained many leading experimental psychologists of the 1950s and 1960s: Hull's intellectual grandchildren. And, of course, Hull's rigorous theoretical system, pristinely mechanistic and eschewing any mysticism about purpose and cognition, was perfectly in tune with the naturalistic–positivistic *Zeitgeist* of American psychology after World War I.

Studies during the 1950s therefore consistently found Hull's impact on psychology to be much greater than Tolman's. For example, as late as the 1960s, a study of which psychologists were most often cited in the leading journals of psychology (Myers, 1970) found that the most cited psychologist was Kenneth Spence, with Hull himself at eighth place. This is especially remarkable considering that Hull had been dead since 1952, and his theory had been subjected to scathing criticism since the early 1950s. Despite the fact that many psychologists saw a cognitive "revolution" taking place in the 1960s, E. C. Tolman, the purposive, cognitive behaviorist, did not place in the top 60.

CONCLUSION: WE'RE ALL BEHAVIORISTS NOW

Hull's colleague, Kenneth Spence, observed in 1948 that few psychologists "ever seem to think of themselves, or explicitly refer to themselves as behaviorists," because behaviorism was "a very general point of view which has come to be accepted by almost all psychologists." Spence noted one exception to his conclusion: Tolman protested perhaps too much that he was a good behaviorist. Spence also recognized that behaviorism took many forms, so that the term "behaviorism" was rather slippery. Still, behaviorism had made progress, Spence thought, because all the neobehaviorisms sharply separated themselves from Watson's early, rather crude formulation of classical behaviorism. Spence tried to tidy up the Babel of behaviorisms by formulating a behaviorist metaphysics along logical positivist lines. He hoped to create a common creed on which all behaviorists might agree. As we shall see in Chapter 13, his hope was misplaced, as the Tolmanians refused to assent.

On the horizon of experimental psychology lay a newly formulated radical behaviorism that after World War II would challenge and then replace all other behaviorisms. B. F. Skinner, a writer turned psychologist, had begun in 1931 to work out a behaviorism in the radical spirit of Watson, but with a new set of technical concepts. Skinner's influence lay in the future, when, after the war, psychologists would again lose confidence in their enterprise and begin to look for a new Newton. Before the war, however, Skinner was not taken too seriously. E. R. Hilgard (1939) said of Skinner's first major theoretical statement, *Behavior of Organisms* (1938), that its narrow conception of psychology would greatly limit its influence.

During the years when academic psychologists came to accept behavioralism as the only legitimate approach to the problems of scientific psychology, other psychologists were beginning to tackle the problems of society. Psychology experienced its greatest growth not in experimental psychology, but in applied psychology.

Note: The bibliographies for Chapters 11 and 12 have been combined following Chapter 12.

REFERENCES

Bode, B. H. (1918). Consciousness as behavior. *Journal of Philosophy 15:* 449–53.

Bridgman, P. (1927). *The logic of modern physics.* New York: Macmillan.

Buckley, K. (1984). *Mechanical man: John B. Watson and the beginnings of behaviorism.* Westport, CT: Guilford Press.

Calkins, M. W. (1913). Psychology and the behaviorist. *Psychological Bulletin 10:* 288–91.

_____ . (1921). The truly psychological behaviorism. *Psychological Bulletin 28:* 1–18.

Chapanis, A. (1961). Men, machines and models. *American Psychologist 16:* 113–31.

Cohen, D. B. (1979). *J. B. Watson: The founder of behaviorism.* London: Routledge and Kegan Paul.

Dashiell, J. F. (1939). Some rapprochements in contemporary psychology. *Psychological Bulletin 36:* 1–24.

Harris, B. (1979). Whatever happened to Little Albert? *American Psychologist 34:* 151–60.

Hilgard, E. R. (1939). Review of B. F. Skinner, Behavior of organisms. *Psychological Bulletin 36:* 121–24.

_____ . (1940). Review of Hull et al. *Psychological Bulletin 37:* 808–15.

Holton, G. (1978). *The scientific imagination: Case studies.* Cambridge, England: Cambridge University Press.

Hull, C. (1917). The formation and retention of associations among the insane. *American Journal of Psychology 28:* 419–35.

_____ . (1920). Quantitative aspects of the evolution of concepts. *Psychological Monographs 28,* no. 123.

_____ . (1930a). Simple trial and error learning: A study in psychological theory. *Psychological Review 37:* 241–56.

_____. (1930b). Knowledge and purpose as habit mechanisms. *Psychological Review 37:* 511–25.

_____. (1931). Goal attraction and directing ideas conceived as habit phenomena. *Psychological Review 38:* 487–506.

_____. (1934). The concept of the habit-family-hierarchy in maze learning. *Psychological Review 41:* 33–54 and 131–52.

_____. (1935). The conflicting psychologies of learning: A way out. *Psychological Review 42:* 491–516.

_____. (1937). Mind, mechanism and adaptive behavior. *Psychological Review 44:* 1–32.

_____. (1943a). The problem of intervening variables in molar behavior theory. *Psychological Review 50:* 273–88.

_____. (1943b). *Principles of behavior.* New York: Appleton-Century-Crofts.

_____. (1951). *Essentials of behavior.* New Haven, CT: Yale University Press.

_____. (1952a). *A behavior system.* New Haven, CT: Yale University Press.

Hull, C. and Baernstein, H. (1929). A mechanical parallel to the conditioned reflex. *Science 70:* 14–15.

Hull, C., Hovland, C., Ross, R., Hall, M., Perkins, D., and Fitch, F. (1940). *Mathematico-deductive theory of rote learning: A study in scientific methodology.* New Haven, CT: Yale University Press.

Hunter, W. S. (1922). An open letter to the anti-behaviorists. *Journal of Philosophy 19:* 307–8.

_____. (1923). Review of A. A. Roback, "Behaviorism and psychology." *American Journal of Psychology 34:* 464–67.

_____. (1925). Psychology and anthroponomy. In C. Murchison, ed., *Psychologies of 1925.* Worcester, MA: Clark University Press.

Jastrow, J. (1927). The reconstruction of psychology. *Psychological Review 34:* 169–95.

Jones, A. H. (1915). The method of psychology. *Journal of Philosophy 12:* 462–71.

Koch, S. (1941). The logical character of the motivation concept. *Psychological Review 48:* 15–38, 127–54.

_____. (1944). Hull's *Principles of behavior:* A special review. *Psychological Bulletin 41:* 269–86.

Langfeld, H. S. (1943). Fifty years of the Psychological Review. Psychological Review 50: 143–55.

Lashley, K. S. (1923). The behavioristic interpretation of consciousness. *Psychological Review 30:* I: 237–72, II: 329–53.

MacDougall, R. (1925). Men or robots? In C. Murchison, ed., *Psychologies of 1925.* Worcester, MA: Clark University Press

McComas, H. C. (1916). Extravagances in the motor theory of consciousness. *Psychological Review 23:* 397–406.

McGeoch, J. A. (1931). The acquisition of skill. *Psychological Bulletin 28:* 413–66.

Myers, C. R. (1970). Journal citations and scientific eminence in psychology. *American Psychologist 25:* 1041–48.

Pepper, S. (1923). Misconceptions regarding behaviorism. *Journal of Philosophy 20:* 242–45.

Perry, R. B. (1921). A behavioristic view of purpose. *Journal of Philosophy 18:* 85–105.

Samelson, F. (1980). J. B. Watson's Little Albert, Cyril Burt's twins, and the need for a critical science. *American Psychologist 35:* 619–25.

_____ . (1981). Struggle for scientific authority: The reception of Watson's behaviorism, 1913–1920. *Journal of the History of the Behavioral Sciences 17:* 399–425.

Schneider, S. M. and Morris, E. K. (1987). A History of the term Radical Behaviorism: From Watson to Skinner. *The Behavior Analyst 10:* 27–39.

Skinner, B. F. (1938). *Behavior of organisms.* New York: Appleton-Century-Crofts.

Smith, L. J. (1986). *Behaviorism and logical positivism: A revised account of the alliance.* Stanford, CA: Stanford University Press.

Spence, K. (1948). Postulates and methods of "behaviorism." *Psychological Review 55:* 67–78.

Stevens, S. S. (1935a). The operational basis of psychology. *American Journal of Psychology 43:* 323–30.

_____ . (1935b). The operational definition of psychological concepts. *Psychological Review 42:* 517–27.

_____ . (1939). Psychology and the science of science. *Psychological Bulletin 36:* 221–63.

Titchener, E. B. (1914). On "Psychology as the behaviorist views it." *Proceedings of the American Philosophical Society 53:* 1–17.

Tolman, E. (1920). Instinct and purpose. *Psychological Review 27:* 217–33.

_____ . (1922). A new formula for behaviorism. *Psychological Review 29:* 44–53.

_____ . (1923). A behavioristic account of the emotions. *Psychological Review 30:* 217–27.

_____ . (1925). Behaviorism and purpose. *Journal of Philosophy 22:* 36–41.

_____ . (1926). A behavioristic theory of ideas. *Psychological Review 33:* 352–69.

_____ . (1932). *Purposive behavior in animals and men.* New York: Century.

_____ . (1935). Psychology vs. immediate experience. Philosophy of Science. Reprinted in E. Tolman (1951/1966) *Behavior and psychological man.* Berkeley: University of California Press.

_____ . (1936). Operational behaviorism and current trends in psychology. In E. Tolman (1951/1966), *Behavior and psychological man.* Berkeley: University of California Press.

_____ . (1948). Cognitive maps in rats and men. *Psychological Review 55:* 189–209.

_____ . (1959). Principles of purposive behaviorism. In S. Koche, ed., *Psychology: A study of a science,* Vol. 2. New York: McGraw-Hill.

Warren, H. (1938). Howard C. Warren. In C. Murchison, ed., *A history of psychology in autobiography,* Vol. 1. Worcester, MA: Clark University Press.

Watson, J. B. (1913a). Psychology as the behaviorist views it. *Psychological Review 20:* 158–177.

_____ . (1913b). Image and affection in behavior. *Journal of Philosophy 10:* 421–28.

_____ . (1916a). The place of the conditioned reflex in psychology. *Psychological Review 23:* 89–116.

_____ . (1916b). Behavior and the concept of mental disease. *Journal of Philosophy 13:* 589–97.

_____ . (1930). *Behaviorism.* 2nd ed. New York: Norton. Original work published 1925.

Watson, J. B. and Rayner, R. (1920). Conditioned emotional reactions. *Journal of Experimental Psychology 10:* 421–28.

Wheeler, R. W. (1923). Introspection and behavior. *Psychological Review 30:* 103–15.

Wickens, D. D. (1938). The transference of conditioned extinction from one muscle group to the antagonistic muscle group. *Journal of Experimental Psychology 22:* 101–23.

Williams, K. (1931). Five behaviorisms. *American Journal of Psychology 43:* 337–61.

Woodworth, R. S. (1924). Four varieties of behaviorism. *Psychological Review 31:* 257–64.

12 *Psychology Takes Off*
Applied Psychology and Society (1896–1950)

Workers assembling telephone relays at the Hawthorne plant of the Western Electric Company. After World War I, applied psychology grew rapidly as psychologists tried to solve the many problems created by urbanization and industrialization. One problem was adjusting workers to repetitive factory work and increasing their productivity. The Hawthorne plant was the site of the single most famous study of worker adjustment, the finding of the so-called "Hawthorne Effect."

Entrance into World War I marked the end of two decades of profound social change, transforming the United States from a rural country of island communities into an industrialized, urbanized nation of everywhere communities. The United States became a great power that could project military might across the Atlantic Ocean and decide the outcome of a European war. Progressive politicians saw a welcome chance to achieve their goals of social control; the war had created a unified, patriotic, efficient nation out of the mass of immigrants and scattered groups created by industrializa-tion. Led by President Wilson, they also saw a chance to bring Progressive, rational control to the whole world. As one Progressive exclaimed, "Long live social control; social control, not only to enable us to meet the rigorous demands of the war, but also as a foundation for the peace and brotherhood that is to come" (quoted by Thomas, 1977, p. 1020).

But the Great War to End All Wars frustrated and then shattered the Progres-sives' dreams. The government created bureaucracies, which accomplished little. Worse, the horrors of the war, in which many European villages lost their entire male populations for a few feet of foreign soil, brought Americans face to face with the ir-rational and left many Europeans with lifelong depression and pessimism. After the armistice, the victorious powers fell to dividing up the spoils of war like vultures, and Wilson became a pathetic idealist ignored at Versailles and then at home, unable to bring America into his League of Nations. World War I did nothing but lay the groundwork for World War II.

The pessimistic, darkly expectant mood of the era was captured in 1920 by William Butler Yeats in the poem "The Second Coming":*

> Turning and turning in the widening gyre
> The falcon cannot hear the falconer:
> Things fall apart; the centre cannot hold;
> Mere anarchy is loosed upon the world,
> The blood-dimmed tide is loosed, and everywhere
> The ceremony of innocence is drowned;
> The best lack all conviction, while the worst
> Are full of passionate intensity.
> Surely some revelation is at hand; . . . .
> . . . what rough beast, its hour come round at last,
> Slouches towards Bethlehem to be born?

Intellectuals and social and political leaders concluded that reason was not enough to achieve social control. Convinced of the wisdom of science, however—for scientism still ran strong in America—American leaders turned to social science, especially psychology, to solve the problems of the postwar world, to give them the tools by which to manage the irrational masses, to reshape the family and the work-place. As Philip Rieff (1966) put it, the Middle Ages, with faith in God, ruled through the church; the progressive nineteenth century, with faith in reason, ruled through the legislature; the twentieth century, with faith in science tempered by recognition of the irrational, rules through the hospital. In the twentieth century, then, psychology would become one of the most important institutions in society; no wonder that psychologists' ideas became more widely applied—the latest scientific marvel, read by leaders for clues to social control and by the masses for insights into the springs of their own behavior.

---

* Reprinted with permission of Macmillan Publishing Co., Inc., from *Collected Poems by William Butler Yeats.* Copyright 1924 by Macmillan Publishing Co., Inc., renewed 1952 by Bertha Georgie Yeats.

THE RISE OF APPLIED PSYCHOLOGY (1896–1918)

Beginnings of Applied Psychology

In 1892, William James wrote, "The kind of psychology which could cure a case of melancholy, or charm a chronic insane delusion away, ought certainly to be preferred to the most seraphic insight into the nature of the soul." James identified a tension in modern psychology—especially modern American psychology—that has steadily increased throughout the twentieth century: the tension between the psychologist as scientist and the psychologist as practitioner of a craft. The tension has been most evident in the history of the American Psychological Association (APA), founded in 1892. The APA was founded to advance the cause of psychology as science, but very quickly its members turned to the application of their science, and the APA found itself embroiled in unwanted problems concerned with defining and regulating the practice of psychology as a technological profession. Especially in America, the development of professional applied psychology was inevitable: Psychology's social circumstances and the philosophies of pragmatism and functionalism required it.

In nineteenth-century Germany, the academicians who controlled the gates of admission to the great universities had needed to be convinced of psychology's legitimacy as a discipline, and in the German Mandarin culture (Chapter 7), pure knowledge was valued above technology. Naturally, Wundt and the other German psychologists founded a discipline strictly devoted to "seraphic insights into the nature of the soul." In the United States, things were very different. American universities were not institutions controlled by a few academicians working for the central state; they were a variegated collection of public and private schools subject more to local needs than central control. As de Tocqueville learned, Americans valued practical success and sought social and personal improvement rather than Platonic knowledge. The tribunal that would pass on psychology's worthiness in America was composed of practical men of business and industry and political leaders interested in techniques of social control. Naturally, then, psychologists came to stress the social and personal utility of their discipline instead of its refined scientific character.

American psychology wanted to be recognized as a science, but especially as a science with practical aims. On the occasion of the twenty-fifth anniversary of the APA, John Dewey (1917) denounced the concept, characteristic of Gall or Wundt, of the mind as a creation of nature existing before society. By placing mind beyond society's control, such a view acted as a bastion of political conservatism, Dewey held. As the proper foundation for experimental psychology, he offered his pragmaticist conception of mind as a social creation. Because, in Dewey's view, mind was created by society, it could be deliberately molded by society, and psychology, the science of the mind, could take as its goal social control, the scientific management of society. Such a psychology would fall in with Progressivism and give American psychology the social utility Wundt's psychology lacked.

American psychologists thus offered a science with pragmatic "cash value." Pragmatism demanded that ideas become true by making a difference to human conduct; so, to be true, psychological ideas would have to show that they did matter to individuals and society. Functionalism argued that the role of mind was to adjust the behavior of the individual organism to the environment. Naturally, then, psychologists would come to be interested in how the process of adjustment played itself out in American life, and they would then move to improve the process of adjustment to make it more efficient and to repair the process of adjustment when it went awry. Adjustment was the great function of mind; therefore, every sphere of human life was opened to the psychological technologist—the child's adjustment to the family; parents' adjustments to their children and to each other; the worker's adjustment to the workplace; the soldier's adjustment to the army; and so on through every aspect of personality and behavior. No aspect of life would finally escape the clinical gaze of professional psychologists.

Interest in these matters appeared as soon as psychology reached America. Central to the first applications of psychology was Cattell's invention of the "mental test" in 1890. At the Columbian Exposition of 1893, psychology first came to the public's attention when people entered an exhibit and took psychological tests. The first "psychological clinic" was opened in 1896 by Lightner Witmer, and many others sprang up in the ensuing years. These clinics used tests to diagnose children with school problems but generally offered no treatment. A related development was the child guidance clinic; the first such clinic was attached to a juvenile court in Chicago in 1909. There, psychologist Grace Fernald gave tests to children brought before the court. The earliest tests used with retarded children were "tests" made up using the brass instruments of the psychological laboratory, but these were soon replaced by the more sophisticated Binet test. The center of this activity was the Vineland Training School for Feeble-Minded Boys and Girls, which opened in New Jersey in 1905; its director, Henry Goddard, introduced the Binet test to the United States. In 1908, Clifford Beers, a former mental patient, started the mental hygiene movement with a book, *A Mind That Found Itself,* endorsed by William James himself. The aim of the mental hygienists was the prevention of psychological problems, and their efforts provided a further impetus to the child guidance clinics, which began to look for problems before they developed. At the McLean Hospital, Chicago, IL, mental patients were tested and became subjects of investigations by psychologists. Finally, psychology was applied to business and industry, beginning with advertising. Walter Dill Scott gave a talk on the psychology of advertising in 1901, and eventually became professor of advertising at Northwestern University in 1915. In the same year, psychologists began to use tests to pick workers for particular jobs.

Just before the United States entered World War I, then, psychologists were actively applying their ideas and techniques—especially tests—to a wide range of social problems. Their efforts, however, were scattered and small scale. When the war came, psychologists enlisted to apply themselves to a truly massive task: the evaluation of men for fitness to serve in the U.S. Army. One year later, psychology had become a permanent part of the intellectual landscape of American life, and its terminology had become part of the American vocabulary.

Psychologists in the Great War

Psychologists, like Progressives, saw the Great War as a great opportunity to show that psychology had come of age as a science and could be put to service. The organizer of psychology's efforts to serve the nation at war was Robert Yerkes, the comparative psychologist. With pride, he explained in his presidential address to the APA just months after the war began:

> In this country, for the first time in the history of our science, a general organization in the interests of certain ideal and practical aims has been effected. Today, American

psychology is placing a highly trained and eager personnel at the service of our military organizations. We are acting not individually but collectively on the basis of common training and common faith in the practical value of our work. (1918, p. 85)

Just as Progressives used the war to unify the country, Yerkes exhorted psychologists to "act unitedly in the interests of defense," bringing psychologists together "as a professional group in a nation-wide effort to render our professional training serviceable" (1918, p. 85).

Only two days after the United States declared war, Yerkes used a meeting of Titchener's "Experimentalists" to begin organizing psychology's war efforts. Following a whirlwind of activity, the APA formed twelve committees concerned with different aspects of the war, ranging from acoustic problems to recreation, but only two committees really accomplished anything: Walter Dill Scott's committee on motivation, which became the Committee on Classification of Personnel of the War Department, and Yerkes's own committee on the psychological examination of recruits, which concentrated on the problem of eliminating the "mentally unfit" from the U.S. Army. There was considerable tension between Yerkes and Scott from the outset. Yerkes came from experimental psychology and brought research interests to the job of testing recruits, hoping to gather data on intelligence as well as serve the needs of the military. Scott's background was industrial psychology, and he brought a practical, management perspective to military testing, aiming above all at practical results. At the wartime organizational meeting of the APA at the Walton Hotel in Philadelphia, Scott said that he "became so enraged at [Yerkes's] points of view that I expressed myself very clearly and left the [APA] council" (von Mayrhauser, 1985). Scott believed Yerkes to be making a power play to advance his own interests in psychology, and he accused Yerkes of concealing self-interest behind sham patriotism. The upshot of the quarrel was that Yerkes and Scott went their own ways in applying tests to the examination of recruits.

Insofar as concrete results welcomed and used by the military were concerned, Scott's committee was the more effective. Drawing on his work in personnel psychology, Scott developed a rating scale for selecting officers. Scott convinced the army of the scale's utility, and he was allowed to form his War Department committee, which quickly became involved in the more massive undertaking of assigning the "right man to the right job" in the army. By the end of the war, Scott's committee had grown from 20 to over 175 members, had classified nearly 3,500,000 men, and had developed proficiency tests for 83 military jobs. Scott was awarded a Distinguished Service Medal for his work.

Yerkes's committee did little for the army—he won no medal—but it did a great deal to advance professional psychology. Its foremost achievement was inventing the group test of intelligence. In May 1918, Yerkes assembled leading test psychologists at the Vineland Training School to write an intelligence test for Army use. Initially, Yerkes believed that group tests of intelligence were unscientific, introducing uncontrolled factors into the test situation, and wanted to test each recruit individually; but associates of Scott's at Vineland persuaded him that individual testing was impossible under the circumstances (von Mayrhauser, 1985). Yerkes's team designed two tests that could be quickly administered to groups of recruits, the Army Alpha test for literate men, and the Army Beta test for presumed illiterates who did badly on the Alpha.

Recruits were graded on a letter scale from A to E, just like in school; "A" men were likely officers, "D" and "E" men were the unfit (see Figure 12–1).

Despite considerable skepticism, in December 1917, the Army approved general testing of recruits. Throughout the war, Yerkes's work was met with hostility and indifference by Army officers who saw Yerkes's psychologists as meddlers, and by Army psychiatrists who feared psychologists might assume some of their roles within the military. Nevertheless, 1,175,000 men were tested before the program was ended in January 1919. With the invention of the group test, Yerkes and his colleagues had invented a tool that greatly expanded the potential scope of psychologists' activities, and multiplied by many times the numbers of Americans who might be scrutinized by the profession.

In concluding his presidential address, Yerkes "looked ahead and attempted to prophesy future needs" for psychology. "The obvious and significant trend of our psychological military work is toward service—the demand for psychologists and psychological service promises, or threatens, to be overwhelmingly great." Yerkes foresaw better than he knew; while speaking only of psychological service in the military, Yerkes's words describe the most important change in institutional psychology in the twentieth century. Before the war, applied psychologists had worked in relative obscurity in isolated settings around the country; during the war, they touched millions of lives in a self-conscious, organized professional effort to apply psychology to a pressing social need; after the war, psychology was famous, and applied psychology grew by leaps and bounds, concerning itself with the "menace of the feebleminded," with immigrants, with troubled children, with industrial workers, with advertising, with problems of the American family. Applied psychology had arrived as an important actor on the American social scene, and its influence has never ceased to grow in the nearly eighty years since Yerkes called psychologists to military service.

Another enduring legacy of the army tests was the enhanced status given to mental tests by their application to war work. Lewis Terman, whose interest in human measurement had begun at age ten, when his "bumps" were read by an itinerant phrenologist, was elected president of the APA, and in his presidential address (Terman, 1924) argued that mental tests were equal to experiments in scientific value, and that, moreover, they were capable of addressing "one of the most important [issues] humanity faces," the relative contributions of nature and nurture to intelligence. Later, Terman (1930) predicted the widespread use of tests in schools, in vocational and educational guidance, in industry, politics, and law, and even in "matrimonial clinics," where tests would be given to couples before they decided to wed. The goals of the phrenological Fowlers would be realized in Terman's world.

Another leading test psychologist, Charles Spearman, grandiosely described the results from intelligence tests as having supplied the "long missing genuinely scientific foundation for psychology, . . . so that it can henceforward take its due place along with the other solidly founded sciences, even physics itself" (quoted by Gould, 1981). Test psychologists were as prone to physics envy as experimental psychologists. Terman's vision appeared to be well on its way to fulfillment. In his report on the army results, Yerkes spoke of "the steady stream of requests from commercial concerns, educational institutions, and individuals for the use of army methods of psychological examining or for the adaptation of such methods to special needs" (quoted in Gould, 1981). With

From *The Camp Sherman News*

FIGURE 12-1 That psychological examination, 1918. In retrospect, we can see that the army tests of intelligence were remarkably silly. This cartoon, from *The Camp Sherman News,* reprinted in *Psychological Bulletin,* 1919, expresses the ordinary soldier's experience of the tests. Groups of men were assembled in rooms, given pencils and response sheets, had to obey shouted orders to do unfamiliar things, and to answer strange questions. The test items that the unfortunate recruit in the cartoon has to answer are but slight exaggerations of the real items. Stephen Jay Gould gave the Beta test to Harvard undergraduates, following the exact procedures used in the war, and found that although most students did well, a few barely made "C" level. Gould's students, of course, were greatly experienced with standardized tests, in contrast with raw draftees under great stress, many of whom had little or no education. One can only imagine how puzzled and confused the average testee was, and can sympathize with the hapless soldier at Camp Sherman.

Terman, Yerkes foresaw a bright future for applied psychology based on mental tests. He (Yerkes, 1923) called psychologists to answer the "need for knowledge of man [which] has increased markedly in our times." Because "man is just as measurable as a bar or a . . . machine," psychologists would find that "more aspects of man will become measurable [and] . . . more social values appraisable," resulting in psychological "human engineering." In the "not remote future," applied psychology would be as precise and effective as applied physics. The goals of Progressive social control would have been reached with the tools of psychology.

PSYCHOLOGISTS IN SOCIAL CONTROVERSY (1917–1940)

As psychologists began to concern themselves with the problems of American society, they naturally became involved in wider social, political, and intellectual controversies outside academia. Ultimately, public attention turned psychology into something of a popular fad in the dozen years following the Great War.

Is America Safe for Democracy? Impact of Army Intelligence Testing

Progressives believed, with E. L. Thorndike (1920), that "in the long run it has paid the masses to be ruled by intelligence." But the results of the Army Alpha and Beta tests suggested that there were alarmingly few intelligent Americans—"A" men—and rather too many feebleminded Americans—"D" and "E" men. Yerkes's massive report on the results of the army tests recorded a mean American mental age of 13.08. Terman's work on translating and standardizing the Binet test had set the "normal" average intelligence at a mental age of 16. Henry Goddard had coined the term "moron" to denote anyone with a mental age of less than 13, so nearly half of the drafted white men (47.3 percent) would have to be considered morons. Performance by recent immigrant groups and Blacks was even worse. Yerkes (1923) told readers of *Atlantic Monthly* that "racial" differences in intelligence were quite real. Children from the older immigrant stock did quite well on the army tests. Draftees of English descent ranked first, followed by the Dutch, Danish, Scots, and Germans. Descendants of later-arriving immigrants did badly. At the bottom of the distribution of intelligence were Turks, Greeks, Russians, Italians, and Poles. At the very bottom were Black African Americans with a mental age on the army tests of just 10.41.

The results appalled people who agreed with Galton that intelligence is innate. In his book's title, psychologist William McDougall (1921) asked, *Is America Safe for Democracy?* and argued that unless action were taken, the answer was no: "Our civilization, by reason of its increasing complexity, is making constantly increasing demands upon the quality of its bearers; the qualities of those bearers are diminishing or deteriorating, rather than improving" (p. 168, italics not reproduced). Henry Goddard, who had helped construct the army tests, concluded that "the average man can manage his affairs with only a moderate degree of prudence, can earn only a very modest living, and is vastly better off when following direction than when trying to plan for himself" (Gould, 1981, p. 223). The Galtonian alarmists were convinced that individual and racial differences were genetic in origin and consequently incapable of being erased by education. For example, Yerkes (1923) noted that Black African Americans living in northern states outscored those living in the southern states by a wide margin, but he claimed that this was because smarter Blacks had moved North, leaving the feebleminded behind. He could, of course, have noted that Black African

Americans were more likely to receive an education in the North than in the South, but he did not even consider such a possibility.

There were critics of the tests and their alleged results, but in the beginning the critics' impact was limited. One insightful critic was the political writer Walter Lippman, who published a devastating critique of the alarmist interpretation of the army results in the *New Republic* in 1922 and 1923 (reprinted in Block and Dworkin, 1976). Lippman argued that the average American cannot have a below-average intelligence. Terman's figure of a "normal" mental age of 16 was based on a reference norm of a few hundred schoolchildren in California; the army results were based on over 100,000 recruits. Therefore, it was more logical to conclude that the army results represented average American intelligence than to stick with the California sample and absurdly conclude that the American average was below average. Moreover, the classification of men into A, B, C, D, and E categories was essentially arbitrary, reflecting the needs of the army, not raw intelligence. For example, the alarmists were reacting to having only 5 percent of the recruits graded as "A" men. Lippman pointed out that the tests were timed so that only 5 percent could be "A" men, because the army wanted to send 5 percent of the recruits to Officer Training School. Had the army wanted only half that number of officers, the tests would have been designed to yield 2.5 percent "A" men, and the alarmists would have been even more worked up. In short, Lippman showed, there wasn't anything in the army results to worry about. Nevertheless, the Galtonian alarmists pressed for political action to fight the supposed "menace of the feebleminded."

Making America Safe for Democracy: Immigration Control and Eugenics

> We can have almost any kind of a race of human beings we want. We can have a race that is beautiful or ugly, wise or foolish, strong or weak, moral or immoral.
>   This is not a mere fancy. It is as certain as any social fact.
>   Albert Edward Wiggam (1924, p. 262)

Galtonians regarded the recent immigrants and the Blacks as Prospero regards Caliban in Shakespeare's *The Tempest:* "a devil, a born devil, on whose nature, nurture can never stick." The army tests, said the Galtonians, demonstrated these groups' irredeemable stupidity, fixed in the genes, which no amount of education could improve. Because education was helpless to improve the intelligence, morality, and beauty of Americans, they concluded, something would have to be done about the stupid, the immoral, and the ugly, were America not to commit "race suicide." Specifically, according to Galtonians, inferior stock would have to be prevented from immigrating to America, and those Americans already here but cursed with stupidity or immorality would have to be prevented from breeding. Galtonians sought, therefore, to restrict immigration to persons whom they regarded as the better sort of people, and to implement negative eugenics by preventing reproduction among the worst sort of people. Although they were only occasionally leaders in the politics of immigration and eugenics, psychologists played an important role in support of Galtonian aims.

The worst Galtonians were outright racists. Their leader was Madison Grant, author of *The Passing of the Great Race* (1916). He divided the supposed "races" of Europe into the Nordic, Alpine, and Mediterranean, the first of which, blond and Protestant, were self-reliant heroes, more intelligent and resourceful than other races. The Nordics, Grant and his followers said, had founded the United States but were in danger of being swamped by the recent influx of immigrants from other racial groups. Yerkes (1923) himself endorsed Grant's fantastic racism, calling for selective immigration laws designed to keep out the non-Nordics, and so fend off the "menace of race deterioration" in the United States. Yerkes wrote the foreword for his student Carl Brigham's *A Study of American Intelligence* (1923), which used the army results to show that because of immigration—and, worse, "the most sinister development in the history of the continent, the importation of the negro"—"the decline of American intelligence will be . . . rapid . . . [unless] public action can be aroused to prevent it. There is no reason why legal steps should not be taken which would insure a continuously progressive upward evolution. . . . Immigration should not only be restrictive but highly selective" (quoted by Gould, 1981 p. 230). Galtonians pressed for action from Congress to stanch the flow of inferior types of people in the United States. Broughton Brandenburg, president of the National Institute of Immigration, testified, "It is not vainglory when we say that we have bred more than sixty million of the finest people the world has ever seen. Today, there is to surpass us, none. Therefore any race that we admit to our body social is certain to be more or less inferior" (Haller, 1963, p. 147). In 1924, Congress passed an immigration restriction act—altered in the 1970s and again in 1991—that limited the number of future immigrants to a formula based on the number of immigrants from each country in 1890, before the flow of non-"Nordic" immigrants increased.

Although the anti-immigration arguments were popular and politically effective, they were pervaded by the crass racism and intellectual snobbery of the whole Galtonian movement in the United States. Its cant and humbug derive not from Darwin or Mendel, but from blind prejudice. In a scientistic age, bigotry adopts the language of science, for the language of heresy will no longer do. By restricting immigration of so-called inferior peoples, racism won a great battle in a nation that 148 years before had pledged its sacred honor to the thesis that "all men are created equal." No longer would the poor huddled masses yearning to breathe free—Polish or Italian, Mexican or Vietnamese—find free entry into the land of the free.

The Galtonians also proposed eugenic policies for dealing with what psychologist Henry Goddard called the "cacogenic"—the "evil gened"—people already in the United States. The army tests did much to further the cause of eugenics in the United States. British eugenics, as we saw in Chapter 9, was concerned with class rather than race—positive rather than negative eugenics—and had little success in obtaining eugenics legislation. American eugenics, however, was fueled by racism and was remarkably successful at getting eugenics programs written into law.

Eugenics in the United States began just after the Civil War. At John Humphrey Noyes's Oneida Community, one of several socialist-Utopian "heavens on earth" created in the nineteenth century, a program called "stirpiculture" was begun in 1869. Based on Noyes's interpretations of Darwin and Galton, the program involved planned matings between the most "spiritually advanced" members of the community; not surprisingly, Noyes fathered more stirpiculture babies than anyone else (Walters, 1978). In the 1890s, the sexual reformer and feminist Victoria Woodhull preached that the goal of the emancipation of women and sexual education was "the scientific propagation of the human race."

Noyes and Woodhull followed Galton in advancing voluntary positive eugenics as the best application of evolution to human betterment. The turn to negative eugenics and to compulsory control of so-called cacogenic people began with the biologist Charles Davenport. With money from the Carnegie Institution, he established a laboratory at Cold Spring Harbor, New York, in 1904, which, with the addition of his Eugenics Records Office, became the center of American eugenics. Davenport was determined to "annihilate the hideous serpent of hopelessly vicious protoplasm" (quoted in Freeman, 1983), and popularized his views with *Eugenics: The Science of Human Improvement by Better Breeding* (1910) and *Heredity in Relation to Eugenics* (1911). Davenport believed that alcoholism, feeblemindedness, and other traits were based on simple genetic mechanisms, and that they in turn caused ills such as pauperism and prostitution. Prostitutes, for example, were morons who were unable to inhibit the brain center for "innate eroticism," so turned to a life of sex. Committed to a belief that various ethnic groups were biologically distinct races, Davenport's writings are full of derogatory ethnic stereotypes supposedly rooted in the genes: Italians were given to "crimes of personal violence"; Hebrews were given to "thieving." Davenport claimed that if immigration from southeastern Europe were not halted, future Americans would be "darker . . . smaller . . . and more given to crimes of larceny, kidnapping, assault, murder, rape, and sex-immorality." Davenport wanted to place "human matings . . . upon the same high plane as that of horse breeding."

The leading eugenicist among psychologists was Henry Goddard, superintendent of the Vineland Training School. Galton had drawn up family trees of illustrious men and women; with help from Davenport's Eugenics Records Office, Goddard drew up a family tree of stupidity, vice, and crime, *The Kallikak Family: A Study in the Heredity of Feeblemindedness*. Goddard presented the Kallikaks as the "wild men of today," possessing "low intellect but strong physiques." Like Davenport, Goddard believed that "the chief determiner of human conduct is a unitary mental process which we call intelligence . . . which is inborn . . . [and] but little affected by any later influences" (quoted by Gould, 1981). Goddard held that "the idiot is not our greatest problem. He is indeed loathsome," but he is unlikely to reproduce on his own, so "it is the moron type that makes for us our great problem." Precisely because these "high grade defectives" can pass for normal, getting married and having families, Goddard feared their influence on American intelligence. Their numbers would swamp the relatively few offspring of the well-to-do, natural American aristocracy.

Davenport, Goddard, and other Galtonian alarmists proposed various eugenics programs. One was education aimed to promote positive eugenics. For example, in the 1920s, state fairs featured Fitter Families contests, sometimes in a "human stock" show, while eugenicists set up charts and posters showing the laws of inheritance and their application to humans. Some eugenicists favored contraception as a means of controlling cacogenics, but others feared it would promote licentiousness and be used mainly by intelligent people able to make plans—that is, the sort of people who should breed more, not less. McDougall (1921) wanted to encourage the fit to breed by giving them government subsidies to support their children. Goddard favored the segregation of morons, idiots, and imbeciles in institutions like his own, where they could live out happy lives in a setting suited to their feeblemindedness, barred only from having children.

The solution favored by Davenport and most other eugenicists was compulsory sterilization of the cacogenic. Voluntary methods were likely to fail, they feared, and permanent institutionalization was rather expensive. Sterilization was a one-time procedure that guaranteed nonreproduction of the unfit at small cost to the state. Sterilizations without legal sanction had begun before the turn of the century in the Midwest; H. C. Sharp invented the vasectomy and performed hundreds on "mental defectives" in Indiana. Compulsory sterilization laws had also been introduced before the Great War. The Michigan legislature was the first to consider one, in 1897, but the motion failed to pass. In 1907, Indiana passed the first sterilization law, but it was overturned by the state supreme court in 1921 and was replaced with an acceptable law in 1923. After the war, state after state passed compulsory sterilization laws; by 1932, over 12,000 people—7,500 of them in California—had been sterilized in 30 states. The conditions warranting sterilization ranged from feeblemindedness (the most common ground) to epilepsy, conviction of rape, "moral degeneracy," prostitution, and being a drunkard or "drug fiend."

The constitutionality of the compulsory sterilization laws was upheld with but one dissenting vote by the U.S. Supreme Court in 1927 in *Buck v. Bell,* a case arising in the state of Virginia, which was second to California in the number of sterilizations performed. Carrie Buck was a black "feebleminded" girl living in the state colony for the feebleminded, who bore an allegedly feebleminded daughter out of wedlock. She was sterilized by court order, and she then sued the state of Virginia. The majority opinion was written by Oliver Wendell Holmes, a justice noted for his sympathy with Progressivism and his willingness to listen to expert scientific opinion in deciding cases. He wrote, "It is better for all the world, if instead of waiting to execute degenerate offspring for crime, or to let them starve for their imbecility, society can prevent those who are manifestly unfit from continuing their kind. . . . Three generations of imbeciles are enough" (Landman, 1932).

There were critics of eugenics and especially of human sterilization. Humanists such as G. K. Chesterton denounced eugenics as a pernicious offspring of scientism, reaching toward "the secret and sacred places of personal freedom, where no sane man ever dreamed of seeing it." Catholics condemned eugenics for "a complete return to the life of the beast," seeing people as primarily animals to be improved by animal means, rather than as spiritual beings to be improved by virtue. Leading biologists, including most notably those who synthesized Darwin and Mendel, condemned eugenics as biologically stupid. For example, because 90 percent of all subnormally intelligent children are born to normal parents, sterilizing the subnormal would have little effect on national intelligence or the rate at which subnormal children were born. Moreover, the "feebleminded" could have normal children. Carrie Buck's child, initially called feebleminded, proved later to be normal, even bright. Civil libertarians such as Clarence Darrow denounced eugenic sterilization as a means by which "those in power would inevitably direct human breeding in their own interests."

In the social sciences, the attack on eugenics was led by anthropologist Franz Boas and his followers. Boas argued that differences among human groups were not biological but cultural in origin, and he taught the "psychic unity of mankind." His teachings inspired psychologist Otto Klineberg to empirically test eugenicists' claims. He traveled to Europe, tested pure Nordics, Alpines, and Mediterraneans, and found no differences in intelligence. In the United States, he showed that northern Blacks did better on intelligence tests by virtue of getting more schooling, not because they were more intelligent. In 1928, Goddard changed his mind, arguing that "feeble-mindedness is not incurable" and that they "do not generally need to be segregated in institutions" (Gould, 1981).

By 1930, eugenics was dying. Thomas Garth (1930), reviewing "Race Psychology" for the *Psychological Bulletin,* concluded that the hypothesis that races differ on intelligence and other measures "is no nearer being established than it was five years ago. In fact, many psychologists seem practically ready for another, the hypothesis of racial equality." The leading spokesmen for eugenics among psychologists, Brigham and Goddard, had taken back their racist views. The Third International Conference of Eugenics attracted fewer than one hundred people. But what finally killed eugenics was not criticism but embarrassment. Inspired by the success of eugenics laws in the United States, the Nazis began to carry out eugenics programs in deadly earnest. Beginning in 1933, Hitler instituted compulsory sterilization laws that applied to anyone, institutionalized or not, who carried some allegedly genetic defect. Doctors had to report such people to Hereditary Health Courts, which by 1936 had ordered a quarter-million sterilizations. The Nazis instituted McDougall's plan, subsidizing third and fourth children of the Aryan elite, and providing S.S. mothers, married or not, with spas at which to bear their superior children. In 1936, marriages between Aryans and Jews were forbidden. In 1939, asylum inmates who had certain diseases began to be killed by state order; next, the order included all Jews, regardless of their mental condition. At first, the Nazis' victims were shot; later, they were taken to "showers" where they were gassed. The "final solution" to the Nazis' eugenics desires was the Holocaust, in which six million Jews perished by order of the state. The Nazis enacted the final, logical conclusion of negative eugenics, and Americans, sickened by the results, simply ceased to preach and enforce negative eugenics. Many of the laws remained on the books, however. Not until 1981 did Virginia amend its eugenics laws, following the revelation of state hospital records detailing many instances of court-ordered sterilization. Moreover, eugenics continues as genetic counseling, in which bearers of genetically based diseases, such as sickle-cell anemia, are encouraged not to have children, or to do so under medical supervision, so that amniocentesis can be used to diagnose any undesirable condition, permitting abortion of "unfit" human beings.

Psychologists at Work

Aside from advertising psychology, which affects everyone with a radio or TV, more people have been affected by industrial psychology—the applications of psychology to business management—than by any other branch of applied psychology. As we have seen, the beginnings of industrial psychology are traceable to the years before World War I; but, as with the rest of applied psychology, its efflorescence occurred after the war.

The goal of Progressives, in business as in government, was efficiency, and the path to efficiency in every case was thought to be through science. The first exponent of scientific management in business was Frederick Taylor (1856–1915), who developed his ideas around the turn of the century and published them in *Principles of Scientific Management* in 1911. Taylor studied industrial workers at work and delineated their jobs into mechanical routines that could be performed efficiently by anyone, not just by masters of a craft. In essence, Taylor turned human workers into robots, mindlessly but efficiently repeating routinized movements. Taylor was not a psychologist, and the shortcoming of his system was that it managed jobs, not people, overlooking the worker's subjective experience of work and the impact of the worker's happiness on productivity. Nevertheless, Taylor's goal was that of scientific psychology: "[U]nder scientific management arbitrary power, arbitrary dictation ceases; and every single subject, large and small, becomes the question for scientific investigation, for reduction to law." And when these laws were understood, they could be applied in the pursuit of greater industrial efficiency.

Gradually, managers recognized that it was not enough to manage jobs; efficiency and profits could be improved only if workers were managed as people with feelings and emotional attachments to their work. After World War I, in the wake of psychologists' apparent success with the large-scale personnel problems posed by the army, industrial psychology became increasingly popular in American business. Perhaps the most influential piece of research demonstrating the usefulness of applying psychology to industry—management via feelings—was carried out in the early 1920s by a group of social scientists led by psychologist Elton Mayo at the Hawthorne plant of the Western Electric Company, in Cicero, Illinois.

The "Hawthorne Effect" is one of the best known of psychological results. It seemed to demonstrate the importance of subjective factors in determining a worker's industrial efficiency. Although the experiments carried out were complex, the results from the relay assembly room are central to defining the Hawthorne Effect. A group of female workers assembling telephone relays were chosen for experimentation. The scientists manipulated nearly every aspect of the work situation, from the schedule of rest pauses to the amount of lighting. They found that virtually everything they did increased productivity, even when a manipulation meant returning to the old way of doing things. The researchers concluded that the increases in productivity were caused not by changes to the workplace, but by the activity of the researchers themselves. They felt that the workers were impressed by the fact that management cared about their welfare, and the workers' improved feelings about their jobs and about the company translated into improved output.

Following a Populist line of thought already articulated by John Dewey's prescriptions for education, Mayo (1933, 1945) thought that, because of industrialization, workers had become alienated from society, having lost the intimate ties of preindustrial life that bound people together in the insular communities of the past. Unlike the nostalgic Populists, however, Mayo, like Dewey, saw that the agrarian world was irretrievably lost, and he urged business to fill the void by creating communities of workers who found meaning in their work. Various measures were instituted to meet workers' apparent emotional needs; one of the first and most obviously psychological was the creation of "personnel counseling." Workers with complaints about their jobs or about how they were being treated by their employers could go to psychologically trained peer counselors to whom they could relate their frustrations and dissatisfactions. Such programs slowly grew in numbers over the following decades.

The Hawthorne results, when reanalyzed, yielded the disconcerting finding that the Hawthorne Effect is a myth (Bramel and Friend, 1981). There is no firm evidence that the workers in the relay room ever felt better about the company as a result of the experiments, and much evidence to suggest that the workers regarded the psychologists as company spies. The improved productivity of the relay assembly team is easily explained as a result of the replacement, in the middle of the experiment, of a disgruntled, not very productive worker by an enthusiastic, productive worker. More broadly, a radical critique of industrial psychology (Baritz, 1960; Bramel and Friend, 1981) argues that industrial psychology produces happy robots, but robots nonetheless. Mayo's personnel counselors were to "help people think in such a way that they would be happier with their jobs"; one counselor reported being trained to "deal with attitudes toward problems, not the problems themselves" (Baritz, 1960). By using psychological manipulation, managers could deflect workers' concerns from objective working conditions, including wages, and turn them instead to preoccupations with feelings, to their adjustment to the work situation. Workers would still carry out the robotic routines laid down by Taylor, but they would do so in a happier frame of mind; they would be prone to interpret discontent as a sign of poor psychological adjustment rather than as a sign that something was really wrong at work.

Flaming Youth and the Reconstruction of the Family

> I learned to my astonishment that I had been involved in a momentous debauch; the campus reeked of a scandal so sulphurous it hung over our beanies for the rest of the academic year. In blazing scareheads the Hearst *Boston American* tore the veil from the excesses tolerated at Brown University dances. At these hops, it thundered, were displayed a depravity and libertinism that would have sickened Petronius, made Messalina hang her head in shame. It portrayed girls educated at the best finishing schools, crazed with alcohol and inflamed by ragtime, oscillating cheek to cheek with young ne'er-do-wells in raccoon coats and derbies. Keyed up by savage jungle rhythms, the abandonnes would then reel out to roadsters parked on Waterman Street, where frat pins were traded for kisses under cover of darkness. . . . [T]he writer put all his metaphors into one basket and called upon outraged society to apply the brakes, hold its horses, and retrieve errant youth from under the wheels of the juggernaut.
>
> S. J. Perelman (1958, pp. 239–40)

Youth was in revolt during the 1920s—the decade of the Jazz Age and the flapper—and the older generation was aghast. Youth seemed to embody the chaos of modernism described by Yeats's "Second Coming." Confused and bewildered, the parents of the 1920s *Flaming Youth*—the title of a best-selling novel pandering to parents' fears, and the object of Perelman's satiric pen—tried to understand what had gone wrong with their children; more importantly, they tried to learn what to do about it. The apparent crisis of the family and its youth created an opportunity for social scientists, including psychologists, to extend the realm of their concern—and of scientific social control—from the public arena of politics and business into the intimate circle of the family.

In social scientists' view, families as traditionally conceived and organized were out of date. In the old island communities, families had been economic units in which father, mother, and child had distinct and productive roles to play. However, in the dawning industrial world, wives and mothers no longer made their families' domestic goods, children were expected to go to school to learn Progressive habits, and husbands and fathers—soon joined by women—left home for the factories that manufactured what wives and mothers had once crafted. The family, it appeared, was no longer a socially functional unit. Indeed, Progressive Deweyites considered the family selfish because parents' concern was for their own children, whereas in the modern, urban world they ought to be equally concerned with everyone's children. Flaming Youth, social scientists said, was but a symptom of a deeper social crisis.

Social scientists offered their expert opinions on the family's future. Raising children should no longer be thought of as something anyone could do without government's help. Government, working through professional social scientists, was to have the leading role in child rearing. As one reformer wrote, "The state is but the co-ordinated parentage of childhood . . . compel[ling] co-partnership, co-operation, corporate life and conscience" (Fass, 1977). In a phrase, motherhood was to become "mothercraft," a profession requiring education and training. The ideal of mother-craft advanced the cause of social science by providing an ideology that justified intervening in family life with "expertise" not possessed by untrained people.

Because the traditional family's role as an economic unit no longer existed, social scientists defined the "new" family's social function: "It does not seem probable that the family will recover the functions it has lost. But even if the family doesn't produce thread and cloth and soap and medicine and food, it can still produce happiness" (Fass, 1977). In the view of reformers, the function of the family was to produce emotional adjustment to modern life. The modern parent, especially the mother, was to become something of a psychotherapist, monitoring children's emotional states and intervening when necessary to adjust their states of mind. The ideas of parent as professional and the family as the producer of emotional happiness mutually reinforced one another. Parents would need, at the very least, training in their new therapeutic roles, and they would probably also need a cadre of experts to call on for advice and to fall back on when acute difficulties arose. Applied psychologists would naturally find a fertile field for professional application of psychology to child rearing, child guidance, and child psychotherapy.

Meanwhile, although youth may have abandoned their parents' values, they were constructing their own, along with new means of social control. Youth found in the culture of their peers a new center for life apart from the family. Central to the youth culture of the 1920s was having a "good personality," learning to be "well rounded," and fitting in with other youth. Youth valued self-expression and sociability, attending to personal satisfaction instead of the production of objective accomplishments. Groups such as fraternities and sororities enforced conformity to the new rules of personality with therapeutic tricks of their own. Deviant youth were forced to participate in "truth sessions" in which their "objectionable traits" and weaknesses were identified and analyzed. Then the offender would make amends, since "the fraternity's group consciousness is the strongest thing. One doing wrong not only disgraces oneself but his fraternity group" (Fass, 1977).

Parents and college youth, then, were not so far apart. Both were being remade by the "triumph of the therapeutic," the modern tendency to define life in psychological terms. Parents were learning that their function was therapeutic: the production of emotionally well-adjusted children. The youth culture similarly valued emotional adjustment and tried to achieve it through therapeutic techniques of its own. The central values of the twentieth century were formed during the 1920s: being true to one's "real" self, expressing one's "deepest" feelings, "sharing" one's personality with a larger group.

Just as the new family and the youth culture were struggling toward a redefinition of life as centered on self, not accomplishment, a visitor came back from the South Seas bearing witness to an idyllic society in which people had little work to do and led peaceful lives of perfect adjustment, harmony, and sexual fulfillment. As in the Enlightenment, when philosophes had felt themselves emerging from centuries of religious repression, there was a longing for the free and easy life—especially the sexual life—apparently to be found in Tahiti. Committed to environmentalism, the philosophes had thought that a Tahitian paradise could be constructed in Europe through social engineering. As twentieth-century intellectuals reacted against Victorian sexual morality and the excesses of eugenics, they felt themselves on the verge of a "new Enlightenment" or, as Watson put it, a "social Renaissance, a preparation for a change in mores" (Freeman, 1983). So they fastened on Margaret Mead's (1928) *Coming of Age in Samoa* as the philosophes had on *Voyage to Bougainvillea:* "Somewhere in each of us, hidden among our more obscure desires and our impulses of escape, is a palm fringed South Seas island . . . a langorous atmosphere promising freedom and irresponsibility. . . . Thither we run to find love which is free, easy and satisfying" (Freeman, 1983, p. 97).

Margaret Mead was a young psychologist and anthropologist who studied under the founder of modern American anthropology, Franz Boas, whose opposition to eugenics we have already noted. Boas and his followers were convinced, with John Dewey, that human nature was, in Dewey's words, a "formless void of impulses" shaped by society into a personality. They agreed with Dewey that mind was a social construction owing nothing to nature and everything to culture. If eugenicists went to one extreme, denying nurture any influence over nature, Boasians went to the other, regarding culture as "some kind of mechanical press into which most individuals were poured to be molded." Agreeing with Watson at his most extreme, Mead wrote how the "almost unbelievably malleable" raw material of human nature was "moulded into shape by culture."

Mead traveled to American Samoa, conducted (rather sloppy) fieldwork, and returned with a description of a society that at once seemed to support the Deweyite and Boasian conception of an infinitely plastic human nature, and to offer the ideal Form of the happy society, in which people experienced "perfect adjustment" to their surroundings, their society, and to each other. Mead limned a society that knew no Flaming Youth in stressful revolt against their parents, a society with no aggression, no war, no hostility, no deep attachment between parent and child, husband and wife, no competition, a society in which parents were ashamed of the outstanding child, and proud of the slowest, who set the pace for the development of every other child.

Most alluring was the idea that the Samoans, far from regarding sex as a sin, thought sexual relations "the pastime par excellence," a "fine art," making "sex [into]-play, permissible in all hetero- and homosexual expression, with any sort of variation as an artistic addition." The Samoan avoidance of strong feelings and deep attachments extended to love: "Love between the sexes is a light and pleasant dance. . . . Samoans condone light love-affairs, but repudiate acts of passionate choice, and have no real place for anyone who would permanently continue . . . to prefer one woman or one man" (Freeman, 1983, p. 91). Samoans regarded jealousy as a sin and did not regard adultery as very serious, Mead reported. Before marriage, Mead said, adolescents experienced a free and easy promiscuity, each boy and girl engaging in many light sexual dalliances of no deep moment. There were no Flaming Youth because what Flaming Youth wanted, condemned by traditional parents, was approved, even encouraged by Samoan society. Samoans also lived the superficial lives of conformity to the group and average well-roundedness that Flaming Youth defined as its norm. Putting it in scientistic terms, one commentator on Mead's book remarked on "the innocent, strangely impersonal, naively mechanistic-behavioristic sexing of the light-hearted youths of far-off Samoa."

Mead's Samoans helped resolve the nature–nurture disputes of the 1920s against the eugenicists and in favor of the Boasians. Mead's work also lifted up a vision of a new Utopia of sexual freedom and perfect happiness, a vision resurrected in the 1960s, by which time Mead had become anthropology's living icon. Finally, it gave psychologists the central role in constructing the new society. Commenting on the work of Boas and his students, Bertrand Russell, familiar with Watson's behaviorism, asserted that "the scientific psychologist, if allowed a free run with children" could "manipulate human nature" as freely as physical scientists manipulated physical nature. Psychologists and other social scientists could ask, even dream, no more than this: to be the architects of a new Western civilization, well adjusted and harmonious, emotionally open and sexually liberated, warm and supporting and not in neurotic pursuit of excellence. Mead's Samoa, a culture entirely outside the traditions of the West, became the social scientists' Holy Grail, a blueprint for them to follow in constructing the New Man of Deweyite, Progressive idealism.

The reality behind Flaming Youth and Samoan society was different, however, from both the Hearst writer's ravings and Mead's more prosaic depictions. Perelman's "orgy" was in fact "decorous to the point of torpor": "I spent the evening buffeting about the stag line, prayerfully beseeching the underclassmen I knew for permission to cut in on their women . . . [frequently] retiring to a cloakroom with several other blades and choking down a minute quantity of gin, warmed to body heat, from a pocket flask. Altogether, it was a strikingly commonplace experience, and I got to bed without contusions" (p. 239). Freeman (1983) has shown that Samoa, far from being the sexual paradise described by Mead, was obsessed with virginity, and rife with rape, aggression, competition, and deep human feelings.

When Psychology Was King

The psychology of introspection held no fascination for the ordinary American. Margaret Floy Washburn, a student of Titchener's, described in her APA presidential address (1922) the reaction of a janitor to her psychological laboratory: "This is a queer place. It somehow gives you the impression that the thing can't be done." By the 1920s, however, psychology had gone behavioral and was proving—in industry, in schools and courts, and in war—that psychology could be done. Contemporary observers remarked on the tremendous popularity of psychology with the public. The first historian of the 1920s, Frederick Lewis Allen (1931, p. 165), wrote, "Of all the sciences it was the youngest and least scientific which most captivated the general public and had the most disintegrating effect upon religious faith. Psychology was king. . . . [O]ne had only to read the newspapers to be told with complete assurance that psychology held the key to the problems of waywardness, divorce, and crime." Another student of Titchener's, Grace Adams (1934), who after abandoning psychology for journalism, had become quite critical of psychology, called the period from 1919 to 1929 the "Period of the Psyche."

Psychology achieved its special place in public attention because of the intersection of the revolution in morals, led by Flaming Youth (Ostrander, 1968), with the apparent triumph of scientism. "The word science," Allen said, "had become a shibboleth. To preface a statement with 'Science teaches us' was enough to silence argument." Religion seemed on the verge of destruction. Liberal theologian Harry

Emerson Fosdick wrote, "Men of faith might claim for their positions ancient tradition, practical usefulness, and spiritual desirability, but one query could prick all such bubbles: Is it scientific?" (Allen, 1931). The faithful responded in two ways: Modernists such as Fosdick strove to reconcile science with the Bible; fundamentalists (the word was coined by a Baptist editor in July 1920) strove to subordinate science, especially Darwinism, to the Bible. Many other people, of course, simply lost their faith. Watson, for example, had been raised as a strict Baptist in Greenville, South Carolina, and had [like 71 percent of early behaviorists (Birnbaum, 1964)] chosen the ministry as his vocation, only to give it up when his mother died. In graduate school, he had a nervous breakdown and abandoned religion completely.

Science undermined religion; scientism bid to replace it. The Flaming Youth of the 1920s were the first generation of Americans to be raised in the urban, industrial, everywhere communities of twentieth-century life. Cut off from the traditional religious values of the vanishing island communities, they turned to modern science for instruction in morals and rules of behavior. Postwar psychology, no longer preoccupied with socially sterile introspection, was the obvious science to which to turn for guidance concerning living one's life and getting ahead in business and politics.

Popular psychology simultaneously accomplished two apparently contradictory things. It provided people with a sense of liberation from the outdated religious morality of the past; this use was stressed by Flaming Youth and their sympathizers yearning for the sexual freedom of a tropical isle. At the same time, it provided new, putatively scientific techniques for social control; this use was stressed by Progressives. As one popularizer, Abram Lipsky, wrote in *Man the Puppet: The Art of Controlling Minds:* "We are at last on the track of psychological laws for controlling the minds of our fellow men" (quoted in Burnham, 1968). Ultimately, the liberating and controlling effects of psychology were not at odds. When Flaming Youth liberated themselves from old values, they chose new, psychological ones, and psychological techniques of control were used to enforce them.

The first wave of popular psychology, and what the general public thought of as the "new psychology" (Burnham, 1968), was Freudianism, used to dissolve Victorian morals. Under the microscope of psychoanalysis, traditional morals were found to be neurosis-breeding repressions of healthy biological needs, primarily sex. Freud seemed to teach that, "The first requirement for mental health is an uninhibited sex life. As Oscar Wilde counseled, 'Never resist temptation!' " (Graves and Hodge, 1940). One convert to Freudian determinism, Lady Betty Balfour, was "not sure that the moral attitude was not responsible for all the crime in the world." Children, vulgar Freudians believed, should be reared with few inhibitions, so they might grow up unrepressed, happy, and carefree like Mead's notional Samoans.

The second wave of popular psychology in the 1920s was behaviorism. The leading popularizer of behaviorism was Watson himself. He had turned to psychoanalysis in the wake of his nervous breakdown and, although impressed with Freud's biological orientation and lack of hypocrisy about sex, came to regard psychoanalysis as "a substitution of demonology for science." The "unconscious" of psychoanalysis was a fiction, Watson held, representing no more than the fact that we cannot verbalize all the influences on our behavior (Watson, 1926c). According to Watson, there was "too little science—real science—in Freud's psychology" for it to be useful or enduring, and he offered behaviorism as the new claimant for popular attention (Watson, 1926a, 1927a).

Watson described behaviorism as representing "a real renaissance in psychology"—an overthrow of introspective psychology, and substitution of science in its place. Watson consistently linked introspective psychology to religion and railed against both. Behaviorists "threw out the concepts of mind and of consciousness, calling them carryovers from the church dogma of the Middle Ages. . . . Consciousness [is] just a masquerade for the soul" (Watson, 1926a). "Churchmen—all medicine men in fact—have kept the public under control" by making people believe in unobserved mysteries such as the soul; science, says Watson the philosophe, is "blasting" through the "solid wall of religious protection" (1926b). Having disposed of the traditional past, both social and psychological, Watson offered strong opinions and advice on the issues of the day.

Watson attacked eugenics. Belief in human instincts, he wrote, has been "strengthened in the popular view by the propaganda of the eugenists," whose programs for selective breeding are "more dangerous than Bolshevism." Watson maintained that there are no inferior races. Taking note of American racism, Watson said that Negroes had not been allowed to develop properly, so that even if a Negro were given a million dollars a year and sent to Harvard, White society would succeed in making him feel inferior anyway (1927b). A human being, Watson told readers of *Harper's,* is "a lowly piece of protoplasm, ready to be shaped . . . crying to be whipped into shape" (1927b) and promised that the behaviorist "can build any man, starting at birth, into any kind of social or asocial being upon order" (1926a).

Because there were no human instincts, human beings could be built to order, and Watson naturally had much advice to give to parents eager for scientific child-rearing techniques. As would Skinner later, Watson maintained that "The home is responsible for what the child becomes" (1926a). Homemaking, including child rearing and sexual technique, should become a profession for which girls ought to be trained. Their training would brook no nonsense about loving children, cuddling them, or putting up with their infantile demands. Watson viewed the traditional family (and the new affectionate family of other family reformers) with scorn. According to Watson, a mother lavishes affection on children out of a misplaced "sex-seeking response." Her own sexuality is "starved," so she turns to cuddling and kissing her child; hence the need for training in sex.

Watson's advice on how to raise children is brutally behavioristic:

> There is a sensible way of treating children. Treat them as though they were young adults. Dress them, bathe them with care and circumspection. Let your behavior always be objective and kindly firm. Never hug and kiss them, never let them sit in your lap. If you must, kiss them once on the forehead when they say good night. Shake hands with them in the morning. . . . Try it out. . . . You will be utterly ashamed of the mawkish, sentimental way you have been handling it. . . .
>
> Nest habits, which come from coddling, are really pernicious evils. The boys or girls who have nest habits deeply imbedded suffer torture when they have to leave home to go into business, to enter school, to get married. . . . Inability to break nest habits is probably our most prolific source of divorce and marital disagreements. . . .
>
> In conclusion won't you then remember when you are tempted to pet your child that mother love is a dangerous instrument? An instrument which may inflict a never healing wound, a wound which may make infancy unhappy, adolescence a nightmare, an instrument which may wreck your adult son or daughter's vocational future and their chances for marital happiness. (1928b, pp. 81–7)

Watson's book (written with the assistance of Rosalie Rayner Watson, his second wife) *Psychological Care of Infant and Child,* from which this advice comes, sold quite well. Even Carl Rogers, founder of client-centered therapy and later a leader of humanistic psychology, tried to raise his first child "by the book of Watson." Occasionally, Watson so despaired of the ability of a mother to raise a happy child—he dedicated the child-care book to the first mother to do so—that he advocated taking children away from their parents to be raised by professionals in a creche (Harris and Morawski, 1979), the solution proposed by Skinner in his utopian novel *Walden II.*

"The behaviorist, then," wrote Watson (1928a), "has given society . . . a new weapon for controlling the individual. . . . If it is demanded by society that a given line of conduct is desirable, the psychologist should be able with some certainty to arrange the situation or factors which will lead the individual most quickly and with the least expenditure of effort to perform that task." In his second career, as an advertising executive, Watson had an opportunity to demonstrate the power of behavioral social control by manipulating consumers (Buckley, 1982). Expelled from academia for his affair with and subsequent marriage to Rosalie Rayner, Watson was hired by the J. Walter Thompson advertising agency, which was looking for the scientific principles that would control the minds of men and women.

It is not surprising that Progressives embraced Watson's behaviorism. In the *New York Herald Tribune,* Stuart Chase, who later coined the phrase "New Deal," exclaimed that Watson's *Behaviorism* was perhaps "the most important book ever written. One stands for an instant blinded with a great hope" (quoted by Birnbaum, 1955). The "great hope" of Progressivism was always that an elite of scientific managers might be empowered to run society, and behaviorism seemed to provide exactly the techniques Progressives needed to control the behavior, if not the minds, of men. Watson himself, it should be said, insisted that the laws of conditioning applied to everyone, whether or not their ancestors had come over on the *Mayflower,* and that anyone could be trained to use behavioral techniques for self-control or the control of others (Birnbaum, 1964).

Within psychology, Watson's popularized behaviorism was welcomed by some but rejected by others. Joseph Jastrow (1929) felt that psychology was degraded by Watson's popularization of himself in magazines and newspapers. What was valuable in behaviorism—the study of behavior—"will survive the 'strange interlude' of . . . behaviorism" and Watson's public antics. Grace Adams ridiculed Watson's behaviorism for sharing "most of the appealing points of psychoanalysis with few of its tedious difficulties," the resulting shallow system being "a cheering doctrine, surely—direct, objective, and completely American." Warner Fite (1918), already depressed by the experimental psychology of 1912, regarded behaviorism as the logical end product of scientism, or, as he put it, in "behavioristic psychology we behold the perfected beauty of the scientific prepossession." Lumping together the effects of psychoanalysis and behaviorism, Fite sarcastically foresaw the psychological society of the later twentieth century: "Doubtless the time is coming, before we are through with the [scientific] prepossession, when all domestic and social intercourse will be made luminous and transparent by the presence of expert psychologists. In those fair days social intercourse will be untroubled by falsehood or insincerity, or even by genial exaggeration" (p. 803).

By 1930, the fad for psychology had run its course. After the crash of 1929, the popular press had pressing economic matters to consider, and the volume of pieces written on psychology diminished noticeably. Grace Adams hoped that its influence was finished, but in fact psychology was only in retrenchment (Sokal, 1983). Psychology continued to grow and expand its areas of application throughout the 1930s, albeit at a slower rate than in the glory years after the Great War. Its reemergence on the popular stage awaited another cue of war.

PSYCHOLOGY TRANSFORMED (1940–1950)

As it had just twenty-four years earlier, world war would profoundly affect psychology. The Great War to End All Wars had helped transform a tiny, obscure academic discipline into an ambitious, visible profession. World War II provided an even greater opportunity for psychologists to act together in pursuit of social good and their own professional interests. Along the way, the war caused psychology to grow at a faster rate than ever, to reunify into a single academic-applied profession, and to invent a new profession-role—the psychotherapist—which quickly became the public role that defined American psychology. After the war ended, psychology fought unsuccessfully to be included among the sciences supported by federal research money. As a profession, however, psychology was more successful. Finding itself in need of mental health professionals, the government embarked on programs to recruit and train new psychological professions, requiring that psychology define itself anew and set standards for its practitioners.

Psychology Divided and Reunited

After the Great War, war psychologists in increasing numbers began practicing applied psychology. At the time, it was called, inappropriately, "clinical" psychology, because of its roots in Witmer's psychological "clinic." In fact, the "clinical" psychology of these years bore little resemblance to today's clinical psychology. The term has come to mean primarily the practice of psychotherapy by psychologists, but, before World War II, "clinical" psychology had mostly to do with giving tests to various populations: children, soldiers, workers, mental patients, and occasional individual clients.

In any event, "clinical" psychologists rarely performed research and were often employed outside universities, working for companies or on their own as psychological consultants. The old guard of scientific psychologists who had founded the APA, for all their apparent commitment to useful psychology, were made uncomfortable by the increasing numbers of "clinical" psychologists. The APA, after all, had been founded to "advance psychology as a science," and it was not at all clear that clinicians were advancing scientific psychology, because they did no research.

During the 1920s and 1930s, the APA vacillated in its treatment of applied psychologists. Entry to the association had for some time depended on having published articles in scientific journals; then a class of associate members was created for the nonscientists, who enjoyed only limited participation in the association. These "clinical" psychologists, whose numbers rapidly swelled, naturally resented their second-class status. During the same period, the APA recognized that, as the official organization of psychologists, it bore some responsibility for ensuring the competence of practicing psychologists, being deeply concerned about charlatans and frauds passing themselves off as genuine psychologists and tarnishing the honor of the science in the eyes of the public. So, for a time, the APA issued expensive certificates, badges of authenticity, to applied—or, as they were officially called, "consulting"—psychologists. The experiment was short-lived, however. Few psychologists bothered to apply for the certificates. The academicians of the APA also were unwilling to exert themselves to attain the proper ends of professionalization by enforcing standards and taking legal action against psychological frauds.

Gradually, applied psychologists got fed up with the APA. They realized that their interest, the creation of a socially accepted and defined practice of psychology on a par with physicians, lawyers, engineers, and other professional practitioners of a craft, could not be realized in an association devoted exclusively to psychology as an academically based science. As early as 1917, applied psychologists tried to form their own association, but the enterprise was controversial and died when the APA agreed to the creation of a clinical section within the association. In 1930, a group of applied psychologists in New York formed a national organization, the Association of Consulting Psychologists (ACP). Beginning with New York, the ACP pressed states to establish legal standards for the definition of "psychologist," wrote a set of ethical guidelines for the practice of psychology, and began its own journal, the *Journal of Consulting Psychology,* in 1937. Despite pleas by professional psychologists for the APA to get involved in defining and setting standards for practitioners of the psychological craft (for example, Poffenberger, 1936), the association continued to fail them. In 1938, the unhappy psychologists of the clinical section of the APA left the parent organization and joined with the ACP to create the American Association for Applied Psychology (AAAP).

Another dissident group was the Society for the Psychological Study of Social Issues (SPSSI), formed by left-wing psychologists in 1936. Although affiliated with the APA, SPSSI psychologists aimed, in contrast to the traditional academicians of the APA, to use psychology to advance their political views. For example, SPSSI psychologists marched in New York's May Day parade carrying banners that read "Adjustment comes with jobs" (it was the depth of the Depression) and "Fascism is the world's worst behavior problem!" (Napoli, 1981). The older APA, devoted as it was to pure research and scholarly detachment, had a hard time finding a place for either the AAAP or SPSSI.

However, it seemed to many psychologists, such as Robert Yerkes and Ernest Hilgard, that the institutional divisions within psychology could and should be overcome. After all, the professionals of the AAAP received their education in academic departments of psychology, and it was the scientific principles of psychology that SPSSI wished to apply to pressing social problems. So, in the years following the break between the AAAP and the APA, informal negotiations were carried on with the aim of reunifying psychologists under a single banner.

The process was greatly accelerated by the coming of World War II. In 1940, even before the United States entered the war, the APA had assembled an Emergency Committee to plan for the inevitable involvement of the United States and its psychologists in the global conflict; in 1941, several months before the Japanese attack on Pearl Harbor, the *Psychological Bulletin* devoted a whole issue to "Military Psychology." In the same year, the APA removed the greatest bar to full participation by applied psychologists in the association—the requirement that a prospective member had to have published research beyond a dissertation was abandoned.

Once the war began, changes came at a faster pace. A Committee on Psychology and War was formed, planning not only for war activities by psychologists, but for a significant postwar social role for psychology as well. The committee noted that, in view of the coming world conflict, psychology should be unified, as it had been in World War I, and to this end it proposed creation of a "general headquarters" for psychology. Such headquarters came into existence in Washington, DC, as the Office of Psychological Personnel (OPP), whose initial job was placing psychologists in government work to aid the war effort.

Creation of the OPP as a "general headquarters" for psychology was a major event in the institutional history of psychology in the United States. Prior to 1941, the APA had no permanent central office: The APA was located in the professorial offices of whoever was its secretary in a given year. The OPP, however, became the central office of the American Psychological Association, located in Washington— fount of funding and locus of lobbying—ever since. Psychologists at the OPP saw an opportunity both to reunify psychology and to advance psychology's role in American society (see Britt, 1943). In 1942, Leonard Carmichael, psychology's representative on the National Research Council, reported to the APA Council that "this office [the OPP] may well mark the initiation of a central agency for psychologists which will have an important and growing effect upon the psychological profession."

Psychologists, listed as "critical profession[als]" by the War Department, were in great demand by the military. As in World War I, psychologists served in many specialized capacities, ranging from test administration to studying the psychological demands made on human performance by new and sophisticated weapons, to the biological control of guided missiles.

The war made human relations in industry more important and emphasized the role of the psychologist in efficient industrial management. Industry faced two problems psychologists could help solve. Producing war matériel required vastly increased rates of production just at the time when experienced factory workers were drafted into the military and replaced with new, inexperienced workers, especially women, who began for the first time to enter the workforce in large numbers. The War Production Board, alarmed by problems of low productivity, absenteeism, and high turnover, appointed an interdisciplinary team headed by Elton Mayo to apply social science techniques to retaining workers and improving their productivity. The business community came to recognize that "the era of human relations" was at hand: "the factors that 'make a man tick' can be described and analyzed with much of the precision that would go into the dies for . . . a Sherman tank" (Baritz, 1960).

Even as the war raged, psychologists prepared for the postwar world by setting their own house in order. The Emergency Committee set up the Intersociety Constitutional Convention, a meeting of representatives of the APA, the AAAP, SPSSI, and other psychological groups, such as the National Council of Women Psychologists. The convention created a new APA along federal lines. The "new" APA was to be an organization of autonomous divisions representing the various interest groups within psychology. New bylaws were written, including, in addition to the APA's traditional purpose as the advancement of psychology as a science, the advancement of psychology "as a profession, and as a means of promoting human welfare." Robert Yerkes, who did more than anyone else to create the new APA, laid out the goals of the organization to the convention: "The world crisis has created a unique opportunity for wisely planned and well directed professional activities. In the world that is to be, psychology will play a significant role, if psychologists can only unite in making their visions realities" (paraphrased by Anderson, 1943, p. 585). In 1944, the various groups voted to create a reunified APA headquartered in Washington and speaking with one voice through the *American Psychologist*. In this new APA, there was a young and growing segment, almost entirely new: the clinical psychologist as psychotherapist.

Redefining Clinical Psychology

"It seems as if the ivory tower had literally been blown out from under psychology" (Darley and Wolfle, 1946). Before the war, psychology had been controlled by the academicians of the APA, despite complaints from and concessions to the AAAP. The war, however, drastically altered the social role of psychologists and the balance of political power in psychology, primarily by inventing a new role for applied psychologists to fill in quickly growing numbers. During the 1930s, applied psychologists continued, as they had in the 1920s, serving primarily as testers and evaluating employees, juvenile offenders, troubled children, and people seeking guidance about their intelligence or personality. However, the war created a pressing demand for a new kind of service from psychologists: psychotherapy, previously the preserve of psychiatrists.

Throughout most of World War II, the most common job performed by psychologists was mental testing, although in a broader range of settings (Sears, 1944). However, soldiers returning from the front needed more psychological services than anyone had anticipated—and more than the existing psychiatric corps could provide. By the end of the war, of 74,000 hospitalized veterans, about 44,000 were hospitalized for psychiatric reasons. Psychologists had heretofore performed diagnostic duties as part of military medical teams, but faced with the overwhelming need to provide psychotherapy, psychologists—however ill-trained—began to serve as therapists, too.

As the war wound down, it became clear that the desperate need for psychological services among veterans would continue. In addition to the hospitalized veterans, "normal" veterans experienced numerous adjustment difficulties. At the very least, men who had been wrenched from their prewar jobs, towns, and families desired counseling about how to make new lives in the postwar world; 65 percent to 80 percent of returning servicemen reported interest in such advice (Rogers, 1944). Others suffered from the World War II equivalent of the posttraumatic stress syndrome of the Vietnam veterans of the 1970s. Secretary of War Henry L. Stimson wrote in his diary about "a rather appalling analysis of what our infantrymen are confronting in the present war by way of psychosis. The Surgeon General tells us the spread of psychological breakdown is alarming and that it will affect every infantryman, no matter how good and strong" (Doherty, 1985, p. 30). Upon return to the United States, veterans felt a "sense of strangeness about civilian life," were often bitter about how little people at home appreciated the horrors of combat, and experienced restlessness, disturbed sleep, excessive emotionality, and marital and family disturbances. Finally, many veterans were handicapped by wounds and needed psychological as well as physical therapy (Rogers, 1944).

The Veterans Administration (VA) acted to provide the services veterans needed. To meet the need for vocational guidance, the VA established guidance centers at universities, where GIs were receiving college educations paid for by the GI Bill of Rights. Psychologists working at these counseling centers continued the development of prewar applied psychology on a larger scale than before, and their activities by and large define the job of today's counseling psychologist. More disturbed veterans, especially those in VA hospitals, needed more than advice, and the VA set out to define a new mental health professional, the clinical psychologist, who could provide psychotherapy to the thousands of veterans who needed it. In 1946, the VA set up training programs at major universities to turn out clinical psychologists whose job would be therapy as well as diagnosis. Because it was the largest employer of clinical psychologists, the VA did much to define the job of the clinical psychologist and how he or she would be trained.

Spurred by the VA, the newly reunified APA, now fully emerged from the ruined ivory tower of academe, undertook the tasks it had avoided for decades: defining the professional psychologist and setting up standards for his or her training. These tasks have not proved easy; to this day, there is widespread disagreement among psychologists about the proper nature of training for the professional psychologist. Since World War II, the APA has established many panels and commissions to look into the matter, but no proposal has satisfied everyone, and controversy about the nature of clinical psychology has been chronic.

The most obvious model of professional training was rejected by the committees appointed after the war to set up professional training in psychology. Typically, schools that train the practitioners of a craft are separate from the scientific discipline to which they are related. Thus, physicians are trained in medical schools, not biology departments, and chemical engineers are trained in engineering schools, not chemistry departments. Physicians learn biology and chemical engineers learn chemistry, but they are not expected to become PhD biologists or chemists.

Psychologists, however, needed to separate themselves from their very close rivals, the psychiatrists, who from the first appearance of "clinical" psychology before World War I had feared that psychologists might usurp their therapeutic duties. So, rather than define themselves as merely practitioners of a craft springing from science, as physicians had, clinical psychologists decided to define themselves as scientist-practitioners. That is, graduate students training to become clinical psychologists were to be taught to be scientists first—carrying out research in scientific psychology—and professionals—practitioners of a craft—second, and they received the scholarly PhD. It was as if physicians were to be trained first as biologists and only secondarily as healers. The appeal of the scheme was that it preserved for clinicians the prestige of being scientists while allowing them to fill the many jobs the VA had open for psychotherapists (Murdock and Leahey, 1986). The model of the clinical psychologist as scientist/professional was enshrined by the Boulder Conference of 1949. As we shall see in later chapters, the Boulder model has not been without its detractors, and periodically the APA has been called on to rethink its approach to professional training. Additionally, from the very first (for example, Peatman, 1949), academic psychologists have been afraid that their discipline would be taken over by professionals, and that they would become the second-class citizens of the APA.

Whatever the trials and tribulations surrounding the redefinition of clinical psychology, it grew rapidly, becoming in the public mind the primary function of the psychologist. In 1954, during the annual meeting of the APA, Jacob Cohen and G. D. Wiebe (1955) asked the citizens of New York who "the people with the badges" were. Of the interviewees, 32 percent correctly identified them as psychologists, although almost as many, 25 percent, thought they were psychiatrists. When asked what the people with the badges did, 71 percent said it was psychotherapy, work scarcely done by psychologists before 1944; 24 percent said "teachers," leaving 6 percent "other" (the percentages are rounded). The founders of the APA had prided themselves on being scientists and had formed their organization to advance the cause of psychology as a science. By 1954, just sixty-two years later, scientific psychology had largely ceased to exist in the public mind, having been replaced by an applied discipline with a remarkably shallow foundation, given what even the best scientific minds in psychology—Hull, Tolman, Thorndike, Watson—had accomplished.

Psychology Fails to Get a Slice of the Big Science Pie

Allied victory in World War II depended in many respects on the successful employment of science, primarily physics, in the pursuit of war aims. During the war, annual federal spending on scientific research and development went from $48 million to $500 million. When the war ended, politicians and scientists recognized that the national interest demanded continued federal support of science, and that control of research monies should not remain a monopoly of the military. However, there was much debate about two questions: How should government money be spent on science? and Who should be eligible to receive it?

The first question has rarely concerned psychology, but it is important for citizens to understand how research funds are alloted in our era of Big Science, in which money can be awarded to only a few of the investigators who want it. Should money be given only to the best scientists, or should it be parceled out on some other basis, perhaps allocating a certain amount of funds within each state? Politicians, worried that only a few states (those with elite research universities) would get the lion's share of research dollars, pushed the latter scheme, but they were defeated by elitists in the scientific ranks and their political allies, who established the grant system by which scientists compete for grants awarded by committees of other scientists ("peer review"). As the system has evolved, most research money is in fact "won" by the elite research universities. As a result, other institutions strive to become research centers, pressuring their faculty to submit and obtain external funding. Universities value their scientists' winning grants because they get "overhead money"—money ostensibly to be spent on electricity, janitors, and other laboratory maintenance—which they in fact spend for new buildings, to hire more staff, to purchase copiers, and many other things they would not otherwise be able to afford.

In 1991, it was discovered that several universities had illegally channeled research overhead money to use for entertainment and other illegitimate purchases (Cooper, 1991). In this system of grants, scientists are not employees of their university; rather, they are its means of support. Scientists, in turn, are compelled to direct their research not to the problems they think are important, but to those the federal funding agencies think are important. Thus, scientists spend much of their time and talent trying to second-guess bureaucrats, who themselves are implementing vague congressional directives.

In an emerging strategy, less prestigious universities get pork-barrel research projects by having their Representatives and Senators put such projects into appropriation bills. Traditional elitists deplore this trend because it bypasses peer review. To defenders of this trend, peer review is an old-boys network by which the well-off become more well-off.

Of direct importance to psychology was whether the funding agency to be created, the National Science Foundation (NSF), should support research in the social sciences. Old Progressives and New Deal liberals included a Division of the Social Sciences in the original NSF bill, but it was opposed by natural scientists and conservative legislators.

A leading supporter of the original bill, Senator J. William Fulbright of Arkansas, argued that the social sciences should be included because they "could lead us to an understanding of the principles of human relationships which might enable us to live together without fighting recurrent wars." Opponents argued that "there is not anything that leads more readily to isms and quackeries than so-called studies in social science unless there is eternal vigilance to protect."

In debate, even Senator Fulbright found little good to say about social science, conceding that "there are many crackpots in the field, just as there were in the field of medicine in the days of witchcraft." He was unable to give an adequate definition of social science and wound up quoting a natural scientist who said that "I would not call it a science. What is commonly called social science is one individual or group of individuals telling another group how they should live." In a letter to Congress, leading physical scientists opposed the Division of Social Science. The original bill mollified them by including special controls "to prevent the Division of Social Sciences getting out of hand," as Fulbright put it on the floor of the Senate. He also said, "It would surprise me very much if the social sciences' division got anything at all" because the NSF board would be dominated by physical scientists. The upshot of the debate was a Senate vote of 46 to 26 to remove the Division of Social Sciences. As sciences, the social sciences did not command universal respect (social scientists might feel that with a friend like Fulbright they did not need enemies), however much their concrete services, such as counseling, psychotherapy, and personnel management, might be needed.

Although the government was not yet sympathetic to supporting psychology and the other social sciences, a new foundation, the Ford Foundation, was. For decades, private research foundations, most notably the Rockefeller Foundation, had made modest grants to support social science. After the war, the Ford Foundation was established as the world's largest, and it decided to fund the behavioral sciences in a big way. The foundation staff saw behavioral sciences as the bright hope for the future, because they might be used to end war and ameliorate human suffering, and proposed to use Ford's immense resources to give "an equal place in society . . . for the study of man as the study of the atom." At the top levels of the foundation, the staff's proposal met the same kind of resistance found in the Senate. The president, Paul Hoffman, said that social science was "a good field to waste billions," and his adviser, Robert Maynard Hutchins, president of the University of Chicago, said that the social science research he had seen—and Chicago had the first school of social science—"scared the hell out of me." Nevertheless, the Ford staff pushed ahead with their ambitious plan and got it approved. At first, the foundation tried to give the money away as grants; but since this didn't get rid of the money fast enough, and took it out of their control, they set up the Center for Advanced Studies in the Behavioral Sciences in California. This center was a place where elite social scientists could go for a few years at a time and, freed from academic pressures, pursue theorizing and research in a congenial climate, sharing their ideas with colleagues from every field.

CONCLUSION

Psychologists Look Ahead to the Psychological Society

By the end of World War II, it was clear to psychologists that their ivory tower had indeed been destroyed. Psychology's links to its ancient roots in philosophy—to "long-haired" philosophers (Morgan, 1947)—were irrevocably severed (and for the good of psychology, according to the newest generation of American psychologists). At an APA symposium on "Psychology and Post-War Problems," H. H. Remmers observed, but did not mourn, psychology's loss of its "philosophical inheritance":

> Our philosophical inheritance has unfortunately not been an unmixed blessing. Deriving from that relatively sterile branch of philosophy known as epistemology and nurtured by a rationalistic science which tended to exalt thought at the expense of action and theory over practice, psychology has too frequently ensconced itself in the ivory tower from which pedants descended upon occasion to proffer pearls of wisdom, objectivity, and logical consistency to their charges without too much concern about the nutritional adequacy of such a diet. (1944, p. 713)

Clifford T. Morgan made the same point more bluntly at a 1947 conference on "Current Trends in Psychology" by observing that, "Biggest [trend] of them all is that in the past thirty years psychology has shortened its hair, left its alleged ivory tower, and gone to work." The world in the making demanded that psychologists be concerned less with abstruse, almost metaphysical, questions inherited from philosophy, and more with questions about how to achieve human happiness.

Psychologists entered their brave new world with anxious hope. Wayne Dennis, speaking at the Current Trends conference, proclaimed that "Psychology today has unlimited potentialities" [sic]. At the same time he worried that psychology had not yet achieved the "prestige and respect" needed to earn a "successful existence as a profession. We cannot function effectively as advisers and consultants, or as researchers in human behavior, without holding the confidence and good opinion of a considerable part of the population." His worries were not misplaced, as the Senate's debate on the Division of Social Sciences in the NSF demonstrated. Dennis (1947) spoke for many when he advocated further professionalization of psychology as the means of achieving public respect. Psychologists, he said, should set their own house in order, tighten requirements for training in psychology, persecute pseudopsychologists, and establish certification and state licensing standards for professional psychologists.

Despite such temporary worries, psychologists saw for themselves a secure and powerful place in the postwar world. Remmers (1944), reflecting the views of many psychologists, defined psychology's new, postphilosophical job: "Psychology in common with all science must have as its fundamental aim the service of society by positive contributions to the good life . . . knowledge for knowledge's sake is at best a by-product, an esthetic luxury." In colleges, psychology should be "placed on a par with the other sciences," and its role should be to teach the undergraduate how "to assess himself and his place in society." More broadly, psychology should help construct a "science of values" and learn to use "journalism, radio, and in the near future, television" to achieve "culture control." Psychology should be more widely used in industry, education ("the most important branch of applied psychology"), gerontology, child rearing, and the solution of social problems such as racism. Remmers failed only to mention psychological psychotherapy among the potential contributions of psychology to human happiness. Psychologists were at last prepared to give people what William James had hoped for in 1892: a "psychological science that will teach them how to act."

Values and Adjustment

There was an unremarked irony in psychology's postwar position. The old psychology of Scottish commonsense philosophy had proudly taken as its ultimate mission the training and justification of Christian religious values. The new psychology of brass-instrument experiments had, in challenging the old psychology, proudly cast off moral, especially religious, values in the name of science. With scientism becoming the new religion of the modern age, however, Remmers could, by 1944, envision psychology as a "science of values." Psychology had come full circle—from serving the Christian God and teaching Christian values, to becoming itself, as John Burnham (1968) put it, a "deus ex clinica" representing the values of scientism.

What were the new values? Sometimes, in keeping with the value-free pose of science, psychology seemed only to offer tools for social control. Watson, for example, saw conditioning as a technique by which psychology might inculcate society's values, whatever they might be, in its citizens. As Remmers put it, the "good life" to be furthered by psychology was "the homeostasis of society"; psychology would keep people from unpleasantly rocking the boat. Emphasis on techniques of social control is symptomatic of the psychology of adaptation's relationship with political Progressivism, and it laid applied psychologists open to Randolph Bourne's criticism of Progressive politicians. Once a Progressive himself, Bourne came to realize that Progressives held no clear values of their own: "They have, in short, no clear philosophy of life except that of intelligent service. They are vague as to what kind of society they want, or what kind of society America needs, but they are equipped with all the administrative attitudes and talents to attain it" (Abrahams, 1985, p. 7).

On the other hand, psychology sometimes held up a positive value of its own, the cult of the self. Psychology's object of study and concern is the individual human being, and its central value became the encouragement of the never-ending growth of individuals. As Dewey had said, "Growth itself is the only moral end." The contradiction between pretending to have no values and holding the value of individual growth was not noticed by American psychologists because their central value was so American as to be transparent. From the time of de Tocqueville, Americans had sought self-improvement more than anything else. Continuing growth and development seem as natural and necessary to Americans as God-centered stasis, the never-changing ideal divine order, had seemed to Europeans of the Middle Ages. In our world of self-made individuals, psychological techniques that fostered continual growth and change appeared value-free: What American society and psychology wanted was individualism.

However, the value of individualism had undergone important changes since the nineteenth century. Character was the concept by which people understood the individual in the nineteenth century. Emerson defined character as "moral order through the medium of individual nature," and the words used to describe character included duty, work, golden deeds, honor, integrity, and manhood. In his or her character, then, a person had a certain relationship, good or evil, to an encompassing and transcendent moral order. Aspiring to good character demanded self-discipline and self-sacrifice; popular psychologists such as the phrenologists offered guides to the diagnosis of one's own and others' character and gave advice on how to improve one's character. In the twentieth century, however, the moral concept of character began to be replaced by the narcissistic concept of personality, and self-sacrifice began to be replaced by self-realization. The adjectives used to describe personality were not moral: fascinating, stunning, magnetic, masterful, dominant, forceful. Having a good personality demanded no conformity to moral order, but instead fulfilled the desires of the self and achieved power over others. Character was good or bad; personality was famous or infamous. Psychologists, having shed the religious values that defined character, aided the birth of personality. Self-growth meant realizing one's potential, not living up to impersonal moral ideals—and potential, that which has not yet become actual, can be bad as often as good. Some potential is for doing bad things. Developing everyone's full potential, then, can be bad for society. Thus, psychology's cultivation of individual growth was at odds with its claim to provide society with tools of social control.

This same essentially moral conflict exists between the psychology of developing potential and the most important concept of the psychology of adaptation, adjustment. Everything in twentieth-century psychology has revolved around the concept of adjustment. In experimental psychology, psychologists of learning studied how the mind and, later, behavior adjusted the individual organism to the demands of its environment. In applied psychology, psychologists developed tools to measure a person's adjustment to his or her circumstances, and, should the adjustment be found wanting, tools to bring the child, worker, soldier, or neurotic back into harmony with society. In the psychological conception, sin was replaced with behavior deviation, and absolute morality was replaced with statistical morality (Boorstin, 1973). In more religious times, one had a problem if one offended a moral norm standing outside oneself and society; now, one had a problem if one offended society's averages as determined by statistical research. In theory, psychology placed itself on the side of individual expression, no matter how eccentric. In practice, by offering tools for social control and by stressing adjustment, it placed itself on the side of conformity.

A new Hellenistic Age was in the making. In the first Hellenistic Age, the natural sciences flourished at Alexandria, supported by the state. People's first desire was personal happiness—*ataraxia*—and they sought out teachers who promised a recipe by which one might find freedom from disturbance. In the modern Hellenistic Age, the natural sciences would again flourish with government support. People's first desire would again be personal happiness—adjustment—and they would seek out psychologists for recipes by which they might find fulfillment, sex, and the right job—things without which the modern person would be greatly disturbed. In both Hellenistic Ages, there remained a deep hunger for more transcendent truths, but in neither were they forthcoming.

BIBLIOGRAPHY

For a general account of American history for the years 1912 to 1950, see John L. Thomas, "Nationalizing the republic" (for the period 1912–1920) and Robert H. Wiebe, "Modernizing the republic" (for the period 1920 and after), both in Bernard Bailyn et al., *The great republic* (Boston: Little, Brown, 1977). For a general account of the period, with an emphasis on social history, including shrewd observations on the role of the social sciences as shapers of modern morality, see Daniel Boorstin (1973); for an emphasis on politics, see Eric F. Goldman, *Rendezvous with destiny: A history of modern American reform,* 3rd ed. (New York: Vintage Books, 1977).

The period between the world wars has been studied a great deal, with emphasis on the 1920s. The first book on the 1920s was Allen (1931); for a more recent interpretation, see

PART III *THE RISE OF BEHAVIORALISM*

Geoffrey Perrett, *America in the twenties: A history* (New York: Touchstone, 1982). Ostrander (1968) provides a brief account of changes in morals in the 1920s. For American religion during these years, see George M. Marsden, *Fundamentalism and American culture: The shaping of twentieth century evangelicalism 1870–1925* (Oxford, England: Oxford University Press, 1980). Graves and Hodge (1940) provide a wonderfully well-written account of the British scene between the wars.

Several important studies of the social movements are discussed in Chapters 11 and 12. On eugenics, the standard history is sure to become Daniel J. Kevles, "Annals of eugenics: A secular faith," which appeared in *The New Yorker,* October 8, 15, 22, and 29, 1984, and as a book, *In the name of eugenics: Genetics and the uses of human heredity* (New York: Knopf, 1985); quotations in the eugenics section are from Kevles unless otherwise noted. Gould (1981) contains useful accounts of American hereditarian attitudes, as well as a critique of intelligence testing and an account of immigration restriction on which I relied and from which I borrowed quotations. On the sterilization movement, the indispensable first source is Landman (1932), which contains valuable details on sterilization legislation and court decisions; Landman was sympathetic to the ideals of the negative eugenicists, but quite critical of their practices. For the applications of social science to industry and other social problems, see Baritz (1960), who focuses on industrial social science, and Napoli (1981), who discusses applied psychology in all its varied roles. On Flaming Youth, the quotations in the text are drawn from Fass (1977), who presents the problems of youth in the 1920s from the perspectives of the youth themselves, popular commentators, and social scientists. A related source is Christopher Lasch's *Haven in a heartless world: The family besieged* (New York: Basic Books, 1977), which concentrates on social scientists' views of the family. An excellent book that touches on many subjects, including American hereditarianism, the reaction against it by American social scientists, and changing conceptions of the ideal family, is Derek Freeman (1983), who dismantles Margaret Mead's romantically naive portrait of the Samoans, first by setting it in its historical context, and then by contrasting it to his own more intimate and prolonged fieldwork. My account of the change from "character" to "personality" is based on Warren I. Susman, "'Personality' and the making of twentieth-century culture," in J. Higham and P. Conkin, eds., *New directions in American intellectual history* (Baltimore: Johns Hopkins University Press, 1979). Finally, the situation of American science after World War II may be found in Daniel J. Kevles, *The physicists: The history of a scientific community in America* (New York: Knopf, 1978). Kevles obviously concentrates on physics, but he provides a general account of the controversy surrounding creation of the NSF.

Moving on to works specifically on psychology, Sokal (1983) and Burnham (1968) offer good broad accounts of psychology in the 1920s, focusing on psychology's social relations, especially in the case of Burnham. For the period after World War II, with some prewar background, consult A. R. Gilgen, *American psychology since World War II: A profile of the discipline* (Westport, CT: Greenwood Press, 1982). On behaviorism in particular, see Birnbaum's works (1955, 1964) as well as David Bakan, "Behaviorism and American urbanization," *Journal of the History of the Behavioral Sciences* (1966, *2:* 5–28); John C. Burnham, "On the origins of behaviorism," *Journal of the History of the Behavioral Sciences* (1968, *4:* 143–52); and Paul G. Creelan, "Watsonian Behaviorism and the Calvinist conscience," *Journal of the History of the Behavioral Sciences* (1974, *10:* 95–118). For the application of intelligence tests to World War I recruits, see Daniel J. Kevles, "Testing the Army's intelligence: Psychologists and the military in World War II," *Journal of American History* (1968, *55:* 565–81); and Franz Samelson, "Putting psychology on the map: Ideology and intelligence testing," in Allan R. Buss, ed., *Psychology in social context* (New York: Irvington, 1979), who draws on archival sources to demonstrate how psychologists were affected by the social and political context of the World War I and postwar years. The sources and results of the clash between Yerkes and Scott are told by von Mayrhauser (1985), as part of his doctoral dissertation at the University of Chicago. There are several useful histories of clinical psychology. The broadest is John M.

Reisman, *The development of clinical psychology* (New York: Appleton-Century-Crofts, 1966). More attention to professional issues is provided by Robert I. Watson, "A brief history of clinical psychology," *Psychological Bulletin* (1953, *50:* 321–46); and Virginia Staudt Sexton, "Clinical psychology: An historical survey," *Genetic Psychology Monographs* (1965, *72:* 401–34). An insider's account of the growth of clinical psychology during and immediately after World War II is given by E. Lowell Kelly, "Clinical psychology," in Dennis (1947). A brief overview of clinical psychology training issues is found in Leonard Blank, "Clinical psychology training, 1945–62: Conferences and issues," in Leonard Blank and Henry David, eds., *Sourcebook for training in clinical psychology* (New York: Springer, 1964).

Psychologists themselves have provided periodic treatments of their immediate history. For the period in question, the broadest and most detailed treatment is given by Jerome S. Bruner and Gordon W. Allport, "Fifty years of change in American psychology," *Psychological Bulletin* (1940, *37:* 757–76), which provided the basis for Allport's APA presidential address, "The psychologist's frame of reference" *Psychological Bulletin* (1940, *37:* 1–28). Earlier relevant surveys include Robert Davis and Silas E. Gould, "Changing tendencies in general psychology," *Psychological Review* (1929, *36:* 320–31); Florence L. Goodenough, "Trends in modern psychology," *Psychological Bulletin* (1934, *31:* 81–97); and Herbert S. Langfeld, "Fifty volumes of the *Psychological Review,*" *Psychological Review* (1943, *50:* 143–55). Later accounts looking back to the period in question are Kenneth E. Clark, "The APA study of psychologists," *American Psychologist* (1954, *9:* 117–20); W. A. Kaess and W. A. Bousfield, "Citation of authorities in textbooks," *American Psychologist* (1954, *9:* 144–48); Russell Becker, "Outstanding contributors to psychology," *American Psychologist* (1959, *14:* 297–98); and Kenneth Wurtz, "A survey of important psychological books," *American Psychologist* (1961, *16:* 192–94).

The narrative account of psychology's preparation for and participation in World War II, including reunification of the APA and AAAP and planning for psychology's postwar role, is based on careful reading of all the *Psychological Bulletins* for the relevant years. The reference to Leonard Carmichael is to his oral report to the meeting of the APA Council (the association did not meet because of the war) in New York on September 3, 1942, beginning in the *Bulletin* at page 713.

Finally, a contemporary account of psychology's place in the postwar competition for research funds is given by Robert Leeper, "An analysis of science legislation in the last Congress," *American Psychologist* (1947, *2:* 127–35). For the debate in the Senate itself, see the *Congressional Record;* Leeper's page references to the *Record* are unaccountably mistaken: One should look up Bill S-1805 in the Index for 1946. The quotations in the text are from p. 8048, and other brief considerations on the social sciences may be found throughout the entire, oft-interrupted, debate. My account of the founding of the Ford Foundation and its interest in behavioral science is based on an Invited Address to Cheiron, the Society for the History of the Behavioral Sciences, June 13, 1985, by Arnold Thackray, "Inventing behavioral science."

REFERENCES

Abrahams, E. (1985, May 12). Founding father of the New Republic. Review of D. W. Levy, *Herbert Croly of the* New Republic: *The life and thought of an American Progressive.* *Washington Post* Book World, p. 7.

Adams, G. (1934). The rise and fall of psychology. *Atlantic Monthly 153:* 82–90.

Allen, F. L. (1931). *Only yesterday: An informal history of the 1920's.* New York: Harper & Row.

Anderson, J. E. (1943). Outcomes of the Intersociety Constitutional Convention. *Psychological Bulletin 40:* 585–88.

Baritz, L. J. (1960). *The servants of power: A history of the use of social science in American industry.* Middletown, CT: Wesleyan University Press.

Beers, C. (1908/1953). *A mind that found itself.* New York: Doubleday.

Birnbaum, L. T. (1955). Behaviorism in the 1920's. *American Quarterly 7:* 15–30.

———. (1964). *Behaviorism: John Broadus Watson and American social thought 1913–33.* Unpublished doctoral dissertation, University of California, Berkeley.

Block, N. J. and Dworkin, G., eds. (1976). *The I.Q. controversy: Critical readings.* New York: Pantheon.

Boorstin, D. J. (1973). *The Americans: The democratic experience.* New York: Vintage Books.

Bramel, D. and Friend, R. (1981). Hawthorne, the myth of the docile worker, and class bias in American psychology. *American Psychologist 36:* 867–78.

Brigham, C. (1923). *A study of American intelligence.* Princeton, NJ: Princeton University Press.

Britt, S. H. (1943). The Office of Psychological Personnel—Report for the second six months. *Psychological Bulletin 40:* 436–46.

Buckley, K. W. (1982). The selling of a psychologist: John Broadus Watson and the application of behavioral techniques to advertising. *Journal of the History of the Behavioral Sciences 18:* 207–21.

Burnham, J. C. (1968). The new psychology: From narcissism to social control. In J. Braeman, R. H. Bremner, and D. Brody, eds., *Change and continuity in twentieth-century America: The 1920's.* Columbus: Ohio State University Press.

Cohen, J. and Wiebe, G. D. (1955). Who are these people? *American Psychologist 10:* 84–85.

Cooper, K. J. (1991, May 6). Universities' images stained by improper charges to government. *Washington Post,* p. A 13.

Darley, J. and Wolfle, D. (1946). Can we meet the formidable demand for psychological services? *American Psychologist 1:* 179–80.

Dennis, W. ed., (1947). *Current trends in psychology.* Pittsburgh: University of Pittsburgh Press.

Dewey, J. (1917). The need for social psychology. *Psychological Review 24:* 266–77.

Doherty, J. C. (1985, April 30). World War II through an Indochina looking glass. *Wall Street Journal,* p. 30.

Fass, P. (1977). *The damned and the beautiful: American youth in the 1920's.* Oxford, England: Oxford University Press.

Fite, W. (1918). The human soul and the scientific prepossession. *Atlantic Monthly 122:* 796–804.

Freeman, D. (1983). *Margaret Mead and Samoa: The making and unmaking of an anthropological myth.* Cambridge, MA: Harvard University Press.

Garth, T. R. (1930). A review of race psychology. *Psychological Bulletin 27:* 329–56.

Gould, S. J. (1981). *The mismeasure of man.* New York: Norton.

Graves, R. and Hodge, A. (1940). *The long week-end: A social history of Britain 1918–39.* New York: Norton.

Haller, M. (1963). *Eugenics: Hereditarian attitudes in American thought.* New Brunswick, NJ: Rutgers University Press.

Harris, B. and Morawski, J. (1979, April). *John B. Watson's predictions for 1979.* Paper presented at the 50th annual meeting of the Eastern Psychological Association, Philadelphia.

James, W. (1892). A plea for psychology as a natural science. *Philosophical Review 1:* 146–53.

Jastrow, J. (1929, April 26). Review of J. B. Watson, *Ways of behaviorism, psychological care of infant and child, battle of behaviorism. Science 69:* 455–57.

Landman, J. H. (1932). *Human sterilization: The history of the sexual sterilization movement.* New York: Macmillan.

Mayo, E. (1933). *The human problems of an industrial civilization.* Cambridge, MA: Harvard University Press.

———. (1945). *The social problems of an industrial civilization.* Cambridge, MA: Harvard Graduate School of Business Administration.

McDougall, W. (1921). *Is America safe for democracy?* New York: Scribner's. Reprint ed. New York: Arno Press, 1977.

Mead, M. (1928). *Coming of age in Samoa.* New York: Morrow.

Morgan, C. T. (1947). Human engineering. In W. Dennis ed., *Current trends in psychology.* Pittsburgh. University of Pittsburgh Press.

Murdock, N. and Leahey, T. H. (1986, April). *Scientism and status: The Boulder model.* Paper presented at the annual meeting of the Eastern Psychological Association, New York.

Napoli, D. S. (1981). *Architects of adjustment: The history of the psychological profession in the United States.* Port Washington, NY: Kennikat Press.

Ostrander, G. M. (1968). The revolution in morals. In J. Braeman, R. H. Bremner, and D. Brody, eds., *Change and continuity in twentieth-century America: The 1920's.* Columbus: Ohio State University Press.

Peatman, J. G. (1949). How scientific and how professional is the American Psychological Association? *American Psychologist 4:* 486–89.

Perelman, S. J. (1958). Cloudland revisited: Sodom in the suburbs. In S. J. Perelman, *The most of S. J. Perelman.* New York: Simon & Schuster.

Poffenberger, A. T. (1936). Psychology and life. *Psychological Review 43:* 9–31.

Rieff, P. (1966). *The triumph of the therapeutic.* New York: Harper & Row.

Remmers, H. H. (1944). Psychology—Some unfinished business. *Psychological Bulletin 41:* 713–24.

Rogers, C. (1944). Psychological adjustments of discharged service personnel. *Psychological Bulletin 41:* 689–96.

Sears, R. R. (1944). Clinical psychology in the military services. *Psychological Bulletin 41:* 502–9.

Sokal, M. M. (1983). James McKeen Cattell and American psychology in the 1920's. In Josef Brozek, ed., *Explorations in the history of psychology in the United States.* Lewisburg, PA: Bucknell University Press.

Taylor, F. (1911). *Principles of scientific management.* New York: Harper Brothers.

Terman, L. M. (1924). The mental test as a psychological method. *Psychological Review 31:* 93–117.

———. (1930). Lewis M. Terman. In C. Murchison, ed., *A history of psychology in autobiography,* Vol. 2. Worcester, MA: Clark University Press.

Thomas, J. L. (1977). Nationalizing the Republic. In B. Bailyn, D. Davis, D. Donald, J. Thomas, R. Wiebe, and W. S. Wood. *The Great Republic.* Boston: Little, Brown.

Thorndike, E. L. (1920). Intelligence and its uses. *Harper's Magazine 140:* 227–35.

von Mayrhauser, R. T. (1985, June 14). *Walking out at the Walton: Psychological disunity and the origins of group testing in early World War I.* Paper presented at the annual meeting of Cheiron, the Society for the History of the Behavioral Sciences, Philadelphia.

Walters, R. G. (1978). *American Reformers 1815–60.* New York: Hill and Wang.

Washburn, M. F. (1922). Introspection as an objective method. *Psychological Review 29:* 89–112.

Watson, J. B. (1926a). What is behaviorism? *Harper's Magazine 152:* 723–29.

_____. (1926b). How we think: A behaviorist's view. *Harper's Magazine 153:* 40–45.

_____. (1926c). Memory as the behaviorist sees it. *Harper's Magazine 153:* 244–50.

_____. (1927a). The myth of the unconscious. *Harper's Magazine 155:* 502–8.

_____. (1927b). The behaviorist looks at the instincts. *Harper's Magazine 155:* 228–35.

_____. (1928a). The heart or the intellect. *Harper's Magazine 156:* 345–52.

_____. (1928b). *Psychological care of infant and child.* New York: Norton.

Wiggam, A. E. (1924). *The fruit of the family tree.* Indianapolis, IN: Bobbs-Merrill.

Yerkes, R. M. (1918). Psychology in relation to the war. *Psychological Review 25:* 85–115.

_____. (1923). Testing the human mind. *Atlantic Monthly 131:* 358–70.

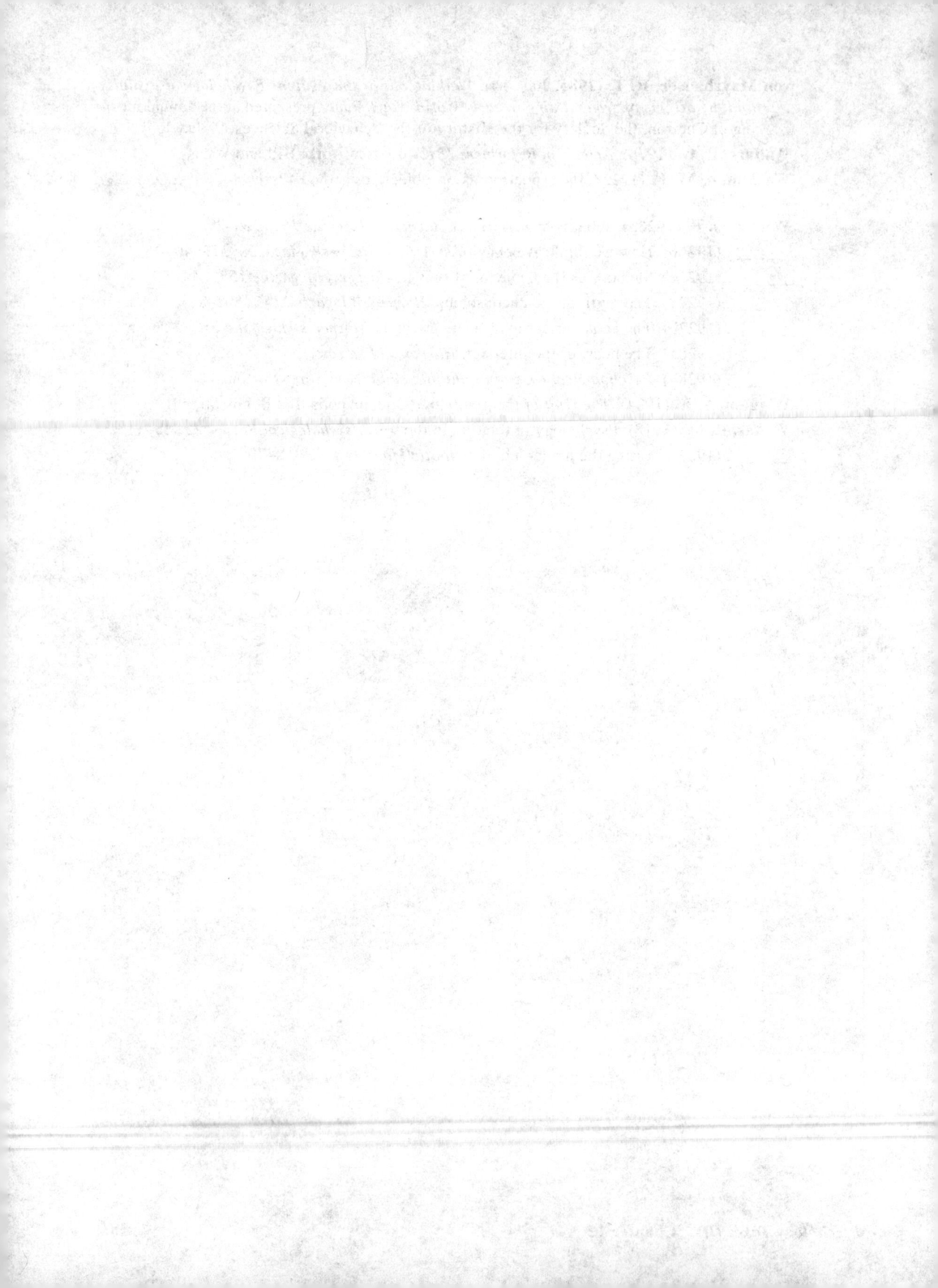

PART IV

PSYCHOLOGY SINCE WORLD WAR II

World War II completed psychology's transformation from a relatively staid science to a profession increasingly concerned with human welfare. Clinical psychology as we know it today—doing psychotherapy—was created by the need for psychological services for returning war veterans. Psychology experienced explosive growth after the war, especially in its applied branches. Scientific psychology grew, too, but at a much slower pace. Growth led to fragmentation. Psychologists divided along professional lines into clinicians, counselors, industrial psychologists, experimental psychologists, and others. In 1988, professional lines became fault lines, and, in a mirror image of 1938's events, academic psychologists split from the APA to form the American Psychological Society.

Within scientific psychology, the divisions of the past continued and new ones were invented. Radical behaviorism was added to the behaviorisms of the 1930s and 1940s. Mediational behaviorism developed out of Hullian behaviorism. Cognitive psychology began in the 1950s, matured into cognitive science in the 1970s, and was challenged by a new *soi-disant* paradigm, connectionism, in the 1980s.

Psychology has become a major institution in modern American life. It is accepted in every college and university as a popular study. Psychologists work in business and industry, and troubled people consult psychologists for help with their problems. Psychological language has become part of everyday life. Some critics say that ours has become a psychological society. Psychology's tremendous growth and increasing influence, along with changes in scientific behavioral psychology, will occupy us in the last three chapters of this book.

13 *Eclectic Psychology (1950-1958)*

After Freud, Burrhus Frederick Skinner is the best-known psychologist. Skinner was the last of the great behaviorist theory-builders. His philosophy of radical behaviorism repudiated all previous approaches to the mind; his experimental analysis of behavior broke new ground in the study of behavior; and his calls for society to renounce notions of free will and accept behavior technology excited some but alarmed more.

TROUBLES WITH BEHAVIORISM (1950–1954)

The most consciously troubled area in psychology after World War II was the core of traditional scientific psychology, experimental psychology, primarily the study of learning. Sigmund Koch, already becoming an effective gadfly to the pretensions of scientific psychology, wrote that "psychology seems now to have entered an era of total disorientation" (1951a, p. 295). In another paper (1951b), Koch asserted: "Since the end of the World War II, psychology has been in a long and intensifying crisis . . . its core seems to be disaffection from the theory of the recent past. Never before had it seemed so evident that the development of a science is not an automatic forward movement." Koch located two causes of the "crisis" in experimental psychology, one internal and one external. Within experimental psychology, Koch identified a decade-long stagnation in the development of the prewar theoretical systems of learning theory. Outside learning theory, clinical and applied psychology were bidding for "social recognition," abandoning theory for practice to take on "social responsibilities." Left out in the rush toward social usefulness, theoretical psychologists had become depressed and were looking for a "new wave" to excite them again.

Koch was not the only critic of traditional behaviorism. In 1950, the distinguished comparative psychologist Frank Beach questioned psychology's reliance on the rat. Comparative psychology, Beach said, was supposed to be genuinely comparative, investigating the behavior of all sorts and conditions of animals. Instead, psychology had focused on a single species, the rat, assuming without question that it could stand in for all other species. Such naïveté, Beach thought, was a dangerous mistake. In 1951, Karl Lashley, Watson's former student and a leader in the study of neuropsychology, attacked the foundation of Watsonian, Thorndikian, and Hullian S–R theory. Implicitly endorsing Tolman's rival view of the mind/brain, Lashley argued that the brain is more than a telephone switchboard making connections between stimuli and responses; it is a central planning agency that maps and controls long sequences of behavior. In this respect, Lashley, like Tolman, anticipated the idea that the mind/brain is a sophisticated computer. In their different ways, Beach and Lashley began to undermine the Spencerian paradigm that had lain at the heart of the psychology of adaptation since the mid-nineteenth century. Beach challenged Spencer's idea that all mind/brains work the same way, and Lashley challenged the idea that the way all mind/brains work is by simple association.

Philosophical Behaviorism

Psychological behaviorism arose out of the problems of animal psychology and in revolt against introspective mentalism. Consequently, behavioristic psychologists never addressed one of the more obvious difficulties that might be raised against their movement—namely, that ordinary people believe they possess mental processes and consciousness. There exists a folk psychology of mind that deserves attention from any psychological program departing from it. It may fairly be asked why, if there are no mental processes—as behaviorists seem to maintain—ordinary language is so rich in descriptions of mind and consciousness? Philosophical behaviorists addressed the problem of reinterpreting commonsense mentalistic psychology into acceptable "scientific" behavioristic terms as part of their more general program of linking claims about unobservables with observables.

As it is usually presented, philosophical or "logical behaviorism is a semantic theory about what mental terms mean. The basic idea is that attributing a mental state (say thirst) to an organism is the same as saying that the organism is disposed to behave in a certain way (for example to drink if there is water available)" (Fodor, 1981, p. 115). According to logical behaviorists, when we attribute a mental statement to a person, we're really just describing his or her actual or likely behavior in a given circumstance, not some inner mental state. In principle, then, it would be possible to eliminate mentalistic concepts from everyday psychology and replace them with concepts referring only to behavior. As stated, logical behaviorism is rather implausible. For example, according to logical behaviorism, to believe that ice on a lake is too thin for skating must mean that one is disposed not to skate on the ice and to say to others that they ought not skate on the lake. However, things are not so simple. If you see someone you thoroughly dislike about to skate out on the ice, you may say nothing, hoping that your enemy will fall through the ice and look foolish. Should you harbor real malice toward the skater—if, for example, he is blackmailing you—you may say nothing, hoping he will drown; indeed, you may direct him to the weakest ice. So, the mental statement "believing the ice is thin" cannot be simply and directly translated into a behavioral disposition, because how one is disposed to behave depends on other beliefs that turn on still others—for example, that the skater is a blackmailer—making any direct equation of mental state and behavioral disposition impossible.

The difficulties of logical behaviorism are relevant to experimental psychology because its doctrines represent the application of operationism to ordinary psychological terms. Logical behaviorism's equation of mental state and behavior or behavioral disposition provides operational definitions of "belief," "hope," "fear," "being in pain," and so on. The example of the thin ice shows that one cannot give an operational definition of "believing the ice is thin," and failure to "operationalize" so simple and straightforward a concept casts doubt on the whole enterprise of operationism in psychology. The British philosopher G. E. Moore, following Ludwig Wittgenstein, refuted the logical behaviorist–operationist treatment of mental terms more bluntly: "When we pity a man for having toothache, we are not pitying him for putting his hand to his cheek" (quoted in Luckhardt, 1983).

Logical behaviorism is so obviously false that it makes an admirable straw man for philosophers of other dispositions, but it is not clear that anyone has actually held the position just sketched. It is typically attributed to Rudolph Carnap, Gilbert Ryle, and Ludwig Wittgenstein, but, in fact, these philosophers held different and more interesting views on the nature of mentalistic folk psychology. We discussed Carnap's "behaviorism" in Chapter 11 in connection with E. C. Tolman, who was for a time under Carnap's influence. Carnap came closest to holding the position of logical behaviorism, but we should bear in mind that, for him, it was just a temporary way station on the road to interpreting mentalistic language as talk about brain states. As we shall see in Chapter 15, Carnap's physicalistic view is fraught with difficulties; but it is possible to separate the idea that mental terms refer to behavioral dispositions from the idea that they refer to brain states.

In *The Concept of Mind* (1949), English philosopher Gilbert Ryle attacked what he called "the dogma of the Ghost in the Machine" begun by Descartes. Descartes had defined two worlds—one material and including the body, the other mental, a ghostly inner stage on which private mental events took place. Ryle accused

Descartes of making a huge "category mistake," treating mind as if it were a distinct thing opposed to the body and somehow lying behind behavior. Here is an example of a category mistake: A person is taken on a tour of Oxford University and sees its college buildings, its library, its deans, its professors, and its students. At the end of the day, the visitor asks, "You've showed me all these things, but where is the university?" The mistake is in supposing that because there is a name "Oxford University," it must apply to some object separate from the buildings and so on, yet be like them in being a thing. Ryle claimed that Cartesian dualism is a category mistake. Cartesians describe behaviors with "mental" predicates such as "intelligent," "hopeful," "sincere," "disingenuous," and then assume that there must be a mental thing behind the behaviors that makes them intelligent, hopeful, sincere, or disingenuous. Here, says Ryle, lies the mistake, because the behaviors themselves are intelligent, hopeful, sincere, or disingenuous; no inner ghost is needed to make them so. Moreover, inventing the Ghost in the Machine accomplishes nothing; if there were an inner ghost, we would still have to explain why its operations are intelligent, hopeful, sincere, or disingenuous. Is there a Ghost in the Ghost? And a Ghost in the Ghost in the Ghost? The Ghost in the Machine, far from explaining mental life, vastly complicates our efforts to understand it.

So far, one might, as Ryle feared, put him down as a behaviorist who is claiming that mind is only behavior. But Ryle held that there is indeed more to mental predicates than simple descriptions of behavior. For example, when we say birds are "migrating" in autumn, we see them flying south, and a behaviorist might say that "migration" is just "flying-south behavior." However, as Ryle pointed out, to say that birds are "migrating" is to say much more than that they are flying south. The term "migration" implies a whole story about why they are flying south, how they will return later, and how it happens every year, and theories about how they navigate. To say birds are "migrating" goes beyond saying that they are flying south, but it does not go *behind* saying that they are flying south. Similarly, to say a behavior is "intelligent" does more than simply describe some behavior. The statement brings in the various criteria we have for saying a course of action is intelligent—for example, it is appropriate to the situation, and it is likely to be successful. But saying a person is acting intelligently does not go behind the behavior to some ghostly inner calculations that make the action intelligent, however much it goes beyond a behaviorist's description of what the person is doing. Ryle rejected dualism, and, although his analysis of mind had some similarities to behaviorism, it was rather different from either psychological behaviorism or logical, philosophical behaviorism.

A difficult and subtle analysis of ordinary psychological language was made by the Viennese (later British) philosopher Ludwig Wittgenstein. Wittgenstein argued that Cartesian philosophers had led people to believe that there are mental objects (for example, sensations) and mental processes (for example, memory), whereas in fact there are neither. Wittgenstein's rejection of mental objects rests on complex, purely philosophical considerations, but his rejection of unconscious mental processes is directly relevant to the claims of cognitive psychology. Consider memory, a topic much studied by psychologists. We remember things all the time, but is there an inner mental process of remembering common to all acts of memory? Wittgenstein thought not. Malcolm (1970) gives the following example: Several hours after you put your keys in the kitchen drawer, you are asked, "Where did you put the keys?" You may remember in any of several ways:

1. Nothing occurs to you, then you mentally retrace your steps earlier in the day and have an image of putting them in the drawer, and say, "I left them in the kitchen drawer."

2. Nothing occurs to you. You have no images, but ask yourself "Where did I put them?" then exclaim, "The kitchen drawer!' "

3. The question is asked while you are deep in conversation with another person. Without interrupting your talk, you point to the kitchen drawer.

4. You are asked while writing a letter. Saying nothing, you walk over to the drawer, reach in, and hand over the keys, all the while composing the next sentence in the letter.

5. Without any hesitation or doubt, you answer directly, "I put them in the kitchen drawer."

In every case, you remembered where the keys were, but each case is quite unlike the others. The behaviors are different, so there is no essential behavioral process of remembering; there is no uniform mental accompaniment to the act of remembering, so there is no essential mental process of remembering; and since there is no common behavior or conscious experience, there is no essential physiological process of remembering. In each case, there is behavior, there are mental events, and there are physiological processes, but no one of them is the same as another, so there is no uniform process of memory. We group these events together under "memory" not because of some essential defining feature of each episode, the way we define "electrons" in terms of uniform defining features, but because they share what Wittgenstein called a "family resemblance." The members of a family resemble one another, but there is no single feature all members possess. Two brothers may share similar noses, a father and son similar ears, two cousins similar hair, but there is no essential defining feature shared by all. Wittgenstein argued that terms referring to mental processes are all family-resemblance terms, having no defining essence that can be captured. "Remembering," "thinking," "intending" are not processes, but human abilities. To the Wittgensteinian, the Würzburg psychologists' efforts to lay bare the processes of thinking had to end in failure, for there are no processes of thought to be found. Thinking, like remembering, is just something people do (Malcolm, 1970).

If Wittgenstein is right, the consequences for psychology are profound. Wittgenstein (1953) had a poor opinion of psychology: "The confusion and barrenness of psychology is not to be explained by calling it a 'young science. . . .' For in psychology there are experimental methods and conceptual confusion" (*Philosophical Investigations II,* Sec. XIV). Psychology's conceptual confusion is to think there are mental objects and mental processes when there are not, and then to seek for explanations of the fictitious objects and processes.

> I have been trying in all this to remove the temptation to think that there "must be" a mental process of thinking, hoping, wishing, believing, etc., independent of the process of expressing a thought, a hope, a wish, etc. . . . If we scrutinize the usages which we make of "thinking," "meaning," "wishing," etc., going through this process rids us of the temptation to look for a peculiar act of thinking, independent of the act of expressing our thoughts, and stowed away in some particular medium. (Wittgenstein, 1958, pp. 41–3)

Wittgenstein's point here is related to Ryle's: There is nothing behind our acts; there is no Ghost in the Machine. Behind the point about psychology, there is a broader point about science: Explanations stop somewhere (Malcolm, 1970). It is no good asking a physicist why an object once set in motion will travel in a straight line forever unless acted on by another force, because this is a basic assumption that allows physics to explain other things. No one has seen an object move that way and the only apparently undisturbed objects we can observe moving, the planets, move (roughly) in circles; indeed, the ancients assumed that an object in space set in motion would naturally move in a circle. Similarly, a physicist cannot explain why quarks have the properties they do, only how, given those properties, their behavior can be explained. Psychologists have all along supposed that thinking, memory, wishing, and so on, required explanations, but Ryle, and especially Wittgenstein, claim that they do not. They are human abilities, and thinking, remembering, and wishing are things we just do without there being some "inside story," mental or physiological, although they are not just behaviors, either. Psychologists went wrong when they framed their question as "What is the process of thinking?" and naturally came up with theories about mental processes. As Wittgenstein remarks:

> We talk of processes and states and leave their nature undecided. Sometimes perhaps we shall know more about them—we think. But that is just what commits us to a particular way of looking at the matter. For we have a definite concept of what it means to learn to know a process better. The decisive movement in the conjuring trick has been made, and it was the very one that we thought quite innocent. (1953, *Philosophical Investigations I,* par. 308)

To Wittgenstein, we cannot scientifically explain behavior, but we can understand it. To understand people's behavior, and the expressions of their thoughts, we must take into consideration what Wittgenstein called human "forms of life." "What has to be accepted, the given, is—so one could say—forms of life" (Wittgenstein, 1958). Luckhardt (1983) introduces a useful analogy to clarify Wittgenstein's point. A painting expresses an artist's conception through the physical medium of paint on canvas. We find it beautiful (or ugly) as we interpret it. Behaviorists and reductionists are like paint salespeople who point out that because the painting is made of paint, its beauty is identical with the arrangements of the paints on the canvas. However, this is obviously absurd; a painting venerated for its beauty among academic painters and audiences in 1875 is likely to be considered tacky kitsch by modernists and their audience. Beauty depends on an interpretation of paint on canvas and is not identical with it. Moreover, how someone interprets the painting depends on the immediate and overall context in which he or she meets it. The gallery-goer may have read art history and criticism, and this knowledge will shape a true appreciation of the picture. He or she will see Frank Stella's latest canvas against the background of Stella's previous work, the works by other artists arranged in the show, and knowledge of the history, ambitions, and techniques of modern and postmodern painting. Simply as paint on canvas, the painting has no meaning and is neither beautiful nor ugly; it takes on meaning only in the eye of an interpretive viewer. All this context is a "form of life"—the form of life of modernism and postmodernism in the arts. A person who knows nothing of modernism is likely to find a Stella work literally without meaning, because that person does not participate in the appropriate form of life. Should he or she take modern art history classes, a new form of life will be learned and the painting will become meaningful.

Wittgenstein's point is that human action is only meaningful within the setting of a form of life. An untutored Westerner is likely to find practices of another culture, or another historical time, without meaning in the same way the naive gallery-goer finds the Stella painting meaningless. The reverse is true: Some African tribesmen came to a city for the first time and were deeply shocked when, in a tall building, they saw two men go into a box and emerge a few seconds later as three women. (They saw an elevator.) If Wittgenstein's claim is correct, then not only can psychology not be a science because there are no mental processes and objects for it to study and explain, but psychology and the other social sciences cannot be sciences because there are no historically permanent and cross-culturally universal principles for understanding human thought and behavior. Psychology, he says, should give up the "craving for generality" and "the contemptuous attitude to the particular case" it has picked up from natural science (Wittgenstein, 1953) and accept the modest goal of explicating forms of life and explaining particular human actions within their historically given forms of life.

Are Theories of Learning Adequate?

Hull and Tolman were not professionally raised on logical positivism and operationism, but the succeeding generation of experimental psychologists, coming into professional maturity after World War II, was. Many of the new generation believed, with Sigmund Koch, that the theoretical debates of the 1930s and 1940s had led nowhere, that the problems of the psychology of learning—the heart of the adjustment process—were not being solved. So, in the later 1940s and through the early 1950s, theoretical psychologists engaged in earnest self-scrutiny, applying the tools of logical positivism and operationism to developing tactics of theory construction in psychology, and applying the criteria of positivism and operationism to the theories of Hull and Tolman.

A central event in the history of behaviorism was the Dartmouth Conference on Learning Theory held in 1950. There, the new generation of learning theorists evaluated learning theories in the light of the logical positivism they took for granted, and which they thought their teachers had accepted. Hull's theory, as the one they believed most closely shared their positivist standards of theory construction, came in for the most devastating criticism. Sigmund Koch, the author of the report on Hull, said, "We have done what may be construed as a nasty thing. We have proceeded on a literal interpretation of some such proposition as: 'Hull has put forward a hypothetico-deductive theory of behavior.' " Proceeding on that interpretation, Koch showed that, judged by positivistic criteria, Hull's enterprise was a total failure. Koch's rhetoric was damning: Hull's theory suffered from "horrible indeterminancy" and "manifold inadequacies" in the definition of its independent variables; it was "empirically empty" and a "pseudoquantitative system"; and it failed to progress from the 1943 formulation to the ones of the early 1950s: "It may be said with confidence that with respect to most of the issues considered . . . there has been no evidence of constructive advance since 1943." The other theories, including those of Tolman, B. F. Skinner, Kurt Lewin (a Gestalt psychologist), and Edwin R. Guthrie (another behaviorist), were variously criticized for failure to meet positivist criteria for good theory.

The older theories of learning were not adequate, at least as judged by the standards of logical positivism. But were the logical positivists' standards necessarily right? At Dartmouth, it was noticed that B. F. Skinner's brand of behaviorism failed to live up to logical positivistic principles because it did not try to. Skinner had set his own standards of theoretical adequacy, and, judged by them, his theory did well. Perhaps, then, change was called for in psychologists' goals, rather than in their continued pursuit of goals set by abstract philosophy. Were theories of learning needed at all?

ARE THEORIES OF LEARNING NECESSARY? RADICAL BEHAVIORISM (1938–1958)

Radical Behaviorism

> Define
> And thus expunge
> The ought
> The should
>
> * * *
>
> Truth's to be sought
> In Does and Doesn't

B. F. Skinner, *For Ivor Richards* (1971)

By far the best known and most influential of all the major behaviorists is Burrhus Frederick Skinner (1904–1990), whose radical behaviorism, if accepted, would constitute a momentous revolution in humanity's understanding of the human self, demanding as it does no less than the complete rejection of the entire intellectual psychological tradition nurtured in philosophy, which we have considered in this book. It would replace this tradition with a scientific psychology grounded in neo-Darwinian evolutionary theory, which looks outside humans for the causes of behavior. Every psychological thinker we have considered, from Thales to Wundt, even to Hull and Tolman, intended psychology to be an explication of internal processes, however conceived—processes that produce behavior or conscious phenomena. Skinner followed Watson in placing responsibility for behavior squarely in the environment. A person does not act at the behest of moral values, the "ought" and "should," the highest guides to action for Plato. For Skinner, people deserve neither praise nor blame for anything they "do" or "don't." The environment controls behavior so that both good and evil, if such exist, reside there, not in the person. To paraphrase Shakespeare's *Julius Caesar:* "The fault, dear Brutus, lies in our contingencies of reinforcement, not ourselves."

Skinner refused to admit the influence in a talk with me in 1985, but Skinner's radical behaviorism may be regarded as a product of neorealism. On the traditional copy theory of cognition found in other theories, there is a mental world of objects—ideas or representations—and that world is the subject matter of psychology. If one denies the validity of the copy theory as neorealism did and as radical behaviorism does, then there is no world of mental objects. We perceive real objects directly, and they directly control our behavior. Interestingly, Skinner gave more credence to conscious experience than did methodological behaviorists, who ruled it out of science as private. In the neorealist conception, however, some of the real objects we respond to are in our bodies, such as damaged nerves that cause pain, and the private stimuli these give rise to must be included in any complete science of behavior.

The heart of radical behaviorism may best be approached by looking at Skinner's attitude toward Freud in his paper "A Critique of Psychoanalytic Concepts and Theories" (1954/1972). For Skinner, Freud's great discovery was that much human behavior has unconscious causes. However, to Skinner, Freud's great mistake was in inventing a mental apparatus—id, ego, superego—and its attendant mental processes to explain human behavior. Skinner believed that the lesson taught by the unconscious is that mental states are simply irrelevant to behavior. We may observe that a student shows a neurotic subservience to her teachers. The Freudian might explain this by asserting that the student's father was a punitive perfectionist who demanded obedience, and that his child incorporated a stern father image that now affects her behavior in the presence of authority figures. Skinner would allow us to explain the current servility by reference to punishments at the hand of a punitive father, but he would insist that the link be direct. The student cowers now because as a child she received punishment from a similar person, not because there is within her any mental image of her father. For Skinner, the inference to an unconscious father image explains nothing that cannot be explained by simply referring current behavior to the consequences of past behavior. The mental link adds nothing to an account of behavior, according to Skinner; in fact, it complicates matters by requiring that the mental link itself be explained. Skinner has extended this criticism of mental entities to encompass all traditional psychologies, rejecting equally the superego, apperception, habit strength, and cognitive maps. All are unnecessary steps in the explanation of behavior.

Skinner's rejection of mental or hypothetical entities as unnecessary fictions was similar to Aristotle's rejection of Plato's Forms. Aristotle argued that the Forms were unseen, fictitious entities introduced into the universe to explain those things that could be seen, but these entities add nothing to our understanding of the observable world and themselves require explaining. Similar, too, was Ockham's rejection of the doctrine of mental faculties. That we remember does not imply the existence of an unobservable faculty of memory. Ockham pointed out that remembering is a mental act, not a faculty. Skinner held that remembering is simply an act, without any reference to mind at all. In Skinner's case, as in Aristotle's and Ockham's, the desire was to simplify our understanding of nature and of the human as a natural creature by eliminating anything not absolutely necessary to scientific explanation, especially any reference to hypothetical, unobservable entities. Aristotle did away with the Forms, Ockham the faculties, and Skinner the mind.

Although radical behaviorism represents a sharp break with any traditional psychology, whether scientific or commonsense, its intellectual heritage can be located. It stands clearly in the empiricist camp, especially with radical empiricism from Ockham to Francis Bacon to Hume to Mach. As a young man, Skinner read Bacon's works, and he often referred favorably to the great inductivist. Like Bacon, Skinner believed that truth is to be found in observations themselves, in "does" and "doesn't," rather than in our interpretations of our observations. Skinner's first psychological paper was an application of Mach's radical descriptive positivism to the concept of the reflex. Skinner concluded that a reflex is not an entity inside an animal, but merely a convenient descriptive term for a regular correlation between stimulus and response. This presages his rejection of all hypothetical entities.

Skinner's account of behavior is also heir to Darwin's analysis of evolution, as Skinner himself often suggested. Darwin argued that species constantly produce variant traits and that nature acts on these traits to select those that contribute to survival, eliminating those that do not. Similarly, for Skinner an organism is constantly producing variant forms of behavior. Some of these acts lead to favorable consequences—are reinforced—and others do not. Those that do are strengthened, for they contribute to the organism's survival and are learned. Those that are not reinforced are not learned, and they disappear from the organism's repertoire, just as weak species become extinct. Both Skinner's analysis of behavior and his values were Darwinian, as we shall see.

Like many innovative scientific thinkers, Skinner received little early training in his discipline. He took his undergraduate degree in English at Hamilton College, intending to be a writer, studying no psychology. However, a biology teacher called his attention to works by Pavlov and the mechanist physiologist Jacques Loeb. The former taught him a concern for the total behavior of an organism, and the latter impressed him with the possibility of careful, rigorous, scientific research on behavior. He learned of Watson's behaviorism from some articles by Bertrand Russell on Watson, whom Skinner then read. After failing to become a writer, Skinner turned to psychology filled with the spirit of Watsonian behaviorism. He initiated a systematic research program on a new kind of behavior, the operant.

The Experimental Analysis of Behavior

The basic goal guiding Skinner's scientific work was stated in his first psychological paper and was inspired by the success of Pavlov's work with conditioned reflexes. Wrote Skinner in "The Concept of the Reflex" (1931), "Given a particular part of the behavior of an organism hitherto regarded as unpredictable (and probably, as a consequence, assigned to non-physical factors), the investigator seeks out the antecedent changes with which the activity is correlated and establishes the conditions of the correlation" (1931/1972, p. 440) The goal of psychology is to analyze behavior by locating the specific determinants of specific behaviors, and to establish the exact nature of the relationship between antecedent influence and subsequent behavior. The best way to do this is by experiment, for only in an experiment can all the factors affecting behavior be systematically controlled. Skinner thus called his science "the experimental analysis of behavior."

A behavior is explained within this system when the investigator knows all the influences of which the behavior is a function. We may refer to the antecedent influences acting on a behavior as independent variables, and the behavior that is a function of them we may call the dependent variable. The organism can then be thought of as a locus of variables. It is a place where independent variables act together to produce a behavior. There is no mental activity that intervenes between independent and dependent variables, and traditional references to mental entities may be eliminated when independent variables have been understood. Skinner assumes that physiology will ultimately be able to detail the mechanisms controlling behavior, but that analysis of behavior in terms of functional relationships among variables is completely independent of physiology. The functions will remain even when the underlying physiological mechanisms are understood.

Thus far, Skinner's account closely followed Mach. Scientific explanation is nothing more than an accurate and precise description of the relationship among observable variables; for Skinner, these are environmental variables and behavior variables. Just as Mach sought to exorcise "metaphysical" reference to unobserved causal links in physics, so Skinner sought to exorcise "metaphysical" reference to causal mental links in psychology. In his early work, Skinner emphasized the descriptive nature of his work, and it is still sometimes called descriptive behaviorism. We may note here the mirror-image nature of Skinnerian and Titchenerian psychology. Titchener also followed Mach by seeking only to correlate variables analyzed within an experimental framework, but of course he wanted a description of consciousness, not behavior. Skinner sometimes concedes the possibility of such a study, but he dismisses it as irrelevant to the study of behavior—as Titchener had dismissed the study of behavior as irrelevant to the psychology of consciousness.

What separates Titchener and Skinner, besides their subject matters, is the importance of control for Skinner. Skinner was Watsonian in wanting not just to describe behavior but to control it. In fact, for Skinner, control is the ultimate test of the scientific adequacy of observationally determined functions between antecedent variables and behavior variables. Prediction alone is insufficient, for prediction may result from the correlation of two variables causally dependent on a third, but not on each other. For example, children's toe size and weight will correlate very highly: The bigger a child's toe, the heavier he or she is likely to be. However, toe size does not "cause" weight, or vice versa, for both depend on physical growth, which causes changes in both variables. According to Skinner, an investigator can only be said to have explained a behavior when, in addition to being able to predict its occurrence, the investigator can also influence its occurrence through the manipulation of independent variables. Thus, an adequate experimental analysis of behavior implies a technology of behavior, wherein behavior may be engineered for specific purposes, such as teaching. Titchener always vehemently rejected technology as a goal for psychology, but it was a concern of Skinner's that became increasingly pronounced after World War II.

The experimental analysis of behavior began with Skinner's first psychological book, *The Behavior of Organisms* (1938), which contains most of the important concepts of the experimental analysis of behavior.In *Behavior of Organisms,* Skinner distinguished two kinds of learned behavior, each of which had been studied before but not clearly differentiated. The first category Skinner called respondent behavior, or learning, studied by Pavlov. This category is properly called reflex behavior, for a respondent is a behavior elicited by a definite stimulus, whether unconditioned or conditioned. It loosely corresponds to "involuntary" behavior, such as the salivary responses studied by Pavlov. The second category Skinner called operant behavior or learning, which corresponds loosely to "voluntary" behavior. Operant behavior cannot be elicited but is simply emitted from time to time. However, an operant's probability of occurrence may be raised if its emission is followed by an event called a reinforcer; after reinforcement, it will be more likely to occur again in similar circumstances. Thorndike's puzzle boxes define an operant learning situation: The imprisoned cat emits a variety of behaviors, one of which, such as pressing a lever, leads to escape, which is reinforcing. With the cat placed back in the box, the probability of the correct response is now higher than before; the operant response, lever-pressing, has been strengthened. These three things—the setting in which the behavior occurs (the puzzle box), the reinforced response (lever-pressing), and the reinforcer (escape)—collectively define the contingencies of reinforcement. The experimental analysis of behavior consists of the systematic description of contingencies of reinforcement as they occur in all forms of animal or human behavior.

These contingencies are analyzed in Darwinian fashion. Emitted behavior is parallel to random variation in species' traits. Reinforcement from the environment follows some operants and not others; the former are strengthened and the latter are extinguished. The environment's selection pressures select favorable responses through the process of operant learning, just as successful species flourish while others become extinct. Skinner considered the experimental analysis of behavior to be part of biology, concerned with explaining an individual's behavior as the product of the environment resulting from a process analogous to that which produces species. There is no room in either discipline for vitalism, mind, or teleology. All behavior, whether learned or unlearned, is a product of an individual's reinforcement history or his or her genetic makeup. Behavior is never a product of intention or will.

Skinner's definition of the operant and its controlling contingencies distinguished him from other behaviorists in three frequently misunderstood ways. First, operant responses are never elicited. Suppose we train a rat to press a lever in a Skinner box (or "experimental space," as Skinner called it), reinforcing the bar press only when a certain light is on above the bar. The rat will soon come to bar-press whenever the light comes on. It may appear that the stimulus of the light elicits the response—but, according to Skinner, this is not so. It merely sets the occasion for reinforcement. It enables the organism to discriminate a reinforcing situation from a nonreinforcing situation, and is thus called a discriminative stimulus. It does not elicit bar-pressing as an unconditioned stimulus or a conditioned stimulus elicited salivation in Pavlov's dogs. Thus, Skinner denied that he is an S–R psychologist, for that formula implies a reflexive link between a response and some stimulus, a link that exists only for respondents. Watson adhered to the S–R formula, for he applied the classical conditioning paradigm to all behavior. The spirit of radical behaviorism is so clearly Watsonian that many critics mistake Watson's analysis of behavior for Skinner's.

There is a second way in which Skinner is not an S–R psychologist. He said that the organism may be affected by controlling variables that need not be considered stimuli. This is clearest with respect to motivation. Motivation was seen by Hullians and Freudians as a matter of drive-stimulus reduction: Food deprivation leads to unpleasant stimuli associated with the hunger drive, and the organism acts to reduce them. Skinner saw no reason for the drive-stimuli. They are examples of mentalistic thinking that may be eliminated by directly linking food deprivation to change in behavior. Depriving an organism of food is an observable procedure that will affect an organism's behavior in lawful ways, and there is no gain in speaking of "drives" or their associated stimuli. A measurable variable, although not conceived in stimulus terms, may be causally linked to changes in observable behavior. The organism is truly a locus of variables, and whether the variables are stimuli of which the organism is aware is irrelevant, which renders the S–R formulation less applicable to Skinner. Intervening variables—operationally defined variables "intervening" between S and R—Skinner saw, were, by the very fact of their being operationally defined, eliminable from science because it is possible to simply replace the name of the intervening variable (e.g., *drive*) with its defining operation (e.g., *not feeding animal for 24 hours*).

The third important aspect of the operant concerns the definition. Behavior for Skinner is merely movement in space. This definition recalls Democritus's statement, "Only atoms and the void exist in reality," but Skinner was careful not to define operants as movements. To begin with, an operant is not a response; it is a class of responses. The cat in the puzzle box may press the escape lever in different ways on different trials. Each is a different response in that its form is different at each occurrence, but all are members of the same operant, for each response is controlled by the same contingencies of reinforcement. Whether the cat butts the lever with its head or pushes it with its paw is unimportant—both are the same operant. Similarly, two otherwise identical movements may be instances of different operants if they are controlled by different contingencies. You may raise your hand to pledge allegiance to the flag, to swear to tell the truth in court, or to wave to a friend. The movements may be the same in each case, but each is a different operant, for the setting and reinforcement (the contingencies of reinforcement) are different in each case. This proves to be especially important in explaining verbal behavior, where one word may have several meanings and one meaning may be expressed in different words. With the exception of Tolman, earlier behaviorists had tried to define responses in purely physical terms as movements, and were criticized for ignoring the meaning of behavior. A word, it was argued, is more than a puff of air; it has meaning. Skinner agrees, but he places meaning in the contingencies of reinforcement, not the speaker's mind.

These are the most important theoretical ideas that guide the experimental analysis of behavior. When Skinner asked, "Are theories of learning necessary?" and answered, "No," he did not intend to eschew all theory. What he rejected was theory that refers to the unobserved hypothetical entities he considers fictions, be they ego, cognitive map, or apperception. He did accept theory in the Machian sense as being a summary of the ways in which observable variables correlate, but no more.

Skinner also defined an innovative and radical methodology in his *Behavior of Organisms*. He created an experimental situation that preserved the fluidity of behavior, refusing to chop it up into arbitrary and artificial "trials." An organism is placed in a space and reinforced for some behavior that it may make at any time. The behavior may be closely observed as it continuously changes over time, not as it abruptly changes with each trial. The experimenter seeks to exert maximal control over the organism's environment, so that the experimenter may manipulate, or hold constant, independent variables and so directly observe how they change behavior. A very simple, yet somewhat artificial response is chosen for study. In Skinner's own work, this was typically either a rat pressing a lever or a pigeon pecking a key to obtain food or water. Choosing such an operant makes each response unambiguous, easily observed, and easily counted by machines to produce a cumulative record of responses. Finally, Skinner defined rate of responding as the basic datum of analysis. It is easily quantified and it has been found to vary in lawful ways with changes in independent variables. Such a simple experimental situation stands in contrast to the relative lack of control found in Thorndike's puzzle boxes or Hull's and Tolman's mazes. The situation is capable of defining precise puzzles for the investigator, because it imposes so much control on the organism. The investigator need only draw on previous research to select what variables to manipulate, and then observe their effects on response rate. There is minimal ambiguity about what to manipulate or measure.

Skinner was unlike all other psychologists in completely dispensing with statistics or statistically dictated experimental designs. He believed statistics are necessary only for those who infer an inner state from behavior. Such researchers see actual behavior as indirect measures of the inner state, contaminated by "noise," and thus they must run many subjects and treat data statistically to get measures of this hypothetical state. Skinner studied behavior itself, so there can be no "noise." All behavior is to be explained; none may be explained away as irrelevant or as "error variance." His experimental paradigm gives such clear-cut results and allows such control that "noise" does not occur. As a result, those who practice the experimental analysis of behavior run only a few subjects (often for long periods) and do not use statistics. The statistics are unnecessary, for one can see in graphic records of behavior how response rate changes as variables are altered; no inference is necessary.

It should be noted that Skinner's followers became isolated within the body of psychology. The experimental analysts began their own Division (25) in the APA. They have established their own journals, the *Journal of the Experimental Analysis of Behavior* (1958), and the *Journal of Applied Behavioral Analysis* (1967). A study of citations in articles appearing in the first has shown that, from 1958 to 1969, writers in the JEAB cited their own journal more and more, and others less and less, indicating a growing isolation of the experimental analysis of behavior from psychology as a whole (Krantz, 1973).

Interpreting Human Behavior

In the 1950s, while other behaviorists were liberalizing their brands of behaviorism, Skinner began to extend his radical behaviorism to human behavior without changing any of his fundamental concepts. Skinner viewed human behavior as animal behavior not significantly different from the behavior of the rats and pigeons he had studied in the laboratory.

His most important undertaking was to interpret language within the framework of radical behaviorism. As a would-be writer, Skinner was naturally interested in language, and some of his earliest, albeit unpublished research was on speech perception. His ideas on language were set forth in a series of lectures at Harvard University and then in a book, *Verbal Behavior* (1957). At the same time, Skinner was concerned with using his radical behaviorism and experimental analysis of behavior as bases for the construction of a utopian society and the reconstruction of existing society. His first extended treatment of these problems came in *Walden II* (1948) and *Science and Human Behavior* (1953).

Although "most of the experimental work responsible for the advance of the experimental analysis of behavior has been carried out on other species . . . the results have proved to be surprisingly free of species restrictions . . . and its methods can be extended to human behavior without serious modification." So wrote Skinner in what he considered his most important work, *Verbal Behavior* (p. 3). The final goal of the experimental analysis of behavior is a science of human behavior using the same principles first applied to animals.

The nature of Skinner's theory of language is well conveyed in an interesting later paper, "A Lecture on 'Having' a Poem" (1971/1972) about how he came to write his only published poem, partially quoted at the beginning of this chapter. In this paper, he draws an analogy between "having a baby" and "having a poem": "A person produces a poem and a woman produces a baby, and we call the person a poet and the woman a mother. Both are essential as loci in which vestiges of the past come together in certain combinations" (p. 354). Just as a mother makes no positive contribution to the creation of the baby she carries, so "the act of composition is no more an act of creation than 'having' the bits and pieces" that form the poem. In such case, something new is created, but there is no creator. Again we see the hand of Darwin: A baby is a random combination of genes that may be selected for survival or may die. A poem is a collection of bits and pieces of verbal behavior, some of which are selected, some of which are rejected, for appearance in the poem. As Darwin showed that no divine Mind was necessary to explain the production and evolution of natural species, so Skinner sought to show that it is not necessary to invoke a non—material mind even to explain language—humans' unique possession, according to Descartes.

His argument was worked out in most detail in *Verbal Behavior,* a complex and subtle book that defies easy summary. Only a few salient points may be discussed here. It is a work of interpretation only. Skinner reported no experiments and sought only to establish the plausibility of applying his analysis to language, not its reality. Further, to say he was analyzing language is misleading; the title of his book is *Verbal Behavior,* behavior whose reinforcement is mediated by other persons. The definition includes an animal behaving under the control of an experimenter; together, they form a "genuine verbal community." It excludes the listener in a verbal interchange, except insofar as the listener reinforces speech (for example, by replies or compliance with demands) or acts as a discriminative stimulus (one speaks differently to one's best friend and to one's teacher). The definition makes no reference to the process of communication we usually assume takes place during speech. Skinner's account may be contrasted with that of Wundt, who excluded animals from consideration, examined the linguistic processes of both speaker and listener, and attempted to describe the communication of a *Gesamtvorstellung* from the mind of a speaker to the mind of a hearer.

Nevertheless, *Verbal Behavior* is basically about what we ordinarily consider language—or, more accurately, speech—for Skinner analyzed only real utterances spoken in analyzable environments, not the hypothetical abstract entity "language." Skinner introduced a number of technical concepts in his discussion of verbal behavior. To show the flavor of his analysis, we will briefly discuss his concept of the "tact," because it corresponds roughly to the problem of universals, and because Skinner considered it the most important verbal operant.

We apply the three-term set of contingencies of reinforcement, stimulus, response, and reinforcement. A tact is a verbal operant response under the stimulus control of some part of the physical environment, and correct use of tacts is reinforced by the verbal community. A child is reinforced by parents for emitting the sound "doll" in the presence of a doll (Skinner, 1957). Such an operant "makes contact with" the physical environment and is called a tact. Skinner reduced the traditional notion of reference or naming to a functional relationship among a response, its discriminative stimuli, and its reinforcer. The situation is exactly analogous to the functional relation holding among a rat's bar-press in a Skinner box, the discriminative stimulus that sets the occasion for the response, and the food that reinforces it. Skinner's analysis of the tact was a straightforward extension of the experimental analysis-of-behavior paradigm to a novel situation.

Skinner extended his analysis to metaphor, metonymy, and the subtleties of "tact" behavior, but we need not pursue them here. Two points deserve further comment. First, Skinner's analysis of the tact was the purest nominalism ever proposed by anyone tackling the problem of universals. A noun is now indeed no more than a puff of air emitted under certain definable contingencies of reinforcement. There is no Platonic Form of cat, no Aristotelian essence of catness, no Ockhamist mental concept of Cat, only a certain verbal habit. Skinner pursued Hume's reduction of knowledge to habit to its final end, substituting purely behavioral for mental habits. The essence of "cat" is no more than the contingencies of reinforcement governing its utterance.

The second point raises an important general aspect about Skinner's treatment of human behavior, his notion of private stimuli. Skinner believed that earlier methodological behaviorists such as Tolman and Hull were wrong to exclude private events (such as mental images, toothaches) from behaviorism simply because such events are private. Skinner held that part of each person's environment includes the world inside her or his skin, those stimuli to which the person has privileged access. Such stimuli may be unknown to an external observer, but they are experienced by the person who has them, can control behavior, and so must be included in any behaviorist analysis of human behavior. Many verbal statements are under such control, including complex tacts. For example: "My tooth aches" is a kind of tacting response controlled by a certain kind of painful inner stimulation.

This simple analysis implies a momentous conclusion. How do we come to be able to make such statements as the private tact? Skinner's answer was that the verbal community has trained us to observe our private stimuli by reinforcing utterances that refer to them. It is useful for parents to know what is distressing a child, so they attempt to teach a child self-reporting verbal behaviors. "My tooth aches" indicates a visit to the dentist, not the podiatrist. Such responses thus have Darwinian survival value. Because these self-observed private stimuli constitute consciousness, it therefore follows that human consciousness is a product of the reinforcing practices of a verbal community. A person raised by a community that did not reinforce self-description would not be conscious in anything but the sense of being awake. The person would have no *self* consciousness.

Self-description also allowed Skinner to try to explain apparently purposive verbal behaviors without reference to intention or purpose. For example, "I am looking for my glasses" seems to describe my intentions, but Skinner (1957) argued: "Such behavior must be regarded as equivalent to When I have behaved in this way in the past, I have found my glasses and have then stopped behaving in this way" (p. 145). Skinner has reduced *intention,* a mentalistic term, to the physicalistic description of one's bodily state.

The last topic discussed in *Verbal Behavior* was thinking, the most apparently mental of all human activities. Skinner continued, however, to exorcise Cartesian mentalism by arguing that "thought is simply behavior." Skinner rejected Watson's view that thinking is subvocal behavior, for much covert behavior is not verbal, yet can still control overt behavior in a way characteristic of "thinking": "I think I shall be going can be translated I find myself going" (p. 449), a reference to self-observed but nonverbal stimuli.

The extreme simplicity of Skinner's argument makes it hard to grasp. Once one denies the existence of the mind, as Skinner did, all that is left is behavior, so thinking must be behavior under the control of the contingencies of reinforcement. The thought of B. F. Skinner was, in his terms, simply "the sum total of his responses to the complex world in which he lived." "Thought" is simply a tact that we have learned to apply to certain forms of behavior, a tact Skinner asked people to unlearn, or at least not teach to our children. For Skinner did not merely wish to describe behavior, human or animal, he wanted to control it, control being a fundamental part of the experimental analysis of behavior. Skinner believed that current control of human behavior, based as it is on mental fictions, is ineffective at best and harmful at worst.

During World War II, Skinner worked on a behavioral guidance system for air-to-surface missiles called "Project ORCON," for *organic control.* He trained pigeons to peck at a projected image of the target that the missile they were imprisoned in was to seek out. Their pecking operated controls on the missile so that it followed its course until it struck the target, destroying target and pigeons alike. Skinner achieved such complete control of the pigeons' behavior that they could carry out the most difficult tracking maneuvers during simulated attacks. The work impressed him with the possibility of a thorough control of any organism's behavior. Skinner's superiors found the project implausible, and no pigeon-guided missiles ever flew. Shortly afterward, however, Skinner wrote his most widely read book, *Walden II,* a utopian novel based on the principles of the experimental analysis of behavior.

In the book, two characters represent Skinner: Frazier (an experimental psychologist and founder of Walden II, an experimental utopian community) and Burris (a skeptical visitor ultimately won over to membership in Walden II). Near the end, Frazier speaks to Burris: "I've had only one idea in my life—a true *idée fixe.* . . . The idea of having my own way. 'Control' expresses it, I think. The control of human behavior, Burris" (p. 271). Frazier goes on to describe Walden II as the final laboratory and proving ground of the experimental analysis of behavior: "Nothing short of Walden II will suffice." Finally, Frazier exclaims: "Well, what do you say to the design of personalities? the control of temperament? Give me the specifications and I'll give you the man! . . . Think of the possibilities! A society in which there is no failure, no boredom, no duplication of effort. . . . Let us control the lives of our children and see what we can make of them" (p. 274).

We have met the *idée fixe* of control before in the history of behaviorism. Frazier's claim to custom-make personalities recalls Watson's claim to custom-make the careers of infants. We have seen how important the desire for social control in Progressivism was to the favorable reaction to Watson's behaviorism. Skinner was heir to the Progressive desire to scientifically control human lives in the interest of society—more specifically, the survival of society, the ultimate Darwinian and Skinnerian value. He was also heir, and consciously so, to the tradition of Enlightenment optimism about human progress. Skinner asked people, in an otherwise disillusioned age, not to give up Rousseau's utopian dream, but to build a utopia on the principles of the experimental analysis of behavior. If pigeons' behavior can be controlled so that the birds guide missiles to their death, so a human being, whose behavior is likewise determined, can be controlled to be happy and productive and to feel free and dignified. *Walden II* was Skinner's first attempt to describe his vision.

THE ROOTS OF COGNITIVE SCIENCE (1943–1958)

While Skinner's radical behaviorism continued the Watsonian tradition of rejecting all inner causes of behavior, most behaviorists, with Hull and Tolman, did not. After World War II, one class of inner cause, cognitive processes, received increasing attention. Psychologists treated cognition from a variety of perspectives, including neo-Hullian "liberalized" or informal behaviorism, and a variety of unrelated theories proposed by American and European psychologists. In the long run, the most important approach to cognition grew out of mathematics and electrical engineering and had little or nothing to do with psychology and its problems. This was the creation of the field of artificial intelligence by the invention of the modern digital computer during World War II.

Informal Behaviorism

Few behavioralists were willing to agree with Skinner that organisms were "empty," that it was illegitimate to postulate, as Hull or Tolman had, mechanisms taking place within the organism linking together stimulus and response. As Charles Osgood (born 1916) put it, "Most contemporary behaviorists [can] be characterized as 'frustrated empty boxers'" (Osgood, 1956). They were aware of the pitfalls of "junkshop psychology," in which mental faculties or entities were multiplied as fast as the behaviors to be explained. Yet they increasingly believed that behavior, especially "the phenomena of meaning and intention, so obviously displayed in human language behavior, entirely escape the single-stage conception" of black-box S–R psychology (Osgood, 1957). It was obvious to psychologists concerned with the human higher mental processes that people possess "symbolic processes," the ability to represent the world internally, and that human responses were controlled by these symbols, instead of being directly controlled by external stimulation. Their problem was avoiding "junkshop psychology": "What is the least amount of additional baggage needed to handle symbolic processes?" (Osgood, 1956).

They solved their problem for a time by building on some of Hull's ideas about covert responses. Hull had proposed that sometimes S–R behavior chains contain covert, that is, unobservable, responses that produce internal, unobservable stimuli. Thus, due to Pavlovian conditioning, an animal running a maze might begin to salivate before it reached the goal box in which it had been fed. In turn, the covert salivation would produce internal stimuli that might cause the animal to turn too soon in anticipation of eating. Or, asked how to tie shoes, a parent might covertly make the hand movements involved, describing them in turn to a child. In both cases, covert responses and stimuli were part of the causal chain from external stimulus to final observable response, and thus mediate between the environment and the organism's response to it.

Osgood and others seized on the concept of mediation as a solution to the problem of human thought. Thinking could be conceived as covert, symbolic pairs of mediating responses and stimuli. "The great advantage of this solution is that, since each stage is an S–R process, we can simply transfer all the conceptual machinery of single-stage S–R psychology into this new model without new postulation" (Osgood, 1956, p. 178). So cognitive processes could be admitted into the body of behavior theory without giving up any of the rigor of the S–R formulation, and without inventing any uniquely human mental processes. Behavior could still be explained in terms of S–R behavior chains, except that now some of the chains took place invisibly within the organism. Behavioralists now had a language with which to discuss meaning, language, memory, problem solving, and other behaviors apparently beyond the reach of radical behaviorism.

The approach described by Osgood had many practitioners. Osgood applied it to language with especial reference to the problem of meaning, which he tried to measure behaviorally with his semantic differential scale. Irving Maltzman (1955) and Albert Goss (1961) applied it to problem solving and concept formation. The broadest program of human psychology in the liberalized vein was social learning theory, led by Neal Miller (born 1909). Miller and others at Hull's Institute for Human Relations at Yale tried to construct a psychology that would do justice to Freud's insights into the human condition but remain within the objective realm of S–R psychology. They downplayed the axioms and quantification of Hull's animal work in order to incorporate humans within the S–R framework, and they added in mediation as a way of talking about mental life in terms more precise than Freud's. Miller's (1959) description of his brand of behaviorism, including the whole neo-Hullian mediational camp, as "liberalized S–R theory" is apt. Social learning theorists did not abandon S–R theory; they only loosened its restrictions in order to be able to encompass human language, culture, and psychotherapy.

The concept of mediation was a creative response by neo-Hullian behaviorists to the challenge of explaining human thought. However, mediationists did not leave S–R psychology intact, because they had to modify Hull's strong versions of peripheralism and phylogenetic continuity to produce a theory capable of doing justice to the human higher mental processes. Hull had envisaged mediating responses as actual, if covert, motor responses that could enter into behavior chains; the mediationists, by contrast, conceived of mediation as taking place centrally in the brain, giving up Watsonian and Hullian muscle-twitchism. Hull had wanted a single set of laws of learning to cover all forms of at least mammalian behavior; mediationists scaled back his ambition, accepting that, while in a general way S–R theory might be universal, special allowances had to be made for species and developmental differences. Nevertheless, changes wrought by neo-Hullians were evolutionary, not revolutionary: Neal Miller was correct in asserting that they had liberalized S–R theory, not overthrown it.

Although it was a major theoretical position in the 1950s, mediational behaviorism ultimately proved to be only a bridge linking the inferential behavioralism of the 1930s and 1940s—Hull's and Tolman's theories—to the inferential behavioralism of the 1980s: cognitive psychology. Diagrams of mediational processes quickly became incredibly cumbersome. More importantly, there was no very good reason to think of mental processes as covert chains of responses and stimuli. The mediationists' commitment to internalizing S–R language resulted primarily from their desire to achieve theoretical rigor and to avoid the apparently unscientific character of "junkshop psychology." In essence, lacking any other language with which to discuss the mental processes in a clear and disciplined fashion, they took the only course they saw open to them. However, when a new language of power, rigor, and precision came along—the language of computer programming—it proved easy for mediational psychologists to abandon their mediating response life raft for the ocean liner of information processing.

Early Cognitive Theories

Not all psychologists interested in cognition worked within the framework of neo-Hullian mediational psychology. In Europe, cognitive development had been studied by the Swiss psychologist Jean Piaget (1896–1980) since the 1920s. In the United States, social psychologists had gradually abandoned the concept of the group mind in the first decades of the twentieth century, gradually defining it as it is today—the study of people in groups. During World War II, social psychologists had been concerned to study attitudes, how persuasion and propaganda change attitudes, and the relation of attitudes to personality. After the war, social psychologists continued to develop theories about how people form, integrate, and act on beliefs. Finally, Jerome Bruner studied how personality dynamics shape people's perceptions of the world.

Genetic Epistemology

Although European psychology in the early twentieth century was quiescent, it was by no means extinct. Piaget was a most important European psychologist. Like Freud and Wundt before him, Piaget had begun with purely biological interests, but he eventually found himself practicing an innovative psychology. In Piaget's case, the influences that drew him away from biology were threefold. First, he maintained a strong interest in the questions of epistemology, although he believed traditional philosophies to be too speculative and unscientific. Second, he experienced psycho-analysis with one of Freud's pupils and studied with Jung's mentor, Bleuler, at Zurich. Third, he worked with Alfred Binet's collaborator, Theophile Simon, administering intelligence tests to children. Out of this eclectic background, Piaget formulated a unique cognitive psychology. The traditional problems of epistemology are important: What is knowledge, and what is human nature that we may have knowledge? To Piaget, these questions should admit of a scientific answer based on sound theory and empirical research. In particular, Piaget felt it should be possible to trace the psychological growth of knowledge in children as they grow up by studying their reactions to intellectual situations, as in intelligence tests, followed up by probing questions as in psychoanalysis. Piaget calls his field of study *genetic epistemology,* the study of the origins of knowledge in child development.

Piaget's approach to epistemology was heavily influenced by Kant. The titles of several of his books are the names of Kant's transcendental categories: *The Child's Conception of Space, The Child's Conception of Number,* and *The Child's Conception of Time,* for example. Moreover, Piaget carried on a distinctly European approach to psychology. Like Wundt, Piaget was interested in the general human mind, not in individuals or their unique lives. Also like Wundt, Piaget was less interested in applied aspects of his work than are Americans, although he sometimes wrote on education. The question of whether training can accelerate the course of cognitive growth Piaget called "The American Question," for it was not asked in Europe. In true pragmatic fashion, Americans want to know how to get knowledge faster and more efficiently.

Piaget began his studies of children's knowledge in the 1920s, but—after a brief flurry of interest—his work was largely ignored in the United States. Only in the 1960s was his work rediscovered. From 1930 to 1960, Piaget's thought was clearly out of step with American behaviorism, and his works consequently went largely unread and untranslated. After 1960, as young psychologists became disenchanted with behaviorism, Piaget would be increasingly read, translated, and researched by students of cognitive development.

Social Psychology

Social psychology is the study of the person as a social being, and so it has roots going back to the Greek political thinkers and to Hobbes's first political science. We have said little about it before because as a field it is exceedingly eclectic, unified by no coherent vision of human nature. It draws our attention now because during the 1940s and 1950s it continued to employ mental concepts of a commonsense sort. We will briefly consider one theory that was widely influential in the 1950s and early 1960s, Leon Festinger's (1919–1989) theory of cognitive dissonance.

Festinger's theory is about a person's beliefs and their interaction. It holds that beliefs may agree with one another, or they may clash. When beliefs clash, they induce an unpleasant state called cognitive dissonance, which the person tries to reduce. For example, a nonsmoker who is persuaded that cigarettes cause lung cancer will feel no dissonance, for her or his belief that smoking causes cancer agrees with and supports her or his refusal to smoke. However, a smoker who comes to believe smoking causes cancer will feel cognitive dissonance, for the decision to smoke clashes with this new belief. The smoker will act to reduce the dissonance, perhaps by giving up smoking. However, it is quite common to manage dissonance in other ways. For example, a smoker may simply avoid antismoking information in order to avoid dissonance.

Festinger's theory provoked much research. One classic study appeared to challenge the law of effect. Festinger and a collaborator, J. Merrill Carlsmith (1959), devised some extremely boring tasks for subjects to perform, such as turning screws for a long time. Then the experimenter got the subject to agree to tell a waiting subject that the task was fun. Some subjects were paid $20 for telling the lie; others were paid only $1. According to the theory, the $20 subjects should feel no dissonance: The large payment justified their little lie. However, the $1 subjects should feel dissonance: They were telling a lie for a paltry amount of money. One way to resolve this dissonance would be to convince oneself that the task was in fact fun, for if one believed this, telling another subject that it was fun would be no lie. After the whole experiment was over, another experimenter interviewed the subjects and discovered that the $1 subjects voted the task significantly more enjoyable than the $20 subjects, as Festinger's theory had predicted. The finding appears inconsistent with the law of effect, for we might expect that a $20 reward for saying the experiment was fun would change one's report about the enjoyability of the experiment more than a $1 reward.

What is most important about the theory of cognitive dissonance for historical purposes is that it was a cognitive theory—a theory about mental entities—in this case, about a person's beliefs. It was not an informal behaviorist theory, for Festinger did not conceive of beliefs as mediating responses, but, in commonsense terms, as beliefs that control behavior. In the 1950s, the theory of cognitive dissonance and other cognitive theories in social psychology constituted a vigorous cognitive psychology outside the orbit of strict behaviorism. Festinger's book, *A Theory of Cognitive Dissonance* (1957), made no reference to behaviorist ideas. Social psychologists rarely challenged behaviorism, but their field was an alternative to it.

The "New Look in Perception"

Shortly after the war, a new approach to the study of perception arose. Dubbed the "New Look" in perception, it was led by Jerome S. Bruner (born 1915). The New Look arose from an attempt to unify several different areas of psychology—perception, personality, and social psychology—and from a desire to refute the prevalent conception, going back at least to Hume (and strongly present in S–R behavior theory), that perception was a passive process by which a stimulus impressed (Hume's term) itself on the perceiver. Bruner and his colleagues (Bruner & Klein, 1960) proposed a view of perception in which the perceiver takes an active role, rather than being a passive register of sense data. Bruner and others (Bruner & Klein, 1960) did a variety of studies to support the idea that a perceiver's personality and social background play a role in affecting what the perceiver sees. The most famous and controversial of these studies concerned perceptual defense and raised the possibility of subliminal perception. Bruner and others in the New Look movement presented words to subjects for brief intervals, as had Wundt in his studies of the span of consciousness. However, these modern researchers varied the emotional content of the words: Some were ordinary or "neutral" words, others were obscene or "taboo" words. Bruner and his associates found that longer exposures are required for a subject to recognize a taboo word than to recognize a neutral word. It appears that subjects somehow unconsciously perceive the negative emotional content of a taboo word and then attempt to repress its entry into awareness. Subjects will see the word only when the exposure is so long that they cannot help seeing it.

Research on perceptual defense was extremely controversial for many years, with some psychologists arguing that subjects see taboo words as quickly as neutral words but falsely deny the experience as long as possible to avoid embarrassment. The controversy grew heated and has never been fully resolved. What is significant for us is that the New Look in perception analyzed perception as an active mental process involving both conscious and unconscious mental activities intervening between a sensation and a person's response to it. The idea of perceptual defense is much closer to psychoanalysis than to behaviorism, a fact in part responsible for the controversy surrounding Bruner's findings. In any event, the New Look was a cognitive alternative to behaviorism.

The investigations and theories of the mediational behavioralists—Piaget, Festinger, and Bruner—demonstrated psychologists' revived interest in human cognitive processes following the war. However, while these research programs were vigorous, their theories were due to be assimilated and eclipsed by a different kind of cognitive psychology, whose roots and conceptions lie almost entirely outside the field of psychology altogether. For during World War II there appeared the thinking machine.

Artificial Intelligence

Ever since Descartes, philosophers of the mind and psychologists had been attracted and repelled by the similarity of human and machine. Descartes thought that all human cognitive processes save thinking were carried out by the machinery of the nervous system, and he based his divisions of human being vs. brute and mind vs. body on his conviction. Pascal feared that Descartes was wrong; it seemed to Pascal that his calculator could think, and he turned to the human heart and its faith in God to separate people from machines. Hobbes and La Mettrie embraced, and de Sade reveled in, the idea that people are no more than animal-machines—an alarming idea to the romantics, who, with Pascal, sought the secret essence of humanity in feeling rather than intellect. Leibniz dreamed of a universal thinking machine, and the English engineer Charles Babbage tried to build one. William James worried about his automatic sweetheart, concluding that a machine could not feel and so could not be human. Watson, with Hobbes and La Mettrie, proclaimed that humans and animals are machines and that human salvation lay in accepting that reality and engineering a perfect future, limned by Skinner in *Walden II*. Science fiction writers and filmmakers began to explore the differences, if any, between human and machine in Rossum's Universal Robots and Metropolis. But no one had yet built a machine that anyone could even hope would emulate human thinking. Until World War II.

Since the time of Newton, the trend of science has been the mechanization of the world picture. As we have seen, in the twentieth century, psychologists had wrestled with the last refuge of teleology—purposive animal and human behavior. Hull tried to give a mechanical account of purpose; Tolman first left it in behavior as an observable, later putting it in the organism's cognitive map room; and Skinner tried to dissolve purpose into environmental control of behavior. None of these attempts to deal with purpose was entirely convincing, but Tolman's failure is the most revealing about the behaviorist enterprise. Tolman could be fairly criticized for committing the

Cartesian category mistake of building a homunculus (or, in the case of a rat, a ratunculus) into a person's head, and explaining that person's behavior as the outcome of the homunculus's decision making. A map implies a map reader; there really was a Ghost in Tolman's machine. Psychologists seemed to be on the horns of a trilemma:

1. They could try to explain purposive behavior by reference to inner events, as the later Tolman did; but this risked inventing a mythical inner Ghost whose behavior was as mysterious as the outer behavior science wanted to explain to begin with.

2. They could try to explain away behavior as purely mechanical, as Hull had, or as subtle and mislabeled environmental control of behavior, as Skinner did; but, while suitably scientific and tough minded, this explanation seemed to deny the obvious fact that behavior is goal-directed.

3. Following the earlier Tolman, Brentano, and Wittgenstein, they could accept purpose as an irreducible truth of human action, neither requiring nor needing explanation; but this denied that psychology could be a science of the same sort as physics, a conclusion unthinkable to psychologists in the grip of physics envy.

Out of scientific work in World War II came the modern high-speed digital computer, bringing with it concepts that made the first alternative more attractive than it had ever been, because these concepts seemed to offer a way around the bogey of the Ghost in the Machine. The most important of these concepts were informational feedback and the computer program itself. The importance of feedback was grasped immediately; the importance of the idea of programming took longer to be realized, but it eventually gave rise to a new solution to the mind–body problem called functionalism. What made the concepts of feedback and programming impressive, even commanding, was their association with real machines that seemed to think.

Given the contemporary rivalry between information-processing psychology and radical behaviorism, there is irony in the fact that the concept of feedback, and hence modern cognitive psychology, arose out of the same war problem that Skinner had worked on in his Pelican project. Project ORCON had aimed at the organic control of missiles. Mathematicians and computer scientists, aiming at the mechanical control of missiles and other weapons, invented the modern digital computer. In 1943, three researchers described the concept of information feedback that lay behind their solution to guiding devices to targets: They showed how purpose and mechanism were not incompatible. As a fact, feedback had been used by engineers since at least the eighteenth century. The achievement of Rosenblueth, Wiener, and Bigelow (1943/1966) was making feedback a scientific concept and describing it in general terms. A good example of a system using feedback is a thermostat and a furnace. You give the thermostat a goal when you set the temperature at which you want to keep your house. The thermostat contains a thermometer that measures the house temperature, and when the temperature falls below the set temperature, it turns on the furnace. As the furnace warms the room, the thermometer registers the change and turns the furnace off when the correct temperature is reached. Here is a feedback loop of information: The thermostat is sensitive to the state of the room, and, based on the information received by its thermometer, it takes action. The action in turn changes the state of the room, which feeds back to the thermostat, changing its behavior, which in turns influences the room temperature, and so on in an endless cycle.

In a simple way, the thermostat and the furnace constitute a purposive organism. Their goal is to maintain a constant temperature, and they are able to respond appropriately to changes in the environment. And there is, of course, no Ghost in the Thermostat. In older times, there would have been a servant who read a thermometer and stoked the furnace when necessary; but he has been replaced by a mere machine, and a simple one at that. The promise of the concept of feedback is that it might be possible to analyze all purposive behavior as instances of feedback: The organism has some goal (for example, to get food), is able to measure its distance from the goal (for example, it's at the other end of the maze), and behaves so as to reduce and finally eliminate that distance. The Ghost in the Machine, or Tolman's cognitive map reader, could be replaced by complex feedback loops. Practically, too, servants and industrial workers might be replaced by machines capable of doing what before only people could do.

So, machines could be purposive. Were they then intelligent, or at least capable of becoming intelligent? Could they emulate human intelligence? Whether computers were or could be intelligent became the central question of cognitive science, and the question was raised in its modern form by the brilliant mathematician A. M. Turing (1912–1954), who had contributed much to the theory of computers during the war. In 1950, Turing published a paper in *Mind,* "Computing Machinery and Intelligence," that defined the field of artificial intelligence and established the program of cognitive science. "I propose to consider the question, Can machines think?" Turing began. Because the meaning of "think" was so terribly unclear, Turing proposed to set his question more concretely "in terms of a game which we call the 'imitation game.'" Imagine an interrogator talking via computer terminal to two respondents, another human and a computer, without knowing which is which. The game consists in asking questions designed to tell which respondent is the human and which is the computer. Turing proposed that we consider a computer intelligent when it can fool the interrogator into thinking it is the human being. Turing's imitation game has since become known as the Turing Test, and it is widely taken to be the criterion of artificial intelligence (AI). Workers in the field of AI aim to create machines that can perform many of the same tasks previously done only by people, ranging from playing chess to assembling automobiles to exploring the surface of Mars.

We have already seen that some psychologists, most notably Hull, had tried to construct learning machines. There were naturally some psychologists, therefore, who were drawn to the computer for a model of learning and purposive behavior. In conversation with Harvard psychologist E. G. Boring, Norbert Wiener asked what the human brain could do that electronic computers could not, moving Boring (1946) to ask the same question as Turing: What would a robot have to do to be called intelligent? After reviewing human intellectual faculties and psychologists' early attempts to mimic them with machines, Boring (1946, p. 192) independently formulated his own version of the Turing test: "Certainly a robot whom you could not distinguish from another student would be an extremely convincing demonstration of the mechanical nature of man and the unity of science." For Boring, a thinking robot could carry much metaphysical baggage, because it would vindicate La Mettrie's declaration that man is a machine and promised to secure psychology a place among the natural sciences. Boring's hopes have become the expectations of contemporary cognitive scientists.

In the early 1950s, various attempts were made to create electronic or other mechanical models of learning and other cognitive processes. The English psychologist J. A. Deutsch (1953) built an "electromechanical model . . . capable of learning mazes and discrimination . . . [and insightful] reasoning." Similar models were discussed by L. Benjamin Wyckoff (1954) and James Miller (1955). Slack (1955) used the similarities between feedback and Dewey's reflex arc to attack Hullian S–R theory. Another English psychologist, Donald Broadbent (1957), proposed a mechanical model of attention and short-term memory in terms of balls being dropped into a Y-shaped tube representing various sensory "channels" of information. Broadbent argued that psychologists should think of the input to the senses not as stimuli but as information (1958). Information-processing concepts were applied to human attention and memory by George Miller in a now classic paper, "The Magical Number Seven, Plus or Minus Two: Some Limits on Our Capacity for Processing Information" (1956). Miller was moving away from an eclectic behaviorist position on human learning and would emerge as one of the leaders of cognitive psychology in the 1960s. In the 1956 paper, Miller drew attention to limitations on human attention and memory and set the stage for the first massive wave of research in information-processing psychology, which concentrated on attention and short-term memory.

In all of these early papers attempting to apply computer concepts to psychology, there was some confusion about what was actually doing the thinking. Encouraged by the popular phrase for the computer, "electronic brain," there was a strong tendency to think that it was the electronic device itself that was thinking, and that psychologists should look for parallels between the structure of the human brain and the structure of electronic computers. For example, James Miller (1955) envisioned a "comparative psychology . . . dealing not with animals but with electronic models," because the actions of computers are "in many interesting ways like living behavior." However, the identification of neural and electronic circuitry was much too simple. As Turing said in his 1950 paper, computers are general-purpose machines (the theoretically ideal general-purpose computer is called a Turing machine). The actual electronic architecture of a computer is unimportant, because what makes a computer behave as it does is its program; the same program may be run on physically different machines, and different programs can run on the same machine. Turing pointed out that a man in a room with an infinite supply of paper and a rulebook for transforming input symbols into output symbols could be regarded as a computer; in such circumstance, his behavior would be controlled only trivially by his neurology. His answers to questions would be dictated by the rulebook, and if one changed the rulebook, his behavior would change. The distinction of computer and program was crucial to cognitive psychology, for it meant that cognitive psychology was not neurology, and that cognitive theories of human thinking should talk about the human mind—that is, the human program— rather than the human brain. A correct cognitive theory would be implemented by the human brain and could be run on a properly programmed computer, but the theory would be in the program, not in the brain or the computer.

What began to emerge in the 1950s was a new conception of the human being as machine, and a new language in which to formulate theories about cognitive processes. People could be described, it seemed, as general-purpose computing devices, born with certain hardware and programmed by experience and socialization to behave in certain ways. The goal of psychology would be the specification of how human beings process information; the concepts of stimulus and response would be replaced by the concepts of information input and output, and theories about mediating R–S chains would be replaced by theories about internal computations and computational states. This new conception of psychology was clearly stated by Allan Newell, J. C. Shaw, and Herbert

Simon in 1958 in "Elements of a Theory of Problem Solving." Since the early 1950s, they had been writing programs that would solve problems, beginning with the Logic Theorist, a program that proved mathematical theorems, and moving on to a more powerful program, the General Problem Solver (GPS). They had previously published their work primarily in computer engineering journals, but, writing now in *Psychological Review,* they defined the new cognitive approach to psychology:

> The heart of [our] approach is describing the behavior of the system by a well-specified program, defined in terms of elementary information processes. . . .
>
> Once the program has been specified, we proceed exactly as we do with traditional mathematical systems. We attempt to deduce general properties of the system from the program (the equations); we compare the behavior predicted from the program (from the equations) with actual behavior observed . . . [and] we modify the program when modification is required to fit the facts.

Newell et al. claimed special virtues for their approach to psychological theorizing. Computers are "capable of realizing programs," making possible very precise predictions about behavior. Additionally, to actually run on a computer, programs must provide "a very concrete specification of [internal] processes," ensuring that theories are precise, never vague and merely verbal. The Logic Theorist and the General Problem Solver represent, Newell et al. conclude, "a thoroughly operational theory of human problem solving."

Newell et al. make stronger claims for their problem-solving programs than Turing made for his hypothetical AI program. Researchers in artificial intelligence wanted to write programs that would behave like people without necessarily thinking like people. So, for example, they write chess-playing programs that play chess but use the brute-force number-crunching ability of supercomputers to evaluate thousands of moves before choosing one, rather than trying to imitate the human chess master who evaluates many fewer alternatives, but does so more cleverly. Newell et al., however, moved from artificial intelligence to computer simulation in claiming that not only did their programs solve problems, but they solved problems in the same way human beings did. In a computer simulation of chess (of which there are a few), the programmer would try to write a program whose computational steps are the same as those of a human master chess player. The distinction of AI and computer simulation is important because pure AI is not psychology. Efforts in AI may be psychologically instructive for suggesting the kinds of cognitive resources humans must possess to achieve intelligence, but specifying how people actually behave intelligently requires more.

While apparently breaking with the past in giving up altogether on S–R theory of any form, GPS was really a continuation of the Hullian impulse in psychology. Like Hull, Newell et al. wanted a theory that was fundamentally mathematical, precise, and well specified; that could predict behavior in detail as deductions from the theory; and that was thoroughly operational. The theory of the GPS hews to the ideal of Newton's *Principia Mathematica* as much as Hull could have wished, and Hull could have fairly seen the implementation of the program on a computer as justification and fulfillment of his own preoccupation with building a learning machine. Newell et al. are simply bringing to the Hullian impulse much better tools with which to theorize, and a much richer language in which to frame behavioralist theories.

Computers were invented by electrical engineers and mathematicians, not psychologists; the concept of programming general-purpose machines was mathematician John von Neumann's and Turing's, not any psychologist's; Newell et al. were from Carnegie-Mellon University, a university outside the circle of leading academic universities at which behaviorism held sway, and closely connected with business, industry, and engineering; and Simon, winner of the Nobel Prize for economics in 1978, was more an economist than a psychologist. Newell et al.'s work, like that of Broadbent, Miller, and the other pioneers in cognitive science, assimilated a powerful tool invented outside psychology to the central program of behavioralism: the description, prediction, and control of human behavior.

PSYCHOLOGY AND SOCIETY (1950–1958)

American psychologists—by the 1950s, psychology had become an American science (Reisman, 1966)—entered the 1950s with a confidence in the future shared by most other Americans. The war had ended, the Depression was only an unpleasant memory, the economy and the population were booming. To Fillmore Sanford (1951), secretary of the APA, the future of psychology lay with professional psychology, and that future was bright indeed, because a new era dawned, "the age of the psychological man":

> Our society appears peculiarly willing to adopt psychological ways of thinking and to accept the results of psychological research. American people seem to have a strong and conscious need for the sorts of professional services psychologists are . . . equipped to give. . . . [T]he age of the psychological man is upon us, and . . . psychologists must accept responsibility not only for having spread the arrival of this age but for guiding its future course. Whether we like it or not, our society is tending more and more to think in terms of the concepts and methods spawned and nurtured by psychologists. And whether we like it or not, psychologists will continue to be a consequential factor in the making of social decisions and in the structuring of our culture. (p. 74)

Sanford argued that psychologists had an unprecedented opportunity to "create a profession the like of which has never before been seen, either in form or content . . . the first deliberately designed profession in history."

By every quantitative measure, Sanford's optimism was justified. Membership in the APA grew from 7,250 in 1950 to 16,644 in 1959; the most rapid growth occurred in the applied divisions, and psychologists, by establishing various boards and committees within the APA, did deliberately design their profession, as Fillmore had hoped. Despite skirmishes with the other APA, the American Psychiatric Association (which was loath to give up its monopoly on mental health care and opposed the legal recognition of clinical psychology), states began to pass certification and licensing laws covering applied—primarily clinical and counseling—psychologists, defining them legally and, of course, acknowledging them as legitimate professionals (Reisman, 1966). Psychology in industry prospered as industry prospered; businesspeople recognized that "we need not 'change human nature,' we need only to learn to control and to use it" (Baritz, 1960). Popular magazine articles on psychology began to appear regularly, often telling people how to distinguish genuine clinical psychologists from psychological frauds.

Psychologists basked in the favorable series on psychology appearing in *Life,* by Ernest Havemann, in 1957. They gave him an award for his series.

Certain troubles remained, however. Within psychology, traditional experimental and theoretical psychologists were becoming unhappy with the increasing numbers and influence of applied psychologists. In 1957, a committee of the Division of Experimental Psychology polled its membership's attitudes to the APA. Although 55 percent approved of the APA, 30 percent were opposed to it; and the committee noted a growing, though still minority, desire for the experimentalists to secede from the APA (Farber, 1957). The first claims were made that clinical psychologists (and psychiatrists) could effectively neither diagnose (Meehl, 1954) nor treat (Eysenck, 1952) their patients. Divided among themselves, psychologists were also divided from the mainstream of American thought in the 1950s. Surveying the social attitudes of twenty-seven leading psychologists, Keehn (1955) found that they were far more liberal than the country as a whole. Compared to most Americans, psychologists were nonreligious or even antireligious (denying that God exists, that survival of bodily death occurs, and that people need religion), were opposed to the death penalty, believed that criminals should be cured rather than punished, and supported easier divorce laws.

Amid the prosperity and general good feelings of the 1950s, there was a small but growing disturbing current, felt faintly within psychology itself and more strongly in the larger American culture: an unhappiness with the ethos and ethic of adjustment. Robert Creegan (1953) wrote in *American Psychologist* that "the job of psychology is to criticize and improve the social order . . . rather than to adjust passively . . . [and] grow fat." Sociologist C. Wright Mills deplored the application of psychology to industrial social control "in the movement from authority to manipulation, power shifts from the visible to the invisible, from the known to the anonymous. And with rising material standards exploitation becomes less material and more psychological" (Baritz, 1960). Psychoanalyst Robert Lindner (1953) blamed psychiatry and clinical psychology for preserving the myth of adjustment by regarding neurotics and other unhappy humans as "sick" when in fact, according to Lindner, they were in healthy but misdirected rebellion against a stifling culture of conformity.

Outside psychology, rebellion against adjustment was more widespread and grew with the decade. In sociology, David Riesman's *The Lonely Crowd* (1950) and William H. Whyte's *The Organization Man* (1956) dissected and attacked the American culture of conformity. In politics, Peter Viereck praised *The Unadjusted Man: A New Hero for America* (1956). Novels such as J. D. Salinger's *Catcher in the Rye* (1951), Sloan Wilson's *The Man in the Grey Flannel Suit* (1955), and Jack Kerouac's *On the Road* (1957) expressed the unease of people caught in a grey world of adaptation and conformity, yearning for lives less constrained and more emotional. The movie *Rebel Without a Cause* portrayed the tragic fate of one whose unease found no constructive purpose. And the fierce, restless energy of the young—whose numbers were growing rapidly— exploded in rock and roll music, the only creative outlet it could find.

At the end of the decade, liberal sociologist Daniel Bell (1960) wrote about the exhaustion of ideas during the 1950s. The beliefs of the past were no longer acceptable to young thinkers, and the middle way of adjustment was "not for [them]; it is without passion and deadening." Bell identified a "search for a cause" moved by "a deep, desperate, almost pathetic anger." The world, to many young minds, was grey and unexciting. In psychology, eclecticism could be boring, for there were no issues to fight over, no battles to be fought as before, when psychology had begun, or when functionalist battled structuralist, and behaviorist battled introspectionist. Psychology was thriving, but to no clear end, apparently happy in its work of adjustment.

All this was about to change.

BIBLIOGRAPHY

Accessible discussions of logical behaviorism may be found in Fodor (1981); Arnold S. Kaufman, "Behaviorism," *Encyclopedia of the social sciences,* Vol. 1 (New York: Macmillan, 1967, pp. 268–73); Arnold B. Levison, ed., *Knowledge and society: An introduction to the philosophy of the social sciences* (Indianapolis: Bobbs-Merrill, 1974), ch. VI; and Norman Malcolm, *Problems of mind: Descartes to Wittgenstein* (New York: Harper Torchbooks, 1971), ch. III. Ryle's *Concept of mind* (1949) is well written, even witty, and quite readable even by someone with no previous knowledge of philosophy. Wittgenstein, on the other hand, is a notoriously difficult philosopher to understand. For our present purposes, his most important works are *The blue and brown books* (1958), a published version of Cambridge lectures delivered in 1933 and 1934, which formed the preliminary studies for the posthumously published *Philosophical investigations* (1953). Wittgenstein wrote in a sort of dialogue style, arguing with an unnamed interlocutor and, like Plato, he tended to develop arguments by indirection rather than outright statement. Further difficulty understanding his philosophy arises from the fact that, in an important sense, he had nothing positive to say, aiming like Socrates at clearing up misconceptions instead of offering his own. As Malcolm put it in the book cited above, "Philosophical work of the right sort merely unties knots in our understanding. The result is not a theory but simply—no knots!" One should not tackle Wittgenstein without guidance. The best book-length introduction is Anthony Kenny's *Wittgenstein* (Cambridge, MA: Harvard University Press, 1973). The best treatment of Wittgenstein's philosophy of mind is Malcolm (1970). Luckhardt (1983) is also helpful and clear, especially concerning Wittgenstein's attitude toward behaviorism.

Papers expounding the positivistic view of psychological theory construction nearly filled the pages of the *Psychological Review* in the late 1940s and early 1950s. Some of them, including Kendler's, are collected in Melvin Marx, ed., *Theories in contemporary psychology* (New York: Macmillan, 1963). A witty reply to Kendler from the realist perspective was given by Tolman's colleague Benbow F. Ritchie, "The circumnavigation of cognition," *Psychological Review* (1953, *60:* 216–21). Ritchie likens Kendler to an operationist geographer who defines problems of navigation purely in terms of the procedures for getting from one point to another on the earth's surface, thereby dismissing the dispute between the "flat-earth theorists" and the "ball theorists" as a pseudoissue because both theories are operationally reducible to statements about movement on the earth's surface, rendering irrelevant any "surplus meaning" concerning the shape of the earth. The "what is learned" debate has been insightfully studied by philosopher Ron Amundson, "Psychology and epistemology: The place versus response controversy," *Cognition* (1985, *20:* 127–55). Anyone interested in the many experiments concerning "what is learned" should consult reviews found under the heading "Learning" in the *Annual review of psychology,* which began publication in 1950. Also useful is Ernest R. Hilgard's (later coauthored with Gordon Bower) text, *Theories of learning,* whose first edition appeared in 1948 (New York: Appleton-Century-Crofts). For an account of the broader issues raised by operationism, see Thomas H. Leahey, "Operationism and ideology," *Journal of Mind and Behavior* (1983, *4:* 81–90).

The works of B. F. Skinner related to this era are fully listed in the references. The best single book of Skinner's to read is *Science and human behavior* (1953), in which he discusses his philosophy of science, explains his scientific work, and goes on to criticize society in light of his conclusions, offering behaviorist remedies for social ills. His autobiography, in three volumes, has been completed and published by Knopf (New York):

Particulars of my life (1976), *The shaping of a behaviorist* (1979), and *A matter of consequences* (1983). A full-scale biography of Skinner is D. Bjork, *B. F. Skinner: A life* (New York: Basic Books, 1993). Richard Evans conducted two interviews with Skinner. *B. F. Skinner: The man and his ideas* (New York: Dutton, 1968) provides a good introduction to Skinner, and *A dialogue with B. F. Skinner* (New York: Praeger, 1981) gives an update. Paul Sagal discusses *Skinner's philosophy* (Washington, DC: University Press of America, 1981). Some of Skinner's later works are cited in Chapter 15.

Neal Miller (1959) provides a good general introduction to informal, "liberalized" behavioralism, although he focuses on his own research and neglects the many other mediational behaviorists, such as Osgood, who were important figures in the 1950s. Miller and his associates, particularly John Dollard, developed their social learning theory over many years and in many publications, beginning with John Dollard, Leonard Doob, Neal Miller, O. Hobart Mowrer, and Robert Sears, *Frustration and aggression* (New Haven, CT: Yale University Press, 1939). Their most important books were Neal Miller and John Dollard, *Social learning and imitation* (New Haven, CT: Yale University Press, 1941); and John Dollard and Neal Miller, *Personality and psychotherapy* (New York: McGraw-Hill, 1950). As the title of the last book implies, Miller and Dollard were pioneers in behavioral psychotherapy, and an excellent summary of their therapeutic methods and comparison with other systems may be found in Donald H. Ford and Hugh B. Urban, *Systems of psychotherapy: A comparative study* (New York: McGraw-Hill, 1963).

Jerome Bruner and George S. Klein (1960) provide an account of the beginnings and guiding concepts of the New Look in perception in "The functions of perceiving: New Look retrospect," in B. Kaplan and S. Wapner, eds., *Perspectives in psychological theory: Essays in honor of Heinz Werner* (New York: International Universities Press, 1960). Jean Piaget wrote many books, most of them very difficult. A comprehensive statement of his theory for the period in question is his *The psychology of intelligence* (Totowa, NJ: Rowman & Littlefield, 1948). Piaget's *Six psychological studies* (New York: Random House, 1964) collects some of his more accessible papers. Secondary sources include Alfred Baldwin, *Theories of child development,* 2nd ed. (New York: John Wiley, 1980); John Flavell, *The developmental psychology of Jean Piaget* (New York: Van Nostrand, 1963); Herbert Ginsberg and Sylvia Opper, *Piaget's theory of intellectual development* (Englewood Cliffs, NJ: Prentice-Hall, 1969); and Thomas H. Leahey and Richard J. Harris, *Human learning* (Englewood Cliffs, NJ: Prentice-Hall, 1985). Finally, Howard Gruber and Jacques Voneche have compiled *The essential Piaget* (New York: Basic Books, 1977), a comprehensive anthology of extracts from all Piaget's major works, including some rare adolescent pieces, and have added their own penetrating commentary.

Boring (1946) is the first paper I know of that addressed the meaning of the World War II computer revolution for psychology, and it included a comprehensive listing of the prewar mechanical models, including Hull's. For Turing, see Alan Hodge, *Alan Turing: The enigma* (New York: Simon & Schuster, 1983). Broadbent (1958) is useful for comparing information-processing and S–R theories. Herbert Simon has written an autobiography, *Models of my life* (New York: Basic Books, 1991). Finally, a book that doesn't fit well anywhere but that documents the revival of interest in cognition in the early 1950s is Bruner et al. (1957), a collection of papers given at the University of Colorado Symposium on Cognition in 1955. The meeting was attended by leading psychologists of cognition, including Charles Osgood (mediation theory), Fritz Heider (social psychology), David Rapaport (psychoanalysis), and Bruner himself. Only one approach was missing: artificial intelligence. Its omission demonstrates that the computer revolution had not yet hit psychology, and that the field of AI developed entirely separately from the psychology of thinking.

A brief survey of general historical developments during the 1950s may be found in the relevant sections of Bernard Bailyn, David Davis, David Donald, John Thomas, Robert Wiebe, and Gordon Wood, *The great republic* (Boston: Little, Brown, 1977). Emphasis on the social, cultural, and intellectual history of the period is in Jeffery Hart, *When the going was good: American life in the fifties* (New York: Crown, 1982). For psychology in the 1950s, see Reisman (1966) and Albert R. Gilgen, *American psychology since World War II: A profile of the discipline* (Westport, CT: Greenwood Press, 1982). Anyone interested in the conflict between the two APAs, psychological and psychiatric, should read the professional journal of the APA, the *American Psychologist.* The year of maximum conflict appears to have been 1953, when the journal was filled with articles, letters, and notes on the struggle of psychologists to win legal approval of their profession over the protests of the psychiatrists. Lindner's (1953) work should be regarded as a symptom of some psychologists' unhappiness with the ideology of adjustment rather than as offering a sound set of analyses or arguments in itself. It depends on a dubious reading of Freud and Darwin, advocates negative eugenics, and is, in general, rather hysterical in its treatment of modern life.

REFERENCES

Baritz, L. J. (1960). *The servants of power: A history of the use of social science in American industry.* Middletown, CT: Wesleyan University Press.

Beach, F. A. (1950). The snark was a boojum. *American Psychologist 5:* 115–24.

Bell, D. (1960). *The end of ideology: On the exhaustion of political ideas in the fifties.* Glencoe, IL: Free Press.

Boring, E. G. (1946). Mind and mechanism. *American Journal of Psychology 59:* 173–92.

Broadbent, D. E. (1957). A mechanical model for human attention and immediate memory. *Psychological Review 64:* 205–15.

———. (1958). *Perception and communication.* Elmsford, NY: Pergamon Press.

Bruner, J. S., Brunswik, E., Festinger, E., Heider, F., Muenzinger, K. F., Osgood, C. E., and Rapaport, D. (1957). *Contemporary approaches to cognition.* Cambridge, England: Cambridge University Press.

Bruner, J. S., Goodnow, J., and Austin, G. (1956). *A study of thinking.* New York: John Wiley.

Bruner, J., and Klein, G. S. (1960). The function of perceiving: A new look retrospect. In B. Kaplan & S. Wapner, eds., *Perspectives in psychological theory.* New York: International Universities Press.

Creegan, R. (1953). Psychologist, know thyself. *American Psychologist 8:* 52–53.

Deutsch, J. A. (1953). A new type of behavior theory. *British Journal of Psychology 44:* 304–18.

Eysenck, H. J. (1952). The effects of psychotherapy: An evaluation. *Journal of Consulting Psychology 16:* 322–24.

Farber, I. E. (1957). The division of experimental psychology and the APA. *American Psychologist 12:* 200–2.

Festinger, L. (1957). *A theory of cognitive dissonance.* Stanford, CA: Stanford University Press.

Festinger, L. and Carlsmith, J. M. (1959). Cognitive consequences of forced compliance. *Journal of Abnormal and Social Psychology 58:* 203–10.

Fodor, J. A. (1981). The mind–body problem. *Scientific American 244:* 114–22.

Goss, A. E. (1961). Verbal mediating responses and concept formation. *Psychological Review 68:* 248–74.

Keehn, J. D. (1955). The expressed social attitudes of leading psychologists. *American Psychologist 10:* 208–10.

Koch, S. (1951a). The current status of motivational psychology. *Psychological Review 58:* 147–54.

———. (1951b). Theoretical psychology 1950: An overview. *Psychological Review 58:* 295–301.

Krantz, D. L. (1973). Schools and systems: The mutual isolation of operant and non-operant psychology. In M. Henle, J. Jaynes, and J. Sullivan, eds., *Historical conceptions of psychology.* New York: Springer.

Lashley, K. S. (1951). The problem of serial order in behavior. In L. A. Jeffress, ed., *Cerebral mechanisms in behavior.* New York: John Wiley.

Lindner, R. F. (1953). *Prescription for rebellion.* London: Victor Gollancz.

Luckhardt, C. G. (1983). Wittgenstein and behaviorism. *Synthese 56:* 319–38.

Malcolm, N. (1970). Wittgenstein on the nature of mind. American Philosophical Quarterly Monograph Series, *Monograph 4:* 9–29.

Maltzman, I. (1955). Thinking: From a behavioristic point of view. *Psychological Review 62:* 275–86.

Meehl, P. E. (1954). *Clinical vs. statistical prediction: A theoretical analysis and review of the evidence.* Minneapolis: University of Minnesota Press.

Miller, G. A. (1956). The magical number seven, plus or minus two: Some limits on our capacity for processing information. *Psychological Review 63:* 81–97.

Miller, J. G. (1955). Toward a general theory for the behavioral sciences. *American Psychologist 10:* 513–31.

Miller, N. (1959). Liberalization of basic S–R concepts. In S. Koch, ed., *Psychology: Study of a science,* Vol. 2. New York: McGraw-Hill.

Newell, A., Shaw, J. C., and Simon, H. A. (1958). Elements of a theory of problem solving. *Psychological Review 65:* 151–66.

Osgood, C. E. (1956). Behavior theory and the social sciences. *Behavioral Science 1:* 167–85.

Reisman, J. M. (1966). *The development of clinical psychology.* New York: Appleton-Century-Crofts.

Rosenblueth, A., Wiener, N., and Bigelow, J. (1943/1966). Behavior, purpose, and teleology. Reprinted in J. V. Canfield, ed., *Purpose in nature.* Englewood Cliffs, NJ: Prentice-Hall.

Ryle, G. (1949). *The concept of mind.* New York: Barnes & Noble.

Sanford, F. H. (1951). Across the secretary's desk: Notes on the future of psychology as a profession. *American Psychologist 6:* 74–76.

Skinner, B. F. (1931/1972). The concept of reflex in the description of behavior. *Journal of General Psychology 5:* 427–58. Reprinted in *Cumulative Record,* 3rd ed. Englewood Cliffs, NJ: Prentice-Hall.

———. (1938). *The behavior of organisms.* Englewood Cliffs, NJ: Prentice-Hall.

———. (1948). *Walden II.* New York: Macmillan.

———. (1953). *Science and human behavior.* New York: Macmillan.

———. (1954/1972). A critique of psychoanalytic concepts and theories. Reprinted in *Cumulative Record,* 3rd ed. Englewood Cliffs, NJ: Prentice-Hall.

———. (1957). *Verbal behavior.* Englewood Cliffs, NJ: Prentice-Hall.

———. (1971/1972). A lecture on "having" a poem. Reprinted in *Cumulative Record,* 3rd ed. Englewood Cliffs, NJ: Prentice-Hall.

Slack, C. W. (1955). Feedback theory and the reflex-arc concept. *Psychological Review 62:* 263–67.

Turing, A. M. (1950). Computing machinery and intelligence. *Mind 59:* 433–60.

Wittgenstein, L. (1953). *Philosophical investigations,* 3rd ed. New York: Macmillan.

_____ . (1958). *The blue and brown books.* New York: Harper Colophon.

Wyckoff, L. B. (1954). A mathematical model and an electronic model for learning. *Psychological Review 61:* 89–97.

14 *Years of Turmoil (1958–1978)*

CHALLENGES TO BEHAVIORISM
  Humanistic Psychology
  Cartesian Linguistics
EROSION OF THE FOUNDATIONS
  The Disappearance of Positivism
  Constraints on Animal Learning
  Awareness and Human Learning
COGNITIVE PSYCHOLOGY ASSERTS ITSELF
  The New Structuralism
  Man the Machine: Information Processing
PSYCHOLOGY AND SOCIETY
  Funding Social Science
  Professional Psychology
  Values

World chess champion Gary Kasparov playing computer challenger Deep Blue in 1996. Beginning in the 1950s a combination of computer scientists, mathematicians, philosophers, and psychologists began trying to understand the mind by building minds in computers; chess-playing was a favorite venue for computerizing intelligence. In the 1970s, seeing the mind as a computer program began to dominate some fields of psychology. As with radical behaviorism, the prospect of computer minds excites some but horrifies others. Here, we see Kasparov deep in battle with the only program he concedes shows real chess intelligence.

By the mid-1950s, behavioralism had settled down into a comfortable eclecticism. Skinnerians, neo-Hullians, and broadly cognitive theorists lived together with disagreement but without serious division. The situation was reminiscent of the years just before World War I, when functionalists, Titchenerians, Wundtians, and others lived together in relative harmony as the new psychologists. In 1913, Watson shattered the atmosphere of eclectic harmony, even though he did not really create the behavioralistic direction American psychology was already taking. Nevertheless, in his wake there was a period of stress and self-inspection. Psychologists grappled with the challenge of behaviorism and came to a conscious redefinition of their field by the 1930s. Similarly, in the late 1950s, angry voices challenged the eclectic status quo and set off a new period of self-examination and inflamed rhetoric. Whether psychology was taken in a revolutionary direction after 1960 any more than it was after 1913 is a question to which we will have to return.

CHALLENGES TO BEHAVIORISM

Humanistic Psychology

Although humanistic psychology did not take off until the late 1950s, its immediate historical roots lay in the post-World War II period. Its most important founders are Carl Rogers (1902–1987) and Abraham Maslow (1908–1970). Both were initially attracted to behaviorism but both became aware of its limitations and staked out similar alternatives. Rogers developed his client-centered psychotherapy in the 1940s and used it with soldiers returning to the United States from service abroad. Client-centered psychotherapy is a phenomenologically oriented technique in which the therapist tries to enter into the worldview of the client, helping the client to work through his or her problems so as to live the life the client most deeply desires. Rogers's client-centered therapy offered a significant alternative to the psychoanalytic methods used by psychiatrists, and thus it played an important role in the establishment of clinical and counseling psychology in the postwar period. Because of his emphasis on empathic understanding, Rogers came into conflict with behaviorism, which treated human beings just as it treated animals—as machines whose behavior could be predicted and controlled, without any attention being paid to subjective consciousness. In 1956, Rogers and Skinner began a series of debates about the relative adequacy of their points of view (Rogers and Skinner, 1956).

Phenomenological psychology is especially appealing to the clinician, for the clinician's stock in trade is empathy, and phenomenology is the study of subjective experience. Rogers distinguished three modes of knowledge. The first is the objective mode, in which we seek to understand the world as an object. The second and third modes of knowing are subjective. One is each person's own subjective knowledge of personal conscious experience, including each person's intentions and sense of freedom. The other mode of subjective knowledge is the attempt to understand another person's subjective inner world. The clinician, of course, must master this last mode of knowing, for, in Rogers's view, only by understanding the client's personal world and subjective self can the clinician hope to help the client. Rogers believes that personal beliefs, values, and intentions control behavior. He hopes that psychology will find systematic ways to know the personal experience of other people, for then therapy will be greatly enhanced.

Rogers argued that behaviorism limits itself exclusively to the objective mode of knowledge and so constrains psychology within a particular set of allowable techniques and theories. It treats human beings exclusively as objects, not as experiencing subjects in their own right. In specific contradistinction to Skinner, Rogers put great emphasis on each person's experienced freedom, rejecting Skinner's purely physical causality. Said Rogers (1964): "The experiencing of choice, of freedom of choice . . . is not only a profound truth, but is a very important element in therapy." As a scientist he accepts determinism, but as a therapist he accepts freedom: The two "exist in different dimensions" (p. 135, in discussion transcript).

Abraham Maslow was humanistic psychology's leading theorist and organizer. Beginning as an experimental animal psychologist, he turned his attention to the problem of creativity in art and science. He studied creative people and concluded that they were actuated by needs dormant and unrealized in the mass of humanity. He called these people self-actualizers because they made real—actualized—their human creative powers, in contrast to most people, who work only to satisfy their animal needs for food, shelter, and safety. Maslow concluded that creative geniuses were not special human beings, but that everyone possessed latent creative talents that could be realized if it were not for socially imposed inhibitions. Maslow's and Rogers's views come together in that they both sought ways to jolt people from comfortable but stultifying psychological ruts and move them to realize their full potential as human beings.

In 1954, Maslow created a mailing list for "people who are interested in the scientific study of creativity, love, higher values, autonomy, growth, self-actualization, basic need gratification, etc." (Sutich and Vich, 1969, p. 6). The number of people on Maslow's mailing list grew quickly, and by 1957 it became clear that more formal means of communication and organization were needed. So Maslow and his followers launched the *Journal of Humanistic Psychology* in 1961 and the Association for Humanistic Psychology in 1963.

Humanistic psychologists deserve the name because, in agreement with the ancient Greek humanists, they believe that "the values which are to guide human action must be found within the nature of human and natural reality itself" (Maslow, 1973, p. 4). But humanistic psychologists could not accept the naturalistic values of the behaviorists. Behaviorists treated human beings as things, failing to appreciate their subjectivity, consciousness, and free will. In the view of humanistic psychologists, behaviorists were not so much wrong as misguided. Behaviorists applied a perfectly valid mode of knowledge—Rogers's objective mode—to human beings, who could only be partially encompassed by this mode of knowing, by ordinary science. Most especially, humanistic psychologists were distressed by behaviorists' rejection of human free will and autonomy. Where Hull, "a near saint of pre-breakthrough [that is, prehumanistic] psychology" treated human beings as robots, humanistic psychologists proclaimed that "Man is aware. . . . Man has choice. . . . Man is intentional" (Bugental, 1964, p. 26).

Humanistic psychologists thus sought not to overthrow behaviorists (first-force psychology), or psychoanalysts (second-force psychology), but to build on their mistakes and go beyond them. "I interpret this third psychology [humanistic psychology] to include the first and second psychologies. . . . I am Freudian and I am behavioristic and I am humanistic" (Maslow, 1973, p. 4). Humanistic psychology, then, while offering a critique of and an alternative to behaviorism, tended still to live with the eclectic spirit of the 1950s. While it thought behaviorism was limited, it thought behaviorism nevertheless valid within its domain, and humanistic psychologists sought to add to behaviorism an appreciation of human consciousness that would round out the scientific picture of human psychology. A more strident, consciously revolutionary voice came from outside psychology, from the field of linguistics.

Cartesian Linguistics

If anyone played Watson to the eclectic peace of the 1950s, it was the linguist Avram Noam Chomsky (born 1928). Chomsky was radical in both politics and linguistics, the study of language. In politics, Chomsky was an early and outspoken critic of the war in Vietnam, and of the United States' support of Israel in the Middle East. In linguistics, Chomsky revived what he took to be Descartes's rationalistic program, proposing highly formal accounts of language as the organ by which reason expresses itself, and resurrecting the notion of innate ideas. Because Chomsky regarded language as a uniquely human, rational possession, he was brought into conflict with behavioral treatments of language.

The Attack on Verbal Behavior

Since the time of Descartes, language has been seen as a special problem for any mechanistic psychology. Hull's student Kenneth Spence suspected that language might render inapplicable to humans laws of learning derived from animals. In 1955, the informal behaviorist Charles Osgood referred to the problems of meaning and perception as the "Waterloo of contemporary behaviorism" and, in response, attempted to provide a mediational theory of language, applicable only to human beings (Osgood, 1957). The philosopher Norman Malcolm (1964), sympathetic to behaviorism, regarded language as "an essential difference between man and the lower animals."

B. F. Skinner, however, was a dissenter from the Cartesian view, shared in part even by fellow behaviorists. The whole point of *Verbal Behavior* was to show that language, although it is a complex behavior, could be explained by reference to only the principles of behavior formulated from animal studies. Skinner therefore denied that there is anything special about language, or verbal behavior, or that there is any fundamental difference between humans and the lower animals. Somewhat as the empiricist Hume raised Kant from his dogmatic slumbers to a defense of the transcendental mind, Skinner's Humean treatment of language roused Chomsky's rationalist counterattack. Behaviorism, said Chomsky, was not merely limited, but completely wrong. Chomsky regarded Skinner's book as a *"reductio ad absurdum* of behaviorist assumptions" and wanted to show it up as pure "mythology" (Jakobovits and Miron, 1967). Chomsky's assault on radical behaviorism began with his lengthy review of *Verbal Behavior* in 1959, perhaps the single most influential psychological paper published since Watson's behaviorist manifesto of 1913.

Chomsky's basically criticized Skinner's book as an exercise in equivocation. Skinner's fundamental technical terms—stimulus, response, reinforcement, and so on—are well defined in animal learning experiments but cannot be extended to human behavior without serious modification, as Skinner claims. Chomsky argued that if one attempts to use Skinner's terms in rigorous technical senses, they can be shown not to apply to language, and if the terms are metaphorically extended, they become so vague as to be no improvement on traditional linguistic notions. Chomsky systematically attacked each of Skinner's concepts, but we will consider only two examples: his analyses of stimulus and of reinforcement.

To any behaviorist, proper definitions of the stimuli that control behavior are important. The difficulty of defining "stimulus," however, is a notorious one for behaviorism, as noted by Thorndike and even some behaviorists. Are stimuli to be defined in purely physical terms, independent of behavior, or in terms of their effects on behavior? If we accept the former definition, then behavior looks unlawful, for very few stimuli in a situation ever affect behavior. If we accept the latter definition, behavior is lawful by definition, for then the behaviorist considers only those stimuli that do systematically determine behavior. Chomsky raised this problem and others specific to Skinner's *Verbal Behavior*. First, Chomsky pointed out that to say each bit of verbal behavior is under stimulus control is scientifically empty; for given any response, we can always find some relevant stimulus. A person looks at a painting and says, "It's by Rembrandt, isn't it?" Skinner would assert that certain subtle properties of the painting determine the response. Yet the person could have said: "How much did it cost?" "It clashes with the wallpaper," "You've hung it too high," "It's hideous!" "I have one just like it at home," "It's forged," and so on, virtually *ad infinitum*. No matter what is said, some property could be found that "controls" the behavior. Chomsky argued that there is no prediction of behavior, and certainly no serious control, in this circumstance. Skinner's system is not the scientific advance toward the prediction and control of behavior it pretends to be.

Chomsky also pointed out that Skinner's definition of stimulus becomes hopelessly vague and metaphorical at a great remove from the rigorous laboratory environment. Skinner speaks of "remote stimulus control," in which the stimulus need not impinge on the speaker at all, as when a recalled diplomat describes a foreign situation. Skinner says the suffix "-ed" is controlled by the "subtle property of stimuli we speak of as action in the past." What physical dimensions define "things in the past"? Chomsky argued that Skinner's usage here is not remotely related to his usage in his bar-pressing experiments, and that Skinner has said nothing new about the supposed "stimulus control" of verbal behavior.

Chomsky next considered "reinforcement," another term easily defined in the usual operant learning experiment in terms of delivered food or water. Chomsky argued that Skinner's application of the term to verbal behavior is again vague and metaphorical. Consider Skinner's notion of automatic self-reinforcement. Talking to oneself is said to be automatically self-reinforcing; that is why one does it. Similarly, thinking is also said to be behavior that automatically affects the behaver and is therefore reinforcing. Also consider what we might call remote reinforcement: A writer shunned in his own time may be reinforced by expecting fame to come much later. Chomsky (1959/1967) argued that "the notion of reinforcement has totally lost whatever meaning it may ever have had. . . . A person can be reinforced though he emits no response at all [thinking], and the reinforcing 'stimulus' need not impinge on the 'reinforced person' [remote reinforcement] or need not even exist [an unpopular author who remains unpopular]" (p. 153).

Adopting a rationalist, Cartesian perspective, Chomsky (1966) believes no behaviorist approach to language can cope with its endless creativity and flexibility. He argues that creativity can be understood only by recognizing that language is a rule-governed system. As part of their mental processes, persons possess a set of grammatical rules that allows them to generate new sentences by appropriately combining linguistic elements. Each person can thus generate an infinity of sentences by repeated application of the rules of grammar, just as a person can generate numbers infinitely by repeated application of the rules of arithmetic. Chomsky argues that human language will not be understood until psychology describes the rules of grammar, the mental structures that underlie speaking and hearing. A superficial behaviorist approach, which studies only speech and hearing but neglects the inner rules that govern speech and hearing, is necessarily inadequate.

As part of his effort to revive Cartesian rationalism in the twentieth century, Chomsky has advanced a nativist theory of language acquisition to accompany his formal, rule-governed theory of adult language. Chomsky (e.g., 1959, 1966) proposes that children possess a biologically given language acquisition device that guides the learning of their native language between the ages of about two and twelve years.

Thus, for Chomsky as for Descartes, language is a possession unique to the human species. In one respect, Chomsky's thesis is even more nativist than Descartes's. Descartes proposed that humans have language because they—alone among the animals—can think and express themselves in language; Chomsky believes that language itself, not the more general ability to think, is a human species-specific trait.

Chomsky's ideas were enormously influential on psycholinguistics, which rapidly and completely eclipsed behaviorist approaches, whether mediational or Skinnerian. Many psychologists, becoming convinced that their behaviorist views were wrong, committed themselves to a renewed study of language along Chomskian lines. Chomsky's technical system, described in *Syntactic Structures* (which appeared in 1957, the year of *Verbal Behavior*), provided a new theory around which to design research. Study after study was done, so that, in only a few years, Chomsky's ideas had generated much more empirical research than had Skinner's. The study of child language was similarly stimulated by Chomsky's controversial nativism. Chomsky's impact was nicely described by George Miller. In the 1950s, Miller had adhered to a behaviorist picture of language, but personal contact with Chomsky convinced him the old paradigm had to be abandoned. In 1962, he wrote, "In the course of my work I seem to have become a very old-fashioned kind of psychologist. I now believe that mind is something more than a four-letter, Anglo-Saxon word—human minds exist, and it is our job as psychologists to study them" (p. 762). The mind, exorcised by Watson in 1913, had returned to psychology, brought back by an outsider, Noam Chomsky. Chomsky's emphasis on the rule-governed nature of language helped shape later information-processing theories that claim all behavior is rule-governed.

EROSION OF THE FOUNDATIONS

Just when humanistic psychologists were challenging behaviorism's dominance in their own way, some of the fundamental working assumptions of behaviorism, and even of behavioralism, were coming into question. Combined with the attacks of critics, doubts thrown on these assumptions helped open the door for the formulation of new theories, some in the tradition of behavioralism, and some more radical.

The Disappearance of Positivism

In the 1930s, logical positivism had provided a philosophical justification for behaviorism, helping to redefine psychology as the study of behavior rather than mind. Positivism modified at least the formulation of the leading learning theories of the era, and it completely captured the allegiance of young experimental psychologists who hitched their stars to operationism, using it as an analytical tool to define which problems were worth studying and which were blind alleys.

However, the methodological view of science became increasingly suspect in the late 1950s and beyond. Since its founding, logical positivism had undergone continuous change that took it further and further away from the simple logical positivism of the 1920s. For example, in the 1930s, it was recognized that theoretical terms cannot be neatly linked to observations by the single step of operational definition, a fact some psychologists acknowledged without abandoning the jargon of operationism. Younger philosophers, though, were less inclined to accept the positivist paradigm even in principle, and, during the 1960s, the movement became moribund. It began to be called "the Received View," like a dead theology, and a symposium on "The Legacy of Logical Positivism" was published in 1969 (Achinstein & Barker, 1969).

Although many criticisms of "the Received View" were offered, perhaps the most fundamental was that its explication of scientific practice was false. Historically oriented philosophers of science, such as Thomas Kuhn and Stephen Toulmin, showed that the supposed objectivity of science was a myth (see Chapter 1). Positivism's postmortem dissection of science as a logically coherent system consisting of axioms, theorems, predictions, and verifications was shown to distort and falsify science as a lively, fallible human enterprise.

Kuhn's views themselves became popular with many psychologists. As cognitive psychology seemed to replace behaviorism in the later 1960s, references to scientific revolutions and paradigm clashes abounded. Kuhn's doctrines seemed to justify a revolutionary attitude: Behaviorism must be overthrown, it cannot be reformed. Many psychologists adopted a kind of scientific revolutionary radical chic paralleling the widespread political revolutionary radical chic of the 1960s. Using Kuhn's *The Structure of Scientific Revolutions* to justify a scientific revolution raises an interesting problem in social psychology. Could the perception of revolution have been a self-fulfilling prophecy? Would there have been a so-called revolution against behaviorism without Kuhn's book? Or, more subtly, could belief in Kuhn's ideas have created the appearance of revolution where there was really only conceptual evolution?

Constraints on Animal Learning

At the other end from philosophy, behaviorism was anchored by empirical studies of animal behavior. Watson began his career as an animal psychologist, and Tolman, Hull, and Skinner rarely studied human behavior, preferring the more controlled situations that could be imposed on animals. Animal experiments were expected to yield general behavioral laws applicable to a wide range of species, including humans, with little or no modification. Tolman spoke of cognitive maps in rats and persons, Hull of the general laws of mammalian behavior, and Skinner of the extension of animal principles to verbal behavior. It was believed that the principles that emerged from artificially controlled experiments would illuminate the ways in which all organisms learn, regardless of evolutionary conditioning. The assumption of generality was crucial to the behaviorist program, for if laws of learning are species-specific, studies of animal behavior are pointless for understanding humanity.

Evidence accumulated in the 1960s, however, that the laws of learning uncovered with rats and pigeons are not general, and that serious constraints exist on what and how an animal learns—constraints dictated by the animal's evolutionary history. This evidence came from psychology and from other disciplines. On the one hand, psychologists discovered anomalies in the application of learning laws in a variety of situations; on the other hand, ethologists demonstrated the importance of innate factors in understanding an animal's behavior in the natural environment its ancestors evolved in.

In developing the pigeon-guided missile, Skinner worked with a young psychologist, Keller Breland, who was so impressed by the possibilities of behavior control that he and his wife became professional animal trainers. As Skinner put it in 1959: "Behavior could be shaped up according to specifications and maintained indefinitely almost at will . . . Keller Breland is now specializing in the production of behavior as a saleable commodity." Skinner's claim for Breland resembles Frazier's boast in *Walden II* of being able to produce human personalities to order.

In the course of their extensive experience in training many species to perform unusual behaviors, the Brelands found instances in which animals did not perform as they should. In 1961, they reported their difficulties in a paper whose title, "The Misbehavior of Organisms," puns on Skinner's first book, *The Behavior of Organisms*. For example, they tried to teach pigs to carry wooden coins and deposit them in a piggy bank. Although they could teach behaviors, the Brelands found that the behaviors degenerated in pig after pig. The animals would eventually pick up the coin, then drop it on the ground and root it, rather than deposit it in the bank. The Brelands reported that they found many instances of animals "trapped by strong instinctive behaviors" that overwhelm learned behaviors. Pigs naturally root for their food, and so they come to root the coins that they have been trained to collect to get food reinforcers. Breland and Breland (1961/1972) concluded that psychologists should examine "the hidden assumptions which led most disastrously to these breakdowns" in the general laws of learning proposed by behaviorism. They were clearly questioning behaviorism's paradigmatic assumptions in the light of experimental anomalies.

They identified three such assumptions: "That the animal . . . [is] a virtual tabula rasa, that species differences are insignificant, and that all responses are about equally conditionable to all stimuli." These assumptions are fundamental to empiricism, and statements of them have been made by the major behaviorists. Although limits on these assumptions had been suggested before, the Brelands' paper seemed to open the floodgates to discoveries of more anomalies under more controlled conditions.

The most important such line of research was conducted by John Garcia (e.g., Garcia, McGowan, and Green, 1972) and his associates. Garcia was a student of Krechevsky, Tolman's major pupil. Garcia studied what he called "conditioned nausea," a form of classical conditioning. Standard empiricist assumptions, enunciated by Pavlov, held that any stimulus could act as a conditioned stimulus, which through conditioning could elicit any response as a conditioned response. More informally, any stimulus could be conditioned to elicit any response. Empirical studies further indicated that the conditioned stimulus and unconditioned stimulus had to be paired within about a half-second of each other for learning to take place.

Using a variety of methods, Garcia let rats drink a novel-tasting liquid and then made the rats sick, over an hour later. The question was whether rats would learn to avoid the place they were sick, the unconditioned stimulus immediately connected with their sickness, or the solution they drank, although it was remote in time from the unconditioned response. The latter uniformly occurred. The usual laws of classical conditioning did not hold. Garcia argued that rats know instinctively that nausea must be due to something they ate, not stimuli present at the time of sickness. This makes good evolutionary sense, for sickness in the wild is more likely to be caused by drinking tainted water than by the bush under which a rat was sitting when it felt sick. Connecting taste with sickness is more biologically adaptive than connecting sickness with visual or auditory stimuli. It appears, therefore, that evolution constrains what stimuli may be associated with what responses. Garcia's research was initially greeted with extreme skepticism and was refused publication in the major journal devoted to animal behavior. However, studies by other researchers demonstrated for many behaviors that an animal's evolutionary inheritance places distinct limits on what it can learn.

The discovery of innate constraints on learning revealed an interesting fact about the influence of Darwin on American psychology. Both functionalists and behaviorists viewed mind and behavior as adaptive processes that adjusted the organism to its environment. We have seen that Skinner's analysis of learning is squarely and consciously based on an extension of natural selection. Yet behaviorism adopted the empiricist assumptions of the Spencerian paradigm of the tabula rasa and species-general laws of learning, and ignored the contribution of evolution to behavior. This was the product of another behaviorist assumption, peripheralism. Behaviorists of course recognized that a dog cannot respond to a tone it cannot hear; nor can it learn to fly. These constraints, however, are only on the organism's peripheral sensory and motor abilities. Because behaviorism denied that central processes exist, it could not recognize evolutionary limits on them. It had to assume that as long as an organism could sense a stimulus, it could be associated with any response it could physically make.

Many of the puzzling phenomena uncovered by researchers, such as the Brelands and Garcia, seemed to involve tastes or sights or sounds an animal can sense but cannot associate with behavior. Such findings seemed to indicate central control over learning—central control that is at least partly determined by heredity. Therefore, although behaviorism, following functionalism, adopted the theory of natural selection as a conceptual tool, it denied the species-oriented implications of evolution because it thought of the brain as a passive connecter of stimuli and responses.

Awareness and Human Learning

Logical positivism and the belief that the laws of learning discoverable with rats and pigeons were applicable without serious exception to all other species, including human beings, were fundamental assumptions of the behaviorist form of behavioralism that had been formulated in the 1930s. Behavioralism rested on a different assumption, that consciousness was of marginal importance in explaining behavior, including human behavior. The motor theory of consciousness and neorealist theories of consciousness viewed consciousness as an epiphenomenon that might at best report some of the determiners of behavior—and not do that very well—but played no role in the actual determination of behavior. Münsterberg, Dewey, and the functionalists placed the determinants of behavior in the environment and in physiological processes, seeing consciousness as merely floating over brain and body, reporting what it saw. Psychology, then, became the study of behavior, not consciousness, although consciousness might be consulted for its occasionally apt insights on why its owner behaved as he or she did. Within this broad framework, behaviorists developed their research programs, using positivism to buttress the behavioralist disdain for consciousness, and turning to rigorous, experimental study of animal learning to find the answer to behavioralism's basic question: What causes behavior?

In its behaviorist form, the causal impotence of consciousness was asserted by the doctrine of the automatic action of reinforcers. The doctrine was contained in Thorndike's Law of Effect in the phrase "stamped in": Reward automatically "stamps in" an S–R connection; it does not lead consciousness to a conclusion on which action is taken. In 1961, the automatic action of reinforcers was forcefully and dogmatically stated by Leo Postman and Julius Sassenrath (1961, p. 136): "It is an outmoded and an unnecessary assumption that the modification of behavior must be preceded by a correct understanding of the environmental contingencies."

A subject might report contingencies accurately, but this only meant that consciousness had observed the causes of the changed behavior, not that consciousness had itself caused behavior to change.

Some experiments seemed to support the view. For example, Greenspoon (1955) was interested in nondirective psychotherapy, in which the therapist merely says "um-hum" periodically during a session. From the behaviorist perspective, this situation could be analyzed as a learning situation. The patient emits behaviors, some of which are reinforced by "um-hum." Therefore, the patient should come to talk about those things that are reinforced, and not others. Greenspoon took this hypothesis to the laboratory. Subjects were brought to an experimental room and induced to say words. Whenever the subject said a plural noun, the experimenter said "um-hum." After a while, extinction was begun; the experimenter said nothing. At the end of the session, the subject was asked to explain what had been going on. Only ten of seventy-five subjects could do so and, interestingly, Greenspoon excluded their data from analysis. His results showed that production of plural nouns increased during training and then decreased during extinction—exactly as operant theory predicts—and in the apparent absence of awareness of the connection between plural nouns and reinforcement. Experiments similar to Greenspoon's found similar results.

In the 1960s, various researchers—disenchanted with behaviorism, and often under Chomsky's influence—challenged the validity of the "Greenspoon effect," or learning without awareness. They argued that Greenspoon's method was inadequate. The questions probing awareness were vague, and they were asked only after extinction, by which time subjects who had been aware of the response-reinforcement contingency could have concluded they had been wrong. Replication of the Greenspoon procedure showed that many subjects held technically incorrect hypotheses that nevertheless led to correct responses. For example, a subject might say "apples" and "pears" and be reinforced, concluding that fruit names were being reinforced. The subject would continue to say fruit names and be rewarded, yet when the subject told the hypothesis to the experimenter, the subject would be called "unaware" (Dulany, 1968).

Those who doubted the automatic action of reinforcers carried out extensive experiments to show the necessity of awareness to human learning. One extensive research program was conducted by Don E. Dulany (1968), who constructed a sophisticated axiomatic theory about types of awareness and their effects on behavior. His experiments seemed to show that only subjects aware of the contingencies of reinforcement could learn, and that subjects' confidence in their hypotheses was systematically related to their overt behavior.

By 1966, the area of verbal behavior was in an apparent state of crisis that called for another symposium. The organizers of the meeting had optimistically planned to gather psychologists from different backgrounds to work out a unified S–R theory of verbal behavior. They called together mediationists such as Howard Kendler, workers in the Ebbinghaus verbal learning tradition, colleagues of Noam Chomsky, and rebellious thinkers such as Dulany. Instead of unanimity, the symposium discovered dissent and disenchantment, ranging from mild displeasure with the current state of verbal learning to a formal proof of the inadequacy of the S–R paradigm's theories of language. In closing the book in which the conference papers were published, the editors' comments reflected the growing influence of Kuhn, identifying behaviorism as a paradigm in crisis (Dixon and Horton, 1968). The last sentence in the book was: "To us, it appears that a revolution is certainly in the making."

COGNITIVE PSYCHOLOGY ASSERTS ITSELF

Because of the attacks on behaviorism and the weakening of its supporting assumptions, cognitive psychology, which had never disappeared, was reinvigorated and attracted more attention and adherents than ever before. Precisely because the situation in experimental psychology was confused and in great flux, several forms of cognitive psychology emerged and vied for center stage. The two most important were structuralism and information processing. Structuralism was associated with the more radical cognitive psychologists, who sought a clear break with the past in American psychology; in particular, they looked to European psychology and continental European philosophical traditions in philosophy, psychology, and the other social sciences. Information-processing psychology was more conservative. It rejected behaviorism, but it nevertheless remained within the behavioralistic tradition of American psychology in the twentieth century. It adopted and adapted the approaches and procedures of artificial intelligence and cognitive simulation to forge a new language in which to cast psychological models from which behavior might be predicted and controlled.

The New Structuralism

The first form of cognitive psychology to emerge was structuralism. This was not a continuation of Titchener's system, with which it shares nothing but the name; it was an independent movement of continental European origin. Structuralism hoped to be a unifying paradigm for all the social sciences, and its adherents ranged from philosophers to anthropologists. Structuralists believed that any human behavior pattern, whether individual or social, may be explained by reference to abstract structures, frequently believed to be logical or mathematical in nature.

In psychology, the leading structuralist was Jean Piaget, who proposed that, at different stages of cognitive development, children's thought is controlled by different systems of logical structures. Some other psychologists are at least partially structuralists. It is sometimes held that Freud was a structuralist because of his revised structural model of the mind, but he lived long before the movement became self-conscious. Noam Chomsky may be regarded as a structuralist for trying to explain language in terms of its formal grammatical structure. In this, Chomsky follows the lead of the French linguist Ferdinand de Saussurre (1857–1913), who many think provided the inspiration for structuralism as a movement.

Structuralism had enormous influence in continental European philosophy, literary criticism, and social science, including psychology. The leading exponents of structuralism, Levi-Strauss, Michel Foucault, and Piaget were French-speaking and carried on the Platonic–Cartesian rationalist attempt to describe the transcendent human mind. As one might expect, given the European rationalist background of structuralism, its impact on American psychology was limited. For example, as they did with Gestalt theory, American psychologists respected Piaget's novel findings about child behavior, but had little use for his arcane logical theory. Chomsky's linguistic theory initially inspired much research, but when Chomsky (1965) proclaimed it had no necessary psychological reality, psychologists began to go their own way. In any event, structuralism has been superseded by a bewildering variety of "poststructuralist" movements (primarily in the humanities, but to some degree in the social sciences), and now seems as stale and passé as polyester leisure suits.

Man the Machine: Information Processing

In 1957, Herbert Simon, coauthor of the General Problem Solver (GPS), prophesied that "within ten years most theories in psychology will take the form of computer programs" (Dreyfus, 1972). But GPS exerted little influence on the psychology of problem solving during the 1960s. In 1963, Donald W. Taylor reviewed the research area of thinking and concluded that although computer simulation of thinking shows "the most promise" of any theory, "this promise, however, remains to be justified." Three years later, Gary Davis (1966) surveyed the field of human problem solving and concluded, "There is a striking unanimity in recent theoretical orientations to human thinking and problem solving . . . that associational behavioral laws established in comparatively simple classical conditioning and instrumental conditioning situations apply to complex human learning"; Davis relegated GPS to one of three other minor theories of problem solving. Ulric Neisser, in his influential text *Cognitive Psychology* (1967), dismissed computer models of thinking as "simplistic" and not "satisfactory from the psychological point of view." On the tenth anniversary of his prediction, Simon and his colleagues quietly abandoned GPS (Dreyfus, 1972).

Yet it was acknowledged by everyone, including its opponents, that cognitive psychology was booming during the 1960s. In 1960, Donald Hebb, one of psychology's recognized leaders, called for the "Second American Revolution" (the first was behaviorism): "The serious analytical study of the thought processes cannot be postponed any longer." In 1964, Robert R. Holt said that "cognitive psychology has enjoyed a remarkable boom." The boom extended even to clinical psychology, as Louis Breger and James McGaugh (1965) argued for replacing behavioristic psychotherapy with therapy based on information-processing concepts. By 1967, Neisser could write that "A generation ago a book like this one would have needed at least a chapter of self-defense against the behaviorist position. Today, happily, the climate of opinion has changed and little or no defense is necessary."

Attempts to turn psychology into a branch of computer science had failed but had brought about a renaissance in cognitive psychology as psychologists accepted "the familiar parallel between man and computer" (Neisser, 1967). It was easy to think of people as information-processing devices that receive input from the environment (perception), process that information (thinking), and act upon decisions reached (behavior). Attempts to write running programs to emulate thought seemed rather boring to psychologists, but the general image of human beings as information processors was immensely exciting. So, although Simon was wrong in predicting that psychological theories would be written as computer programs, the broader vision of artificial intelligence and computer simulation had triumphed by 1967, having far more influence than either of its rivals, structuralism and mentalism.

The reason for the simultaneous failure of computer programs to become the new wave in psychological theory and the success of the general information-processing perspective may be found by continuing the quotations from Hebb and Neisser.

Hebb: "The serious analytical study of the thought processes cannot be postponed any longer. . . . The mediational postulate . . . is a powerful tool, and the time has come to use it" (1960, p. 743).

Neisser: "Today, the climate of opinion is changed and little or no defense is necessary. Indeed, stimulus–response theorists themselves are inventing hypothetical mechanisms with vigor and enthusiasm and only faint twinges of conscience. The basic reason for studying the cognitive processes has become as clear as the reason for studying anything else: because they are there" (1967, p. 5).

It is important to remember the large community of psychologists who fell into the mediational tradition of psychology, whether neo-Hullian or neo-Tolmanian. These psychologists already accepted the idea of processes intervening between stimulus and response, and they had, throughout the 1950s, "invented hypothetical mechanisms," inferred, covert, responses whose internal stimuli linked observable S–R connections into chains of complex behaviors. During the 1950s, neobehaviorist human psychology flourished (Cofer, 1978). Ebbinghaus's study of memory had been revived in the field called "verbal learning," and, independently of computer science, verbal learning psychologists had begun by 1958 to distinguish between short-term and long-term memory. The field of psycholinguistics—an interdisciplinary combination of linguistics and psychology—had begun in the early 1950s under the auspices of the Social Science Research Council. Since the end of World War II, the Office of Naval Research had funded conferences on verbal learning, memory, and verbal behavior. A Group for the Study of Verbal Behavior was organized in 1957. It began, like Maslow's humanistic psychologists, as a mailing list; it became, again like the humanists, a journal, the *Journal of Verbal Learning and Verbal Behavior,* in 1962.

These groups were interconnected, and all the psychologists involved with verbal behavior and thinking took the mediational version of S–R theory for granted. For example, in psycholinguistics, the "grammars [of the pre-Chomsky linguists] and mediation theory were seen to be variations of the same line of thought" (Jenkins, 1968). As late as 1963, Jenkins (Gough and Jenkins, 1963) could discuss "verbal learning and psycholinguistics" in purely mediational terms, but it was clear by 1968 that Chomsky had "dynamited the structure [of mediational psycholinguistics] at the linguistic end" (Jenkins, 1968). Chomsky convinced these psychologists that their S–R theories, even including mediation, were inadequate to explain human language. Looking for a new language in which to theorize about mental processes, they were naturally drawn to the language of the computer, information processing. The "S" of the S → mediating response → R could become "input," the "R" could become "output," and the mediating response could become "processing." Moreover, information-processing language could be used, even without writing computer programs, as a "global framework within which precisely stated models could be constructed for many different . . . phenomena and could be tested in quantitative fashion" (Shiffrin, 1977, p. 2).

Information-processing language gave mediational psychologists exactly what they needed. It was rigorous, up to date, and at least as quantitative as Hull's old theory, without having to make the implausible assumption that the processes linking stimulus and response were just the same as single-stage learning processes in animals. Psychologists could now talk about "coding," "search sets," "retrieval," "pattern recognition," and other information structures and operations, with every expectation that they were constructing scientific theories. Information-processing psychology met psychologists' physics envy better than Hull's had, for information-processing psychologists could always point to computers as the working embodiment of their theories. The theories might not be computer programs, but they were like computer programs in regarding thinking as the formal processing of stored information. Thus, although information-processing theories were independent of computational theories in artificial intelligence, they were conceptually parasitic on them, and cognitive psychologists hoped that at some future point their theories would be programs. Simon's prophecy failed, but his dream remained.

During the 1960s and early 1970s, information-processing theory gradually replaced mediational theory as the language of cognitive psychology, and the fields of artificial intelligence and computer simulation psychology began to merge into a new field distinct from psychology, called cognitive science. Cognitive science defined itself as the science of what George Miller named *informavores* (Pylyshyn, 1984). The idea was that all information-processing systems—whether made of flesh and blood, like human beings, or silicon and metal, like computers, or of whatever materials might be invented or discovered—operated according to the same principles and therefore constituted a single field of study, cognitive science, "converging around the information-processing paradigm" (Simon, 1980).

The proponents of cognitive science were confident perhaps to the point of hubris. Simon (1980) declared: "Over the past quarter-century, no development in the social sciences has been more radical than the revolution—often referred to as the information processing revolution—in our way of understanding the processes of human thinking." Simon dismissed behaviorism as "confining" and "preoccupied with laboratory rats" and praised information-processing theory for helping psychology achieve "a new sophistication" and for creating a "general paradigm, the information processing paradigm," which preserved behaviorism's "operationality" while surpassing it "in precision and rigor." Simon's large claims were reinforced by the Research Briefing Panel on Cognitive Science and Artificial Intelligence (Estes and Newell, 1983), written for government leaders and grant givers. According to the panel, cognitive science addresses a "great scientific mystery, on a par with understanding the evolution of the universe, the origin of life, or the nature of elementary particles" and is "advancing our understanding of the nature of mind and the nature of intelligence on a scale that is proving revolutionary."

In 1979, Lachman, Lachman, and Butterfield attempted, in their often-cited *Cognitive Psychology and Information Processing,* to describe information-processing cognitive psychology as a Kuhnian paradigm. They claimed that "Our [cognitive] revolution is now complete and the atmosphere is one of normal science" (p. 525). They defined cognitive psychology in terms of the computer metaphor: Cognitive psychology is about "how people take in information, how they recode and remember it, how they make decisions, how they transform their internal knowledge states, and how they translate these states into behavioral outputs. The analogy is important. It makes a difference whether a scientist thinks of humans as if they were laboratory animals or as if they were computers" (p. 99).

In discussing an example of "cognitive behavior [sic]," Lachman et al. presuppose that people must process information, thereby legitimating information-processing psychology by assumption. When you drive a car, you must "perceive each familiar landmark anew each time," "have represented the landmark's appearance in your memory," "match up your current perception of the landmark to its stored representation," and so on, though "decid[ing] repeatedly when to shift gears" and where to park (1979, p. 7). Wittgenstein pointed out that how we frame questions about human behavior determines a great deal—probably more than the empirical facts—about the answers we get from our investigations. Lachman et al.'s analysis of driving is a splendid example of this process at work; when they say we must do the things they claim—even if they are out of awareness, as they concede—information-processing psychology is forced on us, and the only possible answers to the question of how we drive or do anything else become information-processing ones. The form of the question dictates the answer.

The explication of the information-processing "paradigm" by Lachman et al. makes clear that information-processing psychology is a form of behavioralism with strong affinity to all but radical behaviorism. Speaking of "cognitive behavior," for example, shows that information processing is the latest form of behavioralism. Their dismissal of introspection as "unreliable and impoverished" and their evaluation of mentalistic introspective psychology as having "reached a dead end" by 1913 are consistent with behavioral views on the psychology of consciousness. They identify the study of consciousness with the study of attention as a stage in information processing, a narrow view of consciousness that Wundt would have rejected.

Lachman et al. themselves recognize that information processing took over much from neobehaviorism: nomothetic explanation, empiricism, focus on the laboratory, operationism, and "the rational canons of natural science." In short, although Lachman et al. specifically deny it, information processing adopted a modified logical positivism from neobehaviorism. This becomes clearest at the end of their book, when the authors become confused about the real existence of the information processes they have discussed for five hundred pages. They would clearly prefer to assert that information processes are real processes that actually take place inside an organism. Yet these processes are generally observable to neither the person within whose mind they are allegedly occurring nor to a neuroscientist observing evidence of brain activity. Information-processing psychology is then forced to define its theoretical terms operationally: "Flowcharts, in a way, have the same status for us that operational definition had for our predecessors" (Lachman et al., 1979, p. 125). But, as we discovered from the "What is learned?" controversy of the 1950s, operationism is antirealistic, treating theoretical terms simply as convenient fictions. The tension between realism and operationism is manifest in the last pages of *Cognitive Psychology and Information Processing,* but its authors do not seem to feel it, lamely concluding that it is too early to tell whether human information processes are real or not.

An important part of the optimism of cognitive scientists, and the conceptual basis of the merger of cognitive psychology and artificial intelligence, was a proposed solution to the mind–body problem called *functionalism.* The basic idea of functionalism is that the relation of mind to body is the same as that of program to computer.

The basic thesis of functionalism derives from the activity of computer programming. Suppose I write a simple program for balancing my checkbook, in a programming language such as BASIC. The program will specify a set of computational functions: retrieving my old balance from memory, subtracting checks written, adding deposits made, and comparing the results to the bank statement. Ignoring minor formatting differences, I can enter and run this program on many different machines: an Apple, an IBM PC or clone, or a mainframe computer. In each case, the same computational functions will be carried out, although the physical processes by which each computer will perform them will be different.

To be able to predict, control, and explain the behavior of a computer, one need not know anything about the electronic processes involved; all one needs to understand is the higher-level computational functions in the system. I am composing these words on a program called AmiPro, and because I understand the programmed functions of AmiPro, I can use it effectively—that is, I can predict, control, and explain my computer's behavior even though I know absolutely nothing about the lower-level computational or electronic functions that compose higher-level functions such as moving paragraphs about.

Functionalism simply extends the separation of program and computer to include human beings. Computers use hardware to carry out computational functions; functionalism asserts that people use neural "wetware" to do the same things. When I balance my checkbook by hand, I carry out exactly the same functions as my BASIC computer program does. My nervous system and my PC's Intel 486 microchip are materially different, but the same program is instantiated as each of us does my accounts. So, functionalism concludes, my mind is a set of computational functions that runs my body in exactly the same way that a computer program is a set of computational functions that controls a computer: My mind is a running program. In this way, psychologists can hope to predict, control, and explain human behavior by understanding the human "program" and without understanding the nervous system and brain. Cognitive psychologists are thus like computer programmers asked to study an alien computer. They dare not fool with the machine's wiring, so they attempt to understand its program by experimenting with its input–output functions.

The attraction of functionalism and information processing is that they offer a solution to the behaviorist's problem: how to explain behavior without any reference to teleology or nonmaterial meanings. Hull, Tolman, and Skinner had tried their own approaches to the problem, but each faced serious difficulties. Hull's theory had foundered on experimental evidence, and in any event was too rigid, mechanistic, and number-bound to work for human beings. Tolman's theory was more traditional in adopting the representational theory of cognition, but left unclear who was reading the maps in the rats' minds: perhaps ghostly rats in the rat machine? Skinner's theory avoided the difficulties of his predecessors, but its denial of the existence of mental processes altogether was too radical for most psychologists' taste.

Functionalism preserved the virtues of Hull's and Tolman's approaches—precisely formulated theories and the appealing notion of mental representation—while seeming to avoid their vices—rigidity and mystery—by invoking the sophisticated and flexible processes of computer programming. Computers carry out their computational functions on internal representations; in the checkbook example, the program directs the computer to manipulate representations of a previous balance, amounts of checks and deposits, and so on. Yet my PC contains no little accountant bent over ledger books doing arithmetic: There is no ghostly accountant in the machine. Rather, the machine applies precisely stated formal rules to the representations, and carries out the computations in a completely mechanistic fashion. From the perspective of functionalism, both Hull and Tolman were right, but it remained for the computational approach to put their insights together. Hull was right that organisms are machines; Tolman was right that organisms build up representations from experience. According to functionalism, computer programs apply Hullian mechanistic rules to Tolmanian representations, and, if functionalism is correct, so do living organisms. Moreover, against Skinner's dismissed mind as a myth, functionalism legitimated the concept of mind by defining it as something familiar and real—a computer program.

Although it's quite different from radical behaviorism, information-processing psychology is a form of behavioralism. It represents a continuing conceptual evolution in the psychology of adaptation, for it views cognitive processes as adaptive behavioral functions and is, in a sense, a reassertion of earlier American functionalism.

The functionalists saw the mind as adaptive but were trapped by the limited metaphysics of the nineteenth century into espousing at the same time a strict mind–body parallelism, engendering a conflict exploited by Watson in establishing behaviorism. The cybernetic analysis of purpose, and its mechanical realization in the computer, however, vindicated the functionalist attitude by showing that purpose and cognition were not necessarily mysterious, and need not involve dualism.

Herbert Simon, one of the founders of modern information-processing psychology, revealed the continuity of information processing with behavioralism, and even its affinity with behaviorism, in *Sciences of the Artificial* (1969, p. 25): "A man, viewed as a behaving system, is quite simple. The apparent complexity of his behavior over time is largely a reflection of the complexity of the environment in which he finds himself." Simon, like Skinner, views human beings as largely the products of the environment that shapes them, since they themselves are simple. In the same work, Simon followed Watson in dismissing the validity of mental images, reducing them to lists of facts and sensory properties associatively organized. Simon also argued that complex behaviors are assemblages of simpler behaviors. Information-processing psychologists share many important behaviorist assumptions: atomism, associationism, and empiricism. On the philosophical side, information processing espouses materialism, holding that there is no independent Cartesian soul, and positivism, continuing to insist on operationalizing all theoretical terms (Simon, 1969).

Watson's and Skinner's behaviorisms were extreme statements of the psychology of adaptation that attempted to circumnavigate the inaccessible—and therefore potentially mythical—reaches of the human mind. The information-processing view follows the steps of William James, Hull, and Tolman in seeing, beneath behavior, processes to be investigated and explained. Behaviorism was one response by the psychology of adaptation to crisis, and information processing is another; but in both we see a deeper continuity under the superficial changes.

PSYCHOLOGY AND SOCIETY

Funding Social Science

The political relations of the social sciences, including psychology, went from disaster to apparent triumph during the 1960s. The disaster was Project Camelot, the largest social science project ever conceived, under which the United States Army, together with the CIA and other intelligence agencies, gave up to $6 million to social scientists at home and abroad to pinpoint potential political trouble spots (for example, incipient guerrilla wars) and to use social scientific expertise to formulate remedies (for example, counterinsurgency actions). However, when in 1965 Project Camelot ceased to be secret, social science was thrown under a cloud. Foreign governments viewed Project Camelot as American meddling in their internal affairs. Their complaints led to a congressional investigation and to the termination of Project Camelot in July 1965. The image of social science was tarnished because social scientists participating in Project Camelot appeared to be tools of the American government rather than disinterested investigators of social phenomena.

However, through the Camelot assignment, social science was able to finally gain a place at the federal research grant trough. As American cities exploded with race riots and street crime in the mid-1960s, and President Lyndon Johnson launched the War on Poverty, members of Congress were moved to ask whether social science could do something about race hatred, poverty, crime, and other social problems. Psychologist Dael Wolfle, an experienced observer of relations between science and government, wrote in *Science* in 1966 that "a call for large scale support of the social sciences was a recurring theme of the 25–27 January meeting of the House of Representatives Committee on Science and Technology" (p. 1177). Wolfle thought that the time "may be ripe for special support of the social sciences," especially in view of recent advances in "quantitative and experimental methodology," so that "within a reasonable time, these disciplines can offer substantially increased help in meeting pressing social problems." As late as 1966, out of $5.5 billion spent by the federal government on scientific research, only $221 million (less than 5 percent) went to social science; but by 1967, the mood in Congress "was to do something generous for the social sciences" (Greenberg, 1967).

What Congress would do, however, remained unclear (Carter, 1966; Greenberg, 1967). In the Senate, liberal Democrats were eager to give social scientists money, and to make them into social planners. Some wanted to create a National Social Science Foundation (NSSF) modeled on the National Science Foundation (NSF); others sought to create a presidential "Council of Social Advisers" who would use their presumed expertise to advise the President on the social consequences of governmental actions and to rationally plan America's future. In the end, a more modest scheme prevailed. The NSF's charter, which precluded support of social science, was rewritten, and it was charged to support social science and to include social scientists on its governing body.

Psychology still had to fight hard through the coming decades for full respectability within NSF and the other government funding agencies. Natural scientists continued to dominate research agendas, and they regarded behavioral scientists as less than "real" scientists. Parity was nearly achieved during the first two years of the Democratic Clinton Administration, but, as this is written in the summer of 1995, the Republican Congress elected in 1994 moved to cut social science funding as part of its promise to balance the federal budget by 2002.

Professional Psychology

In contrast to experimental psychology, where an exciting change from behaviorism to cognitive psychology seemed to be taking place, during the decade 1958 to 1968, professional psychology seemed to be adrift. As Nevitt Sanford (1965) wrote, "Psychology is really in the doldrums right now. . . . The revolution in psychology that occurred during World War II . . . has been over for some time."

There was no doubt that while psychology was growing faster than any other profession (Garfield, 1966), clinical and applied psychology were growing even faster. At the 1963 meeting of the APA, there were 670 openings in clinical psychology for only 123 applicants (Schofield, 1966). The membership in the academic divisions of the APA had grown at a 54 percent rate between 1948 and 1960, the professional divisions had grown at a 149 percent rate, and the mixed academic/professional divisions had grown 176 percent (Tryon, 1963). The relative success of the professional as opposed to the traditional scientific branches of psychology led to increased tension between the two classes of psychologists (Shakow, 1965; Chein, 1966, who coined the labels "scientist" and "practitioner" for the two sides in what he saw as an "irrational" and "destructive" division among psychologists). Echoing the debates of the 1930s, Leonard Small (1963) said that the greatest task facing psychology was "to obtain recognition for its competence," and he hinted that if the APA did not assist professional psychologists in achieving this, they would organize separately.

However, while professional psychology was experiencing tremendous growth, professional psychologists were still somewhat uncertain as to their social and scientific roles. The Boulder Conference on clinical psychology had said that clinical psychologists were supposed to be both scientists and practitioners, but it was becoming obvious that few clinicians were becoming scientists, opting instead for the private or institutionalized practice of psychotherapy (for example, Blank and David, 1963; Shakow, 1965; Garfield, 1966; Hoch, Ross, and Winder, 1966). The Boulder model was increasingly challenged, and psychologists began to think about training psychologists purely as professionals, along the lines of physicians' training (Hoch et al., 1966), and to reflect on their aims as both scientists and professionals (Clark, 1967).

Amid all this self-searching, professional psychologists had reason to worry about their public image. The use of psychological tests in education, business, industry, and government had mushroomed since World War II, including not just intelligence tests, but instruments designed to measure personality traits and social attitudes. Many people began to feel that these tests—inquiring as they often did into sexuality, parent–child relations, and other sensitive areas—were invasions of privacy, products of the morbid curiosity of psychologists, and susceptible to abuse by employers, government, or anyone looking for tools of social control. In 1963, psychologists were upset by the popularity of *The Brain Watchers,* a book by journalist Martin Gross, which assailed the use of personality and social tests by government and industry. The antitest movement culminated in 1965, when some school systems burned the results of personality tests administered to children, and Congress investigated the use of personality tests by the federal government to screen possible employees, and eventually restricted their use. By 1967, psychologists were probably not surprised to learn that their prestige was pretty low. When parents were asked which of six professions they would most like their child to enter, they ranked them as follows, from most preferred to least: surgeon, engineer, lawyer, psychiatrist, dentist, psychologist. Most galling was the finding that parents preferred the clinical psychologist's arch enemy, the psychiatrist, by 54 percent to 26 percent (Thumin and Zebelman, 1967).

Values

In 1960, psychiatrist Thomas Szasz began an effective assault on the entire mental health establishment by analyzing *The Myth of Mental Illness* (Szasz, 1960a, 1960b). Szasz pointed out that the concept of mental illness, a metaphor based on the concept of physical illness, was a bad metaphor with pernicious consequences. Szasz's libertarian analysis quietly drew on Ryle's analysis of the concept of mind. Ryle had argued that the mind was a myth, the myth of the Ghost in the Machine. Szasz concluded that if there is no Ghost in the human machine, the Ghost—the mind—can hardly become ill. Just as according to Ryle we (falsely) attribute behaviors to an inner Ghost who causes them, so, Szasz said, when we find behaviors annoying, we think the Ghost must be sick and invent the (false) concept of mental illness: "Those who suffer from and complain of their own behavior are usually classified as 'neurotic'; those whose behavior makes others suffer, and about whom others complain, are usually classified as 'psychotic.' " So, according to Szasz, "Mental illness is not something a person has [he has no inner, sick Ghost], but is something he does or is" (1960a, p. 267).

Belief in mental illness has evil consequences, Szasz thought. To begin with, psychiatric diagnoses are stigmatizing labels that ape the categories of physical illness, but in reality function to give political power to psychiatrists and their allies in mental health. People labeled "mentally ill" can be deprived of their freedom and locked up for indeterminate periods of time, even though they may have committed no crime; while locked up, they can be given drugs against their will, something that may not be done even to convicted felons in prison: "There is no medical, moral, or legal justification for involuntary psychiatric interventions. They are crimes against humanity" (1960a, p. 268). In a deeper sense, the concept of mental illness undermines human freedom, belief in moral responsibility, and the legal notions of guilt and innocence deriving from human freedom and moral responsibility. Instead of treating a human being who may have offended us or committed a crime as an autonomous agent, we treat him or her as a diseased thing with no will. Because the myth of mental illness is a conspiracy of kindness—we would like to excuse and help people who have done wrong—a person categorized as mentally ill, and therefore not responsible for his or her behavior, will likely come to accept his or her supposed helplessness, ceasing to view himself or herself as a morally free actor. And by contagion, as science sees all action as determined beyond self-control, everyone may cease to believe in freedom and moral responsibility. Hence, the myth of mental illness strikes at the very heart of Western civilization, committed as it is to human freedom and responsibility for one's actions.

Szasz did not say that everything called "mental illness" is a fiction, only that the concept of "mental illness" itself is a fiction. It is obviously possible for a brain to be diseased and to cause bizarre thoughts and antisocial behavior. However, in such a case, there is no mental illness at all, but a genuine bodily disease. But, Szasz held, most of what are called "mental illnesses" are "problems of living," not true diseases. Problems of living are quite real, of course, and a person suffering from them may need professional help working them out, so that psychiatry and clinical psychology are legitimate professions: "Psychotherapy is an effective method of helping people—not to recover from an 'illness,' but rather to learn about themselves, others, and life" (1960a, pp. xv–xvi). Conceived medically, psychiatry is a "pseudoscience"; conceived educationally, it is a worthy vocation.

Szasz's ideas were, and remain, highly controversial. To orthodox psychiatrists and clinical psychologists, he is a dangerous heretic whose "nihilistic and cruel philosophies . . . read well and offer little except justification for neglect" of the mentally ill (Penn, 1985). To others, his ideas are attractive, offering an alternative conception of human suffering that does not needlessly turn an agent into a patient. Szasz and his followers in the "antipsychiatry movement," as it is sometimes called, have had some success in changing the legal procedures by which people can be involuntarily committed to mental hospitals. In many states, such commitments are now hedged about with legal safeguards; no longer is it possible in most places to carry off someone to the local mental ward merely on the say-so of a single psychiatrist, as it was in 1960.

As American society became more troubled in the 1960s—by the struggle for civil rights, by riots and crime, and above all by the Vietnam war and the controversies attending upon it—the value of adaptation—conformity—was decisively rejected by increasing numbers of Americans. The roots of the discontent lay in the 1950s, as we have seen; in the 1960s, criticism of conformity became more open and widespread.

In social science, for example, Snell and Gail J. Putney attacked conformity in *The Adjusted American: Normal Neuroses in the Individual and Society* (1964). In *Civilization and Its Discontents,* Freud had argued that civilized people are necessarily a little neurotic, the psychological price paid for civilization, so that psychoanalysis could do no more than reduce neuroses to ordinary unhappiness. According to Putney and Putney, however, "normal neuroses" are not just ordinary unhappiness but are real neuroses that can and ought to be cured. Adjusted Americans, the Putneys said, have learned to conform to a cultural pattern that deceives them about what their real needs are. Because "normalcy . . . [is] the kind of sickness or crippling or stunting that we share with everybody else and therefore don't notice" (Maslow, 1973), adjusted Americans are ignorant of their deepest yearnings and try to satisfy culturally prescribed rather than real human needs, consequently experiencing frustration and pervasive anxiety. The Putneys rejected the value of adjustment, replacing it with the value of "autonomy, [meaning] the capacity of the individual to make valid choices of his behavior in the light of his needs." Maslow (1961) thought that such views were held by most psychologists: "I would say that in the last ten years, most if not all theorists in psychology have become antiadjustment," and he endorsed the value of autonomy—self-actualization—as a replacement for adjustment.

Autonomy could be gained, humanistic psychologists said, through psychotherapy. Chief exponent of this view was Carl Rogers. His client-centered psychotherapy tried to take clients on their own terms and lead them not to adjustment to the regnant norms of society, but to insights into their real needs, and thence to an ability to meet them. A client who had been through successful psychotherapy became a Heraclitean human. By the end of successful client-centered therapy, Rogers (1958) said, "The person becomes a unity, a flow of motion . . . he has become an integrated process of changingness." Rogers's therapy centered on feelings. The person who came for help, the client (like Szasz, Rogers rejected the metaphor of mental illness and refused to call those he helped "patients"), suffered above all from inability to properly experience and fully express his or her feelings. The therapist worked with the client to open up and experience feelings fully and directly, and to share these feelings with the therapist. So the "flow of motion" within the healthy human was most importantly a flow of feelings immediately and fully experienced. In the Rogerian conception, then, the unhealthy individual was one who controlled and withheld feelings; the healthy person—Maslow's self-actualizer—was one who spontaneously experienced the emotions of each moment and expressed emotions freely and directly.

Rogers, Maslow, and the other humanistic psychologists proposed the new values of "growth" and "authenticity" for Western civilization. Values concern how one should live one's life, and what one should treasure in life. Humanistic psychologists proposed that one should never become settled in one's ways, but instead be always in flux: the Heraclitean human. They taught that one should treasure feelings. Both values derive from psychotherapy as Rogers practiced it.

The value humanistic psychologists called "growth" was the openness to change Rogers hoped to bring about in his clients. A therapist naturally wants to change the client because, after all, the client has come seeking help to improve his or her life. Humanistic psychotherapists make change a basic human value, the goal of all living, whether within or without therapy. Humanistic psychologists agreed with Dewey that "growth itself is the only moral end."

The other new value—"authenticity"—concerned the open expression of feelings characteristic of the person who had been through Rogerian therapy. Maslow (1973) defined authenticity as "allowing your behavior and your speech to be the true and spontaneous expression of your inner feelings." Traditionally, people had been taught to control their feelings and to be careful in how they expressed them. Proper behavior in business and among acquaintances—manners—depended on not expressing one's immediate feelings, and on telling little lies that oiled public social intercourse. Only with one's most intimate circle was free, private, emotional expression allowed, and even then only within civilized bounds. Humanistic psychologists opposed manners with authenticity, teaching that emotional control and deceptive emotional expression—Maslow called it "phoniness"—were psychological evils, and that people should be open, frank, and honest with each other, baring their souls to any and all as they might with a psychotherapist. Hypocrisy was regarded as a sin, and the ideal life was modeled on psychotherapy. The good person (Maslow, 1973) was unencumbered by hangups, experienced emotions deeply, and freely shared feelings with others.

Humanistic psychologists were clear that they were at war with traditional Western civilization and were trying to make a moral as well as a psychological revolution. Maslow (1967) denounced being polite about the drinks served at a party as "the usual kind of phoniness we all engage in" and proclaimed that "the English language is rotten for good people." Rogers (1968) closed an article on "Interpersonal Relationships: U.S.A. 2000" by quoting "the new student morality" as propounded at Antioch College: "[We deny] that nonaffective modes of human intercourse, mediated by decency of manners, constitute an acceptable pattern of human relations."

Rogers's ideas were, of course, not new in Western civilization. Valuing emotional feeling, trusting intuition, and questioning the authority of reason can be traced back through the romantics to the Christian mystics, and to the cynics and skeptics of the Hellenistic Age. Rogers, Maslow, and the others, however, gave expression to these ideas within the context of a science, psychology, speaking with the authority of science. The humanistic psychologists' prescription for ataraxia—feeling and sharing—began to be put into practice in the modern Hellenistic Age. As the troubles of civilization mounted, ordinary life became intolerable for many; and as people had in the ancient Hellenistic world, they sought for new forms of happiness outside the accepted bounds of culture.

Humanistic psychology, a product of the modern Academy, advocated a modern form of skepticism. Maslow (1962) described the "innocent cognition" of the self-actualized person this way:

> If one expects nothing, if one has no anticipations or apprehensions, if in a sense there is no future . . . there can be no surprise, no disappointment. One thing is as likely as another to happen. . . . And no prediction means no worry, no anxiety, no apprehension, no foreboding. . . . This is all related to my conception of the creative personality as one who is totally here-now, one who lives without the future or the past. (p. 67)

Maslow here captured the recipe for ataraxia of the Hellenistic skeptics: form no generalizations, and hence be undisturbed by what happens. The humanistic self-actualizer, like the ancient skeptic, accepts what is without disturbance, "goes with the flow," and is carried without trouble down the constantly flowing stream of change of modern American life.

A much more visible manifestation of the new Hellenism were the hippies, who, like the ancient cynics, dropped out of the conventional society they scorned and rejected. Like humanistic psychologists, they were at war with their culture, distrusted reason, and valued feeling, but they carried their anti-intellectualism and contempt for manners to greater extremes, attempting to actually live lives that were Heraclitean flows of feeling, unconstrained by intellect or manners. The Hippie movement began around 1964 and quickly became a powerful cultural force, described variously as "a red warning light for the American way of life," "a quietness, an interest—something good," or "dangerously deluded dropouts" (Jones, 1967). To explore and express their feelings, hippies turned to drugs. Few had heard of Carl Rogers or Abraham Maslow, though the hippies shared their values; but they had heard of another psychologist, Timothy Leary. Leary was a young, ambitious, and successful Harvard psychologist whose personal problems drove him inward, to his feelings. He began to use drugs, at first peyote and then LSD, on himself and others, to attain the Heraclitean state of being, the "integrated process of changingness" open to new experience and intensely aware of every feeling. The hippies followed Leary into the "psychedelic," mind-expanding world, using drugs (as had Coleridge and other young romantics) to erase individual discursive consciousness (Kant's *Verstand*) and replace it with rushes of emotion, strange hallucinations, and alleged cosmic, transcendental insights (*Vernunft*). For the hippies, as for the post-Kantian idealists, the ultimate reality was mental, not physical; and they believed drugs would open the "doors of perception" to the greater, spiritual world of mind. Even without drugs, hippies and humanistic psychologists were not quite of this world. In a letter, Maslow wrote, "I live so much in my private world of Platonic essences . . . that I only appear to others to be living in the world" (Geiger, 1973).

By 1968, the revolt against traditional Western values, of which humanistic psychology was a part, was at its height. That *annus terribilis* witnessed the assassinations of Martin Luther King and Robert F. Kennedy, violent eruptions from the ghettos of every major American city, and the growing antiwar movement. Never were the words of Yeats's "Second Coming" more true: Things seemed to be falling apart, America's youth lacked all conviction—the hippies dropped out of "straight" society—or were full of passionate intensity against their parents and their nation—the Weather Underground wanted to overthrow the government with bombs and terrorism. Many citizens wondered what rough beast was slouching toward Bethlehem to be born. In its "Prairie Fire Manifesto" the Weather Underground proclaimed, "We live in a whirlwind; nonetheless, time is on the side of the guerrillas."

However, just as information-processing psychology represented no break with behavioralism, the supposed revolutionary nature of humanistic psychology was overstated. Indeed, although humanistic psychology fancied that it offered a radical critique of modern American society, it was at heart profoundly conservative, even reactionary. In his concept of self-actualization, Maslow did no more than refurbish—*tarnish* might be a better word—Aristotle's *scala naturae* with modern psychological jargon. In its cultivation of feeling and intuition, humanistic psychology harked back to the romantic rejection of the Scientific Revolution but was never honest enough to say so. Humanistic psychologists, including Maslow and Rogers, always counted themselves scientists, ignoring the deep conflict between science's commitment to natural law and determinism and their own commitment to the primacy of human purpose. Humanistic psychology is therefore a sort of fraud trading on the good name of science to push ideas entirely at variance with modern science. In the nineteenth century, Dilthey and others of the authentic romantic tradition offered reasons for setting the human sciences—the *Geisteswissenschaften*—apart from physics, chemistry, and the other *Naturwissenschaften*. Twentieth-century humanistic psychologists could only offer barely articulate protests against scientist imperialism. If a case is to be made against the natural scientific, reductionistic image of human beings, it must come from a different, more intelligent, source.

The hippies and their followers, far from providing a radical critique of "Amerika," as they were wont to spell it, embodied every contradiction of the American past. They worshiped simple, preurban lives, yet mostly lived in cities (which were more tolerant of deviance than small towns) and focused their lives on drugs and electronic music, products of the industrial world they feigned to reject. With the humanistic psychologists, they valued feelings and openness to new experience, echoing the romantic poet Blake's cry, "God save us from single vision and Newton's sleep." As humanistic psychology failed to displace behavioralism, so did the hippie movement fail to overthrow straight society. Nor were the hippies and the humanistic psychologists the great nonconformists they made themselves out to be. The hippies lived strange lives, but they demanded conformity to their nonconformism. For them, the great sin was to be "straight," to hold to the values of one's parents and one's natal culture, to work hard, to achieve, to be emotionally "closed." A song by the rock band, Crosby, Stills, Nash, and Young, depicted a member of the counterculture resisting the temptation to cut his hair. Humanistic psychologists did not shed adaptation as a virtue. Maslow (1961) described his utopia, Eupsychia, as a place where "there would be no need to hang onto the past—people would happily adapt to changing conditions." The great therapeutic breakthrough of the humanistic psychologists was the encounter group, in which people supposedly learned to be open and authentic. As Rogers describes it, members were coerced into being authentic:

> As time goes on the group finds it unbearable that any member should live behind a mask or a front. The polite words, the intellectual understanding of each other and relationships, the smooth coin of tact and cover-up . . . are just not good enough. . . . Gently at times, almost savagely at others, the group demands that the individual be himself, that his current feelings not be hidden, that he remove the mask of ordinary social intercourse. (Zilbergeld, 1983, p. 16)

Humanistic psychologists, like the hippies, did not really question the value of adaptation and social control; they just wanted to change the standards to which people had to adapt.

BIBLIOGRAPHY

For histories of humanistic psychology, see Anthony J. Sutich, "Introduction," *Journal of Humanistic Psychology* (1961, *1:* vii–ix); and Sutich and Vich (1969). There are two good collections of articles from the various facets of humanistic psychology: James F. T. Bugental, *Challenges of humanistic psychology* (New York: McGraw-Hill, 1967); and Sutich and Vich (1969). Rogers (1964) is considered by humanistic psychologists to be a representative work (Sutich and Vich, 1969). Maslow (1973) offers a varied selection of his papers.

The most accessible of Noam Chomsky's books is *Language and mind,* enlarged ed. (New York: Harcourt Brace Jovanovich, 1972).

For constraints on animal learning, see M.E.P. Seligman and J.L. Hager, eds., *Biological boundaries of learning* (New York: Appleton-Century-Crofts, 1972), who reprint the most important papers of the period and add useful commentary. Garcia discusses the troubles he had publishing his taste-aversion work in "Tilting at the papermills of academe," *American Psychologist* (1981, *36:* 149–58). The occasion of the address is ironic. It was given upon Garcia's acceptance of a prestigious APA award for his initially rejected work. A similar experience of frustration followed by fame is reported by a pair of other taste-aversion researchers, Paul Rozin and James Kalat, "This week's citation classic: Specific hungers and poison avoidance as adaptive specializations of learning," *Psychological Review* (1971, *78:* 459–86), Current Contents; Social and Behavioral Sciences (August 4, 1980, *31:* 14).

Without question, the best guide to the awareness and learning literature is W. F. Brewer, "There is no convincing evidence for operant or classical conditioning in normal, adult, human beings," in W. Weimer and D. Palermo, eds., *Cognition and the symbolic processes* (Hillsdale, NJ: Erlbaum, 1974).

Collections of the leading research in artificial intelligence and computer simulation for both ends of our period are available in E. A. Feigenbaum and J. Feldman, eds., *Computers and thought* (New York: McGraw Hill, 1963), and M. Minsky, ed., *Semantic information processing* (Cambridge, MA: MIT Press, 1968); Feigenbaum and Feldman also reprint Turing's classic paper (see Chapter 13 References). Hubert L. Dreyfus (1972) provides a history and a penetrating critique of work in AI and computer simulation. Cofer (1978) is a valuable history of the activities of the mediational behaviorists from World War II to 1962. Neisser (1967) is viewed by many psychologists as having created cognitive psychology in its modern form.

A complete autopsy of Project Camelot and the ensuing political fallout may be found in a special issue of *American Psychologist* (1966, *21,* no. 5, May). Good accounts of the maneuvering around the founding of an NSSF as opposed to including social science in the NSF are given by Carter (1966) and Greenberg (1967). The *American Psychologist* published a special issue on the Harris and Mondale bills (1967, *22,* no. 11, November). It reprints both bills, articles by their sponsors (Mondale's has the earnest but mushy and soporific qualities of his presidential campaign speeches), and the testimony given before the committees considering each bill. Digests of the testimony on the NSSF bill may be found in *Transaction* (1968, *5,* no. 1, January–February: 54–76). For the legislative histories of the bill, see the *Congressional Record* for the 90th Congress, Second Session. Mondale's bill is introduced and never heard from again. Harris's bill was discussed on the floor of the Senate, mostly by a cosponsor, Senator Ralph Yarborough, but otherwise languished in committee. Representative Emilio Daddario's bill to revise the NSF is fully discussed in an excellent but anonymously written report entered in the *Record* on pages 14889–95. Complete background on the establishment of the NSF, a legislative history of Daddario's bill, and an accounting of all the changes to NSF that the bill made are included. It is interesting to observe the support of liberal Democrats for social science. Charles G. McClintock and Charles B. Spaulding, "Political affiliation of academically affiliated psychologists," *American Psychologist* (1965, *20:* 211–21), showed that until after World War II, psychologists had voted with the rest of the public—Republican before F.D.R. and Democratic afterward—but they had, unlike the rest of the voting populace, continued to become more Democratic after the war. In the 1952 and 1956 elections, American voters as a whole had supported the liberal and rather intellectual Adlai Stevenson against Eisenhower by only 44 percent and 42 percent, but psychologists had voted for Stevenson by margins of 63 percent and 68 percent. In 1960, a bare majority of voters voted for John Kennedy, while 79 percent of psychologists did so. Psychologists, like their supporters in the Senate, were more liberal than the country as a whole, and social scientists benefited greatly from the rise of political liberalism from 1965 to 1980.

In 1963, *American Psychologist* (*18*) devoted two special issues to the problems of clinical psychology: no. 6, June, and no. 9, September. Alarm over Martin Gross's *The brain watchers* is found in various "Comments" in the no. 8, August, issue of the same year. Political controversies over the use and abuse of tests led to a special issue devoted to "Testing and public policy" (1965, *20,* no. 11, November). The whole fuss was humorously captured by satirist Art Buchwald in a column published in the *Washington Post* (Sunday, June 20, 1965), in which he made up his own personality test. Since 1965, Buchwald's test has been widely circulated among psychologists, many of whom are ignorant of its origin.

Szasz's views were first presented in his book (1960a) and have been elaborated in many books and articles since. Although Ryle's *Concept of mind* is in Szasz's bibliography, he does not in fact derive his own argument from Ryle; nevertheless, the affinity of the two analyses is clear. For a contemporary "straight" view of the hippie movement, see Jones (1967). The movement is best appreciated through its art and music, of which the more lasting has proved to be the music. The Grateful Dead and Jefferson Airplane in particular made records that are still likely to be accessible. Also illuminating is the New Journalism that came out of and at first depended on the movement. My own favorites are Tom Wolfe's *The electric Kool-Aid acid test* (New York: Bantam, 1968) and anything by Hunter S. Thompson, but most relevantly, *Fear and loathing in Las Vegas: A savage journey into the heart of the American dream* (New York: Popular Library, 1971). Wolfe's book is especially interesting in the present context; it centered on the quintessential hippie group, the Merry Pranksters of Ken Kesey, author of a brilliant antipsychiatric novel, *One flew over the cuckoo's nest* (New York: New American Library, 1963). Wolfe became the outstanding observer of the new psychological Hellenistic Age.

For a more detailed argument that no cognitive revolution took place, see T. H. Leahey, "Mythical revolutions in the history of American psychology," *American Psychologist* (1992, *47:* 308–18).

REFERENCES

Achinstein, P., and Barker, S. F., eds., (1969). *The legacy of logical positivism.* Baltimore: Johns Hopkins University Press.

Blank, L. and David, H. (1963). The crisis in clinical psychology training. *American Psychologist 18:* 216–19.

Breger, L. and McGaugh, J. L. (1965). Critique and reformulation of "learning-theory" approaches to psychotherapy and neurosis. *Psychological Bulletin 63:* 338–58.

Breland, K. and Breland, M. (1961/1972). The misbehavior of organisms. *American Psychologist 16:* 681–84. Reprinted in M.E.P. Seligman and J.L. Hager, eds., *Biological boundaries of learnings.* New York: Appleton-Century-Crofts, 1972.

Bugental, J. F. T. (1964). The third force in psychology. *Journal of Humanistic Psychology 4:* 19–26.

Carter, L. J. (1966). Social sciences: Where do they fit in the politics of science? *Science 154:* 488–91.

Chein, I. (1966). Some sources of divisiveness among psychologists. *American Psychologist 21:* 333–42.

Chomsky, N. (1957). *Syntactic structures.* The Hague, The Netherlands: Mouton.

———. (1959/1967). Review of B. F. Skinner's *Verbal behavior. Language 35:* 26–58. Reprinted in L. Jakobovits and M. Miron, eds., *Readings in the psychology of language.* Englewood Cliffs, NJ: Prentice-Hall.

———. (1965). *Aspects of the theory of syntax.* Cambridge, MA: MIT Press.

———. (1966). *Cartesian linguistics.* New York: Harper & Row.

Clark, K. (1967). The scientific and professional aims of psychology. *American Psychologist 22:* 49–76.

Cofer, C. N. (1978). Origins of the *Journal of Verbal Learning and Verbal Behavior. Journal of Verbal Learning and Verbal Behavior 17:* 113–26.

Davis, G. (1966). Current status of research and theory in human problem solving. *Psychological Bulletin 66:* 36–54.

Dixon, T. R. and Horton, D. C., eds. (1968). *Verbal behavior and general behavior theory.* Englewood Cliffs, NJ: Prentice-Hall.

Dreyfus, H. L. (1972). *What computers can't do: A critique of artificial reason.* New York: Harper & Row.

Dulany, D. E. (1968). Awareness, rules, and propositional control: A confrontation with S–R behavior theory. In T. R. Dixon and D. C. Horton, eds., *Verbal behavior and general behavior theory.* Englewood Cliffs, NJ: Prentice-Hall.

Estes, W. K. and Newell A. (Co-chairs) (1983). Report of the Research Briefing Panel on cognitive Science and Artificial Intelligence. In *Research Briefings 1983.* Washington, DC: National Academy Press.

Garcia, J., McGowan, B. K., and Green, K. F, (1972). Constraints on conditioning. In M. E. P. Seligman, and J. L. Hager, eds., *Biological boundaries of learning.* New York: Appleton-Century-Crofts.

Garfield, S. L. (1966). Clinical psychology and the search for identity. *American Psychologist 21:* 343–52.

Geiger, H. (1973). Introduction: A. H. Maslow. In *A. Maslow, The farther reaches of human nature.* New York: Vikins/Esalen.

Gough, P. B. and Jenkins, J. J. (1963). Verbal learning and psycholinguistics. In M. Mary, ed., *Theories in contemporary psychology.* New York: Macmillan.

Greenberg, D. S. (1967). Social sciences: Progress slow on House and Senate bills. *Science 157:* 660–62.

Greenspoon, J. (1955). The reinforcing effect of two spoken sounds on the frequency of two behaviors. *American Journal of Psychology 68:* 409–16.

Hebb, D. O. (1960). The second American Revolution. *American Psychologist 15:* 735–45.

Hoch, E., Ross, A. O., and Winder, C. L. (1966). Conference on the professional preparation of clinical psychologists. *American Psychologist 21:* 42–51.

Holt, R. R. (1964). Imagery: The return of the ostracized. *American Psychologist 19:* 254–64.

Jakobovits, L. and Miron, M., eds. (1967). *Readings in the psychology of language.* Englewood Cliffs, NJ: Prentice-Hall.

Jenkins, J. J. (1968). The challenge to psychological theorists. In T. R. Dixon and D. C. Horton, eds., *Verbal behavior and general behavior theory.* Englewood Cliffs, NJ: Prentice-Hall.

Jones, R. (1967, July 7). Youth: The hippies. *Time,* 18–22.

Lachman, R., Lachman, J., and Butterfield, E. (1979). *Cognitive psychology and information processing.* Hillsdale, NJ: Erlbaum.

Malcolm, N. (1964). Behaviorism as a philosophy of psychology. In T. W. Wann, ed., *Behaviorism and phenomenology: Contrasting bases for modern psychology.* Chicago: University of Chicago Press.

Maslow, A. (1961). Eupsychia—The good society. *Journal of Humanistic Psychology 1:* 1–11.

———. (1962). Notes on being-psychology. *Journal of Humanistic Psychology 2:* 47–71

———. (1967). Self-actualization and beyond. In J. F. T. Bugental, ed., *Challenges of humanistic psychology.* New York: McGraw-Hill.

———. (1973). *The farther reaches of human nature.* New York: Viking/Esalen.

Miller, G. (1962). Some psychological studies of grammar. *American Psychologist 17:* 748–62. Reprinted in L. Jakobovits and M. Miron, eds., *Readings in the psychology of language.* Englewood Cliffs, NJ: Prentice-Hall.

Neisser, U. (1967). *Cognitive psychology.* New York: Appleton-Century-Crofts.

Penn, I. N. (1985, June 24). The reality of mental illness (letter to the editor). *The Wall Street Journal,* 33.

Postman, L. and Sassenrath, J. (1961). The automatic action of verbal rewards and punishments. *Journal of General Psychology 65:* 109–36.

Putney, S. and Putney, G. J. (1964). *The adjusted American: Normal neuroses in the individual and society.* New York: Harper Colophon.

Pylyshyn, Z. W. (1984). *Computation and cognition: Toward a foundation for cognitive science.* Cambridge, MA: MIT Press.

Rogers, C. R. (1958). A process conception of psychotherapy. *American Psychologist 13:* 142–9.

_____ . (1964). Toward a science of the person. In T. W. Wann, ed., *Behaviorism and phenomenology: Contrasting bases for modern psychology.* Chicago: University of Chicago Press.

_____ . (1968). Interpersonal relationships: U.S.A. 2000. *Journal of Applied Behavioral Science 4:* 265–80.

Rogers, C. R. and Skinner, B. F. (1956). Some issues concerning the control of human behavior: A symposium. *Science 124:* 1057–65.

Sanford, N. (1965). Will psychologists study human problems? *American Psychologist 20:* 192–98.

Schofield, W. (1966). Clinical and counseling psychology: Some perspectives. *American Psychologist 21:* 122–31.

Shakow, D. (1965). Seventeen years later: Clinical psychology in the light of the 1947 Committee on Training in Clinical Psychology Report. *American Psychologist 20:* 353–67.

Shiffrin, R. M. (1977). Commentary on "Human memory: A proposed system and its control processes." In G. Bower, ed., *Human memory: Basic processes.* New York: Academic Press.

Simon, H. (1969). *The sciences of the artificial.* Cambridge, MA: MIT Press.

_____ . (1980). The social and behavioral sciences. *Science 209:* 72–8.

Skinner, B. F. (1959). A case history in scientific method. In S. Koch, ed., *Psychology: Study of a science.* New York: McGraw-Hill.

Small, L. (1963). Toward professional clinical psychology. *American Psychologist 18:* 558–62.

Sutich, A. J. and Vich, M. A. (1969). Introduction. In A. J. Sutich and M. A. Vich, eds., *Readings in humanistic psychology.* New York: Free Press.

Szasz, T. S. (1960a). *The myth of mental illness.* New York: Harper Perennial Library. Rev. ed. 1974.

_____ . (1960b). The myth of mental illness. *American Psychologist 15:* 113–19.

Taylor, D. W. (1963). Thinking. In M. Marx, ed., *Theories in contemporary psychology.* New York: Macmillan.

Thumin, F. J. and Zebelman, M. (1967). Psychology and psychiatry: A study of public image. *American Psychologist 22:* 282–6.

Tryon, R. C. (1963). Psychology in flux: The academic-professional bipolarity. *American Psychologist 18:* 134–43.

Wolfle, D. (1966). Social problems and social science. *Science 151:* 1177.

Zilbergeld, B. (1983). *The shrinking of America: Myths of psychological change.* Boston: Little, Brown.

15 *Contemporary Psychology*

The Plaza d'Italia in New Orleans. Psychology was born in the era historians call modernism, the heir to the Enlightenment, in which reason and science held sway, and architecture was austere and pure, continuing a tradition traceable to the ancient Greeks. The Plaza d'Italia, however, is a product of Postmodernism, a playful pastiche of past styles. Some think the Modern Age is past, that we are on the threshold of an imperfectly grasped Postmodern Age, less rational and scientific, less ambitious, more ironic and uncertain. Can psychology, a science born of modernism, survive?

COGNITIVE SCIENCE

Doubts about Cognitive Science

When Herbert Simon, in 1957, prophesied that by 1967 psychological theories would be written as computer programs, he also foresaw that "within ten years a digital computer will be the world's chess champion" and that "within ten years a digital computer will discover and prove an important new mathematical theorem." In 1965, Simon predicted that "machines will be capable, within 20 years, of doing any work that a man can do" (Dreyfus, 1972). By 1995, Simon's forecasts had not come to pass. More important, some psychologists and philosophers had begun to wonder whether they could ever come to pass. The issue is not Simon's credibility as a prophet—others in artificial intelligence made similar claims (Dreyfus, 1972)—but the credibility of the information-processing, computational approach to psychology. If it should turn out that computers in principle cannot do "any work that a man can do," then treating people as computers would be bad psychological theory.

One of the deepest—and most controversial—challenges to the computer model of the human mind comes from a thought experiment proposed by the philosopher John Searle (1980). Imagine that you are seated at a table in an empty room. On the table before you are a book and a supply of paper, and in the wall in front of the table are two slots. Out of the left-hand slot come pieces of paper on which are written Chinese characters. You know nothing about Chinese. When you receive a slip of paper, you examine the string of symbols on it and find the corresponding string in the book. The book tells you to copy out a new set of Chinese figures on one of your pieces of paper and pass it out the right-hand slot. You can do this for any string of characters that comes in the left slot. Unknown to you, Chinese psychologists on the other side of the wall are feeding into the left slot Chinese stories followed by questions about the stories, and they receive answers out of the other slot. From their point of view, the "machine" beyond the wall understands Chinese, because they are able to carry on a conversation with the machine, receiving plausible answers to their questions. They conclude that the machine beyond the wall understands Chinese and has passed the Turing test.

You know that you understand nothing—you are just writing down one set of meaningless squiggles by instructed response to another set of meaningless squiggles. John Searle, whose thought experiment this is, points out that you are functioning in the "Chinese Room" exactly as a computer functions. The computer accepts machine code input (patterns of 0s and 1s), applies syntactic rules to transform these representations into new representations (new patterns of 0s and 1s), and generates output. It is the computer user alone who calls what the computer is doing "understanding stories," "playing chess," "simulating an atomic strike," or whatever, just as it is the Chinese psychologists who say that the machine beyond the wall "understands Chinese." Searle's argument shows that the Turing test is not an adequate measure of intelligence. The Chinese Room passes the Turing test without understanding anything, and its mode of operation is exactly the same as a computer's.

Searle goes on to point out an important peculiarity about cognitive simulation compared to other kinds of simulation. Meteorologists construct computer simulations of hurricanes; economists, of U.S. foreign trade activity; and biologists, of photosynthesis. But their computers do not develop 100-mph winds, create multibillion-dollar trade deficits, or convert light into oxygen. Yet cognitive scientists claim that when and if they simulate intelligence—that is, create a program that passes the Turing test— their machine will really *be* intelligent. In other fields, simulation and real achievement are kept separate, and Searle regards it as absurd to ignore the distinction in cognitive science.

Searle distinguishes between weak artificial intelligence (AI) and strong AI. Weak AI is maintaining the distinction between simulation and achievement, and using computers as other scientists do—as wonderfully convenient calculating devices with which to use and check theories. Strong AI is the claim (refuted by the Chinese Room thought experiment) that simulation of intelligence *is* intelligence. Searle believes that strong AI can never succeed, for the same reason that a computer cannot perform photosynthesis: It's made out of the wrong materials. In Searle's view, it is the natural biological function of certain plant structures to photosynthesize, and it is the natural biological function of brains to think and understand. Machines have no natural biological functions and so can neither photo-synthesize nor understand. Computers may provide tools to help investigate photosynthesis and understanding, but they cannot, Searle concludes, ever actually do either one. Unhappiness with the symbol-system approach to psychology and to artificial intelligence has led to the creation of an alternative approach to both that has gained many followers.

The New Connectionism

For all the doubts and difficulties of the symbol-manipulation paradigm in cognitive science, it remained for two decades "the only game in town," as philosopher Jerry Fodor liked to put it. If thinking wasn't the manipulation of formal symbols following formal rules, what else could it be? Because there was no answer to this question (except from ghettoized Skinnerians and a few other marginalized dissidents), cognitive psychologists remained, perforce, in the information-processing camp. However, in the early 1980s, a rival game set up shop under the name "connectionism," recalling to us (but not to connectionists themselves) the older connectionism of E. L. Thorndike.

A measure of the impact and importance of connectionism was the reception accorded the publication in 1986 of a two-volume exposition of its views and achievements, *Parallel Distributed Processing: Explorations in the Microstructure of Cognition*. The senior author and leader of the PDP (for parallel distributed processing, another name for connectionism) Research Group was David E. Rumelhart, formerly one of the leaders of symbolic paradigm AI. These volumes sold six thousand copies the day they went on the market (Dreyfus and Dreyfus, 1988). Six thousand copies may not sound like much, but in the academic world, where five hundred copies is a respectable sale for a technical book, it's enormous. Shortly afterward, Rumelhart won a MacArthur Foundation "genius grant." Connectionism was soon being hailed as the "new wave" in cognitive psychology (Fodor and Pylyshyn, 1988).

In important respects, connectionism represents the resuscitation of traditions in both psychology and AI that seemed long dead. In psychology, there is a connectionist tradition running from Thorndike to Hull and neo-Hullian mediational theorists (Leahey, 1990). All of them banished symbols and mentalistic concepts from their theories and attempted to explain behavior in terms of the strengthening or weakening of connections between stimuli and responses: This was the central idea of Thorndike's Law of Effect and his and Hull's habit family hierarchies. Mediational psychologists introduced internal processing to Hull's connectionistic ideas by inserting covert connections—the little r-s connections—between external stimulus and overt response.

In AI, connectionism revives a minority tradition in computer science that competed with the symbol manipulation paradigm in the 1950s and 1960s. The symbol manipulation computer architecture is designed around a single complex processing unit performing one computation at a time. Traditional computers gain their power from the ability of CPUs to perform sequential computations at enormous speeds. From the beginnings of computer science, however, there has always existed a rival architecture built around simple multiple processors all hooked up together. With multiple processors working at once, sequential processing of information is replaced by parallel processing. Sequential architecture machines must be programmed to behave, and this is also true for many parallel processing machines. However, some designers of parallel processing computers hoped to build machines that could learn to act intelligently on their own by adjusting the strengths of the connections between their multiple processors depending on feedback from the environment.

Parallel processing computers are potentially much more powerful than single CPU machines, but, for a long time, obstacles stood in the way of constructing them. Parallel machines are more physically complex than sequential machines, and they are vastly more difficult to program, for one must somehow coordinate the work of the multiple processors in order to avoid chaos. With regard to self-programming machines, there is the special difficulty of figuring out how to get feedback information about the results of behavior to interior ("hidden") units lying between input and output units. Because sequential machines were great successes very early on, and the potential power of the parallel architecture seemed unnecessary, work on parallel processing computers virtually ceased in the 1960s. The funeral of early connectionist AI seemed to come in 1969 when Marvin Minsky and Seymour Papert, leaders of the symbolic AI school, published *Perceptrons,* a devastating critique of existing parallel mental models.

In the 1980s, however, developments in both computer science and psychology converged to revive the fortunes of parallel processing architectures. Although serial processors continued to gain speed, designers were pushing up against the limits of how fast electrons could move through silicon. At the same time, computer scientists were tackling jobs demanding ever greater computing speed, making a change to parallel processing desirable. For example, consider the problem of computer vision, which must be solved if household robots are to be built. Imagine a computer graphic made up of 256×256 pixels (dots of light on a TV screen or computer monitor). For a serial computer to recognize such an image, it would have to compute, one at a time, the value of $256 \times 256 = 65,536$ pixels. In contrast, The Connection Machine®, a parallel processing computer containing 256×256 interconnected processors, can assign one to compute the value of a single pixel and so can process the graphic in a tiny fraction of a second (Hillis, 1987). Along with developments in hardware such as The Connection Machine came developments in programming and self-learning that make parallel processing more feasible (Tank and Hopfield, 1987).

In psychology, continued failings of the symbolic paradigm made parallel, connectionist processing an attractive alternative to the old game. In addition to the difficulties with functionalism that we have already discussed, two issues were especially important for the new connectionists. First, traditional AI, although it had made advances on tasks humans find intellectually taxing, such as chess playing, was persistently unable to get machines to perform the sorts of tasks that people do without the least thought, such as recognizing patterns. Perhaps most important to psychologists, the behavior that they had most intensively studied for decades, learning, remained beyond the reach of programmed computers, and the development of parallel machines that could actually learn was quite exciting.

The other shortcoming of symbolic AI that motivated the new connectionists was the plain fact that the brain is not a sequential computing device. If we regard neurons as small processors, then it is obvious that the brain is much more like The Connection Machine than like a PC or an Apple. The brain contains thousands of massively interconnected neurons, all of which are working at the same time. As Rumelhart and the PDP group announced in their book, they aimed to replace the computer model in psychology with the brain model. The interconnected processors of connectionist models function like neurons: Each one is activated by input and then "fires," or produces output, depending on the summed strengths of its input. Assembled properly, such a network will learn to respond in stable ways to different inputs just as organisms do: Neural nets, as such processor assemblages are often called, learn.

At present, connectionist theory is too new to be described in detail or evaluated fairly. But we can address what some observers regard as the deepest issue raised by connectionism: the role of rules in explaining human behavior (Dreyfus and Dreyfus, 1988; Smolensky, 1988). Since the time of Newton, central to scientific explanation has been the positing of laws—rules—that govern the workings of nature. But the notion of rule-governed behavior is ambiguous. Newton's law of gravity precisely describes a force that governs the motions of objects in space. However, the objects governed by gravity do not use Newton's law to calculate their movements. The moon is governed by the Law of Gravity, but it does not follow the Law of Gravity. Computers, like the moon, are governed by the rules in their programs, because their behavior is controlled by the rules the way gravity controls the moon. However, unlike the moon, computers also follow the rules of their programs, since they do use them to calculate their output. If the symbol system approach is correct, then people, like computers, are both rule governed and rule following. Connectionists, however, doubt that humans follow rules, even though our behavior may be described as rule governed.

Consider the following simple example. If I show you a drawing of an unfamiliar animal and tell you it's a "wug," and then show you a picture of two of them, I know you'll say without instruction that there are now two "wugs." Your behavior is consistent with—can be described by—the grammatical rule that, in English, plurals are formed by adding /s/. But did you follow the rule consciously? If not, did you follow it unconsciously? In this case, you might be tempted to say that you learned the rule consciously as a child, and have now applied it unconsciously as an adult. To throw doubt on this hypothesis, consider that you pronounced "wugs" as "wugz." If I had told you the animal was a "wuk," you would have said two of them were "wuks," pronouncing the final /s/ hissingly. In this case, your behavior would be consistent with the phonological English rule to say final /s/ unvoiced following unvoiced consonants and voiced (that is, as /z/) following voiced consonants. But it is unlikely that you were ever taught this rule or used it consciously even in childhood. Your pronunciation is governed by the rule, but you may not have followed it.

The assumption of traditional cognitive science has been that people are like serial processing computers: We learn and then apply rules, at first consciously and then unconsciously. Like the old S–R models, connectionist neural networks, however, do not apply rules to representations: they just modify excitation strengths between their units in accord with feedback about their behavior from the environment. If connectionists are right, the symbol-system information-processing model of the mind is incorrect.

THE STRANGE DEATH OF RADICAL BEHAVIORISM

It is true that radical behaviorism has been somewhat ghettoized, but it would be false to assert, as many have, that it is dead. The radical behaviorists' ghetto is lively indeed. They have their own successful journals, their own division within the APA (Division 25), and their own society, the Association for Behavior Analysis. Radical behaviorists continue to pursue their own research, to develop the conceptual foundations of their discipline, to grapple with cognitive science, and to offer proposals for remaking society.

Beyond Freedom and Dignity

In *Walden II* and *Science and Human Behavior,* Skinner first described his ideal society and its rationale. Against the backdrop of the 1960s, Skinner returned to the problems of society, and again offered radical behaviorism and its technology of behavior as cures for the ills of the modern world. During the 1970s and 1980s, Skinner became preoccupied with spreading his social message, expounded in his book *Beyond Freedom and Dignity* (1972). Skinner argued that it is a great mistake to assume, as everyone does, that people possess free will, and hence moral responsibility and dignity; most psychologists assume, as Skinner did, that humans are not free—after all, cognitive scientists think humans are machines—but few of them talk about (at least in public, as Skinner did) the ethical consequences of determinism. Nor was Skinner depressed by determinism, because he found in the technology of behavior ways to improve human life, and he attacked those who stand in the way of that technology's use.

The consequences of a rigorous determinism for understanding human nature are profound. In general, our own experience and the teachings of our culture tell us there is free will, although from time to time philosophers such as Spinoza have argued otherwise. It appears that one chooses to lift one's arm, that one chooses a profession, that one chooses for whom to vote. To accept a rigorous determinism and apply it to one's own behavior is extremely difficult, requiring the overthrow of a lifetime's habits of thought. Yet such a revolution is required when radical behaviorists ask that we give up the traditional notions of freedom and dignity.

As early as his first paper, Skinner (1931) wrote of the "preconceptions of freedom" that hinder the scientific understanding of behavior. Skinner assumed that all behavior is determined and, consequently, a notion such as freedom is nonsense. In his view, a desire for freedom is always a response to punishment. Skinner drew an important distinction between positive reinforcement and punishment. Positive reinforcement effectively controls behavior without undesirable consequences, because it lets one do essentially what one wants. Punishment, on the other hand, is generally ineffective and produces unfortunate side effects, because organisms, human and otherwise, react emotionally to punishment. Organisms seek to avoid—that is, to be free from—punishment but do not avoid positive reinforcement, which is by definition desirable. Historically, governments have tried to control behavior through punishment. One is told what not to do, not what to do. As an emotional reaction to punishment, a "literature of freedom" has grown up demanding freedom from punishment, but it has also fostered a belief in freedom as a characteristic of life, a false belief according to the scientific assumption of determinism. Now that the early aims of the literature of freedom have been attained in constitutions and so forth, the illusory notion of freedom stands in the way of further progress, for it resists the control of behavior by positive reinforcement as well as by punishment.

Skinner argued that if humanistic goals, the goals of human happiness, are to be reached, it will be done only by controlling behavior through positive reinforcement, for scientific control is more efficient than the haphazard control exerted by the current social environment. It is important to remember again that Skinner assumed all behavior is always completely determined, that there is never freedom of choice.

Therefore, Skinnerians propose that we substitute deliberate, systematic control for inefficient control. If the goal is happiness, it will be reached faster if we apply methodical control, and this cannot be done without first abandoning belief in freedom, which prohibits such control.

The concept of dignity, Skinner argued, depends on belief in free will. We believe that one deserves praise for freely chosen good acts and deserves blame for freely chosen wrong acts. However, Skinner, like Spinoza, argued that praise and blame are equally irrational, because all behavior is determined—for Skinner, by the contingencies of reinforcement, not by an individual's free will. We do not blame the rain for getting us wet or praise the sun for warming our skin (although ancient religions did); we accept each as a natural occurrence beyond the will of any person. Skinner asked us to view human behavior as we view other natural phenomena, not religiously, but scientifically, recalling Watson's linkage of religion and mentalism. The poet is not to be praised for "having a poem," for the poet is merely the site at which external variables operate. A criminal is not to be blamed for "having a crime," for the criminal, too, is a locus of variables that converge on an act society condemns. Desirable behaviors should be strengthened by positive reinforcement, and undesirable behaviors will not be learned, at least in a properly engineered society such as Walden II. Both freedom and dignity are outmoded concepts, Skinner concluded; they are inconsistent with scientific determinism and therefore stand in the way of an effective control of human behavior.

To what end are we to be controlled? The Skinnerian answer is Darwinian. A culture is an experiment in survival, just as a species is an experiment in survival. The ultimate biological value is survival, for the "good" species is the one that survives. Similarly, the "good" society will be the one that survives. Skinner argued that the chances our society will survive will be greatly enhanced should it adopt the methods of the experimental analysis of behavior in pursuit of life, liberty, and happiness. The technology of behavior must be used, say radical behaviorists, if humanity is to survive. The old mentalistic scheme of freedom and dignity is outmoded and must be replaced by his science of behavior.

Skinner's thought stands clearly in the tradition of those who would improve humans by improving their environment. He felt an affinity for Jean-Jacques Rousseau, who, although he believed humans are free, located their faults in the environment: "Man is born free but he is everywhere in chains." In *Emile,* Rousseau proposed that a teacher's student will be happiest if the student feels free but is kept under the teacher's subtle control. Skinner's Walden II was a Rousseauian utopia. Control is benign and hidden, so feelings of freedom and dignity remain, even though they have no referents beyond those feelings.

Skinner was, finally, a humanist in the tradition of the Sophists. Science exists to serve human happiness, not such transcendent Platonic ends as Reason and Truth. For Skinner, the human being, at least as scientifically understood, is the measure of all things. Reason and logic are arbitrary verbal behaviors whose truth lies only in the contingencies of reinforcement, not in a realm of ideas. Freedom and dignity are verbal operants, not linguistic expressions of enduring values. The crisis Skinner set for the modern person is the crisis set for ancient Greeks by the Sophists, and for eighteenth-century Europeans by the Marquis de Sade. Is there anything of value in human affairs beyond feelings, if freedom and dignity mean nothing else? To what can we cling if all tradition is thrown into doubt, if the old center cannot hold? Skinner answers: "The experimental analysis of behavior." He says, "I am all for feelings of causal adequacy as I am for feelings of freedom and dignity. I want people to be adequate, unhampered, successful, and aware of the fact that they are so, and I have suggested ways in which that may be brought about—by changing their environment" (1984a, p. 507).

Critique of Cognitive Science

Skinner, of course, was critical of theories referring to unobserved internal states that cause behavior. Skinner always scorned cognitive science as a "magical term" (1984a) whose popularity "is largely due to the freedom to use a lay vocabulary, not the discovery of an alternative science of comparable rigor to the experimental analysis of behavior" (1984b).

Skinner accused cognitive science of reviving and resting on two (to him) obnoxious doctrines: the copy theory of perception—cognitive science's central concept of mental representations; and the commonsense idea that mental states cause behavior—the concept of the inner person. Against representations, Skinner reasserted his familiar perceptual realism: "What is seen is [a] presentation, not a representation" of an object. Skinner went on to reject the idea that representations are "stored" in a "memory" from which they are "retrieved." Skinner (1985) said these notions depend on a misleading analogy to physical records:

> When physical records are stored, the records continue to exist until they are retrieved, but is that true when people "process information"? A storage battery would be a better model of a behaving organism. We put electricity into a battery and take it out when needed, but there is no electricity in the battery. When we "put electricity in," we change the battery, and it is a changed battery that "puts out electricity" when tapped. Organisms do not acquire behavior as a kind of possession; they simply come to behave in various ways. The behavior is not in them at any time. (pp. 294–5)

Skinner here in his own way stated a criticism of information-processing theory that we have met before: Exactly where does information processing take place? We observe and respond to the environment, we have sensations and thoughts in consciousness, and neuroscientists will one day be able to observe the brain processes behind thought and behavior; but the information-processing psychologists have invented a fictitious level of discourse between consciousness and the brain. If there are no representations, and no storage and retrieval of representations, then there is no information processing and no inner person making decisions on the basis of stored representations. Skinner (1984b) simply denied the validity of the human-computer analogy: "Information processing was devised for, and is useful for formulating, systems which are not analogous to the human organism."

CHALLENGES TO SCIENTIFIC PSYCHOLOGY

From Psychology's Occult Doubles

One of psychology's leaders in the first decades of the twentieth century, Joseph Jastrow, was annoyed by being constantly asked about psychic phenomena, and by the implicit confusion between psychology and psychical research. Today, psychologists are still embarrassed by their links to "occult" disciplines and marginal sciences. Part of the embarrassment stems from psychology's social success. People today look to psychology for advice on all sorts of personal and social problems, so that some practitioners of occult crafts have come to cast their work in a psychological mold. Astrology, for example, is often defended as a means of reading character and a source of advice in love and business, rather than as a prophetic science, its original claim. The clichéd opening line "What's your sign?" is based on the notion that people born under certain signs have certain personalities and will get along well or ill with those born under certain other signs. There is nothing to the claim, but there is a strong parallel to psychological tests that purport to reveal character and suggest interpersonal strategies. In supermarket tabloids and TV ads, psychic "advisors" tout themselves as counselors on relationships, money, and business—subjects shared with professional psychologists.

Experimental psychologists, too, have their occult doubles in the field of psychical research, whose newer name, *parapsychology,* helps tie the fields together in the public mind. Like experimental psychologists, parapsychologists have their own journals and associations. Their work sometimes appears on the program of APA meetings under the auspices of the Division of Humanistic Psychology, and parapsychologists are active in the new transpersonal psychology movement, which bills itself as a "fourth force" in psychology, going beyond humanism to a more cosmic, transcendental psychology.

Mainstream psychologists have a problem differentiating themselves from what they regard as pseudosciences without seeming dogmatically intolerant. Scientifically minded psychologists—not only experimentalists but the vast majority of professional psychologists—try to separate themselves from pseudoscience on formal methodological grounds. The APA has refused to create a Division of Transpersonal Psychology, despite petitions to the APA Council to do so. However, as we saw in Chapter 1, formal "demarcation criteria" do not work very well. The rejection of parapsychology and, *a fortiori,* spiritualism and astrology, rests on their violation of the substantive content of science, not violation of its methods. Parapsychologists do follow the methodological canons of science. They conduct carefully controlled research, they use statistics, they are on the watch for fraud, they replicate their studies more than mainstream psychologists do, and they are outraged when such hard work fails to gain them recognition as scientists.

Occult science has failed to gain scientific recognition because it does not fit in with the content of science. To begin with, psychologists have a hard enough time explaining how people understand natural language, so they get annoyed when parapsychologists badger them about telepathy and clairvoyance. It might turn out in the future that the parapsychologists were on to something, but scientific research is an orderly process focused on current problems, not speculative possibilities. An instructive parallel occurred in the flurry of interest a few years ago in the claim by a science journalist that a human being had been cloned. Biologists dismissed the assertion as wild and ludicrous—not because a human could not in principle be cloned, but rather because it was absurd to attempt it now, and they regarded anyone trying for a human clone as a crank. Method will not save your reputation if your topic of research does not come within the boundaries currently accepted by science.

The real problem with parapsychology is that it violates the oldest and deepest of science's substantive commitments, the commitment to naturalism, to explain happenings in the universe in natural terms. The founders of psychical research and parapsychology were frank in challenging naturalism by hoping to turn the scientific method against scientific content. They hoped to prove with statistics and experiment that spiritual powers and spiritual life existed, that life continued after death. But science in the twentieth century is firmly committed to naturalism and materialism. Naturalism is science's central dogma, without which it could not function, and anyone who challenges this dogma has little hope of gaining a hearing from science.

Some parapsychologists have attempted to steer around these objections by dropping the quasi-religious claims that animated the psychical researchers and by adopting up-to-date scientific vocabulary. Thus, some parapsychologists try to explain psychical wonders in the Alice-in-Wonderland terms of modern quantum physics, and others cast their research and theories in information-processing terms. Their attempt to finally naturalize the supernatural seems to have little chance of success, but it is instructive to ask what would happen if they did succeed. Parapsychology might gain the ear of science, but it would very likely lose the ear of the public. Science has been accepted by many as a substitute religion, but most still want religion, even under the parapsychological guise of science. In a world where religion falls back on "creationist science" to defend faith, which is by definition unscientific, all the borderlines are fuzzy indeed.

Ordinary people do not go to spiritualistic séances, write to psychic advisers, and read astrology books to learn about information-processing mechanisms and ESP (Tart, 1978). They want some sense of how to live their lives. Many people today agree with Frederic Myers, that the Old World sustenance of traditional religion fails to sustain faith in the age of science—the age of nuclear war, the space shuttle, and the ironies of doctors heroically struggling to perform in utero surgery on one fetus only to abort another of the same age. Science has accomplished so much it seems natural to turn to it for answers to ancient moral and religious questions. But it cannot give them. Science gives us the techniques to diagnose fetal abnormalities, and even ways to operate on some of them before the baby is born; it gives us ways to abort fetuses early and late. But it is helpless to tell us which choice to make, to tell us when the fetus becomes a human being, to decide between right and wrong.

Psychology, more than any science, occupies treacherous ground between *is* and *ought*. Physical science reveals the workings of impersonal nature; and although nature can harm and benefit humankind, we would be unreasonable to ask that natural laws also tell us how to use them. Yet psychology, the science of human behavior, purports to reveal the springs of human action; consequently, it seems on the surface not unreasonable to ask psychology how to act, how to make sense of our lives. Psychology writers from Aristotle to Bentham to Skinner have moved from science to morality, pretending to describe the perfect, scientifically engineered community and to prescribe the laws of the land as dictated by human nature. But this urge to ask a science for moral guidance is not legitimate. Operant psychology may help me control my child's behavior, but it cannot tell me how my child should behave. Cognitive psychology may help me construct lessons that my students remember, but it cannot tell me what my students should learn. Science deals with facts, not morals.

Occult psychology—parapsychology, spiritualism, astrology—is a clear manifestation of the confusion of science and values. Each occult system takes on the trappings of science in order to borrow its authority, and then uses that authority to promote various moral and religious values. Practitioners of occult psychology have not been loath to satisfy humankind's spiritual needs. Practitioners of mainstream psychology, however much they try to distance themselves from their occult doubles, have also not been loath to prescribe to troubled humans: in clinical and counseling practices, in industrial psychology, in advertising psychology. We see, then, that psychology, whether mainstream or occult, has been used to meet human needs that science cannot meet. People need to know how they ought to act—they need ethics and morality. People need to find meaning in their lives—they need a form of life, a structure within which to live. Science can meet neither need, and the deepest fraud of psychology's occult doubles is pretending that science can do so. Mainstream psychology itself sits awkwardly astride science and morality. Psychology calls itself a science, yet, with its occult neighbors, it is tempted to become a new religion (Albee, 1977a). Psychological science, like any science, may encompass means, but it can never encompass ends.

From Biology

Depression is the most common psychological disorder of our time (Klerman, 1979). It has long been treated by psychotherapy, but it now seems likely that long-term, nonsituational depression, called endogenous depression, is caused by deficiencies of certain neurotransmitters in the brain (Snyder, 1980), not by early childhood experiences or any other psychological cause. People who suffer from endogenous depression can be effectively treated with antidepressant drugs; after a few weeks, they stop feeling depressed. Therefore, it may be true that "much of the by now entrenched psychodynamic theory is irrelevant or misleading," that treating biological depression psychologically is "tragic . . . since a large fraction of the 30,000 suicides a year in the United States are probably committed by people with [endogenous] depressions" (Wender and Klein, 1981). Faced with this challenge to their practice, clinical psychologists respond by asserting that psychotherapy may nevertheless be useful in helping depressives (and others with biochemical disorders), even if they are also treated with drugs (Peele, 1981). Nevertheless, a challenge remains: A psychological state, depression, has been shown to have a biological cause. A piece of psychology has been reduced to biology. Perhaps psychology will be "cannibalized" by biology, as biologist E. O. Wilson (1975) has predicted.

Reductionism

The idea that one science can reduce another derives from the positivist notion, now called the "unity of science" (Putnam, 1982), that all the sciences can be arranged in a hierarchy from highest to lowest, with each science reducible to a more basic science, until we arrive at physics, the most basic science. According to this theory, psychology is more basic than sociology and can reduce its social concepts to psychological concepts of individual behavior. Psychology's concepts and laws of individual behavior can in turn be reduced to the concepts and laws of neurophysiology, which describes the functioning of individuals' bodies.

A powerful rebuttal of unity-of-science reductionism comes from Donald Davidson's (1980) "anomalous monism." Davidson rejects Cartesian or religious dualism, but he defends a form of materialism in which the psychological concepts of folk psychology cannot be reduced to the laws of neurophysiology even though every mental event is identical with some brain event. If we accept materialism, then we accept that every mental event is also a brain event. However, for psychology to be reduced to neurophysiology, it must be the case that psychological concepts, not just psychological events, must correspond to neurophysiological concepts. When we explain a person's speech or actions psychologically, we do so against a background of assumed beliefs and desires. Most importantly, we assume that a person is rational, that his or her beliefs are reasonably coherent and consistent. If a man says things that are blatantly contradictory, if his actions are inconsistent with his beliefs, we conclude that he is irrational, we give up trying to explain his behavior psychologically, and may banish him from human society by placing him in a psychiatric hospital. Davidson concludes: "But in inferring this system [of interconnected beliefs and desires] from the evidence, we necessarily impose conditions of coherence, rationality and consistency. These conditions have no echo in physical theory, which is why we can look for no more than rough correlations between psychological and physical phenomena" (p. 231). In short, there is no danger that neurophysiology can reduce psychology. Psychological theory is autonomous.

Conclusion: Elimination of Scientific Psychology?

Psychology is not about to be devoured by biology. However, in the minds of some, psychology has no future because it cannot be a science. For example, Paul and Patricia Churchland (P. M. Churchland, 1985; P. S. Churchland, 1986) have argued that neurophysiology will replace and eliminate rather than reduce psychology. From their perspective, Davidson's anomalous monism provides no defense against their claims but instead supports them (Rosenberg, 1983, 1984). The Churchlands claim that folk psychology—and along with it, all forms of intentional, representational psychology such as functionalism—are scientifically false in the same way that Ptolemaic astronomy was false. The failure of psychological concepts to map onto neurophysiology shows that psychological concepts are false, and so they must be replaced by neurophysiological ones. Anomalous monism admits that every mental event is identical with some brain event, claiming only that psychology organizes its talk about mental events in ways irreducible to physical science. The Churchlands urge us to drop psychology altogether and talk only about brain events and the laws of neurophysiology. Precisely because "considerations of rationality, coherence and consistency . . . have no echo in physical theory," they should be eliminated.

The Churchlands' crusade represents scientism at its imperialistic worst. They (like Stephan Stich, 1983) want people to give up talking about hopes, beliefs, desires, and so on, merely because such concepts have no place in science. But their view is like the paint seller's view of art. The aesthetic properties of a painting depend on the physical qualities of its paint, and they are logically independent of the paint's physical properties. Eliminative materialism is like saying that because we cannot map the aesthetic properties of paintings onto the physical qualities of the paint, we should give up aesthetics. If humans adopt the eliminative view, they will have to give up a lot: law (there is no physical difference between killing in self-defense and killing for gain); morality (whether a fetus should be aborted does not depend on physical properties); fiction (Shakespeare and Dickens make constant reference to intentions, beliefs, and so on—even "ER" could not be understood neurophysiologically); politics (science cannot tell fascism from freedom); and, of course, everyday loves, hopes, fears, expectations, and interests.

The eliminativist views folk and intentional psychology as scientific theories and then regards them as false. The lesson to learn from this controversy is that folk psychology is no more a science than aesthetic theory is. Intentional psychology is not an autonomous science; it is not a science at all, and as such it is quite ineliminable. The Churchlands may be right that scientific psychology will one day be purely neurophysiological. It is clear, however, that no human form of life can be built on physical science alone, precisely because science cannot tell right from wrong; and making that distinction, and making meaningful sense of life, is the essence of being human.

Related considerations from evolutionary biology reinforce the conclusion that human psychology is not and cannot be a natural science (Rosenberg, 1980, 1995; Leahey, 1982, 1984; Hull, 1984). Science searches for exceptionless general laws that apply to spatiotemporally unrestricted objects. So physics is not about our solar system, but about stars and planets anywhere and everywhere. It is about quarks and leptons, not chairs and books, though these are made of quarks and leptons. Chairs and books are not suited to scientific laws because they are spatiotemporally local, products of a particular culture in a particular time, and science is universal, applying to all times and places. We can talk intelligibly about furniture, but such talk is not science. There is a craft, and even a practice, of furniture design and making, but a craft is not a science.

From the standpoint of evolution, species are not spatiotemporally unrestricted and so cannot fit into scientific laws. Every species is an individual, a product of a particular history, inhabiting a particular ecological niche. The laws of evolutionary biology apply across species: They should apply to any self-replicating organism anywhere, any time. So just as there cannot be scientific laws about just our sun or just our moon, there cannot be laws about particular species. There will be disciplined studies of the sun and the moon, of gerbils and dolphins, but these studies will produce facts about individual things and species, not general laws. But if there is no science of gerbils or dolphins because they are individuals rather than general entities, so there is also no science of *Homo sapiens*. Psychology is a disciplined study of one species, but it will produce no spatiotemporally unrestricted laws, and so it cannot be a science.

In 1671, Elizabeth Knapp was declared a witch (Demos, 1982). A psychologist reading about her would conclude that she suffered from catatonic schizophrenia: She was alternately sane and insane, and when insane she would hold fixed poses and experience hallucinations and delusions. It is quite likely that a tendency to schizophrenia is a genetic, inherited disposition. A biologist, then, could explain her disease from the standpoint of evolution and genetics, and from the standpoint of neuroscience, but he or she could not tell the whole story. Even if one inherits a tendency to schizophrenia, certain individual experiences are required to cause the disease to actually manifest itself, and personal learning is the province of the psychologist. Moreover, Elizabeth Knapp's hallucinations and delusions centered on the devil: She seemed to see him, to speak in his voice, and she claimed to have signed a compact to serve him. The content of her hallucinations and delusions was determined by her culture, not by the abnormal state of her brain. A modern schizophrenic would be more likely to hallucinate space aliens and have delusions about the CIA. Neuroscience says that Elizabeth Knapp and a modern schizophrenic suffer from the same brain disease, but it cannot explain why Elizabeth saw the devil and moderns see Martians. History, social science, and psychology can, and *only* they can. Physical science can explain, predict, and control the natural world, including the world of our bodies. Humans, however, live not just in the physical world, but, as Johann Herder said in the seventeenth century, "in a world we ourselves create." Our forms of life lie beyond science, but not beyond disciplined inquiry.

From the Humanities

Psychology and the other social sciences are, of course, not the only disciplines concerned with human beings. There are also the humanities. Although the humanities are often honored, the honor generally takes the form of lip service rather than sincere respect. In the modern world, science and technology are revered, and whatever does not fit their mold is deemed eccentric—interesting, perhaps, but decidedly second-rate. Psychologists are not the only people to suffer from physics envy. Hence, since the time of August Comte and John Stuart Mill, psychologists have acted on the assumption that, to quote Mill, "The backward state of the Moral Sciences [today's social sciences] can only be remedied by applying to them the methods of Physical Science, duly extended and generalized." After a hundred years of psychological physics envy, however, it is not at all clear that Mill was right. In Herder's words, "We live in a world we ourselves create," so the study of the human world—the object of the humanities—should be very different from the study of the physical world. The case of Elizabeth Knapp brings the point home. We may know all there is to know about the genetics and biochemistry of schizophrenia, and be able to cure it with sophisticated drugs, but to sympathize with her, to understand her predicament and what it meant to her and her neighbors, requires different tools from the ones science can give us.

According to some poststructuralist psychologists, psychology not only cannot be a science, but should not aspire to science, at least as traditionally conceived. Instead, psychology should emulate the humanities, interpreting rather than explaining or controlling human life. One such movement is called hermeneutics.

Hermeneutics traditionally denotes the field of biblical exegesis: closely examining a text of the Bible and interpreting its meaning. Broadly speaking, it is what is done in the humanities. An English literary critic takes the text of *Macbeth* and tries to set forth and discuss its meaning—for Shakespeare, for Shakespeare's audience, and for us, his modern audience. The critic does not care about the causal processes in William Shakespeare that brought him to write *Macbeth;* instead, he or she tries to grasp the human meaning of the play. A historian considering the case of Elizabeth Knapp does much the same thing. He or she may find useful the scientific hypothesis that schizophrenia is a brain disease, but the historical interest lies in understanding what Elizabeth Knapp and her contemporaries made of her condition. Doing this requires not science, but understanding and the ability to enter into the worldview of another place and time, making rational sense of it, a sense that can then be set down for the historian's readers.

It is possible to regard psychology from a hermeneutical rather than a scientific standpoint. Take, for example, Freud's theory of dreams. One might regard it as a scientific account of how dreams come about in the night: Repressed ideas, released from the shackles of repression, filter up toward consciousness and are reworked as they go by dreamwork into a disguised form suitable for conscious expression. Ideally, in this scientific account of dreams, it ought to be possible to follow the moment-by-moment construction of a dream from repressed impulse in the brain stem to conscious experience in the visual and auditory centers of the cerebral hemispheres.

But the title of Freud's book was *Die Traumdeutung, The Meaning of Dreams,* or, as usually translated, *The Interpretation of Dreams.* If one disregards the theory of his last chapter, one finds that Freud treated dreams primarily as texts to be interpreted:

He practiced hermeneutics (see Chapter 8). Like the critic studying *Macbeth,* Freud took a dream as a text, a meaningful expression of a person's unconscious neurotic problems. Used as a text examined for meaning, it is irrelevant whether the dream was produced as the scientific theory describes, and the process of creation can be ignored much as the critic ignores the process by which Shakespeare wrote *Macbeth.* Working together, therapist and client can recover the underlying meaning of the dream and in so doing reveal something important about the client—and, they hope, relieve him or her of neurotic misery.

It is possible to take hermeneutics as a model for psychology and the social sciences, for we may regard not just dreams but all of behavior as texts to be scrutinized for meaning. Their meaning derives from the form of life we share as human beings in a historical culture—the historian and anthropologist deal with alien forms of life— and the job of the psychologist from the hermeneutical point of view is to make sense of human life in this time and place rather than to predict, control, and scientifically explain it. The hermeneuticist practices *Geisteswissenschaft*—human science—rather than *Naturwissenschaft.* As the word "science" is used today, hermeneutics is no science because it does not aim at universal exceptionless causal laws. Because we live in a scientistic age, labeling something "unscientific" seems to consign it to a junk heap of useless and pointless oddities. If we can free ourselves from physics worship and scientism, however, we can see hermeneutics as only different from science, and value it on its own terms. Moreover, hermeneutics concerns itself with human life—with right and wrong, with love and hate, with what it means to be human rather than animal— and this concern is not obviously inferior to science.

PROFESSIONAL CONTROVERSIES

Clinical Psychology

Clinical psychology was invented just after World War II. By 1968, there were twelve thousand clinical psychologists in the world, and their ranks had swelled to over forty thousand by 1983, with the overwhelming majority located in the United States (Zilbergeld, 1983). Although there was some concern that such rapid growth might be eroding the quality of therapists in training (Strupp, 1976), clinical psychologists could hardly doubt that theirs was a growth field. Nevertheless, clinical psychologists were not completely happy.

To begin with, the question of how best to train clinical psychologists would not go away. The 1950 Boulder model had laid down that clinical psychologists were to be trained as scientific psychologists first and as professional service providers second. However, it was clear that the Boulder model was honored more in the breach than in the observance. By and large, clinical students wanted to help people and to learn how to practice therapy, and they regarded the scientific part of their training as a boring chore. Some clinical psychologists welcomed the seeming death of the Boulder model. George W. Albee (1970), for example, argued that it had been a mistake for clinical psychologists to model themselves on physicians to begin with, when in fact they should be agents of widespread social change. Other clinicians defended the Boulder model (for example, Shakow, 1976). Faced with change that seemed to be slipping out of organized psychology's control, the APA set up another conference on clinical training.

This one met in Colorado, too, at the resort of Vail, in 1973. Despite dissension, it endorsed something that the Boulder conference and other training conferences had rejected: the recognition of a new degree in clinical psychology, the Psy.D., for professionally oriented students. The Psy.D. program would reduce the scientific demands made on students in training and would frankly mint practitioners rather than academicians (Strickler, 1975). Naturally, the proposals proved controversial; some clinicians welcomed the idea (Peterson, 1976), while others (Perry, 1979) denounced the Psy.D. and a related development, the establishment of "freestanding" professional schools, so-called because they were not affiliated with a university. Despite the growth of Psy.D. programs and graduates in the 1980s, delegates to a national conference on clinician training in 1990 held that the scientist practitioner model was "essential" for psychology and "ideal" for practice (Belar & Perry, 1991).

Another problem that would not go away was clinical psychology's status anxiety. On the one hand, mainstream clinical psychologists wanted to assert their superiority over the growing horde of therapy providers who did not hold a Ph.D. or were not trained in psychology, such as clinical social workers, marriage counselors, and psychiatric nurses. The most psychologists could do about them was to keep out of the APA anyone without a Ph.D. On the other hand, clinical psychologists wanted to assert their virtual equality with psychiatrists, who felt disdain for clinical psychologists. Seymour Post (1985) called clinical psychologists and anyone else without an M.D. "barefoot doctors of mental health." "Amazingly," Post went on, "this group of laymen is now clamoring for all the privileges of being a physician, including the right to admit patients to hospitals under their direct management." Worse, "patients come to them with symptoms as they would to a general physician or internist. They are not competent to play such a role. Malpractice is the rule" (p. 21). Throughout the 1980s, organized psychiatry attempted to block the full therapeutic practice of psychologists, maintaining that psychologists are not fully competent to diagnose or treat mental disorders. One psychiatrist, AMA President Paul Fink, seemingly oblivious of the fact that, compared to psychiatrists, psychologists receive many more hours of therapy and diagnosis training, said that psychologists are "not trained to understand the nuances of the mind" (anonymous, 1988, p. 4).

Naturally, psychologists resent such attitudes. Bryant Welch, head of APA's Practice Directorate undoubtedly spoke for many clinicians in saying "organized medicine and psychiatry are a veritable menage of monopolistic personality disorders" (anonymous, 1988, p. 1). Whatever the merits of Post's arguments, however, it is certainly true that clinical psychologists were clamoring, at least on their own behalf, for something approaching the legal status of psychiatrists. Clinical psychologists had won the right to be licensed by the state, despite some well-placed misgivings about whether licenses really served the public interest as opposed to the private interests of psychologists (Gross, 1978). Yet, when a hospital accreditation committee restricted clinical psychologists to hospital practice under an M.D., clinical psychologists were outraged (Dorken and Morrison, 1976). In the 1990s, clinical psychologists fought against psychiatrist's resistance for the right to prescribe psychoactive medication (Squires, 1990; Wiggins, 1992). The biggest dispute between clinical psychology and psychiatry, however, naturally involved money.

Who should pay for psychotherapy? Although the obvious answer is the client or patient, most medical treatment today is paid for by insurance companies or the government, and questions arise about whether psychotherapy should be included in third-party payment plans. A few psychiatrists and clinical psychologists (such as Albee, 1977b) agree with Szasz that there is no such thing as mental illness, and logically conclude that psychotherapy is not really therapy, and so should not be covered under third-party payment schemes. Medical therapy for actual disorders of the nervous system (such as endogenous depression) would be covered. In practice, however, most therapists recognize that if psychotherapy costs had to be borne by clients, their practices would bring in a lot less income. Psychiatrists and clinical psychologists therefore agree that third parties should pay for psychotherapy, but they disagree bitterly about who should be paid.

For many years, much to the resentment of clinical psychologists, insurance companies agreed with psychiatrists that only M.D.s should be paid for medical procedures, and, with certain special limitations that did not apply to organic diseases, they covered psychotherapy only if performed by a psychiatrist. Clinical psychologists rightly viewed this as a monopoly, and they pressed for "freedom of choice" legislation at the state level, to force insurance companies to pay clinical psychologists, too. Psychologists wanted to share the monopoly, not destroy it outright. Already faced with rising costs, insurance companies allied with psychiatry to resist the encroachments of psychology and filed suit (the test case arose in Virginia) alleging improper interference with the practice of medicine and business. Ultimately, freedom of choice laws were upheld in the courts, but the long battle, fueled the long-standing hostility between the APA and the "other" APA, the American Psychiatric Association. The battle was refought in a new arena during the late 1970s and early 1980s, when the federal government considered passing national health insurance. The Reagan Administration's budget reduction programs rendered the issue moot.

Organized psychology had to deal with another means of controlling health care costs: managed care. The phrase managed care encompasses a variety of schemes by which companies and government control patients' access to high-cost specialized care. The APA put forward its own concept of managed care for mental health, called "Paradigm II" (Welch, 1992). Central to Paradigm II is the direct marketing of psychological health care services to the companies who must buy health-care plans for their employees, to ensure psychologists are included. Psychologists and psychiatrists also must market their skills to individuals (Gelman & Gordon, 1987).

Squabbles over insurance and managed care, and the increased marketing of health care like any other product, raised a nasty question that was potentially embarrassing to psychiatrists and clinical psychologists alike: Does psychotherapy work? Private and public health plans do not pay for quackery, so treatments must be proven safe and effective. The first person actually to investigate the outcomes of psychotherapy was the English psychologist Hans J. Eysenck, in 1952. He concluded that getting therapy was no better than just waiting for therapy for the same period of time—the "cure" rate for spontaneous remission was as good as for therapy. This implied that psychotherapy is a fraud. Since then, psychotherapists have challenged Eysenck's conclusion, and hundreds of psychotherapy outcome studies have been done. Naturally, mainstream clinical psychologists eagerly argue that psychotherapy, or at least their kind of psychotherapy, is effective, but the evidence is, at best, extremely mixed. There is a consensus that psychotherapy is probably better than doing nothing for a psychological problem, although the magnitude of improvement is not very great (Smith, Glass, and Miller, 1980; Landman and Dawes, 1982). However, many studies have concluded that professional psychotherapy with a trained therapist may be no more beneficial than amateur therapy or self-help (Prioleau, Murdock, and Brody, 1983; Zilbergeld, 1983). It is also not clear whether psychotherapy is safe. Zilbergeld (1983) quotes estimates that most clinicians are not competent, and he describes numerous cases of people made worse by therapy.

In terms of numbers of practitioners and patients, clinical psychology is a success. But it remains riven by doubts about its identity, its status, and its effectiveness. Carl Rogers, who is the founder of clinical psychology if anyone is, has said: "Therapists are not in agreement as to their goals or aims. . . . They are not in agreement as to what constitutes a successful outcome of their work. They cannot agree as to what constitutes a failure. It seems as though the field is completely chaotic and divided" (Zilbergeld, 1983, p. 114).

Divorced Again: The Academics Walk Out

The tensions between academic psychologists and practitioners that created the AAAP in 1938 were only papered over by the creation of the "new" APA in 1945. Indeed, tensions between the two communities got worse as the balance of practitioners to academics shifted decisively in favor of the former in the 1980s. In 1940, about 70 percent of APA members worked in academia; by 1985, only about 33 percent did. By 1965, scientist-academics were pressing for some restructuring of the APA that would give them a greater voice and interest in an APA they viewed as increasingly devoted to gilding the interests of practitioners, such as getting insurance payments, being able to write prescriptions for psychoactive drugs, and gaining hospital privileges for clinical psychologists on a par with psychiatrists. Efforts to reorganize the APA gained momentum in the 1970s; various committees and commissions were set up to recommend changes in APA structure that would satisfy both academics and practitioners. Repeated failure of every proposal alienated academics, leading to their gradual defection from APA, and an increasing urgency was felt by the reforming academics who remained in APA.

The last attempt to reorganize came in February 1987, when an ambitious restructuring plan was rejected by the association's governing body, the APA Council. Academic reformers formed the Assembly for Scientific and Applied Psychology, whose acronym (ASAP) reflected their sense of a need for immediate change. APA Council created another reorganizing committee, the Group on Restructuring (GOR), chaired by APA past-president and ASAP member Logan Wright. For several months, GOR met in a series of meetings that one member described later as the most unpleasant experience she had ever had. A clinical psychologist quit in the middle, amid great acrimony and bitterness, and in December 1987, GOR approved a rather awkward restructuring scheme by a vote of 11–3.

The plan was debated by APA Council at its winter meeting in February 1988. The emotional debate was marked by accusations of bad faith, conflict of interest, and insincerity. Only because of backstage maneuvering was the plan approved by an APA Council vote of 77–41, and a tepid recommendation was given to the membership to adopt it. Even the distribution of ballots became a source of controversy in the campaigns to win approval or defeat. In the end, at the close of summer 1988, the GOR plan was rejected 2–1 by 26,000 of APA's 90,000 members. In the same election, Stanley Graham was elected President of APA. Graham was a private practitioner who, despite having signed the reorganization document as a member of GOR, reversed his position and campaigned against ratification. In the upshot, many academics, in the words of Logan Wright, felt that "APA has become a guild controlled by small-business people" (Straus, 1988).

ASAP then put into action its backup plan to form a new society dedicated to academic psychologists' concerns, the American Psychological Society (APS). Starting with the initial membership of ASAP (about five hundred), APS had over ten thousand members by February 1990. Rancor between the organizations was strong. Attempts were made in APA Council to oust APS members from APA governance positions on grounds of conflict of interest, but after spirited and bitter debate, nothing came of those efforts. Various APS organizers quit anyway.

As the American Psychological Association celebrated its centennial in 1992, American psychology found itself divided again. The needs and desires of psychological practitioners for a professional society, and of academic scientists for a learned society, have again proved incompatible. The first divorce of practitioners and scientists was reconciled during the heady patriotic days of World War II. Whether psychology will come together again in a single organization without such an external crucible is an open question. Perhaps psychology is simply too large and diverse to be unified. Many psychologists join neither APA nor APS, but interdisciplinary groups related to their research interests, such as the Society for Neuroscience or the Cognitive Science Society.

PSYCHOLOGY AND SOCIETY

Giving Psychology Away

Against the background of turmoil and alienation of the late 1960s, psychology experienced an outbreak of "relevance" in 1969 (Kessel, 1980). Psychologists fretted that they were not doing enough to solve the problems of society. The most widely cited expression of psychologists' impulse to social relevance was George Miller's 1969 presidential address to the APA, in which he stated, "I can imagine nothing we could do that would be more relevant to human welfare, and nothing that could pose a greater challenge to the next generation of psychologists, than to discover how best to give psychology away." Miller asserted that "scientific psychology is one of the most potentially revolutionary intellectual enterprises conceived by the mind of man. If we were ever to achieve substantial progress toward our stated aim—toward the understanding, prediction, and control of mental and behavioral phenomena—the implications for every aspect of society would make brave men tremble." However, Miller said, despite continuous work by applied psychologists, on the whole psychologists "have been less effective than we might have been" in providing "intellectual leadership in the search for new and better personal and social relationships." In considering how to give psychology away, Miller rejected behavioral technology for psychology's playing a part in a broad mutation of human and social values: "I believe that the real impact of psychology will be felt not through . . . technological products . . . but through its effects on the public at large, through a new and different public conception of what is humanly possible and what is humanly desirable." Miller called for "a peaceful revolution based on a new conception of human nature" based on education: "Our scientific results will have to be instilled in the public consciousness in a practical and usable form."

Miller was riding the crest of the wave of public interest in psychology. In 1967, *Psychology Today* began publishing, and in 1969, *Time* inaugurated its "Behavior" department, so psychology was being almost given away in the popular media. Psychologists pushed social relevance as never before. The theme of the 1969 APA meeting was "Psychology and the Problems of Society," and the pages of *American Psychologist* began to fill with articles and notes on student activism, psychology's duty to social responsibility, and hip references to Bob Dylan, the musical poet of youth rebellion. Some Americans, especially conservative ones, did not want what psychologists were giving away. In a widely quoted speech, then Vice President Spiro Agnew (1972) blasted psychologists for proposing "radical surgery on the nation's psyche." Agnew quoted John Stuart Mill, "Whatever crushes individuality is despotism" and added, "we are contending with a new kind of despotism." Conservative columnist John Lofton (1972) contributed to a special issue of *American Psychologist* concerned with the serious overproduction and underemployment of Ph.D. psychologists. From some informal interviews, Lofton concluded that the public believed, "The tight market for Ph.D's is a good thing. There are too many people with a lot of knowledge about unimportant things" (p. 364). People were unsympathetic to psychology, Lofton said, because they were concerned about abuses of behavior-modification technology and tests, and felt traditional American resentment of "lordly Ph.D's, of whatever stripe." Academic psychology, including cognitive psychology, has been similarly castigated from outside: "The discipline continues to traffic in two kinds of propositions: those that are true but self-evident and those that are true but uninteresting. . . . [On] almost any issue that might be considered important for human existence . . . it offers pitifully little that rises above the banal" (Robinson, 1983, p. 5).

The Turn to Service

Despite occasional resistance, psychologists generally seemed to heed George Miller's appeal to get involved with solving social problems. As the 1970s wore on, psychologists were less likely to be found in the haunts of psychology's founders, the classroom and the laboratory, than in settings where they provided services. One of the major changes in the United States in the 1960s and 1970s was the change from a primarily industrial-productive economy to a service-information economy. Between 1960 and 1979, the total U.S. labor force grew by 45 percent, and the service sector grew by 69 percent. The greatest growth occurred in the social sciences, whose ranks grew by an incredible 495 percent; psychology grew by 435 percent.

Increasingly, psychologists were choosing specialties outside the old core area of experimental psychology. Between 1966 and 1980, the increase of new Ph.D.s in experimental psychology averaged only 1.4 percent per year (the slowest growth of all specialty areas). Growth in applied areas was much greater; for example, clinical psychology grew about 8.1 percent per year; counseling, 12.9 percent; and school psychology, 17.8 percent. By 1980, applied psychologists made up about 61 percent of all doctoral psychologists, and traditional experimentalists constituted 13.5 percent. New psychologists were choosing to work outside academia. In 1967, 61.9 percent of new doctoral psychologists took work in colleges or universities; by 1981, the figure was down to 32.6 percent. The most rapidly growing employment setting was self-employment, as a privately practicing clinician or consultant. Self-employed psychologists were not even counted before 1970. In 1970, only 1.3 percent of new doctoral psychologists chose self-employment, but by 1981, 6.9 percent did so. Other rapidly growing employment settings were government, business, and nonprofit institutions. Even psychologists trained in research specialties were increasingly likely to be employed outside academic settings, although nonacademic employment was often forced on them by the limited number of university and college jobs. In 1975, 68.9 percent of new research specialty doctoral psychologists went into academic settings; in 1980, only 51.7 percent did so, for an average annual decline of 8 percent. Because there were offsetting increases in employment outside academia, few psychology Ph.D.s were actually unemployed.

In the 1980s, psychologists could be found virtually everywhere, touching millions of lives. At the Educational Testing Service, psychologists continued to refine the Scholastic Aptitude Test (SAT), familiar to virtually every reader of this book, and pushed testing into new areas. One cannot become a golf pro without taking a multiple-choice ETS test (Owen, 1985). At the Stanford Research Institute, psychologists and others worked on an ambitious marketing program, the Values and Lifestyle Program (VALS). VALS used a technique called "psychographics" to categorize American consumers into several well-defined groups, such as "I-Am-Mes," "Belongers," and "Achievers." Companies and advertising agencies paid for VALS profiles to target their products to the most receptive groups and tune their pitches to the psychological makeup of their audiences (Atlas, 1984; Riche, 1989). Clinical psychologists, despite some official misgivings from the APA, were running radio call-in shows on which people could air their problems and seek advice and comfort from a psychologist (Rice, 1981). Such shows started locally, but, by 1985, a nationwide radio network, Talk Radio, devoted at least six hours a day to the "psych jockeys," and in 1986, the APA created a Division of Media Psychology. People were bringing their troubles to psychologists as never before. Between 1957 and 1976, the percentage of Americans who had consulted a mental health professional rose from 4 percent to 14 percent; among the college-educated, the change was from 9 percent to 21 percent. In fact, the number of people exposed to therapeutic techniques is very much greater; many self-help organizations, such as those for losing weight and stopping smoking, use such techniques (Zilbergeld, 1983). Finally, bookshops have Psychology sections mostly filled with self-help psychology books, and we can add to these most of the books in the Family Life sections, on topics such as sex, intimacy, and child rearing.

By 1985, psychologists were everywhere and were taking themselves seriously as a social force. Charles Kiesler (1979), executive officer of the APA, wrote: "I see psychology, then, as a national force for the future: as a knowledgeable force on scientific issues, on the delivery of human services, and on various human concerns about which we know something."

OUR PSYCHOLOGICAL SOCIETY

Ever since its beginnings in ancient Greece, psychology has perched awkwardly astride the dividing line between science and morals, between what is—how human beings really are—and what ought to be—how human beings should behave. Natural science can rest content with describing nature as it is, giving humans power for good or evil. The other social disciplines, or *Geisteswissenschaften,* describe what human beings have made of themselves across cultures and throughout history. Psychology, however, shares the neo-Platonic tragedy of humankind. People are at once animals, part of the natural world, and, in a sense, divine makers of social worlds, and psychology must come to grips with "*Homo sapiens* the animal" and "human being the creator" of forms of life. Psychology is perennially torn apart by its conflicting obligations, tempted on the one hand by the Newtonian dream of a natural science of humankind, yet likewise tempted to build a better form of life, to remake society in its own image.

Through it all, psychology has remained the study of the individual human being. The human species is studied by biology; human society is studied by sociology and anthropology. In our own time, psychology, as the avowed science of the individual person, has come to replace traditional ways of moralizing about human action with its own perspective, centered on the self and on feelings. In Platonism and traditional religion, the rules by which people live their lives have been thought to come from outside, from a transcendent realm of the Good or from the transcendent world of God. However, as religious and metaphysical traditions have been eroded by mechanistic science, people have turned to science for moral guidance, and this has led them, inevitably, to psychology, the science of individual action. It is quite natural, then, that as transcendental norms fade they should be replaced by scientific ones, and the priest or shaman is then replaced by the clinical psychologist. Psychology, as the study of the individual, must decree that the rules by which we should live life come from within each one of us, rather than from outside, and that these new rules can be discovered by looking within ourselves, by finding out how we really feel about things. In our psychological society, we are told to buy products because if we do we will "feel good" about them, and, even more importantly, about ourselves. Similarly, we are encouraged to share our feelings freely with others—whether they want to hear them or not—because only in this way, psychology says, can we become real human beings.

Psychology, however much behaviorists and cognitive scientists might object, teaches introspection as the final judge of right and wrong and encourages people to undertake an inward journey in search of introspective certainty concerning their real feelings and their supposed secret selves. In the United States, at least, psychology has become a new religion establishing an inner quest for self where before there had been an outer quest for God. The most acute observer of modern America, Tom Wolfe (1977), described the psychological society this way: Americans "plunged straight toward what has become the alchemical dream of the Me Decade. The old alchemical dream was changing base metals into gold. The new alchemical dream is: changing one's personality—remaking, remodeling, elevating, and polishing one's very self . . . and observing, studying, and doting on it. (Me!)" (p. 126, ellipses in original). The Me Decade, the Me Society, is the nearly inevitable result of scientism and psychology. If there is no transcendent truth outside nature, and if psychology is the science of the individual, then the only proper guide to life must come from scientific psychology, and that entails looking within for truth that cannot come from without.

For good or ill, we human beings of the West, especially in the United States, live in a psychological society. We are raised according to the findings of child psychologists, and we raise our children following the newer findings of child psychologists. In business, we turn to psychologists to manage workers and help us sell our products; as consumers, we are vulnerable to appeals crafted by psychologists. When we fall in love, we find ourselves in a "relationship" to be scrutinized in terms of our feelings, and if we find trouble doing that, we phone or visit a psychologist to help us out. We have come to believe the Deweyan notion that there are no fixed rules, that growth is the only moral end. With no outside goals to aim for, only inner ones, only growth and constant change are left to measure our self-worth and our love for each other. As Woody Allen, neurotic spokesman for the psychological society, complains, in *Annie Hall,* "A relationship, I think, is like a shark; it has to constantly move forward or it dies."

BIBLIOGRAPHY

The literature on cognitive science is vast. An excellent introduction to AI is John Haugeland, *Artificial intelligence: The very idea* (Cambridge, MA: MIT Press, 1985). The easiest introduction to functionalism is Jerry Fodor, "The mind–body problem," *Scientific American* (1981, *244,* no. 1, January: 114–23). There are two useful anthologies on foundations and criticisms of cognitive science: John Haugeland, ed., *Mind design* (Cambridge, MA: MIT Press, 1981): and Douglas R. Hofstadter and Daniel C. Dennett, eds., *The mind's eye* (New York: Basic Books, 1981). The latter book is edited by two defenders of formalistic AI, and although they reprint papers critical of cognitive science, such as Searle (1980; also reprinted by Haugeland), they try to defend the AI approach throughout their commentary. It is therefore useful to also read Searle's review of *The mind's eye* in the *New York Review of Books,* April 29, 1982. M. M. Waldrop, The necessity of knowledge, *Science* (1984, *223:* 1278–82), provides a readable account of some of the latest work in AI expanded into a book, *Man-made minds: The promise of artificial intelligence* (New York: Walker, 1987). Owen J. Flanagan, *The science of the mind* (Cambridge, MA: MIT Press, 1984), canvases the field of cognitive psychology, including Freud, James, and Piaget, as well as information processing. An outstanding book on the promise and the limits of AI, including its moral implications, is Joseph Weizenbaum, *Computer power and human reason* (San Francisco: Freeman, 1976). Weizenbaum is an eminent MIT computer scientist who has become revolted by what he regards as "obscene" uses of computers, for example, to do psychotherapy. Finally, although there is no historical connection between modern functionalism and earlier functionalism, there are interesting parallels. For example, John Dewey, in "The realism of pragmatism," *Journal of Philosophy* (1905, *2:* 324–7), describes his instrumentalism as a representational theory of mind.

For the information-processing view of consciousness, see R. Klatzky, *Memory and awareness: An information-processing perspective* (San Francisco: Freeman, 1985), and George Mandler, "Consciousness: Its function and construction," in *Cognitive psychology: A survey of cognitive science* (Hillsdale, NJ: Erlbaum, 1984); for the transpersonal psychology view, see Ronald S. Valle and Rolf von Eckatsberg, eds., *The metaphors of consciousness* (New York: Plenum, 1981); for a variety of scientific approaches, see Kenneth Pope and Jerome Singer, eds., *The stream of consciousness* (New York: Plenum, 1978). The article by R. E. Nisbett and T. D. Wilson, "Telling more than we know: Verbal reports on mental processes," *Psychological Review* (1977, *84:* 231–59), provoked many replies, rebuttals, and elaborations. Two replies to Nisbett and Wilson I find especially interesting: John G. Adair and Barry Spinner, "Subject's access to cognitive processes: Demand characteristics and verbal report," *Journal for the Theory of Social Behavior* (1981, *11:* 31–52); and John Sabini and Maury Silver, "Introspection and causal accounts," *Journal of Personality and Social Psychology* (1981, *40:* 171–9).

Connectionism has generated a lot of literature, most of it highly technical. A good general survey is William Bechtel and Adele Abrahamsen, *Connectionism and the mind* (Cambridge, England: Basil Blackwell, 1990). Also useful is the collection of papers edited by Stephen Graubard, *The artificial intelligence debate: False starts, real foundations* (Cambridge, MA: MIT Press). The papers were ostensibly written for outsiders and contain history, philosophy, and controversy relating to connectionism. The paper by Smolensky (1988) is wide-ranging and thoughtful and is the clearest discussion I've found of the foundational ideas of connectionism, but it is tough going. The standard symbolic paradigm critique of connectionism is Fodor and Pylyshyn (1988). Finally, one of the nice things about connectionist models is that one can get them and build one's own using ordinary computers. The PDP folks have published J. L. McLelland and D. E. Rumelhart, *Explorations in parallel distributed processing: A handbook of models, programs and exercises* (Cambridge, MA: MIT Press, 1988), complete with floppy disks containing most of the models presented in their main work. Using the models, however, requires a modest degree of programming skill. Easier to use are the menu-driven programs one can purchase with the program Brainmaker, published by California Scientific Software in 1988. It comes with easy-to-run prepackaged models, and it's relatively easy to build your own. Moreover, the program comes not only with a manual but a little book, *Introduction to neural networks,* that's a good introduction to connectionism.

In two recent works, Daniel Dennett has attempted to combine symbol-manipulation AI, connectionism, and Darwin into a general theory of the mind: *Consciousness explained* (Boston: Little, Brown, 1991) and *Darwin's dangerous idea* (New York: Simon & Schuster, 1995).

A truly excellent way to understand radical behaviorism and its relations to critics and rival views, especially cognitive science, is to read a special issue of *The Behavioral and Brain Sciences* (1984, *7,* no. 4, December), devoted to the "Canonical papers of B. F. Skinner." The issue reprints Skinner's most important papers and follows them with critical commentary from dozens of philosophers and scientists, followed in turn by Skinner's replies. It should be pointed out that radical behaviorism is no longer Skinner's monopoly, and that others who call themselves behaviorists today formulate the field with different emphases. For instructive examples, see Willard F. Day, "Contemporary behaviorism and the concept of intention," in William J. Arnold, ed., *Nebraska symposium on motivation 1975: Vol. 23. Conceptual foundations of psychology* (Lincoln: University of Nebraska Press, 1976); Charles P. Shimp, "Cognition, behavior, and the experimental analysis of behavior," *Journal of the Experimental Analysis of Behavior* (1984, *42:* 407–20); or Gerald E. Zuriff, *Behaviorism: A conceptual reconstruction* (New York: Columbia University Press, 1985).

For psychology's occult doubles, see Thomas H. Leahey and Grace Evans Leahey, *Psychology's occult doubles: Psychology and the problem of pseudoscience* (Chicago: Nelson Hall, 1983); and Thomas H. Leahey and Grace Evans Leahey, "Occult muddles: Essay review of recent books on the occult," *Journal of the History of the Behavioral Sciences* (1986, *22:* 220–36).

The references cited in the text provide a survey of reductionism. For sociobiology, there are many points of entry. T. H. Leahey and R. J. Harris, *Learning cognition,* 4th ed. (Englewood Cliffs, NJ: Prentice-Hall, 1996) have a one-chapter treatment of sociobiology. David Barash offers the best book-length treatments, including his text, *Sociobiology and behavior,* 2nd ed. (New York: Elsevier, 1982), and his book on human sociobiology, *The whisperings within* (New York: Penguin, 1979). Michael Ruse, *Sociobiology: Sense or nonsense?* (Dordrecht, The Netherlands: D. Reidel, 1979), is a wise introduction to and a balanced evaluation of the field. Recently, sociobiology has given rise to *evolutionary psychology,* see J. Barkow, L. Cosmides, and J. Tooby, eds., *The adapted mind* (Oxford, England: Oxford University Press, 1993).

Hermeneutics is a sprawling, diverse field that has many practitioners. It is primarily a European movement, though recently much interest has been shown in American philosophical and psychological circles. One way to begin to understand hermeneutics is through sources that explicitly contrast it with more familiar ways of thinking. The last part of Dreyfus (1972) contrasts European phenomenology, a branch of hermeneutics, with AI. Kenneth J. Gergen has recently criticized social psychology for not being a science, and his alternative "social constructionism," although not explicitly hermeneutic, is closely related. His most famous paper, which provoked both interest and outrage in social psychology, "Social psychology as history," *Journal of Personality and Social Psychology* (1973, *26:* 309–20), was expanded into a book, *Toward transformation in social knowledge* (New York: Springer-Verlag, 1982). His ideas have been vehemently rejected by mainstream social psychologists. Barry Schlenker reasserted the

Newtonian values of the profession in his reply to Gergen's paper, "Social psychology and science," *Journal of Personality and Social Psychology* (1974, *29:* 1–15). The editors of the *Personality and Social Psychology Bulletin* organized a symposium around the Gergen–Schlenker exchange, including new statements by the combatants; it may be found in *Personality and Social Psychology Bulletin* (1976, *2:* 371–444). Using a lively dialogue form, Gary Gutting contrasts hermeneutics with positivism and mainstream philosophy of science in "Paradigms and hermeneutics. A dialogue on Kuhn, Rorty, and the social sciences," *American Philosophical Quarterly* (1984, *21:* 1–15). The reference to Rorty is to philosopher Richard Rorty, who has incorporated hermeneutics into a reinvigorated pragmatism that has stirred up the same sort of storm in philosophy that Gergen did in social psychology. He analyzes and rejects traditional philosophy and introduces hermeneutics in *Philosophy and the mirror of nature* (Princeton, NJ: Princeton University Press, 1980); he develops his view in *Consequences of pragmatism* (Minneapolis: University of Minnesota Press, 1982), which is briefly summarized in "The fate of philosophy," *The New Republic* (1982, *187,* no. 16, October 18: 28–34). Several books about hermeneutics have been published, but the one I have found to be the clearest is Roy J. Howard, *Three faces of hermeneutics: An introduction to current theories of understanding* (Berkeley: University of California Press, 1982); Howard's book is especially helpful because he connects hermeneutics to English-speaking philosophy, particularly to the followers of Wittgenstein.

On the fuss over insurance, see three special issues of *American Psychologist* devoted to the topic, September 1977 and August 1983, in the "Psychology of the Public Forum" section, and February 1986. The literature evaluating psychotherapy is vast, difficult, and treacherous. Probably the best way to enter the literature is to read Prioleau, Murdock, and Brody (1983). They do a good job of discussing the complex issues involved in evaluating therapy outcomes. Their "Peer Commentary" section gives ample voice to critics who disagree with the article's contention that therapy is ineffective, and their reference section lists all the important works. Zilbergeld (1983) also discusses this literature, more readably but less precisely. See also J. Berman and N. Norton, "Does professional training make a therapist more effective?" *Psychological Bulletin* (1985, *98:* 401–7).

My account of the split between the APA and the APS is based primarily on my own experience as substitute or regular representative on APA Council of Division 24 (Theoretical and Philosophical) from fall 1986 to winter 1989. I have also drawn on a variety of accounts appearing in the newsletter of the APA, the *APA Monitor,* and the APS newsletter, the *APS Observer.* See also S. C. Hayes, "The gathering storm," *Behavior Analysis* (1987, *22:* 41–5); C. Holden, "Research psychologists break with APA," *Science* (1988, *241:* 1036); and C. Raymond, "18 months after its formation, psychological society proves its worth to behavioral-science researchers," *Chronicle of Higher Education,* (1990, June 27, *5:* 9). I should state that I am one of the disgruntled academics of APA. Although I was not a member of ASAP and have not given up my APA membership, I am a charter member of APS, supporting its separation from APA.

The statistics in the "Turn to Service" section are drawn from Georgine M. Pion and Mark W. Lipsey, "Psychology and society: The challenge of change," *American Psychologist* (1984, *39:* 739–54). David Owen's (1985) book on the SAT should be read by everyone who has taken the SAT or is a parent of someone who will take the SAT. Owen really does "rip the lid" off an incredibly corrupt institution that serves no ends but its own and does significant social harm. Anyone who reads the book will agree with Jonathan Yardley of the *Washington Post* that the SAT "is a scam," and with Owen's conclusion that ETS should be abolished.

The outstanding impressionistic portrait of the psychological society is Wolfe (1977). Another, more sardonic, tourist is Shiva Naipul, who reports in "The pursuit of wholiness," *Harper's* (1981, April, *247:* 20–27). The most scientific survey of the psychological society comes from pollster Daniel Yankelovich, "New rules in American life: Searching for self-fulfillment in a world turned upside down," *Psychology Today* (1981, April, *15:* 35–91). The term "psychological society" seems to have been coined by writer Martin L. Gross, *The* psychological society: A critical analysis of psychiatry, psychotherapy, and the psychological revolution (New York: Touchstone, 1978). Gross's book is quite good, if a little heavyhanded at times. Two related books are Peter Schrag, Mind control (New York: Delta, 1978), which is positively Orwellian in tone; and R. D. Rosen, Psychobabble (New York: Avon, 1979), which provides a witty tour of various pop psychotherapies. Several broad critiques of the psychological society exist, and I will mention only those I find especially useful. First, there is an excellent but often overlooked book by Daniel Boorstin, The image: A guide to pseudo-events in America (New York: Harper Colophon, 1964). The first book I know of to specifically address psychology's contribution to a new moral order is Phillip Rieff, The triumph of the therapeutic (New York: Harper & Row, 1966). Concern with the psychological society and the therapeutic sensibility grew more intense in the 1970s, producing Richard Sennett, The fall of public man (New York: Vintage Books, 1976), my own favorite among these books; and Christopher Lasch, The culture of narcissism (New York: Norton, 1979), which has probably had the greatest impact. An excellent book that focuses closely on the therapeutic sensibility encouraged by clinical psychology and psychiatry is Zilbergeld (1983), with the unforgettable title, The shrinking of America. Alasdair MacIntyre, After virtue: A study in moral theory (South Bend, IN: University of Notre Dame Press, 1981) takes a long view of the turn from exterior to interior standards of morality, extending back to the prephilosophic Greeks. Two recent books argue that popularized psychology has undermined traditional ideas of freewill and moral responsibility: Wendy Kaminer, I'm dysfunctional, you're dysfunctional: The recovery movement and other self-help fads (Boston: Addison-Wesley, 1992), and Charles W. Sykes, A nation of victims: The decay of the American character (New York: St. Martin's Press, 1992); see also J. R. Dunlap's review of the Sykes book in American Spectator (1992, December, 25: 72–3). The best actual antidote to the language of feelings is Miss Manners: Judith Martin, Miss Manners' guide to excruciatingly correct behavior (New York: Warner Books, 1982).

REFERENCES

Agnew, S. (1972, January). Agnew's blast at behaviorism. *Psychology Today 5:* 4, 84, 87.

Albee, G. W. (1970). The uncertain future of clinical psychology. *American Psychologist 25:* 1071–80.

_____ . (1977a). The protestant ethic, sex, and psychotherapy. *American Psychologist 32:* 150–61.

_____ . (1977b). Does including psychotherapy in health insurance represent a subsidy to the rich from the poor? *American Psychologist 32:* 719–21.

Anonymous (1988, Summer). AMA and psychiatry join forces to oppose psychologists. *Practitioner Focus, 2:* 1, 4–5.

Atlas, J. (1984, October). Beyond demographics. *Atlantic Monthly, 254:* 49–58.

Belar, C. D. and Perry, N. W., eds. (1991). *Proceedings: National Conference on scientist-practitioner education.* Sarasota, FL: Professional Resource Exchange.

Churchland, P. M. (1985). *Matter and consciousness.* Cambridge, MA: MIT Press.

Churchland, P. S. (1986). *Neurophilosophy.* Cambridge, MA: MIT Press.

Davidson, D. (1980). *Essays on actions and events.* Oxford, England: Clarendon Press.

Demos, J. P. (1982). *Entertaining Satan: Witchcraft and the culture of early New England.* New York: Oxford University Press.

Dorken, H. and Morrison, D. (1976). JCAH standards for accreditation of psychiatric facilities: Implications for the practice of clinical psychology. *American Psychologist 31:* 774–84.

Dreyfus, H. (1972). *What computers can't do: A critique of artificial reason.* New York: Harper & Row.

Dreyfus, H. L. and Dreyfus, S. E. (1988). Making a mind vs. modeling the brain: Artificial intelligence back at a branchpoint. In S. R. Graubard, ed., *The artificial intelligence debate: False starts, real foundations.* Cambridge, MA: MIT Press.

Eysenck, H. J. (1952). The effects of psychotherapy: An evaluation. *Journal of Consulting Psychology 16:* 319–24.

Fodor, J. A. and Pylyshyn, Z. W. (1988). Connectionism and cognitive architecture: A critical analysis. In S. Pinker and J. Mehler, eds., *Connections and symbols.* Cambridge, MA: MIT Press.

Gelman, D. and Gordon, J. (1987, December 14). Growing pains for the shrinks. *Newsweek,* 70–72.

Gross, S. J. (1978). The myth of professional licensing. *American Psychologist, 33:* 1009–16.

Hillis, W. D. (1987, June). The Connection Machine. *Scientific American 256:* 108–15.

Hull, D. L. (1984). Historical entities and historical narratives. In C. Hookway, ed., *Minds, machines, and programs.* New York: Cambridge University Press.

Kessel, F. S. (1980). Introduction to the symposium. In R. A. Kasschau and F. S. Kessel, eds., *Psychology and society: In search of symbiosis.* New York: Holt, Rinehart & Winston.

Kiesler, C. A. (1979). Report of the Executive Officer 1978. *American Psychologist 34:* 455–62.

Klerman, G. L. (1979, April). The age of melancholy? *Psychology Today 12,* no. 11: 36–42, 88.

Landman, J. T. and Dawes, R. (1982). Psychotherapy outcome: Smith & Glass conclusions stand up under scrutiny. *American Psychologist 37:* 504–16.

Leahey, T. H. (1982, April). *Will psychology disappear? The new prospects for reductionism.* Paper presented at the annual meeting of the Eastern Psychological Association, Baltimore.

———. (1984, April). *Evolution, history and cognitive science: Psychology without science or science without psychology.* Paper presented at the annual meeting of the Eastern Psychological Association, Baltimore.

———. (1990, August). *Three traditions in behaviorism.* Paper presented at the annual meeting of the American Psychological Association, Boston.

Lofton, J. (1972). Psychology's manpower: A perspective from the public at large. *American Psychologist 27:* 364–6.

Miller, G. A. (1969). Psychology as a means of promoting human welfare. *American Psychologist 24:* 1063–75.

Minsky, M. and Papert, S. (1969). *Perceptrons: An introduction to computational geometry.* Cambridge, MA: MIT Press.

Owen, D. (1985). *None of the above: Behind the myth of scholastic aptitude.* Boston: Houghton Mifflin.

Peele, S. (1981). Reductionism in the psychology of the eighties: Can biochemistry eliminate addiction, mental illness, and pain? *American Psychologist 36:* 807–18.

Perry, N. J. (1979). Why clinical psychology does not need alternative training models. *American Psychologist 34:* 603–11.

Peterson, D. R. (1976). Need for the Doctor of Psychology degree in professional psychology. *American Psychologist 31:* 792–8.

Post, S. C. (1985, July 25). Beware the "barefoot doctors of mental health." *The Wall Street Journal,* 21.

Prioleau, L., Murdock, M., and Brody, N. (1983). An analysis of psychotherapy versus placebo studies. *The Behavioral and Brain Sciences 6:* 275–310.

Putnam, H. (1982). Reductionism and the nature of psychology. *Cognition 2:* 131–46.

Rice, B. (1981, December). Call-in therapy: Reach out and shrink someone. *Psychology Today, 15:* 39–44, 87–91.

Riche, M. F. (1989). Demographics for the 1990s. *American Demographics 11:* 24–31, 53–4.

Robinson, P. (1983, July 10). Psychology's scrambled egos. *Washington Post* Book World, *13,* no. 28: 5, 7.

Rosenberg, A. (1980). *Sociobiology and the preemption of social science.* Baltimore: Johns Hopkins University Press.

_____ . (1983). Content and consciousness versus the intentional stance. *The Behavioral and Brain Sciences 3:* 375–6.

_____ . (1984, May 1). *Davidson's unintended attack on psychology.* Paper presented at the Conference on the Philosophy of Donald Davidson, New Brunswick, NJ.

_____ . (1994). *Instrumental biology, or, the disunity of science.* Chicago: Chicago University Press.

Rumelhart, D. E., McClelland, J. L., and the PDP Research Group. (1986). *Parallel distributed processing: Explorations in the microstructure of cognition,* 2 vols. Cambridge, England: Cambridge University Press.

Searle, J. (1980). Minds, brains, and programs. *The Behavioral and Brain Sciences 3:* 417–24.

Shakow, D. (1976). What is clinical psychology? *American Psychologist 31:* 553–60.

Skinner, B. F. (1931). The concept of reflex in the description of behavior. *Journal of General Psychology 5:* 427–58.

_____ . (1972). *Beyond freedom and dignity.* New York: Knopf.

_____ . (1984a). Some consequences of selection. *The Behavioral and Brain Sciences 7:* 502–10.

_____ . (1984b). Representations and misrepresentations. *The Behavioral and Brain Sciences 7:* 655–67.

_____ . (1985). Cognitive science and behaviorism. *British Journal of Psychology 76:* 291–301.

Smith, M. L., Glass, G. V., and Miller, T. I. (1980). *The benefits of psychotherapy.* Baltimore: Johns Hopkins University Press.

Smolensky, P. (1988). On the proper treatment of connectionism. *The Behavioral and Brain Sciences 3:* 417–24.

Snyder, S. H. (1980). *Biological aspects of mental disorder.* New York: Oxford University Press.

Squires, S. (1990, July 24). The quest for prescription privileges. *Washington Post,* Health Section, 7.

Stich, S. P. (1983). *From folk psychology to cognitive science: The case against belief.* Cambridge, MA: MIT Press.

Straus, H. (1988, August 12). Psychology field finds itself of two minds: Private practice, research. *Atlanta Journal and Constitution.*

Strickler, G. (1975). On professional schools and professional degrees. *American Psychologist 31:* 1062–6.

Strupp, H. (1976). Clinical psychology, irrationalism, and the erosion of excellence. *American Psychologist 31:* 561–71.

Tank, D. W. and Hopfield, J. J. (1987, December). Collective computation in neuron-like circuits. *Scientific American 257:* 104–15.

Tart, C. (1978, August 31). *Information processing mechanisms and ESP.* Invited address presented at the annual meeting of the American Psychological Association, Toronto, Canada.

Welch, B. L. (1992, September). Paradigm II: Providing a better model for care. *APA Monitor,* 42–3.

Wender, P. H. and Klein, D. F. (1981, February). The promise of biological psychiatry. *Psychology Today 15,* no. 2: 25–41.

Wiggins, J. G. (1992, September). Capitol comments: Time is ripe to seek prescription authority. *APA Monitor,* 3.

Wilson, E. O. (1975). *Sociobiology: The new synthesis.* Cambridge, MA: Harvard University Press.

Wolfe, T. (1977). The Me Decade and the third great awakening. In T. Wolfe, *Mauve gloves and madmen, clutter and vine.* New York: Bantam Books.

Zilbergeld, B. (1983). *The shrinking of America: Myths of psychological change.* Boston: Little, Brown.

ADDITIONAL RECOMMENDED READINGS

Adler, T. (1990, April). Different sources cited in major cognitive texts. *APA Monitor,* 8.

Anderson, J. R. (1978). Arguments concerning representations for mental imagery. *Psychological Review 85:* 249–77.

————. (1981). Concepts, propositions, and schemata: What are the cognitive units? In J. H. Flowers, *Nebraska symposium on motivation 1980: Vol. 28. Cognitive processes.* Lincoln: University of Nebraska Press.

Bandura, A. (1974). Behavior theory and the models of man. *American Psychologist 29:* 859–69.

Boden, M. (1977). *Artificial intelligence and the nature of man.* New York: Basic Books.

————. (1979). The computational metaphor in psychology. In N. Bolton, ed., *Philosophical problems in psychology.* London: Methuen.

Brewer, W. F. and Nakamura, G. V. (1984). The nature and functions of schemas. In R. S. Wyer and T. K. Srull, eds., *Handbook of social cognition.* Hillsdale, NJ: Erlbaum.

Brush, S. G. (1974). Should the history of science be rated "X"? *Science 183:* 1164–72.

Campbell, D. T. (1975). On the conflicts between biological and social evolution and between psychology and moral tradition. *American Psychologist 30:* 1103–26.

Clark, K. (1971). The pathos of power: A psychological perspective. *American Psychologist 26:* 1047–57.

Cleary, T., Humphries, L., Kendrick, S., and Wesman, A. (1975). Educational uses of tests with disadvantaged students. *American Psychologist 30:* 15–91.

Dennett, D. (1978). *Brainstorms.* Cambridge, MA: MIT Press.

————. (1983). Artificial intelligence and the strategies of psychological investigation. In J. Miller, *States of mind.* New York: Pantheon.

————. (1984). Cognitive wheels: The frame problem of AI. In C. Hookway, ed., *Minds, machines, and programs.* New York: Cambridge University Press.

Ericsson, K. A. and Simon, H. (1980). Verbal reports as data. *Psychological Review 87:* 215–51.

Farnham-Diggory, S., ed. (1972). *Information processing in children.* New York: Academic Press.

Flowers, J. H. (1981). *Nebraska symposium on motivation 1980: Vol. 28. Cognitive processes.* Lincoln: University of Nebraska Press.

Fox, J. (1983). Debate on learning theory is shifting. *Science 222:* 1219–22.

Goleman, D. (1983, May). A conversation with Ulric Neisser. *Psychology Today 17,* no. 5: 54–62.

Gottlieb, G. (1984). Evolutionary trends and evolutionary origins: Relevance to theory in comparative psychology. *Psychological Review 91:* 448–56.

Gunderson, K. (1984). Leibnizian privacy and Skinnerian privacy. *The Behavioral and Brain Sciences 7:* 628–9.

Hayes-Roth, F. (1979). Distinguishing theories of representation. *Psychological Review 86:* 376–82.

Hodos, W. and Campbell, C. B. G. (1969). *Scala naturae:* Why there is no theory in comparative psychology. *Psychological Review 76:* 337–50.

Hookway, C., ed. (1984). *Minds, machines, and programs.* New York: Cambridge University Press.

Hulse, S., Fowler, H., and Honig, W., eds. (1978). *Cognitive processes in animal behavior.* Hillsdale, NJ: Erlbaum.

Jackson, G. D. (1975). On the report of the Ad Hoc Committee on Educational Uses of Tests with Disadvantaged Students. Another psychological view from the Association of Black Psychologists. *American Psychologist 30:* 88–93.

Jenkins, J. J. (1981). Can we find a fruitful cognitive psychology? In J. H. Flowers, *Nebraska symposium on motivation 1980: Vol. 28. Cognitive processes.* Lincoln: University of Nebraska Press.

Jensen, A. (1969). How much can we boost I.Q. and scholastic achievement? *Harvard Educational Review 39:* 1–123.

Kasschau, R. A. and Kessel, F. S., eds. (1980). *Psychology and society: In search of symbiosis.* New York: Holt, Rinehart & Winston.

Koch, S. (1980). Psychology and its human clientele: Beneficiaries or victims? In R. A. Kasschau and F. S. Kessel, eds., *Psychology and society: In search of symbiosis.* New York: Holt, Rinehart & Winston.

Leahey, T. H. (1981, April 23). *The revolution never happened: Information processing is behaviorism.* Paper presented at the annual meeting of the Eastern Psychological Association, New York.

———. (1992). Mythical revolutions in the history of American psychology. *American Psychologist,* in press.

Lockard, R. B. (1971). Reflections of the fall of comparative psychology: Is there a lesson for us all? *American Psychologist 26:* 168–79.

Lown, B. A. (1975). Comparative psychology 25 years after. *American Psychologist 30:* 858–9.

Mahoney, M. J. (1977). Reflections on the cognitive-learning trend in psychotherapy. *American Psychologist 32:* 5–13.

McConnell, J. V. (1970, April). Criminals can be brainwashed—now. *Psychology Today 3,* no. 11: 14–18, 74.

Mehler, J. and Franck, S. (1981). Editorial. *Cognition 10:* 1–5.

Meichenbaum D. (1977). *Cognitive behavior modification: An integrative approach.* New York: Plenum.

Miller, G. A. (1972). *Psychology: The science of mental life.* New York: Harper & Row.

———. (1983). The background to modern cognitive psychology. In J. Miller, *States of mind.* New York: Pantheon.

Miller, J. (1983). *States of mind.* New York: Pantheon.

Mischel, W. and Mischel, H. (1976). A cognitive social learning approach to morality and self-regulation. In T. Lickona, ed., *Moral development and behavior.* New York: Holt, Rinehart & Winston.

Neisser, U. (1976). *Cognition and reality.* San Francisco: Freeman.

———. (1982). Memory: What are the important questions? (Preface). In U. Neisser, ed., *Memory observed: Remembering in natural contexts.* San Francisco: Freeman.

———. (1984). Toward an ecologically oriented cognitive science. In T. M. Schlecter and M. P. Toglia, eds., *New directions in cognitive science.* Norwood, NJ: ABLEX.

Newell, A. (1973). You can't play 20 questions with nature and win. In W. G. Chase, ed., *Visual information processing.* New York: Academic Press.

Porter, J., Johnson, S., and Granger, R. G. (1981, December). The snark is still a boojum. *Comparative Psychology Newsletter 1,* no. 5: 1–3.

Pylyshyn, Z. W. (1979). Validating computational models: A critique of Anderson's indeterminacy claim. *Psychological Review 86:* 383–405.

Raimey, C. T. (1974). Children and public policy: A role for psychologists. *American Psychologist 29:* 14–18.

Rheingold, H. (1973). To rear a child. *American Psychologist 28:* 42–46.

Rosch, E. (1977). Human categorization. In N. Warren, ed., *Studies in cross-cultural psychology.* London: Academic Press.

Rose, F. (1985, March). The black knight of AI. *Science 85:* 46–51.

Rubinstein, R. A. (1984). *Science as a cognitive process.* Philadelphia: University of Pennsylvania Press.

Scriven, M. (1980). An evaluation of psychology. In R. A. Kasschau and F. S. Kessel, eds., *Psychology and society: In search of symbiosis.* New York: Holt, Rinehart & Winston.

Skinner, B. F. (1974). *About behaviorism.* New York: Knopf.

———. (1985, August 26). *What is wrong with everyday life in the Western world?* Paper presented at the annual meeting of the American Psychological Association, Los Angeles.

Symons, D. (1987). If we're all Darwinians, what's the fuss about? In C. Crawford, M. Smith, and D. Krebs, eds., *Sociobiology and psychology.* Hillsdale, NJ: Erlbaum.

Tulving, E. (1979). Memory research: What kind of progress? In L. G. Nilsson, ed., *Perspectives on memory research.* Hillsdale, NJ: Erlbaum.

Wasserman, E. A. (1981). Comparative psychology returns. *Journal of the Experimental Analysis of Behavior 35:* 243–57.

Wegman, C. (1984). *Psychoanalysis and cognitive psychology.* New York: Academic Press.

White, M. G. (1985). On the status of cognitive psychology. *American Psychologist 40:* 116–9.

Wispe, L. G. and Thompson, J. N., eds. (1976). The war between the words: Biological vs. social evolution and some related issues. *American Psychologist 31:* 341–84.

Wyers, E. J., et al. (11) (1980). The sociobiological challenge to psychology: On the proposal to "cannibalize" comparative psychology. *American Psychologist 35:* 955–79.

Index

EVENTS IN PSYCHOLOGY			EVENTS IN HISTORY
Freud's *Civilization and Its Discontents*	19	30	
			Pluto Discovered
Hull's First Learning Machine			Stock Market Crash: Depression Begins
			First Talkie/Lindbergh Crosses Atlantic
Terman's "Mental Test as a Psychological Method"			Scopes Trial/First TV Transmission
Freud's *Ego and the Id*			
			Tomb of Tutankhamen Discovered
Wundt's *Völkerpsychologie* Completed	19	20	19th Amendment to Constitution/Women Vote
Yerkes's "Psychology in Relation to the War"			WWI Ends
			U.S. Enters WWI
			WWI Begins
Watson's "Psychology as the Behaviorist Views It"			
			Titanic Sinks
	19	10	*The Firebird* Ballet (Stravinsky)
Freud Lectures in U.S.			
			James's *Pragmatism*
Angells's "Province of Functional Psychology"			
Freud's *Three Essays on the Theory of Sexuality*			Special Theory of Relativity
			British "Physical Deterioration Report"
Gestalt and Würzburg Psychologies Begin			
Freud's *Interpretation of Dreams*	19	00	Picasso's First Major Painting "La Moulin de la Galette"
Titchener's "Postulates of a Structural Psychology"			Spanish-American War
Dewey's "Reflex Arc Concept in Psychology"/Witmer's Psychological Clinic			McKinley Elected U.S. President
			First Professional Football Game
			Panic of 1893
APA Founded			
			Zipper Invented
James's *Principles of Psychology*	18	90	
			Kodak Camera Perfected
American Journal of Psychology			
Ebbinghaus's *On Memory*			
			Huckleberry Finn (Twain)
Romanes's *Animal Intelligence*			Medical Insurance Introduced (Germany)
	18	80	
Wundt's Founding Laboratory			*A Doll House* (Ibsen)
			Telephone Invented
James's Informal Laboratory			
Mind, First Psychology Journal in English			Impressionism Begins
Metaphysical Club			
			Paris Commune
	18	70	
			Professional Baseball Founded
			U.S. Civil War Ends
Sechenov's *Reflexes of the Brain*			Slavery Abolished in U.S.
			U.S. Civil War Begins
Fechner's *Elements of Psychology*	18	60	